THE COLLECTED WORKS
OF HERMAN DOOYEWEERD

Series A, Volume 5

GENERAL EDITOR: D.F.M. Strauss

Reformation and Scholasticism in Philosophy

The Greek Prelude

Series A, Volume 5

Herman Dooyeweerd

PAIDEIA
PRESS

Library of Congress Cataloging-in-Publication Data

Dooyeweerd, H.(Herman), 1884-1977.
    Reformation and Scholasticism in Philosophy
    Herman Dooyeweerd.
        p. cm.
    Includes bibliographical references and index
    ISBN 978-0-88815-215-2 [CWHD A5] (soft)

This is Series A, Volume 5 in the continuing series
The Collected Works of Herman Dooyeweerd
(Initially published by *Mellen Press*, now published
by *Paideia Press*)

ISBN 978-0-88815-304-3

The Collected Works comprise a *Series A,* a *Series B,* and a *Series C*
(*Series A* contains multi-volume works by Dooyeweerd,
Series B contains smaller works and collections of essays,
Series C contains reflections on Dooyeweerd's philosophy
designated as: *Dooyeweerd's Living Legacy,* and
Series D contains thematic selections from Series A and B)

A CIP catalog record for this book is available from the British Library.

The Dooyeweerd Centre for
Christian Philosophy
Redeemer University College
Ancaster, Ontario
CANADA L9K 1J4

©PAIDEIA PRESS 2012
Grand Rapids, MI 49507

Printed in the United States of America

Reformation and Scholasticism in Philosophy

by

Herman Dooyeweerd

Volume I
THE GREEK PRELUDE

Translated by
Ray Togtmann

Initial Editor the Late
Robert D. Knudsen

Final Editor
Daniël Strauss

Editing of All Greek Quotations by
Al Wolters

This is Volume I of a three-volume work. Volume I first appeared in 1949 under the title: *Reformatie en Scholastiek in de Wijsbegeerte* (T. Wever, Franeker – 496 pp.). Parts of Volumes II and III appeared in the Journal *Philosophia Reformata* between 1945 and 1950. Volume III was left uncompleted, but it does contain the main ideas of Dooyeweerd with regard to the theory of enkaptic interlacements and Dooyeweerd's anthropological theory of the complex bodily structure of the human being.

Volume II – Greek and Medieval Philosophy
Volume III – Nature Philosophy and Anthropology

The translation of this book is made possible by a grant from the Free University of Amsterdam, while the Kuyper Foundation of the Netherlands contributed substantially to its publication.

Contents

I

INTRODUCTION

INITIAL SURVEY OF THE RELIGIOUS GROUND-MOTIVES AND THE CONFLICT THEY PRODUCE BETWEEN THE REFORMATIONAL AND SCHOLASTIC SPIRITS IN PHILOSOPHY

v

II

DIORAMA OF THE DIALECTICAL DEVELOPMENT OF THE FORM-MATTER MOTIVE IN GREEK PHILOSOPHY UP TO AND INCLUDING PLATO

Part I

THE DIALECTICAL DEVELOPMENT UP TO PLATO

Part II

THE DIALECTICAL DEVELOPMENT IN PLATO'S THOUGHT UNDER THE PRIMACY OF THE FORM MOTIVE OF THE RELIGION OF CULTURE

Introduction

The Origin of Plato's Theory of Ideas

Chapter One

The Dialectic of the Theory of Ideas from Its Initial Conception to Its Culmination in the *Republic*

Chapter Two

The Dialectic of the Form-Matter Motive in the Crisis of the Theory of Ideas. The *Theaetetus*, the *Parmenides*, the *Sophist*, the *Statesman*, and the Dialectical Portion of the *Phaedrus*

Chapter Three

The Dialectic of the Form-Matter Motive in the Penultimate Stage of Development in Plato's Thought, After the Crisis Has Been Surmounted

Chapter Four

The Dialectic of the Form-Matter Motive in the *Timaeus*, the *Laws*, and the *Epinomis*, and in the Final Stage of Plato's Thought

Commentary on the Text

Index of Subjects

Index of Persons

Foreword

After the appearance of the Dutch edition of his magnum opus, *De Wijsbegeerte der Wetsidee*, in 3 Volumes [1935-1936 – currently available as Volumes 1-4 of the *A Series* in *The Collected Works of Dooyeweerd*, under the title *A New Critique of Theoretical Thought* (NC), 1997], Herman Dooyeweerd deepened and expanded his understanding of the *direction-giving* basic motives operative in the development of Western society and of Western scholarly thinking.

His thesis that the West by and large has been in the grip of *four* ultimate "religious ground-motives" required a more detailed argumentation. On the one hand this need prompted him to develop what has become known as his *transcendental critique of theoretical thought*, and on the other it challenged him to provide an equally penetrating analysis of Greek and medieval thinking, similar to his highly original study of the dialectical development of modern humanistic philosophy (found in the second part of the first Volume of his NC).

This is the first Volume of a more encompassing study of the problem of *Reformation* and *Scholasticism* in philosophy, mainly focused on Greek philosophy up to and including Plato. Although Bram Bos challenges the explanation which Dooyeweerd gave for the *genesis* of the Greek dialectic (see *Dooyeweerd en de wijsbegeerte van de oudheid*, in *Herman Dooyeweerd 1894-1977, Breedte en actualiteit van zijn filosofie*, 1994, Eds. H.G. Geertsema e.a., Kampen: Kok, pp.197-227) by introducing the idea of the "titanic meaning-perspective," he does believe that the value of Dooyeweerd's analysis of the irreconcilable inner dialectic of Greek thought remains intact (p.220).

In the light of the fact that the major part of this first Volume of *Reformation and Scholasticism in Philosophy* is dedicated to the works of Plato, one is automatically reminded of the famous remark made by A.N. Whitehead, namely that the entire history of Western philosophy is to be viewed as *footnotes* to the philosophy of Plato. Anyone reading this work will soon realize that any philosophical investigation of the history of philosophy is at once an exercise in the articulation of a systematic understanding of philosophical problems. Yet, Dooyeweerd is convinced that the historian of philosophy should always attempt to understand historical figures in terms of their own deepest motivation and direction-giving ground motive.

D F M Strauss
General Editor
(University of the Free State
Bloemfontein, South Africa)

Preface

A few years before the outbreak of the Second World War, I received a request from the publisher T. Wever of Franeker to write a booklet on *Calvinism and Philosophy*. Their plan was to include it in a series *Calvinism and the Questions of our Time*. This request came to me at an inopportune moment. My energies were completely taken up with working out my philosophical anthropology. In addition, I was attempting to give my three-volume *Encyclopedia of the Science of Law* a definitive form.

I then conceived the plan of writing, concurrently with the latter work, a smaller book on *Reformation and Scholasticism in Philosophy*. I intended to devote this book in particular to elucidating the questions of anthropology in terms of the opposition between the ground-motive of the Reformation and that of the Scholastic line of thought. This small work would then serve as an introduction to the positive elaboration of my anthropological insights.

I conceived this plan in the face of the deep-seated objections which had been raised immediately preceding the war in certain Reformed theological circles, particularly against the view of the human soul that had been presented in the Philosophy of the Law-Idea. These objections were rooted entirely in traditional Scholastic ideas. In view of this fact, I was eager, first of all, to place them in their appropriate historical setting. By putting them in this light I hoped to provide an explanation as to why this philosophy had so decisively rejected the Scholastic conceptions of the human soul.

Once the theme "Reformation and Scholasticism in Philosophy" had taken hold of me, however, I soon realized that it demanded a much broader treatment than I had originally intended. For the genius of Scholastic thinking can be understood in its opposition to that of the Reformation only when the religious ground-motive of Greek thought has been traced in its radical opposition to the ground-motive of Scriptural revelation.

That there is indeed one common religious ground-motive at the foundation of Greek thought, which gives us the key to understanding the typical dialectical course of development of Greek philosophy, is, however, more easily claimed than actually demonstrated by way of a careful investigation of this development. Such a proof requires not only a thorough study of the religious notions of the Greeks but also a study in depth of the Greek philosophical texts. Every classicist knows that this places almost insurmountable obstacles in the way of a non-classicist. Because of the profound importance of the inquiry, however, I felt obliged to go ahead with it, undeterred by the difficulties. Now, after an involved and time-consuming preparatory study, I am sending forth the first volume of my *Reformation and Scholasticism in Philosophy.*

The introductory section of this work deals with the four religious ground-motives of Western philosophical thought and with the relationship between theoretical and religious dialectic. The major lines of thought of this section have already appeared in an article of mine in the journal *Philosophia Reformata.*[1]

As my study of Greek philosophy broadened and deepened, I became more and more convinced of the accuracy of my original conviction that the background of the Aristotelian form-matter scheme is much broader and has deeper roots than is generally admitted. In fact, as I had suspected, it gives philosophical expression to the dialectical ground-motive which governed all of Greek thought from the beginning.

In this regard the attitude of Aristotle himself should have served as a warning. As one who lived in the Greek world of thought, he construed the entire preceding history of philosophy within this scheme. This of itself should have been enough to alert the modern investigator to the fact that what we have here is far more than a subjective thought-construct of the great Stagirite. Indeed, if this motive had been simply an invention of Aristotle, which did not truly apply to the philosophy before him, it would have been impossible for him to have forced the latter into its mold without provoking opposition. He would have distorted it so badly that the mutilation could not have gone unnoticed by his contemporaries. For it is the very foundations of Greek thought that are at stake here. In addition, the very fact that the form-matter motive so consistently maintained its position throughout later Greek thought and during the entire Scholastic period, controlling the very way in which the philosophical problems were framed, should have served as a second warning against the misconception that what we have here is merely a philosophical invention of Aristotle by which he arbitrarily measured all of his predecessors.

If one penetrates behind the question of terminology, which of itself is insignificant, and concentrates on the actual meaning of Aristotle's form-matter scheme, a thoroughgoing study of Plato and of the so-called

---

1 "De vier religieuze grondthema's in den ontwikkelingsgang van het wijsgerig denken van het Avondland," *Philosophia Reformata*, VI (1941), 161-179.

pre-Socratics will reveal that what is at issue here is indeed a dialectical ground-motive in which the entire Greek community of thought was rooted from the beginning. Once this has taken place, the only remaining task is to lay bare the religious meaning of this ground-motive. At this point, one cannot fail to see that what has been a continual subject of investigation since the Romantic period, the encounter between the pre-Homeric religion of nature and the later culture religion of the Olympic pantheon, is the origin of that deep religious conflict in the Greek consciousness which is embodied in the polar opposition between the form motive and the matter motive. Once one possesses this clue, the entire history of Greek philosophy is bathed in a surprising light. Much within it that had previously appeared inexplicable or internally contradictory is now made clear as it is placed against its proper background. Furthermore, the true meaning of Scholasticism, which tries to construct a bridge between the ground-motive of the Christian religion and the dialectical ground-motive of Greek thought, can now be made fully clear for the first time.

In this way the possibility arises of a true transcendental critique of both Greek and Scholastic philosophy. By this critique, furthermore, the standard portrayal of the history of philosophy as a process of increasing emancipation from the fetters placed upon it by religion is revealed as a radical misconception.

This misconception was rooted in the a priori prejudice that philosophic thought, according to its very nature, is autonomous. Those making this judgment, however, glossed over the fact that in Greek philosophy this presumed autonomy had a completely different meaning from the one it had in Thomistic Scholasticism, and that in both of these its meaning was totally different from the one it has in modern humanistic thought. If fuller account had been taken of this incontrovertible fact, the critical question would have surfaced of its own accord: What is it that has determined the profound differences in the way that this autonomy has been conceived in the course of history? It would then have appeared, as a matter of course, that these differing conceptions were entirely dependent on the religious ground-motives which have undergirded Western thought in its whole development. Then the "axiom" of the autonomy of philosophy would have become a critical problem. Then, too, the philosophic dogmatism which elevated this autonomy to the position of a "dogma" would have had to make way for a transcendental, critical stance, for which philosophic thought itself had the status of a theoretical problem. For only a serious investigation of the inner structure of this thought can provide a truly critical answer to the question as to whether a religiously unprejudiced philosophy in the modern sense of the word is in fact possible.

I initially developed such a transcendental critique of philosophic thought in the first volume of my *Philosophy of the Law-Idea.*[1] There I applied it in a detailed analysis of the dialectical course of development of modern humanistic philosophy. Now the same method will be followed in an investigation of Greek philosophy. And, in conformity with the overall design of this work, it will be the questions of anthropology that stand in the foreground.

In order to help the reader draw his own conclusions as to whether and to what degree this method of approaching Greek philosophy in terms of its own ground-motive does greater justice to Greek thought than the standard one, I have throughout supported my analysis with extensive Greek quotations. Insofar as the sources permit, these are included in the context of the entire argument of the writers themselves. For the benefit of those who do not know the Greek language or who have an insufficient grasp of it, I have placed after each quotation a translation, in which I have attempted as far as possible to avoid prejudicing the philosophical interpretation. The fact that one can never fully succeed in this attempt is known to all who have learned from experience the problems encountered in translating.

By far the greater part of my exposition treats the development of Plato's thought. The justification for this will be found in the design and execution of my method of investigation itself. For, in the philosophy of Plato, all the strands of philosophy before him are gathered together, and it is in the development of his thought that the dialectic of the Greek ground-motive obtains its most representative and, at the same time, its most complicated expression.

At this point I shall make only a few brief comments about the two volumes that are to follow the present one. The second critically investigates the opposition between the Philosophy of the Law-Idea and Scholastic philosophy, more particularly Scholastic anthropology. This volume is now completely finished. It will appear in a short while, as soon as paper becomes available and as soon as there is opportunity to have it printed. This volume will also contain a detailed discussion of the relationship between philosophy and theology, the issue which appears to have been the pivotal one for Christian thought from the beginning. At the same time, by way of a transcendental critique of the Thomistic and Augustinian schools of Scholastic thought, I shall resume my analysis of the dialectical devel-

---

1 *De Wijsbegeerte der Wetsidee* I (Amsterdam: H. J. Paris, 1935). The expanded and altered translation of this work appeared in Enligh in four Volumes between 1953 and 1958. It is currently available in *Series A* as: *A New Critique of Theoretical Thought* (NC), Volumes A1–A4 of *The Collected Works of Herman Dooyeweerd* (1997), General Editor D.F.M. Strauss, published by The Edwin Mellen Press, Lewiston, NY. The translational equivalent for "De Wijsbegeerte der Wetsidee" employed in NC is: "Philosophy of the Cosmonomic Idea."

opment of Greek thought at the point that I temporarily left it after my analysis of Plato. The third volume, which for the greater part has also been brought to completion, will contain an extensive treatment of the problems of anthropology within the framework of the Philosophy of the Law-Idea. This final volume is intended to comprise an important addition to this philosophy, which will make it possible to gain a more precise insight into its overall design and outworking. It is my fervent hope that many misunderstandings which have persisted regarding my earlier published work will thereby be removed.

I

INTRODUCTION

Initial Survey of the Religious Ground-Motives and the Conflict They Produce between the Reformational and Scholastic Spirits in Philosophy

1. The Four Religious Ground-Motives Underlying the History of Western Philosophic Thought

Beginning with the last decades of the nineteenth century, there appeared within Western philosophy three phenomena whose significance and mutual interconnectedness have become clearer to us as the twentieth century has progressed. First, we are struck by the gradual decay of humanistic philosophy. Beginning with the Renaissance, this philosophy had captured the leading role in Western thought. It had found its culmination in German idealism. After the collapse of the latter, however, it became more and more involved in a crisis of foundations which, to the present, it has been unable to surmount. Second, there appeared at the same time within Roman Catholic circles a great Renaissance of Scholastic philosophy, more particularly of Thomism. This renewal was introduced by the encyclical *Aeterni Patris*, issued by Pope Leo XIII in 1879. Third, this same period witnessed the rise of independent philosophical reflection within the Protestant circles that had remained faithful to the basic principles of the Reformation. Here there has been an endeavor to bring about a true reformation of philosophical thought. At this point, however, this endeavor has remained limited to the modern Calvinistic movement inseparably connected to the name of Abraham Kuyper. Most recently, this movement has borne fruit in the appearance of an independent reformational philosophy, called the Philosophy of the Law-Idea. That these three phenomena are closely related cannot be denied. Behind all of them, without doubt, lies the crisis which has shaken modern Western civilization to its foundations.

The spiritual mainsprings of this civilization have been classical culture, Christianity, and humanism. Far from being homogeneous, these spiritual forces have remained in continual tension with one another. Now, such a tension cannot be removed by means of some artificial "balance of powers"; for if cultural development is to have a clear direction, there must be one guiding force.

In classical Greek civilization, this force was the *polis*, the city-state, as the bearer of the new religion of culture. In the classical Roman era, the same position was occupied by the *res publica* and, shortly thereafter, by the emperorship. These served as the bearers of the religious *imperium* idea. The same was true during the Byzantine era, when the idea of the *sacrum imperium* became reconciled in an external fashion with a persecuted Christendom, after the latter had begun to undermine the foundations of the whole of ancient culture.

The Roman Catholic church succeeded in maintaining a position of cultural hegemony during the Middle Ages. Indeed, the next great cultural crisis did not occur until the advent of the modern Renaissance movement. After the way had been prepared by late Scholastic nominalism, this movement began to divert the stream of influence emanating from ancient culture from the power of the church, after having basically reinterpreted it in the spirit of the budding humanism of the day. At the same time the great movement of the Reformation exerted pressure on the ecclesiastically unified culture of Rome from a fundamentally different standpoint.

In the lands which on the whole had remained faithful to the Roman church, Roman Catholicism regrouped its forces in the Counter-Reformation, creating a favorable climate for the reception of Renaissance culture. In the Protestant countries, meanwhile, the cultural leadership passed for a short time into the hands of the Reformation. Gradually, however, a new trend began to emerge within Western civilization, in which both Rome and the Reformation were forced to retreat from their positions of cultural leadership in the face of the advance of modern humanism. That did not mean that either one was thereby eliminated as a major force in the history of the West. They carried on indestructibly in this role, partly in antagonism to the new world and life view, in which Christianity was secularized into a rational religion of personality, and partly in a variety of pseudo-syntheses with the new humanistic ideas which had been able to enter formatively into history. Neither Rome nor the Reformation was any longer in a position, however, to place its own stamp on Western civilization. For two centuries they were forced onto the defensive in the titanic battle that was raging for control of the spirit of our culture. Temporarily, the position of leadership had been taken over by humanism.

Since the last decades of the nineteenth century, however, we have seen the humanistic world and life view as a whole begin to crumble. Now it, itself, has gradually been forced onto the defensive before the onslaught of new, antihumanistic cultural forces. In the arena of world history we are now faced with a violent transitional period. Within it the struggle for the spiritual leadership of our Western culture is not yet finalized.

In this manifestly chaotic time of transition, the two older, spiritually consolidated cultural powers of the West, Roman Catholicism and the

Reformation, now armed with modern weapons, are once again making themselves felt in this great spiritual battle. Their aim is not merely to stand in defense of the Christian foundations of modern civilization; it is to reassert their claim to leadership in the struggle for the future of Western civilization, which, even in its most immediate prospects, remains shrouded in darkness.

This Promethean struggle has also affected the history of philosophy. In its course of development, Western philosophy reveals its historical dependence on the leading cultural powers. By reason of their commanding position in history, these impress on philosophy too their deepest religious ground-motives.

It is predominantly four of these ground-motives that control the history of Western philosophy.[1] Of them, three are clearly dialectical. That is to say, they are torn by an inner dualism, which constantly induces them to spawn positions in which one factor is set irretrievably in diametrical opposition to the other. It is not only the development of theoretical thought that is ruled by these ground-motives, however; as religious dynamics (δυνάμεις), that is to say, as forces that control one's perspective on life, from its center to its entire circumference, they lie at the foundation of Western cultural development as a whole.

These four ground-motives are the following:

(1)   the *form-matter* motive of Greek antiquity;

(2)   the Scriptural ground-motive of *creation, the fall into sin, and redemption through Christ Jesus in the communion of the Holy Spirit;*

(3)   the Scholastic motive of religious synthesis, introduced by Roman Catholicism, that of *nature and grace*, which attempts to reconcile the former two motives;

(4)   the modern humanistic ground-motive of *nature and freedom*, in which the attempt is made to bring all of the earlier motives into an immanent (*diesseitige*) religious synthesis, concentrated in the human personality.

a.   The Greek Form-Matter Motive

The initial motive, which was first given the name "form-matter" (*morphē* and *hulē*) by Aristotle, was the one that governed Greek thought from the very beginning, in accordance with its religious con-

---

1   Whatever influence Jewish and Arabic philosophy and also Eastern religious philosophy have had on Western thought was able to be exerted only within the framework of the ground-motives peculiar to the latter.

tent.[1] It originated in an unresolved conflict within the Greek religious consciousness between the ground-motive of the older telluric, chthonic, and uranic *nature religions*,[2] on the one hand, in which a proto-Greek nucleus was supplemented by many elements both of indigenous pre-Greek (Minoan) and of foreign origin, and, on the other hand, the ground-motive of the newer *culture religion*, the religion of the Olympic pantheon.[3]

The nature religions varied greatly from one locality to the other in their cultic forms and their peculiar beliefs. Especially because of the lack of deciphered written sources, furthermore, there is much guesswork involved in reconstructing exactly what these forms and beliefs were.[4] Nevertheless, a number of features distinguishing pre-Homeric from later religion can now be established with certainty. H. W. Rüssel summarizes these as follows:

> Pre-Homeric religion did not have gods possessing any particularized form, but rather, at most, certain symbols for the deity, which was itself conceived as invisible. Here there are clear traces of a religion of earth and water, whereas the Olympian reli-

---

1 Thus Aristotle was correct, in the first book of his *Metaphysics*, in treating the entire preceding history of Greek philosophy within the framework of this ground-motive. To be sure, one must exercise a proper critical reserve as to his evaluation of his predecessors, and one must discount his typically Aristotelian terminology and his characteristic attempt at synthesis; nevertheless, I shall demonstrate in detail that the view cannot be maintained that the entire form-matter scheme is nothing more than a fabrication of Aristotle himself.

2 The telluric religions focus their attention on "mother earth" as the origin of life; whereas the chthonic religions are directed more to the inorganic soil, and the uranic to the sky and later also to the sea.

3 The presence of this religious conflict, which Friedrich Wilhelm Nietzsche in his youthful work of genius, *The Birth of Tragedy out of the Spirit of Music* (Leipzig, 1872), characterized as the split between the Apollonian and the Dionysian elements, may be regarded as having been definitively established since the investigations of Johann Jakob Bachofen and Erwin Rohde. For one who is not in a position to acquaint himself with the extensive literature on the development of the Greek religions, the book of H. W. Rüssel, *Antike Welt und Christentum* (Amsterdam/ Leipzig, 1941), pp. 48 ff., is a good source of information, although his presentation is strongly influenced by the Roman Catholic synthesis between the ground-motives of the Greek and the Christian religions. The famous smaller book of Albrecht Dieterich, *Mutter Erde* (1905; 3rd ed., 1925), also remains very instructive. Dieterich was a student of Prof. Usener, to whom I shall refer later.

4 Attempts to decipher the Cretan script, which could be a rich source of information concerning the ancient, pre-Greek (Minoan) forms of religion, have to the present consistently met with failure. Even if these efforts should become successful, however, the reconstruction of the pre-Homeric religions, with their strong local differences, would remain hypothetical in many respects, for there are also many other non-Greek elements lying hidden in them.

gion of Zeus would seem to have arisen from the worship of an originally Indo-Germanic sky-god, i.e., a particular individual deity. ... This ancient religion has the character of nature myth, and like nature itself it is wilder, more unpredictable, and often more cruel and demonic than the gods of Homer. On the other hand, it is also filled with a profound ethical seriousness. The pre-Homeric Greek approached his gods with dread, deep humility, piety, and reverence. His gods were gods of the sacred, unbreakable orders of birth, death, blood, the earth, procreation, and growth. Unlike the male gods of Homer, it was here that female deities stood in the foreground and were sought out by men for help, blessing, and deliverance. The mercy which these deities of mother earth displayed in giving help was equalled, however, by the pitilessness and ineluctability of their curse. Whereas for Homer death is a shadowy thing which is no concern to one who is alive and healthy, since his gods are gods of life, the center of pre-Homeric religion is occupied by death, the cult of the dead, and the conviction that there is a continued existence after death. For this reason the dead were here buried in the mother earth, while in Homer cremation was the usual practice.[1]

Nilsson, Cornford, and others have convincingly demonstrated that this last feature mentioned by Rüssel does not in any way imply that primitive Greek nature religion held to a belief in the personal immortality of the soul.[2] It was only later that the belief in individual immortality, which had been present in Orphic and Pythagorean circles and especially among those who had been initiated into the Eleusinian mysteries, came in any real sense to replace the old nature belief in the immortality of the stream of life throughout the cycle of generations. As we shall see later, this change could not have taken place apart from the influence of the individualizing tendencies of the religion of culture. For, whatever remained in pre-Homeric religion of a belief in the personal immortality of rulers and national heroes who were specially favored by the gods and were granted a blessed second life in the "Elysian fields," lay beyond the sphere of nature religion proper. Perhaps such beliefs were based on a tradition descended from the highly developed religious conceptions of Minoan civilization, which probably originated with the Egyptians, a tradition that in any case meant little to the common people.

Within this pre-Homeric religion of nature there was predominantly a single ground-motive at work, which retained a lasting place in the substratum of the Greek mind. This was the motive of *the divine, eternally flowing stream of life.* Arising from mother earth, this stream of life peri-

---

1   H. W. Rüssel, *op. cit.*, pp. 46 ff. (English version by translator.)
2   Cf., e. g., Martin Persson Nilsson, *Geschichte der griechischen Religion* (Munich, 1941), p. 637; esp. p. 640.

odically, in the cycle of time, brings forth everything that has individual form and shape; but then, inevitably, the latter falls prey to blind, unpredictable fate, to dread Ananke (Ἀνάγκη; necessity), in order that the eternally flowing and formless stream of life might continue on with its cycle of birth, death, and rebirth. This divine stream of life, coursing through everything that has bodily form, is a *psychic fluid*, which is not bound to the limits of the bodily form and thus cannot die with the latter, but which is conceived of nevertheless as material and earthly. The deepest mystery of the "psyche" lies in an ecstatic transcending of one's bodily limits in a mystical absorption into the divine totality of life. In the words of Heraclitus, the obscure thinker of Ephesus, "You could not in your going find the ends of the soul... so deep is its law (*logos*; λόγος)."[1]

In Dionysus, who appears in Homer and Hesiod as the wild god of wine vegetation, the ground-motive spoken of here – which I have designated the Greek *matter motive* in its polar opposition to the form motive of the religion of culture – is embodied in its most pregnant form. It is noteworthy that this deity, whose worship had been imported from Thrace,[2] did not receive a fixed cultural form and a developed personality in the Greek pantheon until he was brought into connection with his antipode, the Delphic god Apollo. For, as we shall see later, Apollo became the most pregnant expression of the Greek *form motive*, even though he too was probably non-Greek in origin, and in spite of the fact that, as an oracular god, he had a contrasting, ecstatic side to his personality.

The young Nietzsche, in his brilliant work, *The Birth of Tragedy*, was acute enough to detect the sharp distinction between these contrasting "night" and "light" sides of Greek religion. Through his influence the opposition between the Dionysian and Apollonian elements in the Greek spirit has become commonplace in the subsequent literature. In no way did this mean, however, that insight had been gained into the radical meaning and the true interrelationship between these two opposing religious motives. Indeed, this was impossible, as long as religion was regarded exclusively from the immanence standpoint and the attempt was made to understand it as a psychological phenomenon or to explain it sociologically.

It should be repeated by way of emphasis that in the ancient religion of nature the deity was not conceived and represented in an established form and a personal shape. The deity itself remained fluid and invisible in the eternally flowing stream of life. There was, however, no abstract unity in

---

1   *Translator's note*: Cf. Kathleen Freeman, *Ancilla to the Pre-Socratic Philosophers: A Complete Translation of the Fragments in Diels*, Fragmente der Vorsokratiker (Cambridge, Mass., 1948), p.27.

2   *Translator's note*: The clause regarding Thrace has been interpolated on the basis of a remark in Herman Dooyeweerd's own *corrigenda* and of his *A New Critique of Theoretical Thought*, I (Philadelphia/ Amsterdam, 1953), p. 62.

the conception of the deity. On the contrary, a boundless multiplicity of divine powers was worshiped, in connection with the immense variety of natural phenomena, which were continually embodied in a flowing and variable notion of the deity.

In this situation, it is understandable that the rise of relatively permanent, discrete individual forms and shapes in nature was felt to be an "injustice," for which, in accordance with the mysterious saying of Anaximander, the Ionian nature philosopher, they must "make reparation to one another... according to the arrangement of Time."[1] Likewise, it is clear how in the telluric religion of Gaia, Demeter, and Dionysus, and at first also in the Eleusinian mystery cult, which was connected to the worship of Demeter and at one time became attached to the cult of Dionysus (Dionysus Iacchus), the belief in the continuity of the divine stream of life through the coming and going of the generations could be a source of comfort in the face of the necessary destruction of all individual life that was embodied in a specific visible form and shape.[2]

In later times also, Dionysus remained the deity in whom life and death were united. As a god with a personal form and shape, he differed from the Olympian culture gods in lacking immortality. His grave was even displayed in the sanctuary at Delphi. In the Orphic doctrine, which I shall discuss later, he became, as Dionysus Zagreus, the suffering god who was torn asunder and devoured by the Titans (here the personification of the principle of evil). In the Orphic mysteries, this suffering of the dying god was symbolically reenacted: in orgiastic frenzy animals were torn to pieces and their flesh was consumed raw, in order that the participants might enter into communion with the suffering of Dionysus. Thereupon, the suffering and death of this god was followed by his miraculous rebirth in a new form.

The connection of pre-Homeric religions with the mystery cult of Eleusis and Samothrace, with the Orphic and Dionysian movement during the religious crisis of the transition period of Greek history, and also with the religious ideas of the tragedians (Aeschylus and Sophocles), of Pindar, and of the Greek philosophers (especially Pythagoras, Empedocles, and Plato) was pointed out as early as the famous book *Psyche*,[3] written by Nietzsche's friend Erwin Rohde. Since then, the scientific study of reli-

---

1 *Translator's note*: Freeman, *op. cit*, p.19.
2 Cf. Nilsson, *op. cit.*, pp. 439-40. In this connection, see also the well-known verses of Aeschylus, in which, according to Wilamowitz, the entire Demeter religion can be discerned: καὶ γαῖαν αὐτήν, ἣ τὰ πάντα τίκτεται, θρέψασά δ᾽ αὖθις τῶνδε κῦμα λαμβάνει. [Choephoroi 127].
3 Erwin Rohde, *Psyche: The Cult of Souls and Belief in Immortality among the Greeks* (tr. from the 8th ed.; London/ New York, 1925).

gion in both its philological[1] and ethnological[2] aspects has further broadened and deepened these insights.

The new culture religion was embodied in the official religion of the Greek *polis* (city-state). It created the first national religious center at Mount Olympus. In contrast to the religion of nature, it was the religion of *rational form, measure, and harmony*. It soon received its most typically Greek expression in the Delphic Apollo, the law-giver. The Olympian deities left "mother earth" and became *immortal, radiant form-gods*, who in their supersensible form and personal shape were equivalent to *idealized and personified cultural powers*.

This new religion, which obtained its most brilliant expression in the epic poetry of Homer, attempted to absorb into itself the older religion, both as to its original Greek[3] and as to its imported and its pre-Greek domestic elements. It attempted to adapt it to its own ground-motive of form, measure, and harmony. In particular, it sought to restrain the ecstatic, telluric worship of Dionysus by means of the lawful form principle of the service of Apollo. At Delphi, Apollo and Dionysus became brothers, with the latter losing his indeterminate wildness and appearing in the more serious role of a "shepherd of souls."

In their theogonies, the ancient Greek theological poets (Homer, Hesiod) and the Orphic seers of the archaic transition period attempted to make clear to the people that the Olympian deities had been brought forth by the formless, fluid nature gods themselves. In the process of becoming set forth in Hesiod's theogony, which along with Homer's theogonic constructions exerted great influence on the development of Greek philo-

1   In this connection particular mention is due the school of Herman Karl Usener, whose work *Götternamen*: *Versuch einer Lehre von der religiösen Begriffsbildung* (Bonn, 1896) had a great influence, even though it met with some criticism.
2   Here I mention only Miss J. E. Harrison, *Prolegomena to the Study of the Greek Religion* (Cambridge/ New York, 1903) and *Themis*: *A Study of the Social Origins of Greek Religion* (Cambridge, 1912, with later editions remaining unchanged). In spite of her often speculative combining of Émile Durkheim's positivistic sociological method with the ideas of Henri Bergson, the French philosopher of life, she has nevertheless made a variety of important discoveries with respect to the ancient Greek religions of nature, in particular that of the ἐνιαυτὸς δαίμων, the representative of vegetative life in its death and revival. Mention can also be made of the influential book *From Religion to Philosophy* (London, 1912) by the Cambridge philosopher F. M. Cornford, whose work also has strong ties with Durkheim's sociology. Cf. also the book *Zeus* (I, 1914; II, 1925), by A. B. Cook, who belongs to this same school.
3   The elements belonging to the proto-Greek religion undoubtedly included the original partriarchal service of Zeus, the sky god, of Poseidon, the sea god, of Athena, as a household goddess, and of Hestia, the goddess of the hearth, and also the cult of the forefathers. Cf. Nilsson, *op. cit.*, pp. 313 ff.

sophical thought, the formless confusion of Chaos[1] arises first, and there-after mother earth (Gaia) and the underworld. Simultaneously, there appears *eros* or sexual love, the principle of the divine stream of life and the driving force in the development from chaos to cosmos. From the marriage of Gaia and Uranus, the first sky god, come Cronus and Rhea. The latter, in turn, bring forth Zeus and his two brothers, who subsequently dethrone Cronus.

All of these attempts at synthesis were doomed, however, for three reasons:

(1)   The new culture religion ignored the deepest problems of life and death. The Olympian deities offered protection to man only so long as he was strong and healthy. They withdrew themselves when the dark power of *Ananke* or *Moira*, against which even Zeus, the supreme sky god, was powerless, sounded the death knell over those who were under their protection. In the words of Homer, "Not even the gods can fend it away from a man they love, when once the destructive doom of leveling death has fastened upon him."[2]

(2)   As a mere culture religion, the religion of Olympus in its mythological, Homeric form clashed with the ethical standards of the Greek people. For although the morality of the Greeks stood under the protection and sanction of the Olympian gods, the latter themselves, as Homer presented them, lived "beyond good and evil." They engaged in adultery and theft, and mythology glorified deceit, if only it was contrived "in a divine manner."

(3)   The resplendent divine assemblage of Olympus was too far removed from the ordinary people. In the historical form in which it was cast, the Homeric world of the gods was appropriate to Greek civilization only during the feudal age of Mycenean knighthood, and it lost any real contact with society at large as soon as the role of the knight had been played out. After this, it could find support only in the power of the Greek *polis*. It was precisely during the critical transition period from the era of Mycenean knighthood to the Persian wars, when the Greek *polis* endured its crucial test in splendid fashion, that the religious crisis arose which Nilsson characterizes as the conflict between the ecstatic (mystical) and legalistic tendencies.[3] The former, which came to expression in the

---

1   It appears unacceptable to me that the word "chaos" in Hesiod (Theog. 116) should mean "gaping, immeasurable empty space." An "empty space" cannot procreate; but that is exactly what Hesiod's chaos does (*ibid.*, p.123).
2   Homer, *Odyssey* (Lattimore translation; New York, 1967), p. 57.
3   Nilsson, *op. cit.*, pp. 578 ff.

so-called Dionysian and Orphic movements, which I shall discuss later, was a revival and reformation of the suppressed older religion,[1] while the latter found its typical representative in Hesiod as a defender of the newer religion of culture.

For these reasons, then, it is understandable that the Greeks, while honoring the Olympian deities as the official gods of the *polis*, should have held fast in their private lives to the ancient religions of nature and of life, and that the deeper religious impulses of the masses should have drawn them especially to the mystery cultus, where the problems of life and death stood at the center. Already in the sixth century before Christ, the culture religion, in the mythological form given it by Homer, had been seriously undermined. The criticism to which it was subjected in intellectual circles became increasingly bold, and the Sophist movement, the "Greek Enlightenment," scoffed at it with relative impunity, even though there was a certain amount of reaction which took the form of trials against atheism.

Nevertheless, the *dialectical religious ground-motive* which had been engendered in the Greek consciousness by the encounter between the older nature religions and the Olympian culture religion continued to live on, and after the influence of mythology had been undermined, it was able to undergo modification in philosophical circles, clothing itself in beliefs and ideas that were more appropriate to the religious needs of the time. This dialectical ground-motive, which had come to expression as early as Homer and Hesiod in the opposition between the dark *Moira* and the rational power of Zeus, retained the imprint of this conflict between the eternal flow of all forms, an irrational principle which remained bound to the earth, and the "supermundane" rational and immortal form principle, which is not subject to the stream of becoming.

The matter principle of formless fluidity (which is essentially oriented to the conception of the bio-organic aspect of temporal reality as being "animated" or endowed with soul), in its indissoluble connection with *Anankē*, the threatening, unpredictable power of fate, gives to Greek thought a typically obscure, mystical cast which is foreign to modern, natural scientific thinking. In contrast, the form principle (which in essence is oriented to the *cultural aspect* of temporal reality) continually directs the mind to the supersensible and imperishable form of reality, which does not allow itself to be grasped in a mere concept, but is rather to be intuited in a non-sensible, luminous figure or form. This too is a primeval Greek trait. The Olympian deities were held to be imperishable, luminous fig-

---

1 Concerning this religious reaction, cf. Albert Rivaud, *Le problème du devenir et la notion de la matière dans la philosophie grecque depuis les origines jusqu'à Théophraste* (Paris, 1906), chapter X; cf. also Otto Kern, *Die Religion der Griechen*, II (Berlin, 1935), p. 182.

ures beyond the reach of sense perception. In like manner, the Greek could only conceive that which exists immutably in a shining non-sensible form.

That this form principle is related to the theoretical *intuition of forms* comes to clear expression in the Greek terms *eidos* (εἶδος) and *idea* (ἰδέα), which play a very important role in Platonic and Aristotelian philosophy. Both of these terms are derived from the stem *ΙΔ* (ἰδεῖν, to see, to intuit). They cannot be understood apart from the Greek form motive. The same applies to the Greek idea of theory (*theōria*; θεωρία) to which I shall repeatedly turn in the course of my investigation. *Theōria* too continually involves the activity of observation, which attempts to apprehend the concept in a non-sensible form or figure.

Within the religious ground-motive of Greek thought, however, the principles of form and matter are unbreakably interrelated, in the sense that they mutually presuppose each other. In their dialectical interrelationship they determine the Greek conception of the "nature" (*physis*) of things. At one point, this might well be looked for in the "ensouled" fluid continuum of the matter principle, or, at another point, exclusively in the supersensible rational form principle. For the most part, however, it is sought in a dialectical synthesis of the two. This dialectical ground-motive leads Greek thought into true polar antitheses and causes it to diverge into movements that seem to oppose each other radically. These, however, manifest their underlying affinity within this ground-motive itself. The Greek intellectual community was rooted in this ground-motive, and for this reason it is quite impossible to understand the history of Greek philosophy in its uniqueness without having come to grips with it.

In this first volume I shall present a survey of this development up to and including Plato. My critical investigation of Scholastic philosophy in the second volume will also present the opportunity of examining later Greek and, in particular, Aristotelian philosophy in the light of the Greek ground-motive. In keeping with the overall design of this work, the anthropological questions will stand at the center of inquiry. Thereby, the transcendental critique of Western thought, which I initiated in my *Philosophy of the Law-Idea* (Volume I, part II), will be brought to a provisional completion.

b. The Scriptural Ground-Motive of the Christian Religion:
Creation, the Fall into Sin, and Redemption

The second ground-motive is that of *creation, the fall into sin, and redemption through Christ Jesus in the communion of the Holy Spirit.* Tying in with Old Testament Judaism, the Christian religion introduced this theme into Western thought as a new communal religious motive, which, already in its doctrine of creation, placed itself in diametrical opposition to the ground-motive of ancient philosophy.

As the authentic revelation of God's Word, this motive is distinguished by its *integral* and *radical* character. That is, it penetrates to the *root* of created reality. As the Creator, God reveals himself as the absolute and integral origin of all things. No self-sufficient, equally primordial power stands over against him. For this reason, no expression of a dualistic principle of origin can be found within the created cosmos.

In the powerful words of the 139th Psalm, this integral character of the Scriptural creation motive is expressed in an unsurpassed manner:

Where can I go from your Spirit?
Where can I flee from your presence?
If I go up to the heavens, you are there;
if I make my bed in the depths, you
are there.

If I rise on the wings of the dawn,
if I settle on the far side of the sea,
even there your hand will guide me,
your right hand will hold me fast.

If I say, "Surely the darkness will hide me
and the light become night around me,"
even the darkness will not be dark to you;
the night will shine like the day,
for darkness is as light to you. (NIV)

Truly, the message of this psalm stands at the antipodes of the Greek dualism of the form and matter motives.

In the revelation that he created humankind after his own image, God disclosed humankind to itself in the fundamental religious unity of its creaturely existence, where the entire meaning of the temporal cosmos had been comprehensively focused. According to God's plan of creation, the integral Origin of all things finds its creaturely image in the human heart. The human heart is thus the integral, individual-spiritual fundamental unity of all the functions and structures of temporal reality. Drawn together at the point where human life has its spiritual center, these functions and structures were supposed to be directed towards the absolute Origin, as human beings completely surrender themselves in loving service to God and their neighbor. This revelation had the effect of cutting off at its root the religious dualism of the Greek form-matter motive, which comes to its clearest expression in the religious antithesis found in Greek anthropology between a material body and a theoretical mental substance having the character of pure form.

Inseparably related to the revelation of creation is that of the fall into sin. In the dialectical ground-motives sin has no place in its radical Scriptural sense. Indeed, it cannot play a role there, because one can understand it properly only as he is possessed of the genuine, radical self-knowledge that is the fruit of divine revelation. Within the religious consciousness of the Greeks, the only thing that obtained recognition was the conflict between the principles of form and matter. Modern humanism simply replaced this opposition with that between the world of sense, or nature, which was ruled by the mechanical law of causation, and the "rational autonomous freedom" of human personality. Even in its more profound Kantian conception, the description of this conflict could reach no further than the acknowledgment of an evil moral inclination in man to allow his actions to be guided by his sensual passions rather than by the moral law. In neither case, however, is the opposition one that occurs in the religious root of man's life. In both it takes place only in the temporal ramifications of human existence, where it is merely absolutized in a religious sense. As a consequence, the sense of guilt could not avoid being dialectical in character, consisting in a depreciation of one side of the cosmos in favor of a contrasting, deified side. We shall see later on that the Romanistic conception also eliminated the radicality of the fall by conceiving of sin as nothing more than the loss of a "supernatural gift of grace."

In contrast, the Word of God in its revelation concerning the fall into sin pierces through to the root, the religious center, of human nature. As apostasy from God, the fall took place in the integral center, the heart and soul, of human existence. As alienation from the absolute Source of life, it was spiritual death. The fall, therefore, was radical, and precisely for this reason it affected the temporal cosmos in its entirety, since the latter is brought to its fundamental religious unity only in man. Every conception that denies this radical meaning of the fall, even though it retains the word "radical," as in Kant's ethical teaching concerning the "radical evil" in human nature, stands diametrically opposed to the ground-motive of Scripture and does not know man, nor God, nor the abysmal depth of sin.

The revelation of the fall into sin, for its part, has no room for an autonomous principle of origin standing over against the Creator. Sin is unable, therefore, to introduce an ultimate dualism into the created cosmos. Satan himself is merely a creature who in his created freedom voluntarily apostasized from God.

The Divine Word, whom the Gospel of John declares to have created all things, was made flesh in Christ Jesus. Thus the Word entered into both the root and the temporal ramifications, into the soul and body, of human nature. Just for this reason the redemption accomplished by the Word is a radical one. It was the regeneration of man and thereby of the entire created temporal cosmos, which had been religiously concentrated in man. In his creative Word, through whom all things have been made and who has become flesh in the person of the Redeemer, God also preserves the fallen cosmos through his common grace (*gratia communis*) until the coming of the final judgment. At that time, the redeemed creation will be freed from its participation in the sinful root of human nature and will be allowed to shine in a higher perfection. Then the righteousness of God will radiate even through Satan and his kingdom in confirmation of the absolute sovereignty of the Creator.

Thus, as long as it is understood in its pure, Scriptural sense, this religious ground-motive in no way manifests in itself a dialectical, dualistic character. When it entered into the Hellenistic world of thought, however, it found itself threatened from every direction.

Already by the first centuries of its existence, the Christian church was forced to engage in a life or death struggle in order to prevent the Greek ground-motive from overrunning and conquering that of the Christian religion. In this conflict there was the formulation of the dogma of the oneness of the divine nature (*homoousia*) of the Father and the Son, and shortly thereafter, that of both of these with the Holy Spirit. Moreover, the dangerous influence of Gnosticism within Christian thought was brought to an end. Before this time, the so-called Apologists as well as the Alexandrian school of Clement and Origen had indulged in a form of *Logos* speculation borrowed from the Judaic-Hellenistic synthesis philosophy of Philo. In its conception of the Divine Word (*Logos*) as a demi-god, this line of thinking gave expression to a fundamental denaturing of the Christian ground-motive and transformed the Christian religion into a higher moral doctrine (in the case of the Alexandrians, into a moralistically-tinted religious-philosophical system), wherein a great variety of influences from the ground-motive of Greek philosophy came into play. The Gnostics as well as Marcion (second century A. D.) also attempted to divorce the Old and the New Testaments, and it was above all through its preservation of the unbreakable unity between these that the Christian church under God's direction was able at this time to conquer the religious dualism, introduced by Gnosticism, which drove a wedge between creation and redemption and thereby reverted to a dualistic principle of origin.

In the orthodox Patristics, philosophic thought then reached its high point with Aurelius Augustine, who placed his stamp on Christian philosophy until the thirteenth century and who continued as an important influence even after that time. No one was yet in a position, however, to achieve a sufficiently independent expression of the Christian ground-motive within philosophical thought itself. In particular, there existed at this time great unclarity concerning the relationship of philosophy to dogmatic theology, because the inner connection of philosophic thought to the religious ground-motives had not yet been discovered. The Christian character of philosophy was sought in its relationship of subordination to dogmatic theology,[1] a relationship that was so conceived that all philosophical issues were treated within a scientific theological framework. In this way, Christian philosophy (*philosophia christiana*) and Christian the-

---

1   Here we may already observe that the view that philosophy is the handmaiden of

ology came to be identified, and under the influence of the Greek idea of *theōria*, the threat repeatedly arose of even identifying this theology with the Christian religion. Later on I shall deal with all of these points at length, and in so doing I shall turn my transcendental critique on Christian thought itself.

Under these circumstances, there was no objection to taking over lock, stock, and barrel many important elements from ancient philosophy, for the ground-motive of the latter had not yet been clearly discerned as to its pagan character. Thus theologians resorted to adapting or accommodating heathen thought to the doctrine of the Christian church. As we shall observe later on, this led of necessity to an uncritical reception of a large amount of heathen conceptual matter into Christian philosophy. In turn, theology too was infected at more than one point by the uncritical adoption of Greek philosophical doctrines.

In Augustine's thought, however, at least the Christian ground-motive was on the whole preserved intact. Here then there is no question of a standpoint of a truly religious synthesis, which deliberately aims to unite the Scriptural and the Greek ground-motives.[1]

c. The Romanistic Scholastic Synthesis Motive of Nature and Grace

The attempt to bridge the radical antithesis between the Greek and the Christian ground-motives led in the period of the ecclesiastically unified culture under the sway of Romanism to a new basic dialectical theme, that of nature and grace. It is this motive that placed its distinctive imprint on medieval Scholasticism. With its internally unresolved dualism it also continued to dominate reformational thought to a significant extent. That was the case even though the Reformation had overcome it in principle by returning to the Scriptural doctrine of the radical meaning for human nature of the fall into sin, which had also been defended by Augustine, and to the confession of justification by faith alone. Indeed, the reformational theology of Luther and especially that of Calvin took great initial strides toward freeing the Scriptural ground-motive from its entanglement with Scholastic philosophy; nevertheless, there remained important Scholastic remnants in Reformation theology. And since, as I shall demonstrate, theology as a science cannot do without philosophi-

---

theology (*ancilla theologiae*) is nothing else than a transposition of the Aristotelian concept of the "science of the end of all things and of the good" (i. e., metaphysical theology), as the queen of the sciences, which "...the other sciences, like slave-women, may not even contradict...." Cf. Aristotle, *Metaphysics*, B 996 b 10: "For inasmuch as it is most architectonic and authoritative and the other sciences, like slave-women, may not even contradict it, the science of the *end* and of the *good* is of the nature of Wisdom (for the other things are for the sake of the end)." Aristotle, *Metaphysics* (tr. W. D. Ross; Oxford, 1908; second ed., 1928).

1   In this regard, Augustine's use of the terms "nature" and "grace" is not decisive. He preserves intact the integral and radical character of the Scriptural ground-motive.

cal foundations, and since the way to an inner reformation of philosophy certainly had not yet been found, the "school philosophy" soon regained its influence under Melanchthon. As a consequence, there arose beside that of Rome a Protestant brand of Scholasticism, which shared with its Roman sister the dialectical synthesis motive of nature and grace, even though it gave to this motive a new twist, which was more adapted to the theology of the Reformation.

The dialectical and internally dualistic character of this new ground-motive is latent in the attempt to reconcile the Greek (in particular the Aristotelian) conception of the nature (*physis*) of things, which was completely determined by the dualistic form-matter theme, with the Scriptural conception of the nature of created reality, which is based on the divine order of creation. In the Scholastic views of man, this motive came to pregnant expression in the notion that the relationship of the human soul and body is that between an *anima rationalis*, as substantial form, and a material body. With its affinities to the dialectical form-matter motive, this conception left no room for insight into the fundamental religious unity of created human existence. Neither could it be harmonized, in its consistent elaboration, with the radical meaning of the fall into sin and of redemption.

As long as this ground-motive controlled philosophy, it continually led to the appearance of typically dialectical tensions within Christian thought. At one time, the latter would be driven in a dangerous pagan direction, which ascribed the primacy to nature in its typically Scholastic sense; at another time, it would be driven in a no less perilous mystical direction, which to the neglect of the creation motive identified nature with sin and sought to flee nature in a mystical experience of grace. Yet a third possibility was an outright dualism, which ascribed a complete independence to nature and wanted to make a radical separation between nature and grace. In this process, the way was once again opened in Christian thought for the influence of Gnosticism, as well as for the semi-Pauline theory of Marcion with its dualistic distinction between the imperfect Creator God of the Old Testament and the perfect Redeemer God of the New.

As long as this ground-motive itself was maintained, it was only the Roman ecclesiastical authorities who were in a position to keep this religious pseudosynthesis alive, by officially condemning heresies in the Scholastic philosophy. In this effort, they found their greatest support in the solution offered by Thomas Aquinas, who posited nature as the autonomous but subordinate "preamble" of grace or supernature. Further, the mutual relationship between these was conceived as that between matter and form. Thus Thomas came to his solution with the aid of the same device that had already done service in the Greek intellectual community to bind together two antagonistic religious ground-motives.

In the second volume of this work, this Scholastic synthesis, as it worked itself out within the philosophical thought which it governed, will assume an important place and will be subjected to a transcendental critique. In the present connection our aim is only to obtain a clear insight into the nature of the ground-motive itself. To do this, however, it will be necessary for us to embark on a more detailed investigation of the relationship of what is truly *religious* dialectic to what is called *theoretical* dialectic. This inquiry, in turn, will inevitably drive us to examine more closely the relationship of the synthesis motive of nature and grace to that of form and matter.

d. The Modern Humanistic Ground-Motive of Nature and Freedom

Finally, the fourth major ground-motive is that of *nature* and *freedom*. It arose at the time of the Renaissance out of the modern humanistic religion of personality and of science. This motive sought gradually to assimilate the three older ground-motives into itself, by subjecting them to a complete metamorphosis.

This motive first appeared in Western thought in a specific form at a particular historical juncture. The internal dialectic of the Romanistic synthesis of nature and grace had led the thought of late-medieval Scholasticism into an open dualism between the Christian religion and natural life. Moreover, the ecclesiastically unified culture, which had succeeded in bringing all of the spheres of temporal life under the aegis of the church, had begun to disintegrate. Then there arose a religion of the human personality, which gradually secularized the Christian motive of "freedom in Christ Jesus" into a new ideal of personality. This ideal culminated in the idea of the absolute *autonomy* or self-legislation of the human personality, centered in its reason. It turned with revolutionary fervor against any and all authoritarian restrictions imposed on human thought by the church or by the divine Word-revelation. Within this personality ideal, the creation motive was also secularized. Here it came to signify the domination of reality in its entire extent by a new, "creative" method of thought, which stood in contrast to the purely intuitive approach of Greek and Scholastic philosophy.

Hand in hand with this new *freedom motive* of the humanistic ideal of personality, there developed a new conception of nature. This differed both from the Greek conception of *physis* and from the Scholastic view of nature in a most basic fashion. Here nature was viewed as the macrocosmic reflection of the human personality, as a cosmos that offered infinite possibilities for the deployment of man's creative powers. Nature was emancipated both from the grip of the dark matter-motive of Greek thought and from the Christian motive of the fall into sin. It was regarded as independent of all supernatural powers and influences.

In Renaissance philosophy, Giordano Bruno deified this novel view of nature as "nature naturating" (*natura naturans*). Renaissance art also brought it to clear expression. When shortly thereafter Galileo and Isaac Newton laid the foundations of modern mathematical natural science, thus pointing the way to the control of natural phenomena by means of capturing them in mathematical formulations, within an absolutely determined network of causes, the humanistic personality ideal seized on this new scientific method with true religious zeal and elevated it to the position of the classical ideal of science, which aimed to reconstruct reality in all its aspects according to its own standards. At first this science ideal constructed a new metaphysics. This vaunted its ability to grasp the true nature of reality with the help of mathematically oriented natural scientific thought, placing itself thereby in sharp opposition to the Aristotelian-scholastic metaphysics of substantial forms. Furthermore, even after this metaphysics collapsed under the weight of the criticisms of David Hume and Kant, the deterministic ideal of science continued to assert its right of domain over the whole of nature.

From the beginning, this new science ideal, which was spawned by the personality ideal itself, came into dialectical tension with the latter, a tension which since Kant has generally been described as that between *nature* and *freedom*. According to this view, nature is to be seen as reality conceived, in accordance with the deterministic ideal of science, as a closed chain of cause and effect, which comes to expression in "natural law-conformity" or "natural necessity." Freedom, by contrast, is the personality ideal of free, autonomous self-determination. The latter cannot tolerate the determinism with respect to human activity which is claimed by the natural sciences; it requires that personality govern its own conduct in accordance with norms or rules of propriety which are established by autonomous reason.

Under the influence of the classical ideal of science, Kant continued to view this freedom motive in a rationalistic and individualistic fashion. In Romanticism and within the sphere of what is called "absolute idealism," however, it was given an irrationalistic and universalistic (transpersonalistic) turn. The critical boundary line which Kant had drawn between nature and freedom was no longer respected. Indeed, the freedom motive forced the classical science ideal to retreat even on the terrain of nature. The attempt was made to discover hidden traces of freedom even within nature itself and to arrive at a dialectical synthesis of the two opposing religious motives by the route of theoretical dialectic.

In its new irrationalistic and universalistic form, the freedom motive also gave birth to a new science ideal, one that turned away from mathematical natural science and took its cue from the science of history. Here the concern was no longer to discover universal laws which would make it possible for one completely to determine and govern the course of phenomena; rather, it was to obtain an understanding of the individual, unrepeatable phenomenon, in terms of its historical and super-individual context, according to a method appropriate to the human sciences (a *geisteswissenschaftliche* method).

In attempting to grasp everything in its historical determination, this new science ideal took its point of departure in a historicistic view of reality. Just like the classical science ideal, however, it eventually came into conflict with the freedom motive which had given it birth. In its historicism it destroyed the belief in the eternal validity of the ideas of freedom and humanity. The dialectical pseudo-synthesis which freedom idealism had made between nature and freedom thus dissolved once again into a polar antithesis, and this ultimately led to the undermining of the belief in the value of human personality itself. Historicism, disengaged from freedom idealism, then moved in a positivistic direction, and for a time it allied itself with the evolutionary approach of Darwinism and with modern sociology as the latter took its cue from the natural sciences. In the twentieth century, however, as historicism extended its influence still further, it even undermined the belief in evolution. As a final consequence, both the ideal of science and the ideal of personality became involved in a process of religious uprooting.

In this entire development, the dialectical character of the humanistic ground-motive comes into sharp relief. Until the end of the previous century it had undergirded the thought of the Western community at large. Through its absolute supremacy in modern culture, it had also impressed its conceptual pattern in many ways upon Catholic and reformational thought, at least insofar as these intellectual currents did not want to have themselves banned from the scientific community.

Since in the first volume of my *Philosophy of the Law-Idea* I have already presented such a lengthy analysis of the dialectic of this ground-motive as it has come to expression in the history of modern Western thought, I shall confine myself at the appropriate place in this work to presenting a brief survey in which this development is summarized as incisively as possible. At the same time, this will shed additional light on the causes of the present crisis, which has affected the very foundations of modern philosophy.

In the present context, I need only point out that, after it had secularized the ground-motive of the Christian religion, the humanistic ground-motive gradually attempted to assimilate both the Greek and Scholastic ground-motives as well. For example, both Leibniz and Kant made use of the form-matter motive in this way. Both of these humanistic thinkers, furthermore, introduced the motive of nature and grace into their philosophical systems. As I shall later demonstrate in detail, however, both of these motives were deprived thereby of their original religious content and were transformed into mere intellectual schemata in the service of the humanistic ground-motive of nature and freedom.

2. The Relationship between Religious and Theoretical Dialectic[1]

a. The Communal Character of the Religious Ground-Motives and the Use of the Critical Method in the Investigation of the History of Philosophy

None of the above ground-motives is intrinsically theoretical or scientific. On the contrary, they are all religious in character. That is to say, they have an absolutely central meaning for the whole of life. They exert, therefore, as we have already noted, an influence at the heart of the cultural development and of the entire spiritual and intellectual structure of the West, far beyond the range of philosophic thought. They are, moreover, genuinely communal, for they control the outlook on thought and life of the individual, regardless of whether that person is aware of it or not.

If there is to be a truly critical method for the scientific investigation of the history of Western philosophy, it is above all necessary to trace these four ground-motives, both in their original meaning and in the complicated formal interlacements in which they became involved in their historical development. The philosophical problematics are determined by these ground-motives, and, as I shall demonstrate in detail in my transcendental critique of philosophic thought, any attempt to extricate them from the latter is uncritical and unscientific. Any such attempt could never make it possible to describe the history of philosophy as a purely scientific development; it would only result in one's imposing on an earlier philosophical period the religious ground-motive controlling one's own thinking, whose significance one had not yet understood. In fact, one would have effectively closed the door thereby to a correct understanding of that period.[2]

---

1 In this connection, see my essay "De vier religieuze grondthema's in den ontwikkelingsgang van het wijsgerig denken van het Avondland: Een bijdrage tot bepaling van de verhouding tusschen theoretische en religieuze dialektiek," *Philosophia Reformata*, VI (1941), pp. 161-179.

2 This applies, for example, to a widely accepted interpretation of Greek philosophy, which views it in terms of the modern humanistic ground-motive of nature and freedom. Cf. the discussion of B. J. H. Ovink's final work, *Philosophie und Sophistik* (The Hague, 1940), in my essay "Een tweegesprek met Prof. Ovink over dogmatische en critische wijsbegeerte: Naar aanleiding van *Philosophie und Sophistik* door Prof. Dr. B. J. H. Ovink," *Gereformeerde Theologische Tijdschift* (42nd year, no. 5), pp. 209-227.

b. *The Religious Ground-Motives and the Modern Historicistic Pattern of Thought*

At this point I must hasten to warn against a basic misunderstanding. It is indeed true that modern historicistic thought is readily inclined to admit that each period in the history of philosophic thought must be interpreted in terms of its own ground-motive. It will, however, conceive of these religious ground-motives themselves as dynamic forces of a merely historical-psychological kind, which are accessible as such to theoretical-scientific investigation, free from any religious bias.[1] It might even come to the insight, along with Wilhelm Dilthey, one of the most brilliant and perceptive trailblazers of this school of thought, that "...the religious life is the constant substratum of intellectual development, not a passing phase in the mental development of humankind."[2] Thereupon it will attempt to understand this religious life itself merely in terms of a "fundamental lived experience" (*Erlebnis*), however, in which humanity through its entire course of historical development had the experience of its "personal freedom over against the confines of nature," the experience of "guilt and conscience," and of "the contrast pervading all areas of the inner life between the imperfect and the perfect, the transitory and the eternal, together with the longing of man for the latter." This entire religious lived experience was then thought to be founded on the consciousness of an "absolute dependence of the subject."[3] On this supposition, the various ground-motives could only be the historical manifesta-

---

1   The positivistic sociological school of Émile Durkheim, of course, will attempt to explain these "psychical dynamic forces," which it sees at work in religion, in terms of the historical organization of social life. It too will readily concede, however, that these religious dynamic forces are fundamental historical-social powers, which also determine the direction of thought. Professor Cornford, whom I have already mentioned, also understands Greek philosophy essentially in this way, as "the analysis of religious material." *op. cit.*, p. 125.
2   "das religiöse Leben der dauernde Untergrund der intellektuellen Entwicklung ist, nicht eine vorübergehende Phase im Sinnen der Menschheit...." Wilhelm Dilthey, *Einleitung in die Geisteswissenschaften. Gesammelte Schriften*, I (Leipzig/ Berlin, 1923), p. 38. (English version by translator.)
3   Cf. *ibid.*, p. 137: "Nun sind Erfahrungen solcher Art die Freiheit des Menschen, Gewissen und Schuld, alsdann der alle Gebiete des inneren Lebens durchziehende Gegensatz des Unvollkommenen und Vollkommenen, des Vergänglichen und Ewigen sowie die Sehnsucht des Menschen nach dem letzteren. Und zwar sind diese inneren Erfahrungen Bestandteile des religiösen Lebens. Dasselbe umfasst aber zugleich das Bewusstsein einer unbedingten Abhängigkeit des Subjekts."

tion of this original religious lived experience, which allegedly resides at the foundation of the entire historical process of development.

By this line of reasoning, however, Dilthey actually does away with the religious ground-motives in their true sense. In spite of his many fine observations in his exposition of the development of Western thought since the Greeks, Dilthey does not give adequate account of these religious ground-motives as to their content and their significance for this development. The "psychological analysis" of "fundamental lived experience," which constitutes Dilthey's point of departure, completely overlooks the fact that in their concrete meaning, all of the "experiences" which he ascribes to the content of this feeling are entirely dependent on the religious ground-motives themselves. The latter, in turn, being in themselves neither psychological nor historical in nature, lie at the foundation of every scientific psychological analysis. The concrete religious understanding of such things as "personal freedom" and the "confines of nature," "guilt" and "conscience," "perfection," "transitoriness," and "eternity" is in the last analysis determined by a religious ground-motive, which controls from its very center one's entire perspective on life and thought. For the consciousness of the Greek these were something radically other than for Christian consciousness, which lives out of the ground-motive of the divine Word-revelation. Furthermore, the Roman, Scholastic understanding of these also differed, in the most basic way, from that of modern humanism. In other words, it is precisely in the central sphere of religion, which transcends temporal life, that the antithesis between attitudes concerning life and thought becomes absolute and admits of no synthesis.

c. *The Fundamental Critical Problem in the Study of the History
    of Western Philosophy. The Intellectual Community of the
    West*

This state of affairs gave rise to an extremely difficult and complex problem, which confronts any truly critical study of the history of philosophy. The religious ground-motives which have controlled the course of development of Western philosophy introduce truly radical caesuras into it, because they themselves are not merely historical or psychological but are rather transcendent and religious in nature. If we are not to cut the ground out from under a truly scientific investigation of the history of philosophy, however, we must hold fast to the idea of a common and universally valid *structure* of theoretical thought, as well as to the existence of a *historical* community of *patterns* of thought in the West, and a *historical continuity* in the development of Western philosophy. How can we hold on to both these discontinuities and these continuities without falling into internal contradiction?

In order to give a satisfying answer to this question, I should have to proceed immediately to an exposition of my transcendental critique of theoretical thought in general and of philosophical thought in particular, as it was already developed in germ in my three-volume *Philosophy of the Law-Idea.*[1] The design of this present work requires, however, that I postpone this critique to a later point. At that juncture, I shall be in a position to elucidate the necessity of the central role of the religious ground-motives, by way of an analysis of the structure of theoretical thought itself.

d.   *The Scholastic Approach to This Problem. The Natural*
     Community of Thought Based on the Autonomy of Natural
     Reason

In the present context, I shall confine myself to warning against a frivolous evasion of the problem I have formulated. Thomistic Scholasticism, which is rooted in the ground-motive of nature and grace, thrusts this problem aside with an appeal to the autonomy of natural reason. This reason is judged to be capable of achieving insight into the universally valid truth of nature, independently of religion. Thomistic Scholasticism takes its point of departure, therefore, in a "natural community of thought," which is not susceptible to influence from differences of religious standpoint. This particular view of the problem, however, is completely determined by the Romanistic ground-motive. Scholasticism seeks a foundation for this natural community of thought in a metaphysics. Modern humanism, which just as definitely takes its point of departure in an "autonomous natural intellectual community of mankind," rejects this Scholastic metaphysics as a matter of principle. The upshot of the matter is that the Scholastic conception of the autonomy of natural reason differs in a most basic way both from that of the Greeks and from that of modern humanism. At a later point I shall demonstrate in detail how this fundamental difference is once again completely determined by the respective religious ground-motives.

e.   *Dilthey's So-Called Hermeneutical Method with Respect to*
     This Problem. The "Fundamental Religious Sense" of
     Humanity and "historisch freischwebende Intelligenz"[2]

In the recent crisis of foundations of the Western intellectual community, the historicistic way of thinking, with an air of scientific neutrality,

---

1   *Editorial note*: Dooyeweerd consistently made the claim that this work, *De Wisbegeerte der Wetsidee* (Amsterdam, 1935-1936), contained a transcendental critique, even though it was not formally elaborated. A version of the transcendental critique, in its formal elaboration, appears in the English edition (revised and enlarged) of the above work, *A New Critique of Theoretical Thought* (4 vols.; Amsterdam/ Philadelphia, 1953-1957; The Collected Works of Herman Dooyeweerd, A Series, The Edwin Mellen Press, 1997).

2   *Translator's note*: Intelligence "freely floating" with respect to history, i. e., historically unbound or undetermined.

has also claimed to occupy a position above the diversity of philosophical movements and to be capable of placing itself within every standpoint in an unbiased manner with the aid of an "empathetic hermeneutic." To this a truly critical approach must of necessity respond by inquiring as to the foundation on which this method itself is based.

Once Dilthey's conception of "the religious lived experience of humanity" has been unmasked as a residue of the classical humanistic idea of a "natural religion of humanity," an idea that was completely determined by the ground-motive of humanism, the vicious circle involved in this effort to overcome "intellectual dogmatism" comes into sharp relief. If one concedes with Dilthey that the religious life is the constant substratum of intellectual development, one can no longer share this thinker's expectation that the historical manner of thought "will free scientific thinking from the last remnants of its dogmatic subjection to religious prejudgments." For to accomplish this the thought of the scientific historian would have to be capable of assuming a position above the religious ground-motives, which as a matter of fact determine the entire point of departure and direction of this thought. In fact, if scientific thought cannot even disengage itself from its *historical* fetters, and if even the mere search for a "historisch freischwebende Intelligenz"[1] must be dismissed from the outset as an impossibility, how much less will scientific thought be able to elevate itself above its religious ground-motive, which determines its entire point of departure and direction!

Dilthey seeks a way out of this difficulty by conjuring up an "impersonal cosmic-historical consciousness of humanity," which is supposed to be rooted in a religious lived experience that belongs to one by nature. By entering into this consciousness and abandoning his own individual historical determination, a thinker is supposedly able to give an unbiased interpretation of the cultural development reflected in it, in terms of its unique cosmic life-center. This "impersonal historical consciousness of cultural development," however, which allegedly merely comes to self-reflection in the critical-historical manner of thought, is a quintessential metaphysical construct. This is indeed the case, even though Dilthey himself regards metaphysics as the great obstacle to the development of truly critical thinking. This construction is nothing else than Hegel's metaphysical idea of reason in history (*Vernunft in der Geschichte*), transposed into the framework of a historicistic life-philosophy (*Lebens-*

---

1   I have borrowed this term, with a slight variation, from Karl Mannheim's *Ideology and Utopia: An Introduction to the Sociology of Knowledge* (Second German edition of: *Ideologie und Utopia*, 1930, p.126; English translation, New York, 1968). The book itself speaks of a *sozial freischwebende Intelligenz*, but it means thereby an intelligence that has freed itself of all social-historical determinations.

24

philosophie).[1]

f.   The Absoluteness of the Religious Antithesis

We are still faced with the problem described above, the problem of how a Western community of thought is possible, in the face of the profound divergence of the religious ground-motives which have governed its development. In addition, we cannot get away from the fact that there is an *absolute antithesis* between the Christian ground-motive and two of the others. There is an absolute antithesis between the ground-motive of the Christian religion and that of the Greek religious consciousness. This antithesis holds just as well between the Christian and the humanistic ground-motives, even though in its process of formation the latter passed through the former. For its part, the Romanistic basic theme preserved at least to a degree its connection with the divine Word-revelation. In the face of this divergence and especially in the face of the absolute antithesis between the Christian and the non-Christian ground-motives, what is it that guarantees the existence of a community of philosophic thought in Western civilization?

g.   Is There in the West a Religious Intellectual Community of a Dialectical Kind? Hegel's Conception

One could ask here, first of all, whether the radical religious antithesis does not presuppose a certain community in which there is the possibility of mutual *religious understanding*, apart from which indeed such an antithesis could not even exist. This community, then, would have to be a dialectical one, in which the various ground-motives set themselves over against one another in order to enter into mutual conflict. And once one conceded the necessity of such a dialectical religious community, embracing the whole of Western thought, he would be faced at once with the analogy of the dialectic within it to *theoretical dialectic*, which attempts, of necessity, to bring a theoretical antithesis into a higher synthesis. In this analogy, the mutually opposed antithetical moments appear merely as parts which have been separated in a purely theoretical manner from a higher totality, which embraces both and thus can be absolutely identified with neither. Indeed, these opposed aspects are each other's correlates, and they are therefore incapable of excluding each other in any absolute sense. This kind of solution to the fundamental problem I have posed lies completely in the line of the dialectical thinking of Georg W. F. Hegel.

To be sure, this great thinker knows nothing of religious ground-motives as I have presented them. In his system, as is well known, religion is the second stage in the development of "absolute spirit" (*Geist*), that is,

---

1   See my *Recht en historie: Referaat voor de drie-en-twintigste Wetenschappelijke Samenkomst der Vrije Universiteit*, July 13, 1938 (Assen, 1938), pp. 18 ff.

the level of representation (*Vorstellung*). The first stage of this development, art, is that of intuition (*Anschauung*), whereas the third form, philosophy, in which the former two are brought into a higher synthesis, is that of the concept (*Begriff*).

In line with his theoretical dialectic, however, Hegel now attempts to construct three principal forms of religion, as the three necessary stages of development of representation, which absolute spirit assumes within human consciousness. These are: 1) the religion of nature; 2) the religion of spiritual individuality (*geistige Individualität*), which among the Jews comes to expression as sublimity (*Erhabenheit*), among the Greeks as beauty (*Schönheit*), and among the Romans as utility or practical understanding (*Zweckmässigkeit*); 3) the absolute, or revealed, Christian religion, in which God appears as that which He *is*, that is to say, the Absolute Spirit, which in accordance with the basic dialectical principle must be a Trinity.

In this Trinity, the religions of nature and of spiritual individuality, which were the two earlier forms of development, are brought into an absolute synthesis. For God the Father is nothing other than the eternal idea, which develops itself in the world, i.e., in nature, and which as substantial power "in the reflective determination of causality"[1] is the creator of heaven and earth. God the Son is nothing other than the idea as it has come to consciousness and has entered completely into representation, and which, as concrete individuality and subjectivity, is *spirit* and is one with the Father. And God the Holy Spirit is nothing other than the idea which, as the universal spirit of the church, rules the latter and realizes itself in its external and internal communion, and which is substantially one with the Father and the Son.

In his first major work, *The Phenomenology of Spirit* (*Phänomenologie des Geistes*), Hegel summarizes this dialectical development of religion in "natural, artistic, and manifested (revealed) religion" as follows:

The first form of development is religion

"...as immediate and therefore Natural Religion. In this, Spirit knows itself as its object [it should be noted that the theoretical *Gegenstand* relation, the foundation of all theoretical dialectic, is here transposed to religion!] in a natural or immediate shape. The second reality, however, is necessarily that in which Spirit knows itself in the shape of a superseded natural existence, or of the self. This, therefore, is the Religion of Art; for the shape raises itself to the form of the self through the creative activity of consciousness whereby this beholds in its object its act or the self. Finally, the third reality overcomes the one-sidedness of the first two; the self is just as much an immediacy, as the immediacy is the self. If, in

---

1   *Translator's note*: "in der Reflexionsbestimmung der Kausalität."

26

the first reality, Spirit in general is in the form of consciousness, and in the second, in that of self-consciousness, in the third it is in the form of the unity of both. It has the shape of being-in-and-for-itself; and when it is thus conceived as it is in and for itself, this is the Revealed Religion."

There then follows the passage which Christian Hegelians would be delighted to gloss over, since they do not wish to acknowledge that Hegel claimed to find the highest synthesis of the dialectical oppositions, not in religion, but in philosophy:

"But although in this, Spirit has indeed attained its true shape, yet the shape itself and the picture-thought[1] are still the unvanquished aspect from which Spirit must pass over into the Notion, in order wholly to resolve therein the form of objectivity, in the Notion which equally embraces within itself its own opposite. It is then that Spirit has grasped the Notion of itself, just as we now have first grasped it; and its shape or the element of its existence, being the Notion, is Spirit itself."[2]

Hegel's conception of religion, just as well as his dialectical construction of its three forms of development, is completely determined by the religious ground-motive of humanism, namely, that of *nature* and *freedom*, although in accordance with the new conception of the freedom motive in Romanticism he calls it "nature" and "spirit." This motive stands behind the uncritical circularity of his dialectic. The absolute idea, which in the dialectical process of thesis, antithesis, and synthesis

---

1 *Translator's note*: The German term here, *Vorstellung*, is usually translated "representation."

2 G.W.F. Hegel, *Phenomenology of Spirit* (tr. A. V. Miller, with Analysis of the Text and Foreword by J. N. Findlay; Oxford, 1977), p. 416. The German text reads as follows: "... [Religion] als unmittelbare und also natürliche Religion; in ihr weisz der Geist sich als seinen Gegenstand in natürlicher oder unmittelbarer Gestalt. Die zweite aber ist nothwendig diese, sich in der Gestalt der aufgehobenen Natürlichkeit oder des Selbst zu wissen. Sie ist also die künstliche Religion; denn zur Form des Selbst erhebt sich die Gestalt durch das Hervorbringen des Bewusztseyns, wodurch dieses in seinem Gegenstande sein Thun oder das Selbst anschaut. Die dritte endlich hebt die Einseitigkeit der beiden ersten auf; das Selbst is ebensowohl ein unmittelbares als die Unmittelbarkeit Selbst ist. Wenn in der ersteren der Geist überhaupt in der Form des Bewusztseyns, in der zweiten – des Selbstbewusztseyns ist, so ist er in der dritten in der Form der Einheit beider; er hat die Gestalt des An- und Fürsichseyns; und indem er also vorgestellt ist, wie er an und für sich ist, so ist dies die offenbare Religion. Obwohl er aber in ihr zu seiner wahren Gestalt gelangt, so ist eben die Gestalt selbst und die Vorstellung noch die unüberwundene Seite, von der er in den Begriff übergehen musz, um die Form der Gegenständlichkeit in ihm ganz aufzulösen, in ihm der ebenso dies sein Gegentheil in sich schlieszt. Alsdann hat der Geist den Begriff seiner Selbst erfaszt, wie wir nun erst ihn erfaszt haben, und seine Gestalt oder das Element seines Daseyns, indem die der Begriff ist, ist er selbst." *Phänomenologie des Geistes* (ed. D. Johann Schulze; 2nd ed., 1841), pp. 449-50.

exists in and for itself (*an und für sich*) in the logical activity of thought, and which subsequently "steps outside of itself" as nature in order once again to return from its otherness as nature back to itself in the spirit (as subjective, objective, and absolute spirit, respectively), is in essence nothing other than the religious dialectic in the ground-motive of nature and freedom itself, which governs the entire theoretical dialectic and gives it direction. Hegel's failure to recognize this is simply a consequence of his well-known uncritical transformation of theoretical into metaphysical dialectic, in the course of which the process of theoretical thought is identified with "reality as it truly is." The dogmatic character of metaphysics always hangs on the fact that it does not arrive at a transcendental critique of philosophical thought. That is closed to it, because it is convinced beforehand that theoretical thought and the totality of being are one and the same.

Religious antithesis permits of no genuine synthesis, for the fact that it is religious in nature entails that it is also absolute. The idolatrous ground-motives are not one-sided dialectical moments in the development of religion; they are religious dynamic forces of the spirit of apostasy, which do not allow for any compromise with the spirit of truth.

Now, care must be taken not to apply to the central sphere of religion the dialectical syntheses characteristic of theoretical thought. That must be avoided, if only for this reason, that theoretical dialectic as such can never extend beyond theoretical thinking. If it then turns out that theoretical thought itself is necessarily determined by the religious ground-motives, it follows that any attempt to resolve or mediate the religious oppositions by way of philosophical dialectic must fall by the wayside. The laws of theoretical dialectic do not apply to the radical antithesis which is at work in religion. I shall demonstrate in my transcendental critique that theoretical synthesis can be carried out in a genuine and appropriate fashion only when thought takes its point of departure from the true fundamental religious unity of the moments which have been distinguished and set apart from each other in the theoretical relation.

With this too the question is decided in principle concerning the possibility of religious understanding with respect to the ground-motives. It must be established from the outset that the Christian and the non-Christian starting points do not at all stand in the same position with respect to understanding each other religiously. Certainly from the perspective of the Christian starting point, based on the Scriptures, it is entirely possible to penetrate to the religious meaning of the starting points and ground-motives that stand in opposition to it. For it is only in the light of the Christian starting point that the latter can be revealed in their most profound meaning. The Christian shares, furthermore, in the solidarity of the human race in its fall into sin. Thus the ground-motives in question cannot be alien to him in a religious sense.

It is in the light of the ground-motive of the divine Word-revelation that the true position of the non-Christian ground-motives is established. They are unequivocally a result of the fall. In the redemption accomplished by Christ Jesus the fallen world has been reconciled, not in a speculative and dialectical fashion, but *in reality*. This means that the non-Christian ground-motives are not dialectically mediated in the ground-motive of Scripture. On the contrary, the divine Word-revelation exposes them as fundamentally false and annihilates them as religious starting points, even as it illumines by the light of the divine truth whatever relative moments of truth they may contain. Of themselves the non-Christian ground-motives have nothing to offer the Christian ground-motive by way of complementation. They have no inherent, positive truthfulness to set over against it. The Christian ground-motive, moreover, may not be conceived of as the higher synthesis of all the non-Christian ones; for a synthesis is unable to stand in absolute antithesis to the mutually antithetical elements which it itself has brought to a higher unity.

In its continuing operation, however, the ground-motive of the Christian religion is the only one in a position to guarantee the integrity of the historically determined philosophical community of thought in the West. That is the case, because as a point of departure for philosophy it bars the way to any scientific exclusivism, in which any particular line of thought would seek to elevate its own point of departure, making it the criterion for what does and what does not qualify as science.

If the Christian ground-motive truly has an effect on philosophic thought, it of necessity leads the latter to a radical, transcendental critique, which elucidates the fundamental difference between scientific judgments proper and the supra-scientific pre-judgments which lie at the foundation of their possibility. For this reason the Christian ground-motive refuses to allow any particular philosophical movement to be excluded from the philosophical community because of its point of departure. It relentlessly exposes every scientific dogmatism, which exalts its own religious point of departure to be the criterion for what may qualify as science, and which passes off the so-called autonomy of science as a scientific axiom even though a truly critical inquiry into the structure of scientific thought has never been undertaken. The Christian ground-motive also cuts off at the root the *hubris* of schools of thought which entertain the illusion that they themselves have the monopoly on science and which therefore never engage in truly scientific discussion with those who occupy other standpoints. And, finally, it is in possession of the only real key to understanding those religious ground-motives over against which it has set itself in radical religious antithesis. Therefore, it will allow these [non-Christian] ground-motives to receive their full due in respect of their own significance for the *internal philosophical stance* of the *trend of thought* controlled by them.

At the same time, however, the Christian ground-motive, with its resources for understanding, reaches out beyond the boundaries of the West and lays the only possible foundation for a genuine intellectual community of mankind, because it penetrates beyond all of the temporal distinctions of race and historical culture to the fundamental religious community of the human race. It is this basic community, lying at the religious center of human existence, that at bottom establishes the possibility of the community of philosophic thought. And since the radical antithesis, resulting from the fall and the redemption in Christ Jesus, was made manifest within this basic community itself, as it came into existence through God's creation, the influence of this antithesis must also be felt in the temporal community of thought, as soon as the Christian ground-motive comes into play within it as a spiritual *dunamis*. Nevertheless, just as this absolute antithesis at the spiritual root of humanity does not result in the destruction but rather in the radical preservation of community, it can never lead to the disintegration and dissolution of the historically conditioned philosophic community of thought, as long as the religious dynamic of the Christian ground-motive continues to make itself felt within it. For the Christian religion does not release its grip on fallen man, nor does it leave him out of account; it continually goes in pursuit of him. The radical antithesis it poses is the absolute condition for the preservation of the philosophic community of thought within our sinful society.

Before the outbreak of the Second World War, I presented an argument for all of these points in my essay "The Transcendental Critique of Theoretic Thought: A Contribution toward the Elimination of Exclusivism in Science."[1]

h. The Absence of Reciprocity in the Possibility of Religious
    Understanding between the Christian Starting Point and the
    Points of Departure against Which the Christian Religion
    Sets Itself in Radical Antithesis

From a non-Christian standpoint there exists no true, i.e., religious or spiritual, possibility of understanding with respect to the Christian ground-motive. This possibility cannot exist apart from the life-giving Spirit, who enlightens the spiritual eye and focuses it upon the true center of life, Jesus Christ.

Just for this reason the idolatrous ground-motives will continually seek to ban the *dunamis* of the Scriptural ground-motive from the intellectual community of the West. They constitute, therefore, a constant threat to it in its integral character. They are continually impelled to restrict the intellectual community to the circle of their own actual or presumed adherents. Accordingly, they must present those who engage in philosophy from a Christian standpoint with the choice of either accommodating their philosophic thought to the apostate ground-motive which is temporarily domi-

---

1 Herman Dooyeweerd, "De transcendentale critiek van het wijsgerig denken: Een bijdrage tot overwinning van het wetenschappelijk exclusivisme der richtingen." *Synthese*, IV (July 1939; with an introduction by Prof. Dr. N. Westendorp Boerma), pp. 314-39.

nant in Western culture, or of seeing themselves excluded from the circle of those who have intellectual standing. Since they never arrive at a veritable transcendental critique of theoretical thought, the adherents of these ground-motives are constantly guilty of dogmatically identifying their own supra-theoretical pre-judgments with scientific axioms. As a consequence, misled by the dogma of the autonomy of science, they constantly run the danger of interpreting Western philosophy from its beginnings within the framework of their own modern ground-motives.

In all of these tendencies, they will invariably come to stand in radical antithesis to philosophic thought which is impelled and directed by the Christian ground-motive. For this reason, it has only the appearance of paradox when I assert that the radical antithesis which is posed by the Christian religion is the sole guarantor of the integrity of the intellectual community of the West.

i. *The Origin of the Religious Dialectic. Why the Religious*
    Antithesis Permits No True Synthesis. The Polar Tendency
    in the Dialectical Ground-Motives

There is no higher religious synthesis, therefore, which might serve to bridge the radical antithesis of the ground-motives undergirding the history of Western thought, analogous to the way in which theoretical synthesis embraces a theoretical antithesis in a correlation of partial moments. There is, on the contrary, a *religious dialectic*, which holds sway of necessity within all of the ground-motives in relation to which the Christian religion sets itself in absolute antithesis.

The intrinsic necessity of this religious dialectic resides in the fact that these standpoints are based on an absolutizing of what is relative. Everything that is relative calls forth its *correlata*. Absolutizing something that is relative, therefore, means that these correlates, which now have been cut off from their true fundamental religious unity, will set themselves over against what has first been absolutized with the same presumed absoluteness. For, as I shall demonstrate at a later point, every absolutization is at bottom religious and thus can never be explained merely from theoretical, scientific points of view.

Such absolutization gives rise to a genuine polarity in the religious ground-motive. In it the diametrically opposed elements mutually cancel each other out in their supposed absoluteness. At the same time, because of their necessary correlativity, they mutually determine each other in their religious meaning. This state of affairs assumes, of course, that the two antagonistic motives which have set themselves in opposition to each other in the religious ground-motive have also come to awareness in the religious consciousness or subconsciousness of those whose thought is impelled by them. In view of this, it is understandable that the true meaning of the Greek matter motive first came to light in its opposition to the religious form motive, and vice versa. The same applies to the relationship of nature and freedom in the humanistic ground-motive and to that of nature and grace in the Scholastic motive.

Because of its religious nature a ground-motive cannot be satisfied with a mere correlation of the opposed elements within it. (Such a correlation, in fact, can only exist on the foundation of the absolute fundamental unity of the *correlata*, which is not to be found in a dialectical ground-motive.) Thus philosophic thought is inexorably driven back and forth from the one pole to the other, entangled in a religious dialectic that transforms the correlation into an absolute opposition. By the standards of theoretical dialectic, such a religious dialectic is utterly inexplicable.

In this context a "balance des contraires," in the sense of the French thinker Pierre-Joseph Proudhon,[1] is just as impossible as a resolution of the antithesis in a higher synthesis, in the sense intended by Hegel.

j. The Device of Ascribing the Primacy to One of the Two
Polar Motives Which Appear in the Dialectical Ground-
Motive

Lacking a foundation for a true religious synthesis, religious dialectic will invariably seek a way out by ascribing the primacy or religious priority to one of the antithetical principles which are manifested in the religious ground-motive. Let no one think that he can follow the Hegelian school, therefore, in attempting to employ the method of theoretical dialectic in order to "correct" this religious dialectic, to the extent that it makes itself felt in philosophic thought. This would be a completely uncritical method of philosophizing, for behind this overextension of theoretical dialectic itself there resides a religious dialectic, which remains hidden to the thinker.

k. The Boundaries of Theoretical Dialectic and the Intrusion of
Religious Dialectic into Theoretical Thought

Theoretical dialectic, in the only form in which it is genuine and justified, remains limited to theoretical synthesis in the *Gegenstand* relation, which will be investigated later.[2] Through the theoretical idea this synthesis receives its transcendental directedness, pointing to the supratheo-

---

1 According to Proudhon, the antinomies in philosophical thought, which have their origin, as we have noted, in religious dialectic's control over theoretical dialectic, are not resolved or mediated in a higher synthesis, as Hegel thought, but merely hold one another in equilibrium. For reality itself is supposed to consist of a balance of contradictories.

2 *Translator's note: Gegenstand*, literally, "that which stands opposed," is the standard German word for "object." Dooyeweerd uses this German term in order to bring out the relationship of opposition between thought and its object that is inherent in the theoretical attitude of thought, and also because, for him, the objects of theoretical thought are fundamentally different from the objects of naive experience.

retical fundamental unity and Origin of all the aspects of reality which have been distinguished and set in opposition to one another in the antithetic *Gegenstand* relation.[1] True theoretical synthesis presupposes that theoretical thought is indeed focused on the true, fundamental unity and Origin of the theoretically separated moments of temporal reality. If the religious ground-motive is dialectical in nature, however, the theoretical synthesis itself becomes polar. That is to say, it will look for the higher unity of the terms that have been theoretically opposed to each other in the *Gegenstand* relation in one of the poles of the dialectical ground-motive.

Thus the Greek philosopher Heraclitus, guided by the dialectical ground-motive of Greek philosophy, sought the deeper unity of the forms which stood out in opposition to one another in the process of becoming in the fluidity of the principle of matter, the eternal movement of life which coursed through the contrarily opposed individual forms. Similarly, from an idealistic humanistic standpoint, Hegel sought the deeper unity of nature and freedom (spirit) in the logical self-unfolding of the idea of freedom in the spirit, which incorporates[2] natural necessity, as its logical otherness, within itself as one moment in a higher synthesis. Such a presumed synthesis always entails an unjustified logical relativization of the principle of contradiction (*principium contradictionis*), one that is unjustified because the theoretical antithesis does not permit of a logical resolution or mediation. Indeed, it never comes to resolution in this way. What actually takes place when one goes this route is that the theoretical antithesis is replaced by a polar absolutization.

To state the same thing in a different manner, religious dialectic has intruded into theoretical dialectic. By imposing its own terms, it attempts not merely to unite the theoretical antithesis in a synthesis but to cancel it. The theoretical antithesis may not be cancelled on the theoretical level, however, since it is grounded in the *Gegenstand* relation itself.

1. The Religious Dialectic of the Scholastic Synthesis Motive of Nature and Grace. Two Possible Points of Contact for This Presumed Synthesis

A religious dialectic arises with equal necessity in the ground-motive of philosophic thought when an attempt is made to establish a synthesis

---

In Dooyeweerd, therefore, *Gegenstand* always means "object of theoretical thought." The abstract *Gegenstand* relation between theoretical thought and its object (its *Gegenstand*) always must be distinguished from the concrete *subject-object* relation that belongs to naive experience.

1   This statement will become clear to the reader only after he has studied my transcendental critique of philosophical thought.

2   Dutch: *opheffen*; German: *aufheben*.

between the Christian and the non-Christian points of departure. This simultaneously gives rise to what has the appearance of a community of thought with the non-Christian movements in philosophy, built on a dialectical religious basis. Within this particular synthesis standpoint, however, this community of thought is never grounded in religion, but rather exclusively in the autonomy of natural reason.

The synthesis motive in Western thought that answers to this description is that of nature and grace. It has been employed to effect dialectical syntheses between the Christian ground-motive and both the Greek and the humanistic ground-motives. As such this motive appears to originate in the Scholastic thinking that is characteristic of Roman Catholicism, even when, in conflict with the Scriptural standpoint of the Reformation, it is accepted in Protestant thought.

In this connection, there is no possibility of a genuine religious synthesis which would preserve the Christian ground-motive in its absolute character. As we have noted, this is prevented by the absoluteness of the religious antithesis, which itself can never be of the nature of mere theoretical dialectic. What actually occurs here is that the ground-motives are accommodated to each other. In this process, both of them are partially divested of their original meaning and are thereby rendered capable, in this denatured form, of serving as poles of a religious dialectic.

There are two main directions in which the point of contact for such a dialectical-religious synthesis can be sought. First, it can be sought in the *idea of creation*. Second, it can be sought in the *idea of the fall into sin*.

m. The First Way: The Thomistic Synthesis and the Roman Catholic Standpoint

The first option appears in the Thomistic synthesis, which is brought to expression in the official doctrine of the Roman Catholic church with respect to the relationship between nature and supernatural grace. In the creation idea, nature and supernature are placed over against each other, and in the conception of the nature of created reality, an attempt is made to adapt the Aristotelian Greek form-matter scheme[1] to the Scriptural creation motive. Clearly, the Greek ground-motive is thereby forced to undergo a metamorphosis as to its meaning, for it is now "bracketed" by the new synthesis theme of nature and grace. Grace or supernature is granted religious primacy over nature, in that it is conceived as the supernatural perfecting of the latter as to its form. As it is subordinated to grace within this hierarchical scheme, however, nature is not divested of its intrinsic autonomy; rather, this autonomy is merely relativized. On this standpoint, nature remains centered in the rational form principle, just as God is regarded as the "pure Form" who must be conceived en-

---

1 The fact that the Aristotelian concept of nature is completely controlled by the form-matter motive appears in Aristotle's exposition of this concept in his *Metaphysics, D*, 4. 1015 a.

tirely apart from the matter principle.

This line of thought introduces a true religious dialectic into the idea of creation. "Pure form" has its religious antipode in "pure matter," which is thought of as completely formless. In the Greek ground-motive, the principle of matter cannot have its origin in the principle of form.

Within the nature-grace scheme, however, there was need to correct the form-matter motive of the Greeks, because the Scriptural creation motive will not tolerate any such polarity. In order to avoid dualism, matter was understood to have its origin in the divine creation – but then only the concrete matter of created beings, which is first brought into actual existence as a constitutive principle in composite beings by means of a specific form. This matter was then conceived as a mere possibility, a potentiality, a receptivity for form, and simultaneously as the principle of imperfection, which exists over against the form principle as the principle of perfection. This latter conception is formally connected with the Aristotelian understanding of *hulē* as "potential being" (*dunamei on*). It cannot do away, however, with the autonomy and originality of the Greek matter principle, which also comes to expression in Aristotle in the polar opposition between *Anankē* (blind, unpredictable chance) and the rational causality of the form principle, which operates according to a predictable, purposive plan. The attempt to wed the Greek form-matter motive to the Scriptural idea of creation introduces into the latter an autonomous principle of metaphysical imperfection, which is completely foreign to it.

Can the divine Creator be the origin of imperfection? Indeed, he must be just that if he is the creative author of nature in the Greek sense, something that was never taught by the Greeks themselves. Escape was then sought from this antinomy by regarding "absolute" or "pure" matter as a so-called *sterēsis* or privation of being, which as such is not created.

Centering nature in an autonomous principle of rational form requires, thus, in its turn, a reinterpretation of the Christian doctrine of creation, and the effects of this must also spill over into the understanding of the fall and of redemption. In Thomistic theology, the creative work of God loses its active character, since according to Aristotelian-Thomistic philosophy activity is regarded merely as a natural striving of matter (potentiality, imperfection) toward form (actuality, perfection), a striving that is incompatible with God's essence as "pure Form." In Thomas, therefore, the creation is reduced to a purely one-sided relation *ex parte creaturae*.[1] The *principles* of form and matter are both withdrawn from God's sovereignty as Creator, for the latter only extends to concrete, created things.

The fundamental religious unity of nature is thus left out of account. The Scriptural, Augustinian doctrine that nature has radically fallen into sin must therefore also be abandoned, because the fall now affects only the connection between nature and supernature. It is the loss of the "super-

---

1 I shall return to this point in my critical analysis of Thomistic ontology in volume II of this work, where I shall also give the references to the sources.

natural gift of grace." As a final consequence, redemption in Christ Jesus also loses its radical meaning, according to which it transforms the religious root of fallen nature. The doctrine of the "natural preparation for grace" forms the dialectical capstone in the elaboration of this synthesis motive.

n. The Law of Religious Dialectic: The Operation of the Polar Tendency in the Dialectical Ground Motive. The Dualism between Nature and Grace in Ockham and in Averroistic Nominalism

As we have already noted, it was possible to insulate this typically Romanistic synthesis against the polarizing effects of this dialectic only by the exercise of ecclesiastical authority. As soon as these tendencies were set free to obey the law of religious dialectic, the artificial hierarchical synthesis dissolved into a polar antithesis. This happened with William of Ockham, the leading figure of late-scholastic (fourteenth century A.D.) nominalism. Ockham promulgated the idea that there was a yawning gulf between nature and grace. In the school of nominalism which was influenced by Arabic Averroism (e.g., Siger of Brabant, John of Jandun, a contemporary of Ockham), this gulf had been further widened, even becoming the doctrine of two-fold truth.

Ockham's nominalistic opposition to the reality of the so-called *universalia* (i.e., the universal ontic forms of material things) went hand in hand with his unsuccessful attempt to purge Scholastic theology of the denaturing influence of the Greek principle of rational form by means of his conception of the creative sovereignty of God as a *potentia absoluta*. This attempt was doomed to failure, because the absolute omnipotence of God was not understood in its Scriptural sense, but rather – within the framework of the dialectical ground-motive of Scholasticism – as a lawless, unpredictable arbitrary power, a sort of *Anankē* in the sense of the Greek matter motive, which here was divested of its original religious meaning by being bound to the Christian creation motive. Indeed, the religious depreciation of natural reason and of the validity of all law and form in natural life had its origin in the deification of the principle of matter as it was understood in ancient Greek religion.

o. The Second Way: Lutheranism and the Dialectic of Law and Gospel. Dialectical Theology

The nominalistic dualism between nature and grace had its effects within the Reformation movement itself in Luther's dialectical opposition of *law* and *gospel*. Here the point of contact for a synthesis between the Greek and the Christian ground-motives was sought primarily in the doctrine of the fall. This was the second direction in which there was an attempt at synthesis.

Ockham's view of law was undoubtedly at work in the religious depreciation of the law as the form principle of sinful nature. In the background there also lay Marcion's dialectical antithesis between the God of creation and the God of redemption, an idea which in this thinker from the second century A. D. was accompanied by an opposition to the moralistic-legal view of the gospel and by a pseudo-Pauline emphasis on justification alone *at the expense of the law.*

Nature, which in line with Scholastic theology is still conceived in terms of the rational form principle of Greek thought, is the "kingdom of sin under the law." It is regarded dialectically in polar opposition to grace, the kingdom of the evangelical freedom of the Christian, who breaks through and overcomes the law. "The whore, reason" is tolerated only in the wilderness of sinful nature; covered with shame, it is cast out from "Abraham's tent," the community of faith.

The ground-motive of nature and grace, however, also lends itself very well to a pseudosynthesis between the Scriptural and the humanistic ground-motives, one in which nature is viewed in terms of the polar opposition between nature and freedom. Insofar as this attempt at synthesis issues from the Lutheran conception of nature and grace, it is once again the revelation of the fall that is used to downgrade autonomous nature and to assign it a position diametrically opposed to grace.

In this fashion the humanistic view of temporal reality can also be accepted, even though this view must, of course, be externally accommodated to the Lutheran articles of faith. Along with this, the humanistic ground-motive of nature and freedom, which is still allowed a place of influence in philosophic thought, is invariably disqualified as a typical expression of sinful nature because of its prideful religious root. At the same time, however, every attempt to allow the dynamic power of the Scriptural ground-motive to effect an inner reformation of philosophy as well as scientific thought in general, is sharply rejected from this point of view as a fatal confusion between the Christian life of grace and sinful natural life.

The religious dialectic of the ground-motive of nature and grace as they are here conceived ultimately led, by way of Luther's dualism of law and grace, Kantian criticism, and the more recent irrationalistic philosophy of existence, to what is called "dialectical theology." Here again it expresses itself within theology in polar fashion. In the thought of Karl Barth, there is no point of contact between nature and grace. The influence of Marcion is also unmistakably present in Barth's dialectical theology, although it does not lead here, any more than it did in Luther, to an absolute separation between the Old and New Testaments.

p.   The Dialectic of the Ground-Motive of Nature and Grace
*   in Reformed Scholasticism*

To the extent that the ground-motive of nature and grace is able to establish a beachhead in Calvinistic thought, it will never express itself in a theological way in terms of the polarity characteristic of Lutheranism. The Lutheran dualism of law and gospel is foreign to the Reformed confession. Reformed Scholasticism, which to the present has had results only in theology and which, for reasons I shall explore later, has never been able to elaborate an independent philosophy like that of Thomism, will prefer to go the first way of synthesis. Seizing upon the creation motive, it will seek, just as Thomism does, to accommodate the Greek view of nature to it. In so doing, however, it will reject both the Lutheran dualism between nature and grace and the Thomistic substructure-superstructure theme.

In Reformed Scholasticism, nature can never be conceived of as the antipode of grace or as its relatively autonomous substructure. For, in conformity to Augustine, Reformed Scholasticism always binds the natural light of reason to the light of Scripture. In so doing, moreover, it falls into the same misconception regarding the relationship of theology and philosophy that I pointed out earlier in connection with the great church father. Theology is supposed to take the non-Reformed philosophy of the schools under its wing, in order to accommodate it to orthodox Reformed doctrine and to keep its latent dangerous tendencies under control. It will be very suspicious of a Reformed philosophy that does not bind itself to theology, for it is theology, as the "queen of the sciences" (*regina scientiarum*), that is supposed to come up with the Scriptural principles to which the other sciences must conform.

In the absence of papal ecclesiastical authority, however, all of the theological resources that Reformed Scholasticism can bring to bear will be incapable, even in its own circles, of holding back the influence of the polar tendencies within the ground-motive of nature and grace. Here again, the theologically contrived pseudosynthesis between the Christian and the Greek ground-motives will always be threatened with dissolution. The point of contact for the dualistic separation between nature and grace will be sought, in particular, in the doctrine of *common grace*, which in its relationship to "special grace" can easily degenerate into a doctrine of two separate realms. The Reformed practitioners of the non-theological sciences, finding in Scholastic theology no usable guidelines for their own branches of investigation, will appeal to common grace, in order to justify their alliance with the prevailing, supposedly neutral modes of thought. And insofar as they take care not to trespass on the perilous terrain of theology, Scholastic theology for the most part will not interfere with them.

Indeed, in this view, theology supplies an external link between natural thought and the Scriptures. However, since this connection is completely dominated by the unscriptural ground-motive of nature and grace and cannot lead, therefore, to an inner reformation of scientific thought, the latter will place more and more distance between itself and the Scriptural ground-motive of the Christian religion. In time it will discover that it has even distanced itself completely from the Scholastic way of doing theology.

Within the realm of science, the polarity of this ground-motive will increasingly show up in a separation and even in internal discord between dogmatic theology and the "profane sciences." Within theology itself the accommodated Greek conception of nature will remain in basic tension with the integral and radical ground-motive of the Christian religion.

The dialectic of the synthesis motive of nature and grace is thus always a religious dialectic "of the second power." It contains within itself either the dialectic inherent to the Greek form-matter motive or that of the humanistic ground-motive of nature and freedom. As to both of their poles, these are welded to the Scriptural ground-motive, which in this abortive attempt at synthesis has been robbed of its meaning. In this way, a secondary dialectic is brought into being within the Scriptural ground-motive.

For this reason, a complete understanding of the significance of the Scholastic synthesis motive for philosophy, to which a substantial portion of my investigation in the second volume of this work will be devoted, cannot be achieved without having a clear view of the dialectic inhering in the Greek form-matter theme. I shall now proceed, therefore, to present an in-depth study of the dialectical unfolding of the latter motive in Greek philosophy, up to and including Plato. In this presentation, the philosophy of Plato will occupy the center of attention. For it is Plato who incorporated in his thought the entire preceding history of Greek philosophy. It is also he who brought the dialectic of the Greek ground-motive to its highest and at the same time its most sharply formulated expression.

In presenting this sketch, I do not intend, of course, to write an exhaustive history of Greek thought. Neither shall I emphasize the historical method of approach. Instead, my sole aim here is to investigate the dialectical development of the religious ground-motive in philosophic thought, and this will require the application of a unique transcendental method, which is capable of penetrating to the mainsprings of Greek thinking.

II

DIORAMA OF THE DIALECTICAL DEVELOPMENT OF THE FORM-MATTER MOTIVE IN GREEK PHILOSOPHY UP TO AND INCLUDING PLATO

Part I

THE DIALECTICAL DEVELOPMENT UP TO PLATO

1. **The Dialectic of the Greek Ground-Motive under the Primacy of the Matter Motive in Pre-Socratic Philosophy up to Parmenides**

a. The Conception of Physis (*Nature*) *in the First Phase of Greek Nature Philosophy*

Greek philosophy was born in the archaic transition period which lay between the era of Mycenaean knighthood and the age of prosperity for the Greek *polis* which followed the victorious conclusion of the Persian wars. In the first section of the Introduction, we saw how this transition period was marked by a crisis which affected the whole of Greek culture and society. This crisis came to its focus in a crisis within the religious consciousness of the Greeks. The older religion of nature, which had been placed on the defensive by the newer religion of culture, now rose up in rebellion against it. In many respects this reaction gave the ascendancy in the Greek religious consciousness to the matter motive over the form motive, although it did not render the latter inoperative.

It is understandable, therefore, that Greek philosophy first appeared on the scene in the sixth century B. C. in the form of what is called nature philosophy. This had its origin within the sphere of the Ionian culture of Miletus. It was accompanied by the rudimentary beginnings of the special sciences. Under unmistakable Egyptian, Phoenician, Chaldean, and Babylonian influences, these undertook investigations in mathematics and astronomy, meteorology and geography. What has been brought to light by historical research into the results of these early forays of the Greeks into the special sciences is doubtless of the greatest importance. The view, however, that it is only in terms of its scientific accomplishments that one can penetrate to what lay at the heart of the older Ionian nature philosophy[1] turns matters on their head. It measures Greek philosophy by the standard of the modern humanistic ideal of science.

The question that stands out above all others here is what this Ionian philosophy meant by "nature" or "physis." Any attempt to answer this question should make it clear that the Ionian conception of nature was completely determined by the religious matter motive in its dialectical opposition to the form motive. The Greek philosophy of nature arose in a situation where, within the basic dialectical theme of matter and form, the matter motive had the unmistakable primacy.

*b.   The Religious Primacy of the Matter Motive in Milesian
     Nature Philosophy. Anaximander's* Dikē *Motive*

The Ionian nature philosophers seized upon that which Aristotle was later to designate *hulē* (ὕλη) and which Hesiod had already referred to as Chaos, and they deified it under a variety of names, as it suited them: the *apeiron*, the *rheuston*, the *migma*, the *mixis*, etc. Among most of the Ionian nature philosophers, at least, this was done in close connection with a concrete representation of a movable element – water in Thales of Miletus, air in Anaximenes, fire in Heraclitus. Having deified it, they proclaimed it as the sole origin (*archē*) of all things appearing in a fixed form. This formless and fluid *archē* was identical with what these older Greek thinkers meant by *physis*: an animated divine force, a fluid continuum filled with divine life,[2] which is in eternal, primordial motion, uncaused by any other principle. It is this that is referred to as the "hylozoism" of these thinkers.[3]

The Ionian philosopher Anaximander (sixth century B. C.) designated this *physis* the *apeiron*, the unformed and unbounded disorder. He thereby penetrated behind the concrete representation of the "movable elements," which was still bound to form, to the invisible essence of the matter principle. In the process of eternal separation (*apokrisis*) and reabsorption of all

---

1   This position is taken, e. g., in Ueberweg-Praechter, *Grundrisz der Geschichte der Philosophie*; I: *Das Altertum* (11th ed.; Berlin, 1920), pp. 53-54.
2   Cf. Thales' statement, as reported by Aristotle, in Diels-Kranz, *Fragmente der Vorsokratiker*, I (6th rev. ed., 1951), p. 79; Thales, A. Fragm. 22: πάντα πλήρη θεῶν εἶναι ("everything is full of gods"). Aristotle refers to this statement in *De Anima* A, 5. 411 a 7. In his *Metaphysics* A, 3. 983 b 6, Aristotle states that this *archē* was conceived as *hulē*, and in line 17 of the same passage he also remarks that it was the *mia physis* (the one nature) from which all other living things have proceeded. Aristotle brings Thales' notion of water as the origin of all things into connection with Homer's mythological conception of nature (καὶ πρώτους θεολογήσαντας ... περὶ τῆς φύσεως), according to which Oceanus and Thetis were the progenitors of the entire process of becoming.
3   A compound of ὕλη (matter) and ζώειν (to live).

things having form into the formless *physis*, with its eternal, primordial motion, he discerned a law of justice (δίκη; *Dikē*) at work.[1] In the order of time, which compels all that has form and shape to return to its formless origin, the *Anankē* of the matter principle is manifested as *Dikē*, the principle that also governed the relationships between the patriarchal lineages *(γένη; genē)* in Greek society. Everything, including human social life, was embraced by the divine *physis*.[2]

c. *The Rationalization of* Anankē. *Heraclitus' Conception of the* Logos

Possibly in conjunction with the *Moira* motive of the religion of culture, which I shall discuss presently, the ancient nature philosophy tried merely to rationalize unpredictable *Anankē* to a certain degree, in order that it might be used in giving some kind of theoretical explanation of the origin of things having a definite form which are perceptible to the senses. In the conception of Anaximander fire, earth, water and air (which had been considered to be "elements" since Empedocles) separate themselves from this *apeiron*, this one, formless *physis*. These ele-

---

1 Diels-Kranz I, 89; Anaximander, B. Fragm. 1: ἐξ ὧν δὲ ἡ γένεσίς ἐστι τοῖς οὖσι, καὶ τὴν φθορὰν εἰς ταῦτα γίνεσθαι κατὰ τὸ χρεών. διδόναι γὰρ αὐτὰ δίκην καὶ τίσιν ἀλλήλοις τῆς ἀδικίας κατὰ τὴν τοῦ χρόνου τάξιν. ("That from which existing things arise is also that into which they return at their destruction, as is fitting; for they make just satisfaction and reparation to one another for their injustice, in accordance with the order of time.") With a typically Greek variation on the words of Mephistopheles in Goethe's *Faust* (lines 1339-1340), this statement may be formulated as follows:
  Denn alles, was im Form besteht,
  ist wert dass es zu Grunde geht
  (For all that comes to be
  deserves to perish wretchedly)
Cf. also Diels-Kranz I, 89; Anaximander, B. Fragm. 3: τὸ ἄπειρον (εἶναι) τὸ θεῖον ("the unbounded disorder is the divine") and B. Fragm. 2: ταύτην (sc. ἄπειρον) ἀίδιον εἶναι ("this [unbounded] is invisible").
2 In his book *From Religion to Philosophy,* p. 182, F. M. Cornford maintains that Anaximander and the other Milesian nature philosophers restricted the realm of *Dikē* exclusively to human society. As I shall observe presently, he perceives in this one of the most basic differences between the "scientific" tradition, oriented to the Olympian religion, and the "mystical" tradition, oriented to the Dionysian religion. The latter is supposed to have come to expression, e. g., in the thought of Heraclitus. The fragment from Anaximander cited above clearly demonstrates the contrary, however. Anaximander, like Heraclitus, applied the *Dikē* motive to *physis* in its entirety. The restriction of *Dikē* to human society arose for the first time in Greek philosophical thought with the contrast between *physis* and *nomos* (law in the sense of humanly imposed order). The limitation of *Dikē* to human relationships undoubtedly appears already in Hesiod (*Erga* 276), and it is undeniable that here, just as in Protagoras, the founder of the Sophistic movement, there is an influence of the form motive of the religion of culture. In the thought of the Milesians, however, it is precisely this form motive that occupies the subordinate position.

ments are marked by pairs of mutually opposed, sensible form qualities such as warmth and cold, moistness and dryness, mobility and fixity, and a certain mixing (*mixis*) of them gives rise to the things with form that are accessible to sense perception. The *physis* of these things does not consist in a constant form. Neither does a person have a lasting nature defined by form, for according to Anaximander human beings proceeded from other forms of life.[1]

In order to accomplish the rationalization of the blind power of *Ananke*, Heraclitus of Ephesus in particular used the principle of proportionality between coming into and passing out of existence. As a principle of form, measure, and harmony, this could only have been inspired by the ground-motive of the culture religion.[2] In any case, it has nothing to do with the deterministic and mechanistic concept of causality that is used in the mathematical physics founded by Galileo and Newton, for this was framed in terms of the classical humanistic ideal of science. The vision of nature in these ancient thinkers is not at all mechanistic in the modern sense of the word. The combination of the matter principle with the form principle was rather forced upon theoretical thought by the dialectic of the Greek ground-motive.

This dialectical intrusion of the form motive into the matter motive comes to its clearest expression in Heraclitus' idea of the *logos*. In the process of the eternal flux of the mutually opposed forms of reality, this *logos* maintains a fixed, rational order of measure, proportion, and harmony

---

1 Diels-Kranz I, 83; Anaximander, A. Fragm. 10: ἔτι φησίν, ὅτι κατ᾽ ἀρχὰς ἐξ ἀλλοειδῶν ζῴων ὁ ἄνθρωπος ἐγεννήθη (from Plutarch *Strom*. 2 [D. 579 from Theophrastus]: "he also says that in the beginning human beings were born from other types of living beings.")

2 It is characteristic that in both Anaximander and Heraclitus the principle of measure comes to expression in *Dikē*. Cf., for example, Heraclitus' words in Diels-Kranz, I, 172; B. Fragm. 94: Ἥλιος γὰρ οὐχ ὑπερβήσεται μέτρα· εἰ δὲ μή, Ἐρινύες μιν Δίκης ἐπίκουροι ἐξευρήσουσιν. ("For Helios [the sun] will not transgress his measures; otherwise the Erinyes, the handmaidens of *Dikē*, will find him out.") Here he undoubtedly has in mind the fixed circuit of the sun in its measured course, which may not encroach upon the paths of the other celestial bodies. As Rudolf Hirzel has shown in *Themis, Dikē, und Verwandtes: Ein Beitrag zur Geschichte der Rechtsidee bei den Griechen* (Leipzig, 1907), and also Pierre Guérin in *L'idée de justice dans la conception de l'univers chez les premiers philosophes grecs* (Paris, 1934), *Dikē*, in contrast to *Themis*, has a rational standard of equality that is given pregnant expression in the Greek principle of retribution. Whereas *Themis* was the protectress of the internal order of the community and as such had more of a mystical, ethical-religious than a juridical function, *Dikē* was disclosed precisely in the avenging of injustice in the external relationships among the family lineages. Hesiod thus grants *Dikē* a role in the administration of justice. If only for this reason, Cornford's view that the *Dikē* motive is merely a typical mystical motive of the religion of nature must be regarded as incorrect. The standard of *Dikē* is much too rational and external for this. *Dikē* must rather be considered a rationalized form of *Ananke*.

which makes it possible to state with equal justice that there is nothing that either comes into or passes out of existence.[1] It appears in Diels' first B. fragment that *logos* primarily denotes "divine speech," which can be heard, even though in the realm of their everyday existence humans are unable to understand its meaning. This "speech," however, is the expression of a rational world law, which governs everything that happens and guarantees that the eternally flowing divine *physis* will remain one and the same as it unfolds into antithetical, mutually conflicting forms, maintaining a constant proportionality and harmony (*ἁρμονίη*) throughout all coming into being and passing out of existence.

The dialectic of the Greek ground-motive even leads here to a dialectical "flip-flop" of the matter principle into its religious opposite: the divine fire, the *physis* which flows eternally through all opposed forms, is dialectically one with the *logos*, as world law. In dialectical fashion, the blind, unpredictable *Anankē* of the religious matter motive and the *logos* of the religious form motive are both one and the same and simultaneously polar opposites. As a later disciple of Heraclitus expressed this in the obscure language of the thinker from Ephesus:

> For all things are alike in that they differ, all harmonize with one another in that they conflict with one another, all converse in that they do not converse, all are rational in being irrational; individual things are by nature contrary, because they mutually agree. For rational world-order [*nomos*] and nature [*physis*], by means of which we accomplish all things, do not agree in that they agree.[2]

This Heraclitean dialectical identification of *logos* (as *nomos*) and

---

1 Diels-Kranz I, 157; Heraclitus, B. Fragm. 30–105: *κόσμον τόνδε τὸν αὐτὸν ἁπάντων, οὔτε τις θεῶν οὔτε ἀνθρώπων ἐποίησεν, ἀλλ᾽ ἦν ἀεὶ καὶ ἔστιν καὶ ἔσται πῦρ ἀείζωον, ἁπτόμενον μέτρα καὶ ἀποσβεννύμενον μέτρα.* ("This world-order, which is the same for all beings, was not created by one of the gods or of mankind, but it was ever and is and shall be eternally living fire, kindling in [fixed] measure and going out in [fixed] measure.") See in addition B. Fragm. 31, where this idea of the *logos* as an order of measure and proportion is further elaborated in Heraclitus' doctrine of the coming into being and passing away of the cosmos as a form-world, and also B. Fragm. 90, where the eternal process of coming into and passing out of existence in accordance with the *logos* is compared with the exchange of goods for gold and gold for goods, a comparison that gives clear expression to the principle of equivalency or proportionality.

2 In the writing erroneously ascribed to Hippocrates, *Περὶ διαίτης*, I, xi, 6: *πάντα γὰρ ὅμοια ἀνόμοια ἐόντα καὶ σύμφορα πάντα διάφορα ἐόντα, διαλεγόμενα οὐ διαλεγόμενα, γνώμην ἔχοντα ἀγνώμονα, ὑπεναντίος ὁ τρόπος ἑκάστων ὁμολογεόμενος· νόμος γὰρ καὶ φύσις, οἷσι πάντα διαπρησσόμεθα, οὐχ ὁμολογεῖται ὁμολογεόμενα·*

physis was later adopted in the Stoa, and by this route it also influenced the *logos* speculation of Christian thinkers into the fourth century.[1]

d. Cornford's View of the Religious Orientation of Greek Philosophy. Moira *and the* Dikē *Motive*

In the work referred to above, *From Religion to Philosophy*, Cornford attempts to reveal the presence of a sharp contrast between what he designates the "scientific" and the "mystical" traditions. According to him, the former of these was oriented to the Olympian religion, which in his view was embodied in earlier and later Ionian nature philosophy, whereas the latter took its bearings from the Dionysian mystery religion.

He observes a characteristic difference between the Olympian god and the mystery god. The first originated in the daemon of a particular province of nature. After having left this province and after having been transformed into an immortal Olympian deity, this daemon became separated by sharp boundaries from both *physis* and human society. In contrast, the mystery god remains the daemon of a human social group, living in mystical communion with the latter as the object of a mystical feeling of oneness on the part of its members. He likewise continues to be the animating principle of *physis*.[2]

Cornford believes that the fundamental religious framework in the Olympian conception lies in the *spatial division into territories* (this being directly connected to the polytheistic form of this culture religion), whereas in the mystery religion the same position is occupied by the temporal *cycle of human life and death* and also life and death throughout the whole of nature conceived in accordance with this model. According to him, the former (Olympian) tradition is represented by the Milesian school of Thales, Anaximander, and Anaximenes, which led by way of Anaxagoras to the atomists Leucippus and Democritus. This tradition supposedly was oriented completely to the *Moira* motive, and Cornford appeals to Homer and Hesiod in an attempt to justify his connection of the latter with the territorial partition among the Olympian deities between the three sons of Cronus: Zeus, Poseidon, and Pluto (Hades). The word *Moira*, after all, is closely related to μέρος, which means "part."[3] The scientific tradition, consequently, was allegedly tied to the polytheism of the Olympian religion. Corresponding to this hypothesis, the Cambridge professor conceives the fundamental idea of Ionian nature philosophy to be the territorial partition within *physis* between the four elements that separate themselves from the *archē* – water, air, fire and earth – while the pas-

---

1 The apologist Justin Martyr included Heraclitus as well as Socrates, Abraham, etc., among those who had lived with the logos and were to be considered Christians.
2 Cornford, *op. cit.*, pp. 110 ff.
3 This fact is undeniable, but the etymological derivation of the word is not decisive for the meaning it acquires as it is equated with the *Anankē* of the religion of nature.

sage of one element into the territory of another is then regarded as a transgression of the limits of *Moira*. Furthermore, he establishes here a sharp boundary between *Moira*, on the one hand, which guards against any transgression of the territorial boundaries within *physis*, and *Dikē* or justice, on the other hand, which pertains solely to human society and allegedly there maintains the territorial boundaries, both between the respective family lineages and between humans and gods, by avenging the *hubris* (presumption) which endeavors to transgress these boundaries.

In contrast to this, the mystical tradition – which Cornford sees represented in Heraclitus, Pythagoras, Xenophanes, Parmenides, and to a degree also in Empedocles and Plato – is thought to acknowledge the basic oneness and indivisibility of *physis*. In this *physis*, no less than in the social group, the deity is constantly present as its *daemon*. This tradition thus accepts the existence of just one cosmos, rather than the infinitely many worlds of Anaximander and the atomists. The *polytheistic Moira motive* with its orientation to a spatial territorial division is allegedly supplanted here completely by the *motive of time* and *number* (number as the measure of time), which comes to expression in the cycle of human life and follows the way of *Dikē* as this governs both *physis* and society by one and the same law. The way of *Dikē* is here the way of life, which does not observe any sharply delineated territorial boundaries, but which, in the cycle of time, reconciles all oppositions into a harmonious and proportional relation to their one, indivisible divine origin.

e. Critique of Cornford's Conception

However interesting and suggestive Cornford's elaboration of this hypothesis may be, it does not penetrate to the actual dialectical ground-motive of Greek philosophy. He cannot attain this, because his position, especially with regard to the Olympian culture religion, remains far too much attached to the polytheistic *mythological form*, which must be sharply distinguished from the *religious ground-motive* itself. Furthermore, his interpretation of the *Moira* motive in particular rests upon a shaky foundation. This latter motive is older than that of the Olympian culture religion and is rooted in the *Ananke* of the mystical nature religion itself.

Homer and Hesiod joined the mythological picture of territorial partition to the more ancient motive of *Ananke* with the intent, first of all, to construct a religious synthesis between the newer culture religion and the older nature religion. This synthesis openly reveals the religious dialectic of the religious ground-motive itself in the mere fact that neither of these men succeeded in truly resolving the antithetical relation between *Moira* and the world of the Olympian deities. An opposition between *physis* and *Dikē* first appears in Greek philosophy with Protagoras, the founder of the Sophist movement. As we shall see later, this development was a direct result of the polar tendencies within the dialectical ground-motive, as these worked themselves out when the primacy was granted to the form motive of the culture religion. This opposition is also evident in the poet-theologian Hesiod, the defender of the religion of culture.

The view that Milesian nature philosophy was entirely or even predominantly oriented to the polytheism of the Olympian religious tradition cannot be maintained. All of the Milesian thinkers accept the oneness of the divine Origin, and they conceive this *archē*, in the sense of divine *physis*, as being in polar opposition to the form motive of the culture religion. The explanation of this cannot be, as Cornford supposes, that the Olympian deities were originally *daemons* of specific provinces of nature and that, after their departure from these spatially delimited territories, *physis* was left vacant. From this point of view it would be impossible to account for the fact that the older Milesian nature philosophers conceived of *physis* as a single divine principle of origin. One would rather be led to suspect that they would have held to the existence of a multiplicity of *archai*, each of which would have been set off sharply from the other by *Moira* and have been compelled to remain within its own territory. Cornford himself remarks that the conception according to which "the One can pass out of itself into the manifold, and yet retain its oneness," is a typical "mystical" belief.[1] There is, moreover, nothing to indicate that Anaximander, for instance, held that after the elements had been separated they no longer had a unified divine *physis*. Such a position is first discernible in the case of Empedocles.

What actually appears here is that Milesian nature philosophy was predominantly oriented to the matter principle of Greek nature religion, a principle which Hesiod had already brought to more abstract expression, but which nevertheless, as I have noted in the first section of the Introduction, always retained an obscure mystical cachet. It is also clear that this matter motive remained coupled to the form motive of the religion of culture, for it was only in its dialectical opposition to the latter that the matter motive could drive theoretical thought to a *monistic* conception of the origin of the cosmos. Indeed, in their historical-pistical form, the old nature religions were no less polytheistic than the Olympian culture religion. Nilsson has drawn special attention to the fact that they never arrived at an abstract, monistic conception of the divine continuum of *physis*, for example, in the sense of a universal mana conception. For the Greeks, furthermore, the religion of Dionysus was in no way an exclusive religion of nature which precluded the admission of other divine natural powers. In his Thracian or Lydian-Phrygian origin, Dionysus even belonged to a religion that was undeniably polytheistic. The ground-motive of the nature

---

1 Cornford, *op. cit.*, p. 185.

religions, however, like that of the Olympian culture religion, was not bound to its temporal, mythological form. Indeed, it was precisely in its encounter with the latter motive that it first emerged within the Greek consciousness as a unitary (*einheitlich*) motive. This dialectical awakening of consciousness gave to both of these motives a more profound significance that made it possible for them to overcome their polytheistic form.

The religious ground-motive of Greek thought is *dialectical*. For this reason it may never be divided into an Olympian and a mystical motive, each of which in its own right would have been determinative of an integral movement in Greek thought. Cornford himself, in fact, is unable to maintain such a conception in his treatment of the Greek thinkers. He himself is compelled to admit that a strong mystical trait can be identified, for example, in the thought of Anaximander.[1] In Anaximander's thought the conception of an infinite multiplicity of worlds which periodically return to the womb of the *apeiron* has nothing to do with the polytheistic religion of culture, for he rejects any polytheistic notion precisely with respect to this divine Origin. The same is also true in the case of the other ancient Milesians.

f.   The Motives of Moira *and* Dikē *and Their Relation to* Anankē

Cornford's attempt to contrive an opposition between the *Moira* motive and the *Dikē* motive (in the sense of a justice which applies not merely to human society, as in the Olympian religion, but rather extends equally throughout the entire cosmos) by interpreting the former as Olympian and the later as mystical in character is also unacceptable. Indeed, in spite of this interpretation, he himself must grant, for instance, that in Pindar's most Orphic (i.e., mystical) ode, where time is called the "Father of all things," the "wheel of time" is referred to as that of both *Moira* and *Dikē*.[2] Cornford's construction is decisively refuted by the fact that, in the thought of Anaximander, which Cornford regards as being governed by the *Moira* motive, it is precisely *Dikē* or the law of justice which appears in order to avenge the injustice which he perceives to exist in the rise of all that has delimited form.[3]

---

1   *Ibid.*, p. 147, note 1.
2   *Ibid.*, p. 171.
3   The conception which O. Gigon presents in *Der Ursprung der griechischen Philosophie von Hesiod bis Parmenides* (Basel, 1945), pp. 80 f., is totally unacceptable. In conflict with the texts of both Simplicius and Theophrastus, he denies that Anaximander's *apeiron* was considered the origin of all things and identifies it with Hesiod's conception of Chaos before this had been thought through in a causal-genetic manner. The separation of things having delimited form – a notion which he for some unknown reason calls "un-Greek" – would then naturally no longer be intrinsically unjust. The fact that this conception was in no way un-Greek had already been demonstrated by Rohde, *Psyche, Seelenkult und Unsterblichkeitsglaube der Griechen* (9th and 10th ed.; Tübingen, 1925), p. 119.

In a departure from the traditional conception deriving from Aristotle, Cornford attempts to uncover a sharp contrast between Anaximander and Heraclitus on this point. According to him, the latter regards *Dikē* or "avenging justice" as both the "Way of Life" and "the force that moves along that way," without respect for any boundaries.[1] Heraclitus' doctrine of the harmony of opposites in the eternal flux of the divine *physis* would then be a typical expression of the *Dikē* motive of the mystery religion. Anaximander, by contrast, supposedly thought that all individual existence is unjust because it is produced by the mixing of elements, each of which ought to remain within the boundaries of its own province. In his thought, therefore, "the reign of *Moira* [is] restored." In the extant fragment of Anaximander to which Cornford appeals, however, nothing of the sort can be found. One cannot even find the word *Moira*. For Anaximander, the rise of discrete elements, separated from each other, in itself already constitutes an injustice, because he conceives the deity as formless *hulē*, just as Heraclitus does. For him, furthermore, the way of *Dikē* is identified with the *order of time*. The latter, however, is precisely that which, in Cornford's eyes, must be restricted to the conceptual framework of the mystical tradition. Plato's idea of justice (τὰ ἑαυτοῦ πράττειν), on the other hand, displays typical features of what Cornford would call the *Moira* motif.

In order to bring the contrast between the Heraclitean conception of *Dikē* and the Ionian conception of *Moira* into sharp relief, Cornford appeals especially to Plato's dialogue *Cratylus*, where in a discussion of the origin of the word δικαιοσύνη (*dikaiosunē*; justice) Socrates expounds the conception of the school of Heraclitus, which supposes that the word δίκαιον can be derived from διαϊόν (i. e., "that which passes through [all things]"):

> For this school of thinkers, who suppose that all things are in continual flux, maintains that the great mass of the universe merely moves along, but that there exists something that passes through the entire universe and is the origin of all things that come into being. This is the swiftest and subtlest of all things; for it could not pass through all moving things if it were not the subtlest, so that it cannot be checked by anything else, and if it were not the swiftest, so that other things appear to be stationary with respect to it. Since this element superintends all things by passing through them (διαϊόν), it is rightly called δίκαιον, the consonant "k" being added for the sake of euphony.[2]

Socrates then complains that whereas many thinkers agree up to this

---

1 Cornford, *op. cit.*, p. 190. Cf. Aristotle: *Metaphysics*, A, 3, 984 a 2 ff.
2 Plato, *Cratylus*, 412D (cap. 27): ὅσοι γὰρ ἡγοῦνται τὸ πᾶν εἶναι ἐν πορείᾳ, τὸ μὲν πολὺ αὐτοῦ ὑπολαμβάνουσι τοιοῦτον τι εἶναι, οἷον οὐδὲν ἄλλο ἢ χωρεῖν, διὰ δὲ τούτου παντὸς εἶναί τι διεξιόν, δι' ὃ πάντα τὰ γιγνόμενα γίγνεσθαι· εἶναι δὲ

point, he only receives conflicting answers when he inquires further concerning justice as the fundamental cause of all that has come into existence:

> One would reply that Justice is the sun; for he alone governs nature, passing through and heating it (διαϊόντα καὶ κάοντα, i.e., dia-ka-ion). Another says, it is Fire; another, the Heat that is in Fire. Yet another laughs at all this, and says, with Anaxagoras, that Justice is Mind (nous); for Thinking (divine) Mind has absolute mastery, is mixed with nothing, and orders all things, completely suffusing them.[1]

From this Cornford concludes,

> It is evident that the followers of Heraclitus were puzzled by their master's famous obscurity, and caught at various explanations. In so doing, they introduced new distinctions which... were foreign to the mystical thought of Heraclitus. To him, the living Fire, which, through all the cycle of its transformations, preserved its measures, actually was Reason (another meaning of Logos) and the principle of Justice. Its chief embodiment was the Sun, who "will not overstep his measures, or the Spirits of Vengeance, the ministers of Justice, would find him out."[2]

The suggestive manner in which the Cambridge professor here attempts to support his interpretation of Heraclitus' conception of *Dikē* is not at all convincing, however. In the dialogue to which Cornford appeals, Plato repeatedly pokes fun at the etymological word derivations in which Heraclitus' disciple Cratylus indulges. It is highly questionable whether he thereby does justice to them. Even if we were obliged to take the contested word derivation in all seriousness, however, it would prove nothing with respect to a contrast between the Heraclitean and Ionian conceptions of *Dikē*. Indeed, Plato shows how the Ionian conception of Anaxagoras can be rhymed with the same type of etymological derivation!

In his conception that the divine, eternally flowing *physis*, as the sole *archē*, passes through all opposed forms, Heraclitus does not differ from Anaximander or any of the other Milesians. Anaximander and Heraclitus

---

τάχιστον τοῦτο καὶ λεπτότατον· οὐ γὰρ ἂν δύνασθαι ἄλλως διὰ τοῦ ἰόντος ἰέναι παντός, εἰ μὴ λεπτότατόν τ᾽ ἦν, ὥστ᾽ αὐτὸ μηδὲν στέγειν, καὶ τάχιστον, ὥστε χρῆσθαι ὥσπερ ἑστῶσι τοῖς ἄλλοις. ἐπεὶ δ᾽ οὖν ἐπιτροπεύει τἆλλα πάντα διαϊόν, τοῦτο τοὔνομα ἐκλήθη ὀρθῶς δίκαιον, εὐστομίας ἕνεκα τὴν τοῦ κάππα δύναμιν προσλαβόν. Cf. Cornford, *op. cit.*, p. 189.

1 Cf. *ibid.*
2 *Ibid.*, p. 189.

both understood *Dikē* as involving the principle of measure and proportion. The only point at issue in this connection is whether this principle already lay concealed in the mystical *Anankē* of the earlier nature religions. To this question the answer is decidedly in the negative. The matter motive of the mystical religions of nature knows nothing of rational measure and world order. Whatever form it may take in the first phase of Greek philosophy, *Dikē* is always a partially *rationalized Anankē* in which the ground-motive of the culture religion is already at work. The same is true of *Moira* as this is understood by Homer and Hesiod. Although the *Dikē* motive thus has a mystical root in nature religion, it is rooted just as well in the form motive of the Olympian religion. In other words, it can be understood only in terms of the *dialectical ground-motive* of Greek thought.

There is no support in the literary sources for a contrast, as Cornford conceives it, between Milesian nature philosophy and Heraclitus. Similarly, there is no evidence for his unproved assumption that the thinker from Ephesus included Milesian nature philosophy in the "polymathy" (πολυμαθίη) which he vigorously opposed.[1]

g. What Did Heraclitus Mean by "Polymathy?"

In B. fragment 40, Heraclitus lists among these polymaths only Hesiod, Pythagoras, Xenophanes, and Hecataeus, and in fragment 81 Pythagoras is described as the "father of deceptions." Significantly, Cornford assigns two of these four, Pythagoras and Xenophanes, to the mystical tradition. Hecataeus was the widely traveled countryman of Anaximander, who further worked out the latter's scheme of the celestial globe and the tablet upon which he pictured the inhabited earth; but beyond this there is no evidence that these two thinkers shared the same philosophical views.

The most that can be said is that Heraclitus, whose cosmogenetic conceptions were undoubtedly influenced by the Milesians, was the first person to work out consciously and deliberately the dialectic of the religious ground-motive in philosophical thought itself, and that his metaphysical theory of the oneness of the divine *physis* in the multiplicity of its contrasting phenomenal forms laid a stronger accent on the mystical, indeed Dionysian, character of the matter principle than the Milesians did. Most importantly, in Heraclitus what is placed at the center is the metaphysical philosophy of life, whereas in the case of the Milesians this only formed the background of their scientific endeavors to explain the phenomena of nature.

Cornford's interpretations show that they have suffered from the distorting influence of Durkheim's sociologism, which attempts to explain religious motives in terms of the organization of human social groups. To say this, however, is not to deny the fact that, in spite of these distorted

---

1   *Ibid.*, p.186.

constructions, Cornford often presents very penetrating and fruitful analyses, especially in his elucidation of the mystical features in the thought of Pythagoras, Empedocles, and Plato.

2. The Polar Antithesis between the Principles of Form and Matter in Parmenides' Ontology. The "Uranization" of the Form Motive

Thus, at the beginning, the uncontested hegemony in Greek thought belonged to the principle of matter. However, the internal dialectic of the religious ground-motive involved Greek philosophy, even in the very first phase of its development, in a crisis which drove it to two polarized standpoints. The form and matter principles showed that they could not be reduced to each other, and in the diametrically opposed standpoints of Heraclitus of Ephesus and Parmenides, the founder of the Eleatic school, the opposition of these two principles developed into an exclusive "either-or."[1] It is in this conflict that the Greek metaphysics of form had its birth. This metaphysics attempted, by way of θεωρία (*theōria*; theoretical intuition), to penetrate behind the visible phenomena, which remain subjected to the matter principle, to the hidden, supersensible *ontic form* of reality.[2] In this metaphysics, the primordial dualism in the religious ground-motive of the Greek community of thought presents itself in the garb of the exclusive metaphysical opposition between *being* and *becoming*.

Parmenides of Elea, who was born ca. 540 B.C., denied all true being to the visible world, which in its phenomenal appearance in a multiplicity of forms is subject to the eternal flux of the matter principle. Only being truly *is*, for a non-being cannot be an object of theoretical thought; the latter,

---

1 The polar opposition between these two is a crucial issue for Cornford's interpretation, and likewise for that of Kurt Schilling (*Geschichte der Philosophie* [Munich, 1943], p. 75), both of whom attempt to understand Heraclitus and Parmenides in terms of the same line of thought. For the inner dialectic of the form and matter motives, which appears throughout the religiously determined world of Greek thought, is manifested also at this point. If, as Cornford assumes, Heraclitus and Parmenides belong to the same mystical religious tradition, in which the "way of life" is supposed to respect no fixed boundaries, it would be inexplicable that Parmenides' eternal form of being is held within set boundaries by *Dikē, Anankē*, or even *Moira*, and above all that he should deny all vital movement to that which truly *is*, which he identifies with the divine *physis*. This can only be understood in terms of the internal polarity of the form-matter motive itself; but neither Cornford nor Schilling has come to grips with the latter.

2 It cannot be said that Greek metaphysics as a whole was first brought forth by this conflict, for Anaximander was already a true metaphysician in his conception of the *apeiron* as the invisible origin of all things. His metaphysics, however, like that of Heraclitus, was a metaphysics of the principle of matter.

therefore, as a *μὴ ὄν*, as something which must be repudiated by thought,[1] lacks all valid subsistence. Only *theōria* leads to knowledge of the divine *physis*, which encloses all being within itself, for *theōria* itself is being. For *like is known by like*, a typically Greek notion which we shall later see developed by Empedocles. Here is the clue to the meaning of Parmenides' much-contested pronouncement that theoretical thought and being are identical.[2] This, of course, has nothing to do with the identification of being and thought in the modern logical idealism of the neo-Kantian Marburg school, where being becomes a creation of theoretical thought.

Greek *theōria* thereby consciously and openly took issue with the mythological notions of popular religion; nevertheless, at the same time, it took a position that is opposed in principle to naive experience with its allegiance to the objectivity of sense phenomena. Only theoretical thought can lead to absolute truth, it said. Thus it asserted its *autonomy* over against popular belief and the uncertain opinions of those who put their trust in sense perception. This autonomy, however, was radically different from that which Thomistic Scholasticism or the modern humanistic ideal of personality ascribe to theoretical thought. Parmenides' *theōria* in no way functions as an autonomous substructure for a higher, supernatural knowledge to which it must be accommodated, as is the case in Thomistic metaphysics. It is just as little rooted in the freedom motive of modern humanism. Instead, it presents itself as the sole proclaimer of the true God, *in accordance with the Greek ground-motive.* Indeed, this was also the case with Heraclitus, as well as with Pythagoras, Empedocles, and Anaxagoras, and the thought of Socrates, Plato, Aristotle, and the Stoa is only a continuation of this line of Greek *theōria*.

One must not focus his attention exclusively on the seemingly purely logical method which Parmenides uses in his didactic poem *On Physis*

---

1 Diels-Kranz I, 236; 28 [18] Parmenides, B. Fragm. 8. 8-9: *οὐ γὰρ φατὸν οὐδὲ νοητόν ἔστιν ὅπως οὐκ ἔστι.* ("For it is neither expressible nor thinkable that [what-*is*] is not.")

2 Diels-Kranz I, 231; Parmenides, B. Fragm. 3: *τὸ γὰρ αὐτὸ νοεῖν ἐστίν τε καὶ εἶναι* ("For thinking and being are the same.") The same thought is expressed somewhat differently in B. Fragm. 8. 34 (I, 238): *ταὐτὸν δ' ἐστὶ νοεῖν τε καὶ οὕνεκεν ἔστι νόημα. οὐ γὰρ ἄνευ τοῦ ἐόντος, ἐν ὧι πεφατισμένον ἐστιν, εὑρήσεις τὸ νοεῖν.* ("Thinking and that which forms the ground of thought are the same; for you will not find thinking apart from that being in which it is expressed.") There exists a great variety of conceptions with respect to the meaning of the words *οὕνεκεν ἔστι νόημα*. I follow here the translation of Mullach (Diez), which in my opinion takes the correct viewpoint. The version of Kranz and Fränkel, "the thought that IS is," seems to me insupportable. Cf. also fragment 6. 1 (I, 232): *χρὴ τὸ λέγειν τε νοεῖν τ' ἐὸν ἔμμεναι* ("Speaking and thinking are necessarily something that *is*.") The alternative translation of Burnet strikes me as incorrect. The principle that like is known by like applies also to *doxa*. Cf. fragment 16.4.

(Περὶ φύσεως) in order to demonstrate that the visible world can possess no true being; for the poem opens with a description of Parmenides' journey to the darkness of the underworld.[1] Like Orpheus, the mythological prophet of the religious reform movement of Orphism, he descends thither in order to seek wisdom, being carried in a chariot of the sun escorted by the handmaidens of Helios. He remains alone in the darkness of the "house of night" with the goddess *Dikē,* who has unlocked the "gate of the paths of night and day" to the sun chariot and now presents to him as a divine revelation two ways of knowledge: the *path of Truth,* which alone has certainty, and the *path of uncertain opinion* (δόξα; *doxa*), which is followed by the great majority of mortals. The solemn opening of this didactic poem, written in archaic hexameters, is not mere poetic adornment; it impresses on the entire theory a consecrated and deeply religious character.

The path of Truth is that "of conviction (for this path follows truth); the other path, however, which [suggests to us that] what-is-not is and that non-being has validity, is, I tell you, utterly unexplorable; for you can neither know what-is-not (that is impossible) nor speak of it."[2]

True being is thus being as it is grasped in theoretical thought, which is rooted in conviction, and theoretical thought necessarily has true being as its object. This being is the divine *physis* itself. It is an absolutely single and indivisible, continuous whole. It permits of no fluid unfolding into a

---

1 Parmenides' visit to the goddess is usually viewed as a journey to heaven (cf. Hermann Diels, *Parmenides' Lehrgedicht*, Berlin, 1897), but the fact that it must indeed be considered a descent into the underworld has been shown by O. Gilbert, *Archiv für Geschichte der Philosophie*, XX, 25 ff. In the pseudo-Platonic dialogue *Axiochus* (371 B), the πεδίον Ἀληθείας is similarly located in the underworld. Cornford (*op. cit.,* p. 222, note 3) sees in this a combination of Dionysian and Orphic conceptions regarding the path of the soul, which he thinks can also be found in Plato's *Republic* (616 B ff.). In any case, it remains a problem that Parmenides' search for wisdom in the underworld is difficult to reconcile with his teaching that only the luminous form of being truly *is*. It seems that Cornford has not noticed this contradiction. The text, however, speaks indeed of the δώματα Νυκτός ("the house of Night"), where (ἔνθα) the goddess resides. Similarly, Kranz has "Dort (am Hause der Nacht)."

2 Diels-Kranz, I, 231; Parmenides, B. Fragm. 2: εἰ δ' ἄγ' ἐγὼν ἐρέω, κόμισαι δὲ σὺ μῦθον ἀκούσας, αἵπερ ὁδοὶ μοῦναι διζήσιός εἰσι νοῆσαι· ἡ μὲν ὅπως ἔστιν τε καὶ ὡς οὐκ ἔστι μὴ εἶναι, Πειθοῦς ἐστι κέλευθος (Ἀληθείηι γὰρ ὀπηδεῖ), ἡ δ' ὡς οὐκ ἔστιν τε καὶ ὡς χρεών ἐστι μὴ εἶναι, τὴν δή τοι φράζω παναπευθέα ἔμμεν ἀταρπόν· οὔτε γὰρ ἂν γνοίης τό γε μὴ ἐὸν (οὐ γὰρ ἀνυστόν) οὔτε φράσαις. ("Come then, and I will tell you [you must, however, accept my speech when you have heard it] which ways of inquiry alone can be thought: the one way, that [what-*is*] is and that non-being is not, this is the path of conviction [for it follows Truth]; the other, however, that [what-*is*] is not and that non-being has validity – this path, I tell you, is utterly unexplorable; for you could neither know what-is-not [that is impossible] nor express it.")

multiplicity of phenomenal forms, as the Milesians and Heraclitus had supposed. On the contrary, it is immovable, imperishable, without origination and passing away, without past and future, containing everything within itself exclusively in the *now*.[1] All this is further set forth by way of logical deduction.

a. Parmenides' Conception of the Divine Form of Being as a Sphere

Greek *theōria* is not directed toward an abstract, logical *concept* of being, however. Parmenides' poem deals with the *physis* or nature of the divine unity and totality. In polar opposition to the Milesians and Heraclitus, he grasps this divine *physis*, not in accordance with the eternal flux of the matter principle, but in a particular conception of the supersensible form principle.

Being as it is deduced in a theoretical-logical manner must be intuited in a non-sensible, luminous form or "divine shape," for it is the being of the deity. Parmenides, therefore, conceives it in the mathematical form of a sphere, this clearly being the starry vault of heaven, as had already been done before him by Xenophanes of Colophon.[2] This sphere played an important role in the astronomical speculations of the Greeks as the form of highest perfection. We shall encounter it again in our discussions of Empedocles and Plato. In Aristotle, the sphere of the fixed starry sky (this being made of ether, the fifth element) embraced the entire universe and was the outermost of the fifty-five globes containing the celestial bodies, that of the moon being the closest to earth. For Parmenides, however, the heavenly sphere was a purely mathematical form and was not composed of an element, a view which was also held by Plato's pupil Eudoxus.[3]

One who lives in the modern world is invariably taken aback by the fact

---

1 Diels-Kranz I, 235; B. Fragm. 8. 2-6: ταύτηι δ' ἐπὶ σήματ' ἔασι πολλὰ μάλ', ὡς ἀγένητον ἐὸν καὶ ἀνώλεθρόν ἐστιν, ἐστι γὰρ οὐλομελές τε καὶ ἀτρεμὲς ἠδ' ἀτέλεστον· οὐδέ ποτ' ἦν οὐδ' ἔσται, ἐπεὶ νῦν ἔστιν ὁμοῦ πᾶν, ἕν, συνεχές· ("There are very many signs on this [what-*is*]: because it is unbegotten it is also imperishable, for it is complete and imperturbable as well as without end. And it never was nor will be, since it is altogether present *now* as a single, coherent whole.")

2 Diels-Kranz I, 238; B. Fragm. 8. 42-44: αὐτὰρ ἐπεὶ πεῖρας πύματον, τετελεσμένον ἐστί πάντοθεν, εὐκύκλου σφαίρης ἐναλίγκιον ὄγκωι, μεσσόθεν ἰσοπαλὲς πάντηι·("But since a furthest limit [is present], it is complete from [and toward] all sides, like the body of a well-rounded sphere, equally curved in every direction from the center.") It should be noted that what is intended here is not the sensible form of the sphere, as this may be perceived in a material body, but evidently the non-sensible, purely geometrical sphere. For this reason, the form of being is here only said to be "like" a globe as this is present in sense experience. The celestial globe is likewise imperceptible to the senses; it can only be contemplated by mathematical *theōria* as a non-sensible form.

3 Cf., on this point, Schilling, *Geschichte der Philosophie*, I, 156.

that a Greek thinker who has so emphatically proclaimed theoretical thought to be the sole path to the discovery of truth and who has denied all validity to sense images should nevertheless revert, in a "grossly materialistic" manner, to the image of a "round material body," immediately after his apparently strict logical deduction of the *concept* of being. This, however, indicates only that such a person has not come to terms with the religious ground-motive of Greek *theōria*, but instead has unconsciously judged Parmenides' metaphysics of form by the standard of the modern conception of theory governed by the humanistic ground-motive. Parmenides' metaphysical sphere of being is not a material body, whether in the sense of modern natural scientific thought or in the Greek sense.[1] It is the luminous form of being (ontic form)[2] of the divine *physis*,[3] exalted above all sensible shapes and invisible as the immortal body of the radiant Olympian form-god. Like the latter, it is beyond the reach of the principle of the eternally flowing stream of life, which remains tied to the earth.

Nevertheless, Parmenides' divine form of being is not purely a metaphysical expression of the form motive of the Olympian culture religion. The luminous celestial sphere is no cultural form in which the thinking mind can see a reflection of itself; it is only a mathematical natural form, which as an object of religious contemplation is filled with light and as the geometric form of the starry globe of heaven encloses the supersensible being of the whole of the divine *physis*.

b. The Orphic Religion and Its Influence on Parmenides'
  Conception of the Principle of Form

How is this to be explained? If, as is very likely, Orphic influence was present here,[4] the matter is made somewhat more complex. The Orphic movement, which has already been mentioned in passing in section one,

---

1 This was already seen by Aristotle. In a discussion of Xenophanes' conception of the divine unity (*Met.* A, 5, 986 b 21), he remarks that the latter has not clearly stated his position on the nature of the *one*, with the result that it could not be ascertained whether his single form was eidetic (κατὰ τὸν λόγον) and therefore bounded, as would subsequently be the case with Parmenides, or material and therefore unbounded, as in the later thought of Melissus. In spite of this, Burnet (*Early Greek Philosophy*, p. 208) maintains that Parmenides is the father of all materialism!

2 *Translator's note:* The Dutch term *zijnsvorm* has been translated both as "form of being" and as "ontic form," as syntax allowed. The two terms are equivalent, as is evident from their juxtaposition here.

3 The fact that this is indeed a luminous sphere appears in 28 [18] Parmenides, B. Fragm. 8, 50, which will be discussed further below.

4 This influence came by way of his Pythagorean teachers, Diochaites and Ameinias. Concerning the ancient Pythagorean conception of the divine form as a luminous sphere, see O. Gigon, *op. cit.*, p. 145. Parmenides' sphere was brought into connection with Orphism (the shell of the "world-egg") already by Simplicius (*Phys.* 146. 29).

was a religious reform movement that sought to accomplish an inner reformation of the Thracian and Lydian-Phrygian worship of Dionysus,[1] by harking back to the old uranic religions involving the worship of the celestial bodies, and in particular the sun. Eratosthenes of Cyrene (ca. 276-194 B.C.), the Alexandrian librarian, relates that Orpheus gave honor to Helios the sun god instead of Dionysus: "and rising early in the morning he climbed the mountain called Pangaion, and waited for the rising of the sun."[2] The Dionysus referred to here is the wild Thracian god whose maenads tear apart Orpheus in the myth, and it is therefore apparently this particular form of Dionysus worship that Orpheus opposed. A central role is played in the Orphic religion by the contrast between light and darkness, with light being brought into connection with the starry sky and darkness with the tenebrous earth. Related to this is the Orphic belief in the immortality of the soul. Having originated in heaven, the soul falls to earth and is enclosed in the dark body as in a grave or prison; after having passed through a cycle of reincarnations, which terminates with the completion of the "great world year," it is able to return to its heavenly dwelling in a purified state. An Orphic tablet found at Petelia reads:

> I am a child of the earth and the starry heavens,
> But my origin lies in heaven.[3]

The Dionysus who was worshiped in Orphic circles, in contrast, was no longer the wild god of bacchantic frenzy; he was the deity reborn as Dionysus Zagreus, who, after having been torn to pieces by the Titans as a child, was revived as the son of Zeus and took over the world dominion of the latter.

What is the meaning of this Orphic saga? Following Plutarch, Rohde interprets it as follows: "through wickedness, the one divine being becomes lost in the multiplicity of forms of the world. It arises once again as a unity in the Dionysus who springs anew from Zeus."[4] Although Plutarch presents this interpretation in Platonizing garb, it is in its essentials so far re-

---

1   Concerning the difference between these two forms of Dionysus worship, of which Rohde fails to take note, see Nilsson, *op. cit.*, pp. 532 f. and 545 f. The Orphic representation of the child Dionysus originated, not in Thrace, but in Lydia and Phrygia, where Dionysus would sleep through the winter and reawaken as a child in the spring. The Greeks understood this falling asleep as death and burial.

2   Eratosthenes, *Catast.* xxiv; cf. J. E. Harrison, *Prolegomena*, p. 461, and Cornford, *op. cit.*, p. 177.

3   γῆς παῖς εἰμι καὶ οὐρανοῦ ἀστερόεντος· αὐτὰρ ἐμὸν γένος οὐράνιον Cf. Harrison, *Prolegomena*, p. 661. An English translation of the complete text of the tablet is found in F. M. Cornford, *Greek Religious Thought* (New York, 1923), p. 60.

4   "...durch Frevel verliert sich das Eine Gotteswesen in die Vielheit der Gestalten dieser Welt. Es entsteht als Einheit wieder in dem neu aus Zeus entsprossenen Dionysos." Rohde, *Psyche,* II, 119. (English version by translator)

moved from being dependent on Platonic philosophy that we find its basic idea already in Anaximander. The divine One is not conceived here, however, in terms of the matter principle, as was the case with the Milesians, but rather in accordance with the form principle of the luminous sky. Nevertheless, Dionysus Zagreus himself has entered into the cycle of evil composed of birth, death, and revival. This remains his link with the ancient worship of Dionysus (which the Orphics depreciated) as an ecstatic religion of life. The saga proceeds to tell how the Titans, who had devoured the limbs of the god, were struck with lightning from Zeus. From their ashes arose the human race, and, in accordance with its origin, the good in it which stems from Dionysus Zagreus is mingled with the evil Titanic element. The good element strives to be reunited with the luminous form of its divine origin.

The primitive uranic religion of nature is here enriched by the form motive of the Olympian religion of culture; but it itself is not transformed thereby into a culture religion. The immortal, supersensible form does not enclose an actual Olympian god; rather, the divine, celestial *physis* as a luminous substance is surrounded in its entirety by the immortal form, the round heavenly vault. And since the soul originates in the heavens, it participates in this divine luminous form. In this way, *athanasia*, the supersensible motive of form and immortality in the Olympian religion, is given a naturalistic uranic interpretation. The form motive of the religion of culture is *uranized* and thereby *naturalized*.

According to Aristotle's testimony, Xenophanes (born ca. 580 B. C., in Colophon, Asia Minor), the acute, satirical opponent of the polytheistic mythology of the Olympian religion, had already stated that there is *one* god "looking upon the entire heavenly vault."[1] Whether or not Persian (Zoroastrian) influence is present in this opposition between light and darkness and the identification of this duality with good and evil cannot be known for certain; but it is clear, in any case, that the motive of light and darkness was incorporated into the Greek ground-motive.

c. *The Rejection of the Orphic-Dionysian Conception of the Principle of Matter*

In the second part of his didactic poem, Parmenides himself emphatically brings again to mind this Orphic conception of *physis* and at the same time makes clear at what point he departs from it. When the goddess *Dikē* undertakes to expound to the thinker from Elea the second path of inquiry, which is not the way of truth but rather that of deceptive *doxa*, she begins by saying that two forms (μορφάς) have been given names in the realm of human belief, and that the single form (δέμας) of the divine *physis* has thereby been unjustifiably separated into two op-

---

1 Aristotle, *Metaphysics* A, 5. 986 b 23: εἰς τὸν ὅλον οὐρανὸν ἀποβλέψας τὸ ἓν εἶναί φησι τὸν θεόν.

posed forms with features that set them apart from each other: on the one hand, the ethereal light, which is "everywhere the same as itself"; and, on the other hand, as its diametrical opposite, the lightless night, "a dense and heavy bodily form." The second form, it is expressly stated, ought not to be accepted, for "at this point human opinions have fallen into error."[1]

As the opposite of the luminous form of being, the darkness of the tenebrous earth is naturally a non-being, and a non-being, which cannot be grasped in a theoretical way, has no *valid* subsistence. The doctrine of the cycle of rebirths in an earthly body, which forms the Dionysian background of the Orphic conception, and the individual immortality of the soul as a luminous form-substance as well, are here consigned to the realm of *doxa*;[2] for the one divine *physis*, which fills the non-sensible heavenly globe with immortal being, allows of no multiplicity of form-substances. At the same time, the rigid immobility that had been foreign to the Orphic form principle enters into the divine form of being as a direct consequence of the exclusion of the principle of matter.

---

1 Diels-Kranz I, 239 f.; Parmenides, B. Fragm. 8. 50 ff.: ἐν τῶι σοι παύω πιστὸν λόγον ἠδὲ νόημα ἀμφὶς ἀληθείης· δόξας δ' ἀπὸ τοῦδε βροτείας μάνθανε κόσμον ἐμῶν ἐπέων ἀπατηλὸν ἀκούων. μορφὰς γὰρ κατέθεντο δύο γνώμας ὀνομάζειν· τῶν μίαν οὐ χρεών ἐστιν – ἐν ὧι πεπλανημένοι εἰσίν– τἀντία δ' ἐκρίναντο δέμας καὶ σήματ' ἔθεντο χωρὶς ἀπ' ἀλλήλων, τῆι μὲν φλογὸς αἰθέριον πῦρ, ἤπιον ὄν, μέγ' [ἀραιὸν] ἐλαφρόν, ἑωυτῶι πάντοσε τωὐτόν, τῶι δ' ἑτέρωι μὴ τωὐτόν· ἀτὰρ κἀκεῖνο κατ' αὐτό τἀντία νύκτ' ἀδαῆ, πυκινὸν δέμας ἐμβριθές τε. ("Here I cease to give you my trustworthy account and thought concerning Truth. But learn henceforth the pseudo-opinions of mortals by giving heed to the deceptive ordering of my words. For they have determined to name two forms, one of which ought not to be named – at this point they have fallen into error; and they separated the [one] form [viz., of the divine *physis*] into two opposed [forms] and distinguished their marks from one another. On the one hand, there is the ethereal, luminous fire, gentle, very light, everywhere the same as itself, although not identical to the other. The other also, in itself, is opposite to this: the lightless night, a dense and heavy form.") Cf. in this connection Aristotle's *Metaphysics*, 13. 4. 1091 a 34 f., where he mentions among the *archai* accepted by the earlier poets the Orphic principles of night and heaven (Νύκτα καὶ Οὐρανόν), and also Chaos and Oceanus, the former going back to Hesiod and the latter to Homer. In addition, Aristotle emphatically asserts in *Met.* A, 5. 987 a, that Parmenides considered (warm) fire to belong to what-*is*, and the (cold) earth to what-is-not.

2 The utterance concerning the soul which Simplicius (*ad Arist. Phys.*, p. 39 D) ascribes to Parmenides, viz., that the world-ruling *daemon* "first sends it from the visible into the invisible, and then in the reverse direction," is difficult to evaluate. It seems indeed to point in the direction of the Pythagorean-Orphic conception of the soul, but it in any case lies beyond the framework of Parmenides' ontology. Cf., in this connection, Diels, *Parmenides*, pp. 109 ff., and Rohde, *Psyche*, II, 158.

d. *Xenophanes' and Parmenides' Ideas of God*

If we compare Parmenides' conception of the divine One with that of his predecessor Xenophanes on this point, we must admit that there is a certain resemblance between them, even though Parmenides' metaphysical ontology has nothing further to do with the ideas of the latter. Xenophanes testifies that he left his native city of Colophon in Asia Minor at the age of twenty-five in order to begin his wanderings throughout Hellas, where he supported himself by publicly reciting his poems. At a very advanced age he settled in Elea (Velia), a colony established in southern Italy by the Phocaeans in 540 B.C., where Parmenides set up his school.

Xenophanes opposed the anthropomorphic conception of the gods present in the Olympian culture religion, as they were portrayed by Homer and Hesiod, and taught the all-encompassing oneness of God in the form of the celestial vault. He already denied movement to the deity[1] and propounded the unchangeability and invisibility of the divine form.[2] According to him, the deity is "all mind, all eye, all ear."[3] Diels thinks that these utterances formed part of a poem on *physis*. According to others, they appeared in a collection of satyrical poems (σίλλοι).

Aristotle – for that matter, incorrectly – called Parmenides a pupil of Xenophanes; but he qualified this by adding that the latter had not clearly stated his position concerning the nature of the divine One. Indeed, there is in Xenophanes no evidence of the polar dialectic which stands out in Parmenides' poem and leads there to an absolute antithesis between the uranic form principle and the Dionysian matter principle. He holds that "from earth (and water)" are born all things that are subject to the matter principle of eternal vital movement, humankind included.[4] The deity, on the other hand, "controls everything by the intellectual strength of his mind." A true metaphysical *theōria*, however, which earnestly inquires into the relationship between the form and matter principles and presents itself as the "way of truth," is not to be found in Xenophanes. As an un-

---

1 Diels-Kranz I, 135; Xenophanes B. Fragm. 26: αἰεὶ δ' ἐν ταὐτῶι μίμνει κινούμενος οὐδέν οὐδὲ μετέρχεσθαί μιν ἐπιπρέπει ἄλλοτε ἄλληι. ("He remains always in the same place, not moving at all, and it is not fitting for him to change place from here to there.")

2 Diels-Kranz I, 117: A. Fragm. 28 (from the pseudo-Aristotelian work *De Melisso, Xenophane, Gorgia* c. 3. 977 a 23): ἀίδιον μὲν οὖν διὰ ταῦτα εἶναι τὸν θεόν. ("therefore the deity is invisible").

3 Diels-Kranz I, 135; Xenophanes B. Fragm. 24: οὖλος ὁρᾶι, οὖλος δὲ νοεῖ, οὖλος δέ τ' ἀκούει.

4 Diels-Kranz I, 135; B. Fragm. 27: ἐκ γαίης γὰρ πάντα καὶ εἰς γῆν πάντα τελευτᾶι. ("For all things come from earth, and all things turn back to earth in the end.") Diels-Kranz I, 136; B. Fragm. 29: γῆ καὶ ὕδωρ πάντ' ἐσθ' ὅσα γίνοντ(αι) ἠδὲ φύονται. ("All things that come into being and grow are earth and water.") B. Fragm. 33: πάντες γὰρ γαίης τε καὶ ὕδατος ἐκγενόμεσθα. ("For we were all born from earth and water.")

changeable One which has never come into being, his god is indeed transcendent to nature as this is manifested in the process of becoming; but there is no indication that he denies that nature, in contrast to the divine One, has true reality.[1] Instead, he gives expression to a certain skepticism with regard to all human knowledge: seeming clings to all things, and even our knowledge of the deity is mere *doxa* .[2]

This does not alter the fact that in Xenophanes' idea of God, at least, the form motive has been dissociated from the principle of matter. In this regard he is doubtless the precursor of Parmenides, although he prepared the way even more for Anaxagoras' doctrine of *nous*.

Parmenides' form principle thus remained naturalistic in conception, and a naturalistic conception of the Greek principle of form was continually threatened with being recombined with the principle of matter. This indeed took place, in fact, when his pupil Melissus of Samos once again ascribed the character of an *apeiron* to Parmenides' unchangeable being. Parmenides' notion of the divine *physis* as a single form of being, however, was still arrived at in conscious opposition to the matter principle of the religion of nature. Parmenides *de-deified* the latter precisely as the principle of vital movement and depreciated it as a daemon of *doxa*.[3]

e. *The Theoretical Metamorphosis of* Anankē*: Anankē as the Protectress of the Divine Form of Being and as Logical-Metaphysical Necessity*

Anankē, the unpredictable handmaiden of the matter principle, is transformed by means of *theōria* into the protectress of the divine form of being, which it holds fast "in the bonds of the delimited."[4] It becomes identical with *Dikē* and *Moira*.[5] But here even the latter has lost its char-

---

1   Karl Reinhardt's bold hypothesis that Xenophanes' theology rests upon Parmenides' ontology, a notion which Gigon (*op. cit.*, pp. 192 f.) worked out with greater care, is based on an undoubtedly anachronistic formulation of Xenophanes' doctrine of God in the writing from the Aristotelian corpus which was referred to in an earlier context.

2   Diels-Kranz I, 137; B. Fragm. 34: καὶ τὸ μὲν οὖν σαφὲς οὔτις ἀνὴρ ἴδεν οὐδέ τις ἔσται εἰδὼς ἀμφὶ θεῶν τε καὶ ἄσσα λέγω περὶ πάντων· εἰ γὰρ καὶ τὰ μάλιστα τύχοι τετελεσμένον εἰπών, αὐτὸς ὅμως οὐκ οἶδε· δόκος δ' ἐπὶ πᾶσι τέτυκται. ("And no person has ever seen what is accurate [the truth], and there will also never be someone who knows it about the gods and about all the things which I mention; for even if someone should succeed in the highest degree in speaking perfection, he would nevertheless himself be unaware of it; seeming [*doxa*] clings to all things.")

3   Cf. B. Fragm. 12, 5.

4   Diels-Kranz I, 237-238; Parmenides, B. Fragm. 8, 30-31: κρατερὴ γὰρ 'Ανάγκη πείρατος ἐν δεσμοῖσιν ἔχει, τό μιν ἀμφὶς ἐέργει οὕνεκεν οὐκ ἀτελεύτητον τὸ ἐὸν θέμις εἶναι· ("For powerful *Anankē* holds it in the bonds of the delimitation which encloses it round about, since it is not proper that what-*is* be without boundary.")

5   Diels-Kranz I, 238; B. Fragm. 8, 37-38: ἐπεὶ τό γε Μοῖρ' ἐπέδησεν οὖλον ἀκίνητόν

acter of blind, irrational fate, which in the Olympian religion of culture had been only partially rationalized by the conception of a divine territorial division between heaven, sea, and underworld. *Dikē* and *Moira* now bar the divine form of being from becoming dissolved in the boundless, flowing "non-being" of the matter principle, for *theōria* has declared that this principle has no validity. In this manner, *Anankē* acquires the new theoretical meaning of logical, and simultaneously metaphysical necessity.[1]

The eternal, supersensible form of being cannot have its origin in the principle of matter, for the latter is a *non*-being, and since everything that constitutes an object of thought and speech is something that *is*, a non-being is logically unthinkable.[2] It is only the deceptive appearances of sense perception that lead one to the opinion (*doxa*) that there exists a multiplicity of things which come into being and pass away; for what comes into being is not yet, what passes away is no longer, and all becoming flows through mutually opposed sensible forms, which logically contradict one another. Being admits of no mixing with non-being.

f. The Matter Principle as the Origin of the Form Principle in Heraclitus and the Milesians

The position of Heraclitus is diametrically opposed to this Eleatic standpoint. As we have seen, the thinker from Ephesus denied the existence of an eternal form of being and deified the principle of eternal flux (the *rheuston*) in the religious symbol of ever-moving fire, which in dialectical fashion comes to equal expression in all contrasting forms.[3]

Heraclitus levels trenchant criticism against the religion of culture, against Homer and Hesiod, as well as against the immoral rites present in the worship of Dionysus and in the mystery religions.[4] Nevertheless, in his conception, the *logos* or rational world-order, which is unmistakably

---

τ' ἔμεναι· ("Since *Moira* has bound it so as to be whole and immovable.") Diels-Kranz I, 236; B. Fragm. 8, 13-14, 15: οὔτε γενέσθαι οὔτ' ὄλλυσθαι ἀνῆκε Δίκη ... ἀλλ' ἔχει. ("*Dikē* has given it [what-*is*] liberty neither to come into being nor to pass away... but she holds it fast.")

1 This is one of the meanings that Aristotle ascribes to *Anankē* in the fifth book of his *Metaphysics*.

2 Diels-Kranz I, 235-236; B. Fragm. 8, 7-8: οὐδ' ἐκ μὴ ἐόντος ἐάσσω φάσθαι σ' οὐδὲ νοεῖν ("Nor shall I permit you to speak of or think [the coming into being of what-*is*] from what-is-not.")

3 Diels-Kranz I, 165; Heraclitus, B. Fragm. 67: ὁ θεὸς ἡμέρη εὐφρόνη, χειμὼν θέρος, πόλεμος εἰρήνη, κόρος λιμός, ... ἀλλοιοῦται δὲ ὅκωσπερ <πῦρ>, ὁπόταν συμμιγῆι θυώμασιν, ὀνομάζεται καθ' ἡδονὴν ἑκάστου. ("God is day night, winter summer, war peace, satiety hunger. But he changes just as fire, which, when it is mixed with fragrances, is named after the aroma of each.")

4 B. Fragments 42, 56, and 57 are directed against Homer and Hesiod, and 14 and 15 are directed against the immoral practices of the mystery religions and the cult of

the form principle of measure, proportion, and harmony, springs dialectically from the matter principle itself. According to B. fragment 64, he taught that "fire, endowed with reason, is the *cause* of the entire ordering of the world."[1] The strife (of opposites), he said, is the "father of all things," for the eternal vital movement of the divine *physis* is manifested only in its passage through opposed forms. The individual life of the one form means the death of the other. Milesian nature philosophy also taught that form proceeds from the flux of matter. The impossibility of this, however, is precisely what was demonstrated by Parmenides.

From this point on, pre-Socratic philosophy was increasingly driven toward an *overt dualism in its idea of origin*. In general, there was no longer any attempt to derive the form principle from the matter principle or the matter principle from the principle of form. Instead, both of them were regarded as equally necessary principles of origin (*archai*) for the cosmos. The attempt was simply made, even though it was always in vain, to effect some kind of synthesis between them.

3. The Formalization of the Matter Principle in the Older Pythagorean School

a. The Three Strata in the Original Religious Conception of the Pythagorean Community

Before examining these later developments, however, it is important that we first take cognizance of the remarkable effort of the Pythagorean school to *formalize* the principle of matter by incorporating it into the form principle itself. Our survey of this attempt will take us back to a stage of thought which antedated Parmenides and exerted a demonstrable influence on him.

The thought of Pythagoras, who lived during the sixth century B. C., and who was at the height of his career about 531-532, comprises another part of the religious reform movement which I discussed earlier. This was a movement, as is generally acknowledged, of which Orphism formed the background. With all of the reservations I had to make concerning his sociological method of investigation, it must be said that what Cornford has brought to light concerning the relationship of Orphism and Pythagoreanism belongs without question among the best and most interesting material in his book.

As is known, Pythagoras, who himself came from the island of Samos, founded a religious-ethical community (the Pythagorean order) at Croton, a Greek colony in southwest Italy. In this community, which soon ac-

---

Dionysus.

1 Diels-Kranz I, 165; B. Fragm. 64: λέγει δὲ καὶ φρόνιμον τοῦτο εἶναι τὸ πῦρ καὶ τῆς διοικήσεως τῶν ὅλων αἴτιον ("He says also that this fire is endowed with reason and is the cause of the entire ordering of the world.")

quired great political influence, Greek *theōria* took on the meaning characteristic of it at first, namely, "the path to the true knowledge of god," a significance that we have already come across in Parmenides.

In order to understand this correctly, it is necessary to follow Cornford and to distinguish three strata in the religious conception of Pythagoras: the *Dionysian*, the *Orphic*, and the *Pythagorean* proper, where *theōria* is introduced. The Dionysian substratum provides the conception of the oneness of the divine stream of life and the kinship of all living things in the cycle of birth, death, and rebirth. It is governed by the Greek matter principle, as we found this expressed in Heraclitus' philosophy of life.[1] From Orphism comes the directedness of earthly life in its subjection to the depreciated matter principle toward the eternal form of the luminous heavens, whence the soul has originated. After a cycle of transmigrations into dark earthly bodies, the soul can leave its "prison," after the completion of the "great year" (ten thousand solar years), and return once again in a purified state to the celestial sphere of light.[2] In order to prepare for this return, the soul must observe ascetic practices while it is still on earth. Orphism, however, is still bound to a mythological ritual, the spectacle of the suffering Dionysus, which makes a strong appeal to sensory emotion. In the mystery cult, Dionysus in the symbolic form of an animal is torn to pieces by the savage Titans, before he can be reborn as Dionysus Zagreus. In Pythagoras, this contemplation (*theōria*), which is tied to sensory feel-

---

1 Dicaearchus (in Porphyry, *Vita Pythag.* 19; Diels-Kranz, I, 100, 37; 8a "Life of Pythagoras."), after remarking that it is difficult to attain any certainty with regard to Pythagoras' own ideas, states that his best known doctrines were the following: πρῶτον μὲν ὡς ἀθάνατον εἶναί φησι τὴν ψυχήν, εἶτα μεταβάλλουσαν εἰς ἄλλα γένη ζῴων, πρὸς δὲ τούτοις ὅτι κατὰ περιόδους τινὰς τὰ γενόμενά ποτε πάλιν γίνεται, νέον δ' οὐδὲν ἁπλῶς ἔστι, καὶ ὅτι πάντα τὰ γινόμενα ἔμψυχα ὁμογενῆ δεῖ νομίζειν. ("First he says that the soul is immortal and that it is transformed into other sorts of living beings; further, that whatever has come into being is born anew in accordance with the revolutions of a certain cycle, since nothing is new in an absolute sense, and that everything born with soul in it must be seen as mutually related.") This statement concisely summarizes the originally Orphic and Dionysian motives in Pythagoras. Cf., in this connection, Sextus Empiricus, *Adv. Mathem.* 9: 127: οἱ μὲν οὖν περὶ τὸν Πυθαγόραν καὶ τὸν Ἐμπεδοκλέα καὶ τῶν Ἰταλῶν πλῆθος φασὶ μὴ μόνον ἡμῖν πρὸς ἀλλήλους καὶ πρὸς τοὺς θεοὺς εἶναί τινα κοινωνίαν, ἀλλὰ καὶ πρὸς τὰ ἄλογα τῶν ζῴων. ἐν γὰρ ὑπάρχειν πνεῦμα τὸ διὰ παντὸς τοῦ κόσμου διῆκον ψυχῆς τρόπον, τὸ καὶ ἑνοῦν ἡμᾶς πρὸς ἐκεῖνα. ("Those who follow Pythagoras and Empedocles, as well as most of the Italian philosophers, say that we form some type of community not only with respect to each other and to the gods, but also with respect to non-rational living beings; for [they teach] that one life principle governs the nature of the soul-substance which pervades the entire cosmos and unites us with all living beings.") Cornford observes (*op. cit.*, p. 202) that this is doubtless a sharp description of the originally Dionysian belief in an all-pervading stream of life which forms the substratum of kinship among all living things.

2 See above, p. 58.

ing, is replaced by *philosophical theōria*, which rejects the orgiastic ritual of the Orphic cult of Dionysus and regards the passionless philosophical contemplation of the harmony and measure of the luminous heavens as the only true way to the union of the soul with the deity.

In Pythagoreanism, Dionysus is replaced by Apollo, the luminous Olympian god of science and music; but the form principle, which here assumes the religious primacy, is no more simply that of the religion of culture than the Orphic one was. It is, on the contrary, a "theoreticization" of the Orphic principle. The true deity is not an Olympian culture god; it is the immortal psychic luminous substance, which is enclosed by the imperishable, supersensible form of the celestial vault. It is in this that the soul has its origin.[1] In other words, the form principle here is a theoreticized uranic principle, which has naturalized the form motive of the religion of culture and which continues to manifest its Dionysian basis.

It is in this regard that the Pythagorean philosophy differs basically from the Eleatic standpoint of Parmenides. At least in its origin, the form principle of Pythagoreanism is not static and fixed; it retains a dynamic trait by virtue of its being rooted in the Dionysian conception of the matter principle. As the Pythagoreans understood it, a multiplicity of forms can spring by means of motion from the divine (celestial) oneness of nature. This possibility was later eliminated by Parmenides. Further, for Pythagoras, this dynamism is no longer expressed, as had been the case with the Milesians and Heraclitus, in the symbol of the "movable element" (water, fire, or air). It is rather expressed in an arithmetic process, the rise of the numerical series from a unity as origin; for number contains the measure and harmony of the entire luminous heavens. Pythagoras thus replaces Parmenides' rigid geometric form of being, which excludes the genetic matter principle, with the principle of number as the form of the luminous heavens. This principle of number serves, at the same time, as the *archē* of all genesis, which remains subject to the principle of matter.

In this regard, what Aristotle tells us in the fifth section of the first book of his *Metaphysics* is of the greatest importance:

1　This is clearly enunciated in Empedocles' *Katharmoi* (Purifications), a poetic work that is completely Orphic in spirit. As Empedocles says here (Diels-Kranz I, 365-366; Empedocles, B. Fragm. 134: οὐδὲ γὰρ ἀνδρομέηι κεφαλῆι κατὰ γυῖα κέκασται ... ἀλλὰ φρὴν ἱερὴ καὶ ἀθέσφατος ἔπλετο μοῦνον, φροντίσι κόσμον ἅπαντα καταΐσσουσα θοῆισιν. ("For he [the deity, and Apollo in particular] is not furnished with a human head on his members... but he is only a mind, holy and ineffable, which darts through the whole cosmos with swift thoughts.") This conception of the deity is altogether consistent with the following pronouncements of Xenophanes (Diels-Kranz I, 135; Xenophanes, B. Fragm. 23 and 25: εἷς θεός, ἔν τε θεοῖσι καὶ ἀνθρώποισι μέγιστος, οὔτι δέμας θνητοῖσιν ὁμοίιος οὐδὲ νόημα. ("One god, the greatest among gods and humans, neither in form like unto mortals, nor in thought.") ἀλλ᾽ ἀπάνευθε πόνοιο νόου φρενὶ πάντα κραδαίνει. ("But without toil he stirs all things by the intellectual strength of his mind.")

The Pythagoreans were the first to develop mathematics further, and since they completely immersed themselves in mathematics, they thought that its principles were the principles of everything that is. Since, however, in mathematics numbers are by nature the first, and they believed that they could find in numbers many analogies for what *is* and what *comes into being*, many more than in fire, earth, and water – for one form in which number is manifested is supposedly justice, another is soul and thinking mind, and still other forms are time and opportunity and, so to speak, anything and everything else that exists – and seeing that they furthermore found in numbers the properties and the determinative relationships of musical harmonies – since in fact every other thing clearly seemed to be formed in its entire nature [*physis*] after the model of numbers, and numbers ranked first in all of nature, they held that the elements of numbers are the elements of everything that exists, and *that the entire heaven* [ouranos] *is harmony and number.*[1]

Aristotle then adds to this the following important observation:

Evidently they thought also that number is *archē*, both qua matter [*hulē*] and qua form and habitus of what-*is*, and that the elements of number are the even and the odd. Of these, they held the one to be limited and the other to be unlimited; unity [*monas*], however, consists of both of these, since it is both even and odd; but number consists of unity, and numbers, as has been said, constitute the entire heavens.[2]

Aristotle also remarks that "the decad [the number ten] was held to be *perfect* and to embrace the whole nature of numbers."[3]

What conclusions can we draw from this information in connection with what is known from other sources concerning the role that Pythagoras and his earlier disciples gave to the principle of number?

---

1 Aristotle, *Metaphysics*, A, 5. 985 b and 986 a. I follow here the translation of Rolfes. Italics mine.
2 *Ibid.*, 986 a 21 f.
3 Aristotle, *Metaphysics*, A, 5. 986 a: ἐπειδὴ τέλειον ἡ δεκὰς εἶναι δοκεῖ καὶ πᾶσαν περιειληφέναι τὴν τῶν ἀριθμῶν φύσιν. The following utterance of Philolaus, the first Pythagorean to write a work on *physis* (περὶ φύσεως), agrees with this (Diels-Kranz, I, 411; Philolaus, B. Fragm. 11): θεωρεῖν δεῖ τὰ ἔργα καὶ τὴν οὐσίαν τῶ ἀριθμῶ καττὰν δύναμιν ἅτις ἐστὶν ἐν τᾶι δεκάδι· μεγάλα γὰρ καὶ παντελὴς καὶ παντοεργὸς καὶ θείω καὶ οὐρανίω βίω καὶ ἀνθρωπίνω ἀρχὰ καὶ ἁγεμὼν κοινωνοῦσα ... ἄνευ δὲ τούτας πάντ᾽ ἄπειρα καὶ ἄδηλα καὶ ἀφανῆ. ("One must consider the operations and the essence of number in accordance with the power contained in the number ten. For it is great, bringing all things to their proper end, accomplishing all things, and it is the origin and leader both of divine and heavenly and of human life, participating in [textual corruption at this point]. Without this, everything is unlimited, obscure, and unclear.")

b. The Meaning of the Pythagorean Tetractys

In his biography of Pythagoras, Porphyry, the neoplatonist, relates that the disciples of Pythagoras swore by him as by a god who had given them a symbol that could be used in solving many problems. This symbol is the so-called *tetractys*.[1]

The original *tetractys* appears to have been the *tetractys* of the decad, which is obtained by the addition $1+2+3+4 = 10$. In the absence of numerical symbols, this was represented by a spatial figure consisting of ten points:

According to Theo of Smyrna, a thinker from the so-called middle Platonist school, who lived during the time of the emperor Hadrian and who was strongly influenced by Pythagoreanism, this *tetractys* "is of great importance in music.... But it is not only on this account that it has been held in the highest honor by all Pythagoreans; but also because it is held to contain the nature of the universe. Hence it was an oath by which they swore:

> By him who gave to our soul the *tetractys*, which hath the fountain and root of ever-springing nature (*physis*)."[2]

Theo then proceeds to enumerate other forms of the *tetractys*. The second is that which Plato uses in his dialogue *Timaeus*, in order to symbolize the harmonic constitution of the "world-soul":

$$
\begin{array}{ccc}
 & 1 & \\
2 & & 3 \\
4 & & 9 \\
8 & & 27
\end{array}
$$

According to Theo, these two forms of the *tetractys* comprise the musical, geometric, and arithmetic relationships from which the harmony of the entire cosmos is composed. The later Pythagoreans delighted in using this symbol as the master key for explaining the cosmos. The third *tetractys* is: point, line, plane, solid body; the fourth is: fire, air, water, earth; the fifth is: pyramid, octahedron, icosahedron, cube; the sixth is that of things that grow (τῶν φυομένων): the seed, and growth in length, breadth, and height (the primitive conception of the three spatial dimensions); the seventh is that of societal forms: the individual, the household, the village community, and the state; the eighth is the four levels

---

1 Porphyry, *Vita Pythag.* 20. "Tetra" means "4."

2 Theo[n] of Smyrna, Περὶ τετρακτύος, p. 154, Dupuis (1892), quoted from Cornford. *op. cit.*, pp. 205-206. The Greek text of the oath reads as follows: οὐ μὰ τὸν ἁμετέρᾳ ψυχᾷ (γενέᾳ, al.) παραδόντα τετρακτύν, παγὰν ἀενάου φύσιος ῥίζωμά τ᾽ ἔχουσαν. (I have followed Cornford's translation.) (*Translator's note:* Cornford uses the word "ever-springing," whereas Dooyeweerd's rendering of Cornford's text into Dutch would be better translated "ever-flowing *physis*.")

of cognition: *nous*, knowledge, opinion, sense perception; the ninth is that of the three parts of the soul (in the Platonic conception) and the material body; the tenth is that of the four seasons, by which all things come into being; and the eleventh is the four stages of human development: infancy, youth, manhood, and old age. These later interpretations of the *tetractys* are expressed to a degree in Platonic terms; but, as Cornford has rightly observed, they are in line with the earliest Pythagorean traditions and are typical of the entire original tendency of this school.

The *tetractys* is not merely a symbol of static, formal relationships in the cosmos; it contains within itself just as well the genetic movement of life, which, in subjection to the principle of matter, proceeds to develop the harmonic structure of the cosmos from an original unity (*monas*). As the oath in the text transmitted to us by Theo declares, this symbol is "the fountain of ever-flowing *physis*."[1] At the same time, it is the way to the *true knowledge of deity*, since in accordance with the statement of the Pythagorean Philolaus, number "by its very nature does not partake of falsehood."[2]

Unlike later Pythagorean mathematics, which was static, the original conception of this school did not conceive the development of the series of numbers out of the unity as an addition of abstract mathematical units; instead, it was viewed as dynamic process, containing within itself the genesis of the entire cosmos as a fluid continuum, which is limited by the principle of number and is brought within the bounds of measure and harmony by it. In this process, number lends *bodily form* to things as they come into being, and it also brings about within the soul the correspondence of these things with sense perception, thus making them knowable.[3]

In Orphic fashion, this process is represented as the progressive conquest of the formless and unbounded flowing field (χώρα) of darkness

---

1 Dooyeweerd omits the word "root," which is contained in the original text: "the fountain and root..." (Translator's note).

2 Diels-Kranz, I, 412; Philolaus, B. Fragm. 11, 9: ψεῦδος δὲ οὐδὲν δέχεται ἁ τῶ ἀριθμῶ φύσις οὐδὲ ἁρμονία· ("Falsehood, however, does not at all inhere in the nature of number and in harmony.")

3 *Ibid.*, pp. 411-412; Philolaus, B. Fragm. 11: γνωμικὰ γὰρ ἁ φύσις ἁ τῶ ἀριθμῶ καὶ ἡγεμονικὰ καὶ διδασκαλικὰ τῶ ἀπορουμένω παντὸς καὶ ἀγνοουμένω παντί. οὐ γὰρ ἦς δῆλον οὐδενὶ οὐδὲν τῶν πραγμάτων οὔτε αὐτῶν ποθ' αὐτὰ οὔτε ἄλλω πρὸς ἄλλο, εἰ μὴ ἦς ἀριθμὸς καὶ ἁ τούτω οὐσία. νῦν δὲ οὗτος καττὰν ψυχὰν ἁρμόζων αἰσθήσει πάντα γνωστὰ καί ποτάγορα ἀλλάλοις κατὰ γνώμονος φύσιν ἀπεργάζεται σωματῶν καὶ σχίζων τοὺς λόγους χωρὶς ἑκάστους τῶν πραγμάτων τῶν τε ἀπείρων καὶ τῶν περαινόντων. ("For the nature of number spreads knowledge and is a guide and teacher for everyone in all things that are doubtful or unknown to him. For nothing about things would be clear to anyone, neither in their relation to themselves nor to one another, unless there existed number and its essence. But it brings all things into correspondence with sense perception within the soul and thus causes them to be knowable and mutually corresponding in accordance with the nature of the 'pointer', in that it gives them body and divides the relationships of things into their own groups, whether they be unlimited or limiting.")

(the dark and cold air) by a central nuclear unity, which radiates light and warmth (the central fire or *hestia*).[1] This apriori conception, completely under the influence of the religious ground-motive, led Pythagorean astronomy to the bold step of removing the earth from the central position within the celestial sphere, which it had occupied since the time of Anaximander, in order to make way for the "central fire."[2] Light thus becomes the *peras*, the principle that introduces form and limitation. The flowing darkness, on the contrary, is the *apeiron*, the embodiment of the principle of matter. The principle of number, whose nature is encapsulated in the *tetractys*, is obliged to unite both of these principles within itself, however, if it is indeed to be the fountain of ever-flowing life and, simultaneously, the symbol of the eternal form of the luminous heavens.

c. The Pythagorean Attempt at Synthesis

At this juncture, the attempt to effect a religious synthesis between the antagonistic motives of form and matter begins to make itself felt in Pythagorean mathematics. In the numerical series, the *peras* is conceived as the odd and the *apeiron* as the even,[3] for the odd number places a limit on division by 2. But the unitary origin (the *monas*, to be distinguished from the central fire as τὸ ἕν), which gives rise to the *tetractys* of the decad and therewith to the entire cosmogonic process, is at the same time both even and odd, *peras* and *apeiron*, form and matter, for it is a mixture of both.[4]

Then, furthermore, when the discovery was made within the school of Pythagoras of the well-known theorem that bears his name, according to which the square of the hypotenuse of a right-angled triangle is equal to

---

1 See J. Burnet, *Early Greek Philosophy* (London, 1908, 2nd ed., p.120). Cf. also the astronomical theory of Philolaus, which is discussed below in the text.

2 Diels-Kranz I, 403; Philolaus, A. Fragm. 17, according to Theophrastus: Φιλόλαος ὁ Πυθαγόρειος τὸ μὲν πῦρ μέσον (τοῦτο γὰρ εἶναι τοῦ παντὸς ἑστίαν). ("Philolaus the Pythagorean [held] fire to be the center [of the celestial sphere], for this was according to him the hearth of the universe.")

3 *Ibid.*, p. 406; Philolaus, B. Fragm. 1: ἁ φύσις δ' ἐν τῶι κόσμωι ἁρμόχθη ἐξ ἀπείρων τε καὶ περαινόντων, καὶ ὅλος <ὁ> κόσμος καὶ τὰ ἐν αὐτῶι πάντα. ("But nature was fitted together in the world-order from unlimited and limiting components, both the cosmos as a whole and all [things present] in it.")

4 *Ibid.*, p. 408; B. Fragm. 5: ὅ γα μὰν ἀριθμὸς ἔχει δύο μὲν ἴδια εἴδη, περισσὸν καὶ ἄρτιον. τρίτον δὲ ἀπ' ἀμφοτέρων μειχθέντων ἀρτιοπέριττον. ἑκατέρω δὲ τῶ εἴδεος πολλαὶ μορφαί, ἃς ἕκαστον αὐταυτὸ σημαίνει. ("Number actually has two distinct ontic forms, *odd* and *even*, and a third consisting of the mingling of both: *even-odd*. Each of these two ontic forms, however, takes many shapes, which each [thing] indicates of itself.") *Ibid.*, p. 410; B. Fragm. 7: τὸ πρᾶτον ἁρμοσθέν, τὸ ἕν, ἐν τῶι μέσωι τᾶς σφαίρας ἑστία καλεῖται. ("The first to be fitted together in harmony, the one at the center of the [celestial] sphere, is called hearth [*hestia*].") *Ibid.*, B. Fragm. 8: ἡ μὲν μονὰς ὡς ἂν ἀρχὴ οὖσα πάντων κατὰ τὸν Φιλόλαον (οὐ γὰρ ἕν φησιν ἀρχὰ πάντων). ("The *monas* is the origin of all things, according to Philolaus, [for he does *not* call this *archē* of all that exists *ἕν*].")

the sum of the squares of the sides of the right angle, this also played a role here. Tradition has it that when it became clear that a rational numerical ratio could not always be found between the hypotenuse and the sides, this was regarded as so shameful to the school that a hecatomb was offered in order to atone for its guilt. What confronted the Pythagoreans here were irrational numbers ($\sqrt{2}$, $\sqrt{5}$, etc.), which, when computed in terms of the rational numerical value of the *tetractys*, produced an infinite, unlimited series. Thus, an *apeiron*, which was evidently not bounded by a *peras* (odd number), opened up as an abyss within the principle of number itself.

This, then, explains the above-mentioned statement of Aristotle, that for the Pythagoreans number is the origin or *archē*, both as to (*qua*) matter (ὕλη) and as to (*qua*) form of being. The principle of number, as the form principle of the entire luminous heavens, has assimilated the matter motive. The matter principle has been incorporated within the form principle (the principle of number) itself, and it has thereby been brought within limits. Indeed, in the *monas*, the unitary origin of the divine *physis*, it continues to function as the true root of the form principle. For, as we have seen, it is the oneness of the divine, eternally flowing stream of life (i.e., the oneness of the divine *physis*) that constitutes the Dionysian substratum of the religious conception of Pythagoras.

d. Ten as the Perfect Number

In this unity as *monas*, however, the Dionysian matter principle has been formalized. That is the case because this unity is conceived as the origin of the numerical series. As a result, as Cornford has demonstrated in admirable fashion, the Orphic motive of the descent from the realm of light into darkness was able to come to expression in the *tetractys*.

According to Aristotle, the *tetractys* of the decad is a series of numbers whose sum, ten, is the perfect number, which was thought to embrace the whole nature of numbers. In a statement of Aetius (ca. 100 A. D.), which according to Professor Burnet[1] probably goes back to Pythagoras himself, it is asserted that Pythagoras regarded ten as the "nature" of number because all human beings, Greeks as well as barbarians, count up to ten and, when they reach this number, revert to unity again.[2] The word used here, "revert" (ἀναποδόω), calls to mind a fragment of the Pythagorean Hippodamus, in which it is said that this reversion must be conceived as the revolution of the "wheel of births.":

> All mortal beings revolve under the *Anankē* of *physis* in a wheel of changes.... When they are born, they grow, and when they are grown they reach their height, and they thereafter become old and

---

1 Burnet, *op. cit.*, p. 114. [In the 4th ed. it is p. 103]
2 Aetius i. 3. 8: εἶναι δὲ τὴν φύσιν τοῦ ἀριθμοῦ δέκα· μέχρι γὰρ τῶν δέκα πάντες Ἕλληνες, πάντες βάρβαροι ἀριθμοῦσιν ἐφ, ἃ ἐλθόντες πάλιν ἀναποδοῦσιν ἐπὶ τὴν μονάδα.

eventually die. At an appointed time, nature compels them to reach their end in her sphere of darkness. They then return again in mortal form out of the darkness, through rebirth and repayment on the part of death, in the cycle in which *physis* reverts back upon itself.[1]

The Dionysian motive of the cycle of the eternally flowing stream of life is here given pregnant expression in the symbol of the *tetractys*.

The Orphic motive of the fall of the luminous substance of the soul from the eternal form of the starry heavens to the darkness of the earth, whence it may again revert to its origin in the realm of light, is perceived by Cornford in the typically Pythagorean conception of *harmonia*. With the help of this notion, the development of the numerical series from unity was conceived as a processional movement (προποδισμός)[2] from the one into the many, from light into darkness. According to the Pythagoreans, a harmony is a continuous bond between determinate numerical relationships that is brought about by a principle of unity running through these, namely, the *logos* or *ratio* (1/2 or 1/3), which binds every term to the one preceding it by the same relation. A good example of such a *harmonia* is the *tetractys* from Plato's *Timaeus*, referred to above, where the series 1: 2: 4: 8 and 1: 3: 9: 27 are used to represent the harmonic constitution of the world-soul. Both series arise out of unity, and the numbers within them are bound into a harmony by the ratios 1: 2 and 1: 3, respectively.

The unity unfolds into a manifold, without however entirely losing its oneness (every new number is at the same time a unity in the manifold), and a return from the manifold to the one is secured by the *harmonia*, which runs back and forth through the entire series. In this way it becomes understandable how Pythagoras could regard the "entire luminous heavens" as "harmony and number." The processional movement of the one divine *physis* is here conceived after the model of the soul, which from its original state of union with the divine luminous form falls into the realm of darkness, but nevertheless preserves its connection with the divine One through the mysterious bonds of harmony. It can return again to the One, when a life of ascetic discipline has made it ready through Pythagorean *theōria* and the purifying power of music.

---

1 Hippodamus the Pythagorean, from John Stobaeus (ca. 400 A. D.); *Florilegium* (Anthology) 98, 71: πάντα μὲν ὦν τὰ θνατὰ δι᾽ ἀνάγκαν φύσιος ἐν μεταβολαῖς καλινδεῖται ... τὰ μὲν ὑπὸ φύσιος εἰς τὸ ἄδηλον αὐτᾶς τερματιζόμενα καὶ πάλιν ἐκ τοῦ ἀδήλου ἐς τὸ θνατὸν ἐπισυνερχόμενα, ἀμοιβᾷ γενέσιος καὶ ἀνταποδόσει φθορᾶς, κύκλον αὐταύτας ἀναποδιζούσας.

2 The term προποδισμός is found in Theo of Smyrna, *loc. cit.*, p. 29 (Dupuis): ἀριθμός ἐστι σύστημα μονάδων ἢ προποδισμὸς πλήθους ἀπὸ μονάδος ἀρχόμενος καὶ ἀναποδισμὸς εἰς μονάδα καταλήγων. (Cited by Cornford, *op. cit.*, p. 209.)

e. The Astronomical Theory of Philolaus in the Light of the Religious Ground-Motive

The astronomical theory ascribed to Philolaus[1] is another thing that only becomes clear in terms of this dual role of the *tetractys*. According to him, the universe is composed of the following parts: The central position is occupied by fire, which is designated *hestia* and can be referred to by other mythological names, such as Διὸς οἶκος (abode of Zeus) or μήτηρ θεῶν (mother of the gods). After this comes the so-called counter-earth (ἀντίχθων), which Aristotle says was added so that the number of the celestial bodies (of which only nine were known) would correspond to the sacred number ten. Then comes the inhabited earth, which in revolving around the central fire always stands opposite to the counter-earth, thus concealing the latter from human view. Beyond this are the moon, the sun, and the five planets, and lastly the fixed starry sky. Characteristically, the latter is given the name *Olympos*, for this betrays the fact that Philolaus intends to transform the form motive of the religion of culture in the direction of the uranic form motive of Orphism. The sphere of the planets, the sun, and the moon is designated *kosmos*. The sublunar sphere, in turn, is called *ouranos*. The central fire is the hearth and replenisher of the entire universe; but the sublunar region is subjected to decay from two different sources, namely, the fire streaming down from the sky and the water flowing out from the moon.[2] The fire, which nourishes all of life, can thus once again consume what comes into being upon earth (the sublunar region); but the luminous form of the sky, which is the home of the rational soul, is imperishable and eternal.[3] Here lies the basic difference between the conception of Philolaus and that of Heraclitus, for the latter contains neither a world

---

1   In opposition to August Boeckh, Burnet doubts that this theory comes from Philolaus himself. He acknowledges, however, its early Pythagorean origin. Burnet, *op. cit.*, pp. 281 ff.

2   See Aetius II, 5, 3 (D 333), in Diels-Kranz, I, 404; Philolaus, A. Fragm. 18.

3   This distinction between the changeable sublunar region and the eternal and immutable starry heavens, which Gigon also regards as an old Pythagorean conception (Gigon, *op. cit.*, p.136), comes to pregnant expression in Philolaus B. Fragm. 21 (Diels-Kranz I, 417-18), quoted by Stobaeus (*Ecl.* 1, 20, 2 p.172 [9w]), from Περὶ ψυχῆς (*On the Soul*), a writing attributed to Philolaus. Although the fragment itself has turned out to be spurious, the portion reproduced here unquestionably contains an originally Pythagorean distinction: ἔχει δὲ καὶ τὰν ἀρχὰν τᾶς κινήσιός τε καὶ μεταβολᾶς ὁ κόσμος εἷς ἐὼν καὶ συνεχὴς καὶ φύσει διαπνεόμενος καὶ περιαγεόμενος ἐξ ἀρχιδίου· καὶ τὸ μὲν ἀμετάβλατον αὐτοῦ, τὸ δὲ μεταβάλλον ἐστί· καὶ τὸ μὲν ἀμετάβαλλον ἀπὸ τᾶς τὸ ὅλον περιεχούσας ψυχᾶς μέχρι σελήνας περαιοῦται, τὸ δὲ μεταβάλλον ἀπὸ τᾶς σελήνας μέχρι τᾶς γᾶς. ἐπεὶ δέ γε καὶ τὸ κινέον ἐξ αἰῶνος ἐς αἰῶνα περιπολεῖ, τὸ δὲ κινεόμενον, ὡς τὸ κινέον ἄγει, οὕτως διατίθεται, ἀνάγκη τὸ μὲν ἀεικίνατον τὸ δὲ ἀειπαθὲς εἶμεν· καὶ τὸ μὲν νῶ καὶ ψυχᾶς ἀνάκωμα πᾶν, τὸ δὲ γενέσιος καὶ μεταβολᾶς· καὶ τὸ μὲν πρᾶτόν τε δυνάμει καὶ ὑπερέχον, τὸ δ᾽ ὕστερον καὶ καθυπερεχόμενον· τὸ δὲ ἐξ ἀμφοτέρων τούτων, τοῦ μὲν ἀεὶ θέοντος θείου τοῦ δὲ ἀεὶ μεταβάλλοντος γενατοῦ, κόσμος.

conflagration (ἐκπύρωσις)[1] nor an imperishable form for the luminous heavens.

f. The Antinomy in Pythagoras' Conception of the Form Principle and Philolaus' Attempt at Synthesis

If Cornford's interpretation of the *tetractys* is correct – and it is my belief that it finds strong support in the sources – a consideration of it in the light of the dialectical ground-motive of Greek thought clearly reveals that the primordial dualism of this ground-motive has been transposed here into number itself as the principle of form. On these terms it also becomes understandable why Plato and Aristotle could not accept number in this original Pythagorean conception as a pure form principle, since here it was still laden with matter. If the *Monas* must simultaneously fulfill the roles of *apeiron* and *peras*, of matter principle and form principle, then it has been deprived of the unity that is proper to it as *Origin*.

Philolaus of Croton, in southern Italy, the Pythagorean with whom Diogenes Laertius (III, 6) says that Plato himself came into contact, apparently recognized this when he attempted to discover in harmony a third principle that would effect a synthesis between the *peras* and the *apeiron*.[2] But this attempt misfired, because, in the final analysis, this principle of harmony itself had to be sought in numerical ratios. It could only signify a

---

("The cosmos, as one continuous whole, inspired throughout and turned about by *physis*, also has the origin of motion and change from the very beginning. And one part of it is unchangeable, whereas the other part is changing. And the unchangeable part is given its bounds as far as the moon by the soul that encloses the whole, and the changeable part from the moon to the earth. Since the moving part causes the rotation from everlasting to everlasting, and the part that is moved is disposed as the moving part leads it, it follows necessarily that the one is always moving and the other always passive, the one the abode [?] of reason and the soul, the other that of becoming and change; the one is by its power *primary* and *predominant*, the other *secondary* and *subordinate*. That which consists of both of these [principles], – the divine, which always extends itself in motion, and the mortal, which always changes – is the cosmos.") The elaboration of this Pythagorean distinction in this fragment undoubtedly already betrays Platonic influence, particularly in the notion that the moving soul-substance leads and controls what is moved (the corporeal). The basic distinction between the eternal luminous form and the transitory sublunar region, however, is without question Pythagorean in origin.

1 See Reinhardt, *Parmenides*, pp. 169 f.
2 Diels-Kranz I, 409; Philolaus, B. Fragm. 6: ἐπεὶ δὲ ταὶ ἀρχαὶ ὑπᾶρχον οὐχ ὁμοῖαι οὐδ᾽ ὁμόφυλοι ἔσσαι, ἤδη ἀδύνατον ἧς κα αὐταῖς κοσμηθῆναι, εἰ μὴ ἁρμονία ἐπεγένετο ὡιτινιῶν ἄδε τρόπωι ἐγένετο. ("Since, however, these principles of origin [viz., the *peras* and the *apeiron*] lay at the foundation as unlike and mutually unrelated, it would clearly have been impossible to found a world-order with them if harmony had not been added, however this may have arisen.") The further elaboration of the harmony principle in this fragment makes clear that it was sought exclusively in numerical ratios.

mere relation, therefore, not a deeper original unity.

g. *The Petrifaction of the Pythagorean Motive of Form under
    the Influence of the Eleatic Critique*

Later, when Parmenides' critique, which had irrefutably demonstrated
the impossibility that the eternal flux of life could originate in the principle of the luminous form of being, began to make itself felt within the
Pythagorean school, the numerical principle as a principle of form, measure, and harmony became increasingly disengaged from the Dionysian
matter motive. As a consequence, the Pythagorean theory of numbers
became static and abstract. Then, under Platonic influence, numbers
came to be regarded as eternal formal models or archetypes, of which
temporal things having form, which are subject to the matter principle,
are copies. In spite of the view of Burnet, however, none of this is original to Pythagoreanism.

h. *The Effects of the Dualistic Ground-Motive in the
    Anthropological Conception: The Dualism of Material
    Body and Thinking Soul, in Contrast to the Hylozoistic
    Conception*

Due to the influence of Orphism, the dualism of the religious ground-
motive began to make itself felt within the Pythagorean school also in
its anthropological views. The material body, which remains tied to the
tenebrous earth in the cycle of the stream of life, is conceived as the
"prison" or "tomb" (σῆμα) of the soul, an originally Orphic notion. In
contrast, the soul in its theoretical function of thought, which has in
view the investigation of the mathematical form principle of the divine
luminous substance,[1] is immortal and everlasting.

Alcmaeon of Croton, the physician who according to Aristotle was a
younger contemporary of Pythagoras and whose ideas strongly resembled
those of the Pythagoreans (Diogenes Laertius in 8, 83 calls him a pupil of
Pythagoras), taught that the soul, like the stars, is immortal because it, no
less than the sun, moon, stars, and sky, is in perpetual circular motion.[2]
Related to this is the statement of Alcmaeon, which has come down to us

---

1   It is evident from the fragment of Alcmaeon (Diels-Kranz I, 215; 24 [14] B. Fragm.
    1a), which is preserved in Theophrastus, that humans were distinguished from the
    animals by their theoretical thought function already in the original Pythagorean
    conception. According to Aristotle (*Met.* A, 5. 986 a 29), Alcmaeon was a youth
    during Pythagoras' old age, and he in any case does present an old Pythagorean con-
    ception here. Alcmaeon taught that a human being alone has logical understanding
    (ξυνίησι), whereas every other (living being) only perceives by the senses
    (αἰσθάνεται μέν, οὐ ξυνίησι δέ).
2   Aristotle, *De anima*, A, 2. 405 a 29 (Diels-Kranz I, 213; A. Fragm. 12). *De anima*
    404a 16 f. states that according to some Pythagoreans, the motes suspended in the
    air are souls, since they are in constant motion. This undoubtedly old Pythagorean
    notion of the circular motion of the immortal thinking soul is taken up by Plato in

through Aristotle,[1] that "human beings die because they are not able to join the beginning to the end." Obviously, the meaning of this saying is that human beings in their bodily existence are incapable of holding fast to the circular motion of the starry heavens. In other words, they cannot bring together the beginning and the end of this motion.

Such motion can be attributed only to the thinking soul, and this is the ground of its immortality. According to Orphism, the soul has no essential connection with any material body. As long as it remains chained to the "wheel of births," in its enthrallment to the tenebrous earth, it continually returns in different bodies. The thinking soul, however, which is the vehicle of *theōria*, has its point of origin in the luminous heavens. After the completion of the "great astral year," it is released from the cycle of the stream of life, which constantly subjects it to new incarnations, and it returns again to the place of its origin.

The belief in the individual immortality of the soul, which was based theoretically in the unity-in-multiplicity of the principle of number, found no support in the Dionysian matter motive. In the latter, the wheel of births was never set at rest. No dualism can be detected in the anthropological conceptions of Anaximander and Heraclitus.[2] In these thinkers there is no duality of the thinking soul (as form) and the material body. The basic conception of hylozoism, where the soul itself is viewed as a material stream of life, does not allow for such a duality. Only the eternally flowing origin, the one divine *physis* into which everything that has form must return in an eternal cycle, is immortal. Bodily form, on the contrary, is here merely a transitory phase of the stream of life.

Divine *physis*, as the Milesians and Heraclitus conceived it, is nothing other than a flowing amorphous soul. For, according to the early nature philosophy, which stands under the primacy of the Greek matter principle, the soul is the principle of spontaneous motion, uncaused by any foreign agency. Here, it must be added, motion is conceived not in its original modal sense, but in the analogical sense of vital movement. The body, in turn, is nothing more than a transitory, individual form of the divine "matter-soul," while the latter is in essence impersonal and enters only temporarily into the individual form of a body.

Clearly, Aristotle's criticism of the Milesians for failing to recognize a

---

his *Timaeus*, a dialogue that I shall discuss at a later point in detail. Probably it is present already in his *Phaedrus*.

1   Diels-Kranz I, 215; Alcmaeon, B. Fragm. 2.
2   Reinhardt, *op. cit.*, pp. 192 f., and Gigon, *op. cit.*, p. 236, have recently revived the attempt to construct a Pythagorean theory of the immortality of the individual rational soul on the basis of the portions of Heraclitus' teaching preserved in B. Fragm. 18, 27 and 62. However, after Rohde's definitive critique of the corresponding constructions of Zeller, Pfeiderer, and Schuster, this is no longer deserving of consideration. I need only to point here to Rohde's thorough refutation in *Psyche*, II, 150 f.

principle of motion is completely unfounded.[1] In the Milesian view, the soul is not *form* but rather *matter*, in the typically Greek sense of the word, and the body is its transitory individual form.

In contrast to this, the Olympian religion of culture, with its deification of the principle of form, ascribed a personal immortality (*ἀθανασία*) to the form-gods, who have been separated from *physis* and are no longer in the domain of the principle of matter. Precisely because of their separation from *physis*, however, the culture gods do not possess human life, even though they have been "created in the image of humankind." In Cornford's striking expression, each one of them is in the final analysis nothing more than an *eidos*, a supersensible form which lacks any genuine matter.[2] Or, to put the matter somewhat differently, they are supersensible, deified images or *eidōla* of the living human being, as one who has culture.

i. *The Threefold Homeric Conception of the Soul: Blood-soul,* Thumos, *and* Eidolon

It is of great interest to observe how the encounter between the ground-motives of the nature and culture religions in Homer issued in a three-fold conception of the human soul. The blood-soul is where the true vital force resides. Its vehicle is the blood, which forms a part of the eternal stream of life. In its individual bodily form, this vital soul is perishable. Although the prevailing opinion follows W. F. Otto,[3] in identifying this life-soul with the *thumos* (*θυμός*), R. B. Onians,[4] the Cambridge professor, has shown to the contrary that Homer conceived the latter as a breath-soul, which is endowed with feeling and intelligence, and which has its seat in the lungs (*φρένες*) or the breast (*στῆθος*), but which, like life itself, ceases to exist after death. Nevertheless, according to Homer, humans have yet another soul, the *psychē* as the *eidōla*. This is the recognizable, individual human form, which is impalpable and beyond the realm of the physical. This soul escapes from the mouth of persons at the moment of death, and for a period of time it can appear in dreams to their relatives who survive them.[5] Like the Olympian

---

1 This is also observed by Cornford, *op. cit.*, p. 128.
2 *Ibid.*, p. 115.
3 W. F. Otto, *Die Manen oder von den Urformen des Totenglaubens* (Berlin, 1923), pp. 18 and 26.
4 Richard Broxton Onians, in his important book *Origins of Greek and Roman Thought* (Cambridge, 1937), pp. 85 f.
5 In the book mentioned above, Otto advanced the thesis, which later won general acceptance, that for Homer *psychē* was not the soul released from the body after death, but rather the "ghost of the dead," the shadow of the soulless body, whereas humans while they are alive are animated by the *thumos*, which disappears at the moment of death. Here Otto opposes Rohde, who was strongly influenced by the animistic ethnological theories of Tylor and Spencer, which held sway during his time. In his *The*

form-gods, this *psyche* is a supranatural formal image or *eidōlon*, but it is simultaneously a mere "shadow," which in Hades leads an unreal and disconsolate existence, in actuality the diametrical opposite of the blissful estate of the gods. Only by drinking blood can the *eidōlon* regain consciousness and memory. The "*eidōlon*-soul" as *psychē* is thus the individual, supersensible form of mankind, and in the *Phaedo*, a dialogue of Plato which betrays Orphic influence, it is identified with the thinking subject of knowledge. The blood-soul, in contrast, which belongs to the realm of *physis*, is the same in all human beings and thus lacks true individuality.

j. The Theoretical Antinomy in the Pythagorean Conception of the Soul. The Thinking Soul as Harmony

Orphism could again attribute life to this *eidōlon*, therefore, only because, in keeping with the religious pseudo-synthesis, it regarded the origin of the soul, the immortal form of the luminous heavens, as rooted in the eternally flowing stream of life, the Dionysian principle of *physis*. Pythagorean *theōria* proceeded a step further than this by absorbing the Dionysian matter principle into the form principle of the luminous heavens itself. This meant formalizing it, in the manner described earlier, by means of *theōria*. Precisely for this reason, however, this line of thought was incapable of giving proper philosophical expression to the dualism between the material body and the divine, rational form-soul. It was only capable of conceiving the thinking *psychē* qua *eidos* or *eidōlon* in a theoretical fashion as a *harmonia*, in the previously discussed sense. We remind ourselves here that Philolaus expressly conceived this harmony as a third principle, which was supposed to bring the two antithetical *archai*, the *peras* and the *apeiron*, into a synthesis. The divine luminous substance of the starry heavens is a "harmony" because it is at the same time both *peras* and *apeiron*, both limiting form and limited matter. Or, one might prefer to say, it is harmony because the matter principle is taken up here into the form principle itself. In this way the *psychē* as an *eidōlon* (idol) became a synthesis that could be given philosophical expression only in the harmonic principle of the numerical series. Even though it is a metaphysical construction, it still cannot fail to betray the fact that it is rooted in the matter principle of the Greek conception of

---

Theology of the Early Greek Philosophers (Oxford, 1947), p. 78, Werner Jaeger asks, however, how the term *psychē* could ever have been applied to such a "ghost of the dead." It seems to me that this cannot be explained in terms of the original meaning of the word "breath," for there is no relation between the breath of life and a shadow of the dead. The *eidōlon* is indeed a "dead soul," but as the mere form of the full individual person, not just the shadow of the dead material body. Even in Hades, the shadow remains active. The *eidōlon*, however, is identical with neither the life-soul nor the *thumos*.

physis. The *eidōlon* has life only by the grace of *physis*, as the eternally flowing stream of life. In this situation, it is clear that an unavoidable antinomy arises between Pythagorean *theōria*, which is obliged to conceive the soul as a harmony, and the belief, adopted by Pythagoras from Orphism, that the individual soul is immortal by virtue of its origin in the luminous form of the starry heavens.

In Plato's dialogue *Phaedo*, which I shall discuss later in greater detail, there is an argument about the soul that is based on this idea of *harmonia*. I give attention to this dialogue because in it the dualism in Greek anthropology between an *anima rationalis*, as a pure, thinking form substance, and a material body is given its most pregnant expression. Here the two Pythagoreans, Cebes and Simmias, counter Socrates' proof of the immortality of the soul with several arguments which, especially in the case of Simmias, are based on the conception of the *anima rationalis* as a *harmonia*. Both of these thinkers concede that the soul is of divine origin and that it exists in time before the body; but Simmias expresses doubt as to whether it can exist after the death of the body. For, he argues, it is nothing more than the harmony of the material body.[1]

Socrates, the discussion leader, then exposes the inherent antinomy in this Pythagorean conception. He also attempts to demonstrate that the conception of the soul as a harmony is inconsistent with the ascetic moral doctrines of the Pythagorean school. If the soul were merely the harmony of the material body, it would have to succumb to the body's impulses of hunger and thirst and would never be able to resist them in ascetic fashion. For a harmony can never come to oppose any of its parts; it may never behave differently than the things of which it is composed. It cannot provide guidance to its constituent parts, but is obliged simply to follow them. On the other hand, the Pythagorean conception of the preexistence of the rational soul demands that it cannot be composed of the same elements as the material body. The soul must "remain identical with itself" and can never be "more or less of a soul." This "more or less," however, is precisely what characterizes the impulses of the material body. Accordingly, if the soul is a harmony it will not permit any disharmony, any moral deviation in pursuit of the sensual inclinations of the material body. It therefore would be necessary that all souls without exception be *good*. The Pythagoreans admit, nevertheless, that the soul can be morally evil and without understanding.[2]

Although these arguments may not all be faultless – in particular, the implication that harmony (which in its original meaning is a normative aesthetic figure) could only follow sound waves, without any capability of

---

1 Plato, *Phaedo*, 86 (cap. XXXVI). The theory proposed here, that the soul is a harmonic mixture of the warm and the cold, the dry and the moist, is found already in the physician Alcmaeon (Diels-Kranz I, 215; 24 [14] Alcmaeon, B. Fragm. 4).
2 Plato, *Phaedo*, 92 and 93 f. (caps. XLII and XLIII).

leading or controlling them – it cannot be denied that the antinomy uncovered by Socrates is indeed present in the Pythagorean conception of the soul as *harmonia*. For a *harmonia*, in any case, is unable to be detached from that which it brings into harmony. In the original Pythagorean conception it cannot be detached from *physis*, as the eternally flowing stream of life. In spite of this, however, the rational *psychē* is supposed to be an immortal luminous substance that has originated in the divine luminous form of the starry heavens.

On the basis of this theoretical antinomy, Burnet[1] and other writers have concluded that the conception of the soul as *harmonia* could not have belonged among the original teachings of the Pythagorean school, because it is incompatible with Pythagoras' undeniable belief in the capacity of the soul to exist independently of the material body. Following Cornford, however, I reject this position. I also note the fact that Macrobius states emphatically that this conception stems from Pythagoras himself.[2]

It would appear more correct to assume that, since their conception of the divine *physis* aimed at a conscious formalization of the principle of matter, Pythagoras and his earlier followers considered the idea of the soul as *harmonia* to be compatible with the Orphic belief in the soul's immortality. Even after its fall from the divine celestial sphere of light into the darkness of the sublunar region, the soul continues to maintain a hidden bond with the divine *monas*. This bond is its *harmonia*. The divine *monas* itself, however, is still the eternally flowing source of *physis*, which brings forth the stream of life bound to the tenebrous earth. That is the case, even though it is at the same time the origin of the immortal luminous form of the starry heavens.

In spite of the formalization of the principle of matter, the principle of origin thus continued to be at odds with itself. It was based on a religious pseudo-synthesis. The religious dialectic in the Greek ground-motive, however, did not permit this synthesis. Indeed, under the critique of Parmenides, the latter dissolved once more into a polar antithesis.

Only by going along with this polar antithesis could this belief in immortality come to internally consistent theoretical expression in Greek philosophy. Before this could happen, however, philosophical thought had to enter the path of critical self-reflection, and the form principle of the religion of culture had to be freed from the grip of the Orphic-Pythagorean conception of *physis*, which in the final analysis continued to be rooted in the principle of matter. Within the thought framework of Greek *theōria*, it was only as a pure, rational form-substance that the individual thinking soul could exist independently of the material body and thus possess immortality.

In this development the Orphic dualism between soul and body would

---

1 Burnet, *op. cit.*, p. 295.
2 Macrobius, *Commentarii in Somnium Scipionis*, i. 14, 19.

nevertheless continue to exert great influence. But it was necessary that the Orphic form motive be relieved of its naturalistic tendency and be transformed into the deepened form-motive of the religion of culture.

In the person of Empedocles, however, philosophy would make one more attempt to maintain, in the face of Parmenides' critique, the connection between the form and matter principles in the divine idea of origin. In making this attempt, he entered upon a path different from that of the Pythagoreans.

4. The Formalization of the Earthly Matter Principle in Empedocles' Theory of the Four Elements of *Physis*. The Persistence of the Orphic Dualism in the Principle of Matter

a. The Orphic Dualism in Empedocles' *Καθαρμοί* and the Role of Anankē

Empedocles of Acragas (Agrigentum), who was born ca. 483-482 B. C. and who traveled through the Greek cities in Sicily and Italy as a physician, seer, orator, and miracle worker, is a late representative of the religious reform movement that took its inspiration from Orphism. In his *Katharmoi*, a poem which describes the path of purification of the soul, he displays his close affinity with Orphic teaching. He presents himself as a person honored by all and wreathed with green garlands, who travels about on the earth, no longer as a mortal man but as an immortal god, and as a seer whose oracular utterances and medical advice are sought by all whose cities he visits.

He then goes on, describing in a completely Orphic vein the exile of the soul upon the tenebrous earth, where for the duration of the "great astral year" it is condemned to lead a wandering existence in ever different material bodies, chained to the wheel of births, after the authoritative decree of *Anankē* has forcibly expelled it from its divine origin. In fact, he calls himself such an exile, saying that he has already been born a boy, a girl, a plant, a bird, and a dumb fish in the sea:

> There is an authoritative decree of *Anankē*, a divine edict, ancient, everlasting, and sealed with weighty oaths, that whenever one of the "daemons," whose portion is length of days, has sinfully stained his limbs with the blood of murder, or has followed strife and discord [νεῖκος] and sworn a false oath, he must wander thrice ten thousand seasons far from the blessed, where in the course of time he is born in all possible types of mortal forms, passing from one to the other of the tortuous paths of life.

> For the power of the air pursues them toward the sea, and the sea spews them forth upon the dry land; the earth drives them into the beams of the shining ["indefatigable"] sun, and the sun into the

eddies of the air. The one takes them from the other, but they are accursed by all. Now I too am one of these, banished by the deity and a wanderer, because I put my trust in raging strife.[1]

This description of the "exile of the soul" is in surprising agreement with that presented by Pindar, the great lyric poet, in his second Olympian ode and in the preserved fragment of his *Threnoi* (which was written for Theron of Acragas, the birthplace of Empedocles, when the latter was yet a child).[2] It is completely Orphic in its basic conception and its elaboration.

Empedocles says further:

"[At birth] I wailed when I saw the unfamiliar surroundings."[3]

"From what a rank, from great bliss [have I been cast]!"[4]

"Alas, O wretched and unblessed human race; from such strife and groanings have you been born."[5]

According to him, foolish men stain themselves with the blood of slaughtered animals, not knowing that they thereby murder their own kindred, since everything that has life is mutually related.[6]

If they have followed the path of purification in their earthly life, however, the fallen souls may look forward to leaving the earth at the end of the great year as "prophets, singers, physicians, and princes," when they will be "companions at hearth and table with the other immortals, free of human suffering and indestructible."[7] The wandering of the soul thus begins with its separation from the deity through the influence of *neikos* (en-

---

1   Diels-Kranz I, 357-358; Empedocles, B. Fragm. 115 (*Katharmoi*): ἔστιν Ἀνάγκης χρῆμα, θεῶν ψήφισμα παλαιόν, ἀίδιον, πλατέεσσι κατεσφρηγισμένον ὅρκοις· εὖτέ τις ἀμπλακίῃσι φόνῳ φίλα γυῖα μιήνῃ, <νείκεϊ θ'> ὅς κ(ε) ἐπίορκον ἁμαρτήσας ἐπομόσσῃ, δαίμονες οἵτε μακραίωνος λελάχασι βίοιο, τρίς μιν μυρίας ὥρας ἀπὸ μακάρων ἀλάλησθαι, φυομένους παντοῖα διὰ χρόνου εἴδεα θνητῶν ἀργαλέας βιότοιο μεταλλάσσοντα κελεύθους. αἰθέριον μὲν γάρ σφε μένος πόντονδε διώκει, πόντος δ' ἐς χθονὸς οὖδας ἀπέπτυσε, γαῖα δ' ἐς αὐγὰς ἠελίου φαέθοντος, ὁ δ' αἰθέρος ἔμβαλε δίναις· ἄλλος δ' ἐξ ἄλλου δέχεται, στυγέουσι δὲ πάντες. τῶν καὶ ἐγὼ νῦν εἰμι, φυγὰς θεόθεν καὶ ἀλήτης, νείκεϊ μαινομένῳ πίσυνος.
2   Cf. Rohde, *Psyche* II, 215.
3   Diels-Kranz I, 359; B. Fragm. 118 (*Katharmoi*): κλαῦσά τε καὶ κώκυσα ἰδὼν ἀσυνήθεα χῶρον.
4   *Ibid.*, B. Fragm. 119: ἐξ οἵης τιμῆς τε καὶ ὅσσου μήκεος ὄλβου...
5   *Ibid.*, I, 361; B. Fragm. 124: ὢ πόποι, ὢ δειλὸν θνητῶν γένος, ὢ δυσάνολβον, τοίων ἔκ τ' ἐρίδων ἔκ τε στοναχῶν ἐγένεσθε.
6   Diels-Kranz I, 367; B. Fragm. 137: μορφὴν δ' ἀλλάξαντα πατὴρ φίλον υἱὸν ἀείρας σφάζει ἐπευχόμενος μέγα νήπιος· ("And him who changed his form, his own son, the father raises aloft and slaughters, even accompanying this with a prayer – the great fool!")
7   Diels-Kranz I, 370; B. Fragm. 146: εἰς δὲ τέλος μάντεις τε καὶ ὑμνοπόλοι καὶ ἰητροὶ καὶ πρόμοι ἀνθρώποισιν ἐπιχθονίοισι πέλονται. Ibid., B. Fragm. 147· ἀθανάτοις ἄλλοισιν ὁμέστιοι, αὐτοτράπεζοι ἐόντες, ἀνδρείων ἀχέων ἀπόκληροι, ἀτειρεῖς.

mity), and it ends in reunion with the deity after the soul has completed its cycle of bodily life and death.

b. *Empedocles' Theory of* Physis *and Its Inner Connection with the Teaching of the* Katharmoi

Empedocles' theory of *physis*, which he expounded in another didactic poem, *On Nature* (περὶ φύσεως), cannot be understood without coming to terms with its Orphic religious background in the *Katharmoi*. On this point, therefore, I completely agree with Cornford that to conceive of these two poems as internally unrelated, or even mutually contradictory, is fundamentally in error.[1] Indeed, it follows from my method of investigation that one may not immediately assume that an internal contradiction is present in an author before he has attempted to understand the two, apparently conflicting conceptions in terms of the dialectical ground-motive of Greek thought. Any treatment of a thinker that accuses him solely on the basis of external appearances of harboring such a bifurcation in his thought has to be suspected, for this very reason, of deeply misunderstanding him.

It seems to me, however, that Cornford is wrong in supposing that Empedocles' nature philosophy is simply an attempt to reconcile the Orphic and Pythagorean conception of the soul with the "scientific tradition" of Ionian nature philosophy. For, as we have seen, there is no difference in principle between these two, at least as to the religious ground-motive that was at work behind them. In actual fact, Empedocles wrestled with the same inner antinomy in his idea of origin as Pythagoras did. For him too, the deity is both an eternal luminous substance, exalted above the earthly realm, and the origin, or at least a co-origin, of the eternally flowing *physis* which is bound to the tenebrous earth. Empedocles, however, has encountered Parmenides' dialectical critique. It is against this that he attempts to defend himself in his extensive didactic poem *On Nature*. He refuses to accept the polar either/or of the form and matter principles and seeks for a conception of nature that is compatible with the Orphic notion of god and the soul. If he is to accomplish this, however, he must, on the one hand, deprive Parmenides' form principle of its exclusively static character, and, on the other hand, provide the matter principle with a certain formal substrate in the four elements, which as eternal and immutable forms of being serve as the foundation of the entire process of becoming in the realm of *physis*. Here we have, therefore, yet another attempt to formalize the matter principle bound to the tenebrous earth, not by the Pythagorean route of arithmetization, but by way of a formalization of the elements that had played a role in earlier nature philosophy. These elements thereby undergo a metamorphosis. Or rather, they can now for the first time appear as elements proper. In Empedocles the primal substances are no longer an expression of the matter principle of eternal flux; instead, they take on the

---

1   Cornford, *op. cit*, pp. 224 ff.

static character of intrinsically immutable building blocks of the cosmos as it has come into being. Consequently, they are true forms of *being*.

Already in its outline and form, Empedocles' poem on *physis* has the character of a defense against Parmenides, on the one side, and against the Milesians on the other. He too announces his theory as a divine revelation imparted to him by the "Muse, the white-armed maiden," at the place where he has "secluded himself from those who succumb to the vain delusion that they have full knowledge of the divine totality of life," something that is, of course, not granted to mortals during their wanderings on the tenebrous earth.[1] The sense organs, which Parmenides had deprived of all noetic value, must indeed be relied upon for knowledge of the realm of *physis*, which is subject to the principle of matter; but one may not place more faith in any one of these than in the others.[2] This path, to be sure, does not lead to the discovery of the *whole* truth, since earthly knowledge does not extend to the divine, eternal sphere of light; nevertheless, the standard of mortal wisdom still permits the actual development of a theory concerning the process of becoming that harmonizes with the "path of Truth."

c. *Empedocles' Rejection of Parmenides' Conception of the Eternally Flowing* Physis. *The Four Elements of* Physis *as Static, Corporeal Forms of Being*

The first question that Empedocles raises is directly related to the dilemma set forth by Parmenides: is *physis*, in its subjection to the matter principle of eternal flux, a *non-being*? If the great thinker from Elea were entirely correct on this point, it would indeed be impossible to gain any true knowledge of the process of becoming. Therefore it had to be demonstrated at the outset that the latter is founded on immutable, ungenerated forms of being. There had to be, furthermore, a multiplicity of such forms of being, since Parmenides had shown that from the oneness of the form of being no plurality could arise. That excluded of it-

---

1   Diels-Kranz I, 308-309; B. Fragm. 2 Empedocles, (Περὶ φύσεως) στεινωποὶ μὲν γὰρ παλάμαι κατὰ γυῖα κέχυνται· πολλὰ δὲ δείλ' ἔμπαια, τά τ' ἀμβλύνουσι μέριμνας. παῦρον δ' ἐν ζωῆισι βίου μέρος ἀθρήσαντες ὠκύμοροι καπνοῖο δίκην ἀρθέντες ἀπέπταν αὐτὸ μόνον πεισθέντες, ὅτωι προσέκυρσεν ἕκαστος πάντοσ' ἐλαυνόμενοι, τὸ δ' ὅλον <πᾶς> εὔχεται εὑρεῖν· οὕτως οὔτ' ἐπιδερκτὰ τάδ' ἀνδράσιν οὔτ' ἐπακουστὰ οὔτε νόωι περιληπτά. σὺ δ' οὖν, ἐπεὶ ὧδ' ἐλιάσθης, πεύσεαι οὐ πλέον ἠὲ βροτείη μῆτις ὄρωρεν. ("For narrowly limited are the sense organs ["graspers"], which are spread over the bodily members; and many woes press upon them and blunt their thought. And having beheld in their life only a small part of [the whole of] life, doomed to swift death, they fly away like smoke carried aloft, persuaded only of that upon which each one chanced during his many wanderings; and yet each one boasts of having found the *whole*. So little, however, can this be seen or heard by men, or grasped by the mind. But you, since you have here secluded yourself from them, shall learn – no more than mortal wisdom can attain.")

2   Diels-Kranz I, 309-311; B. Fragm. 3.

self the possibility that the immense diversity of things with form, perceptible to the senses and subject to the matter principle, could have arisen from this source. For this reason, the goddess first makes clear to Empedocles that at the foundation of the whole realm of *physis* (Empedocles explicitly identifies this with the earthly process of the flux of becoming) there are four "root forms" (ῥιζώματα), which neither change nor come into being, namely, the four elements of fire, water, earth, and air. These are here given divine names, which are in part borrowed from the Olympian religion of culture. In Greek nature philosophy, the elements indeed had a mythological origin, but in Hesiod's *Theogony* they were treated as nature deities. From this it appears that the thought of Empedocles too was cradled in a religious framework, the tendency of which was to naturalize the form motive of the religion of culture.[1] The Olympian *athanasia* belongs only to the elements as bodily forms of being, while the immortal soul-substance as such is not a form.

If these elements are indeed eternal forms of being – and Empedocles expressly says that they are[2] – they themselves cannot as such be subject to the matter principle, as the Milesians and Heraclitus had maintained. Nor, in the case of the "movable elements," can they be the symbolic embodiment of this principle. On these terms there cannot *be* any birth or death in the proper sense of these words, for what is referred to as coming into being and passing away is nothing more than a commingling and separation of the immutable elements. Parmenides' dilemma is thereby eliminated. It is indeed impossible for anything to arise from what does not have being at all; likewise, it is "unthinkable and unheard of that what-*is* should pass away."[3] These alternatives, however, do not pertain here.

---

1 Diels-Kranz I, 311-312; B. Fragm. 6: τέσσαρα γὰρ πάντων ῥιζώματα πρῶτον ἄκουε. Ζεὺς ἀργὴς Ἥρη τε φερέσβιος ἠδ᾽ Ἀιδονεὺς Νῆστίς θ᾽, ἣ δακρύοις τέγγει κρούνωμα βρότειον. ("For hear first the four root forms of all things: Zeus, the shining, and Hera, the bringer of life, also Aidoneus and Nestia, who with her tears causes an earthly stream of water to flow.") B. Fragm. 7: ἀγένητα στοιχεῖα (ungenerated elements). B. Fragm. 8: ἄλλο δέ τοι ἐρέω· φύσις οὐδενὸς ἔστιν ἁπάντων θνητῶν, οὐδέ τις οὐλομένου θανάτοιο τελευτή, ἀλλὰ μόνον μίξις τε διάλλαξίς τε μιγέντων ἔστι, φύσις δ᾽ ἐπὶ τοῖς ὀνομάζεται ἀνθρώποισιν. ("But I shall tell you yet another thing. None among all mortal beings has a real coming into existence nor an end in baneful death; but there is only mixing and exchange of the mixed [elements], this being called '*physis*' by men.")

2 Diels-Kranz I, 319; Empedocles, B. Fragm. 21, 2 speaks of the μορφή (form) of the elements, and in Fragment B 17, 13 the elements are explicitly called "unmoved beings" (αἰὲν ἔασιν ἀκίνητοι.) See the next note.

3 Diels-Kranz I, 313-314; B. Fragm. 12: ἔκ τε γὰρ οὐδάμ᾽ ἐόντος ἀμήχανόν ἐστι γενέσθαι καὶ τ᾽ ἐὸν ἐξαπολέσθαι ἀνήνυστον καὶ ἄπυστον· αἰεὶ γὰρ τῇ γ᾽ ἔσται, ὅπῃ κέ τις αἰὲν ἐρείδῃ. ("For from something that in no wise *is*, it is impossible for anything to arise, and it is likewise unthinkable and unheard of that something

d. The Sphere in Empedocles' Poem on Physis

At this point Empedocles takes a position that differs sharply from Parmenides' conception of the static form of being as a sphere or perfectly rounded globe. The course of the world, like the path of the human soul, begins with a state of all-encompassing oneness, a sphere "secured within the close confines of harmony," in which all elements are intimately joined together by the dynamic power of love. Empedocles conceives this sphere as the divine body, understanding "body" in the sense of a supersensible geometric form (δέμας).[1] He does this, just as Xenophanes and Parmenides did, in conscious opposition to the anthropomorphic form of the Olympian culture god.[2] Unlike that of Parmenides, however, his globe of being is not eternal and immutable; it originates from the unifying divine soul-force of love, which combines the four elements (as the actual, static, fundamental forms of all being) into an undivided, corporeal, all-encompassing oneness. As love gradually flows out of the divine globe of being, however, and strife (or enmity) forces its way in from the outside, a process of separation is initiated which culminates in the complete segregation of the elements into four domains. The process is then reversed: love begins to predominate and brings about a reunification which terminates in the restoration of the divine sphere or all-encompassing oneness.

This process of unification, separation, reunification, and renewed separation repeats itself endlessly.[3] "Insofar as the one has learned to arise out of many [elements] and from the sundering of the one a multiplicity once again emerges, to this extent things *come into being* and their life does not remain unchanged; but insofar as their constant exchange [of elements]

---

that *is* should be destroyed; for it will always be there, no matter how much one keeps shifting it about.")

1 Diels-Kranz I, 324; B. Fragm. 27: οὗτως Ἁρμονίης πυκινῶι κρύφωι ἐστήρικται Σφαῖρος κυκλοτερὴς μονίηι περιηγέι γαίων. ("Thus secured in the close confines of harmony lies the sphere, round in form, filled with joyous pride over the solitude round about.")

2 Diels-Kranz I, 325; B. Fragm. 29: οὐ γὰρ ἀπὸ νώτοιο δύο κλάδοι ἀίσσονται, οὐ πόδες, οὐ θοὰ γοῦν(α), οὐ μήδεα γεννήεντα, ἀλλὰ σφαῖρος ἔην καὶ <πάντοθεν>) ἶσος ἑαυτῶι. ("there are not [on the sphere] two branches rising from his back, nor feet, nor swift knees, nor genitals with procreative power; but it was a sphere, equal to itself on every side.") Ibid., B. Fragm. 31: πάντα γὰρ ἑξείης πελεμίζετο γυῖα θεοῖο. ("For all the limbs of the god were shaken in succession [by enmity as the separating principle].") "Limbs" is here a figurative expression of the *corporeal* spherical form itself, which, as the previous quotation shows, actually had no limbs.

3 Diels-Kranz I, 315-316; B. Fragm. 17, 6-8: καὶ ταῦτ' ἀλλάσσοντα διαμπερὲς οὐδαμὰ λήγει, ἄλλοτε μὲν Φιλότητι συνερχόμεν' εἰς ἕν ἅπαντα, ἄλλοτε δ' αὖ δίχ' ἕκαστα φορεύμενα Νείκεος ἔχθει. ("And this continual exchange never ceases; at one time all unites into one through love, then again the individual elements separate themselves in the hatred of enmity.")

never ceases, to this extent they *are* ever unmoved throughout the cycle."[1] "The elements are all of equal power and the same age, but each of them has a different rank (τιμήν) and each its own particular nature; and by turns they gain the upper hand in the circular course of time."[2] Everything is filled with these elements,[3] and "they alone *are*, but by running through one another they *become* different things."[4]

e. Empedocles' Sphere Is No Longer a Static Form of Being

The first thing that strikes one in this exposition is the subjection of Parmenides' divine form of being (the sphere) to the matter principle of eternal flux. Empedocles degrades this "form of being" to the transitory bodily form of the deity, which does not exist as an all-encompassing oneness until the divine soul-force of love fashions it from the four elements as fundamental forms of being. In Empedocles' conception, Parmenides' all-encompassing oneness, in the sense of a divine corporeal unity, thus contains within itself the potential for multiplicity. That is because it itself has arisen from the four elements.

f. The Four Elements Have No Spontaneous Power of Movement. Philia and Neikos as Spontaneously Moving Soul-Forces. The Dissociation from Each Other of the Form and Matter Principles

In the second place, the four elements themselves, as immutable ontic forms of *physis*, have been deprived of the spontaneous, vital power of movement which intrinsically belonged to them in the nature philosophy of the Milesians and of Heraclitus and which was regarded there as the seat of their "divinity." For Empedocles the moving forces are *love* and *hate* (*philia* and *neikos*). He clearly describes these as "daemons" [divine powers], which exist as *fluid continua*.[5] Love is conceived as the fluid *dynamis* of the all-pervading divine soul. In the third book of his *Metaphysics*, Aristotle remarks that Empedocles makes his *philia* the substrate of the (divine) unity in the same sense that Thales does with

---

1 B. Fragm. 17: 9-13: <οὕτως ἧι μὲν ἓν ἐκ πλεόνων μεμάθηκε φύεσθαι> ἠδὲ πάλιν διαφύντος ἑνὸς πλέον᾽ ἐκτελέθουσι, τῆι μὲν γίγνονταί τε καὶ οὔ σφισιν ἔμπεδος αἰών· ἧι δὲ διαλλάσσοντα διαμπερὲς οὐδαμὰ λήγει, ταύτηι δ᾽ αἰὲν ἔασιν ἀκίνητοι κατὰ κύκλον. (translation in the text)
2 Diels-Kranz I, 317; B. Fragm. 17, 27-29: ταῦτα γὰρ ἰσά τε πάντα καὶ ἥλικα γένναν ἔασι, τιμῆς δ᾽ ἄλλης ἄλλο μέδει, πάρα δ᾽ ἦθος ἑκάστωι, ἐν δὲ μέρει κρατέουσι περιπλομένοιο χρόνοιο. (translation in the text)
3 Diels-Kranz I, 318; B. Fragm. 17, 33: πῆι δέ κε κἠξαπόλοιτο, ἐπεὶ τῶνδ᾽ οὐδὲν ἔρημον; ("How too could it [the entirety of the elements] perish, since nothing is empty of them?")
4 Diels-Kranz I, 320; B. Fragm. 21, 13-14: αὐτὰ γὰρ ἔστιν ταῦτα, δι᾽ ἀλλήλων δὲ θέοντα γίγνεται ἀλλοιωπά. (translation in the text)
5 Diels-Kranz I, 333; B. Fragm. 59.

water, Anaximenes with air, and Heraclitus with fire.[1] Indeed, in Empedocles' nature philosophy, the Orphic-Pythagorean dualism, of thinking soul and material body, underwent a remarkable theoretical transposition. To a degree, the matter principle of eternal flux keeps its divine character. It retains the religious primacy it had enjoyed in the Milesians and in Heraclitus. Under the influence of the Eleatic critique, however, it has distanced itself from the form principle, even though Empedocles refused to accept the idea established by Parmenides that they were completely antithetical. The divine soul-substance serves as the vehicle of the matter principle in its unifying function, while form is merely corporeal and remains static only in the four "elements" as corporeal forms of being. The divine corporeal form of the sphere of being is not a form of origin, a form with generative power; on the contrary, it is no less subject to the matter principle of eternal flux than are the earthly corporeal forms.

g. *Empedocles Transposes the Orphic Dualism into the Matter Principle Itself. Plato's* Epinomis

The most important point, however, is that Empedocles transposes the Orphic dualism into the matter principle itself. There are two soul-forces operative as *dunameis* in the process of becoming, and these are in fact in polar antithesis to each other. The dynamic force of divine *philia*, which binds everything into one, is irreconcilably opposed by the dynamic force of the dark *neikos*, which ultimately forces the static ontic forms of the elements apart into four sharply divided realms. This latter process takes place under the dominion of *Anankē*.

The consistent elaboration of this conception necessarily leads to the acceptance of two mutually antagonistic and equally primordial "world-souls," one of which is divine and good and the other anti-divine and evil. We shall see later how Plato, in his *Epinomis* (the supplement to his *Laws*, a dialogue written in his old age), revives this conception in the interest of preserving the soul as the exclusive source of motion. In this, however, he conceives the divine, rational world-soul as a form-soul. Thus it stands in diametrical opposition to the material soul, which is irrational and evil and the source of the unordered motions subject to *Anankē*. For Empedocles, in contrast, the divine world-soul too is a matter-soul. It is a fluid, luminous substance which is in itself formless. Thus, in this conception, the matter principle in one of its poles, has not been de-divinized. This divine soul-substance, however, has a corporeal form, the non-sensible, supermundane sphere or globular shape of the starry luminous sky, and in its cycle of coming into being and passing away, this corporeal form is bound to the four static fundamental ontic forms, i.e., the elements. The one eternal luminous form of Parmenides is thereby broken asunder into a group of four static corporeal forms of being, which are placed at the foundation

---

1   Aristotle, *Met. G*, 996 a 11 f.

of *physis* as the process of becoming. The static form principle is thereby rendered soulless. It is demoted to the level of non-spherical corporeality. It is, furthermore, in the isolated state of the elements that this static principle of form comes to complete expression. It has been taken down from the Orphic sphere of light into the sphere of darkness and turned into the product of *neikos*, the evil daemon of discord and enmity.

The separation between the individual immortal soul and the all-pervading divine soul thus comes to physical expression in the disintegration of the sphere and the eventual dispersal of the static forms of being into the four realms of the elements. The formalization of *physis* as the source of ever-flowing life by way of its embodiment in the four static ontic forms of corporeality involves, therefore, its partial de-deification.

h. The Orphic Dualism Is Also Carried Through in Empedocles' Theory of the Elements

It is noteworthy, in this connection, that Empedocles introduces this dualism even into the elements themselves as ontic forms of corporeality. Even though the elements, as we have seen, all have equal power and are equally primordial, Empedocles holds that each of them has a different rank and that each in turn gains the upper hand in the cycle of time. What is the meaning of this statement? Aristotle observes, in section four of the first book of his *Metaphysics*, that Empedocles was the first to maintain that the elements formed a group of four, "but he nevertheless uses them not as four, but rather as if there were only two, with fire by itself on the one side, and the elements opposed to it – earth, water, and air – together on the other side, as can be seen from the content of his poems."[1]

This comment is indeed very important. Fire is the dominant element in the sphere as the corporeal form of being of the divine luminous substance, which has *philia* as its driving soul-force. The firmament, i.e., the starry heavens (*οὐρανός*) conceived in the shape of a globe, is the corporeal form of the deity. According to Aetius,[2] Orphic tradition regarded the firmament as the "shell of the world egg," and in the Orphic mythological cosmogony (Pherecydes), the universe in its original state had the form of this egg. The firmament consists of air that has been made firm by fire, for Empedocles attributes to the latter a crystalline power.[3] According to Cornford, this astonishing notion that fire has a crystallizing power, which is diametrically opposed to the conception of the Milesians and

---

1 Aristotle, *Metaphysics* 985 a 31: ἔτι δὲ τὰ ὡς ἐν ὕλης εἴδει λεγόμενα στοιχεῖα τέτταρα πρῶτος εἶπεν. οὐ μὴν χρῆται γε τέτταρσιν, ἀλλ᾽ ὡς δυσὶν οὖσι μόνοις, πυρὶ μὲν καθ᾽ αὑτό, τοῖς δ᾽ ἀντικειμένοις ὡς μιᾷ φύσει, γῇ τε καὶ ἀέρι καὶ ὕρατι. λάβοι δ᾽ ἄν τις αὐτὸ θεωρῶν ἐκ τῶν ἐπῶν. (translation in the text)
2 Diels-Kranz I, 292; Empedocles, A. Fragm. 50 (Aetius II, 31, 4).
3 Diels-Kranz I, 293; Empedocles, A. Fragm. 51 (Aetius II, 11, 2): Ἐ. στερέμνιον εἶναι τὸν οὐρανὸν ἐξ ἀέρος συμπαγέντος ὑπὸ πυρὸς κρυσταλλοειδῶς, τὸ πυρῶδες καὶ τὸ ἀερῶδες ἐν ἑκατέρωι τῶν ἡμισφαιρίων περιέχοντα.

Heraclitus, can be explained solely in terms of the close relationship of this element to the unifying and attracting power of *philia*.[1] As we have seen, the latter is the divine luminous substance as a flowing soul-force; and fire, therefore, is nothing other than the basic corporeal form of the divine light, which itself remains formless and fluid.

i.   The Relationship between Light and Fire in the Light-Metaphysics of Augustinian Scholasticism

We shall encounter this conception of the relationship of light to fire as a corporeal element once again in Augustinian Scholasticism. The latter took this over from Empedocles' Orphic doctrine of *physis* by way of Neoplatonism. It developed into a "metaphysics of light," which was accommodated to the biblical story of creation (the divine creative word "Let there be light!"). In Augustinian Scholasticism, however, the application of the form-matter motive is inverted. Here light becomes the supersensible (and in itself incorporeal) primal form of corporeality. Fire is merely its bodily form, which is accessible to sense perception. This light-metaphysics has thus passed through the mold of the Platonic conception of form and matter.

If, in Empedocles, fire is most closely related to *philia* and the divine luminous substance, the cold and dark air is considered to have a direct connection to *neikos*. The elements of water and earth, in turn, which lie between these two poles, have a somewhat more distant relationship to *neikos*. Fire ascends upwards, but the air (ether), in contrast, "sinks down with long roots into the earth."[2]

j.   The Two Hemispheres of Day and Night

As Cornford has shown, there is a perfect correspondence between this polar dualism in Empedocles' theory of the elements and the division of the cosmos into the two hemispheres of day and night, which move around the earth in a circle. Aetius, in particular, gives a detailed description of various aspects of this picture. The first or diurnal hemisphere consists of fire, while the second, nocturnal hemisphere is composed of air (the dark, cold element) mixed with a little fire. Aetius informs us that Empedocles had two suns. The first is the archetypal one, which consists of fire. It fills the one hemisphere of the cosmos and is always situated directly opposite to its reflection (ἀνταυγεία) in the other hemisphere. The second is the sun perceptible to the senses (τὸ φαινόμενον), i.e., the reflection of the original sun in the other hemisphere. The second sun is filled by air mingled with fire, and the rotation of the earth (which is carried along by the motion of the hemisphere

---

1   Cornford, *op. cit*, p. 233.
2   Diels-Kranz I, 332; Empedocles, B. Fragm. 54: αἰθὴρ <δ᾽ αὖ> μακρῆισι κατὰ χθόνα δύετο ῥίζαις.

filled with fire) causes this air to refract the rays of light.[1]

If fire is thus the fundamental bodily form of *philia*, the cold and dark air may justifiably be designated the fundamental bodily form of *neikos*. This means that the Orphic dualism has been extended here to the static ontic forms of corporeality.

k. *Has Empedocles Also Formalized the Divine Matter Principle of* Philia*? The Role of* Harmonia *in Empedocles' System*

It may be asked whether Empedocles has likewise formalized the matter principle in his conception of the divine fluid soul-substance (*philia*). Cornford believes that the *philia* in the divine sphere is in fact the same as the "harmony soul" of Pythagoras, which was simultaneously a numerical proportion (*logos* or *ratio*) and a "mental substance." He also believes that it plays the same role as the fire-*logos* of Heraclitus.

Indeed, as we found earlier, Empedocles states that the sphere lies secured in the "close confines of harmony" and that no discord and strife reigns in its "limbs."[2] Furthermore, in his *De anima*, Aristotle takes issue with the conception of the individual soul as a harmonic proportion of the mixture (of the elements), or λόγος τῆς μείξεως, a view that he ascribes to Empedocles. He argues that because the elements are not mixed in the same proportion in flesh and bone, it would follow that there are several souls in one body, if the proportion that determines the mixture were indeed a harmony, i.e., a soul. Moreover, is the soul then *itself* this proportion, or is it rather something distinct from this? And, finally, is the mixture brought about by *philia* a mixture κατὰ τύχην, i.e., one caused by blind *Anankē*, or is it a mixture in the right proportion? And if the latter is the case, is *philia* then itself this proportion, or is it something distinct from this?[3]

It appears to me that the conclusion that Cornford draws from the above data is in error. In neither of Empedocles' didactic poems is there any trace of a Pythagorean number mysticism. In addition, Heraclitus' conception of the *logos* is incompatible with the Orphic dualism of soul and body, which, as we have seen, was also adhered to by Empedocles.

In the passage referred to, Aristotle is speaking in the first place of the

---

1 Diels-Kranz I, 293; Empedocles, A. Fragm. 56 (Aetius II, 20, 13 [D. 350]): Ἐ. δύο ἡλίους· τὸν μὲν ἀρχέτυπον, πῦρ ὂν ἐν τῶι ἑτέρωι ἡμισφαιρίωι τοῦ κόσμου, πεπληρωκὸς τὸ ἡμισφαίριον, αἰεὶ κατ᾽ ἀντικρὺ τῆι ἀνταυγείαι ἑαυτοῦ τεταγμένον· τὸν δὲ φαινόμενον, ἀνταύγειαν ἐν τῶι ἑτέρωι ἡμισφαιρίωι τῶι τοῦ ἀέρος τοῦ θερμομιγοῦς πεπληρωμένωι ἀπὸ κυκλοτεροῦς τῆς γῆς κατ᾽ ἀνάκλασιν γιγνομένην εἰς τὸν ἥλιον τὸν κρυσταλλοειδῆ, συμπεριελκομένην δὲ τῆι κινήσει τοῦ πυρίνου. (translation in the text) Cf. in this connection the other testimonies of Aristotle, Philoponus, Aetius, and Plutarch (A. Fragm. 57, 58, and 60).
2 Diels-Kranz I, 324; Empedocles, B. Fragm. 27. Cf. p. 87, note 1.
3 Aristotle, *De anima* a. 4, 408 a. 13.

individual human soul that has entered into the earthly body and thus, in Empedocles' conception, has already fallen away from its divine origin. Nowhere does Empedocles call the all-pervading divine soul itself a harmony. Harmony is ascribed, in the first place, solely to the sphere as the "divine body," and it here consists exclusively in the proportional mixing of all four elements into a unity, this being undivided, without *neikos*, and apparently dominated by the element fire. Empedocles' nature philosophy, however, also gives a second role to harmony. To be specific, it appears in his theory about the origin of individual things with form from the mixing and separating of portions of the elements in the earthly process of *physis*.

When the universe is in the state of the sphere, *neikos*, completely separated from the elements, is situated "at the outermost limits of the globe," enveloping it in a cold and dark soul-stream. At the same time *philia* is apparently diffused throughout the entire sphere, as an evenly spread fluid. When, in obedience to the authoritative decree of *Anankē*, *neikos* invades the divine corporeal globe from all sides, *philia* streams out to meet it. As *philia* (or *philotēs*) reaches the center of the vortex which has been created thereby and portions of the elements separate out and mix with one another in definite proportions,[1] these then become men and all kinds of living beings. The assembling of the related bodily parts of a mortal living being (in Empedocles' presentation, these first arise independently and separate from one another)[2] is caused by "the gentle, immortal impulse of love. And straightway what had previously been immortal grew into mortal beings, and what had previously been unmixed became mixed together, a changing of paths."[3]

---

1 Diels-Kranz I, 326-327; Empedocles, B. Fragm. 35, 3: ἐπεὶ Νεῖκος μὲν ἐνέρτατον ἵκετο βένθος δίνης, ἐν δὲ μέσηι Φιλότης στροφάλιγγι γένηται, ἐν τῆι δὴ τάδε πάντα συνέρχεται ἓν μόνον εἶναι, οὐκ ἄφαρ, ἀλλὰ θελημὰ συνιστάμεν᾿ ἄλλοθεν ἄλλα. τῶν δέ τε μισγομένων χεῖτ᾿ ἔθνεα μυρία θνητῶν. ("When strife has reached the lowest depth of the vortex, but love arrives in the middle of it, then all of this unites in her [?] to be a single whole, not all at once, but by coming together at their will, one from here and one from there. From this mixture there sprang countless hosts of mortal beings.") Concerning the harmony in the proportion of the mixture, cf. B. Fragm. 96 and 98: "The white bones are fitted together by the cementing powers of harmony (Ἁρμονίης κόλλῃσιν) with divine beauty." They are mixed from earth, water, and fire in the proportions 2 : 2 : 4.
2 Diels-Kranz I, 333; B. Fragm. 57: ἧι πολλαὶ μὲν κόρσαι ἀναύχενες ἐβλάστησαν, γυμνοὶ δ᾿ ἐπλάζοντο βραχίονες εὔνιδες ὤμων, ὄμματά τ᾿ οἶ(α) ἐπλανᾶτο πενητεύοντα μετώπων. ("On it [the earth] sprang up many jawbones without necks, bare arms wandered here and there without shoulders, and eyes floated about alone without foreheads.") Diels-Kranz I, 336; B. Fragm. 63: ἀλλὰ διέσπασται μελέων φύσις· ("But the origin of the limbs is divided from one another.")
3 Diels-Kranz I, 327-328; B. Fragm. 35, 12: ὅσσον δ᾿ αἰὲν ὑπεκπροθέοι, τόσον αἰὲν ἐπήιει ἠπιόφρων Φιλότητος ἀμεμφέος ἄμβροτος ὁρμή· αἶψα δὲ θνήτ᾿ ἐφύοντο, τὰ

In this process, *philia* brings harmony into being by combining definite portions of the elements. But what arises in this way as an individual being, is a child of both *philia* and *neikos* and is thus defective in its very origin.

l. Blind Ananke *Rules the Entire Earthbound Process of Becoming Which Gives Rise to Individual Beings*

What is noteworthy here is that blind *Ananke* or *Tyche* remains in control of this entire process. This constitutes a second argument against the notion that *harmonia* has the same role in Empedocles' nature philosophy that it had in the doctrine of the Pythagoreans.

Empedocles indeed explicitly states that in the conjoining of the separate members into a mortal body, various monstrosities were formed that had no enduring life, such as creatures with double faces and double breasts, or combinations of human faces with the bodies of oxen, and conversely.[1] Only those combinations were retained that – although they, like the others, were produced by blind chance and unpredictable fate – were nevertheless so constituted that they seemed to have been purposively designed for life.[2] Even the harmony that *philia* creates within mortal beings is thus evidently a product of *Ananke* and not of a thinking divine mind. The all-pervasive divine thinking soul appears to have no power over *physis*, the eternally flowing stream of life, which remains bound to the tenebrous earth, for *physis* is completely subjected to *Ananke,* which follows its course through all the elements.

m. The Problem with Respect to the Immortality of the Soul in Empedocles' Theory of Physis

In the interpretation of Empedocles' theory of *physis*, there arises an extremely difficult problem. Apparently he recognizes no dualism between soul and mortal body in the earthly realm of perishable life; nevertheless, in his *Katharmoi*, he clearly holds to the Orphic doctrine concerning the immortality of the individual soul.

"Out of the elements," he says, "everything is fittingly joined together, and through them do mortal beings think, enjoy, and feel sorrow."[3] He regards the blood coursing round the heart as the seat of human thought.[4] "For we behold earth by means of earth, water by means of water, ether by

---

πρὶν μάθον ἀθάνατ᾽ εἶναι, ζωρά τε τὰ πρὶν ἄκρητα διαλλάξαντα κελεύθους. (translation in the text)

1 Diels-Kranz I, 334; B. Fragm. 61.
2 Aristotle, *Physics* 2. 8. 198 b 29. Aristotle here takes issue with this conception by arguing that the purposively formed organisms do not appear in arbitrary, individual cases, as would be expected if they arose by chance, but ἤ ἀεὶ ἤ ὡς ἐπὶ τὸ πολύ ("either always, or at least in the great majority of cases.")
3 Diels-Kranz I, 351; Empedocles, B. Fragm. 107: ἐκ τούτων <γὰρ> πάντα πεπήγασιν ἁρμοσθέντα καὶ τούτοις φρονέουσι καὶ ἥδοντ᾽ ἠδ᾽ ἀνιῶνται. (translation in the text)
4 Diels-Kranz I, 350; B. Fragm. 105: αἷμα γὰρ ἀνθρώποις περικάρδιόν ἐστι νόημα. (translation in the text)

means of ether, and fire by means of fire; and further, we behold love by our love, and hate by our grievous hate."[1] (Again this is the thesis that played such an important role in Greek philosophy, that like is known only by like.) We are further told that it is by the will of *Tychē* or *Anankē* that all (mortal) beings are endowed with consciousness and partake of thought.[2]

Appealing to the fragment cited above ("we behold earth by means of earth," etc.), Aristotle observes that for Empedocles the individual soul is composed of a mixture of all the elements. Whatever has its origin in a mixture of elements cannot be immortal, however, and it is precisely this that has led to the prevailing opinion that Empedocles' nature philosophy is completely unrelated to his Orphic teaching, expounded in the *Katharmoi*.

n. Cornford's Solution to This Problem Is in Conflict with the Clear Pronouncements of Empedocles

Cornford thinks that this difficulty is removed by regarding Empedocles' human soul as composed of both a mortal and an immortal part. The immortal part allegedly consists solely in a mixture of segments of the soul-forces of *philia* and *neikos* and comprises the actual individuality of the human soul. The mortal part, in contrast, contains the purely sensory faculties, which remain tied to the earthly body. These will then naturally pass away along with this body.[3]

This solution of the difficulty, however, conflicts with the texts cited above. These clearly teach that the human faculty of thought is also derived from a mixture of the elements.[4] Cornford's solution is based upon a hypothetical construction that finds no support in Empedocles' didactic poem on *physis*.

o. The Most Likely Interpretation of Empedocles' Pronouncements on This Point. The Origin of the Thesis That "Like Is Known Only by Like"

In order to understand Empedocles' position correctly, it is necessary to take one's point of departure in his notion that *like* is known only by *like*. In the static interpretation of ontology, this conception goes back to Parmenides, who posited the identity of *being* and *thought* without tak-

---

1 Diels-Kranz I, 351; B. Fragm. 109: γαίηι μὲν γὰρ γαῖαν ὀπώπαμεν, ὕδατι δ' ὕδωρ, αἰθέρι δ' αἰθέρα δῖον, ἀτὰρ πυρὶ πῦρ, ἀίδηλον, στοργὴν δὲ στοργῆι, νεῖκος δέ τε νείκεϊ λυγρῶι. (translation in the text)
2 Diels-Kranz I, 350; B. Fragm. 103: τῆιδε μὲν οὖν ἰότητι Τύχης πεφρόνηκεν ἅπαντα. Diels-Kranz I, 353; B. Fragm. 110, 10: πάντα γὰρ ἴσθι φρόνησιν ἔχειν καὶ νώματος αἶσαν. (translation in the text)
3 Cornford, *op. cit*, p.239.
4 There is here a certain kinship with Parmenides' utterance in B. Fragm. 16 (Diels-Kranz I, 244), which makes the *nous* dependent upon the "mixture of the limbs."

ing account of the theoretical *Gegenstand* relation. Aristotle claims that Heraclitus taught the same thing, [1] but from his own standpoint, according to which what is moved can be known by what is moved. Since Empedocles, as we have seen, dissolved the one static form of being of the Eleatics into the four elements, as four static forms of being, his retention of the Eleatic principle that like is known by like forced him to identify theoretical thought as thought of being with the elements of *physis*. And since these elements are *corporeal* forms of being, thinking itself, as being, also belongs to the realm of corporeality. The elements themselves partake of consciousness and thought, as is expressly stated in the conclusion of Fragment 110: "for know that everything has consciousness and, through *Anankē,* a share (αῖσαν) in thought."[2]

It is thus evident that not merely the powers of sense perception, but even the faculty of thought itself, have their ontic ground in the four basic forms of *physis*. Do they then not belong to the immortal soul? If this question is to be answered in the spirit of the Greek philosopher himself, it must be borne in mind that for Empedocles motion could be imparted to the bodily elements exclusively through the soul-forces. Both the sensory functions and the function of thought, even though as existing things they have been constituted from the elements, can therefore be brought into dynamic activity only by the soul. *Philia* and *neikos*, then, are the two *dunameis* that produce this process. Furthermore, it is only through them that we have knowledge of the "soul-movements" of love and enmity. It is this, therefore, that forms the Heraclitean counterpart in Empedocles' thought to the Eleatic interpretation of the principle that like is known only by like. Thus the actual *movement* in thought is indeed immortal – although, as we shall see, a reservation must be made with respect to its individuality – just as its ontic ground is located in the four basic corporeal forms of *physis*. In spite of this, Empedocles teaches that the thought faculty of mortal man resides in his blood. The human power of thought thus passes away together with the blood-soul.

If this interpretation is correct – and it has the advantage of squaring with both the text of the fragments and the entire spirit of Empedocles' thought – then it would appear that this philosopher, although he maintains the dualism between the form and matter principles, admits of no absolute separation between soul and material body, neither in the divine all-encompassing oneness, nor in the "daemons." With respect to the divine unity, this is evident at once in the description of the sphere. *Philia* as the divine, fluid soul-force is found within the divine globular body, and so long as this sphere (i.e., the supersensible form of the luminous heavens) is not broken asunder by *neikos*, there is no separation of individual souls (daemons) from the all-pervading divine soul enclosed in the sphere. There is likewise at this time no dark terrestrial realm to which the detached souls could fall in order to follow the cycle of incarnation and re-

---

1 Aristotle, *De Anima* 1, 2.
2 Diels-Kranz I, 353; Empedocles, B. Fragm. 110,10.

incarnations in the prison of earthly material bodies.[1] In addition, the thought faculty of the divine mind, which was spoken of in the fragment from the *Katharmoi* cited above, is in truth also not conceived of in isolation from the sphere as the divine bodily form. Even the deity, whose "thoughts dart through the whole cosmos," thinks the elements by means of the elements, i.e., being by means of being.

Just as Pythagoras' divine form principle continued to be rooted in the matter principle (the ever-flowing source of *physis*), so, conversely, Empedocles' divine matter principle – in spite of the fact that it has been distanced from the form principle, which he has restricted to the corporeal realm – is rooted in the four ontic forms of *physis*. It is from the latter that the divine spherical body also arises through the motive force of the divine *philia*.

Empedocles' *Katharmoi* and his didactic poem *On Nature* agree that the separation of individual souls dictated by *Ananke* is produced by the operation of *neikos*, the evil soul-force of strife and discord. The divine *philia* then loses its appropriate corporeal form, and the detached souls likewise fall away from the spherical form of the luminous heavens, i.e., the all-encompassing divine body.

In the continuing exercise of its soul-power, *philia* remains dependent on the four basic corporeal forms, the elements. For without elements there is nothing either to unite or to separate. The same holds for *neikos*, and also for the individual souls born from the mixture of *philia* and *neikos*. These individual souls are also rooted in the four elements. Indeed, it is only through the elements that the soul can think and can experience joy and sorrow.

Like the divine *philia* itself, however, the detached souls that have fallen from the divine all-encompassing oneness no longer have a body that is appropriate to themselves. For this reason they must pass, in subjection to *Ananke*, from one body to the next during their circuit through the earthly realm of *physis*. When eventually *philia* again becomes victorious, they are once more taken up into the immortal, all-pervading divine soul within the sphere, and the divine bodily form is thus restored.

p. Empedocles' Individual Soul is Not Human and Has Immortality Only in a Relative Sense

The individual soul that has fallen away from the deity is, in itself, not human. In the *Katharmoi* it is called only a "long-lived daemon," just as in *Peri physeōs* the gods are called "long-lived."[2] And such a daemon is a flowing soul-substance without fixed form, neither god nor mortal

---

1 In his *Phaedrus*, 246 c 25, Plato likewise says, in conclusion, that one imagines the immortal gods of heaven with soul *and* body, "both joined by nature for all time." According to B. Fragment 115 of the *Katharmoi*, even the daemons have "limbs" (Diels-Kranz I, 357).
2 Diels-Kranz I, 320; Empedocles, B. Fragm. 21, 12.

man. In the cycle of *physis*, the fallen daemon enters into a human body only temporarily, for it assumes other bodily forms just as well. After the completion of the great astral year, it is no longer bound to an earthly body. Then, as Empedocles expressly states, it returns to the divine all-encompassing oneness as an immortal partner, delivered from the power of *Ananke*, which had mingled *philia* with *neikos*.

In both of Empedocles' didactic poems, the individual immortality of the soul is thus only relative. As the product of the activity of *neikos*, individuality can only be preserved for the duration of the cycle of incarnations and reincarnations within the dark, earthly realm, and it of necessity comes to an end when the soul reverts once again to its divine origin.

Even within the conception of Empedocles, therefore, the dualism between material body and immortal thinking soul could not be given suitable philosophical expression. This would not become possible until the form principle of the religion of culture had gained the supremacy in philosophical thought and had been liberated from its naturalistic, pantheistic deformation. The conception of individual immortality was thus first developed in the Olympian culture religion, with respect to the radiant form-gods.

As soon as Greek thought entered the path of *critical* self-reflection, the prototype for the immortality of the individual form-soul could be found in the *athanasia* of the individual form-god; for, as I shall demonstrate in the transcendental critique of philosophic thought, self-knowledge is completely dependent on one's knowledge of God.

q. The Antinomies in Empedocles' Theory of Physis

In its consistent elaboration, Empedocles' endeavor to unite the matter principle with the form principle of the Eleatic ontology inevitably ensnared Greek *theōria* in a complicated web of antinomies. If the divine sphere, as a bodily form produced by the formless flux of *philia*, is truly an all-encompassing *oneness*, how could it have originated from four immutable static elements as forms of being? After its fall from the deity, the soul is able to preserve its individuality only as long as it is pursuing its dark course through all the elements; for if it is reunited with the all-pervading soul, it is absorbed into the latter. But how is it possible for Empedocles to hold that all the diversity of the elements can be annulled in the sphere, when he also explicitly teaches that these four basic forms are eternal and immutable? If the sphere is a harmonious mixture of the elements, it can at most be a unity in the multiplicity of the elements; but the principle of diversity that is simultaneously present in this multiplicity is precisely what is supposed to be foreign to the sphere. Furthermore, unity can never have its origin in a multiplicity, as Empedocles would have it, for even a unity-in-multiplicity is necessarily founded in unity.

In his conception of the sphere, Empedocles apparently wishes to bring the undivided flowing oneness of *philia* to formal expression. In itself, however, *philia* is not a form principle but a divine matter principle.[1] Form is a *peras*, a principle of limit. As such, it contradicts the principle of matter within the dialectical ground-motive. If the sphere is indeed a product of *philia*, the elements within it would have to be eliminated. Only a chaotic, formless *hulē* could remain.

Only a polar antithesis, a complete separation of the form principle from the matter principle, would have sufficed to maintain the independence of the former over against the latter that had been demanded in Empedocles' theory of the elements. This was the course that Anaxagoras would follow. Before he could begin, however, the naturalistic Orphic conception of the form principle, which always retained its root in the Dionysian matter principle, had to be overcome. And this route led to the form principle of the religion of culture in its original, non-naturalized sense.

5. The Primacy of the Form Principle of the Religion of Culture in Anaxagoras' Theory of *Nous*, and the Atomists' Reversion to the Naturalistic Form Principle

a. The Nous *as Divine Form-Giver (Demiurge) Remains Unmixed with Matter, Which It Controls by Its Form-Giving. The Form Motive of the Religion of Culture*

It is in the thought of Anaxagoras of Clazomenae (ca. 499-428 B.C.), a contemporary and friend of the great Athenian statesman Pericles, that the form principle of the religion of culture first began to wrestle free from the grip of the naturalistic uranic motives and to come to expression in its stark opposition to the matter motive of the religion of nature. Anaxagoras elevated *nous*, the theoretical thought operative in θεωρία, to the position of a divine formative principle. In doing so, he released this notion of the deity from its naturalistic mathematical confinement within Parmenides' form of being,[2] and he purified it from any admixture with the matter principle.[3] As the purely thinking *archē* of all form, exalted above all sensory feeling and emotion, *nous* may not be mixed with matter. For if it were, it would not be able to exercise control over matter.[4]

Here there is a clear expression of the ground-motive of the religion of

---

1   Aristotle correctly notes this in *Metaphysics* B, 1 996 a 7.
2   Diels-Kranz II, 37; Anaxagoras, B. Fragm. 12: τὰ μὲν ἄλλα παντὸς μοῖραν μετέχει, νοῦς δέ ἐστιν ἄπειρον καὶ αὐτοκρατὲς καὶ μέμεικται οὐδενὶ χρήματι, ἀλλὰ μόνος αὐτὸς ἐπ᾽ ἑωυτοῦ ἐστιν. ("The rest has a share of everything [i.e., of matter as the chaotic mixture of everything]. The thinking mind, however, is something that is determined by no formal limit [this obviously refers to that of the Eleatics] and is self-ruled and mixed with no material seed, but exists alone by itself.") For the conceptions of ἄπειρον that differ from mine, see Jaeger, *op. cit*, p. 241.
3   See the preceding note.
4   Diels-Kranz II, 37-38; B. Fragm. 12: καὶ ἂν ἐκώλυεν αὐτὸν τὰ συμμεμειγμένα, ὥστε μηδενὸς χρήματος κρατεῖν ὁμοίως ὡς καὶ μόνον ἐόντα ἐφ᾽ ἑαυτοῦ. ("And the

culture in its authentic sense. Culture, after all, is the exercise of control over a given material by means of rational forming according to a free project. At the same time, it is equally clear what the basic difference is between Anaxagoras' view and that of Empedocles. The prevailing opinion wrongly places Empedocles in the same line as Anaxagoras and then lumps them together with the Atomists. For Empedocles, however, the all-pervading divine soul was a fluid continuum, which was conceived entirely in accordance with the Greek matter principle, and the deity lacked all power over the forming process in the cycle of birth, death, and rebirth. The latter remained the exclusive province of *Anankē* or *Tychē*, of blind, irrational fate. In addition, *philia*, as the flowing divine soul-stream, was a true Dionysian *dunamis*, which under the influence of Orphism had merely distanced itself from the form principle, even though it lay enclosed in the divine corporeal sphere.

b. The De-Deification of the Matter Principle

Anaxagoras, in contrast, radically de-deified the realm of matter. He accomplished this by denying to it the spontaneous ever-flowing motion of life. He deprived it, therefore, precisely of that in which the Milesian nature philosophy and Heraclitus had located its divine character.

The situation here is thus completely different from the one we find in Empedocles. The latter's denial of the spontaneous power of motion to the four elements was a direct result of the fact that he dissociated the soul from the body in Orphic fashion. The soul then became the vehicle of the principle of matter, while the elements were not matter in the Greek sense of the word, but rather the basic forms of being from which all corporeal things were constituted and came into being. For his part, Anaxagoras rejected Empedocles' theory of the elements, which was dependent on the Eleatic conception of the eternal form of being. Precisely because he conceived the divine *nous* as the sole form-giving principle of origin and thereby consciously ascribed the religious primacy to the ground-motive of the religion of culture, Anaxagoras was compelled to de-deify per se the matter principle of the religion of nature.

c. Anaxagoras' Conception of Matter as an In-Itself Fixed and Chaotic Meigma of the Seeds of All Things. The So-Called "Homoeomeries"

With this in view, Anaxagoras denies the presence of soul within the realm of matter in itself. Matter becomes fixed and static, although it re-

---

matter-seeds that were mixed with it [viz., the *nous*] would hinder it, so that it could control none of these in the same way as it does when it is alone by itself." In an express appeal to Anaxagoras, this later became one of the main arguments of Aristotle and of Thomas Aquinas for the independence of the activity of theoretical thought from the material body. This anthropological inference is lacking in Anaxagoras, however. B. Fragm. 12: καὶ ὅσα γε ψυχὴν ἔχει καὶ τὰ μείζω καὶ τὰ ἐλάσσω, πάντων νοῦς κρατεῖ. ("And over all things that have soul [life], both the greater and the smaller [beings], *nous* has dominion.")

tains its typical chaotic character. It has become the absolute *meigma*, the chaotic, completely formless mixing together of everything with everything. Here the eternal flux of *physis* is not given a foundation in a group of four static forms of being; instead, matter itself is deprived of its spontaneous power of motion, of its fluid soul-continuum. But matter remains the diametrical opposite of the principle of form. Now it is the realm of chaos, which is instrinsically inert and static. It has become *formlessness*.

For Anaxagoras, movement is in principle form-giving movement, which originates solely in the divine *nous* as demiurge. This *nous* makes out of chaos a cosmos, a form-world, and it knows and determines its entire order.[1] Anaxagoras expressly denies that *Ananke* or *heimarmene Tyche* is the origin of the form-giving process.[2] This does not mean, however, that the chaotic principle of matter has lost its status as a principle of origin independent of the divine principle of form. Chaos does not owe its origin to the divine *nous*. Indeed, following Empedocles, Anaxagoras says that there is no becoming or origination in any absolute sense.[3] In his thought, however, this statement takes on an entirely different meaning than it has in Empedocles. According to Anaxagoras, matter continues to be a chaotic mixture of everything with everything, even when it has been

---

1 Diels-Kranz II, 38; Anaxagoras, B. Fragm. 12, 5: καὶ τῆς περιχωρήσιος τῆς συμπάσης νοῦς ἐκράτησεν, ὥστε περιχωρῆσαι τὴν ἀρχήν. καὶ πρῶτον ἀπό του σμικροῦ ἤρξατο περιχωρεῖν, ἐπὶ δὲ πλέον περιχωρεῖ, καὶ περιχωρήσει ἐπὶ πλέον. καὶ τὰ συμμισγόμενά τε καὶ ἀποκρινόμενα καὶ διακρινόμενα πάντα ἔγνω νοῦς ... πάντα διεκόσμησε ... ("*Nous* also took control of the entire movement of rotation, so that it gave the initial impetus to this. And this rotation first began at some small point [viz., of matter], but the rotating motion extends itself further and will extend further still. And what it therein mingled together and separated out from one another, this all was known by the *nous*... this all was ordered by the *nous*.")
2 Diels-Kranz II, 22; Anaxagoras, A. Fragm. 66.
3 Diels-Kranz II, 40-41; Anaxagoras, B. Fragm. 17: τὸ δὲ γίνεσθαι καὶ ἀπόλλυσθαι οὐκ ὀρθῶς νομίζουσιν οἱ Ἕλληνες· οὐδὲν γὰρ χρῆμα γίνεται οὐδὲ ἀπόλλυται, ἀλλ᾽ ἀπὸ ἐόντων χρημάτων συμμίσγεταί τε καὶ διακρίνεται. ("But the Greeks have no proper notion of coming into being and passing away. For no matter-seed comes into being or passes away, but from existing matter-seeds [things] are mixed and once again decompose.") I continually depart from Diels' translations, because in my view they misrepresent the philosophic content of the text. For example, he translates χρῆμα as "thing." In doing so he imports into the text an indefensible point of view that was certainly not held by Anaxagoras. In Anaxagoras, the word χρήματα often has the pregnant philosophical sense of "primordial principles of *hule*," which he will later also call σπέρματα (seeds). This meaning is already present in fragment 1 (Diels-Kranz II, 32): ὁμοῦ πάντα χρήματα ἦν, ἄπειρα καὶ πλῆθος καὶ σμικρότητα· Here there is a description of the original chaos, in which no things having form exist. Here again, however, Diels translates using the word "thing": "Beisammen waren alle Dinge, grenzenlos nach Menge wie nach Kleinheit." (*Translator:* "All things were together, infinite both in number and in smallness.")

divided and subdivided as far as possible. Precisely for this reason he claims that it contains an infinite number of infinitesimally small *seeds* (σπέρματα or χρήματα) of all things accessible to sense experience (gold, bones, flesh, blood, etc.).[1] It is a formless totality out of which everything that has form and shape is enabled to arise by a movement, produced within it by the divine *nous*, that separates the dissimilar particles and brings together the similar particles.

Anaxagoras regards the four elements of Empedocles not as elementary forms of being, but rather as complexes of matter that are in themselves originally formless and without order and that consist of a mixture of *spermata,* all of which are dissimilar. From such a heterogenous mixture, actual things having form (air, fire, etc.), which are made up predominantly of similar particles, can arise only by way of a process of separation. These similar particles, and also the totalities that are composed of them, later came to be called *homoeomeries* (from ὅμοιος, like, and μέρος, portion).[2] Aristotle contrasted these *homoeomeric* totalities with the *an-homoeomeric* totalities, that is, living organisms, which he considered to be composed of dissimilar parts.

d. *Anaxagoras' Conception of Matter as the Precursor of the Aristotelean Conception. How It Basically Differs from the Latter. The Inner Antinomy in Anaxagoras' Conception of* Hulē *as a Reality Existing Apart from Form*

Anaxagoras' conception of matter, with its infinite number of infinitesimally small components, as the "seed" of all things having form, already foreshadows the Aristotelian conception of *hulē*, which regards matter as the potentiality or possibility of being (δύναμει ὄν). At the same time, however, the inner antinomy which inevitably ensnares theoretical thought when the attempt is made to effect an absolute separation between the form and matter principles also becomes manifest at this

---

1 Diels-Kranz II, 34; Anaxagoras, B. Fragm. 4: τούτων δὲ οὕτως ἐχόντων χρὴ δοκεῖν ἐνεῖναι πολλά τε καὶ παντοῖα ἐν πᾶσι τοῖς συγκρινομένοις καὶ σπέρματα πάντων χρημάτων καὶ ἰδέας παντοίας ἔχοντα καὶ χροιὰς καὶ ἡδονάς. ("Conditions being thus, we must suppose that in all that combines there are many ingredients of many kinds and the seeds of all things [here χρῆμα does mean 'thing having form'], which have manifold forms and colors and tastes [smells].") Concerning the medical character of this theory, see Jaeger, *op. cit*, pp.156 ff.

2 In *Metaphysics* A, 3. 984 a 11, Aristotle calls the totalities which, according to Anaxagoras, arise from the combination of similar seeds ὁμοιομερῆ. In other places, however, he also gives this name to the matter seeds themselves, as parts of a whole. Thus in his *De Caelo G* 3. 202b 1, for example, he says of air and fire: εἶναι ... ἑκάτερον αὐτῶν ἐξ ἀοράτων ὁμοιομερῶν πάντων ἠθροισμένον ("that each of these is an aggregate of all invisible homoeomeries"). Cf. also *De gen. et corr.* A, 1, 314 a 19. Note also Plutarch, *Pericles* c. 4, as an example of the later writers who used the plural form ὁμοιομέρειαι with reference to the primal particles themselves (Diels-Kranz II, 10; Anaxagoras A Fragm. 15).

point. Anaxagoras holds that blood, gold, silver, and all the other substances which he regards as composed of similar particles, contain, just as their material seeds do,[1] all other substances within themselves. The only qualification here is that, in the so-called "homeomeric" totalities, the similar particles predominate.[2]

In Anaxagoras' system, the *spermata* cannot be of the nature of pure, elementary, primordial substances. If they were such, they would have to be unmixed, and they would necessarily take on the character of simple forms of being. Anaxagoras explicitly states, however, that only the divine *nous* is unmixed. The *spermata*, therefore, can have within themselves only the propensity, potentiality, or seed of the distinct forms of being, while as *hulē* they continue to possess the chaotic character of the *meigma*.

In the standard interpretation of Anaxagoras' *spermata*, far too little attention has been paid to this state of affairs, even though Plato already gave an acute analysis of it in his *Parmenides*. As a consequence, the fundamental difference between these *spermata*, on the one hand, and the elements of Empedocles and the atoms of Democritus, on the other hand, has been obscured.[3]

The truth is that, in Anaxagoras' system, the *spermata* can only have the character of pure matter, in which the tendency predominates for the material to take on a specific form. Intimately related to this is his doctrine of the absolute continuity of the *meigma*. The latter contains no *actual* elementary particles, because even the smallest particles are mixed together with all the others in an unbroken continuum. If ultimate *circumscribed* particles were in fact to exist, there would have to be an empty space between them, a notion that the Ionian thinker vigorously combats.

On the other hand, if the *meigma* were composed of pure matter-seeds, they would be completely indistinguishable from one another. On these terms, homeomeries or similar matter-seeds could not exist, since to the Greek way of thinking similarity presupposes a distinguishing form. If, however, they themselves were already *form*-seeds, then the form-giving principle (the *logos*) would have to inhere in the matter principle itself. This position was indeed taken later by the Stoics in their theory of the *logoi spermatikoi*, which was a reversion to the Heraclitean conception of the principle of matter. If Anaxagoras himself had taken this step, however, it would have meant complete failure for his attempt to effect a total separation between *hulē* and the divine *nous* as a principle of form.

---

1 Cf. Aristotle, *Phys.* G 4. 203 a 22: Ὁ μὲν (Ἀναξαγ.) ὁτιοῦν τῶν μορίων εἶναι μεῖγμα ὁμοίως τῷ παντὶ διὰ τὸ ὁρᾶν ὁτιοῦν ἐξ ὁτουοῦν γιγνόμενον ("Anaxagoras declared that each particle [of the original mixture] is a mixture, just like the whole, since he saw everything as arising from everything else.")
2 Diels-Kranz II, 35: Anaxagoras, B. Fragm. 6, 12.
3 Tannery and Burnet already objected to this; nevertheless, they also failed to arrive at a satisfactory conception of the *spermata*.

In order to escape this antinomy, Aristotle later used the stratagem of denying real (actual) existence to pure or primary matter. He taught that matter, as the mere possibility of being, is first brought into real existence by means of form.

Anaxagoras, however, establishes pure *hulē* as an actually existing chaos, which, after initially being in a state of rigid immobility, is formed into a cosmos by the divine motion. According to him, the material *spermata*, by their very nature, have an immutable being, which remains unaffected throughout the process that gives rise to form. And in this absolute separation of what as *correlata* belong inseparably together, namely, matter and form, the genuinely religious dialectic of the Greek ground-motive is once again manifest. As soon as this dialectic is carried through in theoretical thought, it become an inexhaustible source of insoluble theoretical antinomies.

This does not alter the fact, however, that Anaxagoras' theory of *nous* signals a veritable turning point in Greek philosophy. In his conception, the religious priority of the authentic form motive of the religion of culture begins to express itself for the first time in theoretical thought. Here this motive has been deepened by means of θεωρία, and the polytheistic mythological form that Homer and Hesiod had given to it has been decisively overcome. The school of Anaxagoras thus began the attempt to offer an ethical-allegorical interpretation of Homer's mythology (τὴν Ὁμήρου ποίησιν εἶναι περὶ ἀρετῆς καὶ δικαιοσύνης). As the form-giving origin, the divine *nous* has been removed from all human passions and identified with the activity of pure theoretical thought. Indeed, Anaxagoras has purged his notion of the deity from the uranic motives so thoroughly that he calls the stars "lifeless bodies," thus breaking with the ancient uranic religion of the celestial gods (θεοὶ οὐράνιοι).[1]

Nevertheless, Anaxagoras' conception still fails to carry through the primacy of the form motive of the religion of culture in a consistent philosophical manner. The form-giving divine *nous* is only given a role in his philosophy of nature in order to account for the *origin* ("the initial impulse") of motion. When it comes to explaining concrete phenomena of nature it recedes entirely into the background. In fact, Anaxagoras carries on as if the genesis of the world of form were entirely the work of the matter principle, with its blind *Anankē*. Man is supposed to have originated in just the same way as other living beings and inorganic things, through the combination of material *spermata*.[2] Thus the human mental faculty (*nous*) is evidently not regarded as an independent form, divorced from matter. Anaxagoras ascribes this character only to the divine *nous*. In another

---

1 Diels-Kranz II, 9; Anaxagoras, A. Fragm. 12 and II, 25; A. Fragm. 79.
2 Diels-Kranz II, 34; Anaxagoras, B. Fragm. 4, 8-9: καὶ ἀνθρώπους τε συμπαγῆναι καὶ τὰ ἄλλα ζῶια ὅσα ψυχὴν ἔχει. ("And that men also were fitted together [viz., from the matter-seeds of all things] and the other living animated beings.")

fragment he describes this *nous* as "the finest and purest of all *chrēmata.*"[1]

The standard interpretation is completely wrong in taking this statement to mean that Anaxagoras regarded the *nous* as merely a rarefaction of matter.[2] The statement, on the contrary, means that he conceived the divine *nous* as nothing but pure form; for a *chrēma* that is truly unmixed is necessarily formal in character.

It is still possible that Anaxagoras, like Aristotle, regarded the activity of theoretical thought as a universal, divine noetic power which only enters into the human being *from outside* (θύραθεν) and which does not operate within human nature itself (κατὰ φυσίν). This is not likely, however, since fragment 11 expressly states that *nous* is mixed with many other things.

e. *Anaxagoras' Departure from the Notion That Like Is Known by Like. The Metaphysical Interpretation of the* Gegenstand *Relation and Its Influence on the Scholastic Theory of the Soul*

Whatever answer is given to this question, the polar dualism between the form motive of the religion of culture and the matter motive is revealed, in any case, in Anaxagoras' radical departure from the fundamental thesis of Parmenides, Heraclitus, and Empedocles that *like is known by like.* Here Greek philosophy becomes aware for the first time of the *theoretical Gegenstand relation,* and this takes place by way of the metaphysical-theological route of making the theoretical-logical function of thought completely independent, separating it from the "material" field of investigation (the *Gegenstand*). As we shall see later, both Aristotle and the Scholastics will use this metaphysical misconstruction of the theoretical *Gegenstand* relation as their point of departure in demonstrating that the *nous* (or, in Scholasticism, the *anima rationalis*) is a mental substance that is separable from the material body. Divine thought is able to know the matter-seeds of all things, not because it is like them, but precisely because it is mixed with none of them and stands therefore in diametrical oposition to them.[3] The sense organs, in contrast, are too weak to discern the primal constituents of matter truly.[4] Nevertheless, Anaxagoras holds that even sensory knowledge is based on sense experience gained through what is opposed to

---

1   Diels-Kranz II, 38; Anaxagoras, B. Fragm. 12, 2-3: λεπτότατόν τε πάντων χρημάτων καὶ καθαρώτατον.
2   Diogenes of Apollonia was the first to do this, thereby reverting to the conception of Anaximenes (the divine *nous* is conceived as air).
3   Diels-Kranz II, 38; Anaxagoras, B. Fragm. 12, 8-10: καὶ τὰ συμμισγόμενά τε καὶ ἀποκρινόμενα καὶ διακρινόμενα πάντα ἔγνω νοῦς ("All [matter-seeds], both those mingled together and those separated and distinguished, were known by the *nous*.")
4   Diels-Kranz II, 43: Anaxagoras, B. Fragm. 21: ὑπ᾽ ἀφαυρότητος αὐτῶν [sc. τῶν

the object of perception. For example, we only perceive cold through warmth; if something is exactly the same temperature as our sense organ, it makes no impression on it whatsover.[1]

Even though he himself did not carry through the dualism between the theoretical-logical function of thought and its material *Gegenstand* in his anthropology, Anaxagoras was destined to become the spiritual father of one of the major arguments in Aristotelian and Scholastic anthropology for the immortality and spiritual substantiality of the *nous* or thinking soul (*anima rationalis*).

f. The Relationship between Form of Being and Matter in the Atomists

In the atomists Leucippus and Democritus (5th century B. C.), the primacy of the form motive of the religion of culture has disappeared entirely from the scene. That does not mean, however, that they opted for the primacy of the matter motive. They seized on the metaphysical dilemma posed by Parmenides, just as Empedocles did, and, fully aware that the principles of form and matter cannot be reduced to each other, they too sought to effect a synthesis between them.

The atomists accepted Empedocles' solution to the extent that they too took Parmenides' one, indivisible, static form of being and broke it up into a multiplicity of immutable basic forms. For them, however, the latter are not the four elements of *physis*: fire, air, earth, and water. Instead, they are metaphysical entities of stereometric form, in the same sense that we found in Parmenides. Further, the atomists maintained, there is an infinite multiplicity of such basic forms. Each of these possesses the fullness of being and the indivisibility that characterized Parmenides' form of being. Thus they are ἄτομα, atoms, which permit of no further division.

The atomists conceived of matter, by contrast, as an absolutely formless and unbounded (*apeiron*) *kenon* (κενόν), that is, an emptiness or privation of being, in which there prevails nevertheless an eternal, chaotic motion that is imparted to the atoms from outside.

As Burnet has shown in opposition to Zeller,[2] this disorderly motion, which causes a vortex (δίνη) to arise when the atoms collide with one another, cannot be regarded as a consequence of the atoms' "natural weight," in which case there would be only a falling motion. For Leucippus and Democritus weight (βάρος) is not an intrinsic property of the

---

αἰσθήσεων], φησίν, οὐ δυνατοί ἐσμεν κρίνειν τἀληθές,' ("because of their weakness [viz., the sense organs] we are not capable of discerning the true state of affairs.")

1 Diels-Kranz II, 27-28; Anaxagoras, A. Fragm. 92.
2 Burnet, *op. cit,* pp. 342 ff.; cf. p. 343, n.2.

atoms. As both Aetius[1] and Cicero[2] explicitly state, the idea that atoms have weight was first introduced by Epicurus, and this fundamentally altered the original conception of the atoms. According to the original conception, the chaotic, as yet disorderly motion must of necessity be imparted from outside, since it cannot arise from an internal impulse of the atoms themselves. As a consequence, it can only be ascribed to the formless *kenon*, as a matter principle. Apart from a matter principle, an unordered motion was unthinkable to the Greeks, and it is clear from the reliable extant sources that the atoms themselves were conceived of purely as corporeal, mathematical forms of being. What naturally comes to mind here as the source of the atomists' view is the ancient Pythagorean representation of the *kenon* as a flowing stream of dark, cold air. This was the conception of the "void" that Parmenides had in view in his didactic poem and which from his metaphysical-logical point of view he had deprived of any claim to truth. For him the *kenon* is a fluid void, empty of being, which cannot be thought or named.

It is indeed true that later on Empedocles had taken a new position with respect to atmospheric air and had exalted it as a corporeal element to the status of a material form of being. There is no evidence, however, that this led the founders of atomism to regard the *kenon* as an absolutely empty space, a conception that would have been altogether new and that would, in fact, have been incompatible with the Greek matter motive. Burnet, who follows the prevailing view in making this unwarranted assumption, must admit himself that at many points the atomistic cosmology reverted to primitive conceptions which by that time had already become obsolete. It is clear, furthermore, that atomism was strongly influenced by ancient Pythagorean conceptions, just as its cosmology was closely related to that of Anaximenes, the third great figure of Milesian nature philosophy, who regarded flowing air as a formless *archē*.[3]

It is indeed obvious, therefore, that the original chaotic motion in the *kenon* ought to be conceived in Pythagorean fashion as a flowing stream of air in which the atoms are located, and which imparts itself to them ex-

---

1 Diels-Kranz II, 96; Democritus, A. Fragm. 47 (Aetius i, 3, 18). That the *kenon* must be viewed as standing in opposition to Parmenides' form of being, of which he himself says [Diels-Kranz I, 237; Parmenides, B. Fragm. 8, 24]: πᾶν δ' ἔμπλεόν ἐστιν ἐόντος ("it is completely filled with being"), is also confirmed by Democritus, A. Fragm. 38 [Diels-Kranz II, 94], where Simplicius expressly calls Democritus' atoms τὸ πλῆρες ("the filled"), in contrast to the *kenon* ("the empty"): ἀρχὰς ἔθετο τὸ πλῆρες καὶ τὸ κενόν, ὧν τὸ μὲν ὂν τὸ δὲ μὴ ὂν ἐκάλει·

2 Cicero, *De fato*, 20.

3 This does not stand in the way of accepting atoms of air as forms of air-as-matter (Diog. Laert. IX c. 7, 12, 15). According to the atomists, however, there is no matter other than air-matter, this being the boundless and formless *kenon* from which bodies having form arise through a process of "cutting off," or ἀποτομή (Diog. Laert. IX c.6). Thus matter, unlike form, is homogeneous.

ternally, as an atmospheric wind that travels in all directions. It then also becomes understandable that in this conception the "free" soul-atoms, which will be discussed below, are said to be "suspended in air." In no way can this be taken as a reference to *atoms* of air; it must refer to air as *matter*, which is still incorporeal and formless. If one accepts the prevailing conception of the *kenon* as an absolutely empty space, however, the original motion of the atoms remains completely inexplicable. The force of this was not lost on Epicurus, who, having broken with the ancient Pythagorean conception of the void, felt himself obliged to introduce the idea that the atoms have "natural weight," in order to indicate a cause of their motion.

The first atomists apparently felt no need to give a fuller account of their archaic conception of the *kenon*, and this explains why Aristotle, who repeatedly speaks of the conception of the void as "flowing air,"[1] criticizes them nevertheless for failing to specify either the nature or the cause of the motion to which the atoms are subjected.[2]

According to the atomists, the process whereby order is brought into this motion, which enables the atoms to join themselves into relatively lasting, composite things with form that are subject to the principle of matter, does not stem from the matter-motion itself. It is rather a product of the form principle that is inherent in the atoms. Those having like forms are pushed together, and those having unlike forms are pushed apart.[3]

The *kenon*, to be sure, is a μὴ ὄν (non-being), but Leucippus and Democritus differ from Parmenides in conceiving of this non-being as merely a relative and not an absolute nothing. This means that if one considers the fluid matter in itself, that is, attempts to grasp it in detachment from the atoms as immutable forms of being, it indeed cannot become an object of thought and thus does not qualify as being in the theoretical sense of the Eleatics. In relation to the atomic forms of being, however, the fluid matter takes on a relative existence. In fact, one could say that the atoms too have being only in relation to the *kenon*.[4] This is the case because the indivisibility and impenetrability of the atoms presupposes that they are separated from one another by a relative void.

In the relation of the atoms to the void, the logical relation of P to non-P is transformed into a metaphysical ontic relation. Within the scope of the Greek ground-motive, however, there is no way of establishing what the basis of this ontic relation might be; for the dialectical character of this ground-motive does not allow for any integral origin or fundamental unity

---

1 Cf. e.g., *Phys. D*, 6, 213 a 27; *de Part. An.* B, 10, 656b 15; and *de An.* 10, 419b 34.
2 Aristotle, *Phys. Θ* 1, 252 a 32.
3 Diels-Kranz II, 94; Democritus, A. Fragm. 38: πεφυκέναι γὰρ τὸ ὅμοιον ὑπὸ τοῦ ὁμοίου κινεῖσθαι καὶ φέρεσθαι τὰ συγγενῆ πρὸς ἄλληλα ("for by nature [atoms] of like form are moved toward those of like form, and those that are akin are brought to each other.")
4 Plutarch, in *Adv. Col.* 4 p.1108 F (Diels-Kranz II, 174; B. Fragm. 156), attributes the following statement to Democritus: μὴ μᾶλλον τὸ δὲν ἢ τὸ μηδὲν εἶναι ("nothing-ness exists just as much as something-ness").

that would bring together the opposed principles of form and matter. Without question, completely to deprive matter of being in this way is strongly antimaterialistic. It is indeed that, with the proviso that the word "materialism" be understood in its characteristically Greek sense, as an overextension of the matter motive. The atomists regarded matter as, in itself, completely indeterminate (τὸ ἄπειρον). It can be pointed to as the origin of the unordered motion, which is a condition for the coming into being of things that have form; but it has actual existence only in relation to the eternal basic forms of being, namely, the atoms.

The mathematical formal properties of the atoms and their mutual mathematical order (nonsensible geometrical figure, mutual arrangement and positioning) are held to be completely adequate for explaining all the diversity of the phenomena within the cosmos.[1] Because they are entities that are determined essentially by form, it seems that Democritus also refers to the atoms as ἰδέαι.[2] According to him, the qualities present in sense perception, such as sweet and bitter, cold and warm, color and the rest, do not have being, since as conscious phenomena they exist solely *for us*.[3]

g. *The Soul as a Complex of Indivisible Forms of Being (Atoms)
That Are Spread throughout the Entire Body. Not the Soul but
Only Its Constituent Atoms Have Immortality. The Special
Character of the Latter by Virtue of Their Spherical Form*

Democritus also rejoins the soul to the principle of form, where being resides. According to him, the soul consists of the very small, smooth, and round fire atoms that are spread throughout the entire body of what has becomse a living being. As we inhale, we take in soul atoms from the air; as we exhale, we release such atoms back into the air. As long as this process continues, there is life.[4] Sense perception is explained by the atomists, in a causal way, in terms of the emission of atoms by things having form objects. In this manner, formal images (εἴδωλα) are produced, which impinge on our sense organs. Thus Leucippus taught that seeing is caused by the penetration of such *eidōla* into the eye.[5] Thought is the most subtle movement of the fire atoms and is caused by the finest *eidōla*.

There is no place in this atomistic conception for an immortality of the

---

1 Aristotle states in *Metaphysics* A, 4 985 b 14 ff. that the atomists distinguished the atoms only by their form (σχῆμα; according to Aristotle, the atomists themselves used the term ῥυσμός for this), arrangement (τάξις; for the atomists, διαθιγή), and position (θέσις; for the atomists, τροπή).). To illustrate, he gives the letters A and N as an example of difference in form, the sequences AN and NA as an example of difference in arrangement and ⊐ (the older form of Z) and H as an example of difference in position.
2 According to Plutarch, *Adv. Col.* 8 (Diels-Kranz II, 98-99; Democritus A. Fragm. 55, 57). See also Sextus Empiricus, *Adv. math.* VII, 137.
3 Diels-Kranz II, *loc.cit.*, Democritus, A. Fragm. 54, 28, 55, 101.
4 Diels-Kranz II, 78; Leucippus A. Fragm. 28; II, 109; Democritus A. Fragm. 101.
5 Diels-Kranz II, 78-79; Leucippus, A. Fragm. 29; II, 109; Democritus, A. Fragm. 101.

soul in the Orphic sense. Only the *atoms* of the soul are immortal, for they neither come into being nor pass away; but these atoms do not have life. The atomists understand life as a process of motion, and, as we have seen, this process is tied to respiration and thereby to the material body. That the soul-atoms are spherical in shape, this being the form of highest perfection, is the only thing in atomism that is reminiscent of the Orphic regard of the soul as superior to the material body. The fact that this spherical form is also attributed to the fire-atoms indicates that Leucippus and Democritus must still have been influenced to some extent by the light-metaphysics of Orphism. Most likely, this influence came by way of Parmenides' doctrine of the eternal, spherical, luminous form of that which has true being. According to Democritus, the spherical form of the soul-atoms renders them the most mobile and simultaneously makes them most qualified to transmit to the atoms of the body the motion that they receive from outside.

h. The Atoms as the Exact Opposite of Anaxagoras' Spermata

As the infinitely numerous basic forms of being, the atoms must be regarded as the exact opposite of Anaxagoras' infinite number of matter-seeds (*spermata*). In view of this, Cornford is obviously wrong in asserting that Anaxagoras was already halfway on the road to atomism. As we have seen, the *spermata* are pure *hulē* or matter; the atoms, in contrast, are genuine forms of being. As we have also seen, Anaxagoras denies, as a matter of principle, that a void could exist; without such a *kenon*, however, the atoms can have no being. For Anaxagoras, pure matter is a continuous *meigma*, which is infinitely divisible and which, even in its infinitesimally small components, still lacks a limiting form. Even these components are not pure, but retain the chaotic character of the *meigma*. Only the divine *nous* is unmixed.

i. The Anankē of Atomism Is a Metaphysical Formal Necessity.
It Is Neither Teleological nor Mechanistic

The form principle retains indeed the primacy in Atomism; nevertheless, in contrast to the cultural form that this principle took in Anaxagoras, the atomists' conception of it is thoroughly naturalistic. Except for the relic left behind in the view that the soul-atoms are spherical in shape, there is here no further trace of the Orphic conception of the *Sphairos* as the supermundane form of the luminous heavens. In spite of the fact that they are nonsensible *ιδέαι* (figures), the atomic forms become enveloped in the matter principle, in the sense of an unbounded ontic void (i.e., absence of being). They become subject to the original, unordered motion of this *kenon*, even though this motion remains completely external to them. The motions of these atoms, which attract or repel each other depending on whether they are like or unlike in form, eventually give rise to an infinite number of worlds of things with form;[1] but, as Leucippus expressly states, this process does not follow the rational, purposive plan of a form-giving divine *nous*. Instead, it takes place in accordance with *Anankē*. This *Anankē* is to be understood, however, in the metaphysical-logical sense that Parmenides had ascribed to it. It proceeds ἐκ λόγου, that is, according to firm grounds based in the form principle, and does not follow the unpredictable whim of chance (μάτην).[2]

This view of *Anankē* has nothing at all to do with the concept of causality in modern natural science. It must be understood in the context of a naturalistic conception of the Greek form motive, which was framed in an attempt to rationalize the matter principle of ever-flowing, unpredictable becoming. Unlike the classic humanistic ideal of science, it does not have in view the domination of natural phenomena. It belongs, in other words, within the metaphysical conceptual framework of a speculative Greek theory of form, which endeavors to effect a synthesis with the matter principle. It is in essence unrelated to the mechanistic view of nature characteristic of the physics founded by Galileo and Newton. Although some have thought that a relationship between the two conceptual frameworks can be discovered in the fact that both apply the mathematical method to natural phenomena and exclude all final causes, the similarity is only apparent. The domination motive of modern humanistic thought is absent from the mathematical method of the Greek atomists,[3] and their view of *physis* is fundamentally different from the view of nature in modern physics. The modern conception of the laws of nature is as foreign to this context as is the modern, experimental method of inquiry.

j. The "Atheism" of the Greek Atomists

There is a temptation to call Greek atomism "atheistic" and to regard it as a specimen of a so-called "genuinely scientific" way of thought, which allows no place for divine intervention in the natural course of events. If one does this, however, one must be extremely careful in applying such modern designations. Undeniably, the atomists, unlike their predecessors, no longer presented their θεωρία as the path to the true knowledge of God. The atomization of Parmenides' divine form of being was doubtless inspired merely by the scientific endeavor to "sal-

---

1 Cf. Aristotle, *De caelo*, 3, 4. 303 a 4: τῇ τούτων (τῶν ἀτόμων) συμπλοκῇ καὶ περιπαλάξει πάντα γεννᾶσθαι Concerning the infinite multiplicity of worlds that come into being in this manner, cf. Diels-Kranz II, 76; Leucippus, A. Fragm. 21; II, 77; A. Fragm. 24; (89); II, 94 ; Democritus, A. Fragm. [55] 40 (2); II, 95; A. Fragm. 43.

2 Diels-Kranz II, 81; Leucippus, B. Fragm. 2: οὐδὲν χρῆμα μάτην γίνεται, ἀλλὰ πάντα ἐκ λόγου τε καὶ ὑπ' ἀνάγκης. ("nothing happens by chance, but everything for a definite reason and through *Anankē*.")

3 In Plato's dialogue *Euthydemus*, the discussant Clinias undoubtedly expresses the true Greek conception of mathematics when he observes (17, 290C) that the geometer "does not *create* the figures, but merely traces out what already exists," just as a hunter tracks down game.

vage" in a theoretical way the true reality of the world of multiplicity and diversity, which Parmenides had relegated to the status of mere appearance. The question as to whether a place still remained for the deity in all this apparently played no role here. Democritus had no place for immortal gods in the sense of the Olympian religion of culture, but rather only good and evil daemons who lived longer than ordinary mortals and who appeared to men in *eidōla*. It may be recalled how Empedocles, in a similar vein, called "daemons" the souls that had fallen from the divine all-encompassing One.

All of this does not take away the fact, however, that Greek atomism is guided by the same religious ground-motive as the earlier systems of Greek philosophy. For this ground-motive proved to be independent of the particular mythological form that had been given to it by Homer and Hesiod. Anyone who loses sight of this ground-motive exposes himself at every point to modern misinterpretations of Greek *theōria*.

6. Sophism and the Critical Turning Point in Greek Philosophy under the Primacy of the Form Principle of the Religion of Culture

a. The Matter Principle Is Carried Through in Protagoras' Theory of Knowledge

Protagoras of Abdera, who was born ca. 481 B. C. and who reached the height of his career ca. 444-443 B. C., brought Greek thought to a critical turning point. He did this by removing the divine *physis* from the center of attention and replacing it with human beings themselves as cultural beings.

Protagoras became the founder of the so-called sophistic movement and the father of the Greek "Enlightenment." He was active as a teacher of rhetoric in many Greek cities, in particular, Athens. Under the leadership of Pericles, Athens was at that time at the peak of its political and cultural development, although the symptoms of internal decay in the thoroughly democratic form of government which this statesman had instituted would soon come to the surface.

This democracy, which was based on the equality in political rights of all full citizens, created the need for the education of all who wished to obtain a seat in the βουλή, the Athenian public assembly. This was an education particularly in rhetoric, in the art of eloquence, and in political skills; but it also covered the entire encyclopedic range of knowledge, which was considered necessary for the cultivation of the citizenry.

It was the Sophists who rose to meet this need. They presented themselves as the "encyclopedists" of Greece, who wished to disseminate knowledge among the people. They were the first to require a fee for their philosophical instruction, an act which Socrates and Plato considered an unforgivable prostitution of knowledge. The fulminating critique of these two thinkers gave to the name "Sophist" the evil and distasteful connotation which it has retained ever since, but which was entirely inappropriate to it at the beginning. Thus it has come to represent a style of thought that offers a mere semblance of knowledge and that is able to transform a weaker case into a stronger by means of clever trick questions designed to stump the opponent.

Protagoras, who was the founder of this school of thought, did not at all share in this ill repute, however. He called himself *"sophistēs,"* in the serious sense of a "master of wisdom," and he was esteemed as such by all. The pronounced contradictions between the opposing theories about *physis* developed by his predecessors caused him to question seriously whether the human subject is capable of gaining universally valid knowledge about nature. In fact, he came to deny this possibility. He consistently carried through the matter principle (in the Heraclitean sense of the absolute fluidity of *physis*, but without Heraclitus' *logos* idea) both in his critique of human knowledge and in his understanding of the entire world of objective natural phenomena. In this manner, he initiated a crisis at the very foundation of Greek θεωρία.

According to Sextus Empiricus, Protagoras taught that *hulē* is absolutely fluid in nature and subject to continual increase and decrease. Sense perceptions, which the Sophist held to be our only source of knowledge, also are subject to constant change, according to the age and the general condition of the bodies. And since *hulē* contains within itself the grounds of all the phenomena of sense, Protagoras held that it is capable of being, in itself, all things that appear to human beings in sense perception.[1] This testimony of Sextus Empiricus is confirmed entirely by what Plato tells us in his *Theaetetus* concerning Protagoras' theory of knowledge. For Plato too explicitly associates Protagoras' epistemological standpoint with the Greek matter motive, as the principle of the absolute fluidity of *physis*.[2] The application of this matter principle to human knowledge led inevita-

---

1 Sextus Empiricus, *Pyrrh. hyp.* I, 217-218 (Diels-Kranz II, 258; A. Fragm. 14): φησὶν οὖν ὁ ἀνὴρ τὴν ὕλην ῥευστὴν εἶναι, ῥεούσης δὲ αὐτῆς συνεχῶς προσθέσεις ἀντὶ τῶν ἀποφορήσεων γίγνεσθαι καὶ τὰς αἰσθήσεις μετακοσμεῖσθαί τε καὶ ἀλλοιοῦσθαι παρά τε <τὰς> ἡλικίας καὶ παρὰ τὰς ἄλλας κατασκευὰς τῶν σωμάτων. λέγει δὲ καὶ τοὺς λόγους πάντων τῶν φαινομένων ὑποκεῖσθαι ἐν τῆι ὕληι, ὡς δύνασθαι τὴν ὕλην ὅσον ἐφ᾽ ἑαυτῆι πάντα εἶναι ὅσα πᾶσι φαίνεται. ("What this person says is that *hulē* is in flux, that a continual addition arises to counter its effluxions, and that sense perceptions are rearranged and altered in accordance with the age and the other conditions of the bodies. He also says that the grounds of all sense phenomena lie in *hulē*, so that *hulē* can insofar be all things in itself as [it] appears to everyone in sense perception.")

2 In Plato's *Theaetetus*, 152 E, Socrates says: ἔστι μὲν γὰρ οὐδέποτ᾽ οὐδέν, ἀεὶ δὲ γίγνεται. καὶ περὶ τούτου πάντες ἑξῆς οἱ σοφοὶ πλὴν Παρμενίδου ξυμφέρεσθον, Πρωταγόρας τε καὶ Ἡράκλειτος καὶ Ἐμπεδοκλῆς. ("For something never *is*, but is always *becoming*. And with this all wise men, Parmenides excepted, successively agree, Protagoras as well as Heraclitus and Empedocles.") This contradicts

bly to the skeptical conclusion that there is no universally valid norm for truth. Whatever seems true to a person is true. The images that dance before the eyes of a sick person in a feverish dream are no less true for him than it is true for a healthy person that these images are mere illusions.

Protagoras holds that human knowledge is completely dependent on sense perception. Since he also holds that both subjective perception and the very objects of perception undergo constant change and flux, this means that a person's knowledge cannot lay claim to any universally valid norm of truth. It is obvious, then, that from Protagoras' standpoint there was even less room for a theoretical metaphysics of being. For the precise aim of the latter had been to turn away from sense perception entirely and to penetrate to the supersensible essence of things by means of theoretical thought alone. On the basis of his skeptical epistemology, Protagoras drew the conclusion that any affirmative judgment that might be made concerning a state of affairs could be opposed by an equally valid negative judgment.[1] It was in this dialectical method, which was in essence an embodiment of the dialectic of the form-matter motive itself, that the sophistic art of argumentation came to a special focus. Such argumentation was specifically designed to confuse one's opponent, and it made particular use of the ambiguity of words. In this manner, rhetoric was transformed into eristic, the art of disputation.

b. The Meaning of Protagoras' Homo Mensura *Rule*

Protagoras' well-known *homo mensura* rule, "Man is the measure of all things,"[2] is thus in the first place nothing more than a pithy summary of his epistemology, dominated as it was by the matter principle, to the exclusion of any constancy related to the form principle. Here "man" is not understood in the sense of a universal human *nature*, which would entail as a matter of course a universally valid form for knowledge; what is meant here is the completely changeable subjectivity of each individual human being. If only for this reason, this *homo mensura* rule has no intrinsic connection with modern pragmatistic and positivistic notions concerning the value of science.[3]

Remark: In his important work *Protagoras and the Greek Community*

Reinhardt, *op. cit.*, pp. 241 ff., who incorrectly represents Protagoras as a pupil of Parmenides.

1 Diels-Kranz II, 259; Protagoras, A. Fragm. 19. II, 254; A. Fragm. 1 (53).

2 Diels-Kranz II, 263; Protagoras, B. Fragm. 1: πάντων χρημάτων μέτρον ἐστὶν ἄνθρωπος, τῶν μὲν ὄντων ὡς ἔστιν, τῶν δὲ οὐκ ὄντων ὡς οὐκ ἔστιν. ("Of all things the measure is the human being, of [things] that are, how they are, of those that are not, how they are not.")

3 I make this statement in opposition to Ernst Laas, *Idealismus und Positivismus* (Berlin, 1879-84), I, 183, and to Theodor Gomperz, *Griechische Denker* (3rd ed., Leipzig. 1911), I, 361 ff., 472.

(Amsterdam, 1940), p. 53. D. Loenen takes exception to Julius Kaerst, *et al.*, by denying that the *homo mensura* rule has an individualistic tendency. This denial can only be explained by the fact that he has not discerned the ground-motive of Protagoras' thought. He is undoubtedly correct in stating that Protagoras does not use the individual human being as the standard in his view of society. Here the thought of the Sophist is completely determined by the form motive of the religion of culture, whose bearer is the *polis* as a community. In its radical original sense, however, the *homo mensura* rule applies only to human knowledge of the truth and is completely determined by the matter principle. It is evident from Sextus Empiricus' words that Protagoras' intention was precisely to make plain that there exists no constant form for theoretical knowledge which could serve as a norm. For this reason, he indeed conceives this knowledge in an absolutely individual sense, as is indisputably clear from Plato's *Theaetetus*: ὅτι αὐτάρκη ἕκαστον εἰς φρόνησιν ἐποίει (169 D). The notion that human nature is in flux has no place for any fixed genus "man," in the theoretical sense; for this would presuppose the possibility of a universally valid norm of truth. This challenges the statement of Adolf Menzel in his *Beiträge zur Geschichte der Staatslehre*:[1] "One could also say that for Protagoras, the individual human being and humanity as a genus form no contrast."

Protagoras subjects human nature (*physis*), like *physis* as a whole, to the dominion of the pure, unrestrained matter principle. Human nature is submerged in lawless and uninhibited savagery. Rather inconsistently, however, he also concedes that the human being, even in this "natural state," i.e., before the founding of the *polis*, already possessed language, some technical skills, and a certain religiosity.[2]

For the father of Sophism, human nature in itself has no universally valid ontic form that is removed from the matter principle. He denies in principle, therefore, that there is any natural law or right, since justice according to him has no existence in nature.[3] That does not mean, however, that law is subject to the changeable opinion of every individual; it is

---

1 Vienna and Leipzig, 1922, p. 198, note 4. "Man kann auch sagen, dass im Sinne von Protagoras der einzelne Mensch [viz., in the *homo mensura* rule] und der Mensch als Genus keinen Gegensatz bilden." (English version by the translator)
2 See Protagoras' speech in Plato's *Protagoras*, 322.
3 See Plato's *Theaetetus*, 172 B, where Socrates in his rejoinder represents the conception of Protagoras and his adherents as follows: ἀλλ᾽ ἐκεῖ, οὗ λέγω, ἐν τοῖς δικαίοις καὶ ἀδίκοις καὶ ὁσίοις καὶ ἀνοσίοις, ἐθέλουσιν ἰσχυρίζεσθαι, ὡς οὐκ ἔστι φύσει αὐτῶν οὐδὲν οὐσίαν ἑαυτοῦ ἔχον, ἀλλὰ τὸ κοινῇ δόξαν τοῦτο γίγνεται ἀληθὲς τότε, ὅταν δόξῃ καὶ ὅσον ἂν δοκῇ χρόνον. ("But in those cases mentioned by me previously – in what is just or unjust, godly or godless – there we are definitely inclined to maintain that nothing among these things takes its essence from nature, but rather that what seems thus to the state becomes true when and for as

rather a product of the process of positive formation carried on by the *polis*. Nevertheless, this elimination of all constant form in nature, which leads Protagoras also to depreciate and to reject Greek *theōria*, serves merely as the introduction to his exaltation of the formative principle of culture. By means of the latter humans are given a formative education, which inculcates useful opinions that are concerned not with changeable individual insights regarding truth, but rather with the general welfare of the *polis*. Human nature acquires real form only through the civilizing influence of the *polis*, through the free, formative control that it exercises through its legal order and its public moral and religious precepts. It is to this process that the Sophist seeks to contribute by means of his philosophical instruction. For, to Protagoras, justice, morality, and religion are nothing more than useful means for the cultural formation of human beings.

In terms of their truth value, the respective opinions of a sick and a healthy person may indeed be on an equal footing; but that does not mean that they are equally useful. And in matters of justice, morality, and religion, what is useful and what is not are determined by the general opinion of the *polis*.

c. Protagoras' Nominalism in His Conception of the Form Principle of Culture

Protagoras no doubt recognized that this communal opinion of the Greek city-state is also susceptible to change and varies from *polis* to *polis*; nevertheless, it constitutes a formal limit for the fluid nature of human beings. According to him, the form principle is not a metaphysical form of being, as it is conceived by a realistic conception of forms. Protagoras is a thoroughgoing nominalist, and he therefore allows the form principle a place only in subjective human consciousness. Anaxagoras' divine *nous* is also ruled out here as the bearer of this principle. Nevertheless, the seat of the cultural form principle is not located for Protagoras in the individual human consciousness, but rather in the collective consciousness of the *polis*. Thus the *homo mensura* rule loses here its original individualistic character.

Protagoras' form motive is undoubtedly that of the culture religion, which had its seat in the Greek *polis*; but by his own testimony he remained skeptical as to the possibility of a theoretical knowledge of the deity. Both the divine *physis* and the theoretical knowledge pertaining to it are abandoned to the matter principle, and nothing remains in the form principle to counterbalance this. There rules here no measure, proportion, or harmony; nor is there any constant structure and formal limitation to provide stability or any universally valid "path of truth." Within certain limits, even the form principle of culture is for Protagoras subject to the matter principle of eternal flux. It is not rooted in an *eidos* (archetype), an

---

long as it seems thus.")

eternal form of being, as it was later to be in Plato. For the Sophist its sole foundation lies in the general opinion of the *polis*, which is formed in accordance with the democratic principle of majority rule. To be sure, as Plato reports in his *Theaetetus*, Protagoras gives the philosopher the task of criticizing less useful laws and decrees of the democratic regime and thus of influencing public opinion;[1] nevertheless, he can produce no criterion or universally valid norm, which might act as a guide for this criticism.

d. *The Contrast between* Physis *and* Nomos

On the historical level, Protagoras' cultural form principle, which has its seat in the communal consciousness of the *polis*, has clearly distanced itself from *physis* as eternally flowing *hulē*. In terms of its inner nature, however, it has not at all been separated from the matter principle, but is rather construed in evolutionistic fashion as a higher stage of development arising out of the lawless and measureless realm of *physis*. The contrast between *physis* and *nomos*, which some ascribe already to Archelaus, the pupil of Anaxagoras and teacher of Socrates, and in which there is a pregnant expression of the dialectical opposition between the matter principle and the form principle of the religion of culture, is thereby once again relativized.[2] The realm of *physis* has no fixed law, since it consists altogether of *hulē*, the flux of matter. Law and order are based exclusively on the free, constituting power of the *polis*, the bearer of the Greek culture principle. *Nomos* applies solely to the sphere of justice, morality, and belief. It is not grounded in *physis*. Indeed, it cannot be, for Protagoras rejects Heraclitus' dialectical identification of *physis* and *logos* (the latter in the sense of a rational world order) and bases law solely on positive, humanly enacted ordinances. The rule of law is nevertheless higher than the state of nature, since it invests the completely changeable nature of the human being with form, measure, and limitation. In this there is a clear manifestation of the primacy in Protagoras' thought of the form principle of culture.

It must not be forgotten, however, that Protagoras conceives the development of humanity evolutionistically, as proceeding from a state of na-

---

1   Plato, *Theaetetus*, 167 C: ἐπεὶ οἷά γ' ἂν ἑκάστῃ πόλει δίκαια καὶ καλὰ δοκῇ, ταῦτα καὶ εἶναι αὐτῇ. ἕως ἂν αὐτὰ νομίζῃ· ἀλλ' ὁ σοφὸς ἀντὶ πονηρῶν ὄντων αὐτοῖς ἑκάστων χρηστὰ ἐποίησεν εἶναι καὶ δοκεῖν. ("Therefore, whatever seems righteous and beautiful [good] to each *polis* is so, for that *polis*, so long as it holds it to be so. Only, in place of the evil which is present to each *polis*, the wise person brings it about that what is useful both comes to exist and to seem so to it.")
2   With regard to this contrast, cf. Plato's *Gorgias*, 482 E. See also the interesting article by Adolfo Levi, "The Ethical and Social Thought of Protagoras," *Mind*, vol. XLIX (1940), no. 195, p. 284. Levi's conception is the one that most closely approximates my own.

ture, without law and order, and culminating in a cultural existence within the community of the *polis*. In the final analysis, therefore, the form principle arises out of the matter principle, in violation of the Eleatic prohibition. Thus the form principle is deprived of its fixed, independent basis; it even becomes subject to the unpredictable changeableness of *hulē*.

e. Protagoras' Evolutionistic Philosophy of History

Protagoras was the first Greek thinker to develop a kind of evolutionistic philosophy of history, and he thereby reversed the traditional Greek picture of a golden primeval age of harmony, concord, and bliss from which humanity fell by reason of its own guilt. This reversal is intimately bound up with his depreciation of the realm of *physis*, which had hitherto been regarded as divine. In Protagoras, the state of nature becomes the lower, lawless, and wretched original condition of mankind, and it is only through the gradual development of αἰδώς and δίκη (for him the religious-ethical sense and the sense of justice) that mankind is enabled to emerge from this and to make the transition to the democratic rule of law, in the Greek *polis* of the Periclean age.

In Plato's dialogue *Protagoras*,[1] the Sophist gives a mythological presentation of this evolutionistic theory of culture, the material for which was in all likelihood taken over for the most part from Protagoras' own writings. Here αἰδώς and δίκη are represented as gifts of Zeus, which, unlike the other cultural skills such as medicine, he apportions to all persons in equal measure, through the agency of Hermes. This equality of the sense of justice and morality among all normal persons is considered to be the justification for democracy, which is grounded in the political equality of the citizens. At the same time that he makes this distribution, however, Zeus commands that those who prove to be incapable of receiving these gifts should be extirpated from society as a plague.

It is true that Protagoras offers this picture of the origin of αἰδώς and δίκη, which first enable mankind to establish an enduring city-state and thereby to leave the lawless state of nature, merely as a myth and not as a theological *theōria*. Nevertheless, this presentation serves to underscore once again the fact that the form motive of Greek culture religion indeed has the primacy in his thought. In fact, the formative power of culture in the *polis* is granted divine status.

f. The Younger, Radical Wing of Sophism. Its View of the Natural Right of the Strong

Over against this, the younger, radical wing of Sophism (Callicles, Thrasymachus, Polus, Critias, etc.) elevated the matter principle in human nature to a position directly opposite to that of the formative cultural force of the *polis*, turning it into an aristocratic natural right of the one who is strong, who severs all the ties of community and who tramples under foot the "morality of the herd" and the positive laws of the

---

1 Plato, *Protagoras*, 320 C, ff.

polis.[1] In this manner, *physis* in the sense of lawless *hulē* once again assumes the primacy over the cultural form principle.

However much this nihilistic and anarchistic application of the *homo mensura* rule to the terrain of culture, justice, morality, and religion may have stood in conflict with Protagoras' intentions, it was nevertheless difficult to combat from his position, since, as we have seen, he had never succeeded in disengaging the form motive of the religion of culture from its entanglement with the matter principle of *physis*. Thus it is clear that even the Greek "Enlightenment," which is usually regarded as the dawning of the complete emancipation of Greek thought from the fetters of belief and religion, was entirely under the control of the dialectical religious ground-motive in which the whole Greek intellectual community was rooted.

7. The Form-Matter Motive as It Is Illuminated by Critical Self-Reflection and the Ethical-Religious Deepening of the Form Motive in Socratic Dialectic

a. The Central Role of the Maxim γνῶθί σεαυτόν ("Know Yourself") in Socratic Thinking

The subversive influence that Sophism, particularly in the younger, radical wing, exerted upon the Athenian youth in ethical and religious matters called the remarkable, combative figure of Socrates (ca. 469-399 B. C.) to arms against the entire sophistic school of thought. As the first thinker to examine the dialectical ground-motive of Greek philosophy in the light of *critical self-reflection*, Socrates critically deepened the anthropocentric mode of thought that had already been introduced by the Sophists. Along this way of critical self-reflection, he not only ascribed the full religious primacy in his thought to the form motive of the religion of culture, but he also used it to bring criticism to bear on the sophistic capitulation to the matter principle. In doing this, he brought the form motive to expression in a new method of theoretical thinking.

The pronouncement of the Delphic oracle, γνῶθί σεαυτόν ("Know yourself"), whose original purpose was merely to restrain human beings from the *hubris* (arrogance) of overestimating themselves, acquires in Socrates the new meaning of self-introspection by way of *theōria*. He places it, with this meaning, at the very center of philosophical inquiry.

As Plato relates in his dialogue *Phaedrus*, Socrates wishes before all else to know who he himself is. Is he in the core of his being akin to the bestial Typho, the hydra-headed, haughty, savage nature god of destructive storms, or does he partake of a more measured (ἡμερώτερον) and

---

1 With regard to Callicles' natural right of the strongest, see Plato's *Gorgias*, 481 B ff., and Menzel, *op. cit.*, pp. 238 ff. This same dialogue of Plato also deals with Polus' conception of unbridled tyranny as the greatest happiness (470 D, ff.). Concerning Thrasymachus, see book one of Plato's *Republic*. In Callicles' conception (*Gorgias*, 491 C, ff.) that natural right implies total lack of restraint and unlimited freedom in the individual quest for power, the sophistic matter principle comes to clear expression.

simple divine nature?[1] Typho is here a pregnant mythological symbol of the matter principle, with its lack of all measure and formal delimitation. For the sake of this self-knowledge, Socrates willingly abandons both the earlier nature philosophy and metaphysical ontology, not because he is in general agreement with the epistemological skepticism of the Sophists, but because he considers self-knowledge as possessing infinitely greater religious value. Thus he regards all other knowledge as worthless that has not first passed through the crucible of self-knowledge.[2]

For this reason also, he prefers to hold to popular religious beliefs, instead of criticizing them together with the Sophists, who spend much time attempting to give possible explanations, with the help of a "rude wisdom," for the strange and inexplicable creatures of mythology. Socrates exclaims that he has no time for such things. By his own testimony in the above-mentioned dialogue of Plato, he has not yet attained to full self-knowledge, and it seems to him ridiculous "that anyone who does not yet have this knowledge should inquire into things that are of no concern to him."[3]

b. The Continuance of Anaxagoras' Theory of Nous
Socrates carried on the teaching concerning the divine *nous*, of which Anaxagoras had been the first to proclaim that it was the origin of all

---

1 Plato, *Phaedrus*, 230 A: ὅθεν ... σκοπῶ οὐ ταῦτα, ἀλλ᾽ ἐμαυτόν, εἴτε τι θηρίον τυγχάνω Τυφῶνος πολυπλοκώτερον καὶ μᾶλλον ἐπιτεθυμμένον, εἴθ᾽ ἡμερώτερόν τε καὶ ἁπλούστερον ζῷον, θείας τινὸς καὶ ἀτύφου μοίρας φύσει μετέχον. ("Therefore... I do not direct my inquiry to these things, but rather to myself, to discover whether I am a beast with a more complex constitution and wilder nature than Typho, or a tamer and simpler being in which a divine and unpresumptuous nature participates.") As early as Plato's *Charmides* (164 D, 165 D), self-knowledge is described as knowing *that* one does or does not know, although this definition was later rejected as untenable. Cf. also Xenophon's *Memorabilia* IV, ii; where Socrates argues that "self-knowledge is the condition of correct practical activity."
2 See Xenophon, *Memorabilia*, I. i. 11 ff., and IV. vii. 2 ff. Xenophon says here that the reason for Socrates' rejection of earlier nature philosophy and cosmology is that it is proper first to examine human things, which lie closer at hand, and also that the lack of unanimity in the inquiries into these other matters shows that certainty evidently cannot be attained there. The latter statement, of course, does not imply that Socrates agreed with Protagoras' skepticism.
3 Plato, *Phaedrus*, 229 E: αἷς εἴ τις ἀπιστῶν προσβιβᾷ κατὰ τὸ εἰκὸς ἕκαστον, ἅτ᾽ ἀγροίκῳ τινὶ σοφίᾳ χρώμενος, πολλῆς αὐτῷ σχολῆς δεήσει. ἐμοὶ δὲ πρὸς ταῦτ᾽ οὐδαμῶς ἐστι σχολή. τὸ δ᾽ αἴτιον, ὦ φίλε, τούτου τόδε· οὐ δύναμαί πω κατὰ τὸ Δελφικὸν γράμμα γνῶναι ἐμαυτόν· γελοῖον δή μοι φαίνεται τοῦτ᾽ ἔτι ἀγνοοῦντα τἀλλότρια σκοπεῖν. ("If anyone, because he does not believe in these [viz., the strange and inexplicable creatures of mythology], attempts to give a probable explanation of them with the aid of a rude wisdom, he would have to devote much leisure time to it. I, however, have no time at all for such things. And this, my friend, is the reason: I am not yet able to know myself, as the Delphic inscription enjoins, and it seems to me ridiculous that anyone who does not yet have this knowledge should inquire into things that are of no concern to him.")

cosmic form. In an ethical-religious deepening of the form motive of the religion of culture, Socrates now conceived it as the origin of the *kalokagathon*, of the beautiful and good in the cosmos, which is inseparably bound up with the truth sought by *theōria*.[1] It was he who was the first to assert that the true, the good, and the beautiful are indissolubly related to one another in theory. This important point will have to be reviewed extensively in the context of a critical investigation into the so-called "transcendental determinations of being" in Aristotelian and Thomistic metaphysics.

Even though it carried on the idea of the divine *nous*, Socrates' position represented a significant advance over that of Anaxagoras. In Anaxagoras' theory of *physis*, the divine *nous* only provides the "initial impetus" to the kinetic process that transforms the original chaos into a cosmos or form-world. It appears to play no further role in the explanation of the concrete phenomena of nature. In Socrates' theoretical inquiry, however, any satisfactory explanation of things must be teleological. His teleological viewpoint gives constant theoretical expression to the form principle of the religion of culture, which is understood here as the principle of formation by the divine *nous* in accordance with a purposive design.

---

1   This is stated very clearly in Plato's *Phaedo,* 97 B-C, where Plato put what is undoubtedly a genuine Socratic thought into the mouth of his master: Ἀλλ᾽ ἀκούσας μέν ποτ᾽ ἐκ βιβλίου τινός, ὡς ἔφη, Ἀναξαγόρου ἀναγιγνώσκοντος, καὶ λέγοντος ὡς ἄρα νοῦς ἐστιν ὁ διακοσμῶν τε καὶ πάντων αἴτιος, ταύτῃ δὴ τῇ αἰτίᾳ ἥσθην τε καὶ ἔδοξέ μοι τρόπον τιν᾽ εὖ ἔχειν τὸ τὸν νοῦν εἶναι πάντων αἴτιον καὶ ἡγησάμην εἰ τοῦθ᾽ οὕτως ἔχει, τόν γε νοῦν κοσμοῦντα πάντα κοσμεῖν καὶ ἕκαστον τιθέναι ταύτῃ ὅπῃ ἂν βέλτιστ᾽ ἔχῃ. ("But when I once heard someone reading from a book, as he said, by Anaxagoras, and asserting that *nous* is thus the ordering power and the cause of all things, I rejoiced at this explanation, and it seemed to me in some sense right that the cause of everything should be in *nous*. If this is so, I reflected, the ordering mind orders and disposes everything in the way that is best.") Somewhat further on (*Phaedo* 100 B), the good and the beautiful *(καλὸν-ἀγαθόν)*, as supersensible form-powers, are used to demonstrate the ultimate cause of all things, and lastly, the immortality of the rational soul. In this argument, only the elevation of the καλόν and ἀγαθόν to the position of eternal, self-subsistent ideas may be ascribed to Plato, and likewise the conception of the immortality of the human soul as a purely thinking substance (although Socrates probably also believed in personal immortality). Socrates doubtless regarded the concept as the immutable ontic form of human knowledge, exalted above the matter principle, which will lead humans to the discovery of the true, the good, and the beautiful in the cosmos. Xenophon's *Memorabilia*, III, ix. 4 ff., confirms that for Socrates the criterion of wisdom and virtue lay in the knowledge and application of the *kalokagathon*, the good and beautiful. Similarly, in *Memorabilia*, IV, vi. 8, 9, the good is for Socrates identical with the beautiful and the useful *(ὠφέλιμον, χρήσιμον)*. Cf. Plato, *Protagoras*, 333 D; 353 C ff., and *Hippias Major*, 297 A ff.

c. The Socratic Method of Concept-Formation Is Religiously Concentrated on the Divine Formative Power in the Idea of the Kalokagathon. *Socrates' Maieutic Method*

The entire Socratic dialectic, which aims to set limits to the epistemological nihilism of Sophism by means of the rational form of the concept and thereby to deal a mortal blow to the sophistic matter principle in its application to human knowledge, centers in a truly religious fashion on the divine formative power of the *kalokagathon*, the divine idea of the good and beautiful, in accordance with which all things have been formed. Any concept that does not at least set us on the way toward discovering how this idea comes to expression in the cosmos, that does not set forth the end or purpose for which things are good, is in Socrates' view completely worthless. And it is especially to the sphere of human activity that he applies his dialectical method of what is called inductive concept-formation.[1]

Greek *theōria* is thereby given an ethical religious twist, in which even virtue is made to depend on theoretical conceptual knowledge, that is, on *θεωρία* as *epistēmē*, knowledge that aims at the truth.[2] In the final analysis, however, it is the form motive of the religion of culture that remains in control of Socratic ethics.

Plato reports in his *Theaetetus* that Socrates called his dialectical method of concept-formation, which was designed to open up the way to the virtuous life, the *maieutic art (μαιευτικὴ τέχνη)*, i.e., the art of the midwife,[3] a designation in which there was a meaning-laden allusion to the profession of his mother. He often used this analogy, just as he also made meaningful comparisons between his father's work as a sculptor and the "art" of the philosopher. Just as the obstetric art of the midwife helps to bring a living being into the world, Socrates, as Plato has him say in the above-mentioned dialogue, practices an intellectual maieutic or

---

1 See Aristotle, *Metaphysics*, A, 6. 987 b 1 ff.: *Σωκράτους δὲ περὶ μὲν τὰ ἠθικὰ πραγματευομένου, περὶ δὲ τῆς ὅλης φύσεως οὐθέν, ἐν μέντοι τούτοις τὸ καθόλου ζητοῦντος καὶ περὶ ὁρισμῶν ἐπιστήσαντος πρώτου τὴν διάνοιαν....* ("Since, however, Socrates concerned himself with ethical questions and left aside the whole of nature, seeking the universal here [viz., in ethical questions], and was the first to direct his attention to the determination of concepts [definitions]....") See also *Metaphysics*, N, 4. 1078 b 27 ff., and Xenophon, *Memorabilia*, I. i. 16.

2 See Aristotle, *Nicomachean Ethics*, Z, 13, 1144 b 19 f.: *[Σωκράτης] φρονήσεις ᾤετο εἶναι πάσας τὰς ἀρετάς...*; ibid., 1. 30· *λόγους τὰς ἀρετὰς ᾤετο εἶναι·* ("Socrates thought that conceptual insights contained all the virtues... he thought that the virtues were *concepts*.") This report of Aristotle is completely confirmed by what Xenophon and Plato say concerning Socrates' ethical ideas. Cf. Plato's *Protagoras*, 356 D ff., where the art of virtuous living is called *ἐπιστήμη* (knowledge), and the thesis is developed that no one who properly knows the good will choose the evil, while good is seen to lie in what gives pleasure.

3 Plato, *Theaetetus*, 184 B.

midwifery, in which he brings to the light of day thoughts with which his partner in dialogue was already "pregnant." The task of the discussion leader is here essentially to give form to these thoughts with the aid of the method of concept-formation focused on the idea of the good and the beautiful. In the course of the dialogue, which is a true *dia-legein* ("speaking through") of the issue, things which are present in the other person in what are as yet unclear representations are gradually brought into the clear form of a theoretical concept. This process takes place under the condition, however, that the concept must be founded in the direct intuition of the divine idea of the good and the beautiful. In this process, Socrates desires also to learn from his discussion partner. For him dialogue is the path of a *common* search for the good, the true, and the beautiful. He neither offers nor attempts to develop a philosophical system constructed in a one-sided manner, like those of his great predecessors. And although authentic Socratic dialogue never contains a concept that is completely rounded out as a result of the dialectical interchange, Socrates never leaves his pupils in the dark as to the method which, in his judgment, must guide this concept-formation. This method is constantly turned in the direction of the unique source and ultimate unity of virtue, the divine idea of the good and the beautiful, which must serve as the *hypothesis* or foundation of every concept.[1]

d. Socratic Irony

Socrates' critical unmasking of the bogus wisdom of the Sophists plays an important role in his dialectic. In his exchanges, he regularly begins by protesting his own ignorance of the topic under discussion and by appearing to recognize the deeper insight and superior wisdom of the other person. He continues to maintain this attitude until his dialectical investigation of the matter at issue, which inductively measures the general definition presented by the sophistic interlocutor against established concrete examples, exposes the professed knowledge of his partner in dialogue as a mere semblance of wisdom. This is the "Socratic irony," the weapon that was the most feared by the younger Sophists of all those that Socrates used in his disputations with them.[2] Socrates used this procedure in his critical examination of the human being, which in Plato's dialogue *Apology* is called ἐξέτασις.[3] This was the task to which Socrates was convinced that he had been called by the Delphic Apollo, in view of the oracular utterance that he was the wisest of all persons.

---

1   This is the meaning of Xenophon's well-known statement (*Memorabilia*, IV, vi, 13) that Socrates ἐπὶ τὴν ὑπόθεσιν ἐπανῆγεν ἂν πάντα τὸν λόγον ("that he would bring every [*sic*] concept back to its *hypothesis*".)
2   See, for example, Plato's *Republic*, Book I.
3   Plato, *Apology*, 22 E, 23 C ff.

e. Socratic Theōria *as the Path to True Virtue and Piety. The Dynamic Character of the Socratic Concept in Its Directedness toward the Divine Idea of the Good and the Beautiful. Plato's* Euthyphro

By means of the rational form of the concept, Socrates attempts to put a leash on sophistic eristic, which found its inspiration in the fluidity of sense images and the ambiguity of words. Through this conceptual form, *theōria*, as *epistēmē* or *knowledge,* becomes the way to true virtue and piety; for in an intuitive, unitary *(einheitlich)* formal image, it thereby remains focused on the divine form-giving *idea* of the good and the beautiful. The term *ιδέα* first appears in Plato's dialogue *Euthyphro*, and it is without question used there in this authentic Socratic sense.

It is striking that the *Euthyphro* allows for an *ιδέα* of piety as well as of impiety. These are the source of the fixed shape or form present in all particular manifestations of these qualities.[1] As appears from the entire series of the earlier, Socratic dialogues of Plato, such an *idea* is in essence the corresponding intuitive formal image in the human soul of the idea of the good and the beautiful. We shall return to this subject in our discussion of Plato.

Just as the products of human cultural formation possess an *ἀρετή*, a virtue or efficacy toward a certain goal, which belongs to their essence and concept, so the *aretē* or virtue of a person lies in correct conceptual knowledge, which ascends from the fluid sense images subject to the matter principle to their fixed, rational conceptual form.[2] For Socrates, how-

---

1 Plato *Euthyphro*, 5 D: ἢ οὐ ταὐτόν ἐστιν ἐν πάσῃ πράξει τὸ ὅσιον αὐτὸ αὑτῷ· καὶ τὸ ἀνόσιον αὖ τοῦ μὲν ὁσίου παντὸς ἐναντίον, αὐτὸ δ᾽ αὑτῷ ὅμοιον καὶ ἔχον μίαν τιν᾽ ἰδέαν κατὰ τὴν ἀνοσιότητα πᾶν ὅ τι περ ἂν μέλλῃ ἀνόσιον εἶναι; ("Is not piety one and the same as itself in every action, and, on the other hand, is not impiety the opposite of all piety, but also like unto itself, with all that is impious having one distinct *idea* with respect to its impiety?") Euthyphro answers this question in the affirmative, but after he then adduces a particular alleged instance of piety instead of this single *idea* of the pious, Socrates corrects him with the words: "Remember that I did not ask to be taught one or two instances of the many examples of piety, but just that *εἶδος* [this is evidently here still completely identical with *ιδέα*] which makes what is pious pious. For you said that there is one *idea* by which the impious is impious, and the pious pious.... Teach me, then, what this idea is, so that, by looking upon it and using it as an example, I may declare those actions of you or anyone else which resemble it to be pious, and those which do not resemble it not to be pious." *Ibid.*, 6 D, E: Μέμνησαι οὖν, ὅτι οὐ τοῦτό σοι διεκελευόμην, ἕν τι ἢ δύο με διδάξαι τῶν πολλῶν ὁσίων, ἀλλ᾽ ἐκεῖνο αὐτὸ τὸ εἶδος, ᾧ πάντα τὰ ὅσια ὅσιά ἐστιν; ἔφησθα γάρ που μιᾷ ἰδέᾳ τά τ᾽ ἀνόσια ἀνόσια εἶναι καὶ τὰ ὅσια ὅσια. ...Ταύτην τοίνυν με αὐτὴν δίδαξον τὴν ἰδέαν, τίς ποτ᾽ ἐστίν, ἵν᾽ εἰς ἐκείνην ἀποβλέπων καὶ χρώμενος αὐτῇ παραδείγματι, ὃ μὲν ἂν τοιοῦτον ᾖ, ὧν ἂν ἢ σὺ ἢ ἄλλος τις πράττῃ, φῶ ὅσιον εἶναι, ὃ δ᾽ ἂν μὴ τοιοῦτον, μὴ φῶ.

2 See Plato's *Gorgias*, 506 D, and his *Republic*, book I, 352 D ff. Every thing per-

ever, this conceptual form is no static form of being like that of Parmenides. It is not metaphysical in character. It is, instead, the reflection within human thought of a rational world-order that is accepted in faith, an order that originates in the divine *nous* and that forms all things according to a purposive plan and design. The Socratic concept, therefore, is more of a method than a definitive result of thought. It always retains an inner plasticity and dynamic by virtue of its directedness toward the divine, form-giving idea of the good and the beautiful, the goal toward which human knowledge, with all of its limitations, must seek to penetrate more and more.

Socrates wrote no philosophical books or treatises. His living dialogues and his personal presence were the sole means by which he influenced his contemporaries, and his powerful personality made him a conspicuous paragon of a life that conformed to the form motive of the religion of culture, in the more profound ethical-religious sense that he had given it.

f. The Socratic Daimonion *and Its Significance for Post-Socratic Anthropology*

Socrates was firmly convinced that no one who had come to a correct theoretical conceptual knowledge of the good and the beautiful would do what is ethically wrong. By its very nature, virtue is one and is teachable. *Theōria* has both the duty and the ability to form human beings. Anyone who strives after self-knowledge, which in essence consists in knowledge of the good and the beautiful, and who in a methodical theoretical manner directs his thought toward the formative power of the divine *nous*, as this is manifested in a teleological, rational world-order, also hears the voice of this divine *nous* within himself, as a *daimonion* that restrains him from taking wrong courses of action and that instills in him the proper tact in his practical conduct. Socrates himself declared repeatedly that his *daimonion* was a great support to him in life.[1] *Eudaimonia* is the blissful state of the soul in which it lives in harmony with its *daimonion*. Every person has his or her own *daimonion*, as a practical-rational intuition of what is good and beautiful in concrete activity.

We are not presented here with a metaphysical theory of the immortal, rational soul. It is clear, nevertheless, that Socrates' conception of his *daimonion* points to a divine soul-power that actually constitutes the deepest, immortal identity of a person. It is this that imparts to his nature

---

forms its task and vocation through a certain *aretē* or virtue, and so also the human soul, which has as its *aretē* the conceptual knowledge of justice.
1 See Plato, *Apology*, 31 D; *Phaedrus*, 242 B; and Xenophon, *Memorabilia*, IV, viii, 5.

the rational, supersensible form[1] that in its most perfect realization belongs to the deity itself. It can clearly be seen here how Greek *theōria* enters the way of critical self-reflection, relating self-knowledge to a conception of the deity that had been gained by way of a deepening of the form motive of the religion of culture. Even though he did not directly combat the polytheistic beliefs of the people, and in spite of the fact that he continued to participate faithfully in the official cult of the *polis*, Socrates' theoretical contemplation of the teleological world-order nevertheless aligned his thought by and large with Anaxagoras' conception of the one divine *nous* as the demiurge or origin of all form.[2]

g. *Socrates as the "Outstanding Citizen of the Athenian* Polis."
   The Religious Foundation of Obedience to the Laws

Since this religious motive so completely dominated his life, Socrates was fully aware of the obligation which membership in the Athenian *polis*, the vehicle of the culture religion, placed upon him. Unlike Protagoras, he did not regard political ability as the common property of mankind. For him it was only those who had been made wise through their expertise in *epistēmē* who were called to govern. He rejected, therefore, the democratic form of government. Nevertheless, as a matter of heartfelt conviction, he submitted himself, like the Sophist, to the laws of the *polis*. He had much stronger grounds for doing this than Protagoras did, however, for he had completely separated the form motive of the religion of culture from the matter motive of *physis* and, following Anaxagoras, had assigned it its origin in the divine *nous*.

In consequence, Socrates was fully prepared, as Protagoras was not, to accept the full implications of his view of citizenship in the Athenian *polis*. When in the year 399 B. C. the infamous trial was conducted against him, which resulted in his condemnation to drink the poisonous hemlock, he refused to take advantage of the opportunity offered him to escape and save his life. By acquiescing to the death sentence, he wanted to show his judges that he was indeed the "outstanding citizen" of the cultural center of Athens. At the same time, by this act, he threw a glaring light on the internal crisis of the Athenian state, which no longer had a place for its best citizen.

The life of Socrates formed a truly critical turning point in Greek thought, a key factor in which was the powerful influence exerted by his personal example. The way of self-critique had been entered. Thus, even

---

1   See Xenophon, *Memorabilia*, IV, iii, 14. On the meaning of Plato's "eudaemonism," cf. in this connection Julius Stenzel, *Studien zur Entwicklung der Platonischen Dialektik von Sokrates zu Aristoteles* (2nd enlarged ed.; Leipzig and Bern: B. G. Teubner, 1931), p. 12.
2   See Xenophon, *Memorabilia*, I, iv, 5-7. In *Memorabilia*, IV, iii, 13, there appears a certain compromise with polytheism.

when Greek philosophy after Socrates addresses itself again to the problems of *physis* and the metaphysical forms of being, this inquiry no longer has the same form as in pre-Socratic philosophy. There is a continuing influence of the critical tendency of Socratic dialectic, which always places self-knowledge and knowledge of the deity at the center of attention. This dialectic will continue to make itself felt; indeed, it was destined eventually to bring the polar dualism of the religious ground-motive to pregnant philosophical expression also in Greek anthropology.

Part II

THE DIALECTICAL DEVELOPMENT IN PLATO'S THOUGHT UNDER THE PRIMACY OF THE FORM MOTIVE OF THE RELIGION OF CULTURE

Introduction

The Origin of Plato's Theory of Ideas

1. General Description of the Mutually Antagonistic Motives in Plato's Thought. The Socratic Form Motive in the Earliest Dialogues, as the Idea of the Good and the Beautiful

The Socratic standpoint gave rise to various diverging schools that were motivated by a one-sided interest in practical ethical questions. These continued to hold in part to the sophistic *homo mensura* rule within the theoretical realm; nevertheless, in practical, ethical matters, with which they were unduly preoccupied, they sought in various ways to maintain the Socratic idea of self-control and the unity and teachability of virtue and to develop these within their own line of thought. The critical turn-about occasioned by the Socratic teaching also provided the matrix, however, for the trend in Greek thought toward the classical form-realism of Plato and Aristotle, in which it reached its greatest height.

The metaphysical line that had momentarily been interrupted in the Sophists and Socrates is then resumed. The form motive of the culture religion, which has now been deepened by the Socratic idea of the good and the beautiful (the *kalokagathon*), is once again focused on the theoretical comprehension of true being in its opposition to the flux of becoming within the realm of *hulē* or matter. In Socrates, furthermore, *physis* had been pushed into the background. Now it reappears as a theoretical problem. There is a departure from the view of the Sophists, according to which *physis* was regarded as pure *hulē*, in which everything is subject to the flux of becoming. Now the aim is to conceive this *physis* in what has the appearance of a synthesis between the form motive of the culture religion and the matter motive, a synthesis that allows the Socratic idea of the *kalokagathon* to come to full development.

In Plato and Aristotle, the matter principle was emptied once and for all of its divine character. For these thinkers, all that is divine is concentrated in the *nous*, as the form principle of the true, good, and beautiful, which has been purified of any admixture with the chaotic matter principle. For them too, as also for the Pythagoreans, the Eleatics, Heraclitus, and Anaxagoras, philosophical θεωρία (*theōria*) is the only true path along which one may come into religious contact with the deity. In the words which Plato ascribes to Socrates in the *Phaedo*, "To approach the race of the gods, however, is granted to none but the philosophers, who through philosophy strive for wisdom and, completely purified by the latter, depart from life."[1] This *theōria*, however, as Plato and Aristotle conceived it, has traversed the Socratic route of critical self-reflection and has emancipated itself from the naturalistic conceptions of the divine form principle.

Plato and Aristotle were nevertheless unable to abolish the polar dualism in the ground-motive of Greek thought. Already in the initial stage of development of Plato's theory of ideas, this dualism is intensified in an almost unbearable religious tension, which gives new expression to the Orphic-Pythagorean dualism between the heavenly sphere of light and the dark earthly sphere. In this development Plato indeed broke out of the framework of the naturalistic conception; he did not, however, eliminate the dualism. In fact, he went on immediately to elaborate it philosophically in a sharply dualistic anthropology.

Together with his revered teacher Socrates, Plato tracked down the matter principle – like a "hunted animal," to use his own expression in the *Sophist* – in its detested incarnation in the Sophist art of argumentation. He did this, however, only to discover in the end that his quarry had taken refuge in an ἄπορον τόπον, a place where the rights of the *apeiron* cannot be contested.[2]

No previous thinker wrestled through the dialectical tensions of the religious ground-motive of Greek philosophy as Plato did. In this respect, his position within the history of Greek thought corresponds to that in modern times of Immanuel Kant, who grappled with similar intensity with the dia-

---

1 Plato, *Phaedo*, 82 B (cap. 32): Εἰς δέ γε θεῶν γένος μὴ φιλοσοφήσαντι καὶ παντελῶς καθαρῷ ἀπιόντι οὐ θέμις ἀφικνεῖσθαι ἀλλ᾽ ἢ τῷ φιλομαθεῖ.
2 Plato, *Sophist*, 239 C: εἰς ἄπορον ὁ σοφιστὴς τόπον καταδέδυκε. In 236 D of the *Sophist*, Plato speaks of an ἄπορον εἶδος (*aporon eidos*), where the Sophist, who with his pseudo-knowledge remains completely within the *apeiron* or the μὴ ὄν, has taken refuge (καταπέφευγεν).

lectical ground-motive of modern humanistic philosophy, namely, that of nature and freedom.

Plato was born ca. 427 B.C. to a highly distinguished Athenian family, whose paternal line went back to the Attic king Codrus. Drapides, a relative of the renowned statesman Solon, was a maternal ancestor. In Plato's own day, the family was prominent in political affairs in the persons of Critias, who was a member of the government of Thirty, and Charmides, who was one of the ten men of the Piraeus. In his youth, Plato was introduced to the philosophy of Heraclitus by Cratylus, a pupil of the obscure thinker of Ephesus. At the age of twenty, he came into contact with Socrates, although he probably was not accepted into the more intimate circle of the latter's students.[1] He maintained this relationship until the time of his master's death.

The death of Socrates formed the crucial turning point in Plato's life. About 28 years old at the time, Plato first set out with other disciples of Socrates for Megara. There he came into contact with Eucleides, the founder of the so-called Megarian school, who attempted to combine Socrates' idea of the *kalokagathon* with the Eleatic ontology of Parmenides. Thus the influence of Parmenides, which would be of such great importance for the development of his theory of ideas, must already have touched Plato here. After this came his journey to southern Italy and Sicily. In southern Italy he came into more intimate contact with the Pythagorean school, with which he had probably already had some contact in Greece, and this led to a close relationship with the Pythagorean thinker and statesman Archytes. This also was to have decisive significance for the development of Plato's thought in both its mathematical and its mystical-religious aspects. At the same time, his political interests, which, as appears from his seventh letter, were already very strong in his youth, received a powerful stimulus both through his contact with the Pythagorean circle and through his residence at the court of Dionysius, the tyrant of Syracuse, where he struck up a friendship with the latter's brother-in-law Dion and managed to win him over to his own ideas. This first sojourn at the court of the tyrant ended in dramatic fashion with the sale of the approximately forty-year-old thinker in the slave market of Aegina, likely in connection with the hostilities that had broken out between Athens and Aegina. He was, however, ransomed by a certain Anniceris of Cyrene.

After returning to his native city, Plato founded about 387 B.C. his renowned Academy. This was an essentially religious association, which was centered in a communal cult of the Muses. As had also been the case in the Pythagorean order, philosophy and the communal study of the special sciences such as mathematics, astronomy, and physics were also carried on within this religious framework. For the first twenty years after the

---

1   See the Introduction of John Burnet, *Phaedo* (Oxford, 1911), p. xxvi.

founding of the Academy, Plato was able to devote himself without interruption to his school. During this time the latter flourished mightily, also as a training center for statesmen.

Then, about 367 B.C., Plato undertook his second journey to Syracuse, after the younger Dionysius had succeeded his father as tyrant. Dion hoped that through Plato he might influence the youthful ruler to introduce a government based on law, which would guarantee the freedoms of the people. This second journey, however, also ended in failure. The court clique in Syracuse managed to turn the young tyrant against Dion, who was subsequently banished. Plato himself was sent back to Athens, after the outbreak of war in Sicily, with the promise that both he and Dion would be called back to Syracuse after peace had been restored.

It would appear that during this second sojourn at the court of Syracuse Plato had already prepared a scheme of legislation for the Greek cities that were to be newly established in Sicily. It seems that he had also partially drafted the so-called *prooemia* or introductions to the laws, which he later worked out in independent form in the *Laws*, the great dialogue written in his very old age.

The third trip to Sicily then followed between 361 and 360 B.C., and this likewise turned out to be a bitter disappointment for the elderly thinker. It undoubtedly contributed toward his substitution of a more sober, empirically oriented conception of the organization of the *polis* for the vision of the ideal state, framed completely in terms of the theory of ideas, which had been outlined in his *Republic*.

In its development, Plato's philosophy reflects all of the influences which he underwent in the course of his life, as I have briefly summarized it above. Cardinally, there is in his thought a complication and intensification of the tension between the form and matter motives, which is accounted for by his adding to the legacy left him by Socrates.

Although Plato's conception of the form motive was influenced by the Socratic method of concept-formation, which had always retained a dynamic ethical tendency through its religious concentration on the form-power of the *idea* of the true, good, and beautiful in the divine *nous*, this was joined by the influence of the static, mathematical conception of the form principle as this was conceived in the Eleatic school and in the more recent Pythagorean movement, which had followed the Eleatics in this direction. In addition, the Orphic-Pythagorean dualism regarding soul and body had already taken hold of Plato at an early point in his development.

Indeed, through the influence of Socrates, the form motive of the religion of culture, in its deepened ethical-religious sense, attained the uncontested primacy in Plato's thought. This was the case, even though a tension arose within this form motive itself between the dynamic and the static conception of it. Over against this, however, the Heraclitean conception of the matter principle, which Plato had accepted from the time of his youth, continued to dominate the other pole of his thought.[1] Under the influence of Orphism, this led to a polar dualism in his conception of the relation between the form and matter principles, which seemed at first to rule out any attempt at synthesis.

It is only when all these influences have been combined within the compass of Plato's thought that he arrives at the first outline of his theory of ideas. Although he marks out a course all his own here, the various lines of thought continue to stand irreconcilably opposed to one another. From now on, this theory of ideas itself becomes entangled in the religious dialectic of the Greek ground-motive, and as it develops, Plato's thought is driven from one stage to the next, without ever coming to rest in a finished system such as that of his student Aristotle in his final period.

In order to expound his ideas in writing, Plato chose to make use of the dialogue form that Socrates had introduced into verbal philosophical discussion. The only exceptions to this are his *Apology* and those of his letters that have been preserved.

His early works, the *Apology of Socrates*, the *Crito*, the *Ion*, the *Protagoras*, the *Laches*, the *Charmides*, Book I of the *Republic*, the *Euthyphro*, and the *Lysis*, which were probably written shortly after the death of Socrates, merely repeat the Socratic line of thought, giving to it an aesthetic cast and form that is typically Platonic. *Physis* and the problem of the metaphysical forms of being do not yet play a role here.[2] As in Socrates' own thought, *theōria* is wholly concentrated on the deeper unity of virtue, the latter being accessible only to a "conceptual ethics," to borrow a term from Theodor Gomperz,[3] since it can only be learned by way of *theōria*. The ultimate issue in these youthful, Socratic dialogues, however, is not the logical side of definition, its conceptual form as such, no more than this had been the final concern of Socrates himself. That which the conceptual form only approximates inadequately, and, in fact, is never able to define conclusively, must become the object of active contemplation in the *idea* of the good and the beautiful, that is, in an adequate image of the divine idea, which is mirrored in the religious center of the human soul.

The route of the logical concept, indeed, continually leads through diversity. By logic we can only approach virtue in its unity by way of a di-

---

1 Cf. Aristotle, *Metaphysics*, A, 6 987 a, at the end of the section, where he says: "For having already very early in his first period become familiar with Cratylus and with the view of Heraclitus that all sensible things are in constant flux and that there exists no knowledge of them, he [viz., Plato] also held fast to this view in later years." The reader is further referred to this entire sixth chapter for its analysis of the Socratic and Pythagorean lines in Plato's thought and of the Platonic conception of the matter principle.

2 With the exception of an allusion to Empedocles' and Heraclitus' conception of *physis* in the *Lysis* (214 B–216 B, caps. 10-13).

3 *Editorial note (RK)*: In his first period, Gomperz says, Plato comes on the scene as a *Begriffsethiker*. Gomperz, *Griechische Denker*, II, 234.

versity of virtues, e.g., bravery, justice, piety, wisdom. Precisely for this reason, however, such a method of definition, which pulls virtue asunder, can only become fruitful when, in a religious comprehensive vision (synopsis), it fixes its gaze on the divine archetype of the good and the beautiful. This is a vision that transcends the concept; but it is necessary, if we are to know the indivisible essence of virtue in its deeper unity.

At this point in Plato's development, there is as yet no trace of his later theory of ideas, with its characteristic tension between the dynamic-Socratic and the Eleatic-Pythagorean conception of the principle of form. What has been singled out here, especially in the *Euthyphro*,[1] as the first dawning of this theory, is in fact nothing other than the Socratic idea of the good and beautiful. In itself this idea has no relation to the metaphysical conception of the Platonic *eidē*. One can view it as the initial phase of the typically Platonic theory of ideas only if he has confused *idea* and *eidos* in Plato's later thought.

a. The Socratic Idea *in the* Euthyphro

I have already drawn attention to the *Euthyphro*, the dialogue of Plato in which there is the first instance of his use of the terms *eidos* and *idea*. Here there is an attempt to obtain a conceptual definition of the virtue of piety. The path of conceptual determination, however, only leads to a knowledge of the distinguishing features which set piety off from the other virtues. This path must indeed be taken; but so long as it is *merely* the path of logical distinction, it does not lead to the desired goal.

After it has become clear that the attempts of the interlocutor Euthyphro to give a suitable definition of piety are moving aimlessly in a circle, Socrates himself proposes that what is pious be defined as a part of justice. He then invites Euthyphro to ascertain more closely what part of justice it is.[2] When the latter then defines piety as that part of justice which pertains to the θεῶν θεραπεία, the care of the gods, whereas the other part governs one's relations with his fellow men, Socrates points out that the aim of all care is the welfare and the improvement of that toward which it is directed. The gods, however, cannot be benefited or improved by the piety of men. In order to evade this objection, Euthyphro proceeds to take the word θεραπεία in a narrower sense and to define it as a service which one renders to the gods as a slave to his master.[3] All service, however, pertains to some work in which the servant helps his master. But what is the work, Socrates asks, in which those who are pious help the gods? What is the sum of the many noble things that the gods produce by their work? When Euthyphro responds with a rambling exposition that fails to address itself to the question, Socrates remarks: "Surely, dear Euthyphro, you could have told me the sum (τὸ κεφάλαιον) of what I asked for [viz., the noble

---

1   E.g., Ueberweg-Praechter, *Grundriss der Geschichte der Philosophie des Altertums*, p. 250.
2   Plato, *Euthyphro*, 12 E.
3   *Ibid.*, 13 D.

works of the gods toward which the pious contribute] in far fewer words if you had wished. But it is clear that you have no desire to instruct me on this point. For now, when you were right by the goal, you turned away from my question."[1] Had Euthyphro simply answered "the good (and beautiful)," Socrates would have indeed been satisfied with the brand of conceptual definition that was now at last being undertaken.[2]

In this way, by means of relating the distinguishing concept to the divine *idea* of the *kalokagathon*, this concept would have been focused on the essence and deeper unity of all virtue, of which piety would have appeared simply as a particular manifestation. Now, since Euthyphro fails to arrive at the point of focusing the concept on the divine *idea*, but continues to search only for external distinguishing features of virtue, Socrates states that he is compelled, as questioner, to follow the course that Euthyphro himself has set in his answers. Consequently, he proposes that piety be defined as a science of sacrifice and prayer, that is, as a science of giving and asking, a definition that he immediately reformulates with biting sarcasm as "a sort of art of mutual commerce between gods and men."[3] Socrates then relates this definition to one which Euthyphro had already given, namely, that piety consists in that which is pleasing to the gods. This definition had already been refuted by pointing out its circularity. For the quality of being pleasing to the gods cannot define the nature of piety, since, conversely, what is pious can only be pleasing to the gods, and thus form the object of their desire, just because it is pious.

I have given this brief résumé of the method of concept formation employed in this dialogue only because it is typical of nearly all of the dialogues belonging to the first stage of Plato's thought. Furthermore, this method casts light on what the terms *idea* and *eidos*, which are used in this dialogue for the first time, meant during this beginning stage.

It is evident that both terms must be understood in the sense that Socrates tried in vain to make clear to Euthyphro in the course of their discussion. They are the intuitive formal image within the human soul of the one divine *idea* of the good and the beautiful, which first gives to particular expressions of piety the lasting ontic form of virtue. Clearly, therefore, the word *eidos* in 6 D cannot have the meaning of mathematical structure, as Peter Brommer thinks;[4] instead, it must coincide in meaning with the word *idea*. For, from the very beginning, the discussion leader, Socrates, places virtue in sharp opposition to all mathematical and natural scientific concerns. The basic difference between them is seen to lie in the fact that, whereas in scientific discussions of the latter agreement can quickly be reached by means of counting, measuring, and weighing, matters such as

---

1 *Ibid.*, 14 C: καὶ γὰρ νῦν ἐπειδὴ ἐπ᾽ αὐτῷ ἦσθα, ἀπετράπου (the last sentence of the quotation in the text).

2 This is also correctly noted by Ueberweg-Praechter, *op. cit.*, p. 251.

3 Plato, *Euthyphro*, 14 E.

4 Peter Brommer, *ΕΙΔΟΣ et ΙΔΕΑ* : *étude sémantique et chronologique des oeuvres de Platon* (dissertation, University of Utrecht; Assen, 1940), p. 8.

right and wrong, beauty and ugliness, and good and evil are the occasion for differences of opinion that lead to enmity.[1]

b.   The Eidos *as the* Aretē *of the Object of Knowledge*

Julius Stenzel has likewise pointed out that in the original, Socratic phase of Plato's thought, the conception of the *eidos* still coincides with the *idea* of the good and beautiful,[2] and that insofar as there is at this time a multiplicity of *eidē*, these are all joined to the *idea* of the good in the concept of *ἀρετή*. Here the *eidos* is nothing else than the *aretē* of that which forms the object of knowledge. It is that for which the latter is "good," that in which its entire essence is concentrated in an intuitively observable type. In the well-known statement of the *Gorgias*, 503 e, *aretē*, as *τὸ ἑκάστου ἔργον*, that which makes possible a specific accomplishment, is brought into direct connection with the *eidos* as the observable form of a cultural product.[3]

2.   The Rise of the Metaphysical Theory of the *Eidē* and the Dialectical Tension between the Static and the Dynamic Form Motive (*Eidos* and *Idea*). The Dialogues of the Transition Period

a.   The Origin of the Platonic Theory of Ideas Lies in the Conjunction of the Socratic Idea of the Kalokagathon *with the* Eidē *or Static Ontic Forms of Things. The Pregnant Meaning of the Terms* Eidos *and* Idea *in the Platonic Theory of Ideas*

When the theory of ideas comes to actual expression in Plato's thought, *εἶδος* (*eidos*) and *ἰδέα* (*idea*) in their pregnant philosophical sense are no longer identical for him, even though they are not always used terminologically with a fixed meaning. As they are first conceived, the *eidē* are the static ontic forms of things. In Plato's metaphysics, they are transcendent to the changing phenomenal forms of the sense world, which are enclosed in the Heraclitean stream of becoming, and they lie at the foundation of the latter, as their immutable ontic grounds (*αἰτίαι*). These *eidē* are conceived in accordance with the Eleatic model of the form of being, which was naturalistic and geometrical in origin and which became compatible only in the later Pythagorean schools with the conception of number as the invariant ontic ground of the sensible world of forms. By contrast, the *idea* in its pregnant sense continues to preserve the dynamic character of the Socratic dialectic. It is in origin

---

1   Cf. Plato, *Euthyphro*, 7 C ff.
2   Julius Stenzel, *Studien zur Entwicklung der Platonischen Dialektik von Sokrates zu Aristoteles* (Leipzig and Berlin; 2nd ed., 1931), pp. 8 ff.
3   Plato, *Gorgias*, 503 E: *ὥσπερ καὶ οἱ ἄλλοι πάντες δημιουργοὶ βλέποντες πρὸς τὸ αὑτῶν ἔργον ἕκαστος οὐκ εἰκῇ ἐκλεγόμενος προσφέρει ἃ προσφέρει πρὸς τοὖργον τὸ αὑτοῦ, ἀλλ' ὅπως ἂν εἶδός τι αὐτῷ σχῇ τοῦτο, ὃ ἐργάζεται.*

the divine *idea* of the good and the beautiful, in which the entire form-power of the divine *nous* is concentrated, as it were, into the primordial design according to which the cosmos has been formed. The direct, intuitive reflection of this *idea* appears within human thought in the process by which the concept is concentrated on this origin and unity of all form, which comes to expression in an unmediated comprehensive vision of the deeper origin and unity of the objects of definition. Plato also applies the term ἰδέα to this comprehensive vision itself.

Brommer's understanding of this distinction between *eidos* and *idea* is to my mind substantially correct, and this is no small merit of his important dissertation, to which reference has already been made. It seems to me, however, that he takes too little notice of the fact that the divine *idea* is the point of central, original unity. Furthermore, he erroneously locates the origin of the Platonic *eidē* in the purely Pythagorean line of thought.[1] As we have seen earlier, the Pythagorean principle of form, in its original conception, was not at all static; it became this only through the influence of the Eleatic critique. Brommer's view of the *eidos* as a static "structure" also falls short of the truth. By its very nature a structure is a unity in multiplicity, and as such it is not metaphysical in character. The *eidos*, by contrast, is an absolutely unitary (*einheitliche*) ontic form. Just like Parmenides' form of being it excludes all inner diversity, and precisely for this reason it stands in direct relation to theoretical intuition, since the concept cannot reach to the underlying unity of the distinguished features.

Plato's theory of ideas arises only when the *idea*, as the original unity of all cosmic form, is conjoined to the diversity of the self-contained *eidē*. In the pregnant sense of the word, there is only one *idea;* but there are many *eidē*. As Plato first conceived them, the *eidē* are the static forms belonging to the noumenal realm of true being, that is, the world that is accessible only to theoretical thought. They serve as the pattern according to which the world of transitory sense objects is formed. The *idea* of the good and beautiful, in contrast, transcends the diversity of the inherently rigid and inert *eidē*. It does not belong to the world of the static ontic forms; rather, it is in a sense the divine synopsis or unified vision of true being on the part of the divine *nous*, a vision that is focused through one divine proto- or original form to which all the *eidē* are concentrically related. As is evident in both the *Republic* and the *Philebus*, this *idea* is active and effective as the living proto-form of the divine *nous*, in which all sense objects participate in their transitory forms, for it embraces all real being in the comprehensive vision of divine thought and manifests itself as a divine *dunamis* in the purposive, rational world order. It is as such the embodiment of the form motive of the religion of culture in its deepened ethical-religious sense. The *eidē*, by contrast, in their rigidity and inertness,

---

1 Brommer, *op. cit.*, p. 12.

still display some influence of the naturalistic form principle of the Eleatic ontology, which was deprived of all dynamism and life. At least in their original conception, they therefore are not controlled by Anaxagoras' divine *nous*, with its purposive design; they are rather subject to *Anankē* in the metaphysical-logical sense that we have met in Parmenides' ontology. They form the *Gegenstand* of theoretical thought, and they can never be reduced to the theoretical-logical function of thought. In metaphysical fashion, however, Plato ascribes to them an existence in themselves (*καθ' αὑτοῦ*). That is, he absolutizes them to the position of essences that exist independently of the theoretical *Gegenstand* relation. In their rigid self-containment and absolutized status, they mutually exclude one another, and so long as they repose within themselves as static ontic grounds, they can never be reconciled to each other in accordance with the Heraclitean conception of the unity of opposites.

This original tension between *idea* and *eidos* forms the initial source of the internal dialectic of the Platonic theory of ideas. The noumenal world of the *eidē* comes to stand between the Socratic method of concept formation and the *idea*, which forms the *anhypotheton* of all logical concepts. As a supersensible ontic form in its presumed inner fundamental unity, the *eidos* too is an object of direct intuitive contemplation and is the *hypothesis* or foundation of the distinguishing concept. Theoretical concept formation threatens to become rigid, however, if it is focused exclusively on the isolated ontic form in its presumed self-sufficiency. For in its alleged absoluteness, an *eidos* is a form that simply excludes all other *eidē*; moreover, in itself it does not provide any access to the *idea* as the proto- or original form of all being. Mere *"eidetics"* can only disperse theoretical thought in an unreconciled multiplicity of ontic forms which seem to require no origin, and it prevents theory from concentrating its gaze on the original unity of all form in the divine *idea*. Thus it cannot find the way that was pointed out by Socrates in his method of critical self-reflection.

Any retreat to the unity of the form of being (ontic form) as this had been conceived by Eleatic metaphysics was already cut off for Plato, precisely because of the influence of Socrates.[1] For this rigid unity, which excluded in principle any plurality of ontic forms, had been gained by *θεωρία*, only by way of a lack of insight into the nature of the theoretical *Gegenstand* relation. In his *Charmides*, Plato had perceptively examined this relation, in its opposition to the mode of thought which returns into itself.[2] The Socratic route of self-reflection thus brought with it the necessity of abandoning the Eleatic One. The thinking selfhood cannot recog-

---

1 *Translator's note*: I have translated the Dutch term "zijnsvorm" as "form of being" and "ontic form." The two terms are equivalent, which is evident from their juxtaposition here.
2 Plato, *Charmides*, 167 C ff.

136

nize itself in the geometrical, spherical ontic form of being of the celestial vault.

For Plato's theory of ideas, therefore, it became a matter of life and death to suffuse the newly introduced metaphysical world of the *eidē* with the Socratic *idea*. The first question to be asked was whether the *eidē* themselves derive their being from the divine *idea* of the good and beautiful, or whether the divine *nous* finds the *eidē*, as original form-models, standing over against itself as a given reality that is in essence independent of the divine *idea*. The second question was how a synthesis could be effected between the form motive manifested in the world of the *eidē* and the Heraclitean matter principle of eternal flux. These two problems form the major theme of Plato's dialectic whenever this is applied to the metaphysical realm of the *eidē*, and, in this application, the earlier, Socratic conception of dialectic – the common search by means of question and answer for the universally valid conceptual form, which is founded in intuitive contemplation of the divine idea – is given a new metaphysical twist.

The Orphic-Pythagorean dualism between the earthly sphere of eternally flowing *physis* and the supraterrestrial sphere of the luminous starry heavens, which had already obtained a hold on Plato's thought before the development of the theory of ideas proper, introduced a further complication and source of tension into this theory. In Plato's theory of ideas this dualism came to expression in a polar opposition between the noumenal world of the *eidē* and the sense world of transitory objects. On the anthropological level, it was given a sharper focus in the opposition between the thinking, immortal soul, on the one hand, the vehicle of *θεωρία*, which has an inner kinship with the world of the *eidē*, and, on the other hand, the impure, earthly material body, which hinders the soul in its contemplation of the eternal, luminous ontic forms.

This dualism could only heighten the inner tension between *eidos* and *idea*. For, as the divine form-giving principle, the Socratic *idea* is necessarily related to the sensible cosmos, even though it is itself exalted above the matter principle of eternal flux. The Orphic dualism and the dualistic separation of a metaphysical world of *eidē* from a sensory world of phenomena are equally foreign to this *idea*.

To the degree that the theory of the *eidē* has not been completely suffused by the Socratic *idea*, and the kinship between the immortal *anima rationalis* and the fixed metaphysical ontic forms is placed in the foreground, the human soul itself threatens to become petrified into a static *eidos*, a chimerical *eidōlon*, divorced from the ever-flowing living stream of *physis*. Then the original Orphic-Pythagorean form principle, which in spite of everything remained rooted in the Dionysian matter principle, is forced to retreat before the Eleatic conception of ontic form. A dangerous flirtation with the Eleatic thesis that like is known only by like, which Empedocles had worked out in his own fashion, leads Plato to the conclusion that the thinking soul must share in the immobility that characterizes the *eidē* and that applies even to the *eidos* of "life in itself." Hereby, momentarily at least, the path of critical self-reflection seems to have been abandoned. The theoretical thought-function of the soul almost becomes identified in Eleatic fashion with its metaphysically conceived *Gegenstand*, the world of the *eidē*. As soon as *theōria* again concentrates its gaze on the divine *idea*, however, the static conception of the soul is abandoned and the theory of the *eidē* is charged with a new dynamism.

There are six dialogues which belong to Plato's transition period, : the *Gorgias*, the *Meno*, the *Euthydemus*, the *Hippias Minor* and the *Cratylus*. In three of these, the *Gorgias*, the *Meno*, and the *Cratylus*, it is possible to trace the gradual rise of the theory of ideas through the conjunction of all the influences mentioned above.

The *Gorgias*, which starts with the problem of the nature and value of the rhetoric promoted by the Sophists and climaxes by positing a sharp antithesis between the sophistic worldview and Socratic theory, is the first dialogue to evince the influence of Orphic-Pythagorean ideas. Over against the worldview of the later Sophists, who regarded uninhibited pursuit of pleasure as the highest aim, Socratic theory is here described as the pursuit of the good (and beautiful) for its own sake as the final goal. The sophistic matter principle, which pits human *physis* as a chaotic *rheuston* against the *nomos* of the *polis*, is countered by the form principle of the religion of culture, a principle of measure, harmony, and order. Any orator who aspires to influence the human soul must take it upon himself to form it by instilling into it the above virtues. And since a life in accordance with measure, order, and harmony is equivalent to a life in accordance with law (*νόμος*), the task of the orator is to educate the soul for justice and temperance.[1] The perfect good lies in the full embodiment of measure.

This entire exposition is still genuinely Socratic and, taken by itself, does not yet betray any Pythagorean influence. For, as we have seen earlier, the form principle of measure and harmony did not originate in Pythagoreanism; rather, it is the ground-motive of the religion of culture itself. The latter had become deeply rooted in the Greek way of life. All

---

1   Plato, *Gorgias*, 506 D, E: Ἀλλὰ μὲν δὴ ἥ γε ἀρετὴ ἑκάστου καὶ σκεύους καὶ σώματος καὶ ψυχῆς αὖ καὶ ζῴου παντός, οὐχ οὕτως εἰκῆ κάλλιστα παραγίγνεται, ἀλλὰ τάξει καὶ ὀρθότητι καὶ τέχνῃ, ἥτις ἑκάστῳ ἀποδέδοται αὐτῶν .... Τάξει ἄρα τεταγμένον καὶ κεκοσμημένον ἐστὶν ἡ ἀρετὴ ἑκάστου. ("But this virtue of each thing, of an implement, the body, the soul, and also of every living being, is surely not given to it in excellent measure at random, but in accordance with law and rule and the art that is imparted to each of them....Consequently, the virtue of each thing consists in something determined and well-ordered according to a rule.") See further, Gorgias, 506 E: Καὶ ψυχὴ ἄρ᾽ [ἡ] κόσμον ἔχουσα τὸν ἑαυτῆς ἀμείνων τῆς ἀκοσμήτου.... Ἀλλὰ μὴν ἥ γε κόσμον ἔχουσα κοσμία.... Ἡ δέ γε κοσμία σώφρων.... Ἡ ἄρα σώφρων ψυχὴ ἀγαθή. ("And a soul which is well-ordered is better than that which is unordered... But the well-ordered is surely that in which order prevails.... The well-ordered is the temperate, however.... The temperate soul is thus good.")

that the Pythagorean school did was to give it a mathematical character by incorporating it into the principle of number.

At the close of the dialogue, however, this basic Socratic thought is brought into connection with the Orphic-Pythagorean conception of the immortality of the soul as the vehicle of *theōria*, and also with the belief in a supraterrestrial world and a judgment of the souls in Hades in accordance with true justice, which on earth is often confused with a mere semblance of justice.[1] The dualism between the realm of true being and the world of sensory appearance, which will pave the way for the theory of the *eidē*, begins to make itself felt here; but the soul itself is still treated as something visible.[2]

In the dialogue *Meno*, it appears that the Orphic-Pythagorean influence has proceeded further. The doctrine of the immortality and pre-existence of the *anima rationalis* is here developed into a new theory of knowledge, which takes issue with the sophistic thesis that one cannot seek for something that he does not already know. To this end, Plato develops his notion that the acquisition of knowledge is an *anamnēsis* or recollection of what the soul has already beheld in its pre-existent state. This doctrine is not yet announced here, however, as a *theōria* based on firm grounds. With an appeal to priestly wisdom and a verse from the poet Pindar, it is presented only as a notion embodying the truth that the search for knowledge is necessary on ethical-religious grounds.[3] In view of the interconnectedness of all things, it is only necessary to recollect a single item in order to be able to recover all the rest. To illustrate the correctness of this view, Socrates takes a slave who has had no instruction in mathematics and by means of continued questioning elicits from him the solution to a mathematical problem, namely, the proof of the Pythagorean theorem.

---

1 Plato, Gorgias, 523 A ff. It is striking that the immortal soul is portrayed here as something visible. See 524 D: ἔνδηλα πάντ᾽ ἐστὶν ἐν τῇ ψυχῇ, ἐπειδὰν γυμνωσθῇ τοῦ σώματος ("Everything in the soul is visible, once it has been stripped of the garment of the body.") The fact that ἔνδηλα indeed means "visible" here is clear from the entire context. The judge of the underworld inspects the soul and sees in it deformities such as those which, both during life and after death, also can be found on the body. One may not conclude from this, however, that Plato has in mind here visibility to the *senses*. The entire account of the judgment in the underworld, which is related to the ancient tradition of Elysium, the isle of the blessed, is mythological in character and thus does not contain a theoretical conception of the soul, even though Socrates explicitly affirms his belief in its truth.

2 See previous note.

3 Plato, *Meno*, 81 B–C; and 81 C: ἅτ᾽ οὖν ἡ ψυχὴ ἀθάνατός τ᾽ οὖσα καὶ πολλάκις γεγονυῖα, καὶ ἑωρακυῖα καὶ τἀνθάδε καὶ τἀν Ἅδου καὶ πάντα χρήματα, οὐκ ἔστιν ὅ τι οὐ μεμάθηκεν, ὥστ᾽ οὐδὲν θαυμαστὸν καὶ περὶ ἀρετῆς καὶ περὶ ἄλλων οἷόν τ᾽ εἶναι αὐτὴν ἀναμνησθῆναι ἅ γε καὶ πρότερον ἠπίστατο. ("Since the soul is immortal and is born many times [in a body] and has seen what is here below and in Hades, and, in short, all things, there is nothing that it has not learned. It is thus not surprising that, with respect to virtue and the other things, it can call to remembrance that which it formerly knew.")

It is not accidental that Plato, as a preparation for answering the main question in this dialogue, which pertains to the essence and teachability of virtue, conjoins the doctrine of knowledge as *anamnēsis* with the discovery of mathematical states of affairs. For here we already stand at the gateway to the metaphysical theory of the *eidē*. Already in the first part of the discussion, Socrates draws attention to the fact that, just as there is one *ousia* (ontic form) of bees, which is the same in all animals of this species, so there is a single *eidos* which grants to all individual virtues, however many and various they may be, the fixed ontic form of virtue.[1] He proceeds immediately to elucidate this thesis by proving that there is a non-sensory form of the geometrical figure (σχῆμα), which is what imparts the nature of figure both to what is crooked and to what is straight.[2] Thereupon, in a broad exposition, this mathematical ontic form is defined in Pythagorean fashion as the limiting form (*peras*) of a body (στερεόν).[3]

It is indeed no longer the Socratic conception of the *idea* that comes to expression here; rather, the static conception of the metaphysical form of being is already making itself felt. In Eleatic-Pythagorean fashion, the latter is regarded as reposing within itself, even though, in contrast to Parmenides' ontic form, it is as an *eidos* no longer conceived geometrically.

It must be remarked, however, that this dialogue comprises no more than a prelude to the theory of ideas. The question as to the self-contained *eidos* of virtue (τί ποτ' ἔστιν αὐτὸ καθ' αὑτό) is merely raised, but not answered.[4] In the first section of the dialogue, the question as to whether virtue is teachable is not explored by means of the method of inquiry characteristic of the theory of ideas (viz., the metaphysical dialectic focused directly on the *eidē* themselves), but according to the example of the mathematical method *ex hypothesi* (ἐξ ὑποθέσεως).[5] When he is asked whether it is possible to place a particular triangle in a given circle, the mathemati-

---

1   Plato, Meno, 72 C : καὶ εἰ πολλαὶ καὶ παντοδαπαί εἰσιν, ἕν γέ τι εἶδος ταὐτὸν ἅπασαι ἔχουσι δι' ὃ εἰσιν ἀρεταί, εἰς ὃ καλῶς που ἔχει ἀποβλέψαντα τὸν ἀποκρινόμενον τῷ ἐρωτήσαντι ἐκεῖνο δηλῶσαι, ὃ τυγχάνει οὖσα ἀρετή. ("And although they [the virtues] are many and various, they nevertheless all possess one and the same *eidos* which makes them virtues. Therefore, he who would answer this question must look upon this *eidos* when he explains what virtue is.")

2   *Ibid.*, 74 B ff.

3   *Ibid.*, 76 A: στερεοῦ πέρας σχῆμα εἶναι.

4   At the end of the *Meno* (100 B), Socrates remarks: τὸ δὲ σαφὲς περὶ αὐτοῦ εἰσόμεθα τότε, ὅταν πρὶν ᾧτινι τρόπῳ τοῖς ἀνθρώποις παραγίγνεται ἀρετή, πρότερον ἐπιχειρήσωμεν αὐτὸ καθ' αὑτὸ ζητεῖν, τί ποτ' ἔστιν ἀρετή. ("We shall only understand the complete truth (concerning virtue) when, before attempting to discover in what manner virtue is imparted to men, we first try to investigate what virtue is in itself.") This investigation is not pursued here, however.

5   *Ibid.*, 86 E: εἰ μή τι οὖν ἀλλὰ σμικρόν γέ μοι τῆς ἀρχῆς χάλασον, καὶ συγχώρησον ἐξ ὑποθέσεως αὐτὸ σκοπεῖσθαι, εἴτε διδακτόν ἐστιν εἴθ' ὁπωσοῦν. λέγω δὲ τὸ ἐξ

cian makes this possibility dependent on a hypothesis which the triangle must satisfy if this is to be the case. Indeed, he does this before he knows whether the figure actually meets the requirements of the hypothesis. In a similar fashion, Socrates chooses to examine *ex hypothesi* the question as to whether virtue is teachable, before knowing either its ontic form or the mode of existence of its properties. He does this by formulating the question as follows: What conditions must virtue satisfy, if it is to be teachable? The answer then is that in this case it must be a science (ἐπιστήμη),[1] and this thesis is supported by a lengthy argument. This does not at all lead, however, to the conclusion that virtue exists only as a science, and the question as to its *eidos* is at this point left completely unanswered.

Instead, in the further course of the discussion, the argument takes another direction. The position is defended that good ethical action also finds a sufficient basis in ἀληθὴς δόξα (right opinion or true belief and conviction respecting the good) which has not yet been deepened by scientific knowledge of its grounds. Such right opinion is said to be imparted to man as a divine gift (θεία μοῖρα).[2] One can agree with Brommer that this recognition of ἀληθὴς δόξα as being granted to man θείᾳ μοίρᾳ (through divine inspiration) once again signifies the emergence of the Socratic *idea*, which only becomes operative in direct intuitive contemplation of the divine idea of the good and beautiful.[3] It cannot be denied, however, that the manner in which "right opinion" concerning virtue is to some extent made independent here of *epistēmē* or scientific conceptual knowledge evinces a certain departure from the ethical intellectualism of Socrates. In the latter, the intuitive contemplation of the idea of virtue was gained only by way of the proper method of concept formation. Nevertheless, in the *Meno* Plato acknowledges the independent value of ἀληθὴς δόξα only in a very relative sense. For, in the further course of his exposition, Socrates explicitly states that right opinions which are not securely tied down by the knowledge of their grounds – Plato regards this as the essence of *epistēmē* or science – cannot stay put for very long. They escape the human soul, and for this reason they have little value in themselves.

ὑποθέσεως ὧδε, ὥσπερ οἱ γεωμέτραι πολλάκις σκοποῦνται, ... ("Just loosen the reins of your control, if not completely, then only a little, and allow me to examine on the basis of a hypothesis [*ex hypothesi*] whether [virtue] is something teachable, or whether [it can be attained] in another way. I say 'on the basis of a hypothesis' in reference to the manner in which geometers often conduct their investigations.")

1 *Ibid.*, 88 D: κατὰ δὴ τοῦτον τὸν λόγον ὠφέλιμόν γ᾽ οὖσαν τὴν ἀρετὴν φρόνησιν δεῖ τιν᾽ εἶναι. ("According to this argument, virtue, since it is beneficial, must be a kind of scientific insight.") Here φρόνησις is equivalent to ἐπιστήμη.

2 Socrates summarizes this conclusion at the end of the dialogue (100 B), as follows: Ἐκ μὲν τοίνυν τούτου τοῦ λογισμοῦ, ὦ Μένων, θείᾳ μοίρᾳ ἡμῖν φαίνεται παραγιγνομένη ἀρετὴ οἷς παραγίγνεται ("According to this conclusion, dear Meno, virtue seems to us to be imparted by divine lot to those to whom it is imparted.")

3 Brommer, *op. cit.*, p. 21.

Furthermore, it is precisely through *anamnēsis*, the recollection of what the soul has beheld in its pre-existent state, that this securing of the grounds by means of scientific knowledge is accomplished: "But this, my dear Meno, is done by *anamnēsis*, as we agreed earlier. They [right opinions] are tied down, however and only then do they become knowledge and become abiding in nature. This is why scientific knowledge is surely more valuable than a right opinion, and it is in being tied down that scientific knowledge is distinguished from right opinion."[1]

In the *Meno*, *anamnēsis* itself is not yet related to the *eidē* as metaphysical ontic forms, as it will be later on in the *Phaedo*. Here it is merely said that the soul in its pre-existent state has seen everything, both here on earth and in Hades. The thesis that *epistēmē* is based on *anamnēsis* is illustrated, furthermore, only in terms of the knowledge of mathematical forms, which the theory of ideas does not include among the *eidē* proper. These mathematical forms, to be sure, are placed along with the latter in the supersensible world of ontic forms; nevertheless, they are conceived as a type of intermediate form situated between the *eidē* and the sense world of phenomena. As Aristotle observes, they resemble the *eidē* in being eternal and immovable; but like sense objects, they differ from the *eidē* in permitting a plurality within the same form. For example, there are many congruent triangles, but the *eidos* of the triangle is a unity without plurality.[2]

Of the remaining dialogues from the transition period, the *Cratylus*, which is devoted to the problem of the formation of language and its relation to conceptual knowledge, merits special attention. For, in the concluding portion of this work, the dialectical opposition between the Socratic form principle and the Heraclitean matter principle is set forth in sharp relief, with the Socratic idea of the good and beautiful being treated more or less as a static *eidos* (αὐτὸ καλὸν καὶ ἀγαθόν). This idea is ranged alongside of all the other ontic forms which exist in themselves.

The argument proceeds as follows: Knowledge of things cannot be derived from their names, a conception ascribed here to Cratylus. A pupil of Heraclitus, Cratylus had the view that names, precisely through their changing linguistic meanings, embrace the actual *physis* of things in its constant alteration and flux. This cannot be. Natural names must be a representation of something else, which constitutes their eternal archetype or model. Indeed, those who hold that the Heraclitean matter principle comprises the entire nature of *physis* fall into confusion and drag others along with them. Socrates, the discussion leader, says that he has often dreamed that there is a beauty and goodness in itself and an entire world of essences, which are in themselves and always remain identical with them-

---

1 Plato, *Meno*, 98 A: τοῦτο δ᾽ ἐστὶν, ὦ Μένων ἑταῖρε, ἀνάμνησις, ὡς ἐν τοῖς πρόσθεν ἡμῖν ὡμολόγηται. ἐπειδὰν δὲ δεθῶσι, πρῶτον μὲν ἐπιστῆμαι γίγνονται, ἔπειτα μόνιμοι. καὶ διὰ ταῦτα δὴ τιμιώτερον ἐπιστήμη ὀρθῆς δόξης ἐστί, καὶ διαφέρει δεσμῷ ἐπιστήμη ὀρθῆς δόξης. (translation in the text)
2 Aristotle, *Metaphysics* A. 6 987 b.

selves. He believes it quite likely that this world which he has beheld in his dreams actually exists. If these essences themselves were caught up in constant flux, it would be impossible to give things a correct name; one then could signify by means of language neither that they are "this," nor that they are "of a certain kind."[1] For how could anything that has no constant being be *something*? According to Aristotle, Heraclitus considered thought to be the continuous movement of the soul impelled by ever-flowing *physis*.[2] Over against this, Plato set the static *eidos* of knowledge, both as to its subject and its object (*Gegenstand*). If the Heraclitean matter principle were the sole factor here, knowledge, to be sure, would not be possible; because, if the *eidos* of knowledge were itself subject to continuous change, it would therein pass over into another *eidos* of knowledge, and knowledge would have no being. In this case, there would be neither a subject nor an object (*Gegenstand*) of knowledge possessing a constant ontic form.

If, on the contrary, both the subject and the object of knowledge always *are* – if the beautiful, the good, and all the other ontic forms have true *being* – then they cannot possess the nature of incessant flux or motion.[3] For

---

1 Plato, *Cratylus*, 439 C, D: σκέψαι γάρ, ὦ θαυμάσιε Κρατύλε, ὃ ἔγωγε πολλάκις ὀνειρώττω. πότερον φῶμέν τι εἶναι αὐτὸ καλὸν καὶ ἀγαθὸν καὶ ἓν ἕκαστον τῶν ὄντων [οὕτως] ἢ μή; ... Αὐτὸ τοίνυν ἐκεῖνο σκεψώμεθα, μὴ εἰ πρόσωπόν τί ἐστιν καλὸν ἤ τι τῶν τοιούτων, καὶ δοκεῖ ταῦτα πάντα ῥεῖν. ἀλλ᾽ αὐτό, φῶμεν, τὸ καλὸν οὐ τοιοῦτον ἀεί ἐστιν, οἷόν ἐστιν; ("For consider, admirable Cratylus, what I often dream. Shall we say that there are a beauty and a good, and each of the essences [forms] of this nature, that exist in themselves, or not? Let us regard this 'essence in itself,' not asking whether a certain external countenance or anything of this nature is beautiful, or whether this all is involved in constant flux [change]. But shall we not say that beauty in itself always retains the nature that it in truth is?") *Ibid.*, 439 D: Ἆρ᾽ οὖν οἷόν τε προσειπεῖν αὐτὸ ὀρθῶς, εἰ ἀεὶ ὑπεξέρχεται, πρῶτον μὲν ὅτι ἐκεῖνό ἐστιν, ἔπειθ᾽ ὅτι τοιοῦτον; ("If it thus continually slips from our grasp, how can we rightly express in words, in the first place, that it is *this*, and further, that it is *of such a kind?*")

2 Aristotle, *De anima*, 1, 2.

3 Plato, *Cratylus*, 440 A, B: Ἀλλ᾽ οὐδὲ γνῶσιν εἶναι φάναι εἰκός, ὦ Κρατύλε, εἰ μεταπίπτει πάντα χρήματα καὶ μηδὲν μένει. εἰ μὲν γὰρ αὐτὸ τοῦτο, ἡ γνῶσις, τοῦ γνῶσις εἶναι μὴ μεταπίπτει, μένοι τ᾽ ἂν ἀεὶ ἡ γνῶσις καὶ εἴη γνῶσις· εἰ δὲ καὶ αὐτὸ τὸ εἶδος μεταπίπτει τῆς γνώσεως, ἅμα τ᾽ ἂν μεταπίπτοι εἰς ἄλλο εἶδος γνώσεως, καὶ οὐκ ἂν εἴη γνῶσις· εἰ δὲ ἀεὶ μεταπίπτει, ἀεὶ οὐκ ἂν εἴη γνῶσις. καὶ ἐκ τούτου τοῦ λόγου οὔτε τὸ γνωσόμενον οὔτε τὸ γνωσθησόμενον ἂν εἴη. εἰ δὲ ἔστι μὲν ἀεὶ τὸ γιγνῶσκον, ἔστι δὲ τὸ γιγνωσκόμενον, ἔστι δὲ τὸ καλόν, ἔστι δὲ τὸ ἀγαθόν, ἔστι δὲ ἓν ἕκαστον τῶν ὄντων, οὔ μοι φαίνεται ταῦθ᾽ ὅμοια ὄντα, ἃ νῦν ἡμεῖς λέγομεν, ῥοῇ οὐδὲν οὐδὲ φορᾷ. ("Nor can it be reasonably maintained that there is knowledge at all, dear Cratylus, if all things are in transition and nothing remains the same. For if knowledge, precisely because it is knowledge, does not change and thus cease to be knowledge, then it will always remain the same and be knowledge. If there is change in the very *eidos* of knowledge, however, then the latter will pass into another *eidos* of knowledge, and knowledge will not *be*. But if it is

whatever always has the same nature and remains identical with itself can neither change nor move, since it never passes outside of its *idea*.[1] It is evident here that the Socratic *idea* has been almost completely absorbed by the static *eidos* of metaphysical ontology. Although it is true that the passage cited is speaking only of the *idea* of the beautiful (and the good), which the Socratic line of thought regards as the proto-form of the form-power of the divine *nous*, this *idea* is treated here entirely as an ontic form, reposing in itself, that is placed alongside of all the others. Scientific knowledge itself is grounded in a static, self-contained *eidos*.

What is at issue in this exposition, therefore, is indeed the world of the *eidē* in the sense of static, supersensible ontic forms. At this point, however, Socrates does not at all speak of this newly discovered metaphysical world with the certainty of metaphysical *theōria*. He declares only that he has often seen it in a dream.[2] The later dialectical method of investigation has not yet appeared. On the contrary, Socrates says at the end of the discussion, "Perhaps it is so, dear Cratylus, but perhaps not." Cratylus is urged therefore to press on diligently with the investigation.

In spite of this, we can without question endorse the view of Karl Steinhart that this dialogue belongs to a stage of Plato's thought in which the theory of ideas, in the sense of the theory of the *eidē*, was beginning to take shape in Plato's mind, without yet having attained the clarity of his mature conception.[3]

The actual dialectical method used in the *Cratylus* is still Socratic and has not yet developed into the metaphysical dialectic of the theory of ideas. Nevertheless, the world of the *eidē* has already appeared on Plato's intellectual horizon, even if as yet only in a vision, and as a world of immutable ontic forms it places itself squarely in dialectical opposition to the

---

always in transition to something else, there will always be no knowledge. By this reasoning, there would neither be anything that knows, nor anything knowable. But if that which knows and that which is known, and also the beautiful, the good, and every one of the ontic forms, always have *being*, then these things of which we are now speaking seem to me altogether unlike something that is in continual flux or motion.")

1   *Ibid.*, 439 E: εἰ δ᾽ ἀεὶ ὡσαύτως ἔχει καὶ ταὐτό ἐστι, πῶς ἂν τοῦτό γε μεταβάλλοι ἢ κινοῖτο, μηδὲν ἐξιστάμενον τῆς αὐτοῦ ἰδέας; ("But if it is always of the same nature and remains the same, how could it then change and move, since it never passes outside of its *idea*.") The term ἰδέα ἀγαθοῦ has already appeared at an earlier point, e.g., in 418 E: ἀγαθοῦ γὰρ ἰδέα οὖσα τὸ δέον φαίνεται δεσμὸς εἶναι καὶ κώλυμα φορᾶς ("Since one *idea* of the good is the proper, it seems to be a chain and a hindrance of motion.") Here, however, the word *idea* cannot have its pregnant meaning; it can only mean "species." For this passage occurs in the context of some more or less fanciful word derivations, and the ontic forms proper are not yet under discussion.

2   See note 1 on page 143.

3   Karl Steinhart, *Platon's sämmtliche Werke, mit Einleitungen begleitet von K. Steinhart*, (8 vols.; Leipzig, 1850-66), II, *Kratylos*, p. 571.

Heraclitean matter principle of eternal flux. The theory of ideas in its authentic form stands here on the eve of being born.

Chapter One

The Dialectic of the Theory of Ideas from Its Initial Conception to Its Culmination in the *Republic*

1. The *Phaedo*. The Orphic Dualism of Soul and Body and the Static Theory of the *Eidē* in Its Polar Opposition to the Matter Motive

a. The Connection between the Theory of Ideas and the Theory Concerning the Immortality of the Thinking Soul

In the dialogue *Phaedo*, the Platonic theory of ideas appears in its first theoretical conception. Here it has passed from the vague realm of dreams into the sharply contoured terrain of θεωρία. In this famed dialogue, Socrates presents to his students, who are gathered around him in his cell during his last hours, a theoretical account of his conviction regarding the immortality of the soul in the sense of a theoretical mental substance that is separable from the material body.

Insofar as they are regarded as strict, the proofs for immortality that Socrates offers here, which by way of Augustine were in large part taken over by Scholastic anthropology, are so closely intertwined with the new theory of the *eidē* that he regards the two doctrines as inseparable.[1] It is clear, furthermore, that the theory of the *anima rationalis* remained inseparably joined to the theory of ideas throughout the further development of

---

1 Plato, *Phaedo*, 76 D–E (cap.22) : εἰ μὲν ἔστιν ἃ θρυλοῦμεν ἀεί, καλόν τε καὶ ἀγαθὸν καὶ πᾶσα ἡ τοιαύτη οὐσία, καὶ ἐπὶ ταύτην τὰ ἐκ τῶν αἰσθήσεων πάντ' ἀναφέρομεν, ὑπάρχουσαν πρότερον ἀνευρίσκοντες ἡμετέραν οὖσαν, καὶ ταῦτ' ἐκείνῃ ἀπεικάζομεν, ἀναγκαῖον, οὕτως ὥσπερ καὶ ταῦτ' ἔστιν, οὕτως καὶ τὴν ἡμετέραν ψυχὴν εἶναι καὶ πρὶν γεγονέναι ἡμᾶς· εἰ δὲ μὴ ἔστι ταῦτα, ἄλλως ἂν ὁ λόγος οὗτος εἰρημένος εἴη; ἆρ' <οὐχ> οὕτως ἔχει, καὶ ἴση ἀνάγκη ταῦτά (τὰ εἴδη) τ'εἶναι καὶ τὰς ἡμετέρας ψυχὰς πρὶν καὶ ἡμᾶς γεγονέναι, καὶ εἰ μὴ ταῦτα, οὐδὲ τάδε; ("If, as we continually repeat, there is a beautiful and a good, and a whole world of such essences, and if we refer all that we perceive with our sense to this as something that belonged to us formerly and that we now discover as our own, and compare the one with the other, does it then not necessarily follow that, just as these [the *eidē*] *are*, so our soul had *being* even before we were born, whereas if these do not have *being*, our argument would have come out differently? Is this not the situation, and is it not equally necessary that both these *eidē* and our souls *are*, even before we were born, and that if the former have no *being*, this is also not the case with the latter?") *Editorial note – AW*: Note that <οὐχ> is an editorial addition in the text of Plato that Dooyeweerd was using. It is not found in the manuscripts, nor in the editions of Schanz or Burnet. Also note that Dooyeweerd added the words τὰ εἴδη to the Greek text as an explanatory gloss.

147

Plato's thought as well. Because of this, changes in the former left their mark also in the latter, and conversely.

In the *Phaedo*, the rational soul in its pure state, divorced from the body, is conceived as a pure theoretically thinking substance (*οὐσία*), which in this sense is simple, i.e., not composed of various elements, or of any plurality at all. As such it is akin to the eternal form-world of true being, the *eidē*, which exist in themselves, ungenerated and unmoved, and which are divine, eternal, and simple in nature. It is primarily because of this kinship that the thinking soul is considered immortal.[1] The intelligible world of simple and pure *eidē* (transcendent ontic forms) is as such absolutely divorced from the "composite," transitory material things, whose sensible (formal) existence has its ontic ground (*αἰτία*) exclusively in these *eidē*. Whether they be beautiful, good, large or small, like or unlike, visible objects can exist only by way of a certain participation (*methexis, parousia, koinōnia*) in the *eidē*, which have their existence in themselves (*τὸ αὐτὸ καλόν, τὸ αὐτὸ ἀγαθόν, τὸ αὐτὸ μέγεθος*, etc.).[2]

In this *parousia* (presence) *in* or *koinōnia* (communion) *with* sense ob-

---

1 *Ibid.*, 80 A and B: Σκόπει δή, ἔφη, ὦ Κέβης, εἰ ἐκ πάντων τῶν εἰρημένων τάδ᾽ ἡμῖν ξυμβαίνει, τῷ μὲν θείῳ καὶ ἀθανάτῳ καὶ νοητῷ καὶ μονοειδεῖ καὶ ἀδιαλύτῳ καὶ ἀεὶ ὡσαύτως καὶ κατὰ ταὔτ᾽ ἔχοντι ἑαυτῷ ὁμοιότατον εἶναι ψυχήν, τῷ δ᾽ ἀνθρωπίνῳ καὶ θνητῷ καὶ ἀνοήτῳ καὶ πολυειδεῖ καὶ διαλυτῷ καὶ μηδέποτε κατὰ ταὔτ᾽ ἔχοντι ἑαυτῷ ὁμοιότατον αὖ εἶναι σῶμα. ("Then consider, dear Cebes, whether from all we have said we may not draw the conclusion that the soul most resembles that which is divine, immortal, intelligible, uniform, imperturbable, and always remains within itself in the same manner and in the same state, whereas the body is most like that which is human, mortal, unintelligible, multiform, perturbable, and never remains in the same state?") *Ibid.*, 78 C: Ἆρ᾽ οὖν τῷ μὲν ξυντεθέντι τε καὶ συνθέτῳ ὄντι φύσει προσήκει τοῦτο πάσχειν, διαιρεθῆναι ταύτῃ, ᾗπερ συνετέθη· εἰ δέ τι τυγχάνει ὂν ἀξύνθετον, τούτῳ μόνῳ προσήκει μὴ πάσχειν ταῦτα ...; (Is it fitting for what has arisen by compounding and is by nature composite to undergo that, viz., to be [again] decomposed in the same manner in which it was composed? But if something is not composite, is it not fitting for this [simple nature] alone not to undergo that...?")

2 *Ibid.*, 100 D: οὐκ ἄλλο τι ποιεῖ αὐτὸ καλὸν ἢ ἡ ἐκείνου τοῦ καλοῦ εἴτε παρουσία εἴτε κοινωνία ... τῷ καλῷ πάντα τὰ καλὰ γίγνεται καλά. ("Nothing makes this [beautiful thing] beautiful but the presence within it [of] or the communion with the beautiful [as *eidos*]... It is by beauty [as *eidos*] that all beautiful things become beautiful.") *Ibid.*, 100 B: ἔρχομαι γὰρ δὴ ἐπιχειρῶν σοι ἐπιδείξασθαι τῆς αἰτίας τὸ εἶδος, ὃ πεπραγμάτευμαι, καὶ εἶμι πάλιν ἐπ᾽ ἐκεῖνα τὰ πολυθρύλητα καὶ ἄρχομαι ἀπ᾽ ἐκείνων, ὑποθέμενος εἶναί τι καλὸν αὐτὸ καθ᾽ αὑτὸ καὶ ἀγαθὸν καὶ μέγα καὶ τ᾽ ἄλλα πάντα· ἃ εἴ μοι δίδως τε καὶ ξυγχωρεῖς εἶναι ταῦτα, ἐλπίζω σοι ἐκ τούτων τὴν αἰτίαν ἐπιδείξειν καὶ ἀνευρήσειν, ὡς ἀθάνατον ἡ ψυχή. ("What I shall try to demonstrate to you is the *eidos* of the cause, which I have investigated, and I thus return again to what has been much discussed [viz., the *eidē*], and proceed from this with the hypothesis that there is a beauty in itself, and a goodness, and magnitude, and all other [ontic forms that exist in themselves]. If you grant me this and admit that these exist, then I hope from them to demonstrate to you the cause

jects, the *eidē* assume a bodily, sensible shape in which they are no longer seen in their purity.[1] The same applies to the simple, thinking soul when it is incarnated in a material body. Sensory perception, desire, and passion, which pollute the soul and divert theoretical thought from its intuition of the eternal, invisible world of forms, all originate in the material body.[2] The dichotomy between the thinking soul-substance and the material body is here carried through as radically as the metaphysical dichotomy between the intelligible world of the *eidē* and the sense world of *phainomena*.

b. The So-Called Simplicity of the Thinking Soul as a Proof of Its Indestructibility. The Unreconciled Dualism between the Theōria of the Eidē and the Socratic Idea in the Phaedo

Whatever is composite is subject to the *Anankē* of the matter principle of eternal flux and change. Only what has a simple nature shares in the imperishability of the transcendent ontic forms. Since the thinking soul is such a simple *ousia* (substance), it too, like the *eidē* themselves, is indestructible.[3] Here the *eidē* themselves are regarded entirely as static,

---

[ontic ground] of things and to discover that the soul is immortal.")

1 This is expressed most clearly by Plato in the *Symposium*, 211 D, E, which likewise presents the theory of ideas in its initial conception: τί δῆτα, ἔφη, οἰόμεθα, εἰ τῳ γένοιτο αὐτὸ τὸ καλὸν ἰδεῖν εἰλικρινές, καθαρόν, ἄμικτον, ἀλλὰ μὴ ἀνάπλεων σαρκῶν τ᾽ ἀνθρωπίνων καὶ χρωμάτων καὶ ἄλλης πολλῆς φλυαρίας θνητῆς, ἀλλ᾽ αὐτὸ τὸ θεῖον καλὸν δύναιτο μονοειδὲς κατιδεῖν; ("What do we suppose, he said, if it should be granted to someone to see beauty in itself – pure, unsullied, unalloyed, not defiled with human flesh and with the colors and the various other gaudy trifles of mortality – but if he should behold this divine beauty in itself and in its simplicity [uniformity]?")

2 Plato, *Phaedo*, 65 E and 66 A: Ἆρ᾽ οὖν ἐκεῖνος ἂν τοῦτο ποιήσειε καθαρώτατα, ὅστις ὅτι μάλιστ᾽ αὐτῇ τῇ διανοίᾳ ἴοι ἐφ᾽ ἕκαστον, μήτε τὴν ὄψιν παρατιθέμενος ἐν τῷ διανοεῖσθαι μήτε τιν᾽ ἄλλην αἴσθησιν ἐφέλκων μηδεμίαν μετὰ τοῦ λογισμοῦ, ἀλλ᾽ αὐτῇ καθ᾽ αὑτὴν εἰλικρινεῖ τῇ διανοίᾳ χρώμενος αὐτὸ καθ᾽ αὑτὸ εἰλικρινὲς ἕκαστον ἐπιχειροίη θηρεύειν τῶν ὄντων, ἀπαλλαγεὶς ὅτι μάλιστ᾽ ὀφθαλμῶν τε καὶ ὤτων καὶ ὡς ἔπος εἰπεῖν, ξύμπαντος τοῦ σώματος, ὡς ταράττοντος καὶ οὐκ ἐῶντος τὴν ψυχὴν κτήσασθαι ἀλήθειάν τε καὶ φρόνησιν, ὅταν κοινωνῇ; ("Will not the person do this [viz., examine everything through reflection] most purely who approaches each object, as far as possible, only through theoretical thought – not taking recourse to the sense of sight in his thinking, nor availing himself of any other sense perception in his reasoning – but who by using pure thought in itself attempts to pursue each of the ontic forms as it exists pure and in itself, and cuts himself off as much as possible from eyes, ears, and so to speak, from the entire body, since this confuses him when it takes part in this activity and prevents the soul from gaining truth and knowledge?")

3 *Ibid.*, 106 D and E (cap. 56) : Ὁ δέ γε θεός, οἶμαι, ἔφη ὁ Σωκράτης, καὶ αὐτὸ τὸ τῆς ζωῆς εἶδος καὶ εἴ τι ἄλλο ἀθάνατόν ἐστι, παρὰ πάντων ἂν ὁμολογηθείη μηδέποτ᾽ ἀπόλλυσθαι .... Ὁπότε δὴ τὸ ἀθάνατον καὶ ἀδιάφορόν ἐστιν, ἄλλο τι

discontinuous, and self-contained ontic forms which are sufficient to themselves. Contrasting *eidē*, as such, mutually exclude one another and cannot yet be joined together in a single *idea*.[1] Thus the dialectical method of *dihaeresis*, which is developed in a later dialogue, the *Sophist*, and is used to uncover a logical-metaphysical coherence and structure within the world of ontic forms, is still unknown at this point. Indeed, Socrates explicitly relates his *idea* of the good and beautiful to the divine *nous*, which gives form to the visible cosmos.[2] The connection between the divine *idea* and the static *eidē*, however, which will be placed in such a revealing light in the later books of the *Republic*, is left completely in the dark in the *Phaedo*, and in the further course of the discussion the dynamic *idea* recedes entirely into the background.

In the first theoretical conception of Plato's theory of ideas, the influence of the Eleatic-Pythagorean principle of form clearly has the upper hand. The discontinuity present in the later Pythagorean conception of the form principle (i.e., the conception of mutually irreducible numerical forms) is here combined with the unity and simplicity of the Eleatic form of being in its exclusion of all inner plurality and diversity.

ψυχὴ ἦ, εἰ ἀθάνατος τυγχάνει οὖσα, καὶ ἀνώλεθρος ἂν εἴη; ("And thus, said Socrates, I believe that with respect both to the deity and to the *eidos* of life in itself, and also to anything else that might be immortal, it could be admitted by all that they never pass away.... If what is immortal is thus also indestructible, then can the soul, if it is immortal, be other than indestructible?")

1 *Ibid.*, 104 B and C (cap. 52): ἔστι δὲ τόδε, ὅτι φαίνεται οὐ μόνον ἐκεῖνα τἀναντί' ἄλληλα οὐ δεχόμενα, ἀλλὰ καὶ ὅσα οὐκ ὄντα ἀλλήλοις ἐναντία ἔχει ἀεὶ τἀναντία, οὐδὲ ταῦτ' ἔοικε δεχομένοις ἐκείνην τὴν ἰδέαν, ἦ ἂν τῇ ἐν αὐτοῖς οὔσῃ ἐναντία ἦ, ἀλλ' ἐπιούσης αὐτῆς ἤτοι ἀπολλύμενα ἢ ὑπεκχωροῦντα· ἢ οὐ φήσομεν τὰ τρία καὶ ἀπολεῖσθαι πρότερον καὶ ἄλλ' ὁτιοῦν πείσεσθαι, πρὶν ὑπομεῖναι ἔτι τρία ὄντα ἄρτια γενέσθαι; ... Οὐκ ἄρα μόνον τὰ εἴδη τἀναντία οὐχ ὑπομένει ἐπιόντα ἄλληλα, ἀλλὰ καὶ ἄλλ' ἄττα τἀναντία οὐχ ὑπομένει ἐπιόντα. ("But it is the following [that I wish to make clear], that not only these [viz., the *eidē*] do not admit their opposites, but that also those things which, although they are not themselves opposites, always contain the opposite within themselves [e.g., the numbers 2 and 3], naturally do not admit the *idea* that is opposite to the ontic form dwelling within them, but they either pass away when this approaches or they change their position. Or shall we not say that three would sooner pass away or suffer some other fate, than submit to becoming an even number? ... It is thus not only the opposite *eidē* that do not permit each other's approach, but also many other things do not permit the approach of their opposite.")

2 See the earlier citation of *Phaedo* 97 p.121, note 2. See also 99 C, where Socrates takes issue with the pre-Socratic nature philosophers and their conception of the *archē* or *archai*: τὴν δὲ τοῦ ὡς οἷόν τε βέλτιστ' αὐτὰ τεθῆναι δύναμιν οὕτω νῦν κεῖσθαι, ταύτην οὔτε ζητοῦσιν οὔτε τιν' οἴονται δαιμονίαν ἰσχὺν ἔχειν, ("But as for the power to have that position which best suits it [viz., the earth], they neither look into it nor ascribe to it any divine force.")

c. The Orientation of Epistemology to the Theory of the Eidē

At this point Plato's epistemology is also entirely oriented to the theory of the *eidē*. With an appeal to Philolaus the Pythagorean, the aim of the philosopher's whole endeavor is represented here as the mortification of the material body by way of focusing theoretical thought on the eternal world of the *eidē*.[1] If he is to grasp true being in all of its eternal forms as it exists pure and in itself, the philosopher must apply himself to theoretical thought in itself and free himself as much as possible from eyes and ears, indeed, from the entire material body, since the participation of the latter in the act of knowing leads to confusion and prevents the soul from gaining insight and truth. The body is expressly called "despicable" here.[2] The thinking soul, in contrast, is referred to as "divine."[3] In an explicit allusion to the purification mysteries, the true philosopher is characterized in this context as the only real "initiate." It is only he who, purified from the body, enters undefiled into Hades, the realm of the dead. Here, however, "Hades" has become Ἀΐδης,[4] that is, the supersensible realm of the eternal, invisible *eidē*.[5]

The knowledge of these *eidē* obtained by the soul is based on the reawakening in pure theoretical thought of the memory of the eternal, self-subsistent, pure ontic forms that it has beheld in its pre-existent state.[6] Thus the doctrine of *anamnēsis*, which was previously developed in the *Meno*, is now applied to the *eidē*. Among these *eidē*, the following are explicitly mentioned in juxtaposition: "beauty in itself," "goodness in itself," "equality in itself," "justice in itself," "piety in itself," and, further, everything that is said to truly *be*, i.e., that truly possesses immutable *being*. In a later context, we shall witness the introduction of a variety of *eidē* that are logical, mathematical, and physical in nature, and also an *eidos* of "life in itself."

d. The Main Proof for the Immortality of the Soul in the Phaedo

Through the words of Socrates, Plato now argues that the unity of opposites, which Heraclitus claimed was present in the eternal flux of sensi-

---

1 *Ibid.*, 64 A, b (cap. 9).

2 *Ibid.*, 65 D (cap. 10).

3 *Ibid.*, 80 B (cap. 28).

4 *Editor's note – AW:* Dooyeweerd is here referring to the wordplay which Plato makes on Ἀΐδης (= Hades), and ἀειδής (= invisible, unseen).

5 *Ibid.*, 80 D (cap. 29): Ἡ δὲ ψυχὴ ἄρα, τὸ ἀειδές, τὸ εἰς τοιοῦτον τόπον ἕτερον οἰχόμενον, γενναῖον καὶ καθαρὸν καὶ ἀειδῆ, εἰς Ἅδου ὡς ἀληθῶς, παρὰ τὸν ἀγαθὸν καὶ φρόνιμον θεόν, οἷ, ἂν θεὸς ἐθέλῃ, αὐτίκα καὶ τῇ ἐμῇ ψυχῇ ἰτέον ... . ("The soul thus, the invisible, which goes to another place like unto itself, holy, pure, and invisible – to Hades, which [as the Realm of the Invisible] is truly named thus – to the good and rational god, where, if god wills, my soul too must journey without delay.") *Editor's note – AW:* The text Dooyeweerd consulted employed the unusual spelling Ἅδου for 'Hades' in Greek. The normal spelling is Ἅιδου.

6 *Ibid.*, 75 C–D.

ble forms, can never hold true with respect to the *eidē*, such as those of large and small, even and odd, etc. This argument then culminates in the final proof for the immortality of the soul as a pure mental substance.

The soul is that which gives life to the body, and the opposite of life is death. The thinking soul can thus never admit death, for the latter is opposed to what is always inseparably joined to the soul, namely, life.[1] The *eidos* of "life in itself" can neither come into being nor pass away, because it will not permit its opposite to become joined to it.[2] The same is true of the thinking soul, which in accordance with its ontic form has a share in this immutable *eidos*.

e. *The* Parousia *of the* Eidē *in Sense Objects and the Relationship of the* Eidē *to the Thinking Soul in the* Phaedo

It is clear at once that an inner tension must necessarily arise between the discontinuous multitude of fixed *eidē*, on the one hand, which through a sharp accentuation of the logical principle of contradiction have come to stand next to one another without any interconnection, and, on the other hand, the Socratic concentration of all conceptual knowledge on the *idea* of the good, which was given equal emphasis by Plato in an earlier context.[3] In the initial phase of Plato's theory of ideas, this tension could not be eliminated. It is likewise clear that the polar dialectical tension between the form and matter principles is manifest here only in a provisional way. That is the case because at this point the actual relationship between the two, apart from which the theoretical investigation of the *phainomena* would be impossible in Plato's line of thought, is left completely in the dark. The *parousia* and *koinōnia* of the *eidē* in the objects of sense perception was, to be sure, only a mythological picture of the situation. And, as Plato is forced to admit later on in his *Parmenides*, subjecting this picture to analysis ensnares theoretical thought in a maze of antinomies. In the sixth chapter of the first book of his *Metaphysics*, Aristotle remarks that the Platonic *methexis* or "participation" of sense objects in the *eidē* after which they are named is only another word for the μίμησις (*mimēsis*) which the Pythagoreans claimed existed between sense objects and numbers. He adds, however, that both Plato and the Pythagoreans failed to investigate what this *methexis* or *mimēsis* actually is.[4] Cornford has rightly observed that here the word *mimēsis* cannot mean "imitation" in the sense of external resemblance,

---

1 *Ibid.*, 105 E.

2 *Ibid.*, 106 D.

3 *Ibid.*, 97 B.

4 Aristotle, *Metaphysics* A, 6 987 b 9: κατὰ μέθεξιν γὰρ εἶναι τὰ πολλὰ τῶν συνωνύμων τοῖς εἴδεσι. τὴν δὲ μέθεξιν τοὔνομα μόνον μετέβαλεν· οἱ μὲν γὰρ Πυθαγόρειοι μιμήσει τὰ ὄντα φασὶν εἶναι τῶν ἀριθμῶν, Πλάτων δὲ μεθέξει τοὔνομα μεταβαλών· τὴν μέντοι γε μέθεξιν ἢ τὴν μίμησιν ἥτις ἂν εἴη τῶν εἰδῶν ἀφεῖσαν ἐν κοινῷ ζητεῖν. ("For the multiplicity of sense objects bearing the same

for empirical objects resemble neither numbers nor the Platonic *eidē*. The term can only have the older meaning of "embodiment" or "representation," as in a variety of symbols which represent or embody the same sense or meaning.[1] Thus Plato found in sense objects of a specific kind the embodiment of their supersensible *eidos*, just as mortal man for him embodies a divine soul, which is an immortal mental substance.

From this Cornford draws the conclusion that the *eidē*, which he does not distinguish from the *idea*, are actually nothing other than "soul-substances." In fact, he considers them not as individual but as communal souls, which were originally regarded as *daemons* immanent in the respective groups of kindred empirical things. These, however, were later "Olympianized" by Plato and given a transcendent, immortal status, by reason of which they left their groups. Similarly, Pythagoras was at first revered as the *daemon* of his order but later came to be identified with Apollo, the immortal, luminous god of Olympus.

As to its sociological orientation, at least, this explanation is just another example of Cornford's overworking of Durkheim's sociological method in his interpretation of Greek thought. Nevertheless, even if we set aside this sociological reductionism in Durkheim's interpretation of the *eidē*, we must admit that in the *Phaedo*, as we have seen, Plato does strongly emphasize the kinship between the immortal thinking soul and the world of the *eidē*. In this dialogue, however, the *eidē* themselves are not yet conceived of as soul-substances, as would later be the case in the *Sophist*.

Whereas such a soul-substance is active, the *eidē* are static and at rest. The latter are for Plato the true *Gegenstand* (object) of *noēsis* or theoretical thought, and he remains conscious of this *Gegenstand* relation even in the *Phaedo*. Thus, even during this stage of his thought, in which the Eleatic conception of supersensible ontic form became such a dominant influence on the theory of ideas, he never fully reverted to Parmenides' uncritical identification of form-giving theoretical thought with the static form of being. The *Phaedo* teaches nothing more than a kinship between these two. Indeed, their complete identification was ruled out for Plato by the mere fact that he conceived the thinking soul as an individual ontic form, in contrast to the *eidos* as a supra-individual ontic form. As a fruit of Socratic self-reflection, the individuality of the immortal soul has acquired absolute value and significance, overcoming the pantheistic, uranic conception of Empedocles, according to which individuality could only be the result of a fall from the all-pervading divine soul, under the influence of *neikos*. Significantly, Plato grants the individual soul *dominion*

---

name as the *eidē* supposedly exist by participation [in the *eidē*]. The word "participation" was only a new name, however. For the Pythagoreans say that things exist by *mimēsis* of numbers, but Plato says by participation [which is merely another word]. But what this participation in the *eidē* or this *mimēsis* actually is, they have both neglected to investigate.")

1   Cornford, *op. cit.*, p. 254.

over the body, just as the divine in general for him has dominion over what is mortal.[1] From this it is clear that the form motive of the religion of culture indeed retains the primacy in his thought. His conception may be compared with that of Anaxagoras, therefore, and both of these may be contrasted with that of Empedocles.

The source of Plato's theory of ideas is to be found, however, not in his conception of the soul, but in the supersensible form motive. Indeed, this conception of the soul is completely governed by the form-matter motive. Accordingly, the problem he poses in the *Phaedo* is whether the thinking soul is matter, or a supersensible ontic form. And in calling the immortal thinking soul "akin" to the world of pure *eidē*, he implicitly raises the question as to the basic difference between them.

At this juncture, Plato is unable to solve this problem. It is only in the *Philebus* and the *Timaeus*, which belong to the penultimate stage in the development of his thought, that he devises a solution by constructing for the soul an intermediate world located between the world of sense and that of the *eidē*. In the *Phaedo*, however, the soul as an immortal mental substance is still placed alongside the *eidē* within the world of eternal ontic forms. As a consequence, the previously signalized danger arose that the soul might be "Eleaticized" and all but identified with motionless ontic form. Such an identification, however, would have deprived the *anima rationalis* of all vitality, rendering it completely inert. Indeed, Plato's denial of motion to mental substance constituted the initial step in this direction.

Plato recognized this danger in good time. The conviction that the soul is the vital principle of the material body, which had been present in Greek thought from the beginning and which had also been preserved in the *Phaedo*, inevitably led Plato back to the view that the soul contains the principle of motion. The connection of the soul with ever-flowing *physis*, which the Eleatic influence for a moment in the *Phaedo* appeared to have broken, was thus restored. In this way, however, Plato became entangled in the same problem that had frustrated the early Pythagorean school in its attempt to conceive the soul in terms of the form and matter principles simultaneously.

f. Form and Matter in the Eidē *Conceived as Ideal Numbers in the Final Stage of Plato's Thought*

In the final stage of the development of Plato's thought, when the *eidē* in Pythagorean fashion were identified with the so-called "ideal numbers," this same problem emerged within the theory of ideas, and the *eidē* themselves were considered to be composed of both form and ideal matter.[2] This late Platonic conception of the *eidē* was subsequently taken over in neo-Platonism and in Augustinian Scholasticism.

---

1 Plato, *Phaedo*, 80 A.

2 Cf. Aristotle, *Metaphysics*, A, 6 987 b 19 ff.: Ἐπεὶ δ'αἴτια τὰ εἴδη τοῖς ἄλλοις, τἀκείνων στοιχεῖα πάντων ᾠήθη τῶν ὄντων εἶναι στοιχεῖα. ὡς μὲν οὖν ὕλην τὸ

g. *The* Phaedo's *Depreciation of the* Polis *as the Vehicle of the Religion of Culture*

There is no trace of any of this in the *Phaedo*. Here the Eleatic influence on the theory of ideas is predominant. Although, as we saw, Plato essentially holds, even at this point, to the primacy of the form motive of the culture religion, various tendencies are at work here which threaten this primacy. Perhaps the strongest indication of this danger lies in this dialogue's remarkable depreciation of the *polis*, the vehicle of the religion of culture.

In the exposition of the doctrine of the transmigration of souls,[1] it is only the philosophers who are exalted after death "to the race of the gods." The souls of those who have cultivated the popularly esteemed civic virtues of justice and moderation[2] during their earthly existence, in contrast, are reincarnated as one of the animals that form organized societies, such as bees, wasps, or ants, or even as "respectable citizens."

If we compare this valuation of the *polis* and of civic virtue with that given in the earlier, Socratic dialogues, or with that appearing later in the *Republic*, the *Statesman*, and the *Laws*, it is clear that the *polis* as a deified power for the formation of man has receded completely into the background in the *Phaedo*. For the nonce, philosophical *theōria* has been emancipated completely from the *polis*. Only philosophical theory, in its self-sufficient investigation of the world of *eidē*, can lay claim to the task of unfolding the divine form principle in man, and this formative task is fulfilled solely through the gradual dying off of the material body and all earthly bonds. The Orphic-Pythagorean influence, in league with that of the Eleatic school, has for a moment decisively suppressed the Socratic tendency in Plato's thought.

μέγα καὶ τὸ μικρὸν εἶναι ἀρχάς, ὡς δ'οὐσίαν τὸ ἕν· ἐξ ἐκείνων γὰρ κατὰ μέθεξιν τοῦ ἑνὸς [τὰ εἴδη] εἶναι τοὺς ἀριθμούς· τὸ μέντοι γε ἓν οὐσίαν εἶναι, καὶ μὴ ἕτερόν γέ τι ὃν λέγεσθαι ἕν, παραπλησίως τοῖς Πυθαγορείοις ἔλεγε, καὶ τὸ τοὺς ἀριθμοὺς αἰτίους εἶναι τοῖς ἄλλοις τῆς οὐσίας ὡσαύτως ἐκείνοις· ("But since for him [Plato] the *eidē* were the "causes" of the other things, he thought that their elements were the elements of all reality. As matter, the great and small [the Pythagorean *apeiron*] were fundamental principles, but as *ousia* [form-substance], the one [*monas*]; for the *eidē*, or numbers, exist from out of the great and small by participation in the one. In holding that only the *monas* is *ousia*, and that this is not meant as one in the sense that there is yet something other, his teaching indeed agrees with the Pythagoreans, and he also taught, as they did, that the numbers are the causes of the existence of everything else.") It is later said that Plato identified the *monas* with the idea of the good. See *Metaphysics*, N. 4 1091 b 13 ff., and *Ethica Eudem* A, 8 1218 a 25, in connection with the above.

Editor's note – AW: This is as much an interpretive paraphrase as translation – for example, the word *monas* does not occur in the Greek.

1 Plato, *Phaedo*, 81 D ff.(cap. 31).

2 *Editor's note – RK*: The virtues particularly associated with the *polis*.

This is nothing more than a brief intermezzo within the overall development of the theory of ideas, however. The *polis* will quickly regain the central position that it had occupied from the outset in Plato's thought.

2. The Re-emergence of the Socratic Form Motive in the *Phaedrus* and the *Symposium*, and the Revised Conception of the Soul

a. The Doctrine of the World-Soul. The Phaedo's *Static Conception of the Soul Is Abandoned. The Soul as the Principle of Self-Movement.*

In the *Phaedrus*, which examines the relation of rhetoric or the art of eloquence to dialectic, that is, to the science of correct concept formation directed toward the *eidē* and the *idea* (the actual dialectical portion of this dialogue unquestionably belongs to a much later period than the first part), the static conception of the soul present in the *Phaedo* has already been overcome in principle. At the same time, both this dialogue and the *Symposium* once again bring the Socratic central focus in the formation of concepts strongly to the fore in their elaborately developed conception of *erōs* (love). This *erōs* performs the role of mediator between the visible cosmos and the world of the *eidē*, but it culminates in a vision that concentrates on the divine *idea* of the good and the beautiful.

The *Phaedrus* once again places meaningful emphasis on the Socratic demand with respect to self-knowledge.[1] It does this, furthermore, in a manner which makes it clear that Socrates conceives the selfhood in terms of the form motive of the religion of culture. Proof is offered that the soul is immortal, indestructible, and without origin on the ground that it is that which is eternally self-moving. Only that which moves itself never ceases to move, and this also forms the origin and beginning of motion for all that is moved externally by something else. The opposite of the eternally self-moving soul is the material body, which in itself is fixed and motionless and must therefore receive the impulse of motion from the soul. The action of the soul is present, therefore, wherever bodily motion appears in the cosmos. The beginning or origin of motion is transcendent to the realm of becoming, however, for the entire heavens and all coming into being would otherwise be doomed to come to rest and would never find something to bring it back into motion.[2] The influence of Anaxagoras, who denied to matter the principle of motion and ascribed it solely to the form-

---

1 See the previously cited utterance of Socrates in the *Phaedrus*, 230 A (page 120, note 1).

2 Plato, *Phaedrus*, 245 C to E (cap. 24) : Ψυχὴ πᾶσα ἀθάνατος. τὸ γὰρ ἀεικίνητον ἀθάνατον· τὸ δ'ἄλλο κινοῦν καὶ ὑπ' ἄλλου κινούμενον, παῦλαν ἔχον κινήσεως, παῦλαν ἔχει ζωῆς· μόνον δὴ τὸ αὐτὸ κινοῦν, ἅτ' οὐκ ἀπολεῖπον ἑαυτό, οὔ ποτε λήγει κινούμενον, ἀλλὰ καὶ τοῖς ἄλλοις ὅσα κινεῖται τοῦτο πηγὴ καὶ ἀρχὴ κινήσεως. ἀρχὴ δ' ἀγένητον. ἐξ ἀρχῆς γὰρ ἀνάγκη πᾶν τὸ γιγνόμενον γίγνεσθαι, αὐτὴν δὲ μηδ' ἐξ ἑνός· εἰ γὰρ ἔκ του ἀρχὴ γίγνοιτο, οὐκ ἂν <πᾶν> ἐξ ἀρχῆς

power of the divine *nous*, can be clearly discerned here.

The doctrine of the world-soul, which will return later in the *Philebus*[1] and will play a very important role in the *Timaeus*, where it is worked out at greater length, is already implicit in the *Phaedrus*. Just as the rational world-soul is the cause of the entire celestial motion in its subjection to measure and harmony, the individual rational soul is the cause of man's bodily movements. As the first cause and the inception of motion, both of these are fundamentally different from the unmoved, static *eidē*, and their kinship with the latter is no longer emphasized.

b.   The New Source of Difficulty in Plato's Conception of the Soul. The Dualism of the Form and Matter Principles Is Introduced into the Soul Itself. The Doctrine of the Tripartite (Trichotomous) Soul

This development gave rise to a new source of difficulty in Plato's thought, however. In the *Phaedo*, the multiplicity and diversity of the static ontic forms, which exist in themselves and mutually exclude one another, remained in true dialectical tension with the Socratic *idea* of the unity of the form principle in the divine *nous*, as the dynamic form-power of the good and the beautiful. Now, in the *Phaedrus*, the earlier doctrine concerning the simplicity and unity of the soul as a pure theoretical mental substance comes into open conflict with the new conception that the soul is the origin of all motion and that matter in itself is fixed and motionless.

The *nous* can be regarded as the origin only of the motion in the cosmos that has purpose and imparts form. It can never be the source of the chaotic, disorderly motion, which could never be permanently eliminated from the matter principle within the framework of the dialectical ground-motive of Greek thought. If then the soul is the origin of all motions in the cosmos, it can no longer be maintained as a purely thinking

---

γίγνοιτο ... οὕτω δὴ κινήσεως μὲν ἀρχὴ τὸ αὐτὸ αὑτὸ κινοῦν. τοῦτο δ᾽ οὔτ᾽ ἀπόλλυσθαι οὔτε γίγνεσθαι δυνατόν, ἢ πάντα τ᾽ οὐρανὸν πᾶσάν τε γένεσιν συμπεσοῦσαν στῆναι καὶ μήποτ᾽ αὖθις ἔχειν ὅθεν κινηθέντα γενήσεται. ("Every soul is immortal. For what is perpetually moved is immortal; that which moves something else and is moved by something else, however, ceases to live when its motion comes to rest. Only that which moves itself, inasmuch as it does not depart from itself, never stops its motion, but is for the other things that move the cause and origin of motion. But the Origin has not come into being. For everything that has come into being must necessarily come into being from the Origin, but it itself comes into being from nothing. For if the Origin came into being from something [else], then everything would not come into being from the Origin.... That which moves itself is thus the Origin of motion; but this can neither pass away nor come into being, since otherwise the whole heavens and all coming into being would collapse and stand still, and never find something to bring it back into motion.") This final passage can only have in view the "world-soul," which causes the celestial motion.

Editorial note – AW: Note that <πᾶν> is an editorial addition in the Didot edition (not found in current editions of Plato).

1   Plato, *Philebus*, 30 A ff.

form-substance; on the contrary, the dualism of the form and matter principles is bound to appear within the soul itself. As a consequence, it is no longer possible to maintain the simplicity of the soul.

Indeed, beginning with the *Phaedrus*, the doctrine appears that the soul is tripartite. This doctrine is then further developed in Plato's great dialogue the *Republic* in connection with his doctrine of the three classes in the ideal organization of the *polis* that is dedicated to the idea of justice. That the theory of the soul presented in the *Phaedrus* must have been formulated before that of the *Republic* and not after it, as, e.g., Ueberweg-Praechter maintain,[1] seems clear to me from the mere fact that, whereas the *Phaedrus* only adumbrates the new theory in mythological form, the *Republic* works it out in the transparent forms of *theōria*. There is no instance in Plato's works where he takes the mature form of a conception that has already been worked out theoretically and proceeds later to clothe it in the vague, merely allusive form of myth. Where this might seem to take place, the myth is at least immediately given a scientific explanation by means of *theōria* as it has further progressed during the interval.

Beginning with the *Phaedrus*, the *nous* is for Plato only the highest and noblest part of the soul, the *logistikon*, which in a normative sense leads and governs the other parts. It is opposed by the part which is the seat of sensual desire (the *epithumētikon*) and which is controlled as such by the blind matter principle with its lack of form and measure. Intermediate between these two antagonistic parts stands that part of the soul (the *thumo-eidēs*) which is always ready to follow the leadership of the *logistikon* and reacts in anger whenever sensual desire manages to get the upper hand.

c. The Myth of the Soul's Astral Journey

The *Phaedrus* portrays all of this in the beautiful myth of the soul's astral journey following the celestial gods, that is, the twelve celestial bodies known to Plato, which, according to him, are animated by divine spirits that move them in circles. In this mythological picture, the soul is compared with a team of two winged steeds inseparably joined to their driver. In the case of the celestial gods, both steeds are completely will-

---

1   I deliberately restrict this statement to the *Phaedrus'* theory of the soul and thus make no judgment as to the chronological position of this dialogue in its entirety. It is probably impossible to make such a judgment, since this dialogue, which has always been a stumbling block in the way of establishing the chronology of Plato's works, bears clear traces of a later revision of its original design. Thus, for example, the description of the task of dialectic in 265, 266, and 277 is directly related to the mature dialectical line of thought in the *Sophist*, the *Statesman*, and the *Philebus*, whereas the entire first section of the dialogue preserves some features that are clearly Socratic in origin. In addition, the conception of *erōs* is directly connected with the *Symposium*. Concerning the problem of chronology, cf. J. Stenzel, *op cit.*, p. 105. Stenzel's own notion that Plato did not write this dialogue until his final period, intending it as a continuous picture of the development of his thought since the Socratic period, hardly seems plausible to me. There are, in fact, a sufficient number of other dialogues that bear traces of later revision.

ing to obey the guidance of their driver, and the chariot is thus kept in balance without difficulty. In the case of the other souls (*daemones*), however, the two steeds are of different strains. The one is alert and of good stock, while the other is of bad stock and upsets the balance by attempting to pull the chariot down to earth. The journey of all the winged teams follows the harmonious, perfect, spherical motion of the heavens and ascends to the exterior side of the celestial vault. Here in the supra-heavenly realm (τὸν ὑπερουράνιον τόπον) of the eternal ontic forms, the immortal souls behold the "colorless, spatially figureless, impalpable, really existing ontic form" (ἀχρώματός τε καὶ ἀσχημάτιστος καὶ ἀναφὴς οὐσία ὄντως οὖσα),[1] but this can only happen if the soul is led by theoretical thought. For the celestial gods it is sufficient that they see these *eidē* (justice in itself, moderation in itself, knowledge in itself, etc.), free from the process of becoming in its connection with matter, only from time to time, namely, whenever their circuit carries them to the region beyond the heavens. Then they may return to the near side of the celestial vault. This vision is the thinking soul's eternal food, which nourishes its wings and causes them to grow.

Only for the steeds of the gods, however, is this ascent a complete success. Since in the case of human souls the inferior steed seeks to pull the chariot toward earth, the most that the driver can do, even under the most favorable circumstances, is to extend his head into the supra-heavenly realm. Thus the view of the eternal ontic forms largely escapes him. Every human soul has once beheld these *eidē*, however, and the recollection of this enables it to obtain true conceptual knowledge.[2] In the worst case, the soul's entire winged team remains below the celestial vault and feeds on sense images rather than on knowledge of being. Since the soul is then deprived of the nourishment for its wings required by its highest part, it falls to the earth and enters into an earthly material body. In accordance with what they have seen of the world of the *eidē*, the souls are implanted in categories of men distinguished as to value and vocation. Their fate after their bodily death is then determined by what they have done during their earthly existence, with the less worthy being assigned a reincarnation in the body of an animal and a later return to human form.[3]

d. *The Transformation of the Uranic Motives of Orphic Pythagorean Thought in the Theory of Ideas. The* Topos Hyperouranios *of the* Eidē

Two things strike one about this mythical portrayal of Plato's new conception of the soul. In the first place, uranic religious motives are adopted from Orphic-Pythagorean thought and, simultaneously, transformed in terms of the form motive of the theory of ideas. The world of the *eidē* is emphatically said to be located above and beyond the celestial vault in a τόπος ὑπερουράνιος. The souls whose vision remains

---

1   Plato, *Phaedrus*, 247 C.

2   *Ibid.*, 249 B and C.

3   *Ibid.*, 246 A to 249 C.

limited to the area within the celestial vault are deprived of the nourishment of the truly real ontic forms, and they are doomed to fall to earth.

e. The Orphic Dualism of Body and Soul Is Weakened in the Phaedrus

In the second place, one cannot fail to notice that the Orphic dualism between the thinking soul and the material body has been considerably weakened here. Socrates explicitly states that soul and body belong together in a living being.[1] In the immortal heavenly gods, soul and body are by nature united for all time, although Socrates cannot yet offer a theoretical reason for this.[2] It is only in mortal beings that the union between the soul and the material body is merely temporary. Not until the *Timaeus* will Plato attempt in a more precise way to offer a rationale for this basic difference between the earthly human body and the astral heavenly body. He points out the main reason, however, already in the *Phaedrus*. According to Plato, the heavenly bodies are always in orderly motion and move in a circle; and circular motion, as we have seen, was in the Greek view the perfect form of motion. This is an authentic Pythagorean notion, which we already encountered in Alcmaeon.

f. The Aporia of the Origin of the Matter Principle in the Soul. The Theory of the Phaedrus, the Timaeus, the Laws, and the Epinomis, and the Influence of Empedocles on the Latter

What, however, gives rise to the disorderly and unmeasured motions of the sensual feelings and passions in the *epithumētikon* (the appetitive part of the soul)? Surely, these cannot have their origin in the soul's principle of self-movement, for in the *Phaedrus* this is manifestly a form-giving principle. Obviously, they are tied up with the earthly material body. But how then can matter in itself be rigid and motionless?

The continuing influence of the matter principle, both within the human soul and in the entire sublunar region of the cosmos, thus requires a more precise explanation; but Plato does not offer one until the *Timaeus*. There, his only option will be to accept the presence of the ultimate dualism between the form and matter principles within the origin of motion itself. In spite of this, however, in his great dialogue the *Laws* (*Nomoi*) and in its supplement in the *Epinomis*, both of which were written after the *Timaeus*, he will return again to the theory of the *Phaedrus*, which holds

---

1   *Ibid.*, 246 D (cap. 25).

2   *Ibid.*, 246 C and D (cap. 25): ζῷον τὸ ξύμπαν ἐκλήθη, ψυχὴ καὶ σῶμα παγέν, θνητόν τ᾿ ἔσχεν ἐπωνυμίαν· ἀθάνατον δ᾿ οὐδ᾿ ἐξ ἑνὸς λόγου λελογισμένου, ἀλλὰ πλάττομεν οὔτ᾿ ἰδόντες οὔθ᾿ ἱκανῶς νοήσαντες θεόν, ἀθάνατόν τι ζῷον, ἔχον μὲν ψυχήν, ἔχον δὲ σῶμα, τὸν ἀεὶ δὲ χρόνον ταῦτα ξυμπεφυκότα. ("The whole, body and soul combined, is called a living being and is further termed mortal. We call the deity immortal, however, not on any particular well-reasoned basis, but we imagine it without having seen or adequately known it as an immortal living being, possessed of both a soul and a body that are by nature united for all time.")

that the soul is the exclusive origin of motion. As it is worked out there, however, this theory counterposes to the rational and good world-soul another that is irrational and evil. In other words, Plato accepts the existence of a double world-soul: a form-soul and a matter-soul, the former being the cause of the orderly motions and the latter being the cause of those that are disorderly and unmeasured. I have previously called attention to the influence of Empedocles on this late-Platonic theory.

In the *Phaedrus*, however, the polar dualism between the form and matter principles recedes into the background, although it does not actually disappear. Here the Socratic tendency to find the form-giving power of the divine *idea* of the *kalokagathon* throughout the entire cosmos clearly predominates over the dark Orphic-Pythagorean dualism between the earthly material body and the thinking soul-form. *Erōs*, which is directed toward this *idea* of the good and beautiful, serves as a mediator to reconcile sensible *physis* bound to the matter principle with the luminous form-world of the *eidē*.

This *erōs* conception had been developed at length especially in the *Symposium* (the *Banquet*), and it led there to an optimistic, aesthetically and ethically tinted life-and-world view which, in its typically Apollonian character, stands in polar opposition to the pessimistic *physis* conception of the *Phaedo*. These two distinct conceptions of *physis*, the pessimistic view of the *Phaedo*, and the optimistic one of the *Symposium* and the *Phaedrus*, which at first stand in contrast to each other without any inner connection, will soon be combined in Plato's thought and will eventually bring the theory of ideas to a critical stage.

According to the *Phaedrus*, *erōs* is a type of enthusiasm (μανία) that is aroused by the sight of the sensible adumbration of the eternal *eidos* of beauty in material bodies. This awakens within the soul the recollection (*anamnēsis*) of the radiant ontic form of beauty that it has beheld in its pre-existent state. Among all the *eidē*, only beauty in its sensible adumbration has a luster which in its clarity can be apprehended through sight, the clearest of our senses.[1]

This *erōs* causes the wings of the soul to sprout anew. Separation from the sensible image of beauty results in a painful state in which the growth impulse of the wings is checked. One who is ruled by *erōs* longs for the most intimate union with the beloved ideal of beauty. In this situation, the

---

1 Plato, *Phaedrus*, 250 D (cap. 31): περὶ δὲ κάλλους, ὥσπερ εἴπομεν, μετ᾽ ἐκείνων τ᾽ ἔλαμπεν ἰόν, δεῦρό τ᾽ ἐλθόντες κατειλήφαμεν αὐτὸ διὰ τῆς ἐναργεστάτης αἰσθήσεως τῶν ἡμετέρων στίλβον ἐναργέστατα. ὄψις γὰρ ἡμῖν ὀξυτάτη τῶν διὰ τοῦ σώματος ἔρχεται αἰσθήσεων, ᾗ φρόνησις οὐχ ὁρᾶται. ("With regard to beauty, as we said, it shone forth as one among these [eternal ontic forms]; but when we came to this point, we apprehended it, shining most clearly, with the clearest of our senses. For sight seems to us the keenest of the sense perceptions that take place by way of the body, though we do not behold thought with it.")

inferior steed (the appetitive part of the soul), turning against the leadership of *nous* and the better steed that obeys it (the *thumoeidēs*), drives the soul to look for satisfaction in the enjoyment of sensual love and thus fills it with discord. Since beauty also works on the beloved and is answered there as an echo, it arouses an equal longing and the same inner discord and strife within the latter.

If this conflict within the two is brought to rest in an ordered relationship in subjection to the theoretical thought function, *erōs* is "intellectualized" into theoretical or philosophical love for the eternal world of the *eidē*. And since the *eidos* of beauty itself is only fulfilled in the divine *idea* of the good, which is one with beauty, *erōs* then leads to the true ethical-religious manner of life. Such a life makes the philosopher like God, for therein he constantly dwells near to the *eidē* in recollection.[1] Through the self-control and moderation (σωφροσύνη) that it involves, it also grants him true bliss and allows his soul to recover full possession of its wings before the completion of the great astral year (10,000 solar years), more precisely, after a mere 3,000 years, in which it has three times in succession chosen the same manner of life.[2]

In Plato's famed *Symposium*, the Socratic central religious focus that is inherent in this *erōs* is elaborated in even more pregnant fashion. There, the polar tensions between the static *eidē*, on the one hand, and the divine *idea*, on the other hand, and also between the supraterrestrial form principle and the earthly, physical matter principle, are seemingly annulled in a higher synthesis. At the banquet of the acclaimed poet Agathon, after the other guests have sung the praises of love, Socrates delivers the final speech and relates what the prophetess Diotima has revealed to him concerning *erōs*. He begins by observing, in connection with a motif that has already been developed in the Socratic dialogue the *Lysis*, that *erōs* stands between the good and the evil, the immortal and the mortal, the beautiful

---

1   *Ibid.*, 249 C (cap. 29): διὸ δὴ δικαίως μόνη πτεροῦται ἡ τοῦ φιλοσόφου διάνοια· πρὸς γὰρ ἐκείνοις ἀεί ἐστι μνήμῃ κατὰ δύναμιν, πρὸς οἷσπερ ὁ θεὸς ὢν θεῖός ἐστι. ("Therefore it is right that the soul of the philosopher alone is given wings. For he, as much as he is able, always dwells near to memory to those things whose nearness makes the deity divine.")

2   *Ibid.*, 248 E and 249 A (cap. 29): Εἰς μὲν γὰρ ταὐτό, ὅθεν ἥκει ἡ ψυχὴ ἑκάστη, οὐκ ἀφικνεῖται ἐτῶν μυρίων· οὐ γὰρ πτεροῦται πρὸ τοσούτου χρόνου, πλὴν ἡ τοῦ φιλοσοφήσαντος ἀδόλως ἢ παιδεραστήσαντος μετὰ φιλοσοφίας· αὗται δὲ τρίτῃ περιόδῳ τῇ χιλιετεῖ, ἐὰν ἕλωνται τρὶς ἐφεξῆς τὸν βίον τοῦτον, οὕτω πτερωθεῖσαι τρισχιλιοστῷ ἔτει ἀπέρχονται. ("For to the place whence it came a soul does not return for ten thousand years; for before this length of time it cannot obtain wings, except for the [souls] of the philosophers or of those who in a philosophical manner practice pederasty; these, at the third cycle of a thousand years, if they have chosen the same manner of life three times in succession, are thereby provided with wings and depart thence in the three thousandth year.")

and the ugly, the wise and the foolish.[1] *Erōs* is not a god but a *daemon*, a divine impulse of the soul that inspires a person to pursue philosophy, just because it neither yet possesses wisdom nor is it ignorant. In a personification, it itself is called the "philosopher."[2] *Erōs* impels *theōria* toward the vision of the *eidos* of beauty in itself, a vision that is centered, however, on the divine *idea* in which the good and the beautiful have their indivisible original unity. This theoretical concentrating proceeds by way of a step-by-step ascent. The first step is from sensible material beauty, which beams upon us from certain beautiful bodies, to the sensible beauty of all bodies. The next step is beautiful practices or activities; and the step following it is the beauty of the sciences, in particular, mathematics and astronomy. At the end stands philosophical knowledge of the eternal *eidos* of beauty, in its central focus upon the divine form-power of the good and the beautiful. Here the ascent finds its fulfilment.[3]

Erōs thus leads by way of *theōria* to the true ethical-religious manner of life. For, as Julius Stenzel has expressed it in one of his studies of Plato, the idea of the good (*idea tou agathou*), as the highest cause and end of human endeavor, "simultaneously elucidates the actual meaning of absolute beauty in the *Symposium* and therewith the meaning of Plato's *erōs* doctrine."[4] The Apollonian form motive of the religion of culture in the deepened form given it by Socrates seems here indeed to have completely penetrated the Platonic theory of ideas.

It is worthy of note that in Hesiod's theogony *erōs* is the driving force in

---

1   Plato, *Symposium*, 204 (cap. 28).

2   *Symposium*, 204 B (cap. 28): ἔστι γὰρ δὴ τῶν καλλίστων ἡ σοφία, Ἔρως δ᾽ ἐστὶν ἔρως περὶ τὸ καλόν, ὥστ᾽ ἀναγκαῖον Ἔρωτα φιλόσοφον εἶναι, φιλόσοφον δ᾽ ὄντα μεταξὺ εἶναι σοφοῦ καὶ ἀμαθοῦς". ("For wisdom surely belongs among the most beautiful things; but Eros is love directed toward the beautiful; and thus, of necessity, Eros must be a philosopher; but in being a lover of wisdom, he stands between the wise and the ignorant.")

3   *Ibid.*, 211 B and C (cap. 29): τοῦτο γὰρ δή ἐστι τὸ ὀρθῶς ἐπὶ τὰ ἐρωτικὰ ἰέναι ἢ ὑπ᾽ ἄλλου ἄγεσθαι, ἀρχόμενον ἀπὸ τῶνδε τῶν καλῶν ἐκείνου ἕνεκα τοῦ καλοῦ ἀεὶ ἐπανιέναι, ὥσπερ ἐπαναβαθμοῖς χρώμενον, ἀφ᾽ ἑνὸς ἐπὶ δύο καὶ ἀπὸ δυεῖν ἐπὶ πάντα τὰ καλὰ σώματα, καὶ ἀπὸ τῶν καλῶν σωμάτων ἐπὶ τὰ καλὰ ἐπιτηδεύματα, καὶ ἀπὸ τῶν καλῶν ἐπιτηδευμάτων ἐπὶ τὰ καλὰ μαθήματα, ἔστ᾽ ἂν ἀπὸ τῶν μαθημάτων ἐπ᾽ ἐκεῖνο τὸ μάθημα τελευτήσῃ, ὅ ἐστιν οὐκ ἄλλου ἢ αὐτοῦ ἐκείνου τοῦ καλοῦ μάθημα, καὶ γνῷ αὐτὸ τελευτῶν ὃ ἔστι καλόν. ("For surely this is the right way to love, which one must take or be led upon by another, that for the sake of that primal beauty, one climbs from these beautiful things ever upward, step by step, from one to two, and from two to all beautiful bodies; and from bodily beauty on to beautiful practices, from beautiful practices to beautiful sciences, until one finally raises himself from the other sciences to that science which is the knowledge of nothing other than the primal beauty, and one at last knows what the beautiful itself is.") This *idea* of the beautiful is also called καλὸν κἀγαθόν (cf. 204 A).

4   "...erläutert zugleich den eigentlichen Sinn des absoluten Schönen im Symposion und damit den Sinn der platonischen Erotik" (Stenzel, *op. cit.*, pp. 17-18). (English translation by translator.)

the development from chaos to cosmos, conceived in the form of sexual procreation, a notion of which Plato also makes use. According to Socrates, *erōs* even at its lowest sensual level strives to "bring forth in beauty," in order that the perishable image of beauty in the individual body may attain a certain immortality in its progeny. Far above this sensual, sexual propagation, however, stands the intellectual or cultural-political propagation of good notions in one's fellow citizens, and the highest of all is the propagation of intellectual knowledge in one's youthful lovers through philosophical formation, directed toward the world of eternal ontic forms, and its central unity in the divine *idea*.

Nevertheless, the synthesis that Plato sought to achieve in the *Symposium* and the *Phaedrus* with the conception of *erōs* was only a seeming one. This conception, which also had a darker side in Plato's concessions to the common Greek vice of pederasty, did not truly raise *theōria* above the polar dualism of the Greek ground-motive. *Erōs* is not a higher principle of origin standing above the form principle and the matter principle; rather, it only mediates between them. It is itself driven by the discord between these two antagonistic ground-motives from the one pole to the other. In these two dialogues, furthermore, the inner tension between the static world of the *eidē* and the divine *idea* of the good and beautiful is also not satisfactorily overcome. The mutual relationship between the *eidē* is left completely in the dark. That the *eidē* have a central reference to the divine *idea* is in fact implicitly assumed; but it is not yet explicated theoretically. In addition, the basic problem of the Platonic theory of ideas which I formulated earlier, namely, whether the *eidē* themselves derive their being from this divine *idea* of the *kalokagathon*, is passed over without comment. This problem will not be explicitly confronted and solved until that section of the *Republic* which was drafted later, but even there the solution will not prove to be definitive.

3. **The Reconciliation of the Static and the Dynamic Form Motive in the *Republic* (Books II-X). The Socratic Idea as the Origin of the *Eidē***

In books II through X of the *Republic*, the theory of ideas is placed in relation to the *polis*, as the center of Greek life. The *polis*, as the bearer of the religion of culture, thereby again takes the central position in Plato's thought that it had occupied from the very beginning, as is clear from his seventh letter. Further, it is precisely through its being applied to the organization of the *polis* that this theory receives its most far-reaching application to all areas of life. For, as the vehicle of the culture religion, the *polis* is simultaneously the earthly vehicle of the form principle, which governs this religion. *Paideia*, in the sense of the forming of the free Greek into a citizen, meant for the popular Greek mind of classical times, and for Plato as well, the cultural formation of a person in all areas of life. Indeed, according to this view, the *polis* is the all-encompassing sphere of human society, which lays claim to all terrains of human life. The notion that each distinct component of society possesses a sovereignty in its own sphere that is rooted in its internal nature and created structure, a view that arose only from the ground-motive of the Christian religion, is completely foreign to the world of classical antiquity.

In the present context, my inquiry is concerned only with the dialectical development of Plato's theory of ideas in its intimate association with the development of his anthropological views. Thus the wealth of other material in this important dialogue, which indeed would demand separate treatment, will have to be largely passed over.

In the first book of the *Republic*, which belongs to Plato's early period, the subject of inquiry was the virtue of justice; and, as had been the case with all of the Socratic dialogues from this period, the discussion did not arrive at a conclusive concept. In books II through X, this problem is taken up once again. Here justice is placed within the framework of the theory of ideas as it had matured during the interim. It is examined primarily as it is manifested in the ideal organization of the *polis* that conforms to the *eidos* of justice. Both individual ethics and the conception of the human soul are viewed entirely within the context of this idea of the state. The course of Plato's argument here is too well-known to require an elaborate summary; I shall detail only those points that are important for our own discussion.

Following an exposition of the origin and development of the state, which in its attempt to derive the state from totally different societal forms evinces a fundamental lack of insight into the internal structures of the differentiated societal spheres, Plato attempts to give a plausible account of the gradual formation of three distinct classes of citizens, each with a particular calling. These, in their mutual division of labor, provide for the communal needs of the whole.

The oldest class is that which attends to the elemental economic needs of food, housing, clothing, etc. When cultural development causes the above needs to grow and requires an extension of the state's territory, the continual conflicts with neighboring peoples that ensue make necessary the formation of a military class, and the best members of this are recruited to form the class of rulers. There are thus three vocational classes: the farmers and craftsmen (γεωργικοὶ καὶ δημιουργικοί), who have to provide for the needs of the other classes; the guardians (προπολεμοῦντες), who as helpers of the rulers are also called ἐπίκουροι; and the complete guardians or rulers (φύλακες παντελεῖς or ἄρχοντες). Within the *polis*, justice consists of τὰ αὑτοῦ πράττειν (*ta hautou prattein*), according to which each class devotes itself to its own task and only to this, and the strictest division of labor is thus observed in maintaining the separate vocational classes. Plato seeks the criterion for membership in these classes in a person's natural aptitude, and the distinct degree of formative education that the *polis* should provide in each case corresponds to this aptitude.

In order that it may properly carry out its military duties, the second class is to be formed by means of a combined education in gymnastics and music (the latter taken in a broad sense which also includes the study of works of poetry), and since the soul should rule the body, music is given the leading role in this educational process. For the class of rulers, the schooling in music and gymnastics is only propadeutic and is followed by a scientific education that involves the mathematical sciences (including astronomy and the theory of harmony) first of all, and concludes with the study of dialectic, the science of the *eidē*. The aim of this is to make the rulers into nothing less than philosophers, who alone possess knowledge of the truth.[1] If the philosophers do not become kings, or the kings do not become philosophers, there will be no end of disaster in the life of the state and in human life in general.[2] But lest their introduction to the theory of ideas remove them from daily life and leave them without practical skill for conducting the affairs of state, the future rulers' scientific training is interrupted between the ages of 35 and 50 by a period of work in both military and civilian offices, and only after this is their education completed with the *theōria* of the *idea* of the good. Here we have approached the mature conception of the theory of ideas in this stage of Plato's thought.

This conception from the outset places the *idea tou agathou*, the *idea* of the good, at the center of interest, and the centrally focused vision of this divine *idea* comes to be regarded as the actual fulfillment of theoretical knowledge of the *eidē*. A lack of insight into the pregnant sense of *idea* in Plato's theory of ideas has given rise to much misunderstanding in the literature with respect to his exposition of this theory in the sixth and seventh books. In a close examination of the relevant texts, we must pay special attention, therefore, to Plato's exposition here of the relationship between *eidē* and *idea*.

In the course of his detailed investigations, Plato examines the *eidos* of justice and those of the three other so-called cardinal virtues of Greek morality (fortitude, temperance, and prudence) with reference to the three classes of the ideal state and the three parts of the soul. In the sixth book, however, his discussion begins to probe deeper by bringing the idea of the *good* under consideration. Socrates argues that knowledge of this *idea* is the most important and all-controlling knowledge, since it is only through the application of it that the other virtues become useful and beneficial. If the central knowledge of this *idea* is lacking, it avails a person nothing to know everything else very well, just as there is no profit in the possession of anything apart from the good.[3] Although many persons prefer what only seems to be beautiful and just, mistaking the semblance for the real-

---

1   Plato, *Republic*, 484 B ff.

2   *Ibid.*, 473 d.

3   Plato, *Ibid.*, 505 a: Ἐπεὶ ὅτι γε ἡ τοῦ ἀγαθοῦ ἰδέα μέγιστον μάθημα, πολλάκις ἀκήκοας, ᾗ δίκαια καὶ τἆλλα προσχρησάμενα χρήσιμα καὶ ὠφέλιμα γίγνεται. ... εἰ δὲ μὴ ἴσμεν, ἄνευ δὲ ταύτης εἰ ὅτι μάλιστα τἆλλα ἐπισταίμεθα, οἶσθ᾽, ὅτι

ity, with respect to the good no one can be content with the possession of the mere semblance, since here *being* is all-important.[1] If those who are destined to become rulers of the *polis* thus do not know to what extent the beautiful and the just are good, these *eidē* [viz., of beauty and justice] will not have made them into good guardians. For without knowing this, no one can have a sufficient knowledge of the beautiful and the just.[2] It is only as one concentrates his vision of these *eidē* on the divine *idea* that he gains a synopsis of beauty and justice, that is, an *idea* in a subjective, epistemological sense.[3]

a. The Divine Idea of the Good Is Transcendent to the Realm of the Ontic Forms (Ousiai)

When he is asked what the highest good is in itself, however, Socrates replies that he is powerless to define it in a concept, although he had not refused to do this with respect to the *eidē* proper (justice, fortitude, etc.). Instead, he resorts to a comparison taken from the realm of phenomena

οὐδὲν ἡμῖν ὄφελος, ὥσπερ οὐδ᾽ εἰ κεκτήμεθά τι ἄνευ τοῦ ἀγαθοῦ. ἢ οἴει τι πλέον εἶναι πᾶσαν κτῆσιν ἐκτῆσθαι, μὴ μέντοι ἀγαθήν; ("For you have often heard that the most important knowledge is the *idea* of the good, by the application of which justice and the other virtues become useful and beneficial.... But if we do not know it, you are aware that without this, even if we were to know everything else very well, it would profit us nothing, as little as if we should possess all things except the good.")

1 *Ibid.*, 505 D: τόδε οὐ φανερόν, ὡς δίκαια μὲν καὶ καλὰ πολλοὶ ἂν ἕλοιντο τὰ δοκοῦντα, κἂν μὴ ᾖ, ὅμως ταῦτα πράττειν καὶ κεκτῆσθαι καὶ δοκεῖν, ἀγαθὰ δὲ οὐδενὶ ἔτι ἀρκεῖ τὰ δοκοῦντα κτᾶσθαι, ἀλλὰ τὰ ὄντα ζητοῦσι, τὴν δὲ δόξαν ἐνταῦθα ἤδη πᾶς ἀτιμάζει; ("Is it not evident that many would prefer what seems beautiful and just, and even the semblance, although to do and to possess them in this way would be illusory; yet that with respect to the good no one is any longer content to possess what seems good, but they seek what *is* good and all despise the semblance here?")

2 *Ibid.*, 506 A: Οἶμαι γοῦν, εἶπον, δίκαιά τε καὶ καλὰ ἀγνοούμενα ὅπη ποτὲ ἀγαθά ἐστιν, οὐ πολλοῦ τινος ἄξιον φύλακα κεκτῆσθαι ἂν ἑαυτῶν τὸν τοῦτο ἀγνοοῦντα· μαντεύομαι δὲ μηδένα αὐτὰ πρότερον γνώσεσθαι ἱκανῶς. ("I at any rate believe, so I continued, that the just and the beautiful, if it is not known to what extent they are good, will not have secured a very fit guardian in one who does not know this. I suspect that before this no one will know them [the just and the beautiful] adequately.")

3 *Ibid.*, 507 B: Πολλὰ καλά, ἦν δ᾽ ἐγώ, καὶ πολλὰ ἀγαθὰ καὶ ἕκαστα οὕτως εἶναί φαμέν τε καὶ διορίζομεν τῷ λόγῳ. ...Καὶ αὐτὸ δὴ καλὸν καὶ αὐτὸ ἀγαθὸν καὶ οὕτω περὶ πάντων ἃ τότε ὡς πολλὰ ἐτίθεμεν, πάλιν αὖ κατ᾽ ἰδέαν μίαν ἑκάστου ὡς μιᾶς οὔσης τιθέντες ὃ ἔστιν ἕκαστον προσαγορεύομεν. ("We say and determine in our reasoning that much exists that is beautiful, and much that is good, and similarly for everything ... On the other hand, we once again consider the beautiful in itself and the good in itself, and similarly with regard to everything which we formerly posited as a multiplicity, according to the single idea of each of [these] we take them for what they [in truth] are.")

accessible to sense perception, namely, the sun in its relation to both the faculty of sight and visible objects. The sun, he says, has sprung from the divine *idea* of the good and beautiful, as that which corresponds to it in the visible realm.[1]

The eye is able to see objects only by means of light. The faculty of sight is not itself the sun, nor is it the eye, the sense organ with which we see. But as the most "sunlike" of all the sense organs, the eye owes to the sun its power of sight, as something that is beamed upon it from the sun's fullness. The same position that the sun, as a "celestial god," holds within the realm of the visible with respect to the eye's power of sight and the objects that can be seen by the eye, which are only made visible by the sun, is held within the intelligible realm of the eternal ontic forms, which is accessible only to theoretical thought, by the divine *idea* of the good with respect to the faculty of thought and the *eidē* that are its objects.

"Grant, therefore, that it is the *idea* of the good that lends truth to the objects of knowledge and the power of knowing the truth to the knower; think of it as the cause (*aitia*) of knowledge and of truth, and also of the object of knowledge; and if – although these two, knowledge and truth, are already so beautiful – you suppose it to be something still more beautiful than these, then you will think rightly."[2]

When Glaucon shows some surprise at this supreme beauty ascribed to the idea of the good, Socrates explains further: "You will, I think grant that the sun imparts to that which is seen not only the power of being visible, but also generation, growth, and nourishment, although the sun is not itself generation.... Grant then also that through the *idea* of the good the objects of knowledge not only receive their being known, but that also their being and their ontic form (*ousia*) comes to them from it, although the good itself is not an *ousia*, but in dignity and form-power (*dunamis*) is exalted even above the ontic form (*ousia*)."[3]

In their mutual relation, these passages admit of only one interpretation.

---

1 *Ibid.*, 506 E: ὃς δὲ ἔκγονός τε τοῦ ἀγαθοῦ φαίνεται καὶ ὁμοιότατος ἐκείνῳ, λέγειν ἐθέλω ("But what seems to me an offspring of the good and very much like it, this I will tell you.") It is clear from what follows that this is a reference to the sun as a "celestial god."

2 *Ibid.*, 508 E: Τοῦτο τοίνυν τὸ τὴν ἀλήθειαν παρέχον τοῖς γιγνωσκομένοις καὶ τῷ γιγνώσκοντι τὴν δύναμιν ἀποδιδὸν τὴν τοῦ ἀγαθοῦ ἰδέαν φάθι εἶναι, αἰτίαν δ' ἐπιστήμης οὖσαν καὶ ἀληθείας ὡς γιγνωσκομένης μὲν διανοοῦ, οὕτω δὲ καλῶν ἀμφοτέρων ὄντων, γνώσεώς τε καὶ ἀληθείας, ἄλλο καὶ κάλλιον ἔτι τούτων ἡγούμενος αὐτὸ ὀρθῶς ἡγήσει. (translation in the text).

3 *Ibid.*, 509 B (end of cap. 19): Τὸν ἥλιον τοῖς ὁρωμένοις οὐ μόνον, οἶμαι, τὴν τοῦ ὁρᾶσθαι δύναμιν παρέχειν φήσεις, ἀλλὰ καὶ τὴν γένεσιν καὶ αὔξην καὶ τροφήν, οὐ γένεσιν αὐτὸν ὄντα. ... καὶ τοῖς γιγνωσκομένοις τοίνυν μὴ μόνον τὸ γιγνώσκεσθαι φάναι ὑπὸ τοῦ ἀγαθοῦ παρεῖναι, ἀλλὰ καὶ τὸ εἶναί τε καὶ τὴν οὐσίαν ὑπ' ἐκείνου αὐτοῖς προσεῖναι, οὐκ οὐσίας ὄντος τοῦ ἀγαθοῦ, ἀλλ' ἔτι ἐπέκεινα τῆς οὐσίας πρεσβείᾳ καὶ δυνάμει ὑπερέχοντος. ("You will, I think, grant that the sun imparts to the things that are seen not only their power of being

The divine *idea* of the good, to which the highest degree of beauty is ascribed, is explicitly declared to be transcendent to the intelligible realm of the eternal ontic forms, which are here grouped under the general term *ousiai*. The aim of true knowledge is to regard the *eidē* in the light of the divine *idea* and thus to gain an *idea*, a synopsis, of each *eidos* which first makes it fully known (an *idea* of justice, an *idea* of beauty, etc.).[1] The being and essence of the *eidē* are unambiguously derived from the divine *idea* as their origin.

b.   Through Its Idea, *the Divine Nous Is the Origin of the* Eidē

In the tenth book of the Republic,[2] the veil of mystery that has remained hanging over the divine idea of the good is at last fully lifted. Here the discussion leader emphatically argues that the *eidos* of a cultural object such as a couch is not produced by the human craftsman (δημιουργός), who creates only a representation of the *eidos*, but by the divine master workman (θεός). This *eidos* or imperishable ontic form of the couch is called "the couch in the 'nature' of its being" (ἡ ἐν τῇ φύσει οὖσα),[3] and the Eleatic conception of *physis*, in which *physis* is absorbed into the all-encompassing oneness of the unmoved divine form of being, is thereby completely penetrated by the Socratic form motive of the culture religion stemming from Anaxagoras.

There can be no doubt that the term θεός must be understood here in the monotheistic sense of Anaxagoras, namely, as the divine *nous*, conceived

---

visible, but also generation, growth, and nourishment, although it is not itself generation..... Grant therefore also that through the Good the known [ontic forms] not only receive their being known, but that also their being and their ontic form come to them from the same, although the good is not an ontic form, but in its dignity and form-power is exalted even above the latter.") *Ousia* here can only mean ontic or essential form, since a distinction is made between *ousia* and *einai* (being).

1   *Ibid.*, 507 B.

2   *Ibid.*, 596 ff.

3   *Ibid.*, 597 A: *Τί δὲ ὁ κλινοποιός; οὐκ ἄρτι μέντοι ἔλεγες, ὅτι οὐ τὸ εἶδος ποιεῖ, ὃ δή φαμεν εἶναι ὃ ἔστι κλίνη, ἀλλὰ κλίνην τινά;* ("But what of the maker of couches? Did you not just say that he does not make the *eidos* that we call the couch in its true ontic form, but only a particular couch?") *Ibid.*, 597 B: *Οὐκοῦν τριτταί τινες κλῖναι αὗται γίγνονται· μία μὲν ἡ ἐν τῇ φύσει οὖσα, ἣν φαῖμεν ἄν, ὡς ἐγῷμαι, θεὸν ἐργάσασθαι. ... Μία δέ γε, ἣν ὁ τέκτων. ... Μία δέ, ἣν ὁ ζωγράφος.* ("Therefore we get these three [kinds of] couches: one which by its nature is that which I believe we may say is produced by god... one that is the product of the craftsman... one that is the product of the painter [who makes an artistic representation of the couch produced by the craftsman].") *Ibid.*, 597 C: *Ὁ μὲν δὴ θεός, εἴτε οὐκ ἐβούλετο, εἴτε τις ἀνάγκη ἐπῆν μὴ πλέον ἢ μίαν ἐν τῇ φύσει ἀπεργάσασθαι αὐτὸν κλίνην, οὕτως ἐποίησεν μίαν μόνον αὐτὴν ἐκείνην ὃ ἔστι κλίνη· δύο δὲ τοιαῦται ἢ πλείους οὔτε ἐφυτεύθησαν ὑπὸ τοῦ θεοῦ οὔτε μὴ φύωσιν.* ("Now god, either by choice or because he was under some necessity to make but one couch in its natural essence, thus produced only one, viz., that couch which is that by its [natural] being [ontic form]; two or more of this nature were neither made by god, nor could have been made by him.")

as the demiurge or form-giving origin. For the celestial gods (θεοὶ οὐράνιοι) are definitely out of the picture here. Indeed, in the passage cited earlier from the sixth book, they are themselves called a product of the *idea tou agathou*, and in the tenth book,[1] it is said that the "divine master workman" not only can produce all cultural objects, but that he also makes everything that grows on the earth and all that has life, and furthermore, earth and heaven and the gods, and all things in the heavens and under the earth in Hades, i.e., *Aïdēs* ('the invisible realm').[2] If this is the case, however, the *idea tou agathou* can have its seat only in the divine *nous*. It is the central, primal form of the divine mind, the form serving as the origin of the entire intelligible world of the *eidē*.

It does not follow that the *eidē* subsist only within the divine *nous* along with the *idea tou agathou*. This is a later neo-Platonic interpretation that finds no support in the *Republic*. The *eidē* constitute a realm of quiescent ontic forms, which are the imperishable primal models for the things having form in the world of sense. They are, however, also a product of the dynamic activity of the form-giving *idea* in the divine *nous*, an extrapolation from the one *idea* which embraces all ontic form from its very center.

In this way Plato arrived at a provisional solution of one of the most pressing problems of the theory of ideas. The Socratic line of thought has won a decisive victory over the Eleatic-Pythagorean influence.

*c. The Conception of the Idea of the Good as the Highest
  Member of the Realm of the* Eidē *Is Incorrect*

The interpretation is untenable, therefore, which holds that this conception proclaims the *idea* of the good to be the highest member of the realm of the *eidē*.[3] The *Republic* has no realm of intelligible *ideai;* it only has one of eternal ontic forms. And besides the *eidē*, furthermore, this realm includes nothing but non-sensible mathematical forms. The *idea tou agathou* does not itself belong to this intelligible realm and is

---

1 *Ibid.*, 596 C.

2 *Ibid.*, 596 B and C (Book X) : Ἀλλ' ὅρα δὴ καὶ τόνδε τίνα καλεῖς τὸν δημιουργόν. Τὸν ποῖον; Ὃς πάντα ποιεῖ ὅσαπερ εἷς ἕκαστος τῶν χειροτεχνῶν. Δεινόν τινα λέγεις καὶ θαυμαστὸν ἄνδρα. Οὔπω γε, ἀλλὰ τάχα μᾶλλον φήσεις. ὁ αὐτὸς γὰρ οὗτος χειροτέχνης οὐ μόνον πάντα οἷός τε σκεύη ποιῆσαι, ἀλλὰ καὶ τὰ ἐκ τῆς γῆς φυόμενα ἅπαντα ποιεῖ καὶ ζῷα πάντα ἐργάζεται, τά τε ἄλλα καὶ ἑαυτόν, καὶ πρὸς τούτοις γῆν καὶ οὐρανὸν καὶ θεοὺς καὶ πάντα τὰ ἐν οὐρανῷ καὶ τὰ ἐν Ἅδου ὑπὸ γῆς ἅπαντα ἐργάζεται. ("But consider now what name you would give to the Master Workman. Which one? He who makes all the things that each of the craftsmen [produces]. You speak of a very extraordinary and admirable man! Wait a moment, you will soon call him that even more. For this Master Workman is not only able to make all implements, but he also makes everything that sprouts from the earth and produces all that lives, both other things and himself, and in addition earth and sky and gods and everything in the heavens and everything in Hades under the earth.") In this passage, as in the *Phaedo*, Hades is called *Aïdēs*, the invisible realm, which is here understood as the realm of the *eidē*.

3 *Cf.*, e.g. Ueberweg-Praechter, *op. cit*, I (12th ed.), pp. 271-272.

therefore not the object (*Gegenstand*) of a logical concept. It is rather the origin of all ontic forms equally, just as the sun is the origin of the birth and growth of living organisms in the visible world subject to the matter principle.

d. The Epistemological Significance of the Idea

Plato then at once turns, at the close of the sixth book, to work out the epistemological implications of the insight he has gained. There are, he says, two realms. The first is the visible realm (ὁρατὸν γένος) or the realm of becoming (γένεσις). The principle that gives form to this realm resides in the sun (conceived as a celestial god), but the latter owes its origin to the *idea* of the good in the divine *nous*, which Socrates had called the demiurge of the sense organs (τὸν τῶν αἰσθήσεων δημιουργόν).[1] The second is the intelligible realm (νοητὸν γένος), or the realm of the *ousia* or true being. The origin of being in this realm is found in the divine *idea* of the good.

The first realm includes, on its higher level, all natural, visible living beings and all products of human culture; while, on its lower level, it includes the shadows and the reflections of these visible objects in water and upon dense, smooth, clear surfaces. Corresponding in human knowledge to this sensible realm of becoming is *doxa* or opinion, which with respect to sensible objects themselves is manifest as πίστις (belief), and with respect to their shadows and reflections, which have a lesser degree of clarity, is manifest as less certain εἰκασία (literally, the observation of images).[2]

e. The Idea of the Good as the An-hypotheton of Dialectic.
Dianoia and Epistēmē in Their Mutual Relation

Within the second, intelligible realm of the *ousia*, the lower level is assigned to the objects (*Gegenstände*) of mathematical science. The mathematician has to make use of figures perceptible to the senses as images of the nonsensible mathematical ontic forms, and with these sensible images he develops and illustrates his propositions. In so doing, he proceeds from postulates (*hypotheseis*) such as even and odd, straight and crooked, and the angles, and without rendering a theoretical account of these hypotheses by tracking down their ground and cause, he deduces from them his propositions and proofs. His method of investigation moves, therefore, from above to below. It is a method *ex hypothesi*, a hypothetical method, which is directed not toward the *archē* or origin of being, but toward the τελευτή, the end result. The higher level in the realm of the *ousia* is occupied by the *eidē* or ontic forms (Plato here speaks explicitly of *eidē*, not of *ideai*).[3]

Within human knowledge, διάνοια or scientific understanding corre-

---

1 *Ibid.*, 507 C.
2 *Ibid.*, 509 D and E.
3 *Ibid.*, 510 B: Σκόπει δὴ αὖ καὶ τὴν τοῦ νοητοῦ τομὴν ᾗ τμητέον. Πῇ; Ἦ τὸ μὲν αὐτοῦ τοῖς τότε τμηθεῖσιν ὡς εἰκόσι χρωμένη ψυχὴ ζητεῖν ἀναγκάζεται ἐξ ὑποθέσεων οὐκ ἐπ᾽ ἀρχὴν πορευομένη, ἀλλ᾽ ἐπὶ τελευτήν, τὸ δ᾽ αὖ ἕτερον τὸ ἐπ᾽

sponds to the mathematical ontic forms, while *νόησις* in its narrower sense, or *ἐπιστήμη* (here best translated as rational knowledge), corresponds to the *eidē*. Without having to take recourse to the perceptual aid of visible forms, the latter ascends from the *hypothesis* to the *an-hypotheton*, the absolute Origin. Both types of knowledge, *dianoia* and *epistēmē* (or *noēsis* in the narrower sense), are comprised under the broader term *noēsis* and are contrasted with *doxa*.

Within this entire epistemological exposition, found at the end of the sixth book, the following utterance of Socrates is particularly striking: "Understand then, that by the other section of the *noēton* I mean that which logical thought itself apprehends by means of the *dunamis* of dialectic, in that it treats its hypotheses not as principles of origin, but as actual hypothesis, steps and stimulants that enable it to proceed to the absolute [*an-hypotheton*], the origin of all, and having taken hold of this, by again fastening on to that [viz., the *eidē*] which is fastened to this absolute, so to descend to the latter [viz., the *eidē*], not making use of any sense perception, but grasping the *eidē* themselves through themselves and ending with them."[1]

This passage once again confirms what Socrates has already observed earlier, namely, that dialectic, the knowledge of the *eidē* by means of logical thought, should proceed from the divine *idea* of the good as the *an-hypotheton*, in order to apprehend from there the *eidē* in their divine origin and thus to behold them fully in their particular ontic forms. It is the divine *idea*, not the *eidē*, that is the absolute, the *an-hypotheton*. As such it is the divine *archē*, the true dynamic *aitia* or cause which first brings the *eidē* into being. *The eidē*, on their part, are the *teleutē* of dialectic, that is, that with which it ends, not that with which it in an absolute sense begins. Insofar as dialectic begins with conceptual definition of the *eidē*, the latter are still mere hypotheses, which must first be traced back to their *an-hypotheton*.

Precisely for this reason, it is not sufficient to gain a detached concept of the *eidos* of justice. Dialectic must behold this *eidos* in an *idea* (an *idea* of

---

ἀρχὴν ἀνυπόθετον ἐξ ὑποθέσεως ἰοῦσα καὶ ἄνευ ὧνπερ ἐκεῖνο εἰκόνων αὐτοῖς εἴδεσι δι᾽ αὐτῶν τὴν μέθοδον ποιουμένη. ("Consider further how the division of the intelligible is to be performed. How then? In such a way that the soul is compelled to investigate one section of it in terms of hypotheses, by using the section that was previously cut off [viz., the realm of the visible] as images, and proceeding, not back to the origin, but to the conclusion; in the other section, in contrast, it goes back from the assumption to an absolute origin, and does not, as in the first, make use of images, but employs only the *eidē* themselves in its investigations.")

1   *Ibid.*, 511 B: *Τὸ τοίνυν ἕτερον μάνθανε τμῆμα τοῦ νοητοῦ λέγοντά με τοῦτο, οὗ αὐτὸς ὁ λόγος ἅπτεται τῇ τοῦ διαλέγεσθαι δυνάμει, τὰς ὑποθέσεις ποιούμενος, οὐκ ἀρχάς, ἀλλὰ τῷ ὄντι ὑποθέσεις, οἷον ἐπιβάσεις τε καὶ ὁρμάς, ἵνα μέχρι τοῦ ἀνυποθέτου ἐπὶ τὴν τοῦ παντὸς ἀρχὴν ἰών, ἁψάμενος αὐτῆς πάλιν αὖ ἐχόμενος τῶν ἐκείνης ἐχομένων, οὕτως ἐπὶ τελευτὴν καταβαίνῃ, αἰσθητῷ παντάπασιν οὐδενὶ προσχρώμενος, ἀλλ᾽ εἴδεσιν αὐτοῖς δι᾽ αὐτῶν εἰς αὐτά, καὶ τελευτᾷ εἰς εἴδη.* (Translation in the text.)

justice) by following it back to its divine origin in the *idea tou agathou*. Each of the multitude of *eidē* has its own *idea*, which ties the distinctiveness of its nature to the divine *idea* as the form of origin. In this pregnant sense of form of origin, however, there is just one *idea*, for this only becomes a plurality in its relationship as origin to the *eidē*.

f. The Allegory of the Cave

At the beginning of the seventh book, this entire conception of the relationship of the *eidē* to the divine *idea*, and of both of these to the unreal realm of visible things subject to the matter principle, is once again summarized in symbolic form by means of the famous allegory of the cave. There have been men living since childhood in an underground cavern, chained with their backs facing the exit that opens to the daylight in such a manner that they are unable to turn their heads. The light that they do receive comes from a fire burning at a distance behind them. Facing them stands a wall upon which are cast the shadows of images of human beings, other creatures, and all types of cultural objects that men carry past the wall. Of necessity the chained captives will know no other reality than the silhouettes upon the wall, and they will take these to be the only true reality.

If some of them are then unchained and compelled to turn their heads around, to go toward the exit of the cave, and to ascend to where they can see the light, the blinding glare will make it impossible for them at first to discern the real objects of which they had formerly beheld only the shadows of artificial images. If such persons are to be taught to accustom themselves to reality, this will have to be done gradually. At first the shadows will be clearest to them, then the images of men and other things reflected in water, and later on the men and objects themselves in the actual place where they are standing. After they have learned in this way to reaccustom their eyes to the sunlight, they will consider themselves fortunate because of the change that has taken place. If they return to the prisoners in the cave and resume their former position, however, they will need much time to become accustomed once again to the old world of shadows, and the others will thus say that they have returned with their eyesight ruined and that it is not worthwhile to attempt the ascent to the sunlight. The captives will then even try to kill the man who would attempt to unchain someone and lead him to the exit.

This beautiful allegory is then immediately explicated by Socrates in terms of the epistemological theory he has just set forth. The dark cave is the visible world in which man dwells, and the fire that illuminates the cave is the counterpart of the sun in this visible realm. The ascent of the released captives and their observation of the things that are found above corresponds to the elevation of the thinking soul to the *noēton*, the intelligible realm of eternal ontic forms. This realm is irradiated by the pure light of the divine *idea* of the good, which in its gleaming brilliance can itself be known only with great difficulty. If one has beheld this *idea* by means of pure *theōria*, however, he is led to the conclusion that it is the cause (*aitia*) of all that is just and beautiful, giving birth in the visible realm to light and the sun, but reigning sovereign in the realm of the *noēton* by granting truth and giving insight into imperishable being. He must then also conclude that one must have seen this *idea* if he is to act wisely either in his personal life or in the public life of the *polis*.[1]

The formative theoretical training that the *polis* should give to its future rulers must specifically aim, therefore, in the most effective manner possible, to turn the soul toward the realm of eternal being and the *idea* of the good which shines over all, and to turn it away from the unreal realm of becoming in which the matter principle of eternal flux holds sway.[2]

Here correct knowledge of the *eidē* is thus once again made dependent on theoretical vision that is centered on the divine *idea*. In addition, the theoretical thought function is emphatically contrasted with the other faculties of the soul, which the latter acquires through habit and practice only after its union with the body. Theoretical thought is proclaimed to be, above all things, divine in nature. As such, it never loses its *dunamis*, although it can become either useful or harmful depending on whether the theoretical vision is turned toward or away from the intelligible realm.[3]

g. *Plato's Great Epistemological Discovery and Why Its Metaphysical Foundation Left It Unfruitful for Science*
In this whole epistemological conception, Plato is indeed on the track of

---

1 *Ibid.*, 517 B and C : τὰ δ᾽ οὖν ἐμοὶ φαινόμενα οὕτω φαίνεται, ἐν τῷ γνωστῷ τελευταία ἡ τοῦ ἀγαθοῦ ἰδέα καὶ μόγις ὁρᾶσθαι, ὀφθεῖσα δὲ συλλογιστέα εἶναι, ὡς ἄρα πᾶσι πάντων αὕτη ὀρθῶν τε καὶ καλῶν αἰτία, ἔν τε ὁρατῷ φῶς καὶ τὸν τούτου κύριον τεκοῦσα, ἔν τε νοητῷ αὐτὴ κυρία ἀλήθειαν καὶ νοῦν παρασχομένη, καὶ ὅτι δεῖ ταύτην ἰδεῖν τὸν μέλλοντα ἐμφρόνως πράξειν ἢ ἰδίᾳ ἢ δημοσίᾳ. (Translation in the text.)

2 *Ibid.*, 518 C and D. In *Republic* 518 C, the good (not the *idea*) is called τοῦ ὄντος τὸ φαινότατον. This passage cannot disagree in meaning with the unambiguous statements cited earlier in which the divine ἰδέα τοῦ ἀγαθοῦ is declared to be transcendent to *ousia* and *einai*. The reference here is apparently to the shining forth into of the divine *idea* in the realm of being, which makes all being good and thereby imparts to it the brightest splendor. A literal translation would thus be "the most radiant of being." The following term, τἀγαθόν, must then not be translated as *idea* of the good, however, as the text does not warrant this.

3 *Ibid.*, 518 D, E, and 519 A: Αἱ μὲν τοίνυν ἄλλαι ἀρεταὶ καλούμεναι ψυχῆς κινδυνεύουσιν ἐγγύς τι εἶναι τῶν τοῦ σώματος· τῷ ὄντι γὰρ οὐκ ἐνοῦσαι πρότερον ὕστερον ἐμποιεῖσθαι ἔθεσί τε καὶ ἀσκήσεσιν· ἡ δὲ τοῦ φρονῆσαι παντὸς μᾶλλον θειοτέρου τινὸς τυγχάνει, ὡς ἔοικεν, οὖσα, ὃ τὴν μὲν δύναμιν οὐδέποτε ἀπόλλυσιν, ὑπὸ δὲ τῆς περιαγωγῆς χρήσιμόν τε καὶ ὠφέλιμον καὶ ἄχρηστον αὖ καὶ βλαβερὸν γίγνεται. ("Then the other faculties of the soul, as they are called, seem to be akin to those of the body, for as they were indeed not present in it previously, they seem to be produced within it by habit and exercise. That of thought, however, is above all divine in nature, as is fitting, something that never loses its power, but by the direction [which it chooses] becomes something useful and beneficial, or in contrast, something useless and harmful.") With the word περιαγωγή, Plato actually means a "reversal" of thought by which it is directed toward the luminous realm of being and away from the dark world of sense phenomena.

something extremely important. What he has in view is nothing less than the proper relationship between the *concept* and the *idea*. The former is characterized by distinguishing.[1] The latter, without abandoning these conceptual distinctions, redirects the concept of the diversity of the structures of reality, concentrating it upon the origin and unity of all structures. However, in providing a metaphysical foundation for this epistemological insight, which is genuinely Socratic, Plato fails to attain to the central point of departure which is the precondition of its becoming scientifically fruitful. Here too his idea of the origin is still burdened with the polar dualism of the form-matter motive. The *idea tou agathou* is exclusively a form principle and cannot be considered a principle of creation in the sense of the Christian religion.

It is easy to understand that Christian intellectuals believed that they could discern in the above description of the "divine master workman" in the tenth book of the *Republic* a surprising agreement with the Mosaic revelation of divine creation. Indeed, on the terminological level, the agreement is striking. When, however, the conception of Plato is interpreted in terms of its own point of departure in the Greek ground-motive, which is the first requirement of a transcendental, truly scientific interpretation of Greek thought, it can only appear that there is a deep chasm separating Plato's conception of the divine master workman from the Scriptural revelation of the absolute Creator. If philosophy's idea of origin is falsely directed, then its vision of reality will of necessity also be obscured by this idea of origin.

Plato's metaphysical ontology is wholly inspired by the form motive in its polar opposition to the matter motive. Because of this, the seventh book of the *Republic*, which examines in greater detail the scientific training required for the rulers, shows a lack of interest in the phenomena of the visible world. In the plan of education that is outlined there, the first and second positions are assigned respectively to planometry, the science of plane surfaces, and the newly discovered stereometry, which deals with three-dimensional figures. Astronomy, which studies the "movement of depth" (φορὰν βάθους),[2] and the theory of harmony, are given the third and fourth positions. It is explicitly stated here, however, that these investigations should not be directed toward visible celestial phenomena or the tonal harmonic relations perceived by the senses, since in this manner "the

---

1   *Editorial note*: Dooyeweerd uses the term "onderscheidend begrip," which may be translated literally by "distinguishing concept." He means that in concept formation analytical distinguishing has the leading role. The *idea*, in its turn, relates these distinctions, without obliterating them, to a deeper unity. This distinction of *concept* and *idea* is important to Plato and to subsequent thinkers whose epistemology moved in a transcendental direction.

2   *Ibid.*, 528 E: ἀστρονομίαν ... φορὰν οὖσαν βάθους.

natural gift of thought in the soul would be made useless."[1] Just as geometry uses sensible figures merely as perceptual images of its actual, non-sensible field of investigation, astronomy should point the soul beyond sense phenomena to the motions that truly *are*, which "speed in itself" and "slowness in itself" cause within the intelligible realm in true number and the true mathematical figures, and which cannot be apprehended by sense perception but only by theoretical thought.[2] In this manner, Plato resolves the whole of astronomy into an abstract phoronomy (theory of motion) conceived in a priori fashion. At the same time, this repudiation of visible phenomena brings out the fundamental difference between his conception and that of modern natural science. In mathematically oriented *dianoia* as this is conceived in the *Republic*, Plato shows no real interest in empirical phenomena. His *theōria* concentrates its full attention on the metaphysical form-world of true being. The same is the case in the theory of harmony; for the latter, as a particular ontic form (*eidos*) of motion, is resolved for *dianoia* into abstract numerical ratios that are the constant external manifestation of the true essence of harmony.[3]

---

1 *Ibid.*, 530 B and C: Προβλήμασιν ἄρ᾽ ἦν δ᾽ ἐγώ, χρώμενοι ὥσπερ γεωμετρίαν οὕτω καὶ ἀστρονομίαν μέτιμεν, τὰ δ᾽ ἐν τῷ οὐρανῷ ἐάσομεν, εἰ μέλλομεν ὄντως ἀστρονομίας μεταλαμβάνοντες χρήσιμον τὸ φύσει φρόνιμον ἐν τῇ ψυχῇ ἐξ ἀχρήστου ποιήσειν. ("Therefore, I said, as in geometry, we shall make use of astronomy for the sake of problems, but not further concern ourselves with celestial phenomena, if we indeed wish to pursue astronomy in a way that converts the natural gift of understanding in our soul from something useless into something useful.")

2 *Ibid.*, 529 C and D: ταῦτα μὲν τὰ ἐν τῷ οὐρανῷ ποικίλματα, ἐπείπερ ἐν ὁρατῷ πεποίκιλται, κάλλιστα μὲν ἡγεῖσθαι καὶ ἀκριβέστατα τῶν τοιούτων ἔχειν, τῶν δὲ ἀληθινῶν πολὺ ἐνδεῖν, ἃς τὸ ὂν τάχος καὶ ἡ οὖσα βραδυτὴς ἐν τῷ ἀληθινῷ ἀριθμῷ καὶ πᾶσι τοῖς ἀληθέσι σχήμασι φορᾶς τε πρὸς ἄλληλα φέρεται καὶ τὰ ἐνόντα φέρει· ἃ δὴ λόγῳ μὲν καὶ διανοίᾳ ληπτά, ὄψει δ᾽ οὔ. ("These phenomena in the heavens, inasmuch as they are formed in the visible realm, must, to be sure, be regarded as the most beautiful and exact of their kind, but nevertheless as much inferior to the true motions which speed in itself and slowness in itself reciprocally cause in true number and all true figures among them, thus carrying with them what is found therein; but these latter must be apprehended by concept and scientific thought, not by the eye.") *Ibid.*, 529 D: Οὐκοῦν, εἶπον, τῇ περὶ τὸν οὐρανὸν ποικιλίᾳ παραδείγμασι χρηστέον τῆς πρὸς ἐκεῖνα μαθήσεως ἕνεκα. ("We may thus use the manifold phenomena in the heavens only as examples for the sake of the knowledge of those [truly real motions which speed in itself and slowness in itself cause...].")

3 See *Ibid.*, 531 b and c, where disapproval is expressed of those who pursue the theory of harmony as an empirical science: ταὐτὸν γὰρ ποιοῦσι τοῖς ἐν τῇ ἀστρονομίᾳ· τοὺς γὰρ ἐν ταύταις ταῖς συμφωνίαις ταῖς ἀκουομέναις ἀριθμοὺς ζητοῦσιν, ἀλλ᾽ οὐκ εἰς προβλήματα ἀνίασιν ἐπισκοπεῖν τίνες ξύμφωνοι ἀριθμοὶ καὶ τίνες οὔ, καὶ διὰ τί ἑκάτεροι. ("For these do the same thing that the others do in astronomy; they seek for the numbers in such harmonies as they hear with the ear, but they do not raise their consideration to the problems of which numbers create

For the task of *dianoia*, whether in mathematics, in astronomy, or in the theory of harmony, is merely propaedeutic. Its aim is to prepare the soul for metaphysical dialectic, which is directed toward the intelligible realm of the *eidē* by way of a theoretical vision concentrated on the divine *idea* of the good and beautiful. The intent of this dialectic, furthermore, is to teach the soul to turn away from the realm of eternal becoming and toward being and truth. Only in this metaphysical realm can theoretical thought grasp true reality or ontic being, that is to say, ontic form purified from all contamination by the principle of matter.

In all this, however, it is clear that the grand conception of Plato's theory of *ideas* in the *Republic* has not yet arrived at a synthesis between the form and matter principles. In essence the two principles remain in polar opposition to each other, and the earlier-discussed doctrine of *methexis*, *koinōnia*, or *parousia* has not yet made any real progress. In Plato's next period it is precisely this unsolved problem concerning the relationship between the two realms which he so sharply distinguished – the intelligible realm of the eternal ontic forms and the visible realm of phenomena subject to the matter principle – that will plunge the theory of *ideas* into an acute crisis.

h. The Conception of the Soul in the Republic

In the conception of the soul presented in the *Republic*, which, as we have seen earlier, provides the theoretical foundation and elaboration of the tripartition (trichotomy) that had only been described in mythological form in the *Phaedrus*, this essentially unreconciled dualism between the form and matter principles once again stands out in sharp relief. Because of this dualism, Plato is prevented here from grasping the *anima* in its unity, as the fundamental unity that forms the spiritual center of human existence.

In the fourth book of the *Republic*, Plato gave his own description of the path by which he was led to this trichotomistic conception. His intent was undoubtedly to conceive the human soul in full conformity with the example of the ideal organization of the *polis* with its three vocational classes, and this plan is indeed followed here. Nevertheless, in this notion of three classes, there was a deeper religious motive at work, namely, that of form and matter, whose presence is scarcely concealed in the fourth book of the *Republic*. Although, in the *Phaedo*, the dualism between the form and matter principles came to anthropological expression only in the relation between the thinking soul and the material body, we have seen above how, in the *Phaedrus*, the conception of the soul as the origin of all motion compelled Plato to recognize the presence of this dualism within the soul itself.

---

harmony, which do not, and for what reason this is the case with each.") Just before this, Glaucon, with Socrates' approval, had even ridiculed this empirical study of the theory of harmony.

i. The Dialectical Proof for the Tripartition of the Soul and the Path That Led Plato to This Conception

At this point,[1] Plato attempts through his spokesman Socrates to prove that the soul indeed has to have three parts, just as the *polis* has three classes, and that in the functions of each part it is not the entire soul, but only the part under concern that is at work.[2] The starting point for this proof, which follows a completely dialectical route that is expressly described as "difficult," is the thesis that the same thing cannot do or experience opposites at the same time, in the same manner, and in relation to the same thing. Thus, if we find that such indeed seems to be the case, we must conclude that not one and the same element, but a plurality, was present here.[3]

This thesis is first elucidated by means of the following example. If a man is standing still but moving his hands and head, we may not say that he is simultaneously at rest and in motion, but only that one part of the man is at rest and another part in motion. A second example, borrowed from mathematics, is then added to this one, namely, that of a circle which rotates on a fixed point on its tangent.

Plato then applies the thesis to the human soul. Sensual desires, of which hunger and thirst are mentioned as the most conspicuous examples, belong to one *eidos*, "desire in itself," which stands in relation to the object assigned to it by nature, as hunger is particularly related to food, and thirst to drink. The same relation is found in the case of theoretical knowledge. There is one *eidos* of theoretical knowledge, knowledge in itself, which is related to the known in itself, while the particular sciences (belonging to *dianoia*) are each related to a particular object (*Gegenstand*).

In this context, Plato is quick to reject the thesis, which we have discussed earlier, that like is known only by like. Socrates observes that knowledge which is only in itself undoubtedly has as its sole object that which is in itself, whereas a particular science is related solely to a particular object (*Gegenstand*). This does not mean, however, that knowledge

---

1 *Ibid.*, Book I , cap.16 ff.

2 *Ibid.*, 436 A: εἰ τῷ αὐτῷ τούτῳ ἕκαστα πράττομεν, ἢ τρισὶν οὖσιν ἄλλο ἄλλῳ· μανθάνομεν μὲν ἑτέρῳ θυμούμεθα δὲ ἄλλῳ τῶν ἐν ἡμῖν, ἐπιθυμοῦμεν δ' αὖ τρίτῳ τινὶ τῶν περὶ τὴν τροφήν τε καὶ γέννησιν ἡδονῶν καὶ ὅσα τούτων ἀδελφὰ ἢ ὅλῃ τῇ ψυχῇ καθ᾽ ἕκαστον αὐτῶν πράττομεν, ὅταν ὁρμήσωμεν. ("Whether we do everything by means of the same [part of the soul], or, since there are three of these, we do one thing through one, another through another; whether we learn through one, become angry at what goes on within us through a second, and again through a third desire the pleasures of food and sexual procreation and related things, or whether we are active in each of these with our entire soul when we are stimulated to them.")

3 *Ibid.*, 436 B: Δῆλον, ὅτι ταὐτὸν τἀναντία ποιεῖν ἢ πάσχειν κατὰ ταὐτόν γε καὶ πρὸς ταὐτὸν οὐκ ἐθελήσει ἅμα· ὥστε, ἄν που εὑρίσκωμεν ἐν αὐτοῖς ταῦτα γιγνόμενα, εἰσόμεθα ὅτι οὐ ταὐτὸν ἦν, ἀλλὰ πλείω. (Translation in text.)

has the same nature as its object, so that, for instance, the knowledge of what is healthful and what is harmful would itself be healthful and harmful, and the knowledge of evil and good itself evil and good. It means only that knowledge shares the metaphysical or the special scientific character of its field of inquiry.[1]

Returning to the soul, Plato notes that there is an antagonism between the sensual desires, which are directed solely toward their natural objects which they like beasts seek to overpower, and another impulse, which through rational deliberation (*logismos*) restrains the soul from submitting to these desires. By virtue of the earlier thesis that the same thing cannot do or experience opposites at the same time, in the same manner, and in relation to the same thing, it follows that there must be two mutually opposed *eidē* in the soul:[2] that of sensual desire (the *epithumētikon*) and that of theoretical thought (the *logistikon*). The word *eidos*, as Plato uses it here, cannot have its pregnant meaning of "eternal ontic form"; neither may it be translated "faculty," as Steinhart, for instance, renders it. In this context, it must rather be understood in the sense of "specific part," a meaning that it often has elsewhere, particularly in the *Sophist* and the *Statesman*.[3] As is clear from the previous argument, only the *logistikon* in the human soul has a metaphysical foundation in an *eidos* in the sense of a

---

1 *Ibid.*, 438 D and E: Τοῦτο τοίνυν, ἦν δ᾽ ἐγώ, φάθι με τότε βούλεσθαι λέγειν, εἰ ἄρα νῦν ἔμαθες, ὅτι ὅσα ἐστὶν οἷα εἶναί του, αὐτὰ μὲν μόνα αὐτῶν μόνων ἐστί, τῶν δὲ ποιῶν τινῶν ποιὰ ἄττα. καὶ οὔ τι λέγω, ὡς, οἵων ἄν, ᾖ, τοιαῦτα καὶ ἔστιν, ὡς ἄρα καὶ τῶν ὑγιεινῶν καὶ νοσωδῶν ἡ ἐπιστήμη ὑγιεινὴ καὶ νοσώδης καὶ τῶν κακῶν καὶ τῶν ἀγαθῶν κακὴ καὶ ἀγαθή· ἀλλ᾽ ἐπειδὴ οὐκ αὐτοῦ οὗπερ ἐπιστήμη ἐστὶν ἐγένετο ἐπιστήμη, ἀλλὰ ποιοῦ τινός, τοῦτο δ᾽ ἦν ὑγιεινὸν καὶ νοσῶδες, ποιὰ δή τις συνέβη καὶ αὐτὴ γενέσθαι, καὶ τοῦτο αὐτὴν ἐποίησεν μηκέτι ἐπιστήμην ἁπλῶς καλεῖσθαι, ἀλλὰ τοῦ ποιοῦ τινὸς προσγενομένου ἰατρικήν. ("Grant thus, if you have now understood me, that this is what I just meant to say, that of those things which are in relation to something, that which is only in itself is related solely to something that is in itself, but that which is in some [particular] mode is related to something that is in some [particular] mode. And I do not mean that [knowledge] has the same nature as that to which it is related, that therefore knowledge of what is healthful and harmful is itself healthful and harmful, and that of evil and good itself evil and good; but that, since it did not become knowledge of that thing in itself of which it provides knowledge, but rather a science of some particular thing, namely, what is healthful and harmful, it follows that it also became a particular science itself, and this caused it to be no longer called simply science in itself, but through the addition of this qualification, medical science.")

2 *Ibid.*, 439 E: Ταῦτα μὲν τοίνυν, ... δύο ἡμῖν ὡρίσθω εἴδη ἐν ψυχῇ ἐνόντα·

3 The fact that Plato, especially in the *Sophist* and the *Statesman*, often uses the terms εἶδος and μέρος ('part') synonymously (insofar as μέρος signifies a "natural division"), has been rightly observed by Brommer in his dissertation cited earlier (*op. cit.*, p. 117). In the *Sophist* this is at once evident, for what is at issue there is the dialectical method of *diairesis* or dichotomy of the more comprehensive *eidē* into their subordinate parts. As Stenzel has shown, this method also betrays the influence of

self-subsistent ontic form that is transcendent in character.

Between these two completely antagonistic parts of the soul there must be a third, which functions as a mediator in order to assist the *logistikon* in controlling the *epithumētikon*. For it seemed impossible to Plato that the *nous* could directly control the impulse of sensual desire in the soul, since these two are completely opposite to each other in nature and thus remain limited to their respective spheres of activity. This third, mediating part of the soul, which, as we have already noticed, is called the *thumoeidēs*, shares some of the features of the two parts that are the seats of sensual desire and of thought; but it is nevertheless different from both of these. It can perhaps best be represented as "moral sense," which, apart from rational insight, desires what is just and good. This third part of the soul, therefore, is intended to serve as a bridge between the form principle proper in the soul, which resides in the *logistikon*, and the matter principle, which holds sway in the *epithumētikon*.

j. The Unity of the Soul in This Trichotomistic Conception Is Sought in the Pythagorean Principle of Harmony. The Absence of a Metaphysical Foundation for the Latter

This attempt at synthesis had to remain ineffectual, however. Plato teaches that the part of the soul responsible for sensual desire should accept the leadership of the thinking part, and this accords with the original meaning (*archē*) of justice as an inner virtue of the soul. In an earlier context, Plato had expounded civil justice, which prescribed that each person remain strictly within the limits of his own vocational class. He now says, however, that this civil justice is only a shadowy image (*eidōlon*) of inner justice.[1] According to the *idea* of justice, the distinct parts of the soul should agree with one another, even though their proper spheres of activity must be strictly maintained – just as there is an agreement in harmony between the high, middle, and low notes. Moreover, the highest part should lead the lowest.[2] But if, as Plato claims, the part that is the seat of sensual desire indeed can do nothing

---

Democritus, inasmuch as its ultimate aim is the discovery of the ἄτομον εἶδος, i.e., the *eidos* that is not further divisible.

1 *Ibid.*, 443 C: εἴδωλόν τι τῆς δικαιοσύνης ('a certain image of justice'). *Ibid.*: Τὸ δέ γε ἀληθές, τοιοῦτο μέν τι ἦν, ὡς ἔοικεν, ἡ δικαιοσύνη, ἀλλ' οὐ περὶ τὴν ἔξω πρᾶξιν τῶν αὑτοῦ, ἀλλὰ περὶ τὴν ἐντὸς ὡς ἀληθῶς περὶ ἑαυτὸν καὶ τὰ ἑαυτοῦ ("True justice seems to be of this quality, yet not with respect to the external performance of our vocation, but in reality with respect to its internal performance, which concerns ourselves and what belongs to us.")

2 *Ibid.*, 443 D: ξυναρμόσαντα τρία ὄντα ὥσπερ ὅρους, τρεῖς ἁρμονίας ἀτεχνῶς, νεάτης τε καὶ ὑπάτης καὶ μέσης, καὶ εἰ ἄλλα ἄττα μεταξὺ τυγχάνει ὄντα, πάντα ταῦτα ξυνδήσαντα καὶ παντάπασιν ἕνα γενόμενον ἐκ πολλῶν ... ("... bringing the three parts into mutual harmony according to their boundaries, as it were – just like the sounds of the highest, lowest, and middle strings, and whatever else might lie be-

other than strive like a wild "beast" (θηρίον) to satisfy its needs, it hardly seems possible that rational deliberation could exert any influence within its sphere of activity. Instead, this part of the soul is ruled by the blind *Anankē* of the matter principle. We shall later encounter this same problem in the *Timaeus*.

It was of no avail for Plato to introduce the *thumoeidēs* as a mediating principle between the thinking part and the sensual part of the soul. For the *thumoeidēs* too must remain within its own sphere of activity and is not situated above the two antagonistic parts of the soul. Because it lacks any idea of a fundamental, transcendent root-unity located above the diversity of temporal structures, the trichotomistic conception itself prevents Plato from attaining to a true synthesis of the form and matter principles in his view of the soul. In the absence of such a synthesis, he also was unable to grasp in their true nature and coherence the distinct structures within temporal human bodily existence, which he undoubtedly had in view in his doctrine of tripartition. The Greek form-matter motive made it impossible to gain any insight into the soul as the transcendent, spiritual, fundamental unity of human nature, and it compelled *theōria* to locate the soul in an abstraction from bodily existence.

In the trichotomous division, each part of the soul is shut off and made to stand alone, in complete separation from the other two spheres of activity. Apparently taking his cue from the Pythagoreans, Plato resorts in the sixth book to the principle of harmony in order to grant once again a role to the idea of unity. This principle remains completely unfounded in this connection, however, for it presupposes an idea of a unity and totality which the trichotomistic conception lacks and, in fact, excludes in principle.

Plato's basic inability to accept the tripartite soul as a harmonic whole during this stage of the development of his theory of ideas is clearly evident in book X, where he again takes up the problem of the immortality of the *psychē*. Here the Orphic-Pythagorean dualism in the conception of the relation between the thinking soul and the material body, with which we have already become acquainted in the *Phaedo*, again raises its head. The immortality of the soul, which is seemingly demanded by the idea of justice, is now supported by a new proof intended to supplement those advanced in the *Phaedo*.[1] Socrates argues that each thing can only be destroyed by the evil that is specific to itself (the organic body by disease, grain by mildew, wood by rotting, etc.). The special evil of the soul is

---

tween – joined all of this together and in an absolute sense became one out of many [parts] ...") *Ibid.*, 443 E: σοφίαν δὲ τὴν ἐπιστατοῦσαν ταύτῃ τῇ πράξει (... but [calls] wisdom the conduct which leads this activity.")

1 *Ibid.*, 608 ff.

moral wickedness, this being opposed to the four cardinal virtues of wisdom, temperance, fortitude, and justice. Since experience makes clear that these vices do not destroy the soul, the latter must be indestructible; for it could never be killed by an evil foreign to its nature, such as that constituted by the body. This also implies that immortality is individual. In their immortality, the souls always remain the same, and more souls can thus never arise than have existed in the past. For if something immortal should become more numerous, then it would have to originate from what is mortal, and everything would eventually become immortal, which is an absurd notion.

It must be asked, however, whether this individual immortality belongs to the entire tripartite soul that has been under discussion until now. Socrates hints that this would be unthinkable: "It is not easily conceivable that the soul, such as it has appeared to us as something immortal, should be composed of many parts not joined in the fairest composition." [1] "We must regard the soul as it truly is, not as we see it now, disfigured by its association with the body and other evils, but as it is when it has been purified from this...

But what we have just said of it is true of its present appearance." Only "if we focus upon the philosophical endeavor of the soul and consider what it then associates with and yearns to associate with, as being itself akin to what is divine, immortal, and everlasting, then we shall be able to gather what it will become if it should devote itself entirely to this endeavor," and is purified by this impulse from the earthly filth that has encrusted it all around by reason of its union with the material body. "And then one will see its real nature [*physis*], i.e., whether this is multiform [*polueidēs*] or uniform [simple, *monoeidēs*]" [2]

---

1 *Ibid.*, 611 A.ff.: Ἀλλ᾽, ἦν δ᾽ ἐγώ, μήτε τοῦτο οἰώμεθα· ὁ γὰρ λόγος οὐκ ἐάσει· μήτε γε αὖ τῇ ἀληθεστάτῃ φύσει τοιοῦτον εἶναι ψυχήν, ὥστε πολλῆς ποικιλίας καὶ ἀνομοιότητός τε καὶ διαφορᾶς γέμειν αὐτὸ πρὸς αὐτό. ... Οὐ ῥᾴδιον ... ἀΐδιον εἶναι σύνθετόν τε ἐκ πολλῶν καὶ μὴ τῇ καλλίστῃ κεχρημένον συνθέσει, ὡς νῦν ἡμῖν ἐφάνη ἡ ψυχή. ("But this also [viz., that the number of immortal souls should increase] we shall not believe, since reason will not allow it, nor that the soul in its true nature should be such that it is freighted with great diversity and unlikeness and a lack of self-consistency.... Not easily [is it conceivable] ... that the soul, such as it has now appeared to us, viz., as something immortal, should be composed of many parts not joined in the fairest composition.")

2 *Ibid.*, 611 B-612 A: οἷον δ᾽ ἐστὶ τῇ ἀληθείᾳ, οὐ λελωβημένον δεῖ αὐτὸ θεάσασθαι ὑπό τε τῆς τοῦ σώματος κοινωνίας καὶ ἄλλων κακῶν, ὥσπερ νῦν ἡμεῖς θεώμεθα, ἀλλ᾽ οἷόν ἐστι καθαρὸν γιγνόμενον, ... νῦν δὲ εἴπομεν μὲν ἀληθῆ περὶ αὐτοῦ, οἷον ἐν τῷ παρόντι φαίνεται· ... Εἰς τὴν φιλοσοφίαν αὐτῆς, καὶ ἐννοεῖν, ὧν ἅπτεται καὶ οἵων ἐφίεται ὁμιλῶν, ὡς ξυγγενὴς οὖσα τῷ τε θείῳ καὶ ἀθανάτῳ καὶ τῷ ἀεὶ ὄντι, καὶ οἷα ἂν γένοιτο τῷ τοιούτῳ πᾶσα ἐπισπομένη καὶ ὑπὸ ταύτης τῆς ὁρμῆς ἐκκομισθεῖσα ἐκ τοῦ πόντου, ἐν ᾧ νῦν ἐστί ... καὶ τότ᾽ ἄν τις ἴδοι αὐτῆς τὴν

k. The Revision of the Trichotomistic Conception of the Phaedrus

It is clear from this entire exposition that Plato is harking back here again to the conception of the soul presented in the *Phaedo*. In its true and pure nature, the soul is a sheer theoretical mental substance and is thus simple rather than composite. The tripartition of the soul is merely a result of its incarnation in the impure material body, which constitutes an evil for it. Immortality belongs to the soul only in its pure state. It should be noted that Plato is here evidently revising the conception of the trichotomy that the *Phaedrus* had related in mythological form. For in the picture presented there, the soul already had three parts before it was clothed in an earthly body, and it was thus immortal in its entire tripartite nature. The *Republic*, by contrast, reserves immortality solely for the *logistikon*, the thinking part of the soul, although this is done only implicitly. And as we shall see when we turn to the *Timaeus*, Plato from this point on remains faithful to the latter conception, except for the fact that he later modifies his understanding of the nature of this part of the soul.

l. The Inner Antinomy in the Republic's Conception of the Soul. Review of the Present State of the Theory of Ideas

It is evident, however, that the above development led to a distinct antinomy in Plato's theory of the soul. There is, on the one hand, an ethical conception in which justice is manifested within the soul through the harmonious arrangement of its three parts into a good and beautiful whole, following the example of the just state with its three classes. In contrast to this, there is a metaphysical conception which regards the tripartition as a defilement of the soul in its true, simple nature. The first theory is pervaded by the Socratic spirit; the second is suffused by the Orphic-Pythagorean and Eleatic spirit. This antinomy, moreover, has a deeper source in the unreconciled dualism which still prevails in the *Republic* between the religious form motive and the matter motive.

In this dialogue, to be sure, the theory of ideas has reached a stage of development in which the relationship between the divine *idea* and the *eidē* appears to be satisfactorily resolved. The Socratic motive of the divine *nous* as the origin of the good and the beautiful in the visible cosmos has indeed triumphed in this conception. Nevertheless, the conception of the relation between the form principle and the earthly matter principle continues to be essentially determined by the influence of Orphic-Pythagoreanism. The conception of *erōs* as a mediator, presented in the *Symposium* and the *Phaedrus*, has once again been pushed into the background, and the optimistic view of life has departed along with it. As a process of eternal becoming, earthly *physis* defiles the pure *eidē* when they are incar-

---

ἀληθῆ φύσιν, εἴτε πολυειδὴς εἴτε μονοειδής. ... (Translation in the text.)

nated within it (this was in fact also recognized by the *Symposium*). Similarly, the soul in its simple nature as a pure theoretical mental substance is defiled by its association with the earthly material body and deformed into an entity composed of three parts.

At the close of the ninth book, it is emphatically asserted that the ideal state, which forms the model of the virtuous tripartite soul (corresponding to the true *idea* of justice), cannot be found anywhere on earth. The dark power of *Ananke* will always cause the *polis* to degenerate and to fall away from the *idea*. "But in heaven," as Socrates concludes with some resignation, "there is perhaps a model of it for him who desires to see it and, seeing it, to organize his earthly polis in accordance therewith."[1]

The same pessimistic conclusion also seems to emerge with respect to the actualization of the idea of justice in the tripartite soul joined to the matter principle. Will the dark *Ananke* of the matter principle that is at work in the *epithumētikon* ever allow itself to be curbed by the true pursuit of wisdom in the theoretical mental substance? Or will this be granted only to those few who can devote themselves fully to the philosophical *theōria* of the *eidē* and the *idea*, but at the price of turning their gaze away from the visible cosmos in the ascetic way of life recommended in the *Phaedo*? Moreover, are not many, through no fault of their own, predisposed to a bad life by the dark *Ananke* that prevails in the matter principle? Herein lies the problem that will soon be examined in the *Timaeus*, where it will receive a remarkable solution that places the autonomy of the matter principle in the clearest light.

---

1 *Ibid.*, 592 B: Ἀλλ᾿, ἦν δ᾿ ἐγώ, ἐν οὐρανῷ ἴσως παράδειγμα ἀνάκειται τῷ βουλομένῳ ὁρᾷν καὶ ὁρῶντι ἑαυτὸν κατοικίζειν. (Translation in the text.)

Chapter Two

The Dialectic of the Form-Matter Motive in the Crisis of the Theory of Ideas. The *Theaetetus*, the *Parmenides*, the *Sophist*, the *Statesman*, and the Dialectical Portion of the *Phaedrus*

1. The Crisis of the Theory of Ideas and the Continuing Influence of the Religious Dialectic in the New, Dialectical Logic. The *Theaetetus* as a Preparation for the Eleatic Dialogues

The course of development of Plato's thought is faithfully reflected in the evolution of his conception of dialectic. In his first stage, the latter fully preserves the original Socratic features. It is essentially a teleological logic, whose purpose is the apprehension of *aretē* (*ἀρετή*), the true end of men and things, and which is given the form of a dialogue or discussion between two parties. As we have seen, it constantly exhibits the genuinely religious tendency to bring things to a central focus, in that it does not round off the concept in a purely logical definition, but rather relates it to the divine *idea* (*ἰδέα*) of the good and beautiful, the principle of origin of all form, measure, and harmony in the visible cosmos.

When the theory of ideas makes its appearance in Plato's thought, the dialectic takes a metaphysical turn: the logical concept is related to the metaphysical, intelligible world of eternal ontic forms, the *eidē*. The aim of this dialectic is the apprehension of *true being*, which is set in polar opposition to the realm of becoming in its eternal flux (the visible cosmos), and which has to be viewed in complete detachment from sense experience and the temporal world subject to the principle of matter. Plato's metaphysical conception absolutizes these ontic forms into self-subsistent entities, and, as we have seen, it thereby comes into religious conflict with the Socratic idea of origin. The latter was not merely logical; rather, in its philosophic character, it was determined in a way that was distinctly religious. Neither was the solution to this problem offered in the *Republic* a logical one. Since it had to do entirely with philosophy's idea of origin, it could only be a priori and transcendental in character. As I shall later demonstrate at length in my exposition of the fundamentals of my transcendental critique of philosophic thought, this solution had its ground in a religious decision, that is, in a religious choice of a standpoint.

a. The Causes of the Crisis in Plato's Theory of Ideas. The Simplicity of the Eidē as Ideal Ontic Forms Constructed in A Priori Fashion, and the Composite Nature of Empirical Things

In the long run, however, Plato could not remain content with the metaphysical stage at which he had arrived in the evolution of his dialectic. The sharp *chōrismos* (χωρισμός), the absolute separation, between the world of the *eidē* and the visible things subject to the matter principle could not even be reconciled with the Socratic *idea* of the good and beautiful; for the latter had to be operative, as a divine form-power, precisely within the visible cosmos. How then, in the face of this *chōrismos*, could the *eidē* be conceived logically as the effective causes of the visible world of forms?

Plato's increasing interest in empirical phenomena, which can be clearly observed beginning with the *Theaetetus*, also demanded a transformation of the dialectic and a revised conception of the *eidē*. Up to this point the world of the *eidē* had been constructed in a priori fashion as a realm of ideal ontic forms related to the *idea* of the good and beautiful, which shed its light over everything. The mathematical and logical forms, together with the *eidē* of the individual virtues and the *eidos* of beauty, could still be joined to this *idea*, just as the *eidos* of "life in itself" could. To be sure, the metaphysical *eidos* conception had arisen from a mathematical conception of the principle of form and in itself had been completely foreign to the Socratic *idea*. Nevertheless, the Pythagoreans had already introduced the principle of harmony, which was essentially an aesthetic and ethical notion, into the mathematical world of form, and they similarly conceived of the soul as such a *harmonia*. Over against this, the Platonic world of *eidē* had at first no place for the "composite" things in nature, such as men, animals, plants, and inorganic substances. Indeed, the *Republic* had allowed for *eidē* of cultural objects such as tables and reclining couches, since the form motive, which had the primacy there, was essentially that of the religion of culture. However, the *physis* of the "composite" things of nature had as one of its ontic components the matter principle of eternal flux, and the latter itself had been deprived of all divinity and denied any origin in the divine *idea* of the *kalokagathon*.

Thus, if the *Phaedo's* view of the *eidē* as ideal, simple forms was to be maintained, no *eidē* that were composite in nature could be allowed within the confines of the intelligible world. Accepting such composite *eidē* would have demanded, as a first step, the acknowledgment that there was an *eidos* of *hulē*, but this seemed to be excluded by the religious form motive of the religion of culture, as that was embodied in the Socratic *idea*. Motion in the typically Greek sense of continuous chaotic change was incompatible with the ideal ontic form of the eidetic world, at least if this was taken in its pure state. And in this initial metaphysical conception of the realm of ideas, the equally characteristic Greek view of motion as a form-giving power (*dunamis*) proceeding from the rational soul, which ever since Anaxagoras had been reserved for the divine principle of form, also could not be combined with the *eidos*; for, in this conception, the *eidos* was oriented to the static Eleatic view of ontic form.

b. Plato's Growing Interest in Empirical Phenomena Beginning with the Theaetetus. *The Problem of* Methexis *Considered Logically*

To the degree that empirical phenomena as such began to draw Plato's attention, the *eidē* were primarily assigned the task of securing the ontological foundation for these phenomena of the visible cosmos. The demand now arose to "save" the visible world of phenomena (τὰ φαινόμενα διασῴζειν) by granting to all empirical things without exception a share (*methexis*) in the *eidē*. And since within the conceptual framework of the Greek form-matter motive the entire visible cosmos displayed a composite character, it became necessary to make the attempt to achieve within the eidetic world itself a synthesis between the form and matter principles. This meant, first of all, that the earlier discussed problem of *methexis*, which even the *Republic* had left essentially unresolved, had to assume the central position in Plato's dialectic.

Now this problem takes on a new dialectical form: How can the one logically become a plurality? If the *eidos* as a metaphysical, ideal formal unity is indeed the effective cause (*aitia*) of an innumerable multiplicity of individual things having form in the visible cosmos that participate in this *eidos*, how is it to be understood logically that an unlimited multiplicity arises from this one? As long as Plato held to the original Eleatic conception of the *eidos* as an absolute or simple formal unity, this problem had to remain insoluble. Plurality then had to be abandoned to the realm of mere sense appearance as an absolute *ouk on* (οὐκ ὄν) or non-being, and with regard to it there could only be a *doxa*, an unfounded opinion, and not *epistēmē* or truly theoretical knowledge.

In the *Republic* the one and many problem had been raised only with respect to the relationship of the many *eidē* in themselves to the one divine *idea* of the *kalokagathon*. The solution offered to this problem had not been a truly logical one; rather it was a priori and transcendental. The *Republic* taught that the multiplicity of *eidē* derive their being from the one divine *idea*. If this idea of origin was to have any effect on the logical side of Plato's dialectic, however, the rigid isolation of the *eidē* had to be broken through in a logical-dialectical manner. The *eidē* had to be placed in logical relation to one another, and thereby they had to lose their absolute self-containment and monadic character.[1]

---

1 Over against the position of Gottfied Stallbaum and his school, J. Stenzel has convincingly demonstrated in his *Studien zur Entwicklung der platonischen Dialektik von Sokrates zu Aristoteles* (2nd.; Leipzig and Berlin, 1931, p. 48) that there is yet no trace of this in the dialectic of the *Republic*. Indeed, opponents of this position have appealed to *Republic* 454 A and 476 A and have claimed that Plato is here already speaking, respectively, of a διαίρεσις κατ᾽ εἴδη and a κοινωνία τῶν γενῶν; nevertheless, as Stenzel has shown at length, these passages have in fact no connection with the new dialectic that is developed in the Eleatic dialogues (the *Parmenides*, the *Sophist*, and the *Statesman*) and also in the later, dialectical portion

c. *The New, Dialectical Turn of Plato's Logic*

In making this move, Plato clearly intended to preserve the metaphysical character of the *eidē* as transcendent ontic forms. He could do this, however, only at the expense of having his logic become entangled in internal antinomies. It was then forced to enter upon the only path open to a dialectical logic that is rooted in a dualistic ground-motive. It had to think its way through the logical contradictions in a process of thought in order to attain to a higher logical synthesis.

The basic error of such a dialectical mode of thought will not become fully apparent to us until we have been confronted with the transcendental critique of philosophical thought, in which I have subjected the problem of theoretical antithesis and synthesis to a fundamental inquiry. For the present, we must content ourselves with the thesis already set forth in the Introduction, namely, that veritable theoretical synthesis requires a supra-logical point of departure, in which the aspects of reality that are theoretically articulated and set over against one another are actually brought to a central focus in a deeper fundamental unity. A dualistic ground-motive such as that of form and matter, however, definitively excludes such a point of departure; it cannot provide theoretical thought, therefore, with any real foundation for theoretical synthesis. If, as a consequence, logic presumes to take over the task of synthesis itself, it must attempt to overcome the theoretical antithesis in a logical way, and in so doing it must jettison the logical principle of contradiction in the actual *syntheses* at which it arrives.

In the *Phaedo*, it was from this very logical principle that the intrinsic self-containedness of the *eidē* was derived. Mutually opposed *eidē* could not be comprehended logically in a single idea. By virtue of the same logical principle, the metaphysical, supersensible ontic form was of necessity held to exclude the eternal becoming of the matter principle, and, similarly, the absolute unity of the *eidos* could not be synthetically combined with the unlimited multiplicity of the sense objects that participate in it. No foundation could be provided for a synthesis among the *eidē* themselves, and of the *eidē* with empirical reality, unless it were possible to achieve a true synthesis between the form and matter principles. Since the religious ground-motive of Greek thought excluded any such synthesis, however, Plato's dialectical logic could offer nothing but bogus solutions of a metaphysical kind.

d. *The Meaning of the Synopsis in the Original Conception of the* Eidē. *The Evasion of the Logical Contradictions in This Conception*

On the other hand, any attempt to think through the earlier metaphysical conception of the *eidē* in a logical manner could only cause it to dissolve at once in internal antinomies. An absolute formal unity which admits of no inner plurality and diversity transcends every logical concept, which always retains its character as a unity in a multiplicity of distin-

of the *Phaedrus*.

guishing features. Therefore, as soon as the attempt was made to grasp this absolute unity in logical terms as an ontic form, this conception had logically to annul itself; for unity, being, and form must necessarily be distinguished in logical analysis, and a logical diversity permits of only a logical, i.e., a relative, unity, not an absolute unity. Plato's greatness and honesty as a thinker is evident to no small degree in the *Parmenides*, a dialogue in which, without any attempt to disguise what he is doing, he brings to light the logical contradictions in which the earlier conception of the *eide* inevitably had to entangle thought, and thus once again renders the entire theory of ideas problematic.

In the first stage of the development of this theory, which received its mature expression in the *Republic*, there was actually no attempt to comprehend the *eidos* in a concept. The aim here, on the contrary, was only to provide for the method of concept formation a real foundation in the metaphysical ontic form. Like the divine *idea*, the *eidos* itself, as the hypothesis of the logical concept, was understood to fall within the scope of an intuitive, synoptic contemplation of essence. Thus, this synopsis was not based on a logical definition of the general nature of a thing or of a state of affairs; instead, it attempted, without logical analysis, to gain a direct view of the ideal ontic form itself as this is represented in concrete, individual instances. This synopsis had an unmistakable poetic, aesthetic quality. Just as an artist seeks to make an ideal portrayal of what is universally human and to represent this in a concrete figure, the Platonic synopsis seeks to apprehend the ideal ontic form through an intuitive mode of thought, which perceives the direct representation of the ideal type in what is concrete and individual.

In this conception of the *eidos*, the logical concept is given a status that is altogether secondary. According to the theory presented in the *Republic* the logical definition, for example, that of justice as $\tau\grave{\alpha}\ \acute{\epsilon}\alpha\upsilon\tauο\hat{\upsilon}\ \pi\rho\acute{\alpha}\tau\tau\epsilon\iota\nu$ (i.e., that each person perform his own proper task within his class), does not make known the *eidos*, the ideal nature of what is under consideration. The use of such a method of definition was necessary to counter the eristic of the Sophists; nevertheless, if such was to lead to true *episteme*, to theoretical knowledge of true being, it had to be founded in a synopsis which related the *eide* themselves to the one divine idea of the good and beautiful ($\sigma\upsilon\nuο\rho\hat{\alpha}\nu\ \epsilon\acute{\iota}\varsigma\ \mu\acute{\iota}\alpha\nu\ \acute{\iota}\delta\acute{\epsilon}\alpha\nu$). The conception of *episteme* as an *anamnesis*, a recollection of the eidetic world that was beheld by the soul in its pre-existent state, was wholly in keeping with this a priori conception of synopsis and its repudiation of empirical phenomena.

In the new stage of development of Plato's dialectic, in contrast, it is precisely the method of logical definition that comes to the fore. A resolute attempt is made to think through the theory of ideas itself in truly logical fashion, to grasp the *eide* in terms of logical relations, and to conceive them in logical relation to the visible world that had been characterized in the *Republic* as the realm of becoming. The doctrine of *anamnesis* no longer plays a role here.

All of this is accompanied by a quite remarkable suppression of the

Eleatic conception of the *eidos* and an attempt to conceive the latter as a type of active soul-substance. The earlier *chōrismos* between the intelligible world of static ontic forms and the visible world of becoming and change is then almost completely absorbed into the metaphysical dichotomy between the *anima rationalis* and the material body, a dichotomy that does not exclude the union of these two.

e. *The Exaltation of the Principle of Motion in the* Theaetetus.
The Acquisition of Knowledge as κίνησις. *Epistemological Analysis of Existential Judgments*

This new conception makes its bold appearance in the *Theaetetus*, a dialogue that doubtless was written after the *Republic*. This dialogue delivers a frontal attack on Protagoras' theory of knowledge, which, as we have seen, consigned human knowledge altogether to the fluidity of the matter principle, the *rheuston* of individual *sensory* perceptions. Nevertheless, it contains at the same time a remarkable exaltation of the principle of motion in connection with the thinking soul and a depreciation of the inertness and quiescence of the soul-substance.[1] Socrates observes that the acquisition of knowledge, like exercise, is an instance of *kinēsis* or motion; rest, by contrast, that is, the lack of exercise and of a desire to learn, causes the soul to forget what it has once learned. Motion, therefore, is something good with respect to the body and soul, while the other, rest, is just the opposite.

A definitive refutation of Protagoras' position is sought here by way of an epistemological analysis of existential judgments, that is to say, judgments which, for instance, attribute to a sound or color that has been perceived by the senses certain general predicates, such as being or non-being, likeness or unlikeness, identity or difference, unity or plurality, beauty or ugliness, goodness or badness. As Socrates demonstrates, all these predicates belong to that which the thinking soul itself apprehends through itself (αὐτὴ δι᾽ αὑτῆς ἡ ψυχὴ), independently of any sense organ belonging to the material body.[2] In Plato's conception, they are undoubtedly grounded in *eidē*; but in existential judgments these *eidē* are con-

---

1 Plato, *Theaetetus*, 153 B.
2 Plato, *Theaetetus*, 185 A ff.; note 186 A: ΣΩ. Ποτέρων οὖν τίθης τὴν οὐσίαν; τοῦτο γὰρ μάλιστ᾽ ἐπὶ πάντων παρέπεται. ΘΕΑΙ. Ἐγὼ μὲν ὧν αὐτὴ ἡ ψυχὴ καθ᾽ αὑτὴν ἐπορέγεται. ΣΩ. Ἦ καὶ τὸ ὅμοιον καὶ τὸ ἀνόμοιον, καὶ τὸ ταὐτὸν καὶ <τὸ> ἕτερον; ΘΕΑΙ. Ναί. ΣΩ. Τί δαί; καλὸν καὶ αἰσχρόν, καὶ ἀγαθὸν καὶ κακόν; ΘΕΑΙ. Καὶ τούτων μοι δοκεῖ ἐν τοῖς μάλιστα πρὸς ἄλληλα σκοπεῖσθαι τὴν οὐσίαν, ἀναλογιζομένη ἐν ἑαυτῇ τὰ γεγονότα καὶ τὰ παρόντα πρὸς τὰ μέλλοντα. ("Socrates: To which of the two [viz., the thinking soul or the bodily sense organs] do you account knowledge of the ontic form? For this, above all, is present in everything. Theaetetus: I place it among that which the soul itself apprehends through itself. Soc.: And also likeness and unlikeness, sameness and otherness? Theaet.: Yes. Soc.: Where then do you place beauty and ugliness, and good and bad? Theaet.: Also with these, it seems to me that it beholds the essence and the mutual relationships above all in thought, in that it compares within itself the past and the present with the future.")

nected, apparently in the most natural way, with *aisthēsis (αἴσθησις)* or sense perception, even though they themselves transcend sense perception as this takes place through the material body and even though they are apprehended only by the thinking soul itself.

f. Being as the Copula in Existential Judgments and as the Presumed Metaphysical Synthesis between Mutually Opposed Eidē.
The Metaphysical Tendency of Plato's New, Dialectical Logic

The existential judgments place the above-mentioned general predicates in relation to one another, so that every "being" implies a "non-being," and vice versa. Thus the positive judgment "This is an animal" implies countless negative judgments, such as "This is not a plant, a stone, a cultural object." In the judgment, therefore, "being" can be joined both to identity and difference ("A *is* different from B and identical to itself"); both to unity and to plurality ("A tree *is* a unity in plurality"); and likewise both to rest and to motion ("I *am* at rest in the moving vehicle").

What then could have been more natural than to attempt by way of a theory of judgment to relativize the *eidē* logically and to bridge the rigid *chōrismos* between the metaphysical ontic forms and the transitory things of experience, which are subject to the matter principle? In developing this logical theory of judgment, however, which particularly in the *Sophist* and the *Statesman* is founded in a theory of logical definition, Plato failed to limit its reference to temporal reality and to conceive the logical aspect in its proper position within the temporal order of aspects and in its theoretical relation to the non-logical aspects. Had he done so, the theory would never have assumed the typically dialectical character, based upon a logical relativization of the principle of contradiction, that was imposed on it especially in the *Parmenides* and the *Sophist*.

In temporal reality, to which existential judgments refer, motion and static (spatial) rest can never constitute absolute opposites. They are both merely distinct aspects of one and the same reality. For this reason, all spatial rest can only be a state of rest within a reality that is simultaneously in motion. The same is the case with unity and plurality. All temporal unity is necessarily a relative unity within plurality, just as all logical determinations such as identity and difference, likeness and unlikeness, are necessarily correlative in character.

Plato's new dialectical logic, however, has a distinct metaphysical tendency that was impressed on it by his religious ground-motive itself. It sets out to relativize in a logical way the *eidē* themselves in their character as metaphysical ontic forms and to derive number, spatiality, and motion logically from the metaphysical oneness of the *eidos* as an ontic form. Its aim in this is to make understandable how this *eidos* can actually be the *aitia*, the effective ontic ground, of the things within temporal reality that participate in it. The "being" that is the copula in existential judgments is thus not referred merely to temporal existence; it is rather conceived as a metaphysical *eidos* that supposedly unites in itself all the other *eidē*. Motion and rest, identity and difference, unity and plurality, etc., are also expressly conceived as *eidē*, with the intention of annulling in the metaphysical synthesis of the all-embracing *eidos* of being the mutual oppositions by which these qualities would absolutely exclude one another.

g. *The Continuing Influence of the Religious Dialectic in Plato's Dialectical Logic*

In Plato's dialectical logic what is at issue, in the final analysis, is a synthesis between the principles of form and matter. The dialectical ground-motive had placed these in absolute opposition to each other. Now Plato was attempting to synthesize them in a purely dialectical-logical way.

In this kind of theoretical dialectic, as we saw in the Introduction, it is religious dialectic, hiding behind the mask of logic, that is everywhere making its presence felt. This religious dialectic essentially sets aside problems that are theoretical, that is to say, scientific (e.g., those of the relation of numerical unity to logical unity, of the logical movement of thought to physical motion) by substituting them with supra-theoretical prejudgments.

The eternal ontic form, in the metaphysical sense of Plato's theory of the *eidē*, can never be joined logically to the Greek matter principle, because the entire polar dualism between these two is rooted in the dialectic of the Greek ground-motive, which is religious in character, and this religious dialectic is in control of Greek logic itself. An *eidos* of *hulē*, such as the *Sophist* will attempt to introduce, is an internally contradictory, self-destructive notion. And the genuinely dialectical attempt to interpret the logical copula ('is'), which joins subject and predicate in existential judgments, as the higher metaphysical synthesis between logically opposed *eidē* can in fact only undermine the metaphysics of the transcendent ontic forms itself; for if motion and rest can both be joined to an *eidos* of being, as is taught in both the *Parmenides* and the *Sophist*, being in its metaphysical sense is actually deprived of everything that could distinguish it from temporal reality. The *chōrismos* is then broken through, in fact, at the cost of the metaphysical character of the *eidē* as absolute forms of being.

This dialectical logic, of course, was unable to bring the dualism of the Greek ground-motive a single step closer to resolution. It rather only served to entangle the theory of ideas in a fundamental crisis. And as the next stage of development makes clear, this crisis could only be overcome by re-instituting the metaphysical dualism between the eidetic world and the world of phenomena and by no longer allowing this dualism to be resolved into the dichotomy of thinking soul and material body. This does not mean, however, that the new dialectical logic will be abandoned; it merely will be restricted in its application to the eidetic structures of that which comes into being through a mixing process. These structures, furthermore, will not in themselves be identified with the pure *eidē*, but will rather be grounded in a system of dialectical relations between them. This new, restricted conception of the dialectical logic will then be worked out in the *Philebus* and the *Timaeus*.

Plato sets forth his new, dialectical logic in the three so-called Eleatic dialogues: the *Parmenides*, the *Sophist*, and the *Statesman* (*Politicus*). In these dialogues, the discussion leader is no longer Socrates, but rather, either the founder of the Eleatic school, Parmenides, or an unnamed pupil of his. The second part of the *Phaedrus*, however, also contains a description and application of the dialectical logic. The first part of this dialogue proceeded from the theory of ideas as it was conceived in its earlier stage of development and even bears certain features of the original Socratic dialogues. In my opinion, there is every reason to follow Brommer in ascribing the dialectical intermezzo in the second part of the *Phaedrus* to a later revision of the dialogue as a whole.

The *Theaetetus*, which, as I have noted, was undoubtedly written after the *Republic* (books II-X), prepares the way for the Eleatic trilogy.[1] In its frontal attack on the way the Heraclitean matter principle is carried through in Protagoras' theory of knowledge, this dialogue anticipates the fundamental critique of the Eleatic ontology that would be presented later in the *Parmenides* and the *Sophist*. In the *Theaetetus* there is already clear evidence of Plato's ambition to achieve a metaphysical synthesis between the positions of Heraclitus and the Eleatics, which would be sought by way of a fundamental transformation of the theory of ideas.

At this point, I shall subject the *Parmenides* and the *Sophist*, in particular, to a more or less thorough critical analysis in order to shed a clear light on the continuing influence of the religious dialectic in the new dialectical logic.

2. **The Dialectic of the Form-Matter Motive in the *Parmenides* and the New, Logical Function of the Idea. The Dynamization of the *Eidē* as Active Soul-Forces (*Parmenides* and *Sophist*) and the Eideticization of the Matter Principle**

a. *The Three* Aporias *of the Doctrine of* Methexis *in the* Parmenides

In the *Parmenides*, the founder of the Eleatic school, who now leads the discussion, brings three *aporias* or apparent antinomies to the attention of the young Socrates. The latter has been defending the earlier conception of the Platonic theory of ideas. Now Parmenides observes that this conception inevitably entangles theoretical thought in these antinomies, which are intimately connected with the problem of *methexis*. We have already seen that it is precisely this that formed the crux of the earlier conception of the *eidē*. The question of how visible things that are subject to the matter principle of eternal flux can participate in the world of immutable ontic forms poses in essence the genuinely religious-dialectical problem regarding the possibility of a synthesis between the principles of form and matter.

The young Socrates, who in the discussion is undoubtedly defending Plato's earlier position, claims that the theory of ideas is able to escape the

---

1   In his paper "The Course of Plato's Development" (*Mélanges philosophiques: Bibliothèque du Xme Congrès international de philosophie, II* (Amsterdam, 1948), 1-16, p. 8, D.H.Th. Vollenhoven underwrites Schleiermacher's view that the *Theaetetus* was written after the *Parmenides*. His argument for this position, however, has failed to convince me.

antinomies worked out by Parmenides' pupil Zeno. The latter had sought to demonstrate that thought is ensnared in these antinomies if it is assumed that reality contains plurality, diversity, and motion. What Socrates sets forth here is basically the conception of the *eidē* that had been developed in the *Phaedo*. According to this conception, there is one immutable *eidos* of qualititative likeness which stands by itself (αὐτὸ καθ᾽ αὐτό) and one *eidos* of unlikeness that is opposed to this. The multiplicity of things in the sensible world participates in both of these *eidē*. Because of this the things that are subject to constant change are able to have mutually contradictory predicates, for they can share in two different *eidē*. The *eidē* themselves, however, can never turn into their opposites. The same applies to the relationship between the *eidē* of unity and plurality. Although in themselves these *eidē* mutually exclude each other as opposites, they nevertheless permit of a simultaneous *parousia* in transitory things, since the latter participate both in unity and plurality.[1]

At this point, however, Socrates invites Zeno, who is present at the discussion, to apply the dialectical method also to the *eidē*, such as those of qualitative likeness and unlikeness, unity and plurality, rest and motion, and other such qualities, and to demonstrate that these can at the same time be entwined with each other and be set apart from one another in pairs (διαίρεσις). Such a dialectic, which would prove that the world of *eidē* contains the same *aporias* as the world of visible things, would fill him with amazement.[2] This is the first mention of the *diairesis* of the *eidē*, a concern which forms the principal theme of the *Sophist*.

---

1 Plato, *Parmenides*, 129 A, B: οὐ νομίζεις εἶναι αὐτὸ καθ᾽ αὐτὸ εἶδός τι ὁμοιότητος, καὶ τῷ τοιούτῳ αὖ ἄλλο τι ἐναντίον, ὅ ἐστιν ἀνόμοιον, τούτοιν δὲ δυεῖν ὄντοιν, κἀμὲ καὶ σὲ καὶ τἆλλα, ἃ δὴ πολλὰ καλοῦμεν, μεταλαμβάνειν; καὶ τὰ μὲν τῆς ὁμοιότητος μεταλαμβάνοντα ὅμοια γίγνεσθαι ταύτῃ τε καὶ κατὰ τοσοῦτον, ὅσον ἂν μεταλαμβάνῃ, τὰ δὲ τῆς ἀνομοιότητος ἀνόμοια, τὰ δ᾽ ἀμφοτέρων ἀμφότερα; εἰ δὲ καὶ πάντ᾽ ἐναντίων ὄντων ἀμφοτέρων μεταλαμβάνει, καὶ ἔστι τῷ μετέχειν ἀμφοῖν ὅμοιά τε καὶ ἀνόμοια αὐτὰ αὑτοῖς, τί θαυμαστόν; *Ibid.*, 129 B: εἰ δὲ τὰ τούτων μετέχοντα ἀμφοτέρων ἀμφότερα ἀποφαίνει πεπονθότα, οὐδέν ἔμοιγε, ὦ Ζήνων, ἄτοπον δοκεῖ εἶναι, οὐδέ γ᾽ εἰ ἓν ἅπαντ᾽ ἀποφαίνει τις τῷ μετέχειν τοῦ ἑνὸς καὶ ταὐτὰ ταῦτα πολλὰ τῷ πλήθους αὖ μετέχειν· ("Do you not think that there is an *eidos* of likeness, existing in itself, and again, in opposition to this, an *eidos* of unlikeness, and that in these two ontic forms I and you and the other things that we call 'the many' participate? Also, that the things which participate in likeness become alike in that respect and to the degree that they participate [in this *eidos*], those participating in unlikeness become unlike, and those that participate in both become both? But if all things participate in both opposite *eidē* and through their partaking of both are like and unlike one another, what is surprising in that? ... if someone thus proves that things partaking of both [*eidē*] experience both [viz., coming to be like and unlike], this would not seem extraordinary at least to me, Zeno, nor would I be surprised if someone should prove that all is one insofar as it partakes of unity, and that it is again many in that it also partakes of multiplicity.")

2 *Ibid.*, 129 D and E: ἐὰν δέ τις, ὃ νῦν δὴ ἐγὼ ἔλεγον, πρῶτον μὲν διαιρῆται χωρὶς αὐτὰ καθ᾽ αὑτὰ τὰ εἴδη, οἷον ὁμοιότητά τε καὶ ἀνομοιότητα καὶ πλῆθος καὶ τὸ ἓν

The discussion leader, Parmenides, then asks the young Socrates whether he thinks that besides the *eidē* of qualitative likeness and unlikeness, unity and plurality, justice, beauty, goodness, etc., there is an *eidos* of man that stands by itself, or one of fire and water. When Socrates hesitates to commit himself here, Parmenides remarks that one may not despise any of these things and that there is no reason to deny the existence of an *eidos* even of hair or dirt.[1] This remark brings with it the implicit recognition of the need to accept eternal, transcendent ontic forms for all things in the visible cosmos without exception. This also requires, of course, a much closer connection with the empirical world than had been the case with the earlier conception of the *eidē* as ideal forms.

The former Platonic conception of this eidetic world is now confronted with three *aporias*: 1. Do the individual things in the world of phenomena each participate in the entire *eidos*, or only in a part of it? In the first case, the theory becomes involved in the antinomy that what is 'one' cannot be present in a number of things that are separate from one another without being separated from itself.[2] In the second case the antinomy arises that the *eidē* would then themselves be divisible and could no longer be simple in nature, although this is what had been assumed.[3] In addition, things that participate in only part of an *eidos* could no longer be named after the

καὶ στάσιν καὶ κίνησιν καὶ πάντα τὰ τοιαῦτα, εἰτ᾽ ἐν ἑαυτοῖς ταῦτα δυνάμενα συγκεράννυσθαι καὶ διακρίνεσθαι ἀποφαίνη, ἀγαίμην ἂν ἔγωγ᾽, ἔφη, θαυμαστῶς, ὦ Ζήνων. ("But if someone should first set apart in pairs the self-subsistent *eidē* of the things of which I just spoke – for instance, likeness and unlikeness, plurality and unity, rest and motion, and all other such ontic forms – and then prove that they in themselves can be combined with and separated from one another, I would be surprised at this, dear Zeno.") *Ibid.*, 129 E to 130 A: πολὺ μεντᾶν ὧδε μᾶλλον ... ἀγασθείην, εἴ τις ἔχοι τὴν αὐτὴν ταύτην ἀπορίαν ἐν αὐτοῖς τοῖς εἴδεσι παντοδαπῶς πλεκομένην, ὥσπερ ἐν τοῖς ὁρωμένοις διήλθετε, οὕτω καὶ ἐν τοῖς λογισμῷ λαμβανομένοις ἐπιδεῖξαι. ("But I would find it even more amazing if someone could prove that the same perplexity is in any way involved in the *eidē* themselves, and, just as you have shown it in visible things, is also encountered in the [*eidē*] that can be apprehended solely by theoretical thought.")

1 Stenzel, *op. cit,* p. 28, points out that the offense which the young Socrates takes at the thought of *eidē* of hair, dirt, etc., can only be explained in terms of the ethical-aesthetical value which Plato at first ascribed to the *eidos* in connection with the idea of the *kalokagathon*. "Er will von einer ἀρετή des Schmutzes nicht sprechen, von einem εἶδος dass reiner und klarer als der Schmutz auf Erden Schmutz ist" ("He will not speak of an ἀρετή of dirt, an εἶδος that is more purely and clearly dirt than the dirt upon earth" (tr.7).)

2 Plato, *Parmenides*, 131 A and B: Πότερον οὖν δοκεῖ σοι ὅλον τὸ εἶδος ἐν ἑκάστῳ εἶναι τῶν πολλῶν ἓν ὄν; After Socrates' affirmative reply, Parmenides continues: Ἓν ἄρ᾽ ὂν καὶ ταὐτὸν ἐν πολλοῖς χωρὶς οὖσιν ὅλον ἅμ᾽ ἐνέσται, καὶ οὕτως αὐτὸ αὑτοῦ χωρὶς ἂν εἴη. ("Do you think that the whole *eidos* as one ontic form is in each of the many things? ...It will then, as one and the same ontic form, at the same time be wholly present in many separate things, and in this manner it would be separated from itself.")

3 *Ibid.*, 131 C (pertaining to the second case, where individual things only participate

eidos as a whole. 2. A group of many things from the world of sense sharing the same character demands the acceptance of a single *eidos* that corresponds to them (e.g., the many large things correspond to the *eidos* of largeness). The *eidos* of largeness and the many large things that correspond to it, however, require in turn a new *eidos* of largeness of higher order by which the participation of these things in the first *eidos* can be measured. And over and above all of these there must be yet another *eidos* by virtue of which they are all large, and so on *ad infinitum*. Each *eidos* will then no longer be one, but an infinite multiplicity. That is to say, the *eidos* is unable to maintain itself as a simple ontic form, but instead dissolves into the *apeiron*.[1] Socrates attempts to avoid this inference by proposing the hypothesis that the *eidē* are perhaps only subjective *noḗmata* (*noēmata*), subjective mental contents that exist only within the thinking soul. In this case each *eidos* would nevertheless remain one.[2] Parmenides counters this evasive maneuver, however, by pointing out that every *noēma* refers to a real object (*Gegenstand*), and that the *noēma* of an *eidos* thus necessarily presupposes the *eidos* as a single ontic form. The conception of the *eidē* as primal models or paradigms (παραδείγματα) in whose image the objects of sense are fashioned is also rejected, since the resemblance between the *eidos* and the things named after it would again presuppose the standard of an *eidos* of higher order, and so on ad infinitum. 3. In those ideas (*ideai*) which involve an intrinsic correlation (e.g., that of master and slave), the correlation can apply only within the eidetic world and has no bearing on the world of phenomena.[3] Examples of such correlata are

---

in a part of the *eidos*): Μεριστὰ ἄρα, φάναι, ὦ Σώκρατες, ἔστιν αὐτὰ τὰ εἴδη, καὶ τὰ μετέχοντ᾽ αὐτῶν μέρους ἂν μετέχοι, καὶ οὐκέτ᾽ ἐν ἑκάστῳ ὅλον, ἀλλὰ μέρος ἑκάστου ἂν εἴη ... καὶ ἔτι ἓν ἔσται; ("Then, dear Socrates, he said, the *eidē* themselves are divisible, and the things participating in them would participate in only a part, and in each of these there would no longer be the whole [*eidos*], but a part of it ... and will it [the *eidos*] still be one?")

1 *Ibid.*, 132 A and B: Ἄλλο ἄρ᾽ εἶδος μεγέθους ἀναφανήσεται, παρ᾽ αὐτό τε τὸ μέγεθος γεγονὸς καὶ τὰ μετέχοντα αὐτοῦ· καὶ ἐπὶ τούτοις αὖ πᾶσιν ἕτερον, ᾧ ταῦτα πάντα μεγάλα ἔσται· καὶ οὐκέτι δὴ ἓν ἕκαστόν σοι τῶν εἰδῶν ἔσται, ἀλλ᾽ ἄπειρα τὸ πλῆθος. ("Then another *eidos* of largeness will appear that has taken shape alongside largeness in itself and the things that participate in it, and above all of these yet another, by virtue of which they are all large. And each of the *eidē* will no longer be one for you, but an infinite number.")

2 *Ibid.*: Ἀλλά, φάναι, ὦ Παρμενίδη, τὸν Σωκράτη, μὴ τῶν εἰδῶν ἕκαστον τούτων ᾖ νόημα, καὶ οὐδαμοῦ αὐτῷ προσήκῃ ἐγγίγνεσθαι ἄλλοθι ἢ ἐν ψυχαῖς. οὕτω γὰρ ἂν ἕν γ᾽ ἕκαστον εἴη (... "But, dear Parmenides, said Socrates, could not each of the *eidē* be a thought content (*noēma*), which could not properly come into existence anywhere but in the soul? For in this way each could yet be one.")

3 *Ibid.*, 133 C: Οὐκοῦν καὶ ὅσαι τῶν ἰδεῶν πρὸς ἀλλήλας εἰσὶν αἵ εἰσιν, αὐταὶ πρὸς αὑτὰς τὴν οὐσίαν ἔχουσιν, ἀλλ᾽ οὐ πρὸς τὰ παρ᾽ ἡμῖν εἴθ᾽ ὁμοιώματα εἴθ᾽ ὅπῃ δή τις αὐτὰ τίθεται, ὧν ἡμεῖς μετέχοντες εἶναι ἕκαστα ἐπονομαζόμεθα· ("And there-

theoretical knowledge and truth (i.e., true being).[1] Truth in itself, as an *eidos*, thus cannot be an *Gegenstand* (object) of the thought of individual human beings, for the latter refers only to the truth that exists for us.[2] We therefore can have no knowledge of the *eidē* as eternal ontic forms existing in themselves;[3] thus, the ideal knowledge of the *eidē* apparently belongs only to the deity.

If God has possession of this knowledge in itself, however, he can have no knowledge of the individual things in the visible cosmos, for we have seen the correlation between the *eidē* is restricted to the transcendent world of being, along with ideal knowledge. Thus the *eidē* can have no causative efficacy (*dunamis*), no controlling form-power (δεσποτεία), with with respect to sensible things that are an object of knowledge independent of these *eidē*, nor can the reverse be the case.[4] If, therefore, com-

---

fore, those *ideai* which are what they are in relation to one another have their being in relation to each other, not however, in relation to the 'likenesses' [copies], or whatever else they are represented to be, which are found by us, and participating in which we ascribe being to each thing by name.")

1 *Ibid.*, 134 A: Οὐκοῦν καὶ ἐπιστήμη, φάναι, αὐτὴ μὲν ὃ ἔστι ἐπιστήμη τῆς ὃ ἔστιν ἀλήθεια, αὐτῆς ἂν ἐκείνης εἴη ἐπιστήμη; ("Then also, he said, knowledge in itself, of that which is truth in itself, would it not be knowledge of the latter itself?")

2 *Ibid.*: Ἡ δὲ παρ' ἡμῖν ἐπιστήμη οὐ τῆς παρ' ἡμῖν ἂν ἀληθείας εἴη; καὶ αὖ ἑκάστη ἡ παρ' ἡμῖν ἐπιστήμη τῶν παρ' ἡμῖν ὄντων ἑκάστου ἂν ἐπιστήμη συμβαίνοι εἶναι; Ἀνάγκη. ("But would not our knowledge be of the truth that exists for us? And again, would not each item of knowledge present to us be knowledge of each of the things that exist for us? This will, of necessity, be the case.")

3 *Ibid.*, 134 Β: Γιγνώσκεται δέ γέ που ὑπ' αὐτοῦ τοῦ εἴδους τοῦ τῆς ἐπιστήμης αὐτὰ τὰ γένη, ἃ ἔστιν ἕκαστα; Ναί. Ὁ γ' ἡμεῖς οὐκ ἔχομεν. Οὐ γάρ. Οὐκ ἄρ' ὑπό γ' ἡμῶν γιγνώσκεται τῶν εἰδῶν οὐδέν, ἐπειδὴ αὐτῆς ἐπιστήμης οὐ μετέχομεν. Οὐκ ἔοικεν. Ἄγνωστον ἄρ' ἡμῖν ἐστι καὶ αὐτὸ τὸ καλὸν ὃ ἔστι καὶ τἀγαθὸν καὶ πάντα, ἃ δὴ ὡς ἰδέας αὐτὰς οὔσας ὑπολαμβάνομεν. ("But is not each of the real *genē* [i.e., the *eidē* of the *Gegenstände*, brought forth by the divine *idea*] known by the eidos of knowledge in itself? Certainly. Which form we do not possess? No indeed. Then none of the *eidē* is known by us, since we have no part in knowledge in itself. Apparently not. Then beauty in itself, and goodness, and everything that we take as self-subsistent *ideai*, are unknowable to us.") Very soon I shall enter into a more detailed discussion in the text of the use of the term γένη. It is striking that both this and the subsequent term ἰδέαι are directly connected with the immediately following description of the knowledge of the *eidē* that God must possess. In this knowledge, the *eidē* as a matter of course will always be apprehended in genetic relation to the *idea tou agathou*, and they will thereby themselves be conceived as *ideai*, i.e., as *eidē* in their relation to the divine *idea* as origin. For Parmenides' critique here is directed against the theory of ideas in its initial conception, which we have already come to know in its mature form in the *Republic*.

4 *Ibid.*, 134 Ď: μητ' ἐκεῖνα τὰ εἴδη πρὸς τὰ παρ' ἡμῖν τὴν δύναμιν ἔχειν ἣν ἔχει, μήτε τὰ παρ' ἡμῖν πρὸς ἐκεῖνα, ἀλλ' αὐτὰ πρὸς αὐτὰ ἑκάτερα. ("that neither those *eidē* have the *dunamis* that they possess in relation to the things in our world, nor conversely, but each of the two only in relation to itself.")

plete mastery (form-power) in itself (i.e., the *dunamis* of the *eidē*, which are brought forth by the divine form-power of the *idea*) and complete knowledge in itself were to reside with God, this mastery would be unable to rule us as empirical beings, nor could this knowledge know us or anything else in the visible cosmos.[1]

Here then there is an explicit acknowledgment that there was an internal antinomy present between the former (Eleatic) conception of the *eidē* and the form motive of the religion of culture, which was embodied in the Socratic idea as the controlling form of origin of the visible cosmos. Later, Aristotle would point out similar *aporias* in Plato's theory of ideas. Nevertheless, Parmenides concludes, to abandon the *eidē* as eternal ontic forms because of all the difficulties expounded here would cause every *Gegenstand* of theoretical thought to vanish, and the possibility of scientific knowledge, which must always be focused on being in its abiding self-identity, would thereby be eliminated.

When the young Socrates is thrown into deep perplexity by this line of argument, the founder of the Eleatic school advises him to submit to a training in Zeno's dialectical method, and, in particular, repeatedly to pursue the logical consequences of both a positive acceptance and a negation of the *eidos*. At the request of Socrates and Zeno, Parmenides finally declares that he is willing to demonstrate this dialectical method himself as it is applied to the idea of unity. It is noteworthy that he carries this out in dialogue with the young Aristotle, the junior member of the party. Plato no doubt introduces the latter into this discussion because, as the most brilliant of his pupils, he was sure to have raised dialectical objections against the original conception of the *eidē* while he was a member of the Academy.

b. The Use of the Terms εἶδος and ἰδέα in This Section of the
    Dialogue. The Idea *as a Dialectical Correlation of*
    Opposed Eidē

Before we examine more closely Parmenides' dialectical arguments, which often appear at first sight to be sophistical, we should first center our attention on the use of the terms *eidos* and *idea* in the previous sec-

---

1 *Ibid.*: Οὐκοῦν εἰ παρὰ τῷ θεῷ αὐτή ἐστιν ἡ ἀκριβεστάτη δεσποτεία καὶ αὐτὴ ἡ ἀκριβεστάτη ἐπιστήμη, οὔτ' ἂν ἡ δεσποτεία ἡ 'κείνων ἡμῶν ποτ' ἂν δεσπόσειεν, οὔτ' ἂν ἡ ἐπιστήμη ἡμᾶς γνοίη οὐδέ τι ἄλλο τῶν παρ' ἡμῖν. ("If then this highest mastery [i.e., the *dunamis* of the *eidē*] in itself and highest knowledge in itself reside with the deity, the mastery of these [*eidē*] could not rule us, nor could the knowledge [of the *eidē*] know us or any other of the things in our world.") The direct connection between the divine knowledge of the *eidē* and possession of their form-power as the highest mastery is entirely consistent with the thought of Anaxagoras and Socrates.

198

tion of this dialogue. A close study of this makes plain that Plato here uses the term *idea* to denote the higher unity which embraces the correlation between two opposite *eidē*.[1] We shall encounter this same terminology again in the *Sophist*. In the first stage of development of Plato's theory of ideas there was as yet no place for this function of the *idea*, since at that time any correlation at all between the *eidē* was completely out of the picture. In the *Republic* we still find only the theoretical *Gegenstand* relation between ideal knowledge and the *eidos*. The introduction of the above function of the idea into the Eleatic dialogues was a consequence of the new, dialectical turn in the theory of the ideas, which now attempted, insofar as this appeared possible, to think through in a logical manner the relationship between the divine *idea* and the *eidē*, which in the *Republic* had merely been an a priori postulate.[2] Naturally, it its dialectical-synthetical function, the *idea* is not itself the divine *idea* as a primal form; rather, it is only the metaphysical-logical expression or manifestation of the divine form-power of the idea, which brings all of the *eidē* to a single focus within itself and also into logical relation with one another.

It is highly characteristic that within this context Plato should also designate the *eidos* of higher order by the term *genos*,[3] something that has been pointed out especially by Brommer.[4] For the latter term undoubtedly refers in a metaphysical sense to the genetic relation that exists between the *eidē* and the divine *idea*. We have seen in the *Republic* how the *eidos* derives its being from the divine *idea tou agathou*. Thus, in this connection, the word *genos* may not be identified at all with the logical genus.

Lastly, we note that the words $\varepsilon\bar{i}\delta o\varsigma$ and $i\delta\acute{e}a$ can be used, apparently as synonyms, in one and the same passage.[5] I follow Brommer, however, in believing that this synonymity is actually not present. It seems to me that Plato is here using the term *idea* in contrast to *eidos*. *Idea* could denote the subjective synopsis or comprehensive vision of the *eidos*, specifically in its relation to the divine *idea* as the form of origin. Alternatively, the term could denote the *eidos* itself in its concentric, genetic relationship to this *idea*, a relation that Plato explicitly represents as being one of both knowl-

---

1   See the quotation from *Parmenides*, 133 C on page 196.
2   For the reasons given in note 4 on page 197, I hold that Stenzel's claim that the *idea tou agathou* has been completely eliminated in the Eleatic dialogues is entirely wrong. In my opinion we need only refer to the *Sophist*, 254 a, to refute his position, to which I shall refer again at a later point.
3   Cf. the quotation of 134 B on page 197.
4   Brommer, *op. cit.*, p. 159.
5   Cf., for example, *Parmenides*, 134 E and 135 A: Ταῦτα μέντοι, ὦ Σώκρατες, ἔφη ὁ Παρμενίδης, καὶ ἔτι ἄλλα πρὸς τούτοις πάνυ πολλὰ ἀναγκαῖον ἔχειν τὰ εἴδη, εἰ εἰσὶν αὗται αἱ ἰδέαι τῶν ὄντων καὶ ὁριεῖταί τις αὐτό τι ἕκαστον εἶδος· ("These [difficulties], dear Socrates, said Parmenides, and still very many others are indeed necessarily involved with the *eidē*, if these *ideai* of real things [truly] are and one defines each *eidos* individually in itself.")

edge and control.[1] That the *eidos* stands in relation to the *idea* here completely escapes Brommer. Yet, according to Plato, synopsis never focuses on the *eidos* in isolation; it rather always focuses on the *eidos* in its genetic relation to the *idea*, which here has its pregnant meaning of the divine form of origin functioning as a *dunamis* or form-power. What is at work in this notion of the *idea* as the *idea* of an *eidos* is still the Socratic tendency in concept formation to draw things to a central focus. Plato had never abandoned this Socratic motive after his earliest dialogues, and in the *Republic* it takes a significant metaphysical turn in the theory of ideas. A third alternative interpretation of the passage cited above is to conceive the *ideai* as dialectical relations among opposed *eidē*.

c. *The First Path Taken by the Dialectical Argument: The One
    Conceived as Absolute Leads Logical Thought to the Absolute
    Negation of All Predicates*

We now return to Parmenides' dialectical analysis of the one. The first part of this analysis assumes the Eleatic hypothesis that the one truly *is* and that it thus has metaphysical *being*. As this hypothesis is developed, the one is first of all taken in the abstract, absolute sense that had been given to it by the Eleatics (and, in the first place, by Parmenides), that is, as a unity that excludes all plurality, motion, change, becoming, etc.[2]

The discussion leader, Parmenides, shows that a unity of this kind may not be conceived as a whole, since a whole has parts and thus contains a plurality. It then also can have no beginning, middle, or end. And since a beginning and end would impose a *peras* or limit on the one, it would have to be an *apeiron*, a measureless and boundless infinity. Further, the one cannot be conceived in a supersensible geometric form (σχῆμα), as Parmenides himself had done, since the form of the sphere is of necessity a whole having parts. Still further, the predicates of motion or rest may not be attributed to such a one conceived as absolute. Motion is understood here once again in the typically Greek sense, as that is tied in with the matter motive of constant change or flux whether this be in position or in quality. Change of this nature presupposes an infinite multiplicity of states and is thus incompatible with the Eleatic negative conception of the one. "The one, if it were subject to change, could not possibly still be one" [in an absolute sense].[3]

The static rest that the Eleatics ascribed to the one can as little apply to a unity conceived negatively, however; for rest assumes that the one remains always in the same spatial position, and this would only be possible if it were either found in something else that forms its "environment," or if it were enclosed in itself. Neither of these options is acceptable, however, since both presuppose a duality that is excluded by the negative conception of the one.

The predicates of identity and difference, as well as qualitative and

---

1   See above, note 2 on page 198.
2   *Ibid.*, 137 C to 142 B.
3   *Ibid.*, 138 C: Ἀλλοιούμενον δὲ τὸ ἓν ἑαυτοῦ ἀδύνατόν που ἓν ἔτι εἶναι.

quantitative likeness and unlikeness, may also not be attributed to a one of this nature. The absolute one cannot be identical to itself and different from what is other, since identity and difference are something other than the one regarded in itself, and the same applies to qualitative and quantitative likeness and unlikeness. Any relation in which the one might be placed, whether to itself or to something other would divide up this abstract unity into a plurality.

Lastly, such a unity cannot at all participate in time. Therefore, it not only can never have come into being, but it also cannot even be *now*, in the present time. The Eleatics had assumed the latter, and they thereby conceived the eternal simultaneous presence of the one, undivided form of being in terms of the static spatial aspect of time. With a dialectical rigor that leaves nothing out of consideration, Plato now shows, through his spokesman Parmenides, that in reality this conception still places the one that *is* in time.[1] In so doing, however, he fails to make clear, as is done by the Philosophy of the Law-Idea in its analysis of the distinct aspects of time, that what is at issue in the Eleatic conception of the *now* (in the sense of absolute simultaneity) is in fact this static spatial aspect of time.

The outcome of this *beginning* analysis is that the one, in the abstract negative sense that the Eleatic school had given to it, cannot at all participate in *being*. For we can never grasp true being apart from plurality, form, rest or motion, identity or difference, or qualitative likeness or unlikeness, and without relating it to time in some way or other. Similarly, if the oneness of the *eidos* itself is elevated above time, if it does not at least operate as a *dunamis* within the temporal sphere, then it cannot be a cause of visible things.

By means of dialectical argument, the Eleatic thesis that "the one *is*" is thus shown to be untenable so long as unity is taken in the abstract sense that this school gave to it. A unity of this kind breaks down of its own accord in internal antinomies. It cannot be given a name nor can it be apprehended in a concept, and it does not admit of theoretical knowledge, nor perception, nor opinion (*doxa*). With exquisite irony, Plato allows Parmenides here to turn his own conception of the indivisible form of being into its opposite. All of the predicates that the thinker from Elea had ascribed to this indivisible form of being in his didactic poem are now denied to it one by one through a dialectical mode of thought which penetrates into the concept of unity on which it was founded. This analysis applied, by implication, just as well to the original Platonic conception of the *eidē*, however, for these were posited as static "Eleatic ones" of the same sort, each standing alone and unrelated to the others.

---

1 *Ibid.*, 141 E: Τὸ δὲ δὴ ἔστι καὶ τὸ γίγνεται οὐ τοῦ νῦν παρόντος; ... Εἰ ἄρα τὸ ἓν μηδαμῇ μηδενὸς μετέχει χρόνου ... οὔτε νῦν γέγονεν οὔτε γίγνεται οὐτ' ἔστιν ... ("But doesn't 'is' and 'is becoming' still [signify] a participation in what is now present? ...If therefore the one in no way shares in any time,... then it has not now become, nor is it now becoming, nor is it now.")

d. In Making the Absolute Contrast between Unity and Plurality, Plato Is Adhering to the Primordial Dualism of His Religious Ground-Motive

All of this in no way means that Plato is here simply denying the reality of an absolute, undifferentiated, supra-temporal one. For him, this one is present in the divine origin of all ontic form, which as the absolute *archē* lies at the foundation of all relative unity. As we have already seen in the *Republic*, however, this absolute unity is exalted above the eidetic world of ontic forms themselves and can neither be apprehended in any way by human thought in a concept, nor be signified by means of a name.

e. The First, Negative Part of Parmenides' Dialectical Argument as a Negative Theology of the Divine Unitary Origin of All Form. The Second Path of the Dialectical Argument

In other words, this first, negative path of Plato's dialectical analysis of the one is not merely a negative critique of Parmenides' identification of this unity with the form of being. It also constitutes the beginning of what is called negative theology. With the addition of a religious motive borrowed from the Jewish Hellenistic thinker Philo, this theology was to be further elaborated in neo-Platonic thought, in order then by way of Augustine to become an enduring component of Scholastic theology.

After the dialectical analysis of the Eleatic conception of the one has yielded its negative conclusion, the logical consequences of the hypothesis that the one truly *is* are developed in a positive manner. If the one indeed partakes of metaphysical being, it cannot be conceived in purely negative terms.

Unity and being cannot be one and the same; rather, they must be understood as parts that are indissolubly joined together within a whole that embraces them both. And since the whole is determinative of its parts, being and unity must again be indissolubly joined together in each of these parts. At the same time, however, unity and being must be regarded as *different* from each other. If being is thus different from the one, and vice versa, then the one cannot differ from being by virtue of its being one, nor can being differ from the one that *is* by virtue of its being being. Rather, it can only be difference or otherness that differentiates them from each other. Thus difference is coterminous neither with unity nor with being. In the necessary relation of the one to difference, and of difference to being, a twoness is given in the form of pairs, with each of the related terms preserving its intrinsic oneness.

The discussion leader thinks that he has discovered here the metaphysical-logical origin of the even number. He also believes that he has discovered the origin of the odd number as well, for, according to Parmenides, the latter is necessarily given with the threeness of unity, being, and otherness or difference. Otherness forms a kind of mediation or synthesis between the one and being, since it is common to both in their reciprocal relationship. The relationships in which these three simple *eidē* can stand to one another contain in rudimentary form all numbers and numerical relations. To be explicit, they can be combined with one another in pairs and by threes, and from these elementary relationships of one, two, and three both to themselves and to each other, multiplication and increase of exponential power can produce ever new combinations of numbers that can be continued indefinitely. As Parmenides observes, the one in this respect, that is to say, in its relation to being and thus as a *real* unity, seems therefore to be divided within itself into an infinite plurality. Each of these infinitely numerous numbers preserves something of the original one and of being, however, since as parts of the whole constituted by the real one they are determined by this whole. Every number thus participates in both unity and being.

Therefore, if the one *is*, there must also be number. But if number *is*, then there must be an unlimited plurality of things that *are*, all of which participate in being.[1] "Being is thus distributed over all [members] of a plurality of beings,"[2] and there is an infinite number of parts of being. On the other hand, each part of being must itself be a unity and thus participate in the one, and since being is indissolubly joined to the one, the one itself is divided into an unlimited plurality of ones (units). Implicitly, this provides us with the provisional solution to the first *aporia* singled out in Plato's notion of the *methexis* of sensible objects in the *eidē*: number is the first intermediary between the eidetic world and the world of phenomena. It is only through number that the objects of sense perception can participate in the oneness of the ontic form. For in the infinite plurality within the series of numbers, number partakes both of the original unity and of being; but as an infinite series it is nevertheless also an *apeiron*, a plurality that is always coming into being. It is, in its oneness, a *peras*, and in its plurality, an *apeiron*. The *Philebus* will elaborate this Pythagorean notion at greater length.

If then the one is divided by being into an unlimited plurality of parts, it is of necessity also a whole, since without a whole there can be no parts. As a whole, furthermore, the one is necessarily limited, for the parts are embraced by the whole, and that which embraces them forms their limit (*peras*). On this account, the one, as a real unity, is at the same time both one and many, a whole and its parts, limited and – in respect of its infi-

---

1   *Ibid.*, 144 A: Εἰ ἄρ᾽ ἔστιν ἕν, ἀνάγκη καὶ ἀριθμὸν εἶναι ... Ἀλλὰ μὴν ἀριθμοῦ γ᾽ ὄντος, πολλὰ ἂν εἴη καὶ πλῆθος ἄπειρον τῶν ὄντων. ἢ οὐκ ἄπειρος ἀριθμὸς πλήθει καὶ μετέχων οὐσίας γίγνεται ; ("If therefore the one is, there must also be number.... But if number has being, then there can also be plurality and an unlimited multitude of things that are. Or does number not arise by being unlimited in plurality and participating in being?")

2   *Ibid.*, 144 B: Ἐπὶ πάντ᾽ ἄρα πολλὰ ὄντα ἡ οὐσία νενέμηται... (Translation in the text.)

nitely numerous parts – unlimited.[1]

*f. The Dialectical Derivation of Spatiality and Motion from the
    Real One*

If the real one is a whole, however, it must then also have a beginning,
middle, and end. Apart from these three, the discussion leader maintains, there can be no real whole. The middle must be equidistant from
the outermost extremities, since otherwise it would not constitute a middle. A real unity of this nature must then also necessarily have a spatial
form *(schēma),* whether this be straight, curved, or a mixture of both.[2]
Having such a form, the one whole must be situated in something else,
and it is therefore itself a member of a plurality. Insofar as the whole is
the sum of all its parts, however, it must always be enclosed in itself.[3]
Thus, following upon number and numerical relationships, the discussion leader also derives spatial relationships from the metaphysical-logical one, showing that they accompany it by logical necessity.

The dialectical reasoning continues by positing the metaphysical-logical real unity as the origin also of rest and motion. As a self-contained
whole, embracing all its parts, the one must be considered as at rest. As a
whole that is situated in something other, however, it can never be simply
in itself, but is rather in constant motion or change. In other words, as a
self-contained whole the one is always identical to itself; but as an unlimited plurality which as such is located in the other, it always differs from
itself and is thus involved in constant change, becoming, and flowing motion.[4]

The real one, furthermore, as a unity that is identical with itself, is like
itself (qualitatively) as to its nature. At the same time, however, it is like in
nature to the other, since as *eide* that differ from each other both of these
have in common the predicate *difference.* On the other hand, it also differs
in nature from the other, since its very identity constitutes a property that
is opposed to the *eidos* of difference.[5] The same considerations apply to
quantitative likeness and unlikeness in spatial magnitude and in number.

---

1 *Ibid.,* 145 A: Τὸ ἓν ἄρ᾽ ὂν ἕν τέ ἐστί που καὶ πολλά, καὶ ὅλον καὶ μόρια, καὶ
    πεπερασμένον καὶ ἄπειρον πλήθει. (Translation in the text.)
2 *Ibid.,* 145 A and B: εἰ ὅλον, οὐ καὶ ἀρχὴν ἂν ἔχοι καὶ μέσον καὶ τελευτήν; ...
    Ἀλλὰ μὴν τό γε μένον ἴσον τῶν ἐσχάτων ἀπέχει· οὐ γὰρ ἂν ἄλλως μέσον εἴη ...
    Καὶ σχήματος δή τινος ... τοιοῦτον ὂν μετέχοι ἂν τὸ ἕν, ἤτοι εὐθέος ἢ στρογγύλου
    ἢ τινος μικτοῦ ἐξ ἀμφοῖν. (*Editorial note:* paraphrase in text.)
3 *Ibid.,* 145 B: Ἆρ᾽ οὖν οὕτως ἔχον οὐκ αὐτό τ᾽ ἐν ἑαυτῷ ἔσται καὶ ἐν ἄλλῳ; ("If
    things stand thus with it, will not [the real one] be both in itself and in something
    other?") Ibid., 145 E: Ἧι μὲν ἄρα τὸ ἓν ὅλον, ἐν ἄλλῳ ἐστίν· ἧι δὲ τὰ πάντα μέρη
    ὄντα τυγχάνει, αὐτὸ ἐν ἑαυτῷ. ("Then insofar as the one is a whole, it is in some-
    thing other; but insofar as it is the sum of all the parts, it is in itself.")
4 *Ibid.,* 145 E: Οὕτω δὴ πεφυκὸς τὸ ἓν ἄρ᾽ οὐκ ἀνάγκη καὶ κινεῖσθαί καὶ ἑστάναι;
    ("Since this then is the nature of the one, does it not follow necessarily that it is both
    at rest and in motion?")
5 *Ibid.,* 148 C and D: Ταὐτόν τ᾽ ἄρ᾽ ὂν τὸ ἓν τοῖς ἄλλοις, καὶ ὅτι ἕτερόν ἐστι. κατ᾽
    ἀμφότερα καὶ καθ᾽ ἑκάτερον, ὅμοιόν τε ἂν εἴη καὶ ἀνόμοιον τοῖς ἄλλοις. ("Since
    then the one is the same as the others and different from them, in both respects and

In itself, naturally, this line of argument proves nothing more than the logical state of affairs to which I have already called attention. All identity can be only an identity within difference, and all difference only a difference that is founded in a deeper identity. The same state of affairs also applies to likeness and unlikeness and to unity as a unity in multiplicity. This situation is a consequence of the inherent relativity of logical determinations, all of which are necessarily bound to temporal reality.

g. *The Metaphysical Interpretation of Logical Relations Leads to Plato's Deliberate Unearthing of the Theoretical Antinomies Contained in the Metaphysical Concepts of Unity and Being. The Origin of These Antinomies according to the General Theory of the Law Spheres*

The discussion leader, Parmenides, gives a metaphysical twist to these logical determinations, however, by deriving them from being and unity as presumed real *eidē*. At once this dialectical logic deliberately assumes an antinomic character. Over against most of the positive qualities of the real one that he has already noted, Parmenides now reiterates the corresponding negative qualities that he had deduced in his first line of argument from the metaphysical, Eleatic conception of the one. In this manner, the antinomies contained in the metaphysical concepts of unity and being are brought out clearly and in sharp relief.[1]

In its General Theory of the Law Spheres, the Philosophy of the Law-Idea has demonstrated that the attempt to derive number, spatiality, and motion from logical unity, which is always a unity in a logical multiplicity of qualities, necessarily entangles theoretical thought in antinomies. For such a line of thought erases the modal boundaries between the logical aspect and the non-logical aspects that are opposed to it in the theoretical

---

in each singly it will be like and unlike the others.")

1 This occurs expressly in *Parmenides*, 149 C and D, where both the one and the absolute other that is opposed to it are again denied number and spatiality: Εἰ δέ γ᾽ ἓν μόνον ἐστί, δυὰς δὲ μὴ ἔστιν, ἅψις οὐκ ἂν εἴη ... Οὐκοῦν φαμέν, τἆλλα τοῦ ἑνὸς οὔθ᾽ ἕν ἐστιν οὔτε μετέχει αὐτοῦ, εἴπερ ἄλλα ἐστίν ...Οὐκ ἄρ᾽ ἔνεστιν ἀριθμὸς ἐν τοῖς ἄλλοις, ἑνὸς μὴ ἐνόντος ἐν αὐτοῖς ... Οὔτ᾽ ἄρ᾽ ἕν ἐστι τἆλλα οὔτε δύο οὔτ᾽ ἄλλου ἀριθμοῦ ἔχοντα ὄνομα οὐδέν ... Τὸ ἓν ἄρα μόνον ἐστὶν [ἕν], καὶ δυὰς οὐκ ἂν εἴη ... Ἅψις ἄρ᾽ οὐκ ἔστιν, δυοῖν μὴ ὄντοιν ... Οὔτ᾽ ἄρα τὸ ἓν τῶν ἄλλων ἅπτεται οὔτε τἆλλα τοῦ ἑνός, ἐπείπερ ἅψις οὐκ ἔστιν ... Οὕτω δὴ κατὰ πάντα ταῦτα τὸ ἓν τῶν τ᾽ ἄλλων καὶ ἑαυτοῦ ἅπτεταί τε καὶ οὐχ ἅπτεται. ("But if the one is only one, and there is no two, then there can be no [spatial] contact either ... Now, however, as we said, that which is other than the one is neither one nor does it participate in the one, insofar as it is something other ... There is thus no number in the other, if the one is not present in it... The other is therefore neither one, nor two, nor does it have the name of any other number ... The one is thus only one, and there can be no two... Therefore there is no [spatial] contact, since there is no two ... The one thus does not come into [spatial] contact with the other, nor the other with the one, since there is no contact ... Thus, the outcome of all of this is that the one both does and does not come into [spatial] contact with the other and with itself.")

Gegenstand relation, and as a result, the laws which govern the non-logical aspects inevitably come into theoretical conflict with the logical laws of thought, as soon as the attempt is made to reduce them to the latter.

The logical-dialectical derivation of number, space, and motion from the metaphysical oneness of being can give an appearance of plausibility only because, as we shall see in the second volume of this work, the structure of the logical aspect of temporal reality does indeed contain analogies of number, space, and motion. These analogies, however, never take on the original meanings of the non-logical aspects of reality, because they always remain qualified by the nuclear modal meaning of the logical sphere. From this it follows that the aspects of number, space, and motion cannot be reduced to the logical aspect of reality.[1]

At the same time, however, it is clear from this state of affairs that the analogies of number, space, and motion – within the structure of the logical aspect these are manifested respectively as logical unity-in-multiplicity, logical thought-space, and logical thought-movement – always remain founded in the original structures of number, space, and motion, and they thus in fact presuppose the latter. Indeed, in this sense it can be said that number, space and motion (and, to be sure, all the other modal aspects of temporal reality) are given along with the logical aspect, with the result that all these aspects will necessarily be exhibited within the full structure of any *temporal* real unity, at least as soon as it is subjected to a cosmological structural analysis. But temporal reality has no metaphysical or absolute being and no metaphysical or absolute unity; it only displays a unity in multiplicity and a being that is identical in the diversity of its structures.

Over against this, the religious form motive of Greek metaphysics demands a metaphysical or absolute unity of being detached from the matter principle of temporal flux and change, one that is like the *eidos* postulated in Plato's theory of ideas or the rigid, undifferentiated oneness of the form of being postulated in the Eleatic conception. Since the dialectical ground-motive is unable to surmount the dualism between the form and the matter principles, however, this metaphysical oneness of being, which has to be distinguished from Plato's conception of the original unity of all forms, cannot be the central, *fundamental* unity of temporal reality. By reason of its own nature, therefore, it remains trapped within the diversity of the temporal structures of reality, which Plato has hypostatized as supratemporal *eidē*. Because of this, Aristotle, and following him the entire Scholastic movement, will declare this metaphysical unity to be an analogical unity, that is to say, a unity that belongs to different beings in different ways, in conformity with their several natures. I shall later return to this analogical unity at length.

---

1 *Editorial note*: That the various aspects of the cosmic law order cannot be reduced to the logical aspect has been a foundation stone of the philosophy of the cosmonomic idea, reflected in both Dooyeweerd's and Vollenhoven's early criticism of the "logos idea." The logical is not the common-denominator of the aspects; it is itself one side or aspect of reality.

In order that the *eidē* may be understood as the active causes of the forms in the cosmos, Parmenides now attempts by means of dialectical logic to derive the aspects of number, space, and motion in temporal reality from a metaphysical oneness of being of this sort.

*h. Plato's Dialectic in Contrast to the Dialectical Logic of
    Origin of the Marburg School of Neo-Kantianism. The
    Latter's Misconception of Plato's Position*

This line of thought is without question entirely different from that of the so-called logic of origin (*Ursprungslogik*) of the Marburg school of neo-Kantianism. Hermann Cohen, the founder of this school, ascribed creative power to pure logic and assigned it the task of deriving all the categories of mathematics and kinetics in a continuous logical progression from a logical origin. The modern, humanistic science ideal which lies at the foundation of this entire method of thought, however, is altogether foreign to the Platonic dialectic and likewise to the whole Greek conception of logic. Cohen's lavish appeal to Parmenides, Plato and other Greek thinkers in his *Logik der reinen Erkenntnis*[1] is thus completely out of place.

According to Plato, it is not subjective logical thought but rather the metaphysical unity of being as a form principle that implies number, space, and motion, if it is to be apprehended in a concept. It is also the case, however, that it again excludes all of these qualities as soon as it is traced back to its absolute origin. For, in line with Plato's starting point, the absolute original unity always remains transcendent to its temporal manifestations and thus also to human logic, which remains tied to temporal reality. With respect to the absolute, transcendent original unity considered in itself, it is characteristic that Plato is only able to develop a negative logic, whereas all of the positive qualities which his dialectic ascribes to the real oneness of being draw it down into the temporal sphere and thus cause it to turn into its opposite.

i. The Participation (μέθεξις) of Being in Time

The latter emerges most clearly in Parmenides' dialectical argument when he finally grants the real unity even a share in time and thereby, in accordance with Plato's way of thinking, in the eternal flux of the matter principle.[2] As something that *is*, this one is present, given now, and it thus has a temporal character. And since time is a constantly advancing fluid continuum, Parmenides demonstrates that the one becomes both

---

1 Hermann Cohen, *Logik der reinen Erkenntnis. System der Philosophie*, I (3rd ed., Berlin, 1922).

2 *Parmenides* 151 E to 152 A: Τὸ δ᾽ εἶναι ἄλλο τί ἐστιν ἢ μέθεξις οὐσίας μετὰ χρόνου τοῦ παρόντος, ὥσπερ τὸ ἦν μετὰ τοῦ παρεληλυθότος καὶ αὖ τὸ ἔσται μετὰ τοῦ μέλλοντος οὐσίας ἐστὶ κοινωνία; ... Μετέχει μὲν ἄρα χρόνου, εἴπερ καὶ τοῦ εἶναι. ("But is the 'to be' anything other than a participation in the ontic form in the present time, just as the 'was' is a participation in the ontic form in the past, and the "will be" in the future? ... Therefore it [the one] participates in time, if it also participates in being.")

older and younger: older, because of its constant advance in time; younger, because what is older necessarily stands in contrast to something younger, and this can be present nowhere but in the real unity itself.

The one is also always older and younger than itself, however, since at least during the very moment of change (the *now*) whatever advances or becomes must be conceived as something that *is*. As the discussion leader expresses it, "If it is necessary that all that is becoming cannot pass by the *now*, then when it reaches this point, it always brings the becoming to a standstill and then *is* whatever it was at the point of becoming."[1]

j. Zeno's Third Paralogism

The third paralogism of Zeno, the student of Parmenides, which he had formulated in order to disprove the possibility of motion, undoubtedly plays a role in Plato's thought at this point. In this paralogism, Zeno attempted to demonstrate that a flying arrow can in no way be in motion but rather stands still. For in the indivisible moment of the *now*, anything moving must necessarily stand still, since motion is not possible in what is indivisible. Every segment of time, however, consists of an infinite series of such indivisible moments; and since the moving arrow stands still in each of indivisible moments that compose the duration of the movement, the entire movement is actually a standing still.

If Plato had adopted outright this dissolution of motion and its duration into an infinite series of static and, in essence, spatial moments or points, he would have reverted to the rigid Eleatic conception of the oneness of being. This oneness of being could then only consist in the spherical form of the spatial continuum, and the discontinuity of the points, with their relation to numerical order, would have been disclosed as non-being.

The entire course of the dialectical argument, however, makes clear that this is not at all Plato's intention. His dialectic rather aims to achieve, on the basis of the metaphysical oneness of being itself, a true synthesis between the Eleatic and the Heraclitean standpoints. In this way, the form principle basically would be brought into connection with the matter principle. At the same time, Plato must preserve the reality of discontinuity, and thus, of number, since the eidetic world presupposes the discontinuity present in a plurality of ontic forms.

Constant change, in fact, is conceived here as a synthesis between the static being of the Eleatics and Heraclitus' motion, which flows eternally through all contrasting forms. Plato had introduced number as an intermediary between the oneness of the *eidos* and the unlimited plurality of the sensible things that participate in this *eidos*. The actual passage from this one to the many, however, still needed a metaphysical explanation, an explanation that also would have to account for the rise of the numerical series itself from the one. It was Plato's new, metaphysical conception of

---

1 *Ibid.*, 152 C to D: *Εἰ δέ γ' ἀνάγκη μὴ παρελθεῖν τὸ νῦν πᾶν τὸ γιγνόμενον, ἐπειδὰν κατὰ τοῦτ' ᾖ, ἐπίσχει ἀεὶ τοῦ γίγνεσθαι καὶ ἔστι τότε τοῦθ' ὅτι ἂν τύχῃ γιγνόμενον.* (Translation in the text.)

change that opened the way to this explanation. Becoming is indeed, as Heraclitus maintained, a transition from condition A to condition B; but it is at the same time a series of *changes* that come to pass in indivisible moments.

k. The Timeless Moment of Change

"When, then, does the one that *is* change?" asks Parmenides. "For neither while it is at rest nor while it is in motion could it change, nor while it is in time."[1] "The actual change lies in the instant; for the instant (ἐξαίφνης) signifies an indivisible moment in which it changes utterly in both directions."[2] "For it does not change from the state of rest while this is at rest, nor from motion while this is in motion; but this queer instantaneous nature (*physis*), since it occupies no time at all, is situated between rest and motion, and into it and from it what is in motion changes to a state of rest, and what is at rest to motion."[3] "If then the (real) one is both at rest and in motion, it can change in both directions. For only in this way could it do both. But when it changes, it changes instantaneously, and during its change it can occupy no time at all and can then neither be in motion nor at rest."[4] In other words, the actual change of the one that *is* may be conceived neither as spatial rest, nor as motion, but only as an indivisible transition between these two which is conceived as discontinuous. As such, it has to be considered timeless and can then no longer be determined numerically.

The same reasoning applies to all change. "When the one that *is* passes from being to not-being, or from not-being to coming into being, it is then *between* states of rest and motion and has neither being, nor not-being, nor coming into being, nor cessation of being. And, in the same manner, when the one passes into the many or changes from the many back into the one, it is neither one, nor many, nor is it being separated or combined. And in the transition from likeness to unlikeness or from smallness to greatness, and conversely, it is neither like nor unlike, small nor great, nor is it increasing or decreasing," etc. "All these changes can thus happen to the one, if it is a real one."[5]

---

1 *Ibid.*, 156 C: Πότ' οὖν μεταβάλλει; οὔτε γὰρ ἑστὸς ἂν οὔτε κινούμενον μεταβάλλοι οὔτ' ἐν χρόνῳ ὄν. (Translation in the text.)

2 *Ibid.*, 156 D: τὸ γὰρ ἐξαίφνης τοιόνδε τι ἔοικε σημαίνειν, ὡς ἐξ ἐκείνου μεταβάλλον εἰς ἑκάτερον. (Translation in the text.)

3 *Ibid.*, 156 D: οὐ γὰρ ἔκ γε τοῦ ἑστάναι ἑστῶτος ἔτι μεταβάλλει, οὐδ' ἐκ τῆς κινήσεως κινουμένης ἔτι μεταβάλλει· ἀλλ' ἡ ἐξαίφνης αὕτη φύσις ἄτοπός τις ἐγκάθηται μεταξὺ τῆς κινήσεώς τε καὶ στάσεως, ἐν χρόνῳ οὐδενὶ οὖσα, καὶ εἰς ταύτην δὴ καὶ ἐκ ταύτης τό τε κινούμενον μεταβάλλει ἐπὶ τὸ ἑστάναι καὶ τὸ ἑστὸς ἐπὶ τὸ κινεῖσθαι. (Translation in the text.)

4 *Ibid.*, 156 E: Καὶ τὸ ἓν δή, εἴπερ ἕστηκέ τε καὶ κινεῖται, μεταβάλλοι ἂν ἐφ' ἑκάτερα· μόνως γὰρ ἂν οὕτως ἀμφότερα ποιοίη· μεταβάλλον δ' ἐξαίφνης μεταβάλλει, καὶ ὅτε μεταβάλλει, ἐν οὐδενὶ χρόνῳ ἂν εἴη, οὐδὲ κινοῖτ' ἂν τότε, οὐδ' ἂν σταίη. (Translation in the text.)

5 *Ibid.*, 156 E to 157 B: ὅταν ἐκ τοῦ εἶναι εἰς τὸ ἀπόλλυσθαι μεταβάλλῃ ἢ ἐκ τοῦ μὴ

l. Change as a Dialectical Idea

The actual synthesis between the metaphysical ontic form and ever-flowing matter is thus sought in the peculiar moment of change, an instant that in its discreteness and indivisibility (*atomon*) is in fact considered transcendent to time. The indivisible *now* of change may not be understood in the spatial sense of the Eleatic form of being; for, in this case, as I have shown earlier, it would once again have to be a spatial simultaneity. Instead, this *now* transcends space and time. In Plato's thought it becomes a moment of eternity which, when it expresses itself in space and time, displays a continuity that is only apparent, as in a state of otherness. Through change, therefore, being is dialectically one and the same with non-being, and similarly, the one coincides dialectically with the infinite, numerically determinable plurality into which it unfolds, the supratemporal *eidos* with the many temporal objects of sense in which it is present, and the form principle with the matter principle. Or, to put it differently, the metaphysical form principle is identical to the matter principle of eternal flux in its otherness. Here change is conceived as an *idea* in the new, correlative sense that is given to this in the metaphysical dialectic. This dialectical reasoning may give every appearance of being profound. As soon as it is made the object of sober analysis, however, it is no longer able to disguise its inward emptiness.

m. Critical Analysis of the Dialectical Argumentation Uncovers Its Inward Emptiness. The Metaphysical Interpretation of the Logical Relation between Identity and Difference Lacks All Foundation

By means of a similar dialectic, humanistic freedom idealism attempted to abolish the polar dualism in its own religious ground-motive of nature and freedom. What happened here, in fact, was simply that the two poles of the religious ground-motive were set within the logical relation of identity and difference and that this logical relation was then interpreted in metaphysical terms. As long as there was no chance of demonstrating the deeper fundamental unity between form and matter or, in the case of humanism, between nature and freedom, however – and the dualistic character of these religious ground-motives prohibited this – there was no real foundation for theoretical synthesis.

In Plato's dialectic, "change," or the "transition from one state to another," is indeed at bottom nothing more than the above logical relation of

εἶναι εἰς τὸ γίγνεσθαι, μεταξύ τινων τότε γίγνεται κινήσεών τε καὶ στάσεων, καὶ οὔτε ἔστι τότε οὔτ᾽ οὐκ ἔστι, οὔτε γίγνεται οὔτ᾽ ἀπόλλυται; ... Κατὰ δὴ τὸν αὐτὸν λόγον καὶ ἐξ ἑνὸς ἐπὶ πολλὰ ἰὸν καὶ ἐκ πολλῶν ἐφ᾽ ἓν οὐθ᾽ ἕν ἐστιν οὔτε πολλά, οὔτε διακρίνεται οὔτε συγκρίνεται· καὶ ἐξ ὁμοίου ἐπ᾽ ἀνόμοιον, καὶ ἐξ ἀνομοίου ἐφ᾽ ὅμοιον ἰὸν οὐθ᾽ ὅμοιον οὔτ᾽ ἀνόμοιον, οὐθ᾽ ὁμοιούμενον οὔτ᾽ ἀνομοιούμενον· καὶ ἐκ σμικροῦ ἐπὶ μέγα καὶ ἐπ᾽ ἴσον καὶ εἰς τἀναντία ἰὸν οὔτε σμικρὸν οὔτε μέγα οὔτ᾽ ἴσον, οὔτ᾽ αὐξανόμενον οὔτε φθῖνον οὔτ᾽ ἰσούμενον εἴη ἄν ... Ταῦτα δὴ τὰ παθήματα παντ᾽ ἂν πάσχοι τὸ ἕν, εἰ ἔστι. (Translation in the text.)

identity and difference, even though it is immediately interpreted in metaphysical terms as an indivisible, timeless moment that sets being in relation to non-being. There is no way that this can function as a supra-temporal fundamental unity of form and matter, of metaphysical ontic unity and infinite plurality, of static rest and eternal fluid motion.

In point of fact, static (i.e., spatial) rest and motion arc both only distinct modal aspects of temporal reality, which are linked together by time itself. As we shall see in volume II, time in fact lies at the foundation of all the aspects and passes from the one into the other, without thereby erasing the modal boundaries between them. Plato's dualistic starting point in the ground-motive of form and matter, however, precludes this vision of time as the universal substratum of reality. And since this starting point likewise excludes the idea of the true fundamental unity of temporal reality, with its divergence into distinct aspects, Plato has no choice but to ascribe the primacy to the form motive. This means then that the attempt to achieve a synthesis takes place on the basis of the supra-temporal, metaphysical ontic form itself. To this end, change or transition must be elevated beyond time itself and transferred to the discontinuous, supra-temporal eidetic world. Thus it becomes an eidetic predicate of the metaphysical ontic form as a unity. In its changing, being encompasses form and matter, static rest and eternal fluid motion.

What did Plato accomplish here? In fact, he effected only a dynamization of the world of the *eidē*, which now made it possible to conceive the latter logically as formative powers and thus allowed them to function as *aitiai* (αἰτίαι), causes, of transitory objects in their formal aspect. This role had been reserved for the *eidē* ever since the *Phaedo*. During that stage of Plato's thought, however, the static, Eleatic conception of the *eidē* could not be reconciled with their dynamic formative activity in the world of phenomena. In this period, only the Socratic *ἰδέα*, the form-power of the divine *nous*, was able to function as the dynamic cause of the forms appearing in the world of sense perception.

n.   In Dynamizing the Eidē, *Plato Conceives Them as Active Soul-Forces. The Statement about This in the* Sophist

In the *Parmenides*, the new, metaphysical dialectic carries through the conception of the *eidē* as pervaded by the *dunamis* of the divine *idea* in logical terms, even though the actual transcendent content of this *idea* plays no further role in the dialogue. We may observe here that, in having motion and formative power ascribed to them, the *eidē* are now conceived after the model of the thinking soul-force. This situation is thus precisely the reverse of what we had perceived in the *Phaedo*, where the thinking soul, by virtue of its postulated kinship with the fixed, unmoving *eidē*, was nearly, although not completely, identified with such a motionless *eidos*. It is evident that in taking this step Plato has in effect transformed the former *chōrismos* between the eidetic world and the visible world of phenomena into the dichotomy between the thinking soul and the material body. The *parousia* of the *eidos* in visible things, which are united into a group by this ontic form, is thus now conceived after the example of the incarnation of the *anima rationalis* in a material body.

The advantage of this new conception was that in this manner the controlling form-power of the *eidē* with respect to phenomena could be conceived according to the model of the thinking soul's dominion over the material σῶμα, while the *chōrismos* demanded by the form-matter motive could nevertheless still be maintained. Just as Plato's conception of the soul in its condition as pure form completely severed it from its association with the body, the *eidos* as a pure ontic form had to be regarded similarly as detached from the plurality of visible things in which it is embodied.[1] The dialectical logic is unable to apprehend the *eidos* in this *chōrismos*, however, but can rather do so only in its *koinōnia (κοινωνία)* with sensible objects.

The fact that Plato in the *Parmenides* consciously intended to conceive the *eidē* as active form-powers after the model of the thinking soul-substance is convincingly demonstrated by a well-known statement of the *Sophist*. This dialogue, which on the basis of the passage at *Sophist* 217 should almost certainly be placed chronologically soon after the *Parmenides*, is at any rate directly related to the latter. It is remarkably similar to it in its train of thought, even though it undeniably carries through the dialectic in a less complicated fashion. In 248 E - 249 A (cap. XXXV), the discussion leader, an unidentified stranger from Elea, puts the following question to the interlocutor Theaetetus: "Come on now, by Zeus, can we really be so easily convinced that that which *is* completely (τὸ παντελῶς ὄν) lacks motion, life, soul, and thought, that it does not live and think, but rather is something solemn and holy, devoid of mind, fixed and motionless." Theaetetus then answers: "Certainly, O stranger, that

---

1 To a certain extent this was already recognized by K. Steinhardt in his introduction to the *Sophist* (*Platon's sämtliche Werke* [tr. H. Mueller], vol. 3, p. 455), where he observes: "However sharply they (viz., the friends of the ideas) may separate the immutable, eternally self-identical ideas, or the sphere of pure being, from the ever changing and moving world of becoming and appearance, they still cannot avoid recognizing that in man these two worlds come into contact, since the body belongs to the realm of becoming and change, while the mind has communion with the higher sphere by virtue of its ability to think the eternal being of the ideas." (English translation by translator.)

 Steinhart mistakenly restricts this conception of the eternal ontic form, however, to the idea of a "thinking and consciously created Primal Being" (the deity), even though such a restriction is supported by neither the *Parmenides* nor the *Sophist*. The passage cited below from the *Sophist* (248 E – 249 A) speaks of the παντελῶς ὄν, "that which is completely," and we have already learned in the *Republic* that Plato conceived the divine *idea*, and thus by implication the divine *nous* as well, as transcendent to the ontic forms.

would be a bizarre doctrine to accept."[1] The *Sophist* had earlier proposed a general definition of being as *dunamis*, whether this be an active power or a passive capacity to be acted upon.[2] At the same time, the statement cited above was directly aimed at the adherents of the theory of the *eidē*, who attributed to the latter no *dunamis* at all in either an active or a passive sense.[3] Thus, there is no doubt that the earlier passage is concerned with the *eidē*; otherwise, it would be completely out of place in the argument. Philo and the Neoplatonists will later attach themselves to this dynamic conception of the *eidē* as thinking soul-forces.

o. The Antinomy in the New Conception of the Eidē *as
Soul-Forces*

This new conception of the *eidē* also remained saddled with an inner antinomy, however. From the very beginning, the *eidē* had been proclaimed as the true objects (*Gegenstände*) of theoretical dialectical knowledge. They were in fact nothing more than the metaphysical hypostatization of the object (*Gegenstand*), which can exist only in an epistemological relation to the theoretical-logical function of thought. Plato had a keen insight into this *Gegenstand* relation. Indeed, it was this relation that prevented him even in the *Phaedo* from fully identifying the *anima rationalis*, as the logical subject of thought, with the *eidē* conceived as completely static. It had always kept him from accepting the uncritical notion of Parmenides, Heraclitus, and Empedocles, that like is known only by like, and had placed him instead in the line of Anaxagoras, who founded theoretical knowledge squarely on the fundamental unlikeness between the logical subject of thought and its object

---

1   *Sophist*, 248 E to 249 A: ΞΕ. Τί δαὶ πρὸς Διός; ὡς ἀληθῶς κίνησιν καὶ ζωὴν καὶ ψυχὴν καὶ φρόνησιν φρόνησιν ἢ ῥᾳδίως πεισθησόμεθα τῷ παντελῶς ὄντι μὴ παρεῖναι μηδὲ ζῆν αὐτὸ μηδὲ φρονεῖν ἀλλὰ σεμνὸν καὶ ἅγιον νοῦν οὐκ ἔχον ἀκίνητον ἑστὸς εἶναι; ΘΕΑΙ. Δεινὸν μεντᾶν, ὦ ξένε, λόγον συγχωροῖμεν. (Translation in the text.)

2   *Ibid.*, 247 E: τίθεμαι γὰρ ὅρον ὁρίζων τὰ ὄντα, ὡς ἔστιν οὐκ ἄλλο τι πλὴν δύναμις. ("For by this definition I define the things that *are* as nothing but *dunamis* [active power or passive capacity to be acted upon].")

3   *Ibid.*, 248 C: ΞΕ. Ἱκανὸν ἔθεμεν ὅρον που τῶν ὄντων, ὅταν τῳ παρῇ ἡ του πάσχειν ἢ δρᾶν καὶ πρὸς τὸ σμικρότατον δύναμις; ΘΕΑΙ. Ναί. ΞΕ. Πρὸς δὴ ταῦτα τόδε λέγουσιν [sc. φίλοι εἰδῶν], ὅτι γενέσει μὲν μέτεστι <τῆς> τοῦ πάσχειν καὶ ποιεῖν δυνάμεως, πρὸς δ' οὐσίαν τούτων οὐδετέρου τὴν δύναμιν ἁρμόττειν φασίν. ("Did we propose a sufficient definition of the things that *are* when [we held that] they have the *dunamis* of acting or being acted upon even with respect to what is most insignificant? Theaetetus: Surely. Stranger: Against this, they [viz., the friends of the *eidē*] say that becoming does partake of the *dunamis* of being acted upon and acting, but that the *dunamis* of neither of these two is appropriate to the ontic form [the *eidos*].") The connection between this passage (248 C) and what follows [248 E to 249 A] decisively refutes Steinhart's interpretation of the latter (cf. Note 1 on page 212).

(*Gegenstand*). We may recall that, in the *Parmenides*, the discussion leader rejected Socrates' attempt to escape his predicament with the suggestion that the *eidē* are perhaps only *noēmata,* subjective contents of thought, by appealing precisely to the metaphysically interpreted *Gegenstand* relation.

Appeal is now made in the *Sophist* to the very same *Gegenstand* relation in order to counter the static conception of the *eidē*. The thinking soul is the subject of knowledge, while the *ousia* or *eidos* stands in contrast to this as its *Gegenstand*. Insofar as theoretical knowledge is something active, being known is a matter of being acted upon, a passive "suffering." Consequently, since theoretical knowledge comes to know the *eidos*, its *Gegenstand*, according to its nature, this *eidos*, to the degree that it becomes known, must be set in motion when it is acted upon by the knowing activity.[1] This latter thesis relates directly to the conception, developed earlier in the *Theaetetus*, that the process of coming to know is an instance of motion (κίνησις).[2] The statement from the *Sophist* cited above, that what *is* completely cannot lack motion, life, soul, and thought, then immediately follows.

This statement thus actually does not fit in with the immediately preceding argument, for there the *eidē* were only said to be passively moved by the knowing activity. In fact, it immediately threatens to obscure the insight that had been gained into the opposition between the logical subject of thought and its *Gegenstand*. If the *eidē* truly had the same nature as the thinking soul, they could never enter into a *Gegenstand* relation with the logical thought subject. Instead, they would then be accessible only to a supra-theoretical, intersubjective knowledge which actually could consist only in a mental communion between knowing subjects.

This was not Plato's conception, however. Such a position would have come into conflict with the metaphysical foundations of his theory of knowledge and with his entire vision of the eidetic world as an intelligible realm of pure ontic forms. Thus the relationship between the *eidos* and the

---

1 *Sophist*, 248 D and E: ὡς τὸ γιγνώσκειν εἴπερ ἔσται ποιεῖν τι, τὸ γιγνωσκόμενον ἀναγκαῖον αὖ ξυμβαίνει πάσχειν. τὴν οὐσίαν δὴ κατὰ τὸν λόγον τοῦτον γιγνωσκομένην ὑπὸ τῆς γνώσεως, καθ᾽ ὅσον γιγνώσκεται, κατὰ τοσοῦτον κινεῖσθαι διὰ τὸ πάσχειν, ὃ δή φαμεν οὐκ ἂν γενέσθαι περὶ τὸ ἠρεμοῦν. ("If knowing is a sort of acting, it follows necessarily that to be known is to be acted upon. By this reasoning, if the essence [ontic form] is known by knowledge, then this, insofar as it is known, is set in motion by being acted upon, something which we said cannot happen to what is at rest.")

2 *Theaetetus*, 153 b: Ἡ δ᾽ ἐν τῇ ψυχῇ ἕξις οὐχ ὑπὸ μαθήσεως μὲν καὶ μελέτης, κινήσεων ὄντων, κτᾶταί τε μαθήματα...; ("Does not the aptitude in the soul acquire knowledge through learning and mental exercise, which are motions?") It is noteworthy that Socrates here contrasts these motions, which elevate and improve the soul, with rest, as a lack of exercise and of a desire to know, by which already acquired knowledge is lost again. Evidently the theme of motion has gained considerably in estimation at the expense of the Eleatic theme of static rest.

anima rationalis remained a crucial problem area in Plato's theory of ideas that would not be removed until the *Philebus* and the *Timaeus*.

p. The Third Path of the Dialectical Argument. The Introduction of Three New Dialectical Ideai *(the Whole, Individuality, and Limit) That Are Contained in the Supreme Dialectical Idea of the One That Is*

In the third part of his dialectical exposition, Parmenides takes his point of departure in the *eidos* of the *other*, or in the *many*, and inquires into the relationship that this must bear to the one if the hypothesis that the one has *being* is assumed (the one that *is*). All of the mutually contradictory qualities that the second part of the argument had ascribed to the one are now also transferred to the other; but the intent of this is merely to make clear that the many is a necessary correlate of the one.

By means of a trio of *eidē* of higher order (*ideai* in a dialectical sense), all of which contain within themselves the correlation between unity and plurality, the attempt is made here to secure a dialectical identity between unity and plurality and to reduce the plurality to unity. First of all, the other, which is identified here with the many, is conceived as a whole with parts, and as such it is set in opposition to the absolute, indivisible one. As a whole, the other is necessarily a unity in plurality. Apart from unity, plurality is an infinite, boundless, chaotic multiplicity *(plēthos; πλῆθος)* in which everything is thrown together, undifferentiated and formless, and which is beyond the reach of any concept. It is only the one that gives form, measure, and harmony to the many, in that each member of the latter is apprehended as part of an encompassing whole. The *whole* is an *eidos* of higher order (dialectically pervaded by the divine *idea*), an *idea* in the new sense of the dialectical metaphysics, which draws together diverse *eidē* into a unity, pervading all of its parts as a soul-force or *dunamis*. The exposition here is clearly based on Plato's distinction, first introduced in the *Theaetetus*, between a purely *arithmetic totality* (πᾶν), which is nothing more than the sum of its parts, and an *eidetic whole* (holon; ὅλον), the parts of which are all members of a single *idea (μιᾶς τινὸς ἰδέας)*[1] in the sense of a dialectical correlation of unity and plurality.[2]

---

1 *Theaetetus*, 204 A: Ἐχέτω δὴ, ὡς νῦν φαμέν, μίαν ἰδέαν ἐξ ἑκάστων τῶν συναρμοττόντων στοιχείων γιγνομένην ἡ συλλαβή ... ἢ καὶ τὸ ὅλον ἐκ τῶν μερῶν λέγεις γεγονὸς ἕν τι εἶδος ἕτερον τῶν πάντων μερῶν; ("Assume then, as we now say, that the syllable has one idea which arises from its several corresponding elements..... or would you also say that a whole compounded from its parts is one *eidos*, that is different from all the parts?") 204 B: Τὸ δὲ δὴ πᾶν καὶ τὸ ὅλον πότερον ταὐτὸν καλεῖς ἢ ἕτερον ἑκάτερον; ("Do you call the sum and the whole the same, or different from one another?") 204 C: Ταὐτὸν ἄρ', ἔν γε τοῖς ὅσα ἐξ ἀριθμοῦ ἐστι τό τε πᾶν προσαγαρεύομεν καὶ τὰ παντα; ("Therefore, in the case of arithmetic magnitudes, do we mean the same thing by the sum and all the parts?")

2 *Parmenides*, 157 D and E: Οὐκ ἄρα τῶν πολλῶν οὐδὲ πάντων τὸ μόριον μόριον, ἀλλὰ μιᾶς τινὸς ἰδέας καὶ ἑνός τινος, ὃ καλοῦμεν ὅλον, ἐξ ἀπάντων ἓν τέλειον γεγονός, τούτου μόριον ἂν τὸ μόριον εἴη. ("Therefore the part is not part of the many, or of all, but of one *idea* and of a certain unity that we call a whole, which has

The second dialectical *idea* (*eidos* of a higher order in the sense of an eidetic correlation) is that of *individuality* (ἕν ἕκαστον), for this likewise links unity and plurality. The individual part, as soon as it is separated from the indeterminate, chaotic multiplicity in a manner to be grasped by thought, is itself already a unity in plurality, since it too must then be conceived as a whole with parts. The absolute one itself is thus manifested in what is individual (ἕν ἕκαστον) in the necessary correlation of relative unity with relative plurality.[1]

The third dialectical *idea* to be assigned the task of linking together unity and plurality is that of *limit* (*peras*; πέρας). Each discrete part has its own circumscribed being, both with respect to every other part and with respect to the common whole. Thus it has a limit. When the other (since its own nature is opposite to the one, this is in itself an *apeiron*, a limitless *hulē*) is joined to the one, something else arises in the plurality that brings about a reciprocal limitation within it.[2] This limiting principle is the real one itself, which in this instance is conceived as a dialectical *idea* embracing all the *eidē*, an eidetic, metaphysical correlation of unity and plurality.

From within the transcendental framework of his own metaphysical ontology, Plato is no doubt already anticipating here the mature Aristotelian conception of the correlation between form and matter.[3] For the indeterminate, limitless plurality is in fact nothing other than the chaotic *hulē*, which in its eternal flux eludes any and every determination. It is only

become a complete unity composed of all [parts]; of this each part can indeed constitute a part.")

1 *Ibid.*, 157 E to 158 A : Καὶ μὴν καὶ περὶ τοῦ μορίου γ᾽ ἑκάστου ὁ αὐτὸς λόγος. καὶ γὰρ τοῦτ᾽ ἀνάγκη μετέχειν τοῦ ἑνός. εἰ γὰρ ἕκαστον αὐτῶν μόριόν ἐστι, τό γ᾽ ἕκαστον εἶναι ἓν δήπου σημαίνει, ἀφωρισμένον μὲν τῶν ἄλλων, καθ᾽ αὑτὸ δ᾽ ὄν, εἴπερ ἕκαστον ἔσται. ("But surely the same reasoning also holds with respect to each part. For this also must necessarily participate in the one. For if each of these is a part, then 'each' surely signifies something that is separated from the other (parts) and exists in itself, if it is to be an 'each'.")

2 *Ibid.*, 158 C and D: Καὶ μὴν ἐπειδὰν γ᾽ ἓν ἕκαστον μόριον μόριον γένηται, πέρας ἤδη ἔχει πρὸς ἄλληλα καὶ πρὸς τὸ ὅλον, καὶ τὸ ὅλον πρὸς τὰ μόρια ... Τοῖς ἄλλοις δὴ τοῦ ἑνὸς ξυμβαίνει ἐκ μὲν τοῦ ἑνὸς καὶ ἐξ ἑαυτῶν κοινωνησάντων, ὡς ἔοικεν, ἕτερόν τι γίγνεσθαι ἐν ἑαυτοῖς, ὃ δὴ πέρας παρέσχε πρὸς ἄλληλα· ἡ δ᾽ αὐτῶν φύσις καθ᾽ ἑαυτὰ ἀπειρίαν. ("But when each part becomes a part, then they have a limit with respect to each other and with respect to the whole, and likewise the whole with respect to the parts... Naturally for what is other than the one, the result will be that through the combination of the one with something else will come to be in it that brings about a reciprocal limitation; the nature of this other in itself, however, is unlimitedness.")

3 Karl Steinhart has already correctly taken note of this in his Introduction to Plato's *Parmenides* (*op. cit,* vol.3, p. 294). Cf. also his statement on p. 295: "sie ist etwa Das, was Platon in seinen späteren Dialogen als die noch ungeschiedene Materie ὕλη bezeichnet." ("It [viz., the not yet determined plurality] is virtually equivalent to that which, as not yet differentiated matter, Plato calls ὕλη in his later dialogues.")

through the limiting principle of the one that his *hulē* comes to partake of being, and thereby of form and measure. This line of thought will be worked out in greater detail in the *Philebus*; but it will also be made clear there that it applies solely to the world composed of the mixture of form and matter.

q. *The Fourth Path of the Dialectical Argument: The One and the Other as Absolute Metaphysical Opposites. The Negative Dialectic of Absolute* Hulē *as a Counterpart to the Negative Theology of the Absolute Formal Unity*

In the fourth part of the dialectical argument, the one and the other are once again separated from each other in the sharpest possible kind of opposition. Here they are no longer conceived in indissoluble correlation by means of the dialectical *idea*, but are rather opposed to each other as absolute antipodes in accordance with the demands of the dualistic ground-motive.[1]

As an indivisible unity, the absolute one has no parts, and it can therefore be present in the other (here again this refers to the chaotic *hulē*) neither as a whole, nor in parts, if it is indeed separate from the other. Thus the other cannot participate in any way in the absolute one. It itself cannot be one, therefore, nor can it display any trace of oneness within itself. It can then also not be a plurality, however, for it has already been shown that a real plurality is possible only in numerical limitation, which itself is a unity in plurality. This absolute other can thus also be neither distinct from nor identical to the absolute one, nor can it be like or unlike the latter in nature, for if it admitted of these determinations, it would again contain a twoness of mutually opposite qualities. Thus it is equally impossible to conceive it as moving or at rest (spatially), as something that is coming into being or ceasing to be, as greater or smaller, etc. In other words, the other taken in this absolute sense, just like the absolute one in the first part of the argument, can be qualified only in purely negative terms. If the one has true being, however, it is necessarily everything. The absolute other can then have no relation to it, but rather flees from thought into absolute nothingness.[2]

This line of thought, then, forms the exact counterpart of the first portion of the dialectical argument. Just as the negative conclusion of the latter may not be understood as a denial that the absolute formal unity truly exists, the negative conclusion drawn in the fourth section may not be taken as a denial of the existence of absolute *hulē*. Instead, both poles of the religious ground-motive continue to be maintained in their absolutely

---

1   *Parmenides*, 159 B to 160 D.
2   *Ibid.,* 160 B : Οὕτω δὴ ἓν εἰ ἔστι, πάντα τ᾽ ἐστι τό ἓν καὶ οὐδὲ ἕν ἐστι καὶ πρὸς ἑαυτὸ καὶ πρὸς τἆλλα ὡσαύτως. ("For these reasons, therefore, the one, if it *is*, is everything, and it is not one both in relation to itself and to the other in the same manner.")

exclusive character. But a logical concept, representation, or knowledge of absolute *hulē* is no more possible than it was in the case of the absolute one.

Thus this section of the argument is nothing more than the necessary counterpart of the negative theology of the first section. From the point of view of the dialectic, however, the *eidē* can be neither the absolute one itself nor the absolute other itself. As ontic forms they can only be apprehended in relative terms.

r.   The Fifth Path of the Dialectical Argument

In the fifth section, the dialectical line of correlation is once again resumed. Plato's dialectic had attempted in the second part of Parmenides' argument to achieve an eidetic relativization of being and non-being, identity and difference (the self-identical and the other), and ultimately the form principle and the matter principle of eternal flux and becoming, by means of the "peculiar moment of change." In so doing, he sought to introduce a correlation between the latter two principles into the intelligible world of the ontic forms themselves.

The fifth section of the dialectical argument now builds on this accomplishment. The metaphysical one must be able to take leave of its absolute being (which excludes the matter principle) and in the indivisible moment of metaphysical change to turn into its opposite. That is to say, it must be capable of becoming a non-being. This, however, may no longer be conceived as an absolute nothing; instead, it must be a relative nothing (*μὴ ὄν*) that continues to stand in relation to being. The negative logical judgment (A is not B, not C, not D, etc.) points the way here for the metaphysical dialectic.

Democritus had already taken this route when he granted to the matter principle, which for him was the eternally flowing void (devoid of being), a relative existence in relation to the indivisible ontic forms or atoms. The logical relation in the negative judgment was transformed here as well into a metaphysical ontic relation between *on (ὄν)* and *mē on (μὴ ὄν)*, even though no starting point for this synthesis could be demonstrated. The path from the logical to the metaphysical thus proved in this context as well to be a *petitio principii* without any possible justification.

s.   The μὴ ὄν as a Relative Nothing. Relative Negation as a
  Form of Logical Determination

In the fifth part of the argument, Parmenides examines the implications of accepting the hypothesis that the one is not. This not-being, the *μὴ ὄν*, cannot be conceived absolutely, however. The negation in the logical judgment places it in relation to being, and every logical negation is necessarily relative. There is an infinite number of *mē onta (μὴ ὄντα*, predicates that *are not*) that are ascribed to the subject in the negative logical judgment. Such relative negation already contains a relative logical determination, however, for inasmuch as the one is made a subject and has a predicate ascribed to it, even though the latter be negative, it is nevertheless apprehended as an object (*Gegenstand*) that can be understood and spoken of theoretically.[1] Even the one that is not remains one, and we can at least say of it that it is different from its opposite, the other. Since, however, it differs from the other as its opposite, it shares with its opposite the quality of otherness.[2] A correlative relation thus continues to exist between the one that is and the one that is not.

The one that *is not* is indeed *something*, for even if it is only granted the vague predicates of "this" and "that," it becomes an object (*Gegenstand*) of thought.[3] Any *Gegenstand* that is distinguished logically from another, however, no matter how it is qualified, can also have ascribed to it all of the other general qualities that were elaborated earlier. Above all, it must possess the most general of all predicates, namely, being. Even the one that *is not* must partake of being. If it is not to revert to absolute nothingness, it must have a bond (*desmos*; δεσμός) that ties it to its role of not-being, and this bond is the being of not-being. Along the same line, the one that *is* must remain in relation to its own opposite through the not-being of not-being, for it would otherwise not be able to maintain itself as something distinct from the μὴ ὄν.[4] In other words, the two terms of the opposition, the *being* and the *not-being* of the one, must each have both a negative and a positive function. And by way of the logical correlation that is in this manner assumed to exist between being and non-being, Plato thinks he has discovered the higher unity in which these two are identical.

Insofar, then, as both being and non-being belong to the one that *is not*, we must also ascribe to it the possibility of change. For it cannot both be and not be simultaneously, but is rather subject to transition between being and not-being. It therefore shares in all forms of becoming, such as motion, coming into being, and ceasing to be. However, since it is still

---

1   *Ibid.*, 160 d: Ὧδ᾽ ἄρα λεκτέον ἐξ ἀρχῆς, ἓν εἰ μὴ ἔστι, τί χρὴ εἶναι. πρῶτον μὲν οὖν αὐτῷ τοῦθ᾽ ὑπάρχειν δεῖ, ὡς ἔοικεν, εἶναι αὐτοῦ ἐπιστήμην, ἢ μηδ᾽ ὅ τι λέγεται γιγνώσκεσθαι, ὅταν τις εἴπῃ ἓν εἰ μὴ ἔστιν. ("Therefore, we must from the very beginning express ourselves thus: If the one *is not*, what must it then be? In the first place, it must be true of it, as it appears, that there exists a knowledge of it; otherwise one would say he understands nothing when someone says, 'if the one is not'.")

2   *Ibid.*, 160 D: Καὶ ἑτεροιότης ἄρ᾽ ἐστὶν αὐτῷ πρὸς τῇ ἐπιστήμῃ ("Otherness, therefore, belongs to it [viz., the one that is not] in addition to the knowledge of it.")

3   *Ibid.*, 160 E: Καὶ μὴν τοῦ γ᾽ ἐκείνου καὶ τοῦ τινὸς καὶ τούτου καὶ τούτῳ καὶ τούτων καὶ πάντων τῶν τοιούτων μετέχει τὸ μὴ ὂν ἕν. ("And assuredly, the one that *is not* also participates in the 'that', the 'something', the 'this', the 'relatedness to this', and all such things.")

4   *Ibid.*, 162 A: Δεῖ ἄρ᾽ αὐτὸ δεσμὸν ἔχειν τοῦ μὴ εἶναι τὸ εἶναι μὴ ὄν, εἰ μέλλει μὴ εἶναι, ὁμοίως ὥσπερ τὸ ὂν μὴ ὂν ἔχειν μὴ εἶναι, ἵνα τελέως αὖ εἶναι ᾖ. ("Therefore, if it [viz., the one that *is not*] is not to be, it must have its *being* that which *is not* as a bond with non-being, in the same manner as that which *is* must have its *not-being* that which *is not*, in order that, for its part, its being may be complete.")

conceived as something that *is not*, and can thus nowhere occupy a spatial position, it is by its own intrinsic nature deprived of all spatial qualification and can therefore in this respect neither move nor change, neither come into being nor cease to be.

According to its own nature, that which is not thus remains an *apeiron*. Only through its connection with the one that *is* does it receive a limitation in terms of real number, and by means of the latter it also comes to partake of the qualities of space and motion. Relative non-being as an *apeiron* is nothing other than the possibility of formal limitation. All of the mutually contradictory predicates that were ascribed to the one that *is* thus also belong to the one that *is not*, and the latter is likewise only accessible to thought in a correlation of *peras* and *apeiron*.

t.   The Sixth Path: The Second Contribution to the Negative Dialectic of Absolute Hulē

In the sixth section of the argument, the not-being of the one is understood in an absolute sense, that is to say, apart from any relation to the one that is. All possibility of predication with respect to the μὴ ὄν then vanishes at once, and the possibility of scientific concepts is therefore eliminated as well. This section thus forms another contribution to the negative dialectic of *hulē*.

Now the one question which the discussion leader must yet answer is whether the hypothesis that the one *is not* still leaves room for the other and, if so, what the nature of the latter would then have to be.

u.   The Elaboration of the Negative Dialectic in the Seventh Path. Plato's Critique of Anaxagoras' Conception of the Spermata

This question forms the theme of the seventh part of Parmenides' argument. The other, conceived without any unity, can only be pictured as an unordered mass in the manner of the indeterminate plurality spoken of in the third section. It is the unformed chaos in which nothing is combined into a unity with anything else, but in which everything dissolves into an infinite mass of completely different masses, each of these in itself being a similar *apeiron* that is always something other with respect to anything other.

This argument can be regarded as an implicit critique of Anaxagoras' theoretical conception of *hulē* as an absolute *meigma*, which in its independent existence over against the form-power of the divine *nous* constituted an object of thought. Plato shows in this part of the argument that the above conception is saddled with an inner antinomy. For since nothing can become an object of thought apart from form and limit, one is able to frame some concept of such a chaotic mixture of everything with everything only by distinguishing discrete elements within it and thus introducing a process of division and separation. In this manner, one can ascribe to the one that is absolutely other approximately the same qualities that were given to the one that *is*.

Since, however, the *principle* of separation, distinction, and limitation – that is, the one as a dialectical *idea* – nevertheless remains absent, all of these qualities are immediately deprived of their foundation and appear as mere products of fantasy. Apart from oneness, everything is mere semblance, comparable to a dream world of vague, fleeting, ever-changing images.[1] A *hulē* of this sort would have to contain an infinite multiplicity of masses. Although each of these would seem like a one, they would not in fact really be such, since it has been assumed that there is no one. Because there would be an infinite multiplicity of them, each such mass would appear to us as a number. If there is no one, however, even and odd have no place here, and there is thus no basis for any real numeration. All that remains is the semblance of number and the semblance of oneness. Although every mass in the *hulē* will seem to be infinitesimally small in relation to the infinite multiplicity of masses, it will in turn be an infinitely large multitude in relation to its own infinite divisibility. Even the likeness and unlikeness of the masses as well as their mutual limitation will be nothing more than semblance.

Here Anaxagoras' conception of the *spermata* has indeed been dealt a mortal blow. Given the infinite divisibility of this *hulē*, theoretical thought cannot find a single stable reference point or foothold, for there is a complete lack of any principle of formal limitation. In other words, if the oneness of the *eidos is not*, all of the qualities that theoretical thought seeks to ascribe to a *hulē* of this sort are without any real foundation.

v. The Eighth Path of the Dialectical Argument

In the eighth and final section of his argument, Parmenides concludes from this conception that "if the one *is not*, then there is [in truth] nothing."[2] For it is only the real one, as an eidetic ontic form, that can exist as the *aitia* (αἰτία) or real cause of the world of sensible things having form. If this *aitia* is absent, the visible cosmos disintegrates into a world of mere semblance that has no foundation in being.

---

1 *Ibid.*, 164 C and D: Κατὰ πλήθη ἄρ᾽ ἕκαστα ἀλλήλων ἄλλα ἐστί. καθ᾽ ἓν γὰρ οὐκ ἂν οἷά τ᾽ εἴη, μὴ ὄντος ἑνός· ἀλλ᾽ ἕκαστος, ὡς ἔοικεν, ὁ ὄγκος αὐτῶν ἄπειρός ἐστι πλήθει, κἂν τὸ σμικρότατον δοκοῦν εἶναι λάβῃ τις, ὥσπερ ὄναρ ἐν ὕπνῳ φαίνεται ἐξαίφνης ἀνθ᾽ ἑνὸς δόξαντος εἶναι πολλὰ καὶ ἀντὶ σμικροτάτου παμμέγεθες πρὸς τὰ κερματιζόμενα ἐξ αὐτοῦ. ("As to the multitudes, each is thus another in relation to another. For as to unity, they cannot be such, since there is no one; but it seems that every [formless] mass [L. *moles*] of them is unlimited in multitude, even if someone should take what seems to be the smallest; as in a dream in sleep, it suddenly, in place of what seemed to be one, appears as many, and in place of what was smallest, as very great in relation to the [innumerable] fragments of it.")

2 *Ibid.*, 166 C: ἓν εἰ μὴ ἔστιν, οὐδέν ἐστιν (translation in the text). The dialogue concludes shortly thereafter with the well-known, at first sight sophistical and sceptical utterance: ὅτι, ὡς ἔοικεν, ἓν εἴτ᾽ ἔστιν εἴτε μὴ ἔστιν, αὐτό τε καὶ τἆλλα καὶ πρὸς αὑτὰ καὶ πρὸς ἄλληλα πάντα πάντως ἐστί τε καὶ οὐκ ἔστι, καὶ φαίνεταί τε καὶ οὐ φαίνεται. ("...that, as it seems, whether the one *is* or is *not*, it itself and the others, both in relation to themselves and to one another, are and are not all things in all ways, and appear thus and do not appear thus.")

w. Summary of Our Analysis of the Parmenides

If we summarize our analysis of this important dialogue, the following points become evident. The avowed purpose of the dialogue is to dynamize the eidetic world in order to render a satisfactory logical account of the fact that the *eidos* can function as an *aitia* (αἰτία) or formative power, active within the visible cosmos, and thereby to provide a logical solution for the problem of *methexis*. This endeavor had a twofold motivation. On the one hand, it was motivated by the Socratic tendency in Plato's thought, which postulated the divine *idea* as the origin of all form, measure, and harmony in the cosmos and focused all logical conceptual knowledge on this *idea*. On the other hand, it was motivated by Plato's increasing interest in empirical phenomena, which now had to be subjected to a rigorous process of definition with the help of the new, dialectical logic.

To this end, the new eidetic or metaphysical-logical dialectic introduces dialectical *ideai* that establish a correlation between *eidē* that are opposite in nature, while all *eidē* are now conceived as active soul-forces. These *ideai* are gleaned mainly from the correlation of logical determinations in the affirmative and the negative judgment; but they are then metaphysically interpreted as *eidē* of higher order that bring *eidē* of opposite character, which in themselves are mutally exclusive, into a higher unity.

The same procedure also produces a dialectical *idea* whose purpose is to reconcile the principle of form and matter within the intelligible world of the ontic forms themselves. This *idea* is that of the timeless instant of change or transition between unity and plurality, being and non-being, rest and motion, limiting form and measureless *apeiron*, and to it are joined several other *ideai* (totality, individuality, and limit), all of which contain the correlation between unity and plurality and are comprehended in the real one itself. The later then functions as the supreme dialectical *idea*, which contains all the others – even that of change – within itself and embraces everything that has true being.

Furthermore, the principle of number is introduced in semi-Pythagorean fashion as the intermediary between the pure form-world of the *eidē* and the plurality of things in the cosmos present to sense perception that participate in a particular *eidos*.

From the very beginning of Parmenides' dialectical argument, the primordial religious dualism of the form-matter motive is maintained. It can be seen winding as a common thread through all his positive dialectical demonstrations. As soon as the opposition between unity and plurality, being and becoming, form and matter, is taken in an absolute sense, that is, in the sense that it has as religious origin, thinking these terms through dialectically leads to completely negative results. For both the divine idea as the unitary origin and form-giving principle, on the one hand, and pure *hulē*, considered apart from all unity, form, and limitation, on the other hand, are inaccessible to theoretical thought. They can only lead thought to a negative theology , which applies also to *eidē* as absolute ontic forms, considered apart from any connection with the visible world, and to the dialectical counterpart of this in a negative conception of absolute matter. Both of these, however, remain the ultimate hypotheses, in the sense of *an-hypotheta*, of the theoretical dialectic, since they are the final presuppositions, irreducible to any higher origin, of a dialectical theory of the *eidē* that seeks to secure the participation of the visible comos in true being. They are necessary because, according to the Greek conception of Plato, the visible cosmos is formed out of *hulē* through the *dunamis* of the eternal *eidē*, and because the latter, in turn, as the *Republic* demonstrates, owe their own being to the divine *idea*, the principle of origin of all form. *Hulē* itself is not a product of the divine form-power, however, but is rather the eternal antipode of the *idea*.

3. The Temporary Suppression of the Socratic Form Motive in the Eleatic Dialogues and the *Diairesis* of the *Eidē* (the *Sophist*, the *Statesman*, and the Dialectical Portion of the *Phaedrus*)

a. The Diairesis *or Dichotomization of the* Eidē *in the* Sophist, *the* Statesman, *and the* Phaedrus

The *Sophist*, a dialogue in which Plato sets out to elucidate the fundamental difference between the teaching of the Sophists and true philosophy, and along with this between sophistical and philosophical dialectic, introduces into the new, dialectical logic the famed method of *diairesis*, the logical 'cutting in two' (*dichotemnein*; διχοτέμνειν) of the *eidē*, which is intended to lead to the final definition of the Sophist. This method of diairesis, which is elaborated in the *Statesman* and in the later-inserted dialectical portion of the *Phaedrus*, presupposes the logical relativization of the *eidē* that I have already analyzed in detail in the *Parmenides*. It also presupposes the dialectical *ideai*, which as higher *eidē* of correlation are intended to bring together the lower *eidē* (these being opposed to one another in the logical relatin of identity and difference) into a synthesis (*sumplokē*; συμπλοκή). The method of *diairesis* thus forms the true capstone of the logicization of the *eidē*.

The passage at 253 D, where the method of *diairesis* is summarized in pregnant fashion, offers the key to this entire dialogue. This passage has presented grave difficulties to commentators and has given rise to sharply divergent interpretations. Stenzel unquestionably deserves credit, therefore, for having analyzed this text so clearly that a bright light has been cast on the entire method of *diairesis*.

The discussion leader, an unidentified stranger from Elea, first asks Theaetetus: "Dividing in two *(διαιρεῖθαι)* according to genera *(γένη)*, and not taking the same ontic form *(εἶδος)* for another *(ἕτερον)*, nor another for the same *(ταὐτόν)*, shall we not call this the task of the science of dialectic?"[1] After Theaetetus responds affirmatively to this question, the discussion leader describes the task of dialectic more fully in a four-part passage. The first two parts take their point of departure from the principle of the separation of each of the *eidē*, in order to proceed from this to their synthesis or conjunction in an encompassing dialectical *idea*. The latter two move in the reverse direction, descending from the encompassing *idea* to the final result of the *diairesis*, that is, to say, an *atomon eidos* (ἄτομον εἶδος) that cannot be divided further. Such an *atomon eidos* is separated from all the others as a rigorously defined unity, but because it is systematically determined by all the higher *eidē* that embrace it, it nevertheless reveals itself as a true *sumplokē eidōn (συμπλοκὴ εἰδῶν)* (intertwinement of *eidē*).[2]

---

1   *Sophist*, 253 D: ΞΕ. Τὸ κατὰ γένη διαιρεῖσθαι καὶ μήτε ταὐτὸν εἶδος ἕτερον ἡγήσασθαι μήτε ἕτερον ὂν ταὐτόν, μῶν οὐ τῆς διαλεκτικῆς φήσομεν ἐπιστήμης εἶναι; (Translation in the text.)

2   *Ibid.*, Οὐκοῦν, ὅ γε τοῦτο δυνατὸς δρᾶν, μίαν ἰδέαν διὰ πολλῶν, ἑνὸς ἑκάστου κειμένου χωρίς, πάντῃ διατεταμένην ἱκανῶς διαισθάνεται, καὶ πολλὰς ἑτέρας ἀλλήλων ὑπὸ μιᾶς ἔξωθεν περιεχομένας, καὶ μίαν αὖ δι᾽ ὅλων πολλῶν, ἐν ἑνὶ ξυνημμένην, καὶ πολλὰς χωρὶς πάντῃ διωρισμένας· τοῦτο δ᾽ ἔστιν, ᾗ τε κοινωνεῖν ἕκαστα δύναται, καὶ ὅπῃ μή, διακρίνειν κατὰ γένος ἐπίστασθαι. ("He who is therefore able to do this discerns adequately one [correlative] *idea* extending over the many *eidē*, each of which lies separate from the others as a unity, and how many [*eidē*], different from one another, are embraced from without by one [*idea*]; and again, how one [viz., the *atomon eidos*] is connected through the many [eidetic] wholes into a single unity [viz., the intended *definiendum*], and many [*eidē*] are [thereby] completely separated and marked off from it. This, however, is to know and to distinguish the genera, to what degree the individual [*eidē*] can associate, and to what degree they cannot.") Paul Natorp understood the first part of this passage to be speaking only of the most elementary application of a concept in its unity to the multiplicity of discrete, individual, sensible *Gegenstände*. Over against this, Apelt and most other commentators have believed that the reference here can only be to *eidē*, not sensible things, "quae in mundo mutationis fluctibus obnoxio posita et a dialectica aliena sunt" ("[sensible things] that are situated in the world of change, subject to flux, and foreign to dialectic"). In my opinion, this part of the passage indeed speaks only of the *eidē*; but among these, the *atomon eidos* must be regarded as the actual ontic content of the individual object of sense perception. The same view is shared by Stenzel, *op.cit.*, p. 65. There is a surprising agreement between the above passage from the *Sophist*, 253 D, and the description of the task of dialectic given in the *Phaedrus*, 265 D and E: Εἰς μίαν τ᾽ ἰδέαν συνορῶντ᾽ ἄγειν τὰ πολλαχῇ διεσπαρμένα, ἵν᾽, ἕκαστον ὁριζόμενος, δῆλον ποιῇ περὶ οὗ ἂν ἀεὶ διδάσκειν ἐθέλῃ .... Τὸ πάλιν κατ᾽ εἴδη δύνασθαι τέμνειν κατ᾽ ἄρθρα, ᾗ πέφυκεν, καὶ μὴ ἐπιχειρεῖν καταγνύναι μέρος μηδὲν κακοῦ μαγείρου τρόπῳ χρώμενον. ("To comprehend in the synopsis of one *idea* that which is dispersed in many directions, in order that, by defining each individually, he makes clear what it is he wishes to teach about in each instance ... The converse ability to cut asunder, following *eidē* and natural articulations, and not to try to break apart in pieces in the manner of a poor cook.") One may also compare the summary given in *Phaedrus*, 266 B:

The *atomon eidos*, as Stenzel observes,[1] is the bearer of as many predicates as are "bound together" in it. The wish that Socrates had expressed in the *Parmenides*,[2] that someone show by means of dialectic how, even within the eidetic world itself, a single subject can without contradiction unite different qualities, thus indeed finds its fulfillment here.

b. The Atomon Eidos *and the Individual Things of the Sense World*

In the *atomon eidos*, the ontic form that is not further divisible, the eidetic world is brought into the closest conceivable connection with the individual thing (ἓν ἕκαστον) in the visible cosmos. According to Plato, a rigorous dialectical definition that lays hold of the *atomon eidos* is equivalent to the eidetic determination of individuality itself, that is, of everything in individuality that has true being. Whatever lies beyond this is *apeiron* and *mē on*. *Logos* and *aisthēsis*, logical-eidetic definition (this must still always partake of the supersensible contemplation of the *eidē*, since the Greek conception of the ontic form invariably has a visual foundation) and sense observation, are here brought so close together that Plato could indeed think that he had found in this new dialectical method the appropriate means for grasping empirical phenomena themselves in a completely logical manner.

Stenzel observes in this regard:

"Plato procures for himself in his διαίρεσις the organon for the formation of a conception of knowledge that also embraces empirical reality. He regards it as the means for descending, in propositions of thought that are in his view independent of experience, to objects which αἴσθησις and the δόξα which results from it also present in some way, except that it is only by means of the additional factor of the λόγος, the definition, that a judgment can be made about the truth or falsehood of the object perceived by the senses or reproduced in imagination."[3]

Τούτων δὴ ἔγωγε αὐτός τε ἐραστής, ὦ Φαῖδρε τῶν διαιρέσεων καὶ συναγωγῶν, ἵνα οἷός τε ὦ λέγειν τε καὶ φρονεῖν .... καλῶ δὲ οὖν μέχρι τοῦδε διαλεκτικούς. ("I myself am also a lover of such divisions and collections, dear Phaedrus, so that I might be able to speak and to think ... [those who are able to do this] I have hitherto called dialecticians.") Cf., in addition, *Statesman*, 287 C: Κατὰ μέλη ... οἷον ἱερεῖον διαιρώμεθα ("following their limbs ... we must dissect them [viz., the offices in the state besides kingship] like a sacrificial animal.")

1 Stenzel, *op. cit.*, p. 61.
2 *Parmenides*, 129 E.
3 "Platon schafft sich in der διαίρεσις das Organon für die Bildung eines das Empirische mitumfassenden Wissensbegriffes. Er sieht in ihr das Mittel in – wie er glaubt – erfahrungsfreien Setzungen des Denkens herabzusteigen zu Objekten, die die αἴσθησις und die aus ihr sich ergebende δόξα ebenfalls irgendwie darbieten, nur dass erst durch den hinzukommenden λόγος, die Definition, ein Urteil über Wahrheit und Irrtum des sinnlich gegebenen oder in der Vorstellung reproduzierten Gegenstandes gefällt werden kann." Stenzel, *op. cit.*, pp. 73-74. (English version by translator.)

c. Has All Relation between the New Dialectic and the Idea Tou Agathou *Disappeared in the Eleatic Trilogy?*

It may be asked whether, in the *Sophist* and the related dialogues, the dialectic proper has completely lost its relation to the absolute divine *idea* of the good and the beautiful. Although Stenzel claims that this is in fact the case,[1] I believe that he is in error. We have already observed that in the *Parmenides* the absolute opposition between the divine form of origin in its unity (the ἰδέα τοῦ ἀγαθοῦ) and pure *hulē* ran as common thread through the entire dialectical argument of the discussion leader. It is true that the dialectical logic was able to grasp neither of these as such in a concept, but Plato nevertheless continued to maintain both as the *an-hypotheta*, the absolute religious presuppositions, of his entire dialectic. We also observed that for Plato the new correlative dialectical *idea* could be nothing other than the logical-metaphysical expression of the mutual coherence that exists among all the *eidē* in their central reference to the divine *idea* as origin.

The *Sophist* contains a statement about the philosophical enterprise which confirms this understanding. Immediately after the passage in 253 D cited above, where the task of the new logic is described, there follows the remark that it can be undertaken only by true philosophers. Plato then observes that it is no less difficult to discern the nature of the philosopher than that of the Sophist, although in each case the reason is different. "The latter, fleeing into the darkness of non-being, continually occupied and in contact with this, is difficult to perceive because of the darkness of this place ... The philosopher, in contrast, who through logical reasoning is always wedded to the *idea* of being, is also not at all easy to see because of the brightness of this region; for the eye of the common soul cannot endure to gaze steadfastly upon the divine."[2] This statement harks back to the *Republic's* depiction of the blinding glare of the divine *idea*; it can in no way apply to the new logical-dialectical function of the *idea*. The *idea* spoken of here is the divine form of origin, which, like the sun, spreads its blinding glare over the realm of the *eidē*. Apart from this *idea*, the new, dialectical logic would lose its true philosophical meaning for Plato, for it must remain rooted in the ultimate religious synopsis of this *idea* and receive from there its *dunamis* for tracing the mutual intertwinements of the *eidē*.

It must be granted, however, that what stands at the center of interest in

---

1 *Ibid.*, p. 72.
2 *Sophist*, 254 A: Ὁ μὲν ἀποδιδράσκων εἰς τὴν τοῦ μὴ ὄντος σκοτεινότητα, τριβῇ προσαπτόμενος αὐτῆς, διὰ τὸ σκοτεινὸν τοῦ τόπου κατανοῆσαι χαλεπός ... Ὁ δέ γε φιλόσοφος, τῇ τοῦ ὄντος ἀεὶ διὰ λογισμῶν προσκείμενος ἰδέᾳ, διὰ τὸ λαμπρὸν αὖ τῆς χώρας οὐδαμῶς εὐπετὴς ὀφθῆναι· τὰ γὰρ τῆς τῶν πολλῶν ψυχῆς ὄμματα καρτερεῖν πρὸς τὸ θεῖον ἀφορῶντα ἀδύνατα. (Translation in text.)

the Eleatic dialogues is not this ultimate, centrally focused synopsis, but rather the dialectical-logical separation and combination of the *eidē*. Here the relgious synopsis is subordinated to the endeavor to render the world of *eidē* transparent to logic and serviceable for the definition of all empirical phenomena.

d. The Temporary Suspension of the Transcendental Qualification of Being as Good and Beautiful

Directly related to this is the fact that the Eleatic dialogues temporarily leave aside the transcendental qualification of being as good and beautiful. Furthermore, this also means that the teleological character of conceptual definition – the statement of the *aretē* (*ἀρετή*) of the subject of definition, the end toward which it is good or appropriate – is also abandoned for the time being. Plato nevertheless did not abandon the Socratic *idea*, even in the crisis of his theory of ideas, and precisely for this reason, the logicization of the *eidē* and the extension of these into ontic forms for all empirical phenomena without exception actually led to a new dialectical tension between this *idea* and the *eidē*.

The earlier tension between these two had been resolved logically by the dynamization of the *eidē*. Now that the former a priori character of the theory of the *eidē* has been replaced by a greater emphasis on empirical reality, however, Plato at present seems unable to answer the question of how the *eidē*, as active soul-forces, can actualize the good and the beautiful throughout the visible cosmos. What could mud, for example, be good for? Not until the *Timaeus* will Plato make a serious attempt completely to penetrate the new, logical-dialectical conception of the *eidē* with the earlier conception of the *eidos* as *aretē*, thus making it serviceable for a comprehensive teleological explanation of the forms in the visible cosmos. The path to this new attempt at synthesis is prepared already in the *Philebus*, however.

e. Diairesis *as the λόγον διδόναι of Empirical Phenomena.* Epistēmē *as ἀληθὴς δόξα μετὰ λόγου*

The *diairesis* of the *eidē*, which culminates in the definition of the *atomon eidos* of an individual phenomenon in the sense world, is Plato's means to the *logon didonai* (*λόγον διδόναι*), the "theoretical accounting," for empirical phenomena. In practical terms this is equivalent to the formation of definitions according to the method of the so-called *genus proximum* and *differentia specifica*. In a sense that differs fundamentally from Plato's conception, this method of definition plays a very central role in Aristotle's logic. I shall later subject this method to a fundamental critique in my analysis of the Aristotelian-Thomistic concept of substance.

It is this *logon didonai*, the rigorous definition of the generic and specific ontic distinguishing features of a thing, that first elevates *alēthēs doxa* (*ἀληθὴς δόξα*; right opinion) to the status of *epistēmē* or scientific knowledge. In the *Republic*, *doxa* and *epistēmē* were still separated by an unbrideable gulf, and at the close of the *Theaetetus* (which already has a strong empirical orientation), the definition of *epistēmē* as *alēthēs doxa meta logou* (ἀληθὴς δόξα μετὰ λόγου) hopelessly foundered upon the lack of a correct notion of the generic element in the *logos* as definition. With the help of the method of *diairesis*, however, Plato is now able in the *Sophist* and the *Statesman* to bridge the gap between eidetic knowledge and sensory representation.

f.   The Highest Eidē *according to the* Statesman *and in the*
      Sophist. *Their Inability to Be Represented as a*
      Sensory Eidōlon

According to the *Statesman*,[1] the whole of *diairesis* is actually founded in the investigation of the dialectical separations and conjunctions among the highest and noblest *eidē* (κάλλιστα ὄντα καὶ μέγιστα). These are not themselves embodied (ἀσώματα) in sensible images (εἴδωλα), and for this reason they can only be clarified in a dialectical-logical definition (λόγῳ μόνῳ). In contrast to this, the numerous subordinate *eidē* are indeed capable of being embodied in such *eidōla*. These can thus be apprehended in direct synopsis, apart from the toilsome route of dialectical definition (χωρὶς λόγου), since the sensible objects under their purview are easily recognizable by the visible images that we grasp in *eidōla*.[2] The *eidos* is represented here in the *eidōlon* of an individual visible thing.

The discussion leader thus makes the observation here that no reasonable person would pursue the dialectical-diairetic investigation of the art of weaving, which served as an introduction to the definition of the states-

---

1   *Statesman*, 285 D and E.
2   *Ibid.*, 285 D to 286 A: Ἦ που τὸν τῆς ὑφαντικῆς γε λόγον αὐτῆς ταύτης ἕνεκα θηρεύειν οὐδεὶς ἂν ἐθελήσειε νοῦν ἔχων, ἀλλ᾽, οἶμαι, τοὺς πλείστους λέληθεν, ὅτι τοῖς μὲν τῶν ὄντων ῥαδίως καταμαθεῖν αἰσθηταί τινες ὁμοιότητες πεφύκασιν, ἃς οὐδὲν χαλεπὸν δηλοῦν, ὅταν αὐτῶν τις βουληθῇ τῷ λόγον αἰτοῦντι περί του μὴ μετὰ πραγμάτων ἀλλὰ χωρὶς λόγου ῥαδίως ἐνδείξασθαι· τοῖς δ᾽ αὖ μεγίστοις οὖσι καὶ τιμιωτάτοις οὐκ ἔστιν εἴδωλον οὐδὲν πρὸς τοὺς ἀνθρώπους εἰργασμένον ἐναργῶς, οὗ δειχθέντος τὴν τοῦ πυνθανομένου ψυχὴν ὁ βουλόμενος ἀποπληρῶσαι, πρὸς τῶν αἰσθήσεών τινα προσαρμόττων, ἱκανῶς πληρώσει. διὸ δεῖ μελετᾶν λόγον ἑκάστου δυνατὸν εἶναι δοῦναι καὶ δέξασθαι· τὰ γὰρ ἀσώματα κάλλιστα ὄντα καὶ μέγιστα, λόγῳ μόνῳ, ἄλλῳ δ᾽ οὐδενὶ σαφῶς δείκνυται, τούτων δ᾽ ἕνεκα πάντ᾽ ἐστὶ τὰ νῦν λεγόμενα. ("No reasonable man would want to pursue the definition of the art of weaving for its own sake. But I think it escapes most people that with things that are easily knowable, sensible images naturally present themselves which are not difficult to clarify if one simply points these out to someone who wishes an account of them, without much trouble and without logical definition; on the other hand, with the greatest and most excellent [*eidē*], there is no image manifestly suited to man's intelligence, to which he who wishes to appease the soul of the inquirer may point, and, by fitting this image to a sense perception, may satisfy him. Therefore, one must through practice acquire the ability to give and to understand a definition of each thing. For the incorporeal, noblest, and greatest ontic forms are clearly explained only by logical definition, and nothing else, and all that we have discussed up to now relates to them.")

man, merely for its own sake. In the final analysis, the entire investigation focuses exclusively on the highest and noblest *eidē*, which are incapable of sensible representation and are thus "incorporeal."[1]

The *Sophist* sets forth five of these supreme *eidē*: rest, motion, being, *the other* (τὸ θατέρον), and *the same* (τὸ ταὐτόν). Of these five, the first two are in themselves incapable of being combined with each other logically. Motion can never be rest, and rest can never be motion. In contrast, the three other *eidē*, among which being is the one that is all-embracing, are genuine *ideai* in the sense of the new dialectic, for they are intended to establish a mutual relation between all *eidē* that are logically opposite to each other. Being functions here, moreover, as the supreme dialectical *idea* in which all of the others must participate.[2] It is only in what has individual being (the individual ontic form) that being is distinct from the four other *eidē*. As an all-embracing *idea*, however, it extends over the other genera.

---

1 See the final part of the previous footnote.

2 *Sophist*, 254 C: τὸ δὴ μετὰ τοῦτο ξυνεπισπώμεθα τῷ λόγῳ τῇδε σκοποῦντες, μὴ περὶ πάντων τῶν εἰδῶν, ἵνα μὴ ταραττώμεθ᾽ ἐν πολλοῖς, ἀλλὰ προελόμενοι τῶν μεγίστων λεγομένων ἄττα, πρῶτον μὲν ποῖα ἕκαστά ἐστιν, ἔπειτα κοινωνίας ἀλλήλων πῶς ἔχει δυνάμεως, ἵνα τό τ᾽ ὂν καὶ μὴ ὂν εἰ μὴ πάσῃ σαφηνείᾳ δυνάμεθα λαβεῖν, ἀλλ᾽ οὖν λόγου γ᾽ ἐνδεεῖς μηδὲν γιγνώμεθα περὶ αὐτῶν, καθ᾽ ὅσον ὁ τρόπος ἐνδέχεται τῆς νῦν σκέψεως , ἐὰν ἄρ᾽ ἡμῖν πῃ παρεικάθῃ τὸ μὴ ὂν λέγουσιν ὡς ἔστιν ὄντως μὴ ὂν ἀθῴοις ἀπαλλάττειν. ("Let us next continue our argument in such a way that we do not extend it to all ontic forms, lest we get confused in the multitude of these, but rather select a few of them that are called the highest, and first consider the nature of each of these and then what capacity they have to be combined with one another, in order that, although we are not able to apprehend being and non-being with full clarity, we at least do not fall short of our logical investigation of them insofar as the method of our present speculation allows, and see if we may succeed in escaping unscathed when we assert that what *is not* really *is* what *is not*.") *Ibid.*, 254 D: Μέγιστα μὴν τῶν γενῶν, ἃ νῦν δὴ διῇμεν τό τ᾽ ὂν αὐτὸ καὶ στάσις καὶ κίνησις . ... Καὶ μὴν τώ γε δύο φαμὲν αὐτοῖν ἀμίκτω πρὸς ἀλλήλω. ... Τὸ δὲ γ᾽ ὂν μικτὸν ἀμφοῖν· ἐστὸν γὰρ ἄμφω που. ("The greatest of the genera [*eidē*], which we were just now discussing, are surely being itself, rest, and motion ... And in truth, we said that the [latter] two cannot be combined [blended] with one another ... But being is compatible with both, for both surely are?") *Ibid.*, 255 C, D, and E: Τέταρτον δὴ πρὸς τοῖς τρισὶν εἴδεσιν εἶδος τὸ ταὐτὸν τιθῶμεν; ... Πέμπτον δὴ τὴν θατέρου φύσιν λεκτέον ἐν τοῖς εἴδεσιν οὖσαν ἐν οἷς προαιρούμεθα... καὶ διὰ πάντων γ᾽ αὐτὴν αὐτῶν φήσομεν εἶναι διεληλυθυῖαν· ἓν ἕκαστον γὰρ ἕτερον εἶναι τῶν ἄλλων οὐ διὰ τὴν αὐτοῦ φύσιν, ἀλλὰ διὰ τὸ μετέχειν τῆς ἰδέας τῆς θατέρου. ("We will thus accept a fourth *eidos* besides the three *eidē* [mentioned], that of sameness ... The fifth among the *eidē* we have selected must then be called the nature of the other ... And we shall say that this extends over all of them, for each individually is different from the others not by its own nature, but by participating in the *idea* of otherness.") *Ibid.*, 256 E: Περὶ ἕκαστον ἄρα τῶν εἰδῶν πολὺ μέν ἐστι τὸ ὄν, ἄπειρον δὲ πλήθει τὸ μὴ ὄν. ("... With respect to each of the *eidē* there is a multiplicity of being and an unlimited plurality of non-being.")

It is clear at once that the selection of these five highest *eidē* relates directly to Plato's endeavor, which began in the *Theaetetus*, to find a dialectical-logical synthesis between the Eleatic ontology and Heraclitus' doctrine of eternal flux. The polar opposition between Parmenides' conception of the static ontic form and the Heraclitean theory of eternal motion is to be resolved by the new dialectical *idea* into a higher synthesis.

g. *The Idea of Otherness as the Ontic Form of the μὴ ὄν, the*
   Hulē of the Sophists

On this point, then, the *Sophist* moves exactly in the same direction as the *Parmenides*. It is noteworthy, however, that in the *Sophist*, the ontic form of otherness [the other] as a dialectical *idea* (ἰδέα τοῦ θατέρου) is explicitly designated as the *eidos* of non-being (the μὴ ὄν).[1] This μὴ ὄν was nothing other than the ever-flowing *hulē* (the matter principle), where the Sophist retreated into an *aporon topon* (ἄπορον τόπον) at every attempt to define his nature and to capture him in this definition "like a hunted animal."

The discussion leader had begun the process of definition by ascertaining the total *eidos* of art (τέχνη).[2] Following the method of *diairesis*, this total *eidos* (ὅλον εἶδος) was then repeatedly subdivided into increasingly specific pairs of types. The first subdivision yielded two contrasting types (εἴδη δύο) of art, the first of these being concerned with the production of something new, and the second with the mere acquisition of what already exists. In the end, the *diairesis* proceeded to the division of the *eidos* of imitative art (μιμητικὴ τέχνη), into two formal types, namely, those of representative and of phantastic art (εἰκαστική and φανταστική). Both of these types are qualified as *eidōla-* (sensible image) making (εἰδωλο-ποιική); but the *eidōla* of the former are *eikona* (εἰκόνα),[3] representations of actually existing things, while those of the latter are phantasms, images that bear no likeness to real objects. The art of the Sophists is then naturally subsumed under the *eidos* of phantastic *technē*.

Having arrived at this point in his inquiry, the discussion leader, the

---

1 *Sophist*, 258 D: Ἡμεῖς δέ γ᾽ οὐ μόνον ὡς ἔστιν τὰ μὴ ὄντα ἀπεδείξαμεν, ἀλλὰ καὶ τὸ εἶδος ὃ τυγχάνει ὂν τοῦ μὴ ὄντος ἀπεφηνάμεθα· τὴν γὰρ θατέρου φύσιν ἀποδείξαντες οὐσάν τε καὶ κατακεκερματισμένην ἐπὶ πάντα τὰ ὄντα πρὸς ἄλληλα, τὸ πρὸς τὸ ὂν ἕκαστον μόριον αὐτῆς ἀντιτιθέμενον ἐτολμήσαμεν εἰπεῖν ὡς αὐτὸ τοῦτ᾽ ἐστὶν ὄντως τὸ μὴ ὄν. ("We have, however, not only shown that things which are not *are*, but we have also brought to light what the *eidos* of non-being is; for in proving that the nature of the other [the different] extends over all the ontic forms in their mutual relationship, we ventured to say that the part of it which is opposed to each ontic form really is precisely 'that which is not'.")

2 *Editorial note*: The Dutch word translated here is "kunstvaardigheid," which more than the word "art" bespeaks a high degree of skill in artistic production. In translating, the choice has been made, for simplicity's sake, of the short but vaguer term "art."

3 *Editorial note – AW*: Dooyeweerd here mistakenly quotes the Greek εἰκόνα as though it were a neuter plural; the correct form of the plural is εἰκόνες.

stranger from Elea, observes that the attempt to 'capture' the Sophist in this definition runs the danger of bogging down in the *aporia* of non-being. For any attempt to define the Sophist as a maker of phantasms, which as such actually *are not*, necessarily ascribes a certain *being* to non-being. As an embodiment of what *is not*, the phantastic image is, after all, *really* an image.[1]

A closer examination reveals that the *eidos* of being is itself burdened with many *aporia* and is thus no less difficult to grasp than that of the μὴ ὄν.[2] This is demonstrated first of all in terms of the relationship between being, the one, and the whole which was already discussed in the *Parmenides*, in the course of which a fundamental critique is leveled both at the Eleatic and the Heraclitean positions, and also at the entire Ionian nature philosophy. In the second place, it is demonstrated once again in terms of the dialectical conception, already developed in the *Parmenides*, of the *idea* of being as the highest *eidos*, which admits of a connection with both rest and motion and by its own nature can thus itself be neither at rest nor in motion, but must rather be something different from either of these.

h. The Dialectical Ideai *of Being and Non-Being Are for Plato Not Identical with the Absolute Ontic Form and Absolute* Hulē. *Plato's Own Statement on This in the* Sophist

The discussion leader explicitly states that this conception of being is not at all easy to grasp: "for how can something that is not in motion be other that at rest? or how can it be conceived that what is never at rest is not in motion?" And yet, "being is revealed to us as lying beyond the bounds of rest and motion."[3]

---

1 *Ibid.*, 239 C and D: Τοιγαροῦν εἴ τινα φήσομεν αὐτὸν ἔχειν φανταστικὴν τέχνην, ῥᾳδίως ἐκ ταύτης τῆς χρείας τῶν λόγων ἀντιλαμβανόμενος ἡμῶν εἰς τοὐναντίον ἀποστρέψει τοὺς λόγους, ὅταν εἰδωλοποιὸν αὐτὸν καλῶμεν, ἀνερωτῶν τί ποτε τὸ παράπαν εἴδωλον λέγομεν. ("If we therefore say that he possesses a certain art of creating phantasms, he will easily trap us through our use of words and turn our statements into their opposites, when we call him a maker of phantasms.")

2 *Ibid.*, 250 D and E: ΞΕ: Μῶν οὖν ἐν ἐλάττονί τινι νῦν ἐσμὲν ἀπορίᾳ περὶ τὸ ὄν; ΘΕΑΙ: Ἐμοὶ μέν, ὦ ξένε, εἰ δυνατὸν εἰπεῖν, ἐν πλείονι φαινόμεθα. ("The stranger from Elea: Are we now in a lesser perplexity with respect to being [than with respect to non-being]? Theaetetus: To me at least, dear stranger, if this can be said, we seem to be in one still greater.")

3 *Ibid.*, 250 C and D: Κατὰ τὴν αὐτοῦ φύσιν ἄρα τὸ ὂν οὔθ᾽ ἕστηκεν οὔτε κινεῖται ... Ποῖ δὴ χρὴ τὴν διάνοιαν ἔτι τρέπειν τὸν βουλόμενον ἐναργές τι περὶ αὐτοῦ παρ᾽ ἑαυτῷ βεβαιώσασθαι; ... Οἶμαι μὲν οὐδαμῶσ᾽ ἔτι ῥᾴδιον. εἰ γάρ τι μὴ κινεῖται, πῶς οὐχ ἕστηκεν; ἢ τὸ μηδαμῶς ἑστὸς πῶς οὐκ αὖ κινεῖται; τὸ δ᾽ ὂν ἡμῖν νῦν ἐκτὸς τούτων ἀμφοτέρων ἀναπέφανται. ("By its own nature, therefore, being is neither at rest nor in motion ... Whither then should someone turn his thoughts who wishes by himself to reach some clear conclusion about being? ... I think this will not be easy in any direction. For if something is not in motion, how is it then not at rest? Or conversely, how is what is in no wise at rest not in motion? And yet being is

When the stranger from Elea asks whether this can be regarded as possible, Theaetetus answers emphatically in the negative. The discussion leader then explicitly allows this *aporia* – which evidently results from the attempt to grasp the nature of absolute being *in itself* (apart from rest and motion) – to stand as an unresolved problem, in order that he may henceforth limit his logical investigation solely to the dialectical relations *between* being and non-being, as in themselves equally obscure entities. In taking this route, he holds out the hope that, "if we are unable to know either of these in itself, we can at least direct the logical investigation upon both at once [i.e., in their mutual relationship] in the best possible manner."[1]

This passage is extremely important. Here, as I have already established in my analysis of the *Parmenides*, it is once again made clear that Plato does not identify the absolute ontic form and absolute *hulē* (*μὴ ὄν*) – only these two are mentioned in this context – with the dialectical, purely correlative *ideai* of being and non-being. The former are rather *an-hypotheta* that are inaccessible to logical-dialectical investigation. The new dialectic can indeed extend no further than the sphere of logical relations, and it is thus never in a position to bridge the polar dualism in the religious ground-motive. The dialectical *ideai* do indeed have real eidetic being, but they nevertheless do not fathom the absolute nature which the transcendent ontic forms that they bring into relationship have in themselves. The *Sophist* contains only one statement on this absolute nature, and I have already cited this in my analysis of the *Parmenides*. There it appears that at this time Plato actually conceived the absolute ontic forms (the *παντελῶς ὄν*) as thinking soul-substances in accordance with the prototype of the divine *nous*. This statement, however, only brings to light the *religious conviction* of Plato that lay at the foundation of his actual dialectic of the ontic forms, a conviction that he did not for a moment consider to

---

now revealed as lying beyond the bounds of both.")

1 *Ibid.*, 250 E: *Τοῦτο μὲν τοίνυν ἐνταῦθα κείσθω διηπορημένον. ἐπειδὴ δ' ἐξ ἴσου τό τ' ὄν καὶ τὸ μὴ ὄν ἀπορίας μετειλήφατον, νῦν ἐλπὶς ἤδη, καθάπερ ἂν αὐτῶν θάτερον εἴτ' ἀμυδρότερον εἴτε σαφέστερον ἀναφαίνηται, καὶ θάτερον οὕτως <ἂν> ἀναφαίνεσθαι· κἂν αὖ μηδέτερον ἰδεῖν δυνώμεθα, τὸν γοῦν λόγον ὅπηπερ ἂν οἷοί τ' ὦμεν εὐπρεπέστατα διωξόμεθ' οὕτως ἀμφοῖν ἅμα.* ("Let this then remain here as an unresolved difficulty. Since, however, being and non-being are burdened with the same *aporia*, the hope remains that if one of them is revealed to us in a clearer or dimmer light, the other will be *revealed* in the same manner; and again, if we can get sight of neither, we will at least thus be able to investigate as best we can the logical relationship of both at once in some manner or other.") Cf. also the passage cited earlier, in note 2 on page 229, from *Sophist*, 254 C: *ἵνα τό τ' ὄν καὶ μὴ ὄν εἰ μὴ πάσῃ σαφηνείᾳ δυνάμεθα λαβεῖν, ἀλλ' οὖν λόγου γ' ἐνδεεῖς μηδὲν γιγνώμεθα περὶ αὐτῶν.*

be susceptible of scientific proof. Rather it clearly strikes one as a *cri de coeur*, which gives vent to the thinker's religious protest against his own former position, namely, the Eleatic conception of the *eidē* as rigid, inanimate, lifeless abstractions. This same observation has already been made by Cornford.

i. *The Idea of Otherness as the* Principium Individuationis.
    Plato and Augustinian Scholasticism

According to the discussion leader, the dialectical, relative *ideai* of being and non-being may not be conceived as ontic forms that are opposite, but only as different from one another.[1] In this sense, non-being is nothing else than otherness (i.e., *being* other), and in accordance with its *eidos* it thus participates in being. As the supreme *eidos*, being can be apprehended by the dialectic only in a relative *idea*, in which it is a unity and at the same time a whole possessing a plurality of parts. The situation is no different in regard to the *idea* of non-being as otherness. Otherness alway relates solely to a part of being that differs from all other parts and therefore *is not* these others.

Ultimately, the *atomon eidos*, a part of being that cannot be further divided, thus becomes the ontic form of individuality precisely through its connection with the *idea* of otherness. As the discussion leader expresses this: "And that which *is*, for us *is not*, in as many respects as the *other* is. For in not being that, it is itself an indivisible unity, while again it is not the countless other."[2] In medieval Augustinian Scholasticism, this conception of the *principium individuationis* will be taken up particularly by the Flemish thinker Henry of Ghent.

j. *The Relationship between the Dialectical* Idea *of the Other*
    (ἰδέα τοῦ θατέρου) and the Idea of Change in the Parmenides

It may be asked whether the *idea* of the other, in which the *Sophist* locates the *eidos* of non-being, coincides with the *idea* of change or transition in which the *Parmenides* had sought to achieve a dialectical synthesis between being and non-being. It is most likely that this is not the case and that Plato replaced the latter with the former. The *Timaeus*, at least, speaks solely of the *idea* of the other (τὸ θάτερον), and even the *Sophist* itself nowhere mentions the *idea* of the transition between being and non-being. In this *idea* of change, Plato had attempted to grasp the *eidos* of eternal flux or motion in a dialectical-logical manner. Over against this, he uses the *idea* of otherness to apprehend non-being, which embraces both rest and motion, in its relation to being. In the

---

1   *Ibid.*, 257 B: Ὁπόταν τὸ μὴ ὂν λέγωμεν, ὡς ἔοικεν, οὐκ ἐναντίον τι λέγομεν τοῦ ὄντος, ἀλλ᾽ ἕτερον μόνον. ("Whenever we speak of that which *is not*, it seems we are not speaking of something opposite to that which *is*, but only of something [that is] different from it.")

2   *Ibid.*, 257 A: Καὶ τὸ ὂν ἄρ᾽ ἡμῖν, ὅσαπερ ἐστὶ τἆλλα, κατὰ τοσαῦτα οὐκ ἔστιν· ἐκεῖνα γὰρ οὐκ ὂν ἓν μὲν αὐτό ἐστιν, ἀπέραντα δὲ τὸν ἀριθμὸν τἆλλ᾽ οὐκ ἔστιν αὖ. (Translation in the text.)

Parmenides,[1] however, motion was nevertheless conceived eidetically as the real unity's being "always in the other," or "different from itself," with the result that the *idea* of change, at least in this dialogue, also fulfilled as a matter of fact the role of the *Sophist's idea tou thaterou* (ἰδέα τοῦ θατέρου).

In any case, Plato's intention in both cases was to logicize *hulē*, grasping it in a dialectical *idea* and introducing it into the eidetic world itself. Although it is true that the absolute antithesis between the principles of form and matter continues to be maintained as the religious presupposition of the dialectic, in the dialectic itself it must nevertheless be resolved into the metaphysical-logical relation between the same and the other (identity and difference), both of which participate in being.

k. *The Inner Antinomy in the Attempt of the Dialectic to Capture
    the Matter Principle Itself in an* Eidos. *The Crisis in the
    Theory of Ideas Can Only Be Overcome by Limiting the
    Scope of the New, Dialectical Logic*

However, the matter principle, the region of darkness where the Sophist has sought refuge, could not be captured in a dialectical *idea* of otherness, for in the religious ground-motive of Greek thought, this principle was nothing less than the absolute antipode of the form principle. For this reason, the dialectical logic, which was itself completely controlled by this ground-motive, necessarily became ensnared in antinomies when it attempted to introduce *hulē* into the eidetic world. These antinomies, moreover, threatened to be the internal undoing of the metaphysical ontology itself. It was therefore of critical importance to the theory of ideas that the scope of the new dialectical logic be restricted.

The world of the *eidē* had been introduced in the *Phaedo* as an intelligible world of pure and absolute, simple ontic forms. The new dialectic had deprived the *eidē* of this purity and simplicity, however. The advantage of this was that a logically comprehensible account had now apparently been rendered of how the ontic forms could become embodied in *hulē* and could function as active causes in the visible cosmos. However, an *eidos* that becomes embodied in an immense multiplicity of sensible things subject to the matter principle is no longer the pure ontic form of the intelligible world proper. Like the *nous* when it becomes incarnated in a material body, it is now mingled with *hulē*, and, in this condition, has relinquished its simplicity and its purely formal character.

l. *Pure* Eidē *and* Eidē *Mixed with Matter. In Plato's Next
    Period, Only the Latter Can Be Retained as* Genē *Related
    to the Divine* Idea *as Origin*

If the theory of ideas was thus to continue as a metaphysical *theoria* of pure ontic forms, a sharp distinction had to be introduced once again be-

---

1   *Parmenides*, 146 A.

tween the world of pure *eidē* and the *composite* or *mixed* world in which the *eidē* are incarnated in *hulē*. The *Republic* had already characterized the latter as the realm of what has come into being. It was thus natural to regard the *eidē* as *genē* (γένη), ontic forms of becoming, only in their composition or mixture with the matter principle. The earlier conception of the *Republic*, which held that the *eidē* in themselves derive their being from the divine form-power of the *idea* of the good and beautiful, would then be restricted to the real of what is mixed or composite. This was also entirely consistent with the original Socratic viewpoint, which placed the divine *idea* in direct relation to the visible cosmos and had no need to reckon with a metaphysical world of eternal ontic forms. Such a metaphysical world, of course, was unknown to Socrates.

The pure *eidē* would once again have to be set over against the divine *nous* as independent, ungenerated, eternal models, and the character of active soul-forces which they had acquired in the *Parmenides* and the *Sophist* would have to be abandoned. In themselves, then, they are not brought into being by the divine *nous*, but instead repose from eternity in the intelligible world of being. It is only in the cosmos present to sense perception, the world of what is mixed and composite, that the divine form-power is causally active. The claims of the new dialectic introduced in the Eleatic dialogues would then henceforth have to be restricted to the sphere of mixed being, and its task there would be to track down the structural principles grounded in eidetic relations.

These eidetic relations do not extend to the inner, simple and indivisible nature which belongs to the ontic forms as *ousia* or substance. Instead, they apply only to the structures of mixed being, which do in fact have their origin in the form-power of the divine *nous*. We shall find this clearly enunciated in the *Timaeus*.[1] At this point, the recognition that the dialectical logic cannot penetrate to the nature of absolute being and absolute non-being, which we have found to be at least implicitly present already in the *Parmenides* and the *Sophist*, will thus be sharpened considerably.

When Plato's thought takes this new turn, the crisis of the theory of ideas will be surmounted. We shall then be presented with one of the last stages in the development of this theory, the chief dialogues in which this is expressed being the *Philebus* and the *Timaeus*. Nevertheless, however much the elderly philosopher's interest in empirical phenomena may increase, these dialogues will still reveal the primordial dualism of the ground-motive in all of its religious intensity. We shall also see that Plato was unable to arrive at the modern conception of empirical science by this route.

---

1   *Timaeus*, 35 A.

Chapter Three

The Dialectic of the Form-Matter Motive in the Penultimate Stage of Development in Plato's Thought, After the Crisis Has Been Surmounted

1. The Theory of Ideas in the *Philebus* and the Dialectical Theory of the Mixture of the Principles of Form and Matter

a. The Dialectical Theory of the Mixture of the Principles of Form and Matter

The *Philebus* once again takes up an early Socratic theme of inquiry, the question as to the highest good. It is thus no accident that the leading role in the discussion is once more entrusted to Socrates himself. The great crisis of the theory of ideas has now been surmounted. During this crisis the dialectical logic had been temporarily dissociated from the Socratic *idea* of the good as the divine form of origin, although as a presupposition this *idea* had never been abandoned. This had been done so that exclusive attention could be focused on the endeavor to break through, in a logical manner, the rigid Eleatic *chōrismos* between the world of *eidē* and the phenomenal world. Now this crisis has been left behind. The *idea* of the good and beautiful resumes its central position as origin in Plato's thought, and in conformity with the Socratic position it is set in relation to the visible cosmos. The new, logical dialectic has shown how this cosmos can be understood as an incarnation of the *eidē* in *hulē*.

Now the only thing that remains is to establish once again a sharp boundary between this *mixed* and *composite* world and the world of the pure *eidē* and to pose unambiguously, with the aid of the method of the new dialectic, the question as to the highest good for the former world, to which the human being as a composite being most certainly belongs.

The *Philebus*, therefore, has a direct connection with the dialectical problem that was formulated in the *Parmenides*: How can the unity of the *eidos* as an ontic form become a plurality? The young Philebus had defended the hedonistic position of the post-Socratic Cyrenaic school, that pleasure is the highest good. In contrast, Socrates at first defended the view that the supreme good resides in knowledge or *phronēsis*. Now, as the discussion leader, Socrates undertakes an inquiry into the correctness of these two views. His partner in this is the young Protarchus, who for the most part assumes the role of his friend Philebus in the dialogue. At the very outset, Socrates draws Protarchus' attention to the problem formulated above, this being present in both positions.

According to Socrates, neither pleasure nor knowledge can be appraised as the highest good without further consideration. There are numerous types of each of these which must first be properly distinguished from one another in a dialectical manner and then be once again synthetically combined into a unity. Only then will it become possible to determine which of the two deserves the title of the highest good, or if perhaps this honor must rather be conferred upon some third thing (what Socrates has in mind here is a harmonic combination or mixture of particular types of each).

b. The Number of Intermediate Links between the Unity of the Genus and the Apeiron

In this connection, Socrates once again takes issue in passing with the Eleatic conception of unity and plurality, which had already been combated in the *Parmenides* and the *Sophist*. Over against absolute unity and plurality, the Eleatics had placed the *apeiron* or unlimited. As a plurality that was utterly devoid of unity, the latter was inaccessible to logical thought and therefore had to be dismissed as absolute non-being. According to Plato's new dialectic, however, unity is joined to the *apeiron* by means of numerous intermediate links. That is to say, between the most comprehensive *eidos*, which forms the genus proper, and the individual thing in the visible cosmos, whose individuality is not susceptible to further logical determination and thus constitutes an *apeiron* for logical definition, there lies a large number of formal types (species) that become increasingly specific and are arranged in a descending series under the genus. The logical tracking down of these species in accordance with the method of *diairesis* terminates in the definition (*logos*) of the earlier discussed *atomon eidos*. If one is to obtain a correct logical definition, therefore, he must determine the precise number of these specific ontic forms that lie between the unity of the genus and the *apeiron* of the individual phenomenon.

This is the meaning of Socrates' obscure utterance in the *Philebus*, 16 C-E:

It was a gift of the gods to men, so it seems to me, flung down[1] by some Prometheus together with an exceedingly bright fire. And the ancients, who were better than ourselves and dwelt nearer the gods, handed it down to us as an oracle, that all things which are said always to *be* consist of a one and a many and therefore by nature combine in themselves limit (πέρας) and unlimitedness (ἀπερίαν). Since these things are so ordered, it is necessary, they said, that we therefore always assume one *idea* in every individual thing and search for it, for we shall find it contained therein; then, if we have laid hold of this, we must after the

---

1   *Translator*: The Greek has: "flung down from the gods."

one [*idea*] look for two [*eidē*] – at least if they are present – or if not, for three or some other number; and we must again deal with each of these individually in the same manner, until it is seen that the original one is not only a one, a many, and unlimitedness, but is also a definite number. But we are not to apply the *idea* of the unlimited to the many before we have discerned the total number lying between the one and the unlimited. Only then may we abandon each individual thing, apart from all unities, to the unlimited and regard it as done with.[1]

c. The Use of the Term Idea Is Again Perfectly Consistent with the Dialectical Logic

The use of the term *ἰδέα* is here again perfectly consistent with the framework of the new dialectical logic. This dialectical *ἰδέα* is a unity in plurality, but its unity is a metaphysical rather than a purely logical one. In spite of the fact that it belongs to the realm of the *eidē* and is thus transcendent in character, this unity has become a plurality in the visible world by way of the eidetic relations. And now, with the aid of the *diairetic* method of the dialectic, it must be gathered up from this plurality and combined again into a unity.

The dialectical *ἰδέα* always retains the supersensible, intuitive character that belongs to the ontic form. Nevertheless, the synopsis takes place here on the basis of logical analysis and combination. It does not function here, as it still did in the *Republic*, independently of logical analysis and synthesis. Just as the *Republic* had apprehended all of the *eidē* in their concentric relation to their origin in the one divine *idea* of the good and the beautiful, the new dialectic grasps the plurality of sensible phenomena in their concentric relation to their dialectical genus; but it herein proceeds by way of the step-by-step method of *diairesis* and *synairesis*.[2]

The passage quoted above also makes clear that Plato did not wish to

---

1 *Philebus*, 16 C-E: Θεῶν μὲν εἰς ἀνθρώπους δόσις, ὥς γε καταφαίνεται ἐμοὶ, ποθὲν ἐκ θεῶν ἐρρίφη, διά τινος Προμηθέως ἅμα φανοτάτῳ τινὶ πυρί. καὶ οἱ μὲν παλαιοί, κρείττονες ἡμῶν καὶ ἐγγυτέρω θεῶν οἰκοῦντες, ταύτην φήμην παρέδοσαν, ὡς ἐξ ἑνὸς μὲν καὶ ἐκ πολλῶν ὄντων τῶν ἀεὶ λεγομένων εἶναι, πέρας δὲ καὶ ἀπειρίαν ἐν αὑτοῖς ξύμφυτον ἐχόντων· δεῖν οὖν ἡμᾶς τούτων οὕτω διακεκοσμημένων ἀεὶ μίαν ἰδέαν περὶ παντὸς ἑκάστοτε θεμένους ζητεῖν· εὑρήσειν γὰρ ἐνοῦσαν. ἐὰν οὖν καταλάβωμεν, μετὰ μίαν δύο, εἴ πως εἰσί, σκοπεῖν, εἰ δὲ μή, τρεῖς ἤ τιν' ἄλλον ἀριθμόν, καὶ τῶν ἓν ἐκείνων ἕκαστον πάλιν ὡσαύτως, μέχρι περ ἂν τὸ κατ' ἀρχὰς ἓν μὴ ὅτι ἓν καὶ πολλὰ καὶ ἄπειρά ἐστι μόνον ἴδῃ τις, ἀλλὰ καὶ ὁπόσα· τὴν δὲ τοῦ ἀπείρου ἰδέαν πρὸς τὸ πλῆθος μὴ προσφέρειν, πρὶν ἄν τις τὸν ἀριθμὸν αὐτοῦ πάντα κατίδῃ τὸν μεταξὺ τοῦ ἀπείρου τε καὶ τοῦ ἑνός· τότε δ᾽ ἤδη τὸ ἓν ἕκαστον τῶν πάντων εἰς τὸ ἄπειρον μεθέντα χαίρειν ἐᾶν. (Translation in text.)

2 The logical preparation for the synopsis is formulated most clearly in *Philebus*, 18 A: ὥσπερ γὰρ ἓν ὁτιοῦν εἴ τίς ποτε λάβοι, τοῦτον, ὥς φαμεν, οὐκ ἐπ' ἀπείρου φύσιν δεῖ βλέπειν εὐθὺς ἀλλ' ἐπί τιν' ἀριθμόν, οὕτω καὶ τοὐναντίον ὅταν τις τὸ ἄπειρον ἀναγκασθῇ πρῶτον λαμβάνειν, μὴ ἐπὶ τὸ ἓν εὐθὺς ἀλλ' ἐπ' ἀριθμὸν αὖ

adhere in a doctrinaire fashion to the method of dichotomy (*diairesis*), the bipartite division of genus and species. Already in the *Statesman*, which was written after the *Sophist*,[1] he had acknowledged both that it is not always possible to divide into two and that a dismemberment into three or more lower formal types can at times prove necessary.[2] Nevertheless, the term *diairesis* is still retained in these latter cases.

Lastly, the passage speaks once again of an *idea* of the *apeiron*, which for Plato is in fact identical with *hule* or matter in its eternal flux. According to him, individuality, insofar as this lies beyond the *atomon eidos*, the formal type that cannot be subdivided further, has its locus in this *apeiron*. In the *Parmenides*, the *apeiron* had been apprehended in the *idea* of the indivisible moment of change, while in the *Sophist* the *idea* of otherness served this same purpose. The *Philebus* makes a new attempt to logicize the *apeiron*, a point to which we shall soon return.

It has now become self-evident what the conclusion of the above-quoted passage means in saying that "we abandon each individual thing ... to the unlimited." The dialectic must first ascertain the precise number of intermediate links lying between the genus and the individual thing from the visible comos that is subsumed under it. In this manner, it follows the *eidos* as it embodies itself in the *apeiron*, in its stepwise approach to individual phenomena all the way to the *atomon eidos*. Once this has been accomplished, the individuality that remains, which lies beyond the reach of all further formal limitation and therefore cannot be embraced by the *atomon eidos*, may be left to the *apeiron*. The task of logical definition is finished once it has analyzed all the eidetic formal links of a phenomenon and combined these into a unity in a single *idea*.

Socrates argues that the new, dialectical method must therefore be applied both to the diverse feelings of pleasure and to the various types of knowledge. At the outset he observes, however, that it may become evident that the supreme good for man lies in neither of these, but rather in

---

τινὰ πλῆθος ἕκαστον ἔχοντά τι κατανοεῖν, τελευτᾶν τ᾽ ἐκ πάντων εἰς ἕν. ("Just as when someone has grasped any unity, as we said, he must not immediately turn his eyes to the nature of the unlimited, but to some number, so conversely, if someone were compelled to consider the unlimited first, he must not immediately turn his mind to the one, but again to a certain number, which in every case contains a plurality, and only come to the one last of all.")

1 That the *Statesman* must have been written after the *Sophist* is evident from *Statesman* 284 B (the only place where Plato quotes his own words), where there is explicit reference to an argument from the *Sophist*.

2 *Statesman*, 287 B-C: Οἶσθ᾽ οὖν ὅτι χαλεπὸν αὐτὰς τεμεῖν δίχα; ... Κατὰ μέλη τοίνυν αὐτὰς οἷον ἱερεῖον διαιρώμεθα, ἐπειδὴ δίχα ἀδυνατοῦμεν· δεῖ γὰρ εἰς τὸν ἐγγύτατα ὅτι μάλιστα τέμνειν ἀριθμὸν ἀεί. ("Do you know, then, that it is difficult to divide these [viz., the other offices in the state besides kingship] in two? ... Following their joints, therefore, we must dissect them like a sacrificial animal, since we cannot do it in two parts. For we must always, if possible, divide them into the next smallest number.")

some third thing that differs from both and that should be preferred to both.

Pleasure that is unaccompanied by understanding, knowledge, memory, judgment, or any other intellectual activity, befits an animal and is comparable to the life of a mollusc or an oyster. On the other hand a life endowed with thought, understanding, and memory, but devoid of all feelings of pleasure and pain can also not be considered good and felicitous for a person. It is only in the case of the deity, a being that is absolutely and purely formal in nature, that thought coincides with the absolute good. The human being, however, like everything else in the cosmos as the realm of what has come into being, has a mixed or composite nature, and for this very reason, the supreme good for a person can only be found in a mixed mode of life.

d. *The Distinction between the Realm of Pure or Absolute Being and the Realm of Being That Is a Mixture of* Peras *and* Apeiron. *The Four* Genē *(Genera) of the Latter*

The realm of pure, absolute, simple being is now sharply distinguished from the realm of mixed being. Socrates divides the latter into three *eidē* or genera, namely, that of the *peras* (the limited), that of the *apeiron*, and that of the unity that is a mixture of these two (ἐξ ἀμφοῖν τουτοῖν ἕν τι ξυμμισγόμενον). The fact that he indeed restricts this analysis of being solely to those things that have come into being and are found within the cosmos is clearly evident from his words in 23 C: "Let us divide all that *now exists in the universe* into two, or rather, if you will, into three parts."[1] These three parts are *genē*. In their mixture, they are ontic forms of what has come into being, and this mixture requires an origin or active cause. As Protarchus puts it, summarizing Socrates' exposition, "I see. It seems to me that you mean that, when these [*genē*] are mixed with one another, certain generations arise from every mixture of them."[2] Socrates then hastens to add a fourth genus to the first three that he has mentioned, namely, the *cause of the mixture* (τῆς ξυμμίξεως τούτων πρὸς ἄλληλα τὴν αἰτίαν).[3]

---

1 *Philebus*, 23 C: Πάντα τὰ νῦν ὄντα ἐν τῷ παντὶ διχῇ διαλάβωμεν, μᾶλλον δ᾽, εἰ βούλει, τριχῇ. (Translation in text.)

2 *Ibid.*, 25 E: Μανθάνω· φαίνει γάρ μοι λέγειν, μιγνὺς ταῦτα, γενέσεις τινὰς ἐφ᾽ ἑκάστων αὐτῶν συμβαίνειν. (Translation in text.)

3 *Ibid.*, 23 D: Τετάρτου μοι γένους αὖ προσδεῖν. ... Τῆς ξυμμίξεως τούτων πρὸς ἄλληλα τὴν αἰτίαν ὅρα, καὶ τίθει μοι πρὸς τρισὶν ἐκείνοις τέταρτον τοῦτο. ("I still need a fourth genus ... Consider the cause of the mixing of these with each other and add this as a fourth to these three.") *Ibid.*, 27 b: Τὸ δὲ δὴ πάντα ταῦτα δημιουργοῦν λέγωμεν τέταρτον, τὴν αἰτίαν, ὡς ἱκανῶς ἕτερον ἐκείνων δεδηλωμένον; ("Shall we then not name that [power] which fashions all this, the cause, as a fourth [genus], something that has been adequately clarified in its distinctness from the others?")

e. The New Dialectical Idea *of the Unlimited. The Influence of Heraclitus' Conception of the Matter Principle*

Socrates now attempts to establish, first of all, that the dialectical *idea* of the *apeiron* is a multiple unity. Indeed, the entire dialectical correlation between unity and plurality that was set forth in the *Parmenides* serves as the foundation for this attempt. In this process, theoretical thought once again becomes entangled in the antinomy I described earlier, namely, that the *apeiron* as such resists every attempt to grasp it in the unity of an ontic form and is nothing less than the utter absence of form, measure, and limit. We have already determined, however, that the dialectical *idea* does not actually penetrate to the absolute nature of the ontic form and to the ever-flowing *hulē*. Instead, its role is simply to establish a correlation between these two antipodes. The *idea* that is intended to introduce unity into the infinite multiplicity of manifestations of the *apeiron* is the genetic, fluid relation of more and less, stronger and weaker, larger and smaller, and other contrasts that are in the class of the "more and less."[1] Thus, for example, colder and hotter as such have no definite measure and limit. They are in a state of constant fluid progression and becoming, and as such they have no permanent being.[2] It is only number, as the manifestation of limit and measure, that brings the continuous flux of the "more and less' to rest and thereby grants it empirical (i.e., mixed) being.

On this point, the *Philebus* without question brings the *idea tou apeirou* into sharper relief than the *Parmenides* and the *Sophist* did. As we have seen, the *Parmenides* still identified the idea of the unlimited with the dialectical *idea* of change, which at that juncture contained within itself the *idea* of otherness (difference). The *Sophist*, for its part, identified it with the *idea* of otherness. The *Philebus* now attempts to capture in the *idea* of

---

1   *Ibid.*, 24 E-25 A: Ὁπόσ' ἂν ἡμῖν φαίνηται μᾶλλόν τε καὶ ἧττον γιγνόμενα καὶ τὸ σφόδρα καὶ ἠρέμα δεχόμενα καὶ τὸ λίαν καὶ πάνθ' ὅσα τοιαῦτα, εἰς τὸ τοῦ ἀπείρου γένος ὡς εἰς ἓν δεῖ πάντα ταῦτα τιθέναι, κατὰ τὸν ἔμπροσθε λόγον, ὃν ἔφαμεν, ὅσα διέσπασται καὶ διέσχισται συναγαγόντας χρῆναι κατὰ δύναμιν μίαν ἐπισημαίνεσθαί τινα φύσιν, εἰ μέμνησαι. ("Whatever appears to us as becoming more or less, and admitting of terms like "strongly," "slightly" [a very intense or mild degree], "excessively," and all such things, we must subsume all of this under the genus of the unlimited as in one [*idea*]; this would conform to our previous argument, where, if you remember, we showed that one must combine all that is separated and divided asunder and, as far as possible, designate them with one nature.")

2   *Ibid.*, 24 D: οὐ γὰρ ἔτι θερμότερον οὐδὲ ψυχρότερον ἤστην ἂν λαβόντε τὸ ποσόν· προχωρεῖ γὰρ καὶ οὐ μένει τό τε θερμότερον ἀεὶ καὶ τὸ ψυχρότερον ὡσαύτως, τὸ δὲ ποσὸν ἔστη καὶ προϊὸν ἐπαύσατο. ("For [hotter and colder], if they took on a definite degree, would no longer be hotter and colder. For 'hotter' is in constantly progressing flux, and is not permanent, and likewise 'colder'; but a definite degree has come to rest and has ceased flowing further.") It may be noted that Plato here, apparently by design, uses the same term for '*apeiron*' that appears in the statement he ascribes to Heraclitus in the *Cratylus* (402 A): πάντα ῥεῖ (προχωρεῖ) καὶ οὐδὲν μένει ("everything is in constant flux; nothing has permanent being").

the unlimited itself the moment of eternal flux passing through opposite formal states, a notion that had been expressed most pregnantly in Heraclitus' conception of the matter principle. In the *Sophist*, the *idea* of otherness, even though it was identified with the *idea* of the unlimited, had to serve simultaneously as a synthesis between the unity of the ontic form and the unlimited. Now, we have already seen that the dialectical *idea* always possesses a correlative character. It is impossible, therefore, for an *idea* of the unlimited to be anything else than an *idea* of the *relative apeiron*. It cannot be an *idea* of absolute *hulē*, for the *Parmenides* has demonstrated that the latter can only lead the dialectical logic to the negation of all predicates.

f. Plato's Dialectical Idea *of the Unlimited and Aristotle's Conception of Matter as Potential Being (δυνάμει ὄν)*

In the new conception of this *idea* as well, the relationship to ontic form, measure and limit is obvious. For all things that admit of more or less, larger or smaller, stronger or weaker, etc., are susceptible to a limitation in degree and are thus oriented in principle to such a limitation in degree. For this reason Aristotle will later conceive *hulē* as δυνάμει ὄν, "potential being," which can only be brought into actual existence through the ontic form (μορφή) and therefore can only be separated from the form *in abstracto*.

The fact, moreover, that the *idea* of otherness also continues to play an essential role in Plato's new conception of the *idea* of the *apeiron* is clearly evident from the immediately following description of what is involved in the *idea* of the *peras*.[1] According to Socrates, the latter, as a multiple unity, embraces all that is the opposite of the *apeiron*: in the first place, the equal and equality (τὸ ἴσον καὶ ἰσότητα), and then, the double, and everything that is a ratio of numbers or measures. In the *Parmenides* and the *Sophist*, the "other" (τὸ θάτερον) was always treated as the dialectical opposite of equality or identity, although to the degree that it participated in being it nevertheless had to remain identical to itself.

Socrates then combines the plurality that is subsumed under the *idea* of the *peras* back into a unity by means of the genus of *law and order* (νόμος καὶ τάξις). In Heraclitean fashion, this is identified with the harmony of opposites in which the correlation of *peras* and *apeiron* is once again manifest.[2]

---

1 *Ibid.*, 25 A-B: Οὐκοῦν τὰ μὴ δεχόμενα ταῦτα, τούτων δὲ τἀναντία πάντα δεχόμενα, πρῶτον μὲν τὸ ἴσον καὶ ἰσότητα, μετὰ δὲ τὸ ἴσον τὸ διπλάσιον καὶ πᾶν ὅ τί περ ἂν πρὸς ἀριθμὸν ἀριθμὸς ἢ μέτρον ἢ πρὸς μέτρον, ταῦτα ξύμπαντ᾽ εἰς τὸ πέρας ἀπολογιζόμενοι καλῶς ἂν δοκοῦμεν δρᾶν τοῦτο ... ; ("Then that which does not admit of these, but rather admits of the opposites of all this – in the first place, the equal and equality, and after the equal the double, and everything that is the ratio of a number to a number or of a measure to a measure – would we not seem to do well if we reckoned all this together to the *peras*... ")

2 *Ibid.*, 26 B-C: ὕβριν γάρ που καὶ ξύμπασαν πάντων πονηρίαν αὕτη κατιδοῦσα ἡ

g. *The Pure* Eidos *of the* Peras *and the Dialectical* Idea *of the* Peras
Are Not Identical

It is characteristic of Plato's restricted conception of the dialectical *idea* in the *Philebus*, however, that soon after this (26 D) he denies any plurality to the pure, unmixed nature of the *peras* or form principle and that he represents it as a multiplicity only in the process of becoming.[1] At

---

θεός, ὦ καλὲ Φίληβε, πέρας οὐδὲν οὔθ᾿ ἡδονῶν οὔτε πλησμονῶν ἐνὸν ἐν αὐτοῖς νόμον καὶ τάξιν πέρας ἔχοντ᾿ ἔθετο· καὶ σὺ μὲν ἀποκναῖσαι ἔφησθ᾿ αὐτήν, ἐγὼ δὲ τοὐναντίον ἀποσῶσαι λέγω. ("For since this goddess perceived the wantonness and every sort of wickedness of all creatures, fair Philebus, and that there was among them no limit to pleasures and self-indulgence, she instituted law and order as things that contain limit. And you maintain that these are a vexation to them; but I say, in contrast, that they preserve them.")

1 *Ibid.*, 26 D: Καὶ μὴν τό γε πέρας οὔτε πόλλ᾿ εἶχεν οὔτ᾿ ἐδυσκολαίνομεν ὡς οὐκ ἦν ἓν φύσει. ("But the *peras* contained no plurality, nor did it make us suspicious that it was not one in the world of becoming.") The first part of this passage, in its striking contrast with 25 A-B (cited above) and 23 E (cited below), decisively refutes Léon Robin's notion (*Platon*; Paris: Librairie Felix Alcan, 1935, pp. 155-156) that, in his *Philebus*, Plato also includes the intelligible world of the *eide* in its detachment from the process of becoming in the sphere of that which is mixed or composite. Robin supports this position by arguing that Plato used the same method in this dialogue as in the *Sophist*, where he was indeed concerned with demonstrating the intertwinement of the genera. "For the rest," Robin says, "if the domain of the mixed were exclusively the world of experience, it would be necessary to restrict to this world the two principles from whose union this mixture was produced. However, they clearly extend much further than this. The unlimited is in point of fact the same as the Other, which is the Platonic non-being; and the non-being of the Other is diffused, as is well known, among all of the essences. Moreover, we have learned from Aristotle that sensible things are not constituted in any other way than the intelligible things and that irrespective of its stage of existence, whether it be in the intelligible or in the sensible, there is no being at all that is not a mixture." There are several objections to this argument: 1. It proceeds from the assumption, which has proven to be incorrect, that the *Philebus* retains the exact position of the *Sophist* in regard to the theory of the *eide*. Beginning with the *Philebus*, the *eide* are conceived as *gene* (genera) only in their impure or mixed state. In the *Parmenides* and the *Sophist*, by contrast, the predominance of the logical dialectic threatened to become the complete undoing of the world of pure *eide*. 2. Plato never conceives the genus of otherness as anything but an *idea* of the dialectical logic. As such, it is intended to bring the *eide* into logical correlation; but the apprehension of the intrinsic nature of the pure *eide* is precisely what is forbidden to it. A comparison of 26 D with 23 E and 25 A-B makes clear that the *Philebus* once again introduces a sharp distinction between the pure *eide*, on the one hand, and the *eide* in their incarnation in the *apeiron* as constant structural principles of the world of what has come into being, on the other hand, and that it also has no place for the μὴ ὄν in the world of the *eide* in themselves. 3. It is precisely the world of the pure *eide*, as this is once again conceived in the *Philebus*, that is left untouched by Aristotle's testimony. Instead, the latter relates only to the final stage of Plato's development, where the *eide* are iden-

first sight, it appears somewhat rash to conclude from the first part of this passage, which Socrates leaves completely unexplained in its seeming flagrant contradiction of the former description of the *peras*, that Plato here does in fact again introduce the *eidos* as a simple and indivisible unity, thus reverting to this extent to the original conception of his theory of ideas. We shall discover in the sequel, however, that this passage does not stand alone in the *Philebus*, but is rather supported by later statements of Socrates.

It is crucial therefore to seek other evidence which will give us a more secure basis for forming a clear notion of what Plato could have meant at this stage of the development of his theory of ideas by the "simple and indivisible *peras*." It is also important to obtain a clear notion of how he conceived the relationship between this pure *eidos* and the quantitative numbers (the main elements of the plurality subsumed under the genus of the *peras*).

h. The Eidetic Numbers and the Mathematical Numbers.
The Eidos Number as Indivisible and Incommensurable
(ἀσύμβλητος)

It can scarcely be doubted that we are here confronted with the typically Platonic conception of the so-called eidetic or ideal number in its contradistinction to the mathematical number. Although the general identification of *eidos* and ideal number belongs only to the final stage of the theory of ideas, which came to expression in Plato's unpublished lecture *On the Good* (περὶ ἀγαθοῦ), the recognition of eidetic numbers as the metaphysical, eidetic foundation of the mathematical or quantitative numbers is unmistakably present already in the *Phaedo*.[1] Ever since Léon Robin's groundbreaking book *La théorie platonicienne des idées et des nombres*,[2] which for the first time could make use of the monumental Greek Aristotle commentaries prepared by the Berlin Academy, it has been known that the account which Aristotle gives in his *Metaphysics* (M 6, 1080 a 30-35) of the Platonic conception of the ideal number is incorrect. Its error lies in the fact that it creates the impression that the ideal number, like the mathematical, consists of units. Aristotle's view is incorrect in this regard, even though he acknowledges that the Platonic idea numbers differ from the mathematical numbers in being mutually independent.[3]

---

tified with the so-called ideal numbers. Robin himself, in the end, has to admit that all the examples which the *Philebus* gives of what is mixed refer exclusively to the empirical cosmos. In addition to all of this, in *Philebus* 23 C, the distinction between *peras* and *apeiron* is expressly restricted to the things "that now exist in the universe."

1 *Phaedo* 96 D-97 B; 101 B-C.

2 Léon Robin, *La théorie platonicienne des idées et des nombres. Étude historique et critique* (Paris: F. Alcan, 1908).

3 Aristotle, *Metaphysics*, M 6, 1080 a 30-35: διὸ καὶ ὁ μὲν μαθηματικὸς ἀριθμεῖται

In Plato's conception, the principal difference between these two domains of number is that the former are not aggregates and thus contain no plurality, and further, that there exists only one exemplar of each idea number.[1] In contrast to this, the mathematical number consists of units that are completely identical to one another and that exist only as objects of thought. Plato holds that both the mathematical and the ideal numbers are independent and separate from perceptible things. This view stands in sharp contrast to Aristotle's conception, which eliminates the ideal numbers and regards the mathematical numbers merely as an abstraction from perceptible things. According to Plato, however, the ideal numbers are genuine *eidē* and are not themselves quantities. In his view, their numerical character is based exclusively on the fact that they are positioned in a fixed, immutable, non-temporal sequence of earlier and later.[2] The mathematical numbers (the numbers in themselves, *καθ' αὑτῶν*) then do not derive their positional value in the series from the addition of new units, as Aristotle taught, but rather, as the *Phaedo* explains, solely from their

---

μετὰ τὸ ἓν δύο πρὸς τῷ ἔμπροσθεν ἑνὶ ἄλλο ἕν, καὶ τὰ τρία πρὸς τοῖς δυσὶ τούτοις ἄλλο ἕν, καὶ ὁ λοιπὸς δὲ ὡσαύτως· οὗτος δὲ μετὰ τὸ ἓν δύο ἕτερα ἄνευ τοῦ ἑνὸς τοῦ πρώτου, καὶ ἡ τριὰς ἄνευ τῆς δυάδος, ὁμοίως δὲ καὶ ὁ ἄλλος ἀριθμός. ("Therefore the mathematical numbers are counted as follows: after the one, two, i.e., in addition to the previous one another one, and three, in addition to these two existing ones another one, and the remaining numbers in like manner. With the others [viz., the idea numbers], however: after the one, two other ones without the first one, and the three without the two, and likewise also the other numbers.")

1 As Robin says, "Each of these numbers [viz. the idea numbers], ... far from being a composite of units which can be formed in a variety of ways, and as often as one desires, is alone within its kind ..." According to Robin, Aristotle always assessed Plato's doctrine of the idea numbers "in terms of the teachings of Xenocrates" (à travers la doctrine de Xénocrate"). Xenocrates, one of Plato's own pupils, held that the idea numbers were identical to the mathematical numbers, and he thus diverged sharply from his teacher on this point. Cf. W. Vander Wielen, *De idee-getallen van Plato* (dissertation: Amsterdam, 1941), p. 51, and further, W.D. Ross, ed. *Aristotle's Metaphysics* (Oxford: Clarendon Press, 1924, 1953), X, I (Introduction) pp. lxxi-lxxvi. With regard to the idea numbers, Ross also observes (*loc. cit.*, lii): "From their nature as Ideas it follows that they are specifically distinct and incomparable, i.e., incapable of being stated as fractions one of another. Twoness is not half of fourness. Nor is a natural number [i.e., idea number] an aggregate of units."

2 Aristotle, *Metaphysics*, M 6, 1080 b 11-14: Οἱ μὲν οὖν ἀμφοτέρους φασὶν εἶναι τοὺς ἀριθμούς, τὸν μὲν ἔχοντα τὸ πρότερον καὶ ὕστερον τὰς ἰδέας, τὸν δὲ μαθηματικὸν παρὰ τὰς ἰδέας καὶ τὰ αἰσθητά, καὶ χωριστοὺς ἀμφοτέρους τῶν αἰσθητῶν. ("Some then say that both kinds of number exist – on the one hand, the number that possesses the relation of earlier and later, the ideas, on the other hand, the mathematical number alongside the ideas and perceptible things – and that both are distinct from perceptible things.") Concerning this passage and the seemingly conflicting statement in *Ethica Nicomachea*, A 4, cf. Vander Wielen, *op.cit.*, pp. 65 ff.

methexis or participation in the idea numbers.[1]

In this connection, we need not yet concern ourselves with Plato's conception of the so-called origin of these ideal numbers, since this evidently belongs to the final stage of development of the theory of ideas.[2] Indeed, it does not appear at all in Plato's dialogues. Our exclusive source of knowledge regarding this conception lies in Aristotle's writings and the testimony of the commentators on Plato and Aristotle.

i. The Pure, Indivisible Peras *Is Not a Genus of Mixed Being.*
    Stenzel's Unsuccessful Attempt to Derive the Eidetic
    Numbers by the Method of Diairesis

At this point we are interested only in the fact that Plato, ever since the *Phaedo*, has conceived the idea numbers as pure, indivisible, eternal ontic forms, which according to Aristotle's reliable testimony were put forward as mutually incommensurable (ἀσύμβλητοι) units.[3] By itself this is enough to establish that, in the *Philebus*, the *peras* (in the sense of idea number) cannot belong to the realm of mixed being as this was expounded in the dialectical logic of the Eleatic trilogy. For we learned as early as the *Parmenides* that the "real one" can only be apprehended dialectically as a whole with parts. As a consequence, an indivisible ontic form that is not composed of units lies in the nature of the case be-

---

1 *Phaedo*, 101 B-C: ἑνὶ ἑνὸς προστεθέντος τὴν πρόσθεσιν αἰτίαν εἶναι τοῦ δύο γενέσθαι ἢ διασχισθέντος τὴν σχίσιν οὐκ εὐλαβοῖο ἂν λέγειν; καὶ μέγα ἂν βοῴης, ὅτι οὐκ οἶσθ᾽ ἄλλως πως ἕκαστον γιγνόμενον ἢ μετασχὸν τῆς ἰδέας οὐσίας ἑκάστου οὗ ἂν μετάσχῃ, καὶ ἐν τούτοις οὐκ ἔχεις ἄλλην τινὰ αἰτίαν τοῦ δύο γενέσθαι ἀλλ᾽ ἢ τὴν τῆς δυάδος μετάσχεσιν καὶ δεῖν τούτου μετασχεῖν τὰ μέλλοντα δύο ἔσεσθαι, καὶ μονάδος, ὃ ἂν μέλλῃ ἓν ἔσεσθαι, τὰς δὲ σχίσεις ταύτας καὶ προσθέσεις καὶ τὰς ἄλλας τὰς τοιαύτας κομψείας ἐῴης ἂν χαίρειν, παρεὶς ἀποκρίνασθαι τοῖς ἑαυτοῦ σοφωτέροις. ("Would you not guard against saying that when one is added to one, the addition is the cause of the two's coming into being, or when one is divided, the division? And you would loudly proclaim that you know of no other way in which anything can come into being than by participation in the *idea* of the essence proper to each, and that in these cases you know no other cause of the two's coming into being than participation in twoness, and that whatever is to be two must participate therein, and whatever is to be one, in oneness. But you would dismiss these divisions and additions and the other niceties of this sort, leaving the answer to those wiser in this.")

2 This is likewese the view of Ross, *loc.cit.*, p. xli, who in this connection also expressly mentions the *Philebus*.

3 This testimony is found in *Metaphysics*, M 8, 1083 a 31-36: εἰ δέ ἐστι τὸ ἓν ἀρχή, ἀνάγκη μᾶλλον ὥσπερ Πλάτων ἔλεγεν ἔχειν τὰ περὶ τοὺς ἀριθμούς, καὶ εἶναι δυάδα πρώτην καὶ τριάδα, καὶ οὐ ἀσυμβλήτους εἶναι τοὺς ἀριθμοὺς πρὸς ἀλλήλους. ("If the one is a principle, it is rather necessary that things stand with the numbers as Plato said, and that there is an eidetic twoness and threeness and the numbers are not commensurable with one another.") In translating δυάδα πρώτην καὶ τριάδα as "eidetic [ideal] twoness and threeness," I follow Vander Wielen, *op.cit.*, p. 62. The reference here is naturally not to mathematical numbers.

yond the reach of this dialectic.

Stenzel's attempt to generate the idea numbers by means of the *diairetic* method[1] stands condemned by this same consideration. The method of *diairesis* belongs only within the framework of a dialectical logical conception of the *eidos* that proceeds from the *genos*, as an encompassing whole with pairs of opposite parts that descend from it stepwise. Anything that is essentially indivisible permits of no *diairesis*.

If it is indeed the case that in the *Philebus* the pure *peras* is the idea number, it is immediately clear why it is placed in opposition to the *peras* as a genus dispersed in a plurality. *Peras* in this latter sense embraces the mathematical numbers, which the early Pythagoreans identified outright with the *peras* and which they, in contrast to Plato, did not conceive of as detached from perceptible things.[2] Only the mathematical numbers can comprise a plurality. The ideal numbers, on the contrary, are indivisible units, whose being is absolutely pure and unmixed in character.

This eidetic theory of numbers, which was developed most distinctly in the *Phaedo*, was never abandoned by Plato. Not until his lecture *On the Good* did he attempt to derive the ideal numbers, following the ideal unity, dialectically from a combination of *peras* and *apeiron* as constitutive principles, and his pupils who attended this lecture (one of whom was Aristotle) apparently took this to be a completely new theory. Plato had evidently not yet arrived at such a theory during the stage of his development when he wrote the *Philebus*.

In any case, according to this later dialogue, the ontic form of limit can be a dialectical plurality only in its incarnation in the *apeiron* (the everflowing *hulē*). The dialectical *idea* apprehends only the unity that has become a plurality, that is to say, the formal unity in its development in limitless matter. Further, as the *Parmenides* sought to demonstrate, this process gives rise to (mathematical) number in the fluid substrate of the *apeiron*. Still further, the dialectical *idea* apprehends this multiple-unity solely in the eidetic relations, which serve to express the constant structures of temporal reality.

Socrates expounds this clearly in *Philebus*, 25 D ff. He invites Protarchus to combine the *apeiron*, which had been gathered up into a single *idea* in the dialectical relation of the "more or less," with the genus of the *peras*. For, as he observes, even though they should have gathered the latter into a single *idea*, just as they did earlier with the *apeiron*, they did not do it. "Perhaps the result will also be the same now, however. For by combining these two the third genus [i.e., that of the mixture of the two] will also become clear."[3] It is, however, only through the combination of *peras* and *apeiron* that they arrive at the single *idea* of the *peras* as a ge-

---

1   J. Stenzel, *Zahl und Gestalt bei Platon und Aristoteles*, 2nd edition, 1933, p. 31.

2   In the *Parmenides*, the *peras* is conceived only as a dialectical *idea*, i.e., as the relation between unity and the intermediate plurality of the *apeiron*.

3   *Philebus*, 25 D: Ἦν [viz., τοῦ πέρατος γένναν] καὶ νῦν δὴ, δέον ἡμᾶς, καθάπερ

nus, this being the *idea* of law, order, or harmony in the contrasts of the "more or less."[1]

From the above it is obvious that this genus cannot be identical to the *peras* as an indivisible unity lacking all plurality. Thus too it is evident why Socrates assigns the *peras* and the *apeiron* as genera exclusively to the realm of mixed being, the mode of being which belongs to the cosmos as a product of becoming.

j. *The Idea of Composite Being as a γένεσις εἰς οὐσίαν. The Teleological Element Is Once Again Introduced into the Definition of That Which Has Come into Being*

The third *idea*, that of being as a mixture or composition of *peras* and *apeiron*, is conceived, in addition, as a γένεσις εἰς οὐσίαν, that is, as a coming into being of something that *is*, as a result of a limiting of the *apeiron*. This limitation imparts measure to the *apeiron* and thereby brings its random flux to rest.[2]

In this third *idea*, the correlation between form and matter immediately

---

τὴν τοῦ ἀπείρου συνηγάγομεν εἰς ἕν, οὕτω καὶ τὴν τοῦ περατοειδοῦς συναγαγεῖν, οὐ συνηγάγομεν. ἀλλ᾽ ἴσως καὶ νῦν ταὐτὸν δράσει· τούτων ἀμφοτέρων συναγομένων καταφανὴς κἀκείνη γενήσεται. ("That [*viz.*, the genus of the limit] which we – although, just as we combined the genus of the unlimited into one, we should likewise now also have combined that of the limit – did not [yet] combine into it. But perhaps it will also perform the same service now. For by combining these two that third genus will also become clear.")

1 The fact that this *ἰδέα* too is indeed a dialectical multiple unity, and not, like the pure *eidos* of the *peras* (spoken of in *Philebus*, 26 D), a simple unity, is convincingly demonstrated by Socrates' words in *Philebus*, 23 E: Πρῶτον μὲν δὴ τῶν τεττάρων τὰ τρία διελόμενοι, τὰ δύο τούτων πειρώμεθα πολλὰ ἑκάτερον ἐσχισμένον καὶ διεσπασμένον ἰδόντες, εἰς ἓν πάλιν ἑκάτερον συναγαγόντες νοῆσαι πῇ ποτ᾽ ἦν αὐτῶν ἓν καὶ πολλὰ ἑκάτερον. ("By first setting apart three of these four, then, let us attempt – since we see two of them [*viz.* the *peras* and the *apeiron*, see 24 A below] each dispersed and torn apart into a plurality – to comprehend, after we have gathered up each of the two back into one, to what extent each of them is one and many.") *Ibid.*, 24 A: Λέγω τοίνυν τὰ δύο, ἃ προτίθεμαι, ταῦτ᾽ εἶναι ἅπερ νῦν δή, τὸ μὲν ἄπειρον, τὸ δὲ πέρας ἔχον. ("I therefore say that the two [genera] that I propose are those of which I just spoke, viz., the unlimited and the limited.") As is evident from 25 D above, the πέρας ἔχον cannot be identical to the third genus. In spite of its unclear qualification, this must rather be the *peras* itself.

2 *Ibid.*, 26 D: ἀλλὰ τρίτον φάθι με λέγειν, ἓν τοῦτο τιθέντα τὸ τούτων ἔκγονον ἅπαν, γένεσιν εἰς οὐσίαν ἐκ τῶν μετὰ τοῦ πέρατος ἀπειργασμένων μέτρων. ("Say, however, that I admit a third [genus], in that I reckon all the offspring of these [viz., of *peras* and *apeiron*] as a unity, i.e., as a becoming that issues in being, resulting from the relations of measure achieved with the aid of the *peras*.") It is evident from *Philebus*, 27 a, that the *peras* can indeed act only by virtue of the "cause" (the divine *nous*) and is only the instrument of the latter in this activity. In itself, the *peras*, as a genus, has no active power. The text thus reads not διά but μετὰ τοῦ πέρατος.

impresses itself on one. As a matter of fact, however, this correlation was already presupposed in the two other *ideai*. For, according to Plato, the mathematical number, which is subsumed under the *idea* of the *peras*, first arises through the combination of the ontic unity with the *apeiron*, and as the Pythagorean theory brought to light, it contains in itself both *peras* and *apeiron*.

The teleological element, which had temporarily dropped out of the picture during the crisis of the theory of *ideas* is now reintroduced into the conception of the cosmos as a product of becoming. This takes place, as a matter of course, because of the new understanding of mixed or composite being – as produced by the combination of form and matter, limitation and unlimitedness – in terms of a *genesis eis ousian*. For, in this manner, genesis or becoming is given a goal. As Socrates explains, "I thus maintain that it is for the sake of coming into being that all instruments and tools and all matter (ὕλη) are provided to anyone; but that every instance of becoming takes place for the sake of another particular form of being (ἄλλης οὐσίας τινὸς ἕνεκα), and the totality of coming into being for the sake of the totality of being."[1] "If pleasure is thus an instance of becoming, it must of necessity come to be for the sake of some particular being."[2] "But that which is the goal of what always comes to be for the sake of something else belongs in the class (ἐν μοίρᾳ) of the good, while that which comes to be for the sake of something else, excellent friend, must be placed in another class."[3] It therefore follows from this that feelings of pleasure as such can never be something good.[4]

It is evident from the first statement quoted above that the conception of mixed or composite being as a *genesis eis ousian*, which Aristotle would soon develop in his own manner in his theory of the relation between form and matter in composite being, is unambiguously oriented to the ground-motive of the religion of culture. The attempt is herein made to conceive *hulē* as material for a divine δημιουργεῖν, a divine form-giving activity, and in this way to surmount the antagonism between the princi-

---

1 *Ibid.*, 54 b, C: Φημὶ δὴ γενέσεως μὲν ἕνεκα φάρμακά τε καὶ πάντ᾽ ὄργανα καὶ πᾶσαν ὕλην παρατίθεσθαι πᾶσιν, ἑκάστην δὲ γένεσιν ἄλλην ἄλλης οὐσίας τινὸς ἑκάστης ἕνεκα γίγνεσθαι, ξύμπασαν δὲ γένεσιν οὐσίας ἕνεκα γίγνεσθαι ξυμπάσης. (Translation in text.)

2 *Ibid.*, 54 C: Οὐκοῦν ἡδονή γ᾽ εἴπερ γένεσίς ἐστιν, ἕνεκά τινος οὐσίας ἐξ ἀνάγκης γίγνοιτ᾽ ἄν (Translation in text.)

3 *Ibid.*, Τό γε μὴν οὖ ἕνεκα τὸ ἕνεκά του γιγνόμενον ἀεὶ γίγνοιτ᾽ ἄν, ἐν τῇ τοῦ ἀγαθοῦ μοίρα ἐκεῖνό ἐστι· τὸ δὲ τινὸς ἕνεκα γιγνόμενον εἰς ἄλλην, ὦ ἄριστε, μοῖραν θετέον. (Translation in text.)

4 *Ibid.*, 54 D:᾽Αρ᾽ οὖν ἡδονή γ᾽ εἴπερ γένεσίς ἐστιν, εἰς ἄλλην ἢ τὴν τοῦ ἀγαθοῦ μοῖραν αὐτὴν τιθέντες ὀρθῶς θήσομεν; ("Then if pleasure is a becoming, shall we be correct in placing it into a class other than that of the good?") (Translation supplied by translator.)

ples of form and matter. In this process, the relation between the cosmos that has come into being and the formative power of the divine *nous* with its *idea* of the good and beautiful is placed as a matter of course in the hands of the new dialectic. At the same time, the *erōs* motive, developed in the *Symposium* and the *Phaedrus*, is able to receive a dialectical-logical elaboration.

k. The New Dialectic's Physico-Teleological Proof for the Existence of God

Theōria need no longer appeal solely to the religious synopsis when it proclaims the existence of a divine *nous* as the origin of all form in the cosmos. From now on it can establish its case on the purported dialectical proof for the deity. The so-called physico-teleological proof for God's existence would henceforth be a permanent picture in metaphysical theology, with the result that it would take a place of honor in what is called natural theology (*theologia naturalis*), particularly in Scholastic thought.

2. The New Conception of the Soul as a Mixture of Form and Matter (a Product of Becoming)

It is of great importance to study how this teleological proof is carried out in the *Philebus*. This is the case, because as he elaborates it here Plato also sets forth his new conception of the soul. In the *Timaeus* this conception will be worked out more fully. The latter dialogue will also go further by determining the position of the soul in relation to both the world of the *eidē* and the world of phenomena. But it is in the *Philebus* that this new conception is set forth for the first time.

After Socrates has won Protarchus' acquiescence to his conclusion that pleasure as such belongs to the genus of the *apeiron* (the unlimited), he proceeds to take up the problem of assigning *nous*, understanding, and knowledge to one of the three remaining genera. Reacting to Protarchus' perplexity at his questioning, Socrates remarks: "Yet surely the answer is easy. For all the wise agree, thereby in reality exalting themselves highly, the *nous* is our ruler and that of heaven and earth, and perhaps they are right."[1] It is then agreed that over all things, and over that which is called the universe, there does not reign the power of irrational *Tuchē* (the ancient, unpredictable *Anankē*), as a 'terribly clever man' (δεινὸς ἀνήρ; the reference is probably to Democritus) had claimed, but that on the contrary, as their predecessors maintained, *nous* and a wondrous understanding orders and guides it.[2] Socrates thereupon takes note that the bodies of

---

1 *Ibid.*, 28 C: Ἀλλὰ μὴν ῥᾴδιον. πάντες γὰρ συμφωνοῦσιν οἱ σοφοί, ἑαυτοὺς ὄντως σεμνύνοντες, ὡς νοῦς ἐστι βασιλεὺς ἡμῖν οὐρανοῦ τε καὶ γῆς. καὶ ἴσως εὖ λέγουσι. (Translation in text.)

2 *Ibid.*, 28 D: Πότερον, ὦ Πρώταρχε, τὰ ξύμπαντα καὶ τόδε τὸ καλούμενον ὅλον ἐπιτροπεύειν φῶμεν τὴν τοῦ ἀλόγου καὶ εἰκῇ δύναμιν καὶ τὸ ὅπῃ ἔτυχεν, ἢ

all living beings are by nature constituted from the four elements: fire, earth, air, and water. Each of these elements is present in our own bodies only in a scant and insignificant quantity and in an impure state, and possesses a power that is in no way proportionate to its nature. Protarchus need merely compare the small quantity of fire in the human body with the fire that is present in the world-body of the universe, which in its abundance, its beauty, and its enormous power is a cause of wonder. Rational consideration makes plain that our bodies are sustained and brought into existence by this world-body, and not the other way around. For imperfection cannot be the source of perfection.[1]

Observing that the human body has a soul, Socrates next asks whence it could have gotten this if the body of the universe, which contains the same elements as ours and in a manner much fairer, were not endowed with a

---

τἀναντία, καθάπερ οἱ πρόσθεν ἡμῶν ἔλεγον, νοῦν καὶ φρόνησίν τινα θαυμαστὴν συντάττουσαν διακυβερνᾶν· *Ibid.*, 28 E-29 A: *Βούλει δῆτά τι καὶ ἡμεῖς τοῖς ἔμπροσθεν ὁμολογούμενον ξυμφήσωμεν, ὡς ταῦθ᾽ οὕτως ἔχει, καὶ μὴ μόνον οἰώμεθα δεῖν τἀλλότρια ἄνευ κινδύνου λέγειν, ἀλλὰ καὶ συγκινδυνεύωμεν καὶ μετέχωμεν τοῦ ψόγου, ὅταν ἀνὴρ δεινὸς φῇ ταῦτα μὴ οὕτως ἀλλ᾽ ἀτάκτως ἔχειν·* ("Shall we say, dear Protarchus, that over all things, and that which is called the universe, there reigns the power of un-reason, randomness, and chance, or on the contrary, as our predecessors maintained, that *nous* and a wondrous understanding orders and guides it? ... Are you then willing that we also should assent to what was agreed by our predecessors, that this is the way all these things are [i.e., that they are governed by *nous*], and that we not only should think we must state a view of others without risk to ourselves, but should also share the risk and the blame with them when a terribly clever person asserts that things are not like this, but are rather devoid of order?")

1 *Ibid.*, 29 B-C: *σμικρόν τε τούτων ἕκαστον παρ᾽ ἡμῖν ἔνεστι καὶ φαῦλον καὶ οὐδαμῇ οὐδαμῶς εἰλικρινὲς ὂν καὶ τὴν δύναμιν οὐκ ἀξίαν τῆς φύσεως ἔχον. ἐν ἑνὶ δὲ λαβὼν περὶ πάντων νόει ταὐτόν. οἷον πῦρ ἔστι μέν που παρ᾽ ἡμῖν, ἔστι δ᾽ ἐν τῷ παντί. ... Οὐκοῦν σμικρὸν μέν τι τὸ παρ᾽ ἡμῖν καὶ ἀσθενὲς καὶ φαῦλον, τὸ δ᾽ ἐν τῷ παντὶ πλήθει τε θαυμαστὸν καὶ κάλλει καὶ πάσῃ δυνάμει τῇ περὶ τὸ πῦρ οὔσῃ. ...τί δαί; τρέφεται καὶ γίγνεται ἐκ τούτου καὶ ἄρχεται τὸ τοῦ παντὸς πῦρ ὑπὸ τοῦ παρ᾽ ἡμῖν πυρός, ἢ τοὐναντίον ὑπ᾽ ἐκείνου τό τ᾽ ἐμὸν καὶ τὸ σὸν καὶ τὸ τῶν ἄλλων ζῴων ἅπαντ᾽ ἴσχει ταῦτα;* ("In us each of these elements is present only in a small quantity, an insignificant measure and a state that is in no way pure, and with a power that is not proportionate to its nature. If you observe this in one of them, think the same of all the others. How, for example, fire is in us [in our bodies] and is present in the universe. ... Is not that which is present in us small in quantity and weak and insignificant, but that which is in the universe wondrous in its vast quantity and its beauty, and in all the power that dwells within it? ... And further? Is the fire in the universe nourished by that in our body, does it arise from there and have its origin there, or on the contrary does mine, and yours, and that of all other living beings owe all of this to the former?")

soul.[1] In the universe there is much that is unlimited, but with an adequate formal limitation (*peras*), and over this reigns an 'exalted cause' which orders and regulates the years, seasons, and months, and has every right to the names wisdom and *nous*.[2] Wisdom and thought cannot exist apart from soul, however, and it may therefore be said that "in the nature of Zeus a ruling soul and a ruling intelligence have come to be by virtue of the power of the cause, but in that of the other gods, other fair attributes which they are pleased to have attributed to them."[3] This statement obviously refers to the celestial gods (θεοὶ οὐράνιοι) or the celestial bodies conceived as ensouled. These, as members of the realm of becoming, must be clearly distinguished from the divine *nous* as demiurge.

If the divine *nous* or intelligence thus exercises dominion over the universe, it can be concluded that *nous* belongs to the fourth of the genera that compose mixed being, namely, the genus that has been designated the "cause."[4] Shortly thereafter, Socrates expresses himself more guardedly by saying "that *nous* is 'akin' to the cause and 'approximately' (σχεδόν) of the genus of the latter, while in contrast, pleasure is in itself unlimited and measureless, and of the genus that in itself and of itself neither has, nor will have, beginning, middle, or end."[5] The first statement obviously has the pure, divine *nous* in mind, and the second, the human *nous*; for the

---

1 *Ibid.*, 30 A: Τὸ παρ' ἡμῖν σῶμα ἆρ' οὐ ψυχὴν φήσομεν ἔχειν; ... Πόθεν, ὦ φίλε Πρώταρχε, λαβόν, εἴπερ μὴ τό γε τοῦ παντὸς σῶμα ἔμψυχον ὂν ἐτύγχανε, ταὐτά γ' ἔχον τούτῳ καὶ ἔτι πάντῃ καλλίονα; ("Shall we not say that our body has a soul? ... From where, friend Protarchus, did it get this, if the body of the universe were not possessed of soul, since it has the same [elements] as our body and in a manner much fairer still?")

2 *Ibid.*, 30 C: Οὐκοῦν εἰ μὴ τοῦτο, μετ' ἐκείνου τοῦ λόγου ἂν ἑπόμενοι βέλτιον λέγοιμεν, ὡς ἔστιν, ἃ πολλάκις εἰρήκαμεν, ἄπειρόν τ' ἐν τῷ παντὶ πολὺ καὶ πέρας ἱκανόν, καί τις ἐπ' αὐτοῖς αἰτία οὐ φαύλη κοσμοῦσά τε καὶ συντάττουσα ἐνιαυτούς τε καὶ ὥρας καὶ μῆνας, σοφία καὶ νοῦς λεγομένη δικαιότατ' ἄν. (Translation largely in text.)

3 *Ibid.*, 30 C-D: Σοφία μὴν καὶ νοῦς ἄνευ ψυχῆς οὐκ ἄν ποτε γενοίσθην. ... Οὐκοῦν ἐν μὲν τῇ τοῦ Διὸς ἐρεῖς φύσει βασιλικὴν μὲν ψυχήν, βασιλικὸν δὲ νοῦν ἐγγίγνεσθαι διὰ τὴν τῆς αἰτίας δύναμιν, ἐν δ' ἄλλοις ἄλλα καλά, καθ' ὃ φίλον ἑκάστοις λέγεσθαι. (Translation in text.) Just like the human soul, the soul of Zeus, the celestial god, has thus come into being through the power of a cause that originates in the highest divine *nous* as demiurge. See the following note.

4 *Ibid.*, 30 D-E: Τῇ δέ γ' ἐμῇ ζητήσει πεπορικὼς ἀπόκρισιν, ὅτι νοῦς ἐστι γένους τοῦ πάντων αἰτίου λεχθέντος τῶν τεττάρων, ὦν ἦν ἡμῖν ἓν τοῦτο. ("It [the preceding argument] has also provided an answer to my question [viz., to which of the genera *nous* and understanding must be reckoned], viz., that *nous* belongs to that one of the four genera called the cause of all things, which for us constituted one of these.")

5 *Ibid.*, 31 A: ὅτι νοῦς μὲν αἰτίας ἦν ξυγγενὴς καὶ τούτου σχεδὸν τοῦ γένους, ἡδονὴ δ' ἄπειρός τ' αὐτὴ καὶ τοῦ μήτ' ἀρχὴν μήτε μέσα μήτε τέλος ἐν ἑαυτῷ ἀφ' ἑαυτοῦ ἔχοντος μηδ' ἕξοντός ποτε γένους. (Translation in text.) We see here a reserve similar to that in the *Phaedo*, where Plato called the human thinking soul "akin" to the

former applies directly to *nous* as the ruler of the universe, while the latter refers to *nous* in its dialectical opposition to pleasure, something that is altogether absent in the deity.[1]

a. The Human Anima Rationalis *and the Rational World-Soul
Are Restricted to the Realm of Generated or Mixed Being*

In the above discussion, one is immediately struck by Plato's explicit acknowledgment that the human soul and the souls of the celestial gods belong to the realm of what has come into being. This implies that they are of necessity composite in nature and that their being has a mixed character. As a consequence, the soul is once and for all fundamentally distinguished from the world of pure ontic forms. Thus too, the latter, in their absolute and simple nature, can themselves no longer be conceived as active soul-forces, that is, as efficient causes, as had still been done in the *Sophist* and, implicitly, in the *Parmenides*. On the other hand, it is equally impossible to return to the conception of the soul presented in the *Phaedo*, where the rational soul was said to be akin to the world of pure *eidē* and was allowed to share in their unmoved and ungenerated nature. Plato has also broken here with the standpoint of the *Republic*, which ascribed a composite nature to the human soul exclusively in its union with the material body and reserved for the *anima rationalis* a pure state in which it could possess the simple character that had been granted to it in the *Phaedo*.

That the soul must be composite and mixed can be clearly seen in *Philebus*, 47 d to 51 a (beginning in chap. 29 and running into the first part of chap. 31), where Socrates undertakes an inquiry into the mixture of feelings of pleasure and pain that are displayed by the soul itself (αὐτὴν τὴν ψυχὴν αὐτῇ), independent of the material body. As examples of such feelings, he adduces anger, longing, sadness, fear, love, and jealousy. Socrates concludes by remarking – in connection with the mixed emotional state which the soul experiences during laments and both staged and real tragedies and comedies, for in every case these produce a mixture of feelings of pain and pleasure – that he is only giving these examples so that Protarchus may recognize "that both the body without the soul and the soul without the body, and likewise the two in their mutual association, are filled in their inner states with a feeling of pleasure that is mingled with feelings of pain."[2]

---

eidē without venturing to identify these completely.

1   *Ibid.*, 33 B: ΠΡΩ· Οὔκουν εἰκός γ᾽ οὔτε χαίρειν <τοὺς> θεοὺς οὔτε τοὐναντίον. ΣΩ· Πάνυ μὲν οὖν οὐκ εἰκός· ἄσχημον γοῦν αὐτῶν ἑκάτερον γιγνόμενόν ἐστιν. ("*Protarchus*: It is therefore not likely that the gods experience either pleasure or its opposite. *Socrates*: It is not at all likely, of course, for each of the two proved to be formless.")

2   *Ibid.*, 50 D: ὅτι καὶ σῶμα ἄνευ ψυχῆς καὶ ψυχὴ ἄνευ σώματος καὶ κοινῇ μετ᾽

Thus, there are mixed feelings which belong to the soul in itself. Along with these, however, there are also pure, unmixed feelings of the soul, and in this category Socrates lists the aesthetic feelings of pleasure that are attached to beautiful colors, beautiful mathematical forms, harmonious sounds, most sensations of smell, and above all, the feelings that pertain to knowledge. These pure feelings are tied to measure and are called "true" and "beautiful." Over against them, the intense feelings, which always have a mixed character, are classed in the genus of the *apeiron* and the measureless, which extends over both body and soul.

Since in the human *anima rationalis* everything depends on achieving a harmonious mixture between pure or true feelings and rational knowledge, which belong to different genera, it is abundantly clear that, in the *Philebus*, Plato no longer accepts the abstraction of an *anima rationalis* wholly absorbed in the activity of theoretical thought as an ethical-metaphysical ideal of philosophical θεωρία. This immediately follows from the new shift in Plato's anthropological notions. In the *Phaedo* and also the *Republic*, the Orphic-Pythagorean motif was predominant. Accordingly, earthly life was considered to be a fallen state and a contamination of the thinking soul. Even during its present existence, therefore, the thinking soul had to strive to die to the world of phenomena, in order to devote itself wholly in pure *theōria*, the mode of life proper to philosophy, wholly to the contemplation of the pure *eidē* and, ultimately, of the divine *idea* of the good and beautiful.

After he has once again established that the perfect good for a person can lie neither in pleasure alone nor in pure knowledge, Socrates argues in the *Philebus* that the path leading to the good can be discovered only if one has first ascertained the abode where man is at home. "Just as someone who is looking for a man, if he has first ascertained the house where he lives, would surely have a great advantage in finding him for whom he is looking."[1]

The place where the human being is at home, to be sure, is not the world of pure *eidē*, as the *Phaedo* had taught; instead, it lies in the realm of mixed and generated being. This, however, does not prevent knowledge of the pure, unmixed *eidē* or ontic forms from occupying the highest rank among all the various kinds of knowledge, as the knowledge which is completely reliable and true.[2] Theoretical intuition of the eternally self-identical, intelligible world of being is thus again explicitly acknow-

---

ἀλλήλων ἐν τοῖς παθήμασι μεστά ἐστι συγκεκραμένης ἡδονῆς λύπαις; (Translation in text.)

1 *Ibid.*, 61 A-B: Καθάπερ εἴ τίς τιν᾽ ἄνθρωπον ζητῶν τὴν οἴκησιν πρῶτον ὀρθῶς ἵν᾽ οἰκεῖ πύθοιτ᾽ αὐτοῦ, μέγα τι δήπου πρὸς τὴν εὕρεσιν ἂν ἔχοι τοῦ ζητουμένου. (Translation in text.)

2 *Ibid.*, 58 A: τὴν γὰρ περὶ τὸ ὂν καὶ τὸ ὄντως καὶ τὸ κατὰ ταὐτὸν ἀεὶ πεφυκὸς πάντως ἔγωγ᾽ οἶμαι ἡγεῖσθαι ξύμπαντας, ὅσοις νοῦ καὶ σμικρὸν προσήρτηται,

ledged as the foundation, also for the new dialectic. For it cannot be maintained, as Robin thinks, that Plato has in mind here only a system of relations apprehended in dialectical *ideai*, that is to say, ontic forms that are mingled with *hulē* and have thereby become a plurality. It is true that, just as in the *Republic*, abstract numerical theory and abstract geometry are here included in the category of true knowledge, since these are most nearly akin to knowledge of the pure *eidē*. Nevertheless, the bare fact that in the *Philebus* Plato restricts the knowledge of true being to that which remains forever self-identical, without the slightest admixture, and that he once again adduces the knowledge of "justice in itself" (ὅτι ἔστι) as an example of knowledge of the pure ontic forms, is of itself enough to show that he does not have in mind here first of all the new, dialectical logic developed in the Eleatic dialogues. In Plato's line of thought, "justice in itself" is not at all a dialectical relation, although it must be admitted that he also includes the dialectical relations as such among the constant *eidē*.

Theoretical knowledge of the pure *eidē*, according to the *Philebus*, occupies the most exalted place among all the sciences, but it can no longer be identified with the highest good for man. In order to "find the way home," more is necessary than that intuitive knowledge embody itself, with the aid of dialectical logic, in a proper logical definition (λόγον ἐπόμενον τῷ νοεῖν) and that it descend from its sphere of purity to the uncertain phenomena of the visible cosmos, which, as things that have come into being, cannot become the objects of exact science;[1] for this knowledge must also be mingled with pure and true feelings of pleasure, if that mode of life is to be attained which for a human being constitutes the high-

---

μακρῷ ἀληθεστάτην εἶναι γνῶσιν. ("For the whole body of those who have even a grain of common sense hold, I believe, that the knowledge of what really *is*, of that which by nature always remains the same, is by far the truest knowledge.") *Ibid.*, 59 C:'Ως ἢ περὶ ἐκεῖνα ἔσθ' ἡμῖν τό τε βέβαιον καὶ τὸ καθαρὸν καὶ τἀληθὲς καὶ ὃ δὴ λέγομεν εἰλικρινές, περὶ τὰ ἀεὶ κατὰ ταὐτὰ ὡσαύτως ἀμικτότατα ἔχοντα, ἢ [δεύτερος] ἐκείνων ὅτι μάλιστ᾽ ἐστὶ ξυγγενές. ("That, for us, knowledge which is reliable and pure and true and, as we say, unalloyed, refers to those things that always remain just so, in the same manner and without the slightest admixture, or to what is most akin to these.")

1   There can be no *epistēmē* here, but only ὀρθὴ δόξα, correct, but always hypothetical, opinion, which can never lead to firmly established truth. It is evident here how Plato's fundamental dualism once again prevents him from attaining to the modern conception of empirical science. See 59 B: Οὐδ' ἄρα νοῦς οὐδέ τις ἐπιστήμη περὶ αὐτά ἐστι τὸ ἀληθέστατον ἔχουσα. ("Concerning these things there is then no reflection, no pure science, which contains that which fully corresponds to the truth.") What Plato has in mind here is the knowledge of "nature" (δόξαι περὶ φύσεως), the visible cosmos, which always involves the question of how the latter has come into being and what changes it undergoes and brings about (59 A). All of this has no bearing upon the conceptual division of phenomena into classes and species via the method of *diairesis* developed in the *Sophist* and the *Statesman*.

est good. In this mixture, truth, proportion (ξυμμετρία), and beauty are necessary partners, and the second of these, right measure and proportion, is called the cause (αἰτία – here this does *not* mean efficient cause) which lends the highest value to any mixture, since the absence of this is the ruin of both the mixture and its ingredients.[1] Socrates concludes this part of his argument as follows: "If we therefore are unable to track down the highest good in a single *idea*, by grasping it in three – namely, beauty, proportion, and truth – let us declare that in these [three], as in one, we with full justice seek the cause of the value of the mixture, and that by virtue of this the latter has become good."[2]

The new dialectic thus apprehends the divine *idea* of the good, the absolute form of origin, in a tri-unity of *eidē* only in its limited manifestation within the cosmos. In their mixture together, these *eidē* not only constitute the supreme good for the composite life of a human being; they also embody the teleological norm for the entire cosmos. The actual reason why the good for composite or mixed being cannot be pure and absolute in nature resides in the fact that soul and body are conjoined, with the former in control of the latter, both in human existence and in the cosmos as a whole.[3] One cannot imagine a clearer expression than this of the distance that lies between the anthropological conception of the *Phaedo* and the *Republic*, on the one hand, and that of the *Philebus*, on the other hand.

b. Causality as a Separate Genus

We should take special note of the fact that the *Philebus* elevates causality, in the sense of efficient cause, to a separate genus that is brought within the reach of the new, dialectical logic. The *aitia*, as efficient causality,[4] is herein conceived as a rational formal cause (consistent with Socrates' thought and in connection with Anaxagoras' doctrine of *nous*)

---

1 *Ibid.*, 64 D: Καὶ μὴν καὶ ξυμπάσης γε μίξεως οὐ χαλεπὸν ἰδεῖν τὴν αἰτίαν δι᾿ ἣν ἢ παντὸς ἀξία γίγνεται ἡτισοῦν ἢ τὸ παράπαν οὐδενός ... Ὅτι μέτρου καὶ τῆς ξυμμέτρου φύσεως μὴ τυχοῦσα ἡτισοῦν καὶ ὁπωσοῦν ξύγκρασις πᾶσα ἐξ ἀνάγκης ἀπόλλυσι τά τε κεραννύμενα καὶ πρώτην ἑαυτήν. ("And with every mixture it is not difficult to see the cause which lends to each of them the highest value or deprives it of all value ... That every mixture, whatever kind it be, if it does not share in the nature of right measure and proportion, necessarily destroys both its ingredients, and first of all itself.")

2 *Ibid.*, 64 E-65 A: Οὐκοῦν εἰ μὴ μιᾷ δυνάμεθ᾿ ἰδέᾳ τἀγαθὸν θηρεῦσαι, σὺν τρισὶ λαβόντες, κάλλει καὶ ξυμμετρίᾳ καὶ ἀληθείᾳ, λέγωμεν ὡς τοῦτο οἷον ἓν ὀρθότατ᾿ ἂν αἰτιασαίμεθα [ἂν] τῶν ἐν τῇ ξυμμίξει, καὶ διὰ τοῦθ᾿ ὡς ἀγαθὸν ὂν τοιαύτην αὐτὴν γεγονέναι. (Translation in text.)

3 *Ibid.*, 64 B: ἐμοὶ μὲν γὰρ καθαπερεὶ κόσμος τις ἀσώματος ἄρξων καλῶς ἐμψύχου σώματος ὁ νῦν λόγος ἀπειργάσθαι φαίνεται. ("For to me it appears that our argument has been carried out like an incorporeal order which rules in a fair manner over a body possessed of a soul.")

4 The fact that the *aitia* here indeed constitutes a *causa efficiens* is evident from 26 E: Οὐκοῦν ἡ τοῦ ποιοῦντος φύσις οὐδὲν πλὴν ὀνόματι τῆς αἰτίας διαφέρει, τὸ δὲ

and is recognized exclusively as the cause of composite being.

c. *According to the* Philebus, *Neither the Pure* Eidē *nor* Hulē
    Originates in the Divine Nous *as Efficient Cause. The
    Scholastic Accommodation of This Platonic Conception
    (Later Adopted by Aristotle) to the Christian
    Creation Motive*

For this reason, in the view of the *Philebus*, neither the *eidē*, as pure
ontic forms, nor *hulē* can be attributed to the divine *nous* acting as cause
(*aitia*). The doctrine *ex nihilo nihil fit* (nothing can arise from nothing),
which was the final outcome of Greek metaphysics in its subjection to
the dialectical form-matter motive, permits of no exception even in the
case of the divine demiurge. In the Aristotelian ontology as well, ontic
form and matter are in themselves ungenerated.

Scholastic philosophy will later take over this conception, even though
it is opposed to the Scriptural motive of creation. Combining Plato and
Aristotle, it will attempt to accomodate it to the creation motive by placing
it within the framework of the religious synthesis motive of nature and
grace.

Because the efficient cause is sharply distinguished as a genetic *eidos*
from the *peras* and the *apeiron*, the conception of the other *eidē* as active
soul-forces, which belonged to the crisis period of the theory of ideas, has
been rendered superfluous. Insofar as there is yet mention of an ἔκγονον
(offspring) that arises from the combination of *peras* and *apeiron*, these
latter genera are expressly qualified as instruments of the *aitia* in its activity of bringing into being [compare the way the relevant Greek phrase is
translated in note 1, and on page 260] (τὸ δουλεῦον εἰς γένεσιν αἰτίᾳ).[1]
The *aitia*, in contrast, is called the demiurge.[2] Only this causative genus is
still conceived as an active soul-force, since it originates in the divine
nous, which itself is borne by a divine soul as its vital principle.

Is this divine soul and the causative form-power of the *nous* identical to
the world-soul? One might momentarily be tempted to think so, because

---

ποιοῦν καὶ τὸ αἴτιον ὀρθῶς ἂν εἴη λεγόμενον ἕν; ("Then does not the nature of
the agent differ only in name from the cause, and may not the agent and that which
causes rightly be called one?")

1   *Ibid.*, 27 A: Ἄλλο ἄρα καὶ οὐ ταὐτὸν αἰτία τ' ἐστὶ καὶ τὸ δουλεῦον εἰς γένεσιν
    αἰτίᾳ. ("Therefore the cause and that which is subservient to it when it brings into
    being are different and not the same.")

2   *Ibid.*, 27 A-B: Οὐκοῦν τὰ μὲν γιγνόμενα καὶ ἐξ ὧν γίγνεται πάντα τὰ τρία
    παρέσχετο ἡμῖν γένη; ... τὸ δὲ δὴ πάντα ταῦτα δημιουργοῦν λέγωμεν τέταρτον,
    τὴν αἰτίαν, ὡς ἱκανῶς ἕτερον ἐκείνων δεδηλωμένον; ("Then did not the things that
    have come to be, and that out of which everything comes to be [viz., *peras* and
    apeiron], furnish our three genera? ... Shall we therefore name the cause, that which
    [as demiurge] gives form to all these, as the fourth, something whose difference
    from the others has been adequately clarified?")

Socrates says that the human body owes its origin to the world-body, and the human soul to the world-soul.

d. The Nous *Which Reigns over the Universe Is Not Identical to the* Nous *in the World-Soul*

The *Timaeus*, however – and its developement of this point is based wholly on the *Philebus* – explicitly teaches that the universe, both in its body and in its rational soul, belongs to the realm of what has come into being and has its origin in the divine δημιουργός, the divine architect. Cornford and Stenzel, and others, are of the opinion that this demiurge is a purely mythological repesentation of the world-soul itself; but this is clearly refuted by the *Timaeus's* description of the latter as something that is in fact itself mixed in nature and which therefore, according to the *Philebus*, requires a cause of its coming into being. The former dialogue also sheds light on the passage in the *Philebus* which says that the body and soul of man are derived only from the world-body and the world-soul. In our discussion of the *Timaeus*, we shall inevitably be brought back to these matters.

e. The Philebus *and the* Timaeus *Both Admit Only One Causality: That Which Originates in the Rational Soul*

In attributing the causality that brings the cosmos into being exclusively to the rational soul, the *Philebus* has taken over, in this regard, the position of the *Phaedrus*. In so doing, however, it simultaneously took on the *aporia* that I already mentioned in my discussion of the latter dialogue (where it remained completely unsolved), namely, the problem of how the ascription of causality exclusively to the rational soul comports with the primordial dualism between the motives of form and matter. Is it not necessary that *hulē* (the *apeiron* of the *Philebus*) be granted its own genus of causality if one indeed wishes to give a full account within the framework of the Greek ground-motive of the origin of the things that have come into being? The *Timaeus* will answer this question in the affirmative, and the single idea of causality will thereby be abandoned once more.

f. Do the Philebus *Genera Correspond to the Five Highest* Eidē *in the* Sophist?

There is also a question as to the relationship between the four *genē* or dialectical *ideai* of the *Philebus* and the five highest *eidē* of the *Sophist*. Ever since antiquity, numerous attempts have been made to discover a direct connection between these two groups, and recently Léon Robin,[1] the noted French Plato scholar, and C. Ritter,[2] professor at Tübingen, and others, have made the same endeavor. It must be emphasized, however, that any attempt at this must come to terms with the new develop-

---

1 Léon Robin, *Platon* (Paris: F. Alcan, 1935).

2 C. Ritter, *Die Kern-gedanken der platonischen Philosophie* (Munich, 1931), pp. 156 ff.

ment that the *Philebus* introduced into Plato's theory of ideas. Apparently, neither Robin nor Ritter was cognizant of this.

We must observe at the outset that, without exception, the four *genē* of the *Philebus* are all dialectical *ideai* in the previously delineated sense. Among the five supreme ideas (*megista eidē*) of the *Sophist*, in contrast, motion and rest definitely lack this character, since they are mutually exclusive opposites. The comparison must therefore be confined to the *Sophist's* three dialectical *ideai* – individual being, otherness (τὸ θάτερον), and sameness (ταὐτόν) – and, as we have seen, all of these can in fact be regarded as dialectical functions of the all-embracing *idea* of being. The latter was defined in a general way as *dunamis* in both an active and a passive sense, that is, active power and the capacity to be acted upon.[1] In the *Philebus*, the *genē* or dialectical *ideai* of the *peras* and the *apeiron* can likewise be regarded as dialectical functions of mixed or generated being, and they thus correspond respectively to the *ideai* of sameness and otherness in the *Sophist*. Robin maintains that the *peras* is the counterpart of the *Sophist's* active function of being and that the *apeiron* is the counterpart of the passive function. The *idea* of the cause as a function of mixed being, in turn, has a special correspondence to the active function of being in the *Sophist*.[2]

This construal contradicts the clear text of the *Philebus*, however. In this dialogue, the *peras* as such is nowhere called an active *dunamis* nor the *apeiron* a passive *dunamis* of mixed being. In *Philebus*, 27 A, the contrast that is made between the activity which by nature leads and controls (ἡγεῖται μὲν τὸ ποιοῦν ἀεὶ κατὰ φύσιν) and that which is passively acted upon and comes into being (ποιούμενον γιγνόμενον) applies only to the cause and that which this cause brings into being from the mixture of *peras* and the *apeiron*. Further, the *aitia* is sharply distinguished from that "which is subservient to it in the activity of bringing into being" (τὸ δουλεῦον εἰς γένεσιν αἰτίᾳ).

We have already observed that the *Philebus* represents both the *peras* and the *apeiron* in themselves merely as subordinate instruments of the aitia and that it does not conceive the peras as such as an active power.[3] Between the *Sophist* and the *Philebus* came the shift in Plato's conception of the *eidē*. In the *Philebus*, unlike the *Sophist*, the *eidē* can no longer be

---

1   *Sophist*, 247 D-E.

2   Robin, *loc.cit.*

3   *Philebus*, 27 A: ΣΩ· Ἆρ᾽ οὖν ἡγεῖται μὲν τὸ ποιοῦν ἀεὶ κατὰ φύσιν, τὸ δὲ ποιούμενον ἐπακολουθεῖ γιγνόμενον ἐκείνῳ; ΠΡΩ· Πάνυ γε. ΣΩ· Ἄλλο ἄρα καὶ οὐ ταὐτὸν αἰτία τ᾽ ἐστὶ καὶ τὸ δουλεῦον εἰς γένεσιν αἰτίᾳ. ("*Socrates*: Is not then that which acts by nature always leading, but that which is acted upon, as coming into being, [passively] following this? *Protarchus*: Most certainly. *Socrates*: Then also the cause and that which subserves the cause in bringing into being are different and not the same.")

conceived as active soul-forces, since the *aitia* as an efficient cause has been sharply distinguished from the other genera and identified with the form-power (the δημιουργεῖν) of the divine *nous*.

This observation also contradicts Ritter's position. He too places the *Sophist's* general definition of being as *dunamis* at the foundation of the four genera of the *Philebus* and maintains that in the latter dialogue Plato ascribes active power to both *peras* and *apeiron* as constituents of reality.

The *Philebus*, in fact, speaks of yet a fifth genus. When Socrates has first enumerated the four genera, Protarchus asks: "Will you not in addition need yet a fifth which has the ability to separate (διάκρισίν τινος δυναμένου)?" Socrates answers: "Possibly, but not, I think, at present. But should it appear necessary in any way, you will surely agree with me if I go in pursuit of a fifth."[1] As the dialogue unfolds, this fifth genus indeed proves necessary, even though it is not explicitly mentioned as such. Once the need for a mixture of pleasure and knowledge has been established, Socrates asks which of these two components has a claim to the higher rank within the realm of mixed being. Shall all feelings of pleasure without exception, even the gross sensual desires and passions, be admitted into the mixed mode of life which merits the title of the highest good for the human being? This would be a mistake, because the diverse kinds of pleasure must first be distinguished and individually judged as to their ethical value. The various kinds of knowledge can indeed all be admitted; but here too a διάκρισις, a distinction according to value, is necessary. This διάκρισις, the correlative selection of the pleasures and types of knowledge permitted in the good, mixed mode of life, thus indeed seems to be added as a fifth genus of sorts to the four mentioned previously.

There is no possibility, however, of finding a counterpart for this fifth genus in the *Sophist*. Its introduction in the *Philebus* is rather the best proof of the distance that separates this dialogue from the *Parmenides* and the *Sophist*, for it indicates that the effects of the *idea tou agathou* are felt within the logical dialectic itself. Over against this, during the period of crisis in the theory of ideas, it appeared that this *idea*, in its supralogical character, could exert no influence on the new logical dialectic itself, but instead remained in unreconciled tension with the latter. We have seen, however, that in the *Philebus* the *idea tou agathou* is directly manifest only in its dialectical expression within the genus of what is mixed. As a consequence, one observes on this point as well a great difference between this dialogue and the *Republic*.

All this does not mean that the genera established in the *Sophist* have lost their significance for the later dialogues. On the contrary, we shall encounter the dialectical *ideai* of being, otherness, and sameness again in the *Timaeus*. We shall also find the *eidē* of motion and rest there. These then will have to conform, however, to the framework of the genus of mixed

---

1   Ibid., 23 D-E: *Τάχ' ἄν· οὐ μὴν οἶμαί γ'ἐν τῷ νῦν· ἐὰν δέ τι δέῃ, συγγνώσει πού μοι σὺ μεταδιώκοντι πέμπτον.* (Translation in text.)

being developed in the *Philebus*, in its stark difference from the pure being of the intelligible world of *eidē* and of the divine *idea* of the good and
beautiful, which lights this intelligible world with its rays.

Chapter Four

The Dialectic of the Form-Matter Motive in the *Timaeus*, the *Laws*, and the *Epinomis*, and in the Final Stage of Plato's Thought

1. The Polar Dualism in the *Timaeus* between the *Eidos* as Formal Model for the Visible Cosmos and Absolute *Hulē*

In its conception of the theory of ideas and of the soul, the *Timaeus* displays the closest affinity with the *Philebus*. Nevertheless, the former dialogue recognizes, much more acutely than the latter, the impotency of the logical dialectic in its effort to bridge the primordial dualism between the motive of form and matter. In the *Philebus*, it was still the case that there was an *eidos* of the *apeiron*, which was to be grasped in a single dialectical *idea*, namely, that of the fluid relation between the more and the less.

a. Ideal Matter and Hulē *in Its Original Meaning*

Ever since the *Parmenides*, Plato had endeavored in his new dialectic to eideticize *hulē* and to introduce it into the eidetic world itself as a kind of "ideal matter." His avowed intention in this had been to annul the primordial dualism of the religious ground-motive in a higher synthesis, at least within the scope of the dialectical logic, in order to meet the demand of the *logon didonai* with respect to the world of phenomena. As we have seen, Plato remained well aware that this strategem was unable to nullify the effects of *hulē* in its original religious sense. Moreover, the *Philebus* had already recognized that the new, dialectical conception of the *idea* as a multiple-unity, combining in itself the principles of form and matter, could not do away with the conception of the pure or simple *eidos* demanded by the religious ground-motive.

In this latter dialogue we have seen the old Socratic *idea tou agathou* revived. During the crisis of the theory of ideas it had been temporarily superseded by the new, dialectical logic; but it now worked its way into this logic itself, as its controlling motive. The conception of the *aitia* as the rational, purposive form-power of the divine *nous* once more came to control logical definition, but now enriched with the gains won for the theory of ideas by the new, dialectical mode of thought.

b. The Timaeus *Breaks Through the Unity in the Concept of Causality. The New Problem for Plato's Dialectic*

The new, logical dialectic was able to constitute a gain for the theory of ideas, however, only insofar as it proved capable of actually rendering the latter fruitful for giving a logical account of empirical phenomena. To this end, more would be needed than the simple classification of phenomena, with the aid of the diairetic method, under a hierarchy of mixed ontic forms, dialectically set asunder and again conjoined into a unity.

The *Philebus* had distinguished the *aitia*, understood as efficient causality, sharply from the remaining genera, and these other *eide* then could no longer be conceived as active causes in the sense of soul-forces. It was therefore inevitable that *hule* would eventually assert itself, as a dark *Ananke* or an unpredictable, material efficient cause, over against the rational, formal cause of the divine *nous*. Thereby it would again seriously rupture the synthesis that had been artificially contrived by the logical dialectic. If *hule*, as an original efficient cause, could not be reduced to the form principle as *aitia*, then the whole endeavor to eideticize *hule* would stand revealed as an evasion of the basic dilemma which the Greek form-matter motive had imposed upon theoretical thought.

In the forum of experience, the form motive of the religion of culture had proved incapable of eliminating the matter principle as an autonomous efficient cause. Thus, in deliberately resisting the temptation to construct a logically tight, monistic system in the *Timaeus*, Plato once again revealed his greatness and honesty as a thinker.

c. *The Conception of Eidetic or Ideal Matter Is Restricted, Not Abandoned. The Influence of This Conception on Augustinian Scholasticism*

Now, as before, Plato does not correct his course by abandoning the earlier achieved results of the new dialectic. In the *Timaeus* he retains the conception of an "ideal matter" present in all mixed ontic forms. Ever since the *Parmenides* this had remained as a fixed component of the Platonic theory of ideas. Later, by way of neo-Platonism, it would pass into Augustinian-Platonic Scholasticism, becoming one of the outstanding points of disagreement between it and Aristotelian-Thomistic Scholasticism. The scope of this dialectical conception, however, is now restricted to the eidetic sphere of mixed forms of being, a sphere with which Plato's logic can no longer rest content. Over against *hule* as an *eidos*, the dialectical correlate of the ontic form, *hule* once again asserts itself in its original sense as the dark, unpredictable antipode of the absolute form principle. As such it is no longer merely a presupposition of the dialectical logic, something which the latter can henceforth disregard; rather, it becomes a unique factor that breaks though the logical unity of the very concept of causality, since it is the metaphysical antipode of the *nous* as the divine formal cause.

We shall now examine the way in which the *Timaeus* attempts to solve the new problems confronting Plato's dialectic because of this develop-

ment. We shall also examine the influence that all this has on his conception of the soul.

This dialogue is the first to assign the leading role in the discussion to a
Pythagorean. Doubtless, Plato did this in order gratefully to acknowledge
the increasing significance of Pythagorean philosophy for the development of his own thought. The theme of inquiry is now no longer the
eidetic world itself, but rather the *genesis* or coming into being of the cosmos; and each of the empirical sciences will have its contribution to make
to the inquiry.

The *Philebus* had earlier acknowledged that the dialectical logic, with
its method of classification, can give no answer to questions about the origin and the continual changes of the visible cosmos, since this logic is oriented to the constant eidetic structural relations of mixed being.[1] Moreover, this dialogue had already restored the sharp dualism which the *Republic* postulated between the world of *genesis*, accessible only to sense
perception and *doxa*, and the world of the eternal, imperishable ontic
forms, to which only *theōria* (θεωρία) or infallible *epistēmē* can gain entrance. To be sure, the *Philebus*, following the *Sophist* and the *Statesman*,
accepted a synthesis between *doxa* and *epistēmē* in *orthē doxa* (ὀρθὴ
δόξα: right opinion), which joins sense perception to correct logical definition (λόγος) in consequence of the diairetic method; and this *orthē doxa*
was ranked as equal in value to *technē* and *epistēmē*, all three being exclusive possessions of the rational soul.[2] Nevertheless, the scientific character of this *orthē doxa* was to be found in its dialectical-eidetic component
alone, and, in the end, this was once more concerned invariably with the
relations between immutable ontic forms. The problems of Greek nature
philosophy, which stemmed from the matter principle in its original sense
of fluid becoming, lay in principle beyond the eidetic field of vision of the
dialectical logic.

d. The Relation between Belief and Truth

At this point, the *Timaeus* has nothing to add to the position of the
Philebus. It takes its point of departure in the fundamental dualism between hypothetical *doxa* (unprovable belief and opinion) and securely
established *epistēmē* (theoretical knowledge), and, like the *Republic*, it
finds a metaphysical foundation for this contrast in the antithesis between the world of eternal ontic forms and the world of fluid genesis.
The discussion leader, Timaeus, declares (29 C) that "as the eternal

---

1 *Philebus*, 59 B.
2 *Philebus*, 66 B-C: Ἆρ᾽ οὖν οὐ τέταρτα, ἃ τῆς ψυχῆς αὐτῆς ἔθεμεν, ἐπιστήμας τε
καὶ τέχνας καὶ δόξας ὀρθὰς λεχθείσας, ταῦτ᾽ εἶναι τὰ πρὸς τοῖς τρισὶ τέταρτα,
εἴπερ τἀγαθοῦ γ᾽ ἐστὶ μᾶλλον [ἢ] τῆς ἡδονῆς ξυγγενῆ; ("Then are not the fourth in
rank those things which we reckoned as belonging to the soul itself – we called them
sciences and arts and right opinions – which come after the first three, since they are
more akin to the good than pleasure is?")

ontic form [*ousia*] is to the flux of becoming [*genesis*], so is truth [*alētheia*] to belief [*pistis*]."[1]

He thus begins his exposition by distinguishing between that which always *is*, having no genesis or coming into being, and that which becomes and never has being. The former, which always remains identical to itself, can be apprehended solely through theoretical thought by means of a concept (μετὰ λόγου). The latter can only be the object of an opinion (δόξα) formed by means of direct sensory perception apart from any logical concept (μετ᾿ αἰσθήσεως ἀλόγου), and as such it is perceived as something that comes into being and passes away, but in no way has real being (ὄντως δὲ οὐδέποτε ὄν). Moreover, everything that comes into being must necessarily proceed from a cause.[2] The eternal ontic form is also called the everlasting pattern (παράδειγμα) to which the divine demiurge looked when he brought forth the visible world in both its form (ἰδέα) and its power (δύναμις).

e. The Timaeus *and the Four Genera of the* Philebus. *The Eternal* Eidos *Is Again the* Paradeigma *for the Visible Cosmos. The* Republic *and the* Parmenides

One is immediately tempted to draw a comparison here with the four *genera* under which the *Philebus* sought to comprehend "all that now exists in the universe." At the beginning of *Timaeus'* exposition, however, the dialectical logic apparently has not yet come up. The realm of mixed being is not yet under consideration.

For the present, Plato's only concern is to reintroduce the old *chōrismos* between the eidetic world and the visible world of *genesis*, as this had been set forth in the *Republic*. Even in the terminology that is used, there

---

1 *Timaeus*, 29 B-C: τοῦ μὲν οὖν μονίμου καὶ βεβαίου καὶ μετὰ νοῦ καταφανοῦς μονίμους καὶ ἀμεταπτώτους, καθ᾿ ὅσον τε ἀνελέγκτοις προσήκει λόγοις εἶναι καὶ ἀκινήτοις, τούτου δεῖ μηδὲν ἐλλείπειν· τοὺς δὲ τοῦ πρὸς μὲν ἐκεῖνο ἀπεικασθέντος, ὄντος δὲ εἰκόνος εἰκότας ἀνὰ λόγον τε ἐκείνων ὄντας· ὅτι περ πρὸς γένεσιν οὐσία τοῦτο πρὸς πίστιν ἀλήθεια. ("Statements about what is abiding and certain and accessible to theoretical thought must be constant and unalterable, and indeed, as far as possible, irrefutable and incontrovertible, lacking nothing in this respect. But those pertaining to what has been formed on the pattern of that [abiding being], which is only an image in relation to the former, are merely probable: for as the ontic forms are to becoming, so is truth to belief.")

2 *Ibid.*, 28 A: παντὶ γὰρ ἀδύνατον χωρὶς αἰτίου γένεσιν σχεῖν, ὅτου μὲν οὖν ἂν ὁ δημιουργὸς πρὸς τὸ κατὰ ταὐτὰ ἔχον βλέπων ἀεί, τοιούτῳ τινὶ προσχρώμενος παραδείγματι τὴν ἰδέαν καὶ δύναμιν αὐτοῦ ἀπεργάζηται, καλὸν ἐξ ἀνάγκης οὕτως ἀποτελεῖσθαι πᾶν. ("For the universe cannot come into being without a cause. Now whenever the maker of anything, looking constantly to that which always remains self-identical [viz., the everlasting ontic form], fashions its form and motive power after such a pattern, it must necessarily be made beautiful in its entirety.")

is a conspicuous affinity with the vision that had been detailed there concerning the relation between the eternal ontic form and the transitory sense world. We may recall that the *Parmenides*, when it sought to approach the problem of *methexis* in a dialectical-logical manner, rejected the conception of the *eidos* as a *paradeigma* or model for transitory things.

At the same time, the difference between the *Republic*'s and the *Timaeus'* conception of the *eidē* also stands out clearly. Whereas, in the former dialogue, even the *being* of the *eidē* had its origin in the divine *idea* of the good, the *Timaeus* reverts here to the *Phaedo's* conception of the *eidē*, according to which they are ungenerated, eternal proto-forms which as such constitute a given reality even for the divine *nous*. We have seen that this return to the earlier conception was already noticeable in the *Philebus*, since, as a separate genus, the *aitia* was there distinguished sharply from the other *eidē*, and was set in relation solely to the products of becoming as "composite being." On this point the *Timaeus* thus links up directly with the latter dialogue.

f. The Idea of the Good and Beautiful as the Origin of the Cosmos in the Timaeus. Did Plato Really Believe That the Cosmos Has Come into Being?

Here, no less than in the *Philebus*, the *idea* of the good and beautiful remains, as the *dunamis* of the divine *nous*, the *aitia* or origin of all form in the cosmos that has come into being.[1] Moreover, from the very beginning, Timaeus' account of the origin of the cosmos is founded in the basic notion of the *Philebus* that all becoming can be understood only as a *genesis eis ousian*, a "becoming that issues in being," where being is indissolubly connected to the good and beautiful. The Socratic trait in Plato's thought, which derived ultimately from Anaxagoras' doctrine of *nous*, thereby receives its most comprehensive cosmological expression. What Plato could not yet attain in the Eleatic trilogy – the conjunction of the new, logical dialectic with the *idea tou agathou* – had become possible with the *Philebus*. Now Plato will attempt to exhibit the good and beautiful as the goal of becoming in all particular species of what has come into being. The divine *nous* is the demiurge or form-giver.

---

1 *Ibid.*, 29 E: Λέγωμεν δή, δι᾽ ἥτινα αἰτίαν γένεσιν καὶ τὸ πᾶν τόδε ὁ ξυνιστὰς ξυνέστησεν· ἀγαθὸς ἦν, ἀγαθῷ δὲ οὐδεὶς περὶ οὐδενὸς οὐδέποτε ἐγγίγνεται φθόνος· τούτου δ᾽ ἐκτὸς ὢν πάντα ὅτι μάλιστα γενέσθαι ἐβουλήθη παραπλήσια ἑαυτῷ. ταύτην δὴ γενέσεως καὶ κόσμου μάλιστ᾽ ἄν τις ἀρχὴν κυριωτάτην παρ᾽ ἀνδρῶν φρονίμων ἀποδεχόμενος ὀρθότατα ἀποδέχοιτ᾽ ἄν. ("Let us then demonstrate for what cause the Orderer of all genesis and of this universe ordered it. He was good, and in the good no envy can ever arise in any respect. Being far from this, He desired that all things should come to resemble himself as much as possible. One thus has every right to accept the claim of wise men, who declare this to be the supreme origin of becoming and of the cosmos.")

"Since he desired that all things should be as good as possible, and that evil should be restrained as much as could be, finding all that is visible not at rest, but in unmeasured and disorderly motion, he brought the chaos from disorder into order, since the latter seemed to him better than the former."[1]

Various modern Plato scholars[2] have held that Plato's notion of this divine *nous* as the fashioner of the world (the demiurge) was purely symbolic or mythological in intent, and that he actually considered the cosmos to be without origin. Such a view, however, which was in fact already in circulation in antiquity,[3] simply cannot be squared with the Platonic dialectic. Its proponents have apparently been led astray by the fact that Timaeus offers his theory on the origin of the cosmos not as *epistēmē* or rigorous science, but only as a likely opinion (*doxa*).

Several observations are in order. First, the identification of *doxa* in its Platonic sense with myth will not pass muster. Second, it is forgotten here that the sharp distinction between the eternal world of being and the world of becoming is an indispensable element in Plato's theory of ideas. Third, these thinkers apparently overlook the fact that, ever since the *Philebus*, Plato's dialectical logic itself identified the *aitia* (cause), as a logical-metaphysical genus, with the divine *nous* as form-giver.

Timaeus' entire subsequent exposition is grounded throughout in the dialectical logic. Even by itself this is enough to distinguish it fundamentally from the purely mythological images that Plato presents in various

---

1 *Ibid.*, 30 A: βουληθεὶς γὰρ ὁ θεὸς ἀγαθὰ μὲν πάντα, φλαῦρον δὲ μηδὲν εἶναι κατὰ δύναμιν, οὕτω δὴ πᾶν ὅσον ἦν ὁρατὸν παραλαβὼν οὐχ ἡσυχίαν ἄγον, ἀλλὰ κινούμενον πλημμελῶς, καὶ ἀτάκτως, εἰς τάξιν αὐτὸ ἤγαγον ἐκ τῆς ἀταξίας, ἡγησάμενος ἐκεῖνο τούτου πάντως ἄμεινον. ("For since God desired that everything should be good and, as far as possible, not bad, finding all that is visible not at rest, but in unmeasured and disorderly motion, he brought it from disorder to order, since the latter seemed to him in every way better than the former.")

2 See, e.g., F.M. Cornford, *Plato's Cosmology: The Timaeus of Plato Translated with a Running Commentary* (London, 1937), p. 37: "We shall be led to the conclusion that both the Demiurge and chaos are symbols," and p. 40: "the creator god, as such, is a mythical figure." This conclusion is based on the conviction that, in Plato's thinking, "chaos" is not created. This is no doubt correct; but Plato's divine *nous* is not a creator, but rather a demiurge who, as Plato explicitly states, only brings form and order into the chaos. Cornford's view is also shared by Stenzel and Ritter.

3 Cf. Plutarch, *De animae procreatione in Timaeo Platonis*, 3, 1013 A. Here Plutarch observes that Xenocrates, his pupil Crantor, and also other pupils, regarded the soul as ungenerated and claimed that Plato postulated its origin only for the sake of theoretical explanation (θεωρίας ἕνεκα). Plutarch then continues by noting that they spoke likewise concerning the origin of the cosmos (οὐρανός). Plato supposedly knew well that this has not come into being, but since he realized that those who did not frame an hypothesis concerning the origin of the cosmos could not easily grasp its structure, he used such an hypothesis to clarify this structure for them.

dialogues. Thus too the doctrine that the divine *nous* is the origin of the cosmos is based entirely upon the so-called physico-teleological proof for the deity that has been worked out in the *Philebus*, although it must be admitted that, in the *Timaeus*, Plato only allows this proof the status of a probable inference (*κατὰ λόγον τὸν εἰκότα*). There is just as little support for the mythological hypothesis in the fact that Plato uses the image of the "mixing bowl" a few times, in describing the divine formation of the world-soul and the immortal part of the human soul. Already in the *Philebus*, this image has appeared in the middle of a strict dialectical argument concerning the mingling of pleasure and knowledge.[1] One can no doubt point out mythological elements in *Timaeus'* narrative, but in no instance can these stamp the Platonic idea of the origin of the cosmos as something purely mythological.

The conception of the divine *nous* as demiurge originated in Anaxagoras' nature philosophy, and it passed by way of the Socratic notion of virtue (*aretē*) into Plato's sphere of thought and became an integral component of the latter. Plato observes only that it is "difficult to find the Origin and Father of this cosmos, and, once one has found him, impossible to speak of him in a manner understandable to all."[2] Following Anaxagoras completely, he regards the divine *nous* as the source of all ordering or form-giving motion. But he no longer tries, as he had still done in the *Phaedrus*, to remain with the Ionian thinker in his denial that *hulē* has its own autonomous *dunamis* or motive power. *Timaeus'* great discourse has scarcely begun when the principle of disorderly, chaotic motion makes its appearance,[3] as a dark, unpredictable *Anankē*, an autonomous power that will stand opposed to the divine *nous* and its *idea* of the good and the beautiful. And in the further course of the dialogue, Plato will give a truly dramatic account of this conflict in his principle of origin.

2. The Formal Model of the Visible Cosmos and the Theory of Idea-Numbers in the Final Stage of Development of Plato's Thought

a. *The* Eidos *of the Living Being according to the Dialectical-Logical Conception of the* Timaeus. *The Conception of This as an Indivisible Unity in the Oral Lecture* On the Good.

The everlasting model to which the demiurge looks as a pattern when he forms the visible cosmos as an ordered universe is the intelligible ontic form of the complete living being (*τὸ παντελῶς ζῷον*). This *eidos* com-

---

1 *Philebus*, 61 B-C.
2 *Timaeus*, 28 C: *τὸν μὲν οὖν ποιητὴν καὶ πατέρα τοῦδε τοῦ παντὸς εὑρεῖν τε ἔργον καὶ εὑρόντα εἰς πάντας ἀδύνατον λέγειν·* (Translation in text.)
3 *Ibid.*, 30 A.

prehends, as its parts within a single whole, all the intelligible forms of living things, both as to their *atomon eidos* and as to their diverse genera (καθ' ἕν καὶ κατὰ γένη), just as the visible cosmos contains all visible living things, namely, the "celestial gods" (the earth, the planets, and the fixed stars), human beings, and the plant and animal kingdoms.[1]

It is thus evident that Plato at once places this intelligible model of the visible cosmos within the framework of the Eleatic dialogues' dialectical logic and its diairetic method. Precisely because, as a paradigm, this is set in relation to the visible cosmos, logic can only grasp it as a whole with parts, that is, as a multiple-unity, in a single dialectical *idea*. For as a pure, indivisible (ἀμέριστον), simple *eidos*, it is beyond the reach of the logical dialectic in this stage of Plato's thought.

Aristotle declares in *De anima* that, in the final stage of development of the theory of ideas, represented by the oral lecture *On the Good*, Plato attempts to conceive the *living being in itself*, independent of its relation to the cosmos that has come to be. He relates that "in what are called the lectures on philosophy, it was set forth that the living being in itself consists of the *idea* itself of the one and the primary [i.e., eidetic] length, breadth, and depth."[2] As Léon Robin observes, the lectures of Plato referred to here are most likely the group to which the discourse *On the Good* belonged.[3]

In *De anima*,[4] Aristotle establishes a direct connection between the conception of the living being in itself set forth in these lectures and the construction of the soul that Plato presents in the *Timaeus*. Moreover, he believes that both of these are based on Empedocles' thesis that like is known

---

1 *Timaeus*, 30 C-D: Τούτου δ' ὑπάρχοντος αὖ τὰ τούτοις ἐφεξῆς ἡμῖν λεκτέον, τίνι τῶν ζῴων αὐτὸν εἰς ὁμοιότητα ὁ ξυνιστὰς ξυνέστησε. τῶν μὲν οὖν ἐν μέρους εἴδει πεφυκότων μηδενὶ καταξιώσωμεν· ἀτελεῖ γὰρ ἐοικὸς οὐδέν ποτ' ἂν γένοιτο καλόν· οὗ δ' ἔστι τἆλλα ζῷα καθ' ἕν καὶ κατὰ γένη μόρια, τούτῳ πάντων ὁμοιότατον αὐτὸν εἶναι τιθῶμεν. τὰ γὰρ δὴ νοητὰ ζῷα πάντα ἐκεῖνο ἐν ἑαυτῷ περιλαβὸν ἔχει, καθάπερ ὁ κόσμος ἡμᾶς ὅσα τε ἄλλα θρέμματα ξυνέστηκεν ὁρατά. ("After this beginning, we must now further state in the likeness of what living being the demiurge framed it [the universe]. No being that by its nature falls under the *eidos* of the part shall we deem worthy of this, for nothing that resembles an incomplete being will ever become something beautiful. Let us rather suppose that it above all resembles that of which everything that lives, both in its individual [indivisible] unity and in its genera, is a part; for this comprehends in itself all conceivable living things, just as the cosmos contains us and all other visible living beings.")

2 Aristotle, *De anima* A 2, 404 b 18-21: ... ἐν τοῖς Περὶ φιλοσοφίας λεγομένοις διωρίσθη [ὁ Πλάτων], αὐτὸ μὲν τὸ ζῷον ἐξ αὐτῆς τῆς τοῦ ἑνὸς ἰδέας καὶ τοῦ πρώτου μήκους καὶ πλάτους καὶ βάθους ... (Translation in text.)

3 Léon Robin, *La théorie platonicienne des idées et des nombres d'après Aristote* (Paris, 1908), pp. 307-308

4 Aristotle, *De anima* A 2 404 b 16-27.

by like.[1] We shall return very soon to this point as we examine the theory of the soul presented in this dialogue. But however this may be, the conception of the αὐτὸ τὸ ζῷον (ὁ νοητὸς κόσμος, the intelligible cosmos, according to Themistius and Simplicius) in the final stage of development of Plato's theory of the ideas differs fundamentally from the dialectical-logical conception of the *Timaeus*. The former no longer operates with the dialectical concept of the whole and its parts as a multiple-unity, but rather with the indivisible, absolute idea-numbers as pure forms. When these are thought through dialectically – in order to perform its genetic derivation this process requires an eidetic *apeiron* as a substratum for "becoming" – they give rise to the pure dimensions (αὔξαι)[2] of eidetic space (primary length, breadth, and depth), which serve as the foundation for both mathematical space and the space perceived by the senses. In the same passage, Aristotle relates that, as an idea-number, the absolute unity corresponds to *nous*, while the idea-number two corresponds to *epitēmēe* or dialectical science, the idea-number three to *doxa*, and the idea-number four to sense perception.[3]

It appears from other statements of Aristotle[4] that the eidetic straight line, as primary length, is either identical to the idea-number two, or else arises from it in connection with the *apeiron* "long and short"; further, that the eidetic plane surface (primary breadth) is either identical to the idea-number three, or arises from it in connection with the *apeiron* "broad and narrow"; and finally, that the eidetic solid body, as primary depth, is either

---

1   *De anima* A 2, 404 b 16 ff.: τὸν αὐτὸν δὲ τρόπον καὶ ὁ Πλάτων ἐν τῷ Τιμαίῳ τὴν ψυχὴν ἐκ τῶν στοιχείων ποιεῖ· γινώσκεσθαι γὰρ τῷ ὁμοίῳ τὸ ὅμοιον, τὰ δὲ πράγματα ἐκ τῶν ἀρχῶν εἶναι. ("In the same way [viz., as Empedocles] Plato too, in the *Timaeus*, constructs the soul out of the elements; for [according to him] like is known by like, and things are composed of the *archai* [principles].") This passage is immediately followed by the one from which I quoted above (*De anima* A 2, 404 b 18-21): ὁμοίως δὲ καὶ ἐν τοῖς περὶ φιλοσοφίας λεγομένοις διωρίσθη, etc. ("In like manner, it was set forth in what are called the lectures on philosophy that ...")

2   Plato himself uses the term αὔξη (literally, "augmentation") in the sense of "dimension" in the *Republic*, VII, 528 a-b (μετὰ δευτέραν αὔξην τρίτην λαμβάνειν) and in the *Laws*, X, 894 a.

3   *De anima*, A 2, 404 b 21-27: ἔτι δὲ καὶ ἄλλως, νοῦν μὲν τὸ ἕν, ἐπιστήμην δὲ τὰ δύο· μοναχῶς γὰρ ἐφ᾽ ἕν· τὸν δὲ τοῦ ἐπιπέδου ἀριθμὸν δόξαν, αἴσθησιν δὲ τὸν τοῦ στερεοῦ. οἱ μὲν γὰρ ἀριθμοὶ τὰ εἴδη αὐτὰ καὶ αἱ ἀρχαὶ ἐλέγοντο, εἰσὶ δ᾽ ἐκ τῶν στοιχείων· κρίνεται δὲ τὰ πράγματα τὰ μὲν νῷ, τὰ δ᾽ ἐπιστήμῃ, τὰ δὲ δόξῃ, τὰ δ᾽αἰσθήσει· εἴδη δ᾽ οἱ ἀριθμοὶ οὗτοι τῶν πραγμάτων. ("And then also in other terms: *nous* is the one; *epitēmēe* is the two, for it moves in a straight line toward the one; the [idea] number of the plane surface is *doxa*, and sense perception is the [idea] number of the solid body. For the [idea] numbers were called the *eidē* themselves and the *archai* [principles], but they still consist of the elements. Things are judged partly by the *nous* [intuitive rational contemplation], partly by dialectical science [*epitēmēe*], partly by *doxa*, partly by sense perception; and these [idea] numbers are the *eidē* of things.")

4   *Metaphysics*, Z 11 1036 b 13-17; A 9, 992 a 10-13; M 9, 1085 a 7-12.

identical to the idea-number four, or else arises from it in connection with the *apeiron* "high and low."[1] In this way then, Plato in his last period has allegedly conceived the living being in itself as an eidetic unity of soul and body.

In addition, it deserves special attention that the Aristotle commentators Themistius, Simplicius, and Philoponus all conclude that *nous* corresponds to the idea-number one because it beholds the essence of things in one indivisible act. This agrees so closely with what we earlier ascertained concerning Plato's original conception of the subjective *ἰδέα* (as the direct unitary vision of the divine *idea* of the good and beautiful), that we may properly regard it as a faithful representation of Plato's own view. It is evident from Aristotle's report that Plato identified the absolute unity as an idea-number with the good. In the previously cited passage from *De Anima*, Aristotle also observes that *epistēmē* or dialectical science corre-

---

1 *Metaphysics*, Z 11, 1036 b 13-17: καὶ τῶν τὰς ἰδέας λεγόντων οἱ μὲν αὐτογραμμὴν τὴν δυάδα, οἱ δὲ τὸ εἶδος τῆς γραμμῆς, ἔνια μὲν γὰρ εἶναι τὸ αὐτὸ τὸ εἶδος καὶ οὗ τὸ εἶδος (οἷον δυάδα καὶ τὸ εἶδος δυάδος), ἐπὶ γραμμῆς δὲ οὐκέτι. ("And of those who speak of the ideas, some say that the two is the line itself, others that it is the ontic form [*eidos*] of the line; for according to them in some cases the ontic form and that of which it is the form are the same (e.g., two and the ontic form of two), but with the line this is no longer so.") Here Aristotle is speaking of the Platonic school in general, and it is not made clear which of the two conceptions was Plato's own. *Metaphysics*, A 9, 992 a 10-13: βουλόμενοι δὲ τὰς οὐσίας ἀνάγειν εἰς τὰς ἀρχὰς μήκη μὲν τίθεμεν ἐκ βραχέος καὶ μακροῦ, ἔκ τινος μικροῦ καὶ μεγάλου, καὶ ἐπίπεδον ἔκ πλατέος καὶ στενοῦ, σῶμα δ' ἐκ βαθέος καὶ ταπεινοῦ. ("When we [viz., in accordance with the theory of idea-numbers] wish to reduce the ontic forms to the *archai* [principles], we hold that the [eidetic] lengths arise from short and long, i.e., from a kind of small and great, the [eidetic] plane surface from broad and narrow, and the [eidetic] solid body from high and low.") *Metaphysics*, M 9, 1085 a 7-12: ὁμοίως δὲ καὶ περὶ τῶν ὕστερον γενῶν τοῦ ἀριθμοῦ συμβαίνει τὰ δυσχερῆ γραμμῆς τε καὶ ἐπιπέδου καὶ σώματος. οἱ μὲν γὰρ ἐκ τῶν εἰδῶν τοῦ μεγάλου καὶ τοῦ μικροῦ ποιοῦσιν, οἷον ἐκ μακροῦ μὲν καὶ βραχέος τὰ μήκη, πλατέος δὲ καὶ στενοῦ τὰ ἐπίπεδα, ἐκ βαθέος δὲ καὶ ταπεινοῦ τοὺς ὄγκους. ("Similarly, difficulties arise also with regard to the genera [classes] which come later than the [idea]-number. For some construct these out of the *eidē* [ideal kinds of matter] of the great and small, e.g., [eidetic] lengths out of long and short, eidetic planes out of broad and narrow, and [eidetic] solids out of high and low.") As W. Vander Wielen has shown (*De idee-getallen van Plato*, p.149), it is clear from *Met.* N 3, 1090 b 36 to 1091 a 2, that this in fact applies also to Plato's own view, for the words that immediately precede this passage reveal that it was aimed directly at Plato. In his commentary, Ross observes at *Met.* Z 11, 1036 b 13-17 (quoted above) that Plato could have been one of those who identified [eidetic] length with the eidetic two, while Vander Wielen thinks otherwise (p.146). In my view, both of these conceptions can equally be attributed to Plato. In the direct synopsis of intuitive contemplation, eidetic length is the idea-number two itself, while in the discursive, dialectical thought of *epistēmē*, a construct made from idea-number and eidetic *apeiron* is needed. See below in the text.

sponds to the idea-number two because it moves in a straight line (μοναχῶς) towards one. Themistius, Simplicius, and Philoponus all take this to mean that *epistēmē* moves from the premises along a single path to the one correct conclusion, and thus, by establishing as it were the shortest connection between two points, move in a straight line.[1]

The latter interpretation sounds more Aristotelian than Platonic. The *Timaeus* never conceives the movement of thought as rectilinear, but rather as a circle. It therefore seems plausible to me that, for Plato, the eidetic twoness of *epistēmē* is based on the necessary duality of the *archai* or principles of origin with which every attempt dialectically to derive the ontic forms coming after the one is compelled to operate.

From this evidence we may then draw the following conclusion. Plato's account of the *auto to zōon* (the eidetic living being) in his oral lectures on philosophy proceeds from the indivisible unity of the absolute living being in itself, a unity that can be grasped only by the *nous* in its intuitive contemplation of essence. However, he needed the duality of *peras* and eidetic *apeiron*, or form and eidetic matter, for his dialectical-scientific derivation of the idea-numbers that come after one and of the eidetic forms (which lie at the foundation of geometric figures) that come after the idea-numbers. For it is indeed reasonable to suppose that Plato presented his entire dialectical account of the origin of the idea-numbers posterior to the absolute unity, as they arise from this one (as form or pure *peras*) in connection with an eidetic matter, only for the sake of instruction and dialectical understanding (διδασκαλίας χάριν), since *epistēmē* cannot escape the duality of *archai* (principles of origin).[2]

b. The Idea-Numbers and the Pythagorean Tetractys.
The Living Being in Itself as an Eidetic Decad

All the same, within this whole conception of the living being in itself there lurks a problem that we may not simply pass by. For, although Aristotle's testimony indicates that Plato did not introduce this conception until his final stage of development, the problem appears to have an oblique bearing on the interpretation of the eternal model of the visible cosmos in the *Timaeus*.

It is clear at once that this conception must be most intimately related to the Pythagorean number mysticism that we encountered earlier in the sa-

---

1 See Vander Wielen, *op.cit.*, p. 163.
2 On the basis of his study of the various sources (*testimonia*), Vander Wielen likewise concludes: "It is therefore plausible that Plato has produced the idea-numbers (the world and the soul need not be considered further) τοῦ θεωρῆσαι ἕνεκεν or διδασκαλίας χάριν" (p.96). In other words, the entire genetic derivation of the "idea-numbers posterior to the one" – and, as I have added, also of the pure ontic forms "posterior to the idea-numbers" – this being accomplished by means of the influence of the one (or, respectively, the other idea-numbers) as pure *peras* upon an eidetic *apeiron*, did not at all detract in Plato's mind from the indivisible unity of the *eidē*. Rather, he presented this derivation for the sole purpose of making the pure *eidē* accessible to the dialectical understanding of his students.

cred symbol of the *tetractys*, the "ever-flowing fountain of physis." According to Theon of Smyrna, we may recall, the original form of the *tetractys* was $1 + 2 + 3 + 4 = 10$; the second *tetractys*, that which Plato uses in the *Timaeus* to symbolize the harmonic constitution of the world-soul; the third: point, line, plane, and solid body; and the eighth, namely the four levels of cognition: *nous*, knowledge, *doxa*, and sense perception.

Now, Aristotle also reports in various places that Plato limited the series of idea-numbers to the number ten (the decad). We must conclude, therefore, that this conception of the living being in itself amounts to nothing other than a transformation of the original Pythagorean *tetractys* in terms of the conceptual scheme of the Platonic theory of ideas. This then simultaneously explains why the only idea-numbers mentioned by Plato are the one, two, three, and four. After all, the *tetractys*, as the term expresses, is always a tetrad or foursome. It also explains why he has primary length corresponding to the two, primary breadth to the three, and primary depth to the four. In addition, the cognitive series of *nous*, *epistēmē*, *doxa*, and sense perception is explained in this same way as an unfolding of the *tetractys* in the soul.

This Platonic transformation of the Pythagorean *tetractys*, however, brings about fundamental alterations in the Pythagorean conception and leads to internal contradictions. In Plato's conception, first of all, the unity and origin (*monas*) cannot be a union of *peras* and *apeiron*, form principle and matter principle, as it had been in the original Pythagorean conception. For Plato, the absolute unity is pure *peras*. But if the *apeiron* does not originate in this *monas*, the idea-numbers posterior to one cannot arise from the latter in any real sense. That is because, in both the Pythagorean and the Platonic conceptual schemes, genesis presupposes a combination of *peras* and *apeiron*. This then would explain why Plato's theory concerning the generation of the idea-numbers posterior to one was framed exclusively for the sake of instruction and dialectical understanding. The thought, therefore, that what we have here is a veritable return to the theory of the *Republic*, with its attribution of the *being* of the *eidē* to the divine *idea* of the good, is simply out of the question.

In the second place, the first form of the Pythagorean *tetractys* is based upon a *quantitative* conception of numbers, which, as we have seen, cannot apply to Plato's idea-numbers. We may recall, however, that our study of the original Pythagorean theory of numbers made clear that the development of the numerical series from one is not conceived there as in the later, static Pythagorean conception, as an enumeration of abstract arithmetical units. Rather, it is a dynamic process that contains within itself the genesis of the entire cosmos, this being regarded as a fluid continuum that is limited and brought within the confines of measure and harmony by the principle of number. In view of this, it follows that we should attach no great importance to the purely additive form of the first *tetractys*. Plato's dialectical theory concerning the generation of the subsequent idea-numbers, and primary length, breadth, and depth, from out of unity is without doubt most intimately related to the original Pythagorean conception. It simply does not apply, however, to the ungenerated world of pure, indivisible *eidē* as this is understood both in the *Timaeus* and in the conception of the *eidos* as idea-number.

If it is indeed the case – and this can hardly be doubted – that Plato understands the living being in itself to be the consummation of the eidetically conceived *tetractys* 1, 2, 3, 4, it must then correspond to the decad as the complete number. Already in the *Timaeus*,[1] Plato does in fact call the αὐτὸ τὸ ζῷον the παντελὲς ζῷον or "complete living being." As the idea-number ten it is then a pure, indivisible, and incommensurable *eidos*. Aristotle relates that the decad was thought by the Pythagoreans to embrace the whole nature of numbers (πᾶσαν τὴν τῶν ἀριθμῶν φύσιν).[2] Transformed in terms of the Platonic theory of idea-numbers, this would thus mean that the living being in itself unites within itself the nature of all the idea-numbers. It is in keeping with this that Themistius and Simplicius identify the living being in itself, as this was conceived in Plato's lectures on philosophy, with the κόσμος νοητός (the intelligible world). In his commentary, Philoponus understands it as the "*eidos* of the living being."

Although Van der Wielen thinks otherwise, this latter explanation in no way contradicts that of the first two Aristotle commentators, nor does it run counter to the drift of Aristotle's argument in the passage quoted above from *De Anima*.[3] For what is under consideration here is indeed the *eidos* of the living being, which apparently is tantamount to the pure ontic form of the body-soul unity. By virtue of being the complete idea-number of the decad the latter combines within itself the nature of all the idea-numbers in an indivisible unity, and in this capacity it must therefore indeed be equivalent to the *kosmos noētos*.

The internal inconsistency in which this conception is entangled, inasmuch as it contradicts Plato's notion of the mutual incommensurability of the idea-numbers, is due solely to the fact that in the final stage of the Platonic theory of ideas the Pythagorean conception of the *tetractys* has undergone a metamorphosis. In the Pythagorean conception, the decad is indeed the complete unfolding of the unity and origin, since the latter unites within itself both *peras* and *apeiron*. In Plato's conception, by contrast, the *monas* or idea-number one is only pure *peras*, pure form principle. In the nature of the case, the later idea-numbers are incapable of being generated from this *monas*, since they are incommensurable, ungenerated, and indivisible units.

3. The Relationship between the Socratic *Idea*, the *Eidos*, and the Visible Form of the Cosmos in the *Timaeus*

In the *Timaeus* as well, the living being in itself is in no way a product of the divine ἰδέα τοῦ ἀγαθοῦ.

---

1   *Timaeus*, 31 B.
2   *Metaphysics*, A 5, 986 a.
3   *De Anima*, A 2, 404 b, 16-17.

a. The Conception of the Visible Cosmos in the Timaeus and the Teleological Explanation of Genesis

Returning to this dialogue, we should observe that Plato regards the visible cosmos, which the divine *nous* as demiurge has fashioned after the eternal model of the living being in itself, as an indissoluble unity of *nous*, soul, and body (ζῷον ἔμψυχον ἔννουν).[1]

Nothing in the cosmos that is a product of the divine form-power of the good and beautiful can therefore be devoid of soul or exempt from the control of reason. And the reason for this, as Plato adds by way of explanation, is that the divine demiurge wanted to make the visible cosmos conform to its eternal eidetic model as closely as possible. In view of this, he rejects the notion that there exist more than one, or even an infinite number of worlds. Since there is but one eternal model of the cosmos, containing all conceivable living things as its parts, the visible replica (*Abbild*) of this must also be a single whole that embraces all visible living things.[2] This is not because it would be inherently impossible for a plurality of copies of the one eternal model to exist, a conclusion that would be patently incorrect in terms of Plato's thinking. Rather, the reason is only that the demiurge desired that the visible cosmos resemble the eternal model also in its singularity.

This entire conception of the visible cosmos as an ensouled, bodily whole governed by *nous* – Plato expressly characterizes it as a "deity that

---

1 *Timaeus*, 30 A-B: λογισάμενος οὖν εὕρισκεν ἐκ τῶν κατὰ φύσιν ὁρατῶν οὐδὲν ἀνόητον τοῦ νοῦν ἔχοντος ὅλον ὅλου κάλλιον ἔσεσθαί ποτε ἔργον, νοῦν δ' αὖ χωρὶς ψυχῆς ἀδύνατον παραγενέσθαι τῳ. διὰ δὴ τὸν λογισμὸν τόνδε νοῦν μὲν ἐν ψυχῇ, ψυχὴν δὲ ἐν σώματι ξυνιστὰς τὸ πᾶν ξυνετεκταίνετο, ὅπως ὅτι κάλλιστον εἴη κατὰ φύσιν ἄριστόν τε ἔργον ἀπειργασμένος. οὕτως οὖν δὴ κατὰ λόγον τὸν εἰκότα δεῖ λέγειν τόνδε τὸν κόσμον ζῷον ἔμψυχον ἔννουν τε τῇ ἀληθείᾳ διὰ τὴν τοῦ θεοῦ γενέσθαι πρόνοιαν. ("Through reflection upon this, then, he [viz., the demiurge] discovered that among things that are by nature visible, nothing without intelligence would as a whole ever be more beautiful than the whole endowed with intelligence, and, moreover, that intelligence can be present in nothing apart from soul. By virtue of this reasoning, he placed intelligence in the soul and the soul in a body, and from this fashioned the universe, in order that the work which he completed might be by nature as good and beautiful as possible. In this manner, therefore, as we must say according to probable reasoning, this cosmos has in truth come into being by God's providence as a living being endowed with soul and reason.")

2 *Ibid.*, 30 D: τῷ γὰρ τῶν νοουμένων καλλίστῳ καὶ κατὰ πάντα τελέῳ μάλιστα αὐτὸν ὁ θεὸς ὁμοιῶσαι βουληθεὶς ζῷον ἓν ὁρατόν, πάνθ' ὅσα αὐτοῦ κατὰ φύσιν ξυγγενῆ ζῷα ἐντὸς ἔχον ἑαυτοῦ, ξυνέστησε. ("For God ordered it [the universe] in this way, because he wished to make it as much as possible like in form to that which is the most beautiful of all intelligible things and in every respect complete – a single visible living being that contains in itself all living beings whose nature is akin to its own.")

comes to be" (ἐσόμενον θεόν)[1] – is fully appropriate to the conception of the absolute, divine *nous* as the *aitia* or first, active formal cause of the universe. It is the basis for the teleological explanation of the cosmos that has come to be, although in the second part of the dialogue this mode of explanation will prove to be limited by the autonomous efficient causality of *hulē*.

b. *The Elements as Primary, Mathematically Formed Bodies. The Mathematical Corporeal Form as the Condition for the Visibility and Tangibility of the Elements*

Plato argues that the cosmos that has come to be, as a visible and tangible copy of the eternal model, of necessity must have a bodily structure in which fire and earth are joined to each other. For without fire nothing can be visible, and without earth (as the most solid elementary body), nothing can be tangible.[2] As early as Chapter 8,[3] fire, earth, air, and water are conceived by Plato, in part following Empedocles, as primary bodies,[4] and the supersensible mathematical structures of the latter will be explicated further in chapter 20.

It is very important that we take note of this, since it will prove to have crucial significance for the conception that Plato has in this dialogue of *hulē*, with its autonomous efficient causality. Body never exists apart from form, and according to Plato the primary corporeal forms are mathematical in character. This means, therefore, that for Plato the sensible qualities of visibility and tangibility are themselves ultimately dependent on mathematical, non-sensible structural properties of bodies, an insight that in itself is unquestionably profound and correct, and is obscured only by Plato's metaphysical separation between the eternal, intelligible ontic form and the visible world of becoming.

c. *The Harmonic Mathematical Structure of the World-Body*

Now fire, as the most mobile element, and earth, as the most fixed, cannot be joined together without some third thing; for between the two a connecting bond (δεσμός) must arise. The most beautiful of all bonds is one that makes itself and what it joins as nearly as possible a unity, and this is achieved best by a geometric relation or proportion (ἁρμονία)

---

1 Ibid., 34 A-B: Οὗτος δὴ πᾶς ὄντος ἀεὶ λογισμὸς θεοῦ περὶ τὸν ποτὲ ἐσόμενον θεὸν λογισθεὶς λεῖον καὶ ὁμαλὸν πανταχῆ τε ἐκ μέσου ἴσον καὶ ὅλον καὶ τέλεον ἐκ τελέων σωμάτων σῶμα ἐποίησε. ("This whole course of reasoning of the eternal God with respect to the god who was to come to be caused him to make the latter smooth and uniform and in every direction equidistant from the center, a body whole and complete, consisting of complete bodies.")

2 *Ibid.*, 31 B: χωρισθὲν δὲ πυρὸς οὐδὲν ἄν ποτε ὁρατὸν γένοιτο, οὐδὲ ἁπτὸν ἄνευ τινὸς στερεοῦ, στερεὸν δὲ οὐκ ἄνευ γῆς· ("For nothing would become visible without fire, nor tangible without a solid body, and nothing is a solid body without earth.")

3 *Timaeus*, 32 A-B.

4 The mathematical foundation of this conception is completely Pythagorean. Aether first appears as the fifth element in the *Epinomis*.

having three terms. The proportion is constructed in such a way that, as the first term is to the middle, so is the middle to the last, and conversely, as the last is to the middle, so is the middle to the first, while "the middle term in the proportion also can become first and last, and the last and first terms both the middle."[1]

The numerical series 2, 4, 8 can serve as the simplest example of such a proportionality. These terms can first of all be joined in the proportion 2:4 = 4:8 (the first: the middle = the middle:the last); then in the proportion 8:4 = 4:2 (the last : the middle = the middle:the first); and finally in the two proportions 4:8 = 2:4 (the middle:the last = the first:the middle) and 4:2 = 8:4 (the middle:the first = the last:the middle). Thus each of the three terms in the proportion can occupy the first, middle, and last positions alike, and in this manner, according to Plato, the unity that they form will be as complete as possible.

If the world-body is to be constructed according to a mathematical proportion such as will lend it internal unity, however, three terms are not sufficient. For all bodies, whether primary or the world-body constructed from these, have three dimensions, and Plato maintains that two different middle terms are necessary in order to join together two primary bodies like fire and earth. The demiurge therefore inserted water and air between fire and earth, and he joined them all together, as far as was possible, in the

---

1 *Ibid.*, 31 B-32 A: δύο δὲ μόνω καλῶς ξυνίστασθαι τρίτου χωρὶς οὐ δυνατόν· δεσμὸν γὰρ ἐν μέσῳ δεῖ τινὰ ἀμφοῖν ξυναγωγὸν γίγνεσθαι. δεσμῶν δὲ κάλλιστος ὃς ἂν αὑτὸν καὶ τὰ ξυνδούμενα ὅτι μάλιστα ἓν ποιῇ. τοῦτο δὲ πέφυκεν ἀναλογία κάλλιστα ἀποτελεῖν. ὁπόταν γὰρ ἀριθμῶν τριῶν εἴτε ὄγκων εἴτε δυνάμεων ὡντινωνοῦν ᾖ τὸ μέσον, ὅτιπερ τὸ πρῶτον πρὸς αὐτό, τοῦτο αὐτὸ πρὸς τὸ ἔσχατον, καὶ πάλιν αὖθις, ὅτι τὸ ἔσχατον πρὸς τὸ μέσον, τὸ μέσον πρὸς τὸ πρῶτον, τότε τὸ μέσον μὲν πρῶτον καὶ ἔσχατον γιγνόμενον, τὸ δ᾽ ἔσχατον καὶ τὸ πρῶτον αὖ μέσα ἀμφότερα, πάνθ᾽ οὕτως ἐξ ἀνάγκης τὰ αὐτὰ εἶναι ξυμβήσεται, τὰ αὐτὰ δὲ γενόμενα ἀλλήλοις ἓν πάντα ἔσται. ("It is impossible, however, to join two [elements] alone in a fair manner without a third; for between the two a bond of union must come into being. The most beautiful of all bonds is the one that makes itself and what it joins as nearly as possible a unity, and it is of the nature of a mathematical proportion to accomplish this best. For whenever, of three numbers, the middle between two that are either numbers of solid bodies or of planes is such that, as the first is to the middle, so is the middle to the last, and conversely, as the last is to the middle, so is the middle to the first – while the middle term in the proportion also can become the first and the last, and again, the last and the first both the middle – then in this manner all will of necessity play the same role toward one another, and in so doing, they will all be a unity.") In my translation of the much-disputed words ὁπόταν γὰρ ἀριθμῶν τριῶν εἴτε ὄγκων εἴτε δυνάμεων,, etc., I have followed Cornford (*Plato's Cosmology*, p. 44) who himself in the main follows Sir Thomas Heath (*The Thirteen Books of Euclid's Elements*; tr. with an introduction and commentary by Sir T. L. Heath, Cambridge: 1926; II, 294; and *Greek Mathematics*; Oxford, 1921; I, 89). The arguments for this may be found in Cornford. "Numbers of planes" indicate square numbers such as p^2 and pq, and "numbers of solid bodies" are cubic numbers (e.g., p^3 and p^2q).

same proportion (fire:air = air:water, and water:earth = air:water).[1]

In this way, then, Plato attempts to prove that the foursome of elements from which the Greeks imagined the world-body to be constructed itself has a rational cause in the divine *nous*, in conformity with its *idea tou agathou* (ἰδέα τοῦ ἀγαθοῦ). According to him, this foursome is necessary in order that a unity that is indestructible (for any other than the demiurge) might arise from it in the geometric proportionality of the terms. For in Plato's view, the world-body, in contrast to the body of a person, is imperishable, and this is precisely why it was formed by the divine demiurge himself.

As the totality of all elements and as the complete body that contains all others within itself, the world-body has been given the form of a sphere. We have already observed more than once that the Greeks regarded this as the most perfect form. Since the demiurge made the world-body in such a way that it indeed comprises all that is visible and corporeal, it cannot be attacked by corporeal forces that would act on it from outside. It cannot become old, and it is not susceptible to sickness and death.[2] It is immortal

---

1 *Ibid.*, 32 A-B: εἰ μὲν οὖν ἐπίπεδον μέν, βάθος δὲ μηδὲν ἔχον ἔδει γίγνεσθαι τὸ τοῦ παντὸς σῶμα, μία μεσότης ἂν ἐξήρκει τά τε μεθ' ἑαυτῆς ξυνδεῖν καὶ ἑαυτήν· νῦν δὲ – στερεοειδῆ γὰρ αὐτὸν προσῆκεν εἶναι, τὰ δὲ στερεὰ μία μὲν οὐδέποτε, δύο δὲ ἀεὶ μεσότητες ξυναρμόττουσιν· οὕτω δὴ πυρός τε καὶ γῆς ὕδωρ ἀέρα τε ὁ θεὸς ἐν μέσῳ θεὶς καὶ πρὸς ἄλληλα καθόσον ἦν δυνατὸν ἀνὰ τὸν αὐτὸν λόγον ἀπεργασάμενος ὅτιπερ πῦρ πρὸς ἀέρα, τοῦτο ἀέρα πρὸς ὕδωρ, καὶ ὅτι ἀὴρ πρὸς ὕδωρ, ὕδωρ πρὸς γῆν, ξυνέδησε καὶ ξυνεστήσατο οὐρανὸν ὁρατὸν καὶ ἁπτόν. ("Now, had it been necessary that the body of the universe come to be a plane surface without depth, a single mean would have been sufficient to join its companions and itself; but now – since the form of a solid body was appropriate for the world and solid bodies are never connected by one, but always by two means – God accordingly inserted water and air between fire and earth and brought them mutually, as far as was possible, into the same proportion to one another, so that as fire is to air, so is air to water, and as air is to water, so is water to earth, and thus he joined and put together the visible and tangible cosmos.") From this passage, I must emphasize, it once again becomes evident that, for Plato, the visibility and tangibility of the cosmos are dependent on a mathematical (invisible) structure.

2 *Ibid.*, 32 C to 33 A: τῶν δὲ δὴ τεττάρων ἓν ὅλον ἕκαστον εἴληφεν ἡ τοῦ κόσμου ξύστασις. ἐκ γὰρ πυρὸς παντὸς ὕδατός τε καὶ ἀέρος καὶ γῆς ξυνέστησεν αὐτὸν ὁ ξυνιστάς, μέρος οὐδὲν οὐδενὸς οὐδὲ δύναμιν ἔξωθεν ὑπολιτών, τάδε διανοηθείς· πρῶτον μὲν ἵνα ὅλον ὅτι μάλιστα ζῷον τέλεον ἐκ τελέων τῶν μερῶν εἴη, πρὸς δὲ τούτοις ἕν, ἅτε οὐχ ὑπολελειμμένων ἐξ ὧν ἄλλο τοιοῦτο γένοιτ' ἄν, ἔτι δὲ ἵνα ἀγήρων καὶ ἄνοσον ἦ, κατανοῶν, ὡς ξυστατῷ σώματι [σώματα] θερμὰ καὶ ψυχρὰ καὶ πάνθ' ὅσα δυνάμεις ἰσχυρὰς ἔχει, περιιστάμενα ἔξωθεν καὶ προσπίπτοντα ἀκαίρως λύει καὶ νόσους γήρας τε ἐπάγοντα φθίνειν ποιεῖ. ("Now the structure of the cosmos took up within itself the number of each of these four [elements]; he who put it together compounded it out of all the fire and water and air and earth, leaving no part or power of any one of them outside; and his intent in this was: first, that it might be in full measure a living being whole and complete, consisting of complete

and self-sufficient, a typically divine predicate that Xenophanes and Parmenides had already conferred upon the divine *Sphairos*.[1] And as Plato argues, following Xenophanes' and Empedocles' description of the spherical "god of heaven" and departing from Pythagorean cosmology, it had no need of sense organs, limbs, or digestive organs, since it does not have to take in anything from outside itself.[2] Only one motion was assigned to the world-body, namely, the circular motion which always returns to itself, this being the truest likeness of the self-identical, eternal ontic form, and also of the movement of thought in the *nous*, which likewise returns to itself. Because it has this motion, as Plato observes following Empedocles, the world-body also needed no feet or legs.[3]

d. *The Demiurge Uses the Celestial Deities as Intermediaries*
   in the Composition of Perishable Beings. Plato's Influence
   on the Later Logos *Theory and Scholasticism*

The demiurge itself gives form directly only to that which, like the divine *nous* itself, has been granted immortality, namely, to both the soul and body of the universe and of the individual celestial deities, but in

---

parts, and moreover, that it might be a single [universe], since nothing was left over from which another such could come into being; further, that it might be free of aging and sickness; for he perceived that if hot and cold things and all things that have strong powers should act upon a composite body and attack it from without, they would decompose it prematurely and prepare its ruin by causing old age and sickness.")

1 *Ibid.*, 33 D: ἡγήσατο γὰρ αὐτὸ ὁ ξυντιθεὶς αὔταρκες ὂν ἄμεινον ἔσεσθαι μᾶλλον ἢ προσδεὲς ἄλλων. ("For he who framed the universe judged that, if it were self-sufficient, it would be better than if it needed something else.")

2 *Ibid.*, 33 C: ὀμμάτων τε γὰρ ἐπεδεῖτο οὐδέν· ὁρατὸν γὰρ οὐδὲν ὑπελείπετο ἔξωθεν· οὐδ᾽ ἀκοῆς· οὐδὲ γὰρ ἀκουστόν· πνεῦμά τε οὐκ ἦν περιεστὸς δεόμενον ἀναπνοῆς. οὐδ᾽ αὖ τινος ἐπιδεὲς ἦν ὀργάνου σχεῖν, ᾧ τὴν μὲν εἰς ἑαυτὸ τροφὴν δέξοιτο, τὴν δὲ πρότερον ἐξικμασμένην ἀποπέμψοι πάλιν. ("For it had no need of eyes, since there was nothing visible outside of it, nor of ears, since there was nothing outside to be heard; no air necessary for breathing surrounded it; and it also needed no organ for taking food into itself or, once it had digested this, for discharging it again.")

3 *Ibid.*, 34 A: κίνησιν γὰρ ἀπένειμεν αὐτῷ τὴν τοῦ σώματος οἰκείαν, τῶν ἑπτὰ τὴν περὶ νοῦν καὶ φρόνησιν μάλιστα οὖσαν. διὸ δὴ κατὰ ταὐτὰ ἐν τῷ αὐτῷ καὶ ἐν ἑαυτῷ περιαγαγὼν αὐτὸ ἐποίησε κύκλῳ κινεῖσθαι στρεφόμενον, τὰς δὲ ἓξ ἁπάσας κινήσεις ἀφεῖλε καὶ ἀπλανὲς ἀπειργάσατο ἐκείνων. ἐπὶ δὲ τὴν περίοδον ταύτην ἅτ᾽ οὐδὲν ποδῶν δέον ἀσκελὲς καὶ ἄπουν αὐτὸ ἐγέννησεν. ("For he assigned to it the motion proper to its bodily [i.e., spherical] form, namely, that of the seven motions which above all belongs to *nous* and understanding; accordingly, he caused it to revolve along the same track in the same place and within its own limits, and made it turn round in a circle; but he took from it the other six [i.e., rectilinear] motions and gave it no part in their wanderings. And since for all this revolution it needed no feet, he made it without feet or legs.")

the case of human beings only to the immortal part of the soul. The demiurge delegates responsibility for the composition of the mortal human body and the mortal parts of the human soul, and also for the mortal animals and plants in their totality, to the celestial deities, particularly, as the *Epinomis* specifies, to the sun.[1] As early as the *Republic*, the foremost position among the visible celestial gods had been conferred upon the sun as the "source of the good in the visible world, which most resembles its divine form-giver," and "the cause of the birth, growth, and sustenance of visible living beings."[2] The thought that the divine *nous* uses intermediary beings in order to give form to what is perishable is thus found as early as Plato. The reason for this is that the divine *nous* apparently may not come into direct contact with the earthly matter principle of ever-flowing *physis*, just as the immortal Olympian culture gods who had departed from the mother earth shunned contact with the realm of the dead. The speculative *logos* theory of Philo of Alexandria and of the so-called Middle and Neo-Platonic schools would later tie in with this view, and, as we have seen earlier, this *logos* theory would also infect Christian thought of the early centuries through its subversion of the scriptural creation motive. The influence of Plato's notion that the divine demiurge leaves the generation of mortal beings to the celestial deities – particularly the sun – extends still much further than this, however. Its effects are found even in the adage *Homo generat hominem et sol* ("Man and the sun generate man"), which was accepted by the whole of medieval Scholasticism, both in its Augustinian-Platonic and in its Aristotelian-Thomistic schools. Aristotle works out this principle in his *De generatione animalium*.[3] We shall encounter it once again, at a later point, in our critical investigation of Scholastic anthropology.

The demiurge implants the rational world-soul at the center of the spherical world-body. "And he caused it to spread throughout the whole and further to surround the body on the outside; and so he formed the one universe, existing alone, a sphere revolving in a circle, which by its own power is able to fecundate (ξυγγίγεσθαι) itself and needs nothing else besides itself, but is sufficiently acquainted and befriended with itself. Thus he brought into being a deity that on all these accounts is blessed.")[4]

---

1 *Epinomis*, 986 E.
2 *Republic*, 508 B, 509 B.
3 Aristotle, *De generatione animalium*, 716 a ff.
4 *Ibid.*, 34 B: ψυχὴν δὲ εἰς τὸ μέσον αὐτοῦ θεὶς διὰ παντός τε ἔτεινε καὶ ἔτι ἔξωθεν τὸ σῶμα αὐτῇ περιεκάλυψε ταύτῃ, καὶ κύκλῳ δὴ κύκλον στρεφόμενον οὐρανὸν ἕνα μόνον ἔρημον κατέστησε, δι᾽ ἀρετὴν δὲ αὐτὸν αὐτῷ δυνάμενον ξυγγίγνεσθαι καὶ οὐδενὸς ἑτέρου προσδεόμενον, γνώριμον δὲ καὶ φίλον ἱκανῶς αὐτὸν αὐτῷ. διὰ πάντα δὴ ταῦτα εὐδαίμονα θεὸν αὐτὸν ἐγεννήσατο. (Translation in text.)

e. Plato's and Empedocles' Descriptions of the sphairos. *For Plato the Body Has an Innate Mathematical Form, Independent of the Soul. The Influence of This Conception on Augustinian Scholasticism*

This entire description of the implanting of the world-soul in the spherical world-body is in many ways reminiscent of Empedocles's description of *philia*, which joins all the elements, as the primary corporeal forms, into a unity within the spherical whole of the world-body. Like him, Plato says that the universe is "befriended" to itself. But there are fundamental differences between Plato's and Empedocles' conceptions. Unlike that of Empodocles, Plato's world-body does not owe its spherical form to *philia* as an active, fluid soul-force. For Plato the form of the world-body, like the *sphairos* in the Eleatic conception, is indestructible. There is an innate harmonic structure in the proportionate combination of the four corporeal elements and an innate original form that is mathematical in nature, which belong to the body independently of the rational soul. And, as we shall see, the latter unites in itself both the form and matter principles.

Plato applied this conception of the innate formal character of the body to the world-body and to the human body, although in different senses. This conception came to be passed on to the whole of the Augustinian-Platonic school in Scholasticism. There it was to remain one of the essential points of difference with the Aristotelian-Thomistic conception in regard to the relation between soul and material body, namely as form and matter.

4. The Place of the Soul in the Intermediate Realm. Has Plato Reverted in the *Timaeus* to the Uncritical Position That Like Is Known by Like?

a. According to Timaeus 35 a, *the Being of the Rational Soul Has a Form Intermediate between the Eidetic Ontic Forms and Visible, Corporeal Forms*

Like the *Philebus*, the *Timaeus* considers the soul to be something that has come into being. This pertains both to the world-soul endowed with *nous* and to the individual rational soul of a human being. The *Timaeus*, therefore, clearly distinguished the soul from the eternal world of the *eidē*.

Restoring the rational soul to the world of becoming had given rise to a new problem within the compass of Plato's thought, however. The *Republic* had identified the realm of becoming with the genus of the visible (ὁρατὸν γένος), and the intelligible realm (νοητὸν γένος) of *ousia* (that which truly *is*) was set over against this.

282

Ever since the *Philebus*, however, the soul could not be assigned to either of these two realms. Once Plato had abandoned the conception, which had been introduced in the *Parmenides* and the *Sophist*, of the *eidē* as active soul-forces, and also the *Phaedo's* conception of the soul's eternal, unoriginated mode of existence, it no longer fit within the world of the eternal *eidē*. But, on the other hand, it was no more possible for it to find a home in the ὁρατὸν γένος or visible realm. The soul is invisible, and at least in this respect it belongs to the intelligible realm. Nevertheless, it is still something that has come into being. In Plato's line of thought there was therefore no choice but to assign it to an intermediate realm.

The composition of the world-soul by the divine demiurge is described in the *Timaeus*.[1] Plato argues first of all that the soul, both in its origin (*genesis*) and in the value of its nature (*aretē*), is prior to and older than the body. It was formed, he reasons, by the divine demiurge to be the mistress and governess of the body. The manner of its composition is as follows: "From the indivisible and ever unchanging mode of existence of the intelligible ontic form [τῆς ἀμερίστου καὶ ἀεὶ κατὰ ταὐτὰ ἐχούσης οὐσίας] and the divisible mode of existence which becomes in bodies, he [i.e., the demiurge] blended a third form of being [τρίτον οὐσίας εἶδος]; and, again, looking to the nature of the self-identical and that of the other, he also by this standard compounded a third lying between the modes of existence of these two, namely, that which is undivided and that which is divisible in bodies; and then, taking these three modes of being [καὶ τρία λαβὼν αὐτὰ ὄντα], he blended them together into one *idea*, by forcibly uniting the nature of the other, hard to mix as it was, with that of the self-identical, and mixing both together with [the mode of existence of] the pure ontic form [μιγνὺς δὲ μετὰ τῆς οὐσίας]."[2]

---

1   *Timaeus*, 35 A ff.
2   *Ibid.*, 34 B, C to 35 B: *Τὴν δὲ δὴ ψυχὴν οὐχ ὡς νῦν ὑστέραν ἐπιχειροῦμεν λέγειν, οὕτως ἐμηχανήσατο καὶ ὁ θεὸς νεωτέραν· οὐ γὰρ ἂν ἄρχεσθαι πρεσβύτερον ὑπὸ νεωτέρου ξυνέρξας εἴασεν· ἀλλά πως ἡμεῖς πολὺ μετέχοντες τοῦ προστυχόντος τε καὶ εἰκῇ ταύτῃ πῃ καὶ λέγομεν, ὁ δὲ καὶ γενέσει καὶ ἀρετῇ προτέραν καὶ πρεσβυτέραν ψυχὴν σώματος ὡς δεσπότιν καὶ ἄρξουσαν ἀρξομένου ξυνεστήσατο ἐκ τῶνδέ τε καὶ τοιῷδε τρόπῳ. τῆς ἀμερίστου καὶ ἀεὶ κατὰ ταὐτὰ ἐχούσης οὐσίας καὶ τῆς αὖ περὶ τὰ σώματα γιγνομένης μεριστῆς τρίτον ἐξ ἀμφοῖν ἐν μέσῳ ξυνεκεράσατο οὐσίας εἶδος, τῆς τε ταὐτοῦ φύσεως αὖ πέρι καὶ τῆς τοῦ ἑτέρου, καὶ κατὰ ταῦτα ξυνέστησεν ἐν μέσῳ τοῦ τε ἀμεροῦς αὐτῶν καὶ τοῦ κατὰ τὰ σώματα μεριστοῦ, καὶ τρία λαβὼν αὐτὰ ὄντα συνεκεράσατο εἰς μίαν πάντα ἰδέαν, τὴν θατέρου φύσιν δύσμικτον οὖσαν εἰς ταὐτὸν ξυναρμόττων βίᾳ, μιγνὺς δὲ μετὰ τῆς οὐσίας. καὶ ἐκ τριῶν ποιησάμενος ἓν πάλιν ὅλον τοῦτο μοίρας ὅσας προσῆκε διένειμεν, ἑκάστην δὲ ἔκ τε ταὐτοῦ καὶ θατέρου καὶ τῆς οὐσίας μεμιγμένην.* ("The soul was not, however, as we are now attempting to speak of it

In order to understand this obscure passage, we must first of all observe that here the divine demiurge's mixture of the world-soul is presented in two distinct stages. In the first place, a mixture is brought about between the *indivisible* (eidetic) and the *divisible* (corporeal) modes of being. The product of this first mixture is a third mode of existence that stands midway between these two. In the second place, a mixture is brought about between the indivisible and the divisible (corporeal) modes of the *self-identical*. The product of this second mixture is a third (mixed) genus of the self-identical. In the third place, there is a mixture between the indivisible and the divisible (corporeal) modes of the other. The product here is a third (mixed) genus of the other. From the three ingredients that have arisen as the products of these first mixtures, the world-soul is then finally compounded.

The diagram that Cornford gives in his commentary on the *Timaeus*[1] can serve to clarify this:

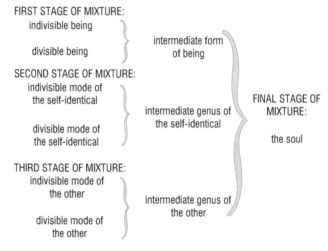

FIRST STAGE OF MIXTURE:
indivisible being

divisible being

intermediate form of being

SECOND STAGE OF MIXTURE:
indivisible mode of the self-identical

divisible mode of the self-identical

intermediate genus of the self-identical

THIRD STAGE OF MIXTURE:
indivisible mode of the other

divisible mode of the other

intermediate genus of the other

FINAL STAGE OF MIXTURE:

the soul

b. Timaeus *35* A *and the Dialectical* Ideai *of the* Sophist

The real meaning of this passage can be understood only in the light of

later, constructed by God as the younger product [i.e., younger than the body]; for he never would have suffered that the elder should be ruled by the younger to which he joined it. But as we are often dependent on chance and likelihood, we now express ourselves thus; whereas he fashioned the soul – which in its origin and in the excellence of its nature is prior and older – as the governess and mistress over the body subject to it, from the following elements and in such matter ..." [the remainder of the translation appears in the text].) In the punctuation after μιγνὺς δὲ μετὰ τῆς οὐσίας, I have followed the edition of Jackson, who established that these words belong with the preceding ξυναρμόττων, not with the following aorist ποιησάμενος. Cornford also adopts this reading (*Plato's Cosmology*; 1937, p. 60).

1   Cornford, *op.cit.*, p. 61.

the *Sophist*, where we have seen Plato distinguish five fundamental forms (highest *eidē*): (individual) *being, motion, rest, identity* (the self-identical), and *difference* (the other). Of these five, three (i.e., being, the self-identical, and the other) proved to be dialectical *ideai* or genera that extended over the entire intelligible world of forms in its relation to the visible cosmos. In this way, they made it possible for the dialectical logic to join together the individual *eidē*, which in themselves are mutually opposed (as, e.g., those of motion and rest), in a true existential judgment which as such can be related to temporal reality. We have observed that the concern here was always with ontic forms that have become incarnated in a plurality of corporeal things, and therefore have lost their pure, simple character.

In the *Philebus*, the theory of mixture was introduced with the two basic principles of the *peras* and the *apeiron*. *Peras* and *apeiron* were treated exclusively as genera of generated being (*genesis eis ousian*), and this was held to include both visible things and the soul. The difference between the modes of existence of these two was not explicitly treated here, however.

c. The Theory of Mixture Is Worked Out Anew. The Testimony of Proclus

In the *Timaeus*, the theory of mixture receives a special development in respect of the soul. The visible body too is a product of mixture between (mathematical) *peras* and *apeiron*, but it falls as such in the ὁρατὸν γένος (the realm of the visible products of becoming) of the *Republic*.

The soul, however, is the product of another mixture, namely, a mixture of the mode of being, identity, and difference of the pure, indivisible *eidos* with the mode of being, identity, and difference of what is divisible in bodies, which itself can exist only as a mixture of *peras* and *apeiron*. In consequence of this new mixture, the soul is assigned an intermediate form of being that actually makes it into the connecting link between the two realms that in the *Republic* had been separated by a rigid *chōrismos*. It is incorrect, therefore, to say that the soul belongs to both realms.[1] In accordance with its ἰδέα (the single, effective divine plan according to which the divine *nous* formed it), it rather belongs to neither. Its place is an intermediate realm.

Proclus, the neo-Platonist, has elucidated this clearly in his commentary on the *Timaeus*, where he speaks continually of the soul as an intermediate entity compounded from the intermediate kinds of being, identity, and difference.[2] He distinguishes three modes of being in the *Timaeus*: (1) intelligible, things that have not come into being; (2) sensible, things that have

---

1 As, e.g., Cornford maintains, *op.cit.*, p. 63.

2 Proclus, *In Platonis Timaeum commentaria* (ed. E. Diehl) ii, 137: ἐπεὶ οὖν ἡ

come into being; (3) intermediate things that are both intelligible and have come into being. The first are all simple (not composite) in nature and indivisible. They are ungenerated, therefore, and have not come into being. The second are composite and divisible. Therefore, they have come into being. The intermediate things are intelligible and have come into being, and by nature they are both indivisible and divisible, simple and composite, although in ways that differ from the first two.[1]

Proclus then writes: "That Plato meant by 'indivisible mode of being' the intelligible being that partakes as a whole in eternity, and by 'divisible mode of being in bodies' the mode of being that is inseparable from bodily extension and is inserted within the whole of time, he makes clear himself by speaking of the former as 'unchangeable,' of the latter as 'coming into being,' in order not only to call the soul at once indivisible and divisible, but also 'intelligible' (*νοητόν*) and 'the first among things that come into being'."[2] "There is a difference between the everlastingness that is eternal and the everlastingness that is extended in the infinitude of time; and there is still another, composed of both, such as belongs to the soul. For in its being the soul is unchangeable and eternal, but in respect of its thoughts it is changing and temporal."[3] We shall see that this latter statement is not entirely correct.

d. Indivisible Being as Idea-Number? The Testimony of Xenocrates

We should take note of the fact that, in the passage under consideration, Plato's notion of the *being* of the *eide* once more accords with the original conception of the theory of ideas put forward in the *Phaedo*. They are thus conceived as simple, indivisible, and without origin. This contrasts distinctly with the conception of the *eidos* in the logical dialectic of the *Parmenides*, where *eidos* in the sense of the "real unity" was always understood as a whole with parts. *Timaeus* 38 A further accentu-

---

ψυχικὴ οὐσία μέση δέδεικται τῶν ὄντων, ἐκ τῶν μέσων εἰκότως ἐστὶ γενῶν τοῦ ὄντος, οὐσίας, ταὐτοῦ, θατέρου. *Ibid.*, iii, 254[3]: ψυχή ἐστιν οὐσία μέση τῆς ὄντως οὔσης οὐσίας καὶ γενέσεως, ἐκ τῶν μέσων συγκραθεῖσα γενῶν. He also speaks similarly in numerous other places. My quotations here follow Cornford, *op.cit.*, p. 63, note 1.

1 Proclus, ii, 117[14].

2 Proclus supports this by referring to *Timaeus*, 36 e, where the soul is called "invisible" and "the best of the things that have come into being." In this connection, he remarks (ii, 293[13]) that the soul belongs simultaneously to both classes of being – namely, things that are eternal, and things that have come into being – and that, because of its participation in time, it occupies the lowest position in the first class. But this remark reveals, by its very convolutedness, that it cannot be correct to assign the soul equally to both realms.

3 Proclus, ii, 147[23].

ates this contrast. It does so by denying to the living being in itself, as an eternal *eidos*, all motion and temporal qualification and by ascribing these exclusively to what comes into being.[1]

In this passage from the *Timaeus*, therefore, Plato is obviously speaking again of the intrinsic ontic nature of the pure *eidos*, independent of its relation to the plurality of sensible things that correspond to it. Herein we can ascertain once more a definite approach to the Eleatic conception. It is impossible to establish for certain whether this indivisible being, like the pure *peras* in the *Philebus*, must here be understood as idea-number; but this is indeed likely. For according to Plutarch's report, in his *On the Origin of the Soul in the Timaeus*,[2] Plato's pupil Xenocrates explicitly observed that indivisible being is the unity, divisible being the plurality, and that the soul is the number which arises in the limitation of the plurality by the unity, once the latter has entered into a second mixture with identity (ταὐτόν) and difference (τὸ θάτερον). In full accord with the text of the *Timaeus*, Xenocrates' interpretation of Plato's conception of indivisible being thus clearly distinguishes between unity as an idea-number and identity and difference as dialectical *ideai*. The pure being of the *eidos* as

---

1 *Timaeus*, 38 A: Τὸ δὲ ἦν τό τ᾽ ἔσται περὶ τὴν ἐν χρόνῳ γένεσιν ἰοῦσαν πρέπει λέγεσθαι· κινήσεις γάρ ἐστον. τὸ δὲ ἀεὶ κατὰ ταὐτὰ ἔχον ἀκινήτως οὔτε πρεσβύτερον οὔτε νεώτερον προσήκει γίγνεσθαι διὰ χρόνου οὐδὲ γενέσθαι ποτὲ οὐδὲ γεγονέναι νῦν οὐδ᾽ εἰσαῦθις ἔσεσθαι, τὸ παράπαν τε οὐδὲν ὅσα γένεσις τοῖς ἐν αἰσθήσει φερομένοις προσῆψεν, ἀλλὰ χρόνου ταῦτα αἰῶνα μιμουμένου καὶ κατ᾽ ἀριθμὸν κυκλουμένου γέγονεν εἴδη. (" 'Was' and 'will be' are properly [only] spoken in respect of becoming, which proceeds in time. For they are motions. But that which is forever immovably in the same state cannot become older or younger by lapse of time, nor can it at some time or other have come to be, or be now, or come to be in the future; and in general nothing belongs to it of all that becoming attaches to moving things in sense perception; but these have come into being as forms of time, which images eternity and moves in a circular path according to number.") It may be concluded that in the *Timaeus* the conception of the pure *eidos* is again Eleatic, at least in principle. To come to this conclusion one need only compare this exposition in regard to the fundamental difference between the eternal and unmoved *eidos* and the *genesis* that is moving in time with the dialectial-logical expositions of the *Parmenides* and the *Sophist*, in which real being is dialectically related to movement and rest (and in the *Parmenides* even with time and spatiality). By way of this comparison, it may also be concluded that the dialectical synthesis between the standpoints of Parmenides and Heraclitus in regard to the pure eidetic sphere of being that is found in the Eleatic dialogues has again been abandoned. Plato's adoption of Parmenides' position naturally had to stop short of the latter's mathematical-spatial conception of the ontic form, however. In the *Timaeus*, the absolute *eidos* is probably already to be understood as an idea-number. See the testimony of Xenocrates below in the text.

2 Plutarch, Περὶ τῆς ἐν Τιμαίῳ ψυχογονίας (*De animae procreatione in Timaeo*), c. 21, 1012 e.

idea-number is to be equated with neither the self-identical nor the other. For both of these dialectical qualifications belong to the domain of eidetic relations, which do not concern the intrinsic unity of the ontic form as an idea-number.

If Plato indeed conceives the soul's mode of being in the *Timaeus* in terms of number, however – and we shall see that this is explicitly taught later in the dialogue – then number is in any case not to be understood here in the sense of idea-number. Rather, it must be regarded as a mathematical, harmonic proportion, and we have seen that plurality is inherent in this. For the soul has a mode of existence that is intermediate between the *eidos* and corporeal, perceptible things, and the *Republic* teaches that mathematical numbers and figures do indeed occupy an intermediate position between the two realms of pure *eidē* and visible things.

All of this will show itself to be of fundamental significance for answering the question as to whether Plato has in fact, as Aristotle believed, reverted in the *Timaeus* to the uncritical position of earlier Greek nature philosophy and metaphysics, that like is known by like.

Finally, the parallel distinction between indivisible, divisible (in bodies), and intermediate kinds of identity and difference is explained only by the fact that, as dialectical qualifications of the three kinds of being, they conform to the latter. The identity of the indivisible ontic form, therefore, must of necessity itself be indivisible, since there exists only one instance of the latter. On the other hand, the identity of the ontic form distributed among diverse bodies is divided into a plurality of instances of the same kind. The same then holds also for difference.

e.   The Division of the World-Soul into Harmonic Intervals

The demiurge has combined the three mixed structural elements of the soul mentioned above into a unity. Continuing its description of the formation of the world-soul, the *Timaeus* states that the demiurge now divides this whole into as many parts as correspond to the intervals of a musical scale (*harmonia*) that expresses the harmonic relationships of the cosmos (the Pythagorean harmony of the spheres?). Each of these parts is in turn a mixture of ontic form, identity, and difference. The division starts from a series of numbers that form two geometric proportions of four terms each – 1, 2, 4, 8 and 1, 3, 9, 27 – in other words, two forms of the *tetractys*, both of which start from unity.[1]

The *tetractys* intended here is clearly mathematical, and not eidetic (i.e.,

---

1   *Timaeus*, 35 B-C: Καὶ ἐκ τριῶν ποιησάμενος ἓν πάλιν ὅλον τοῦτο μοίρας ὅσας προσῆκε διένειμεν, ἑκάστην δὲ ἔκ τε ταὐτοῦ καὶ θατέρου καὶ τῆς οὐσίας μεμιγμένην. ἤρχετο δὲ διαιρεῖν ὧδε· μίαν ἀφεῖλε τὸ πρῶτον ἀπὸ παντὸς μοῖραν, μετὰ δὲ ταύτην ἀφῄρει διπλασίαν ταύτης, τὴν δ' αὖ τρίτην ἡμιολίαν μὲν τῆς δευτέρας, τριπλασίαν δὲ τῆς πρώτης, τετάρτην δὲ τῆς δευτέρας διπλῆν, πέμπτην δὲ τριπλῆν τῆς τρίτης, τὴν δ' ἕκτην τῆς πρώτης ὀκταπλασίαν, ἑβδόμην δ'

that of the four idea-numbers), since what is spoken of is the division of a whole into quantitative portions. In respect of the mathematical *tetractys*, Plato had no difficulty in accepting the Pythagorean notion that unity contains in itself both *peras* and *apeiron*, both odd and even. The two series, both proceeding from unity, then unfold via the first even (2) and the first odd (3) number to the squares and then to the cubes of these, ending in 8 and 27 respectively.

Plato thus constructs the soul in this manner as a Pythagorean *harmonia*. This is not, however, a *harmonia* that results from the material proportion in the body (the conception refuted in the *Phaedo*), but an intelligible harmony which, as an autonomous structure of the soul, is formed independently of the body and is intended to rule the latter.

f. The Circular Motion of the Self-Identical and the Other in the World-Soul

The demiurge constructs the world-soul in such a manner that it contains in its self-movement the prototype for the whole corporeal motion of the heavens, of which it is of course the "cause." This self-movement of the world-soul proceeds in accordance with the basic forms of the self-identical and the different (the other). As an ordered motion it has the form of a circle, and it is constructed in two rings. The outer of these represents the motion of the sphere of the fixed starry sky, and the inner the motion of the planets. The outer revolution in Plato's picture is the circuit of the self-identical. It corresponds with the movement of the universe around its own axis without change in position, and it has the supremacy over the inner ring of motions. The inner ring of divisions is divided into seven unequal circles moving in opposite directions, these forming the circuit of the different (the other). They represent within the soul the motions of the seven planets, which according to Plato have unequal circles (i.e., differing in diameter) that can thus fit inside one another around a common center.[1]

Cornford rightly observes in his commentary, referring explicitly to

ἑπτακαιεικοσιπλασίαν τῆς πρώτης. μετὰ δὲ ταῦτα συνεπληροῦτο τά τε διπλάσια καὶ τριπλάσια διαστήματα ... ("And after he had made a unity of these three, he again divided this whole into as many parts as was fitting, each part being blended from the self-identical, the other [the different], and the ontic form. And he began the division in this way: first he took one portion (1) from the whole, and next the double (2) of this; the third (3), in turn, one and a half times as much as the second and three times the first; the fourth (4) the double of the second; the fifth (9) the triple of the third; the sixth (8) eight times the first; and the seventh (27) twenty-seven times the first. After this he filled up both the double and the triple intervals ...")

1 *Ibid.*, 36 B-D: ταύτην οὖν τὴν ξύστασιν πᾶσαν διπλῆν κατὰ μῆκος σχίσας μέσην πρὸς μέσην ἑκατέραν ἀλλήλαις οἷον χῖ προσβαλὼν κατέκαμψεν εἰς ἓν κύκλῳ, ξυνάψας αὐταῖς τε καὶ ἀλλήλαις ἐν τῷ καταντικρὺ τῆς προσβολῆς, καὶ τῇ κατὰ ταὐτὰ ἐν ταὐτῷ περιαγομένῃ κινήσει πέριξ αὐτὰς ἔλαβε, καὶ τὸν μὲν ἔξω, τὸν δ᾽ ἐντὸς ἐποιεῖτο τῶν κύκλων τὴν μὲν οὖν ἔξω φορὰν ἐπεφήμισεν εἶναι τῆς ταὐτοῦ φύσεως, τὴν δ᾽ ἐντὸς τῆς θατέρου. τὴν μὲν δὴ ταὐτοῦ κατὰ πλευρὰν ἐπὶ δεξιὰ

Proclus, that Plato's division of the inner ring of revolutions into seven unequal circles is not meant to indicate that the motion of the other (the different) within the world-soul itself is actually divided into seven orbits. As he writes, "The meaning can only be that a single motion – the motion of the Different – is, from the physical point of view, distributed among all the seven orbits where it actually takes place (with additional modifications)."[1] In other words, within the world-soul there is only one motion of the other, and that is not corporeal in nature. Regarded from the physical point of view, however, this motion has its counterparts in the circular motions of the seven celestial bodies: the sun, Venus, Mercury, the moon, Mars, Jupiter, and Saturn, which because of his still-primitive knowledge of astronomy Plato calls the "seven planets." That this indeed must be Plato's intention is evident from *Timaeus* 36 C, 37 B, and 38 C, where the circuit of the other in the world-soul continues to be regarded always as a single motion, this only being imparted to the planets by its distribution over seven circles.

If the circuit of the self-identical be taken only as a motion of the world-soul, detached from the physical motions of the world-body, its "supremacy" over the circuit of the other must then also be understood "psychologically" as the supremacy of reason (*nous*), which regulates the other motions in the soul (judgments and desires). By means of this structure, the world-soul is able to know both the eternal, self-identical order of

περιήγαγε, τὴν δὲ θατέρου κατὰ διάμετρον ἐπ᾽ ἀριστερά. κράτος δ᾽ ἔδωκε τῇ ταὐτοῦ καὶ ὁμοίου περιφορᾷ· μίαν γὰρ αὐτὴν ἄσχιστον εἴασε, τὴν δ᾽ ἐντὸς σχίσας ἑξαχῇ ἑπτὰ κύκλους ἀνίσους κατὰ τὴν τοῦ διπλασίου καὶ τριπλασίου διάστασιν ἑκάστην, οὐσῶν ἑκατέρων τριῶν, κατὰ τἀναντία μὲν ἀλλήλοις προσέταξεν ἰέναι τοὺς κύκλους, τάχει δὲ τρεῖς μὲν ὁμοίους, τοὺς δὲ τέτταρας ἀλλήλοις καὶ τοῖς τρισὶν ἀνομοίως, ἐν λόγῳ δὲ φερομένους. ("He then divided this entire construction lengthwise into two halves; and joining the center of one to that of the other in the form of the letter X, he bent them around and connected them into a unity in a circle, making each meet itself and the other at a point opposite that where they touched each other. And he enclosed them in the uniform motion that circles in the same place and made the one the outer, the other the inner circle. He directed that the outer motion have the nature of the self-identical, but the inner nature of the other. The motion of the self-identical he carried around by way of the side to the right, the motion of the other to the left by way of the diagonal. But he gave the ascendancy to the revolution of the self-identical and the like; for this alone he left one and undivided, whereas he divided the inner revolution six times into seven unequal circles, each corresponding with the double and triple intervals, of each of which there were three. And he ordained that the circles should move in opposite directions to one another, three with equal speed, but the other four with speeds different from one another and from that of the first three, although in accordance with a ratio.") For a more detailed explanation of the circles in the world-soul, cf. Cornford, *op.cit.*, pp. 72 ff.

1   Cornford, *op.cit.*, p. 78.

the world of ontic forms (*eidē*) and the visible order of the world of changeable, divisible things subject to the matter principle.

g. Has Plato Reverted in Timaeus 35 A ff. to the Position That Like Is Known by Like?

Thus, we are indeed confronted here with the problem as to whether in the *Timaeus* Plato has reverted – as the prevailing view maintains following Aristotle – to the uncritical position that like is known only by like. In the passage quoted earlier from *De anima*,[1] one is struck by the direct connection that Aristotle draws between Plato's and Empedocles' view as to how the soul is constructed. He states that "in the same manner [i.e., as Empedocles] Plato too, in the *Timaeus*, constructs the soul out of the elements; for according to him like is known by like, and things are composed of the *archai* [of all that is]." Nevertheless, it is clear that the elements from which Plato builds the soul are completely different in nature from those of Empedocles' cosmogony. He does not construct the soul out of fire, air, water, and earth as primary, corporeal forms of being, and one would search in vain in the *Timaeus* and in the other dialogues as well for any statement attributable to him that like is known by like. On the contrary, we found that he explicitly rejects this thesis in various earlier dialogues. Moreover, the *Timaeus'* entire conception of the soul absolutely excludes it in the uncritical sense in which it was accepted by the earlier nature philosophy and metaphysics. For if, as Plato emphatically declares in *Timaeus* 36 E, the soul belongs to the realm of what is invisible and has come into being, in contrast to the visible body, and if its mode of being is neither that of the *idea*, nor that of corporeal, perishable things, but is rather intermediate between both, then it is out of the question that Plato has reverted to the old, uncritical epistemological maxim. The latter, whether in its Eleatic or Heraclitean version, or as interpreted by Empedocles, is incompatible with his new conception of the soul.

One might suppose nevertheless that in the *Timaeus* Plato would subscribe at least to the Pythagorean conception of like knowing like. For according to this conception, numbers are the *archai* of all things, the soul included, and the latter can thus obtain knowledge of the cosmos only because it consists of the same *archai*. Even this Pythagorean version of the maxim was unacceptable to Plato, however, since he makes a fundamental distinction in the number themselves between eidetic, mathematical, and perceptible or concrete numbers.[2] The numerical nature of the soul as harmony differs in principle from the numerical nature of the pure *eidē* and that of corporeal objects.

When Proclus observes in the above-quoted comment that the soul is unchangeable and eternal in its being but changing and temporal in re-

---

1 Aristotle, *De anima*, A 2, 404 b 16-27.
2 *Theaetetus*, 195 E to 196 B and 198 A to 199 C; *Philebus*, 55 D to 57 A; *Republic*, VII, 525 C to 526 B; and the passages cited earlier from the *Phaedo*, 96 D to 97 B and 101 B-C.

spect of its thoughts, we must at once add to this that the soul cannot have the same being as the *eidē*. For according to Plato, the soul's mode of being places it in the realm of becoming, and this mode of being is the result of a mixture between that which is indivisible (simple) and that which is divisible (composite). On Plato's view, souls that have come into being are not eternal. Eternity belongs solely to the *eidē* and the divine *nous*.

The question as to precisely what Plato intended by constructing the soul from the mixed structural elements of *ousia*, the self-identical, and the other remains extremely difficult to answer. One thing is certain, however. *Timaeus* 37 A-B establishes a direct link between these structural elements and the cognitive activity of the soul. Beginning at 36 E, near the end, the text in my view is best rendered as follows: "And the body of the universe came into being visible, but the soul as something invisible, which, taking part in theoretical thought and in harmony, is the best of intelligible, everlasting things that have come into being, brought forth by the best [artificer]. Seeing, then, that the soul is blended from these three ingredients, namely, the nature of the self-identical, the other, and the ontic form, and is divided and bound together in due proportion, and returns to itself in its circular motion, the soul, whenever it apprehends something having an ontic form either divisible or indivisible, in both cases is spontaneously moved throughout its whole being and declares to itself whether something is the same as or different from any given thing, and in what relation precisely, and in what way, and how far, and when it comes about that things are severally related and experience an effect, both among things that come into being and among those what always remain self-identical. Now whenever this reasoning [λόγος] – which is equally true whether it takes place concerning what is different or what is self-identical, and is carried on without speech or sound in the self-moving soul by this soul itself – is about what is perceptible to the senses, and the circle of the other, moving rightly, sends its message through the entire soul, then opinions and beliefs arise that are reliable and true. But whenever it is about that which is intelligible [τὸ λογιστικόν], and the circle of the self-identical, running smoothly, makes this known to it, the necessary outcome is rational thought and science [ἐπιστήμη]"[1]

---

1 *Timaeus*, 36 E, 37 A-C: καὶ τὸ μὲν δὴ σῶμα ὁρατὸν οὐρανοῦ γέγονεν, αὐτὴ δὲ ἀόρατος μέν, λογισμοῦ δὲ μετέχουσα καὶ ἁρμονίας ψυχή, τῶν νοητῶν ἀεί τε ὄντων ὑπὸ τοῦ ἀρίστου ἀρίστη γενομένη τῶν γεννηθέντων. ἅτε οὖν ἐκ τῆς ταὐτοῦ καὶ τῆς θατέρου φύσεως ἔκ τε οὐσίας, τριῶν τούτων συγκραθεῖσα μοιρῶν, καὶ ἀνὰ λόγον μερισθεῖσα καὶ ξυνδεθεῖσα αὐτή τε ἀνακυκλουμένη πρὸς αὑτήν, ὅταν οὐσίαν σκεδαστὴν ἔχοντός τινος ἐφάπτηται καὶ ὅταν ἀμέριστον, λέγει κινουμένη διὰ πάσης ἑαυτῆς, ὅτῳ τ᾽ ἄν τι ταὐτὸν ᾖ καὶ ὅτου ἂν ἕτερον, πρὸς ὅτι τε μάλιστα καὶ ὅπη καὶ ὅπως καὶ ὁπότε ξυμβαίνει κατὰ τὰ γιγνόμενά τε πρὸς ἕκαστον ἕκαστα εἶναι καὶ πάσχειν καὶ πρὸς τὰ κατὰ ταὐτὰ ἔχοντα ἀεί. λόγος δὲ ὁ κατὰ ταὐτὸν ἀληθὴς γιγνόμενος περί τε θάτερον ὂν καὶ περὶ τὸ ταὐτόν, ἐν τῷ κινουμένῳ ὑφ᾽ αὑτοῦ φερόμενος ἄνευ φθόγγου καὶ ἠχῆς, ὅταν μὲν περὶ τὸ

h. Timaeus 37 A-B *Can Only Be Understood in Terms of the Old Platonic Problem of* Methexis

In my opinion, we cannot at all come to grips with this obscure passage in terms of the essentially un-Platonic maxim that like is known by like. For this we must turn instead to the problem that occupied Plato in his early thought, that of *methexis*. We have seen Plato wrestling with this problem ever since the first stage of development of his theory of ideas. The soul participates in two worlds, the eidetic world and the sensible world; but it does not itself belong to either of these. The soul's cognitive activity presupposes this *methexis* in that it can obtain no knowledge of a world in which it does not participate. It participates in both the divine *nous* and the world harmony. But for Plato *methexis* never means that that which participates is identical, either wholly or in part, with that in which it participates. The *methexis* of sensible objects in the *eidē* after which they are named can never mean therefore that they are like in kind to the *eidē*. Likewise, the *methexis* of the soul in the *eidē*, on the one hand, and in the world perceptible to the senses, on the other hand, can never mean that it belongs to both worlds. This would of necessity have been the case, however, if Plato had accepted the principle of the knowledge of like by like.

The self-identical and the other are represented in the soul by certain circular motions which are not corporeal, but rather symbolize cognitive activity. They are typical movements of the soul which cause the harmonic motions of the corporeal, fixed starry heavens and the planets, and they serve as the "psychic" prototype of the latter.

Plato portrays the soul as being in "sympathetic contact" with the eidetic and the visible worlds. In the psychic circuit of the self-identical (this apparently is the theoretical thought movement of dialectic), which corresponds to the circular motion of the fixed starry heavens, it has contact with the eternal, unchangeable and unoriginated world of the *eidē*. In the circuit of the other, which corresponds to the seven planetary orbits, it has contact with the visible world of change.

i. *How Aristotle and the Prevailing View Which Followed Him Came to the Wrong Interpretation of Plato's Conception*

It is of course obvious how, following Aristotle's example, the maxim that the subject and the object (*Gegenstand*) of knowledge are identical came to be read into Plato's understanding of how the soul is con-

---

αἰσθητὸν γίγνηται καὶ ὁ τοῦ θατέρου κύκλος ὀρθὸς ὢν εἰς πᾶσαν αὐτοῦ τὴν ψυχὴν διαγγείλῃ, δόξαι καὶ πίστεις γίγνονται βέβαιοι καὶ ἀληθεῖς· ὅταν δὲ αὖ περὶ τὸ λογιστικὸν ᾖ καὶ ὁ τοῦ ταὐτοῦ κύκλος εὔτροχος ὢν αὐτὰ μηνύσῃ, νοῦς ἐπιστήμη τε ἐξ ἀνάγκης ἀποτελεῖται. (Translation in text.)

structed. The primary elements from which the soul was mixed by the demiurge are indeed members of both the eidetic and the visible worlds. However, these elements belong to two totally different worlds that are separated from each other by a *chōrismos*, and the result of their primary mixture is the origin of intermediate kinds of *ousia*, the self-identical, and the other. This by itself reveals that Plato actually is not working within the conceptual framework of the traditional maxim to which I referred above. Already in the *Parmenides* he had implicitly brought out into the open the destructive consequences of this view for the theory of the *eidē*. If like could be known only by like, then for mankind the *eidē* would be unknowable in principle, and then, moreover, the divine *idea* of the good and the beautiful could not be active in the visible cosmos.

It is precisely the theory of mixture that Plato uses in the *Timaeus* in order to make clear how the soul can obtain knowledge of both the visible-corporeal and the eidetic realms, even though it is fundamentally unlike either of them. Plato's conception, as it is expounded in the passage cited above from the *Timaeus*, holds in essence that such knowledge is possible only through the *sympathetic contact* that the soul has in its intermediate sphere with the world of the *eidē* and with the visible, corporeal world. This correspondence is based upon the principle of harmony, which comes to expression within the three spheres in numerical relationships that are peculiar to each.

The soul is able to grasp the indivisible oneness of the *eidē* only in "psychical" synopsis, that is, in the intuitive, intelligible contemplation of *nous*, which itself corresponds to the idea-number one. In *epistēmē* or dialectical logic, however, it has to divide these *eidē* logically and grasp them in eidetic relations, even though by their nature they are indivisible and absolute. The visible multiplicity of corporeal objects can be apprehended by the soul only in the conjunction of logical concept and *aisthēsis* (sense perception),[1] as this relates the mathematical relationships of number to *hulē*, the material of the sensible cosmos. This conjunction of *aisthēsis* and logical concept gives rise in the world-soul to *alētheis doxai* and *pisteis*, true opinions and beliefs.

j. The Homoiōsis *of the Object of Knowledge to the Knowing Soul*

Plato holds, however, that throughout this entire cognitive activity the thinking soul remains in the *Gegenstand* relation to the object of know-

---

1   In Plato's description, the world-soul has no sensory organs, since there is no world external to it that would have to be taken in by means of sense impressions. This soul also is not pure *nous*, however. Since it is united with a visible body, it has internal affective motions (emotions) which grant it internal perception (*aisthēsis*) Cf. Cornford, *op.cit.*, p. 96, where he refers to the *Theaetetus*, 156 B.

ledge. Nevertheless, the soul makes this object in a certain sense like unto the object by taking it into its own intermediate sphere. This is the theory of ὁμοίωσις (*homoīosis*) or "making like," which Aristotle will later develop in his own way in his theory of knowledge. In Plato this theory comes out most clearly in the dialectical logic or *epistēmē*. Here, the *eidē*, which in themselves (i.e., in their absolute nature) are inaccessible to the logical concept, are nevertheless adapted to the latter, by being divided asunder in accordance with the *diairetic* method and by being gathered back into unity in a dialectical *idea*.

In another context I shall demonstrate that this theory of *homoīosis* could not really solve the problem of the *Gegenstand* (object of theoretical thought). Here my only concern has been to shed light upon its fundamental difference from the uncritical epistemological standpoint of earlier Greek metaphysics and nature philosophy.

The fact that our understanding of the connection which Plato draws between the structure of the rational world-soul and its knowledge of the two worlds must indeed be correct is, in my view, convincingly demonstrated by the following observation. Plato conceives the world-soul's entire cognitive activity as the *incorporeal circular motions* of the self-identical and the other, respectively, and these motions proceed in time. The *eidē*, on the other hand, are motionless and *eternal*, while sensible objects, on their part, are *corporeal*.

The elements from which the structure of the world-soul is built have in fact been *transformed* by the divine act of mixture, and they therefore are no longer actually existent in the world-soul as such. In its *ousia* or form of being as well, the soul differs in principle from the *eidos*, on the one hand, and from corporeal objects, on the other. As we have seen, the conception introduced in the *Parmenides* and the *Sophist* of the *eidē* as active soul-forces had already been abandoned in the *Philebus*. Moreover, the conception of the soul as an unmoving and unoriginated *ousia*, which was advanced in the *Phaedo*, was discarded once and for all when in the *Philebus* Plato came to the fundamental recognition that the soul is a mixed product of becoming.

k. Time as a Circle in the Timaeus. The Conception of Time in the Timaeus and the Parmenides

The view of time that Plato developed in the *Timaeus* cancelled out all previous attempts to obscure in one sense or another the fundamental difference between the eidetic world and the rational soul. One can easily ascertain that there is a marked difference between this view of time and the one that had previously been worked out in the *Parmenides*.

Timaeus continues his narrative by relating that "when the father who had brought it [the universe] into being saw how it was in motion and alive, having become an *agalma* [sacred dwelling] for the everlasting [celestial] gods, he rejoiced and in his gladness took thought to make it even more like its model. Just as that model, then, is the living being that has *eternal* being, he sought also in this respect to make this universe as much as possible like it. Now the nature of this model was eternal, and to attach this character in its perfection to the thing brought into being was not possible. But he took thought to make, as it were, a moving likeness of eternity, and at the same time that he set in order the universe, he made of eternity, which abides in unity, an everlasting likeness moving according to [the measure of] number, namely, that which we have given the name *time.*"[1]

Time, according to Plato, is thus a product of the form-power of the divine *nous*. It has come into being *together with* the universe as an everlasting, ensouled, corporeal being. This means that the universe has always been in time and will always remain in time, without beginning or end.[2] Moreover, the motion of time is spherical.[3] This is the most perfect formal movement, which embraces both the motion of the world-soul and that of the world-body. According to Plato, therefore, the world-soul, too (and *a fortiori* the human soul), is also contained in time, the reason being that it is a product of becoming.

It is characteristic of the Greek view that it conceives time as a circle and not, like Newton, as a continuum that moves in a straight line. In the fourth book of his *Physics*, Aristotle mentions that this was the prevailing opinion. He calls it a "common saying" that human affairs form a cycle and that there is a cycle in all other things which have a natural movement

---

1 *Timaeus*, 37 C-D: ὡς δὲ κινηθὲν αὐτὸ καὶ ζῶν ἐνόησε τῶν ἀϊδίων θεῶν γεγονός ἄγαλμα ὁ γεννήσας πατήρ, ἠγάσθη τε καὶ εὐφρανθεὶς ἔτι δὴ μᾶλλον ὅμοιον πρὸς τὸ παράδειγμα ἐπενόησεν ἀπεργάσασθαι. καθάπερ οὖν αὐτὸ τυγχάνει ζῷον ἀΐδιον ὄν, καὶ τόδε τὸ πᾶν οὕτως εἰς δύναμιν ἐπεχείρησε τοιοῦτον ἀποτελεῖν. ἡ μὲν οὖν τοῦ ζῴου φύσις ἐτύγχανεν οὖσα αἰώνιος. καὶ τοῦτο μὲν δὴ τῷ γεννητῷ παντελῶς προσάπτειν οὐκ ἦν δυνατόν, εἰκὼ δ᾽ ἐπενόει κινητόν τινα αἰῶνος ποιῆσαι, καὶ διακοσμῶν ἅμα οὐρανὸν ποιεῖ μένοντος αἰῶνος ἐν ἑνὶ κατ᾽ ἀριθμὸν ἰοῦσαν αἰώνιον εἰκόνα, τοῦτον, ὃν δὴ χρόνον ὠνομάκαμεν. (Translation in text.) In my translation of the difficult passage τῶν ἀϊδίων θεῶν γεγονὸς ἄγαλμα, I have followed Cornford.

2 *Ibid.*, 38 B-C: τὸ μὲν γὰρ δὴ παράδειγμα πάντα αἰῶνά ἐστιν ὄν· ὁ δ᾽ αὖ διὰ τέλους τὸν ἅπαντα χρόνον γεγονώς τε καὶ ὢν καὶ ἐσόμενος. ("For the model *is* through all eternity. But it [the universe] has come into being, and is, and will be perpetually, through all time.") *Ibid.*, 38 B: χρόνος δ᾽ οὖν μετ᾽ οὐρανοῦ γέγονεν ἵνα ἅμα γεννηθέντες ἅμα καὶ λυθῶσιν, ἄν ποτε λύσις τις αὐτῶν γίγνηται. ("Time therefore came into being with the universe, in order that, as they came into being together, they may also come to an end together, if ever their dissolution should come about.")

3 *Editor's note – RK*: Given the spherical nature of the invisible body of the universe, all kinds of circular motion are possible.

and which come into existence and then pass away. "This is," he says, "because all these things are distinguished by time and have their beginning and end, as it were, in a kind of circle; for even time itself is thought to be a kind of circle."[1]

Cornford brings this notion of time as a circle into connection with life, which moves in the cycle of time as it comes into being and passes away. What we have here then is the ancient notion of the wheel of birth, growth, maturation, decay, death, and rebirth. This indeed must be the *origin* of the conception in question. But the *Timaeus* takes this circular conception of time, which stands in such flagrant contrast to the Christian and the modern, humanistic conceptions, and orients it in Pythagorean fashion to the form principle.[2] Here it no longer takes its bearings primarily from the matter principle with its unpredictable *Ananke*, as did the old nature philosophy and apparently still the exposition in the *Parmenides* which we discussed earlier. For in the *Timaeus* the circular movement of time has its prototype in the circuit of the rational world-soul, and the construction of this soul, like that of time itself, is attributed to the divine *nous* as the origin of all form. If then the soul is the principle of life, this means that Plato no longer regards the stream of life as primarily a work of unpredictable *Ananke*. Rather, it is the work of rational form-giving. We shall see, however, that in the case of mortal beings *Ananke* is assigned an antagonistic role in the circle.

In the above development we find the reason why the Augustinian-Platonic wing of Scholasticism approached time primarily in terms of the rational soul. At the appropriate place, we shall observe how this conception also clearly influenced Thomas's view of time. Nevertheless, it was also Augustine who was the first to break in principle with the paganistic conception of the Greeks that time is a circle.

We should note, however, that for Plato time only comes into complete existence through the periodic revolutions of the sun, moon, and "five other planets" within the universe. As Timaeus explicitly remarks, these were formed by the divine Artificer "in order to define and preserve the numbers of time."[3]

According to Plato, there was a special purpose to this in that the human

---

1 Aristotle, *Physics*, IV, 223 b.

2 See above p. 75.

3 *Timaeus*, 38 C: ἐξ οὖν λόγου καὶ διανοίας θεοῦ τοιαύτης πρὸς χρόνου γένεσιν, ἵνα γεννηθῇ χρόνος, ἥλιος καὶ σελήνη καὶ πέντε ἄλλα ἄστρα ἐπίκλην ἔχοντα πλανητὰ εἰς διορισμὸν καὶ φυλακὴν ἀριθμῶν χρόνου γέγονε. ("By virtue, then, of this plan and this intent of God for the birth of time, in order that time might be brought into existence, sun, moon, and the five other stars, called planets, came into being to delimit and preserve the numbers of time.")

being, by observing the regular, periodic revolutions of these celestial bodies, would discover number and be spurred on to the study of all nature and to philosophy.[1]

The actual objective measure of time is thus oriented to the corporeal motions of the "celestial gods"; but this does not erase the fact that the real foundation and unity of the existence of time lies only in the rational soul of the universe, of the celestial gods, and of the human being. For the corporeal formal movement has its cause in the cyclical motion of the soul within the two spheres of the self-identical (identity) and the other (difference).

l. The Anima Rationalis *as the Immortal Part of the Human Soul Is Not Pure* Nous, *but Mixed in Nature*

After treating the formation of the immortal celestial gods as ensouled bodies (the fixed stars, the planets, and the earth), the discussion turns to the formation of the immortal part of the human soul. We have already observed that the divine demiurge himself brings only the immortal part into existence. He leaves it to the celestial gods "to mingle the immortal with the mortal and to make from this living beings [humans], bringing them to birth, feeding them, and causing them to grow."[2] It is noteworthy, however, that Plato describes this immortal part of the human soul in the *Timaeus* as an "individual soul in itself," produced by the division of a whole which, with a slight reservation, is compounded in the same manner as the divine world-soul.[3]

This means that Plato no longer conceives the immortal part of the soul as a pure thinking soul or *nous*, as he did in the *Phaedo* and the *Republic*. Rather, it is also possessed of internal emotive functions, which enable it

---

1 *Timaeus*, 47 A-B: ὄψις δὴ κατὰ τὸν ἐμὸν λόγον αἰτία τῆς μεγίστης ὠφελείας γέγονεν ἡμῖν, ὅτι τῶν νῦν λόγων περὶ τοῦ παντὸς λεγομένων οὐδεὶς ἄν ποτε ἐρρήθη μήτε ἄστρα μήτε ἥλιον μήτε οὐρανὸν ἰδόντων. νῦν δ' ἡμέρα τε καὶ νὺξ ὀφθεῖσαι μῆνές τε καὶ ἐνιαυτῶν περίοδοι μεμηχάνηνται μὲν ἀριθμόν, χρόνου δὲ ἔννοιαν περί τε τῆς τοῦ παντὸς φύσεως ζήτησιν ἔδοσαν, ἐξ ὧν ἐπορισάμεθα φιλοσοφίας γένος, οὗ μεῖζον ἀγαθὸν οὔτ' ἦλθεν οὔτε ἥξει ποτὲ τῷ θνητῷ γένει δωρηθὲν ἐκ θεῶν. ("Sight, then, in my judgment has become the cause of the greatest benefit to us, since not a word of our present discourse on the universe could have ever been uttered had we never beheld the stars, the sun, and the sky. But now the sight of day and night, of months and the revolution of years, has caused the discovery of number and bestowed the knowledge of time and the study of all nature; whence we have procured for ourselves entrance to philosophy, than which no greater good ever has come or will come to the race of mortals from the gods.")

2 *Timaeus*, 41 D.

3 *Ibid*. This passage describes the blending of the part of the soul that is fashioned by the demiurge himself, and is thus immortal: Ταῦτ' εἶπε καὶ πάλιν ἐπὶ τὸν πρότερον

298

to perceive changeable things. That is, it has *aisthēsis*, in the sense of internal sensation unmediated by sense organs. As Plato conceives it, a pure *nous* would have nothing more than the sphere of motion of the self-identical. We have seen, however, that the immortal soul also has a circuit of the other. On this account, it not only has the ability to gain dialectical knowledge (*epistēmē*) of the eternal ontic forms, but it also has the ability to form for itself opinions (*doxai*) and beliefs (*pisteis*) concerning the changeable, visible world and the origin of the cosmos and the celestial gods. *Timaeus* 43 D reveals that the *anima rationalis*, the immortal part of the soul, is divided into mathematical proportions having the same *harmonia* as the rational world-soul, and that it too is allotted the motions of the self-identical and the other.

m. The Laws of Heimarmenē in the Combination of the Immortal with the Mortal

As Timaeus describes the situation, however, it appears that the human immortal souls are mixed from elements that are less pure than those of the world-soul. That is to say, they have a lower degree of perfection, since they are capable of acting wrongly by their own will. The human immortal souls are equal in number to the stars, and this number is finite. Each soul is placed in a particular star as in a chariot – an obvious allusion to the astral journey of the soul in the *Phaedrus* – and the demiurge shows it the nature of the universe and declares to it the laws of destiny (νόμους τοὺς εἱμαρμένους), "in order that he might bear no guilt for the future wickedness of any of them."[1]

κρατῆρα, ἐν ᾧ τὴν τοῦ παντὸς ψυχὴν κεραννὺς ἔμισγε, τὰ τῶν πρόσθεν ὑπόλοιπα κατεχεῖτο μίσγων τρόπον μέν τινα τὸν αὐτόν, ἀκήρατα δ' οὐκέτι κατὰ ταὐτὰ ὡσαύτως, ἀλλὰ δεύτερα καὶ τρίτα. ("Thus he spoke, and into the former mixing bowl, in which he had blended and compounded the soul of the universe, he once more poured what was left over from before, blending this in much the same way, only the ingredients were no longer in like manner pure to the same degree, but only to the second or third.") In Plato's view, the human soul is thus of a lower order than the world-soul, since in contrast to the latter it is capable of going wrong. The words ἀλλὰ δεύτερα καὶ τρίτα pertain to the distinction between the male and the female soul. The next sentence then reads: ξυστήσας δὲ τὸ πᾶν διεῖλε ψυχὰς ἰσαρίθμους τοῖς ἄστροις ἔμεινέ θ᾿ἑκάστην πρὸς ἕκαστον ... ("And when he had compounded the whole, he divided it into souls, equal in number to the stars, and assigned to each a separate star.")

1 *Ibid.*, 41 E: καὶ ἐμβιβάσας ὡς εἰς ὄχημα τὴν τοῦ παντὸς φύσιν ἔδειξε νόμους τε τοὺς εἱμαρμένους εἶπεν αὐταῖς. ("And mounting them there as in a chariot, he showed them the nature of the universe and declared to them the laws of destiny.") 42 D: ἵνα τῆς ἔπειτα εἴη κακίας ἑκάστων ἀναίτιος ("in order that he would be guiltless of the wickedness of each of them, which might arise later.")

According to these laws, the souls would undergo a first incarnation that would be the same for all, so that no one of them would initially be found in a less favorable condition than the others. After this, they would be sown in the planets and the earth as "instruments of time" and "born as the most god-fearing of living beings."[1]

> In accordance with *Anankē* they must be implanted in bodies, upon which material forces act from without, and for this reason will necessarily be born in them: first sensory perception, the same for all, which arises from violent impressions; secondly, sensual desires blended from pleasure and pain; and in addition, fear and anger and all feelings that accompany these and all that are of a contrary nature. And if they should master these emotions, they would live righteously, but if they should be mastered by them, unrighteously.[2]

If a soul should live well during its allotted time, it would return to the abode of its designated star and there lead a happy life corresponding to its previous existence. Failing in this, however, it would be given the body of a woman at its second incarnation; and if in this condition it still did not renounce its wickedness, then in accordance with the worsening of its character, it would be incarnated in a beast of like nature. And the "wheel of birth and rebirth" would no sooner come to rest for it "until the motion of the self-identical, ruling within it, should draw into its circular course the throng of chaotic, turbulent and irrational motions, which only has arisen in it later from fire and water and air and earth, and mastering these by reason, it should return again to the form [*eidos*] of its first and best condition."[3]

---

1   *Ibid.*, 41 E: ὅτι γένεσις πρώτη μὲν ἔσοιτο τεταγμένη μία πᾶσιν, ἵνα μή τις ἐλαττοῖτο ὑπ᾽ αὐτοῦ, δέοι δὲ σπαρείσας αὐτὰς εἰς τὰ προσήκοντα ἑκάστοις ἕκαστα ὄργανα χρόνων φῦναι ζῴων τὸ θεοσεβέστατον ... (Translation in text.)

2   *Ibid.*, 42 A: ὁπότε δὴ σώμασιν ἐμφυτευθεῖεν ἐξ ἀνάγκης, καὶ τὸ μὲν προσίοι, τὸ δ᾽ ἀπίοι τοῦ σώματος αὐτῶν, πρῶτον μὲν αἴσθησιν ἀναγκαῖον εἴη μίαν πᾶσιν ἐκ βιαίων παθημάτων ξύμφυτον γίγνεσθαι, δεύτερον δὲ ἡδονῇ καὶ λύπῃ μεμιγμένον ἔρωτα, πρὸς δὲ τούτοις φόβον καὶ θυμὸν ὅσα τε ἑπόμενα αὐτοῖς καὶ ὁπόσα ἐναντίως πέφυκε διεστηκότα· ὧν εἰ μὲν κρατήσοιεν, δίκῃ βιώσοιντο, κρατηθέντες δὲ ἀδικίᾳ. (Translation in text.)

3   *Timaeus*, 41 E, 42 A-D; note 42 C-D: ἀλλάττων τε οὐ πρότερον πόνων λήξοι, πρὶν τῇ ταὐτοῦ καὶ ὁμοίου περιόδῳ τῇ ἐν αὐτῷ ξυνεπισπόμενος τὸν πολὺν ὄχλον καὶ ὕστερον προσφύντα ἐκ πυρὸς καὶ ὕδατος καὶ ἀέρος καὶ γῆς, θορυβώδη καὶ ἄλογον ὄντα, λόγῳ κρατήσας εἰς τὸ τῆς πρώτης καὶ ἀρίστης ἀφίκοιτο εἶδος ἕξεως. (Translation in text.)

n. Heimarmenē *and* Anankē

The mention of laws of *Heimarmenē* in this context makes it evident that the latter is not identical with *Anankē* in its original sense as the ground-motive of the religion of nature. Plato himself makes a clear distinction between them, since he expressly declares in *Timaeus*, 46 E that *Anankē* is completely destitute of reason and produces its effects according to *tuchē* and without order.

Heimarmenē is identical with the *Moira* of the religion of culture. As we have already seen, this *Moira* evinces a partial rationalization of the ancient *Anankē* for the purpose of achieving a synthesis between the motives of form and matter. Plato makes clear that the laws of *Heimarmenē* are also laws for conjoining the rational soul, which has its origin in the heavens, with the impure, earthly material body, which as such is subject to *Anankē*. Thus here again we find ourselves in the midst of the mythological, Pythagorean-Orphic notions of the transmigration of the soul that we already encountered in earlier dialogues, particularly in the *Phaedrus*.

5. The Polar Dualism between the Form-Power of the Divine *Nous* and the *Anankē* of the Matter Principle in the *Timaeus'* Conception of the Soul

One cannot fail to notice that it is just here, where the discussion turns to the addition of the mortal parts to the *anima rationalis*, that *Anankē* begins to make its entry as an irrational, unpredictable efficient cause. It is also here that the great conflict with the form-motive of the culture religion, which was already announced at the beginning of Timaeus' exposition, first makes its presence felt.

There was no question of such a conflict between the motives of form and matter so long as the dialogue dealt with those immortal things that were the handiwork of the divine demiurge alone. There the principle of harmony had made it possible for the rational form principle to gain complete control of the matter principle. To be sure, it is no doubt the Orphic religious motive that continues to work in this antithesis. The original dwelling place of the soul lies in the heavens (*ouranos*) with its harmony of the spheres. The dark, earthly sphere is the place where the soul has fallen and been subjected to *Anankē* in the cycle of its incarnations. But the Orphic-Pythagorean motives have been wholly adapted here to the rational form motive of the religion of culture. Here again, the Platonic theory of ideas, with the *idea tou agathou* as its idea of origin, has purified the uranic motives from their naturalistic, pantheistic tendencies. This part of the dialogue, therefore, already anticipates the second part, where the autonomous operation of the πλανωμένη αἰτία, i.e., the errant, incalculable causality of *Anankē*, will be set forth.

a. The Condition of the Soul at the Birth of Human Beings

An extremely graphic preliminary illustration of the operation of this "errant cause" follows immediately in Timaeus' portrayal of the condiion in which the human soul finds itself directly after its first incarnation in a material body. The celestial gods, having received from the hands of the demiurge "the immortal principle of a mortal being," mix at their divine Father's command portions of fire and earth, water and air "which they have borrowed from the universe, on condition that these again should be repaid" (a clear allusion to the notion of *dikē* in Ionian nature philosophy).[1] The undoubtedly mythological presentation goes on to tell how they fastened these elements together, "not with the indissoluble bonds by which they were themselves held together, but fastened them with numerous pegs, too small to be seen, thus making each body a unity of all the portions; and they tied the circuits of the immortal soul to the body with its ebb and flow."[2]

In other words, this means that the earthly body lacks the *harmonia* of the world-body and the celestial bodies. It is subjected to the *Anankē* of the matter principle and is therefore taken up into the current of the constant flux of all earthly, visible things. At the birth of man, the immortal soul, being tied to a "mighty river," is in its circular motions unable to control the body. These circuits are rather subjected to violent influences, so that the whole living being is set moving, and, led by unpredictable chance (*tuchē*), advances without order or reason in all the six directions of motion. "For it went forward and backward, and again to right and left, up and down, and every which way in all the six directions. For great as is the flood and ebb of the tide which brings nourishment, still greater tumult is nevertheless caused by the assaults of the sense qualities [παθήματα] of things, when someone's body collides with alien fire from without, or with the solidity of earth and softly gliding waters, or is seized by the tempest of air-borne winds, and when the motions caused by all this attack the soul by way of the body (for this reason these motions were later called 'sense impressions,' a name they still bear)."[3]

---

1 *Ibid.*, 42 E: πυρὸς καὶ γῆς ὕδατός τε καὶ ἀέρος ἀπὸ τοῦ κόσμου δανειζόμενοι μόρια ὡς ἀποδοθησόμενα πάλιν. (Translation in text.)

2 *Ibid.*, 43 A: εἰς ταὐτὸν τὰ λαμβανόμενα ξυνεκόλλων οὐ τοῖς ἀλύτοις, οἷς αὐτοὶ ξυνείχοντο, δεσμοῖς, ἀλλὰ διὰ σμικρότητα ἀοράτοις πυκνοῖς γόμφοις ξυντήκοντες, ἓν ἐξ ἁπάντων ἀπεργαζόμενοι σῶμα ἕκαστον, τὰς τῆς ἀθανάτου ψυχῆς περιόδους ἐνέδουν εἰς ἐπίρρυτον σῶμα καὶ ἀπόρρυτον. (Translation in text.)

3 *Ibid.*, 43 A-C: βίᾳ δ' ἐφέροντο [viz., τῆς ἀθανάτου ψυχῆς περίοδοι] καὶ ἔφερον ὥστε τὸ μὲν ὅλον κινεῖσθαι ζῷον, ἀτάκτως μὴν ὅπη τύχοι προϊέναι καὶ ἀλόγως, τὰς ἓξ ἁπάσας κινήσεις ἔχον· εἴς τε γὰρ τὸ πρόσθε καὶ ὄπισθεν καὶ πάλιν εἰς δεξιὰ καὶ ἀριστερὰ κάτω τε καὶ ἄνω καὶ πάντη κατὰ τοὺς ἓξ τόπους πλανώμενα προήειν. πολλοῦ γὰρ ὄντος τοῦ κατακλύζοντος καὶ ἀπορρέοντος κύματος, ὃ τὴν τροφὴν παρεῖχεν, ἔτι μείζω θόρυβον ἀπειργάζετο τὰ τῶν προσπιπτόντων παθήματα ἑκάστοις, ὅτε πυρὶ προσκρούσειε τὸ σῶμά τινος ἔξωθεν ἀλλοτρίῳ περιτυχὸν ἢ καὶ στερεῷ γῆς ὑγροῖς τε ὀλισθήμασιν ὑδάτων, εἴτε ζάλη πνευμάτων ὑπ' ἀέρος φερομένη καταληφθείη, καὶ ὑπὸ πάντων τούτων διὰ τοῦ σώματος αἱ

Timaeus thus shows in his archaic and graphic manner of presentation how the circular motions of the soul are deformed and driven from their courses by the violent action of the constantly advancing and receding flood of nourishment and sense impressions. The circle of the self-identical is then completely hampered in its sovereignty over the circuit of the other, while the circuit of the other is disturbed. In other words, at the birth of a human being the rational activity of the soul is brought to a complete standstill. To be sure, the harmony of the immortal, rational soul cannot be destroyed, since it is the imperishable work of the divine architect. Nevertheless, both the intervals in the two *tetractys* and the circles of motion are deformed and disturbed in every way possible, and their movements thus become irregular and without order. ⌐ "It was as if a man stood on his head, resting it on the earth, and thrust his feet aloft by holding them against something; in such a case right and left, both of the man and of the spectators, appear reversed to the other party. The same and similar effects manifest themselves with great intensity in the revolutions of the soul; and when they come in contact with something in the outside world that falls under the genus of the self-identical (identical) or of the other (the different), they call it the same as a given thing and different from it, contrary to the truth".[2]

In consequence of all these external influences, the soul is at first, when it is confined in a mortal body, born in an irrational condition [*ἄνους*]. "But when the current of growth and nourishment flows in less strongly, and the motions of the soul, taking advantage of the ensuing claim, can go their own way and take an even steadier course as time passes, then the revolutions are corrected to the form that belongs to the several circles in their natural motion."[3] "And now, if the right [intellectual] nourishment contributes toward education" – it appears from 47 C that this refers to the

---

κινήσεις ἐπὶ τὴν ψυχὴν φερόμεναι προσπίπτοιεν· αἳ δὴ καὶ ἔπειτα διὰ ταῦτα ἐκλήθητάν τε καὶ νῦν ἔτι αἰσθήσεις ξυνάπασαι κέκληνται. (Translation in text.)

1 *Ibid.*, 43 d: ὥστε τὰς τοῦ διπλασίου καὶ τριπλασίου τρεῖς ἑκατέρας ἀποστάσεις καὶ τὰς τῶν ἡμιολίων καὶ ἐπιτρίτων καὶ ἐπογδόων μεσότητας, καὶ ξυνδέσεις, ἐπειδὴ παντελῶς λυταὶ οὐκ ἦσαν πλὴν ὑπὸ τοῦ ξυνδήσαντος, πάσας μὲν στρέψαι στροφάς, πάσας δὲ κλάσεις καὶ διαφθορὰς τῶν κύκλων ἐμποιεῖν ("Accordingly, the intervals of the double and triple, three of each sort, and also the intermediate tones and connecting links of the ratios 3/2 and 4/3 and 9/8 – since they could not be dissolved completely except by him who bound them together – were twisted by them [i.e., the sense impressions] in every way, and all possible fractures and deformations of the circular motions were caused.")

2 *Ibid.*, 43 E-44 A: οἷον ὅταν τις ὕπτιος ἐρείσας τὴν κεφαλὴν μὲν ἐπὶ γῆς, τοὺς δὲ πόδας ἄνω προσβαλὼν ἔχῃ πρός τινι, τότε ἐν τούτῳ τῷ πάθει τοῦ τε πάσχοντος καὶ τῶν ὁρώντων τά τε δεξιὰ ἀριστερὰ καὶ τὰ ἀρίστερα δεξιὰ ἑκατέροις τὰ ἑκατέρων φαντάζεται. ταὐτὸν δὴ τοῦτο καὶ τοιαῦτα ἕτερα αἱ περιφοραὶ πάσχουσαι σφόδρως, ὅταν τέ τῳ τῶν ἔξωθεν τοῦ ταὐτοῦ γένους ἢ τοῦ θατέρου περιτύχωσι, τότε ταὐτόν τῳ καὶ θάτερόν του τἀναντία τῶν ἀληθῶν προσαγορεύσουσι ψευδεῖς καὶ ἀνόητοι γεγόνασιν. (Translation in text.)

3 *Ibid.*, 44 B: ὅταν δὲ ... αἱ περίοδοι λαμβανόμεναι γαλήνης τὴν ἑαυτῶν ὁδὸν ἴωσι

observation of the undisturbed circuits in the heavens, which leads one to philosophy and teaches him to reduce to settled order the errant [πλανωμένας] motions in himself – "then he who receives this becomes an unblemished and perfectly healthy person, having escaped the greatest malady. But he who neglects this," as Timaeus states in terms borrowed from the mystery ritual, "after having limped down the path of life, goes back to Hades uninitiated and without understanding."[1]

The overall plan of the dialogue dictates that Plato interrupt his further account of the structure of the human soul – this will involve the two mortal parts and their connection with the material body – in order first to pursue what things in the genesis of the cosmos must be attributed to blind and incalculable *Anankē*. Before he does this, he gives a brief description of the structure which the celestial gods gave to the human body, which is possessed of sensory organs and of all the emotions that accompany sense perception. Although even at this point the working of *Anankē* cannot be ignored, the entire emphasis falls here upon the rational purpose which the gods have in view in their formative work.

Timaeus thus sets forth how the immortal part of the soul receives its seat in the head, which is fashioned by the celestial gods in imitation of the spherical shape of the world-body (the celestial vault).[2] Being the seat of the two circuits of the *anima rationalis*, the head is "the most divine part of the body and ruler of all the others." The gods then gave it the entire body, once they had assembled it, as a servant, a vehicle [ὄχημα] by which it could move in all directions.[3]

It is evident from 69 C that Plato conceives the material body likewise as a 'vehicle' in this sense for the immortal soul itself.[4] This notion would

---

καὶ καθιστῶνται μᾶλλον ἐπιόντος τοῦ χρόνου, τότε ἤδη πρὸς τὸ κατὰ φύσιν ἰόντων σχῆμα ἑκάστων τῶν κύκλων αἱ περιφοραὶ κατευθυνόμεναι (Translation in text.)

1 *Ibid.*, 44 B-C: ἂν μὲν οὖν δὴ καὶ ξυνεπιλαμβάνηταί τις ὀρθὴ τροφὴ παιδεύσεως, ὁλόκληρος ὑγιής τε παντελῶς τὴν μεγίστην ἀποφυγὼν νόσον γίγνεται· καταμελήσας δέ, χωλὴν τοῦ βίου διαπορευθεὶς ζωήν, ἀτελὴς καὶ ἀνόητος εἰς Ἅδου πάλιν ἔρχεται. (Translation in text.)

2 *Ibid.*, 44 D: Τὰς μὲν δὴ θείας περιόδους δύο οὔσας τὸ τοῦ παντὸς σχῆμα ἀπομιμησάμενοι περιφερὲς ὂν εἰς σφαιροειδὲς σῶμα ἐνέδησαν, τοῦτο, ὃ νῦν κεφαλὴν ἐπονομάζομεν, ὃ θειότατόν τέ ἐστι καὶ τῶν ἐν ἡμῖν πάντων δεσποτοῦν. ("Copying the round shape of the universe, they [i.e., the celestial gods] tied up the two divine circular motions in a spherical body – the head, as we now call it – which is the most divine and rules everything in us.")

3 *Ibid.*, 44 D: ᾧ καὶ πᾶν τὸ σῶμα παρέδοσαν ὑπερεσίαν αὐτῷ ξυναθροισαντες θεοί, κατανοήσαντες, ὅτι πασῶν ὅσαι κινήσεις ἔσοιντο μετέχοι. ("To this the gods gave the entire body, once they had assembled it, for its service, reflecting that it would take part in all the motions that were to be.") *Ibid.*, 44 E: ὄχημα αὐτῷ τοῦτο καὶ εὐπορίαν ἔδοσαν. ("They gave it the body as a vehicle and for ease of movement.")

4 *Ibid.*, 69 C: οἱ δὲ [viz., θεοὶ] μιμούμενοι, παραλαβόντες ἀρχὴν ψυχῆς ἀθάνατον,

later become common currency in Augustinian Scholasticism, where it will form one of the salient points of diference between the Aristotelian Scholastic conception of the relation between soul and body.

Timaeus then presents a brief account of the significance of the organs of sight and hearing. This account is given here because these sense organs above all reveal to mankind the harmany of the cosmos. Only after this comes Timaeus' great exposition concerning those things in the cosmos that are attributable to the blind working of *Ananke*. The further account of the mortal parts of the soul and their bodily organs does not follow until 69 D.

b. The Two Mortal Parts of the Soul and Their Seats in the Body

We shall now turn to this latter account first, in order to obtain a comprehensive overview of Plato's conception of the soul in this dialogue. The two mortal parts of the soul which, according to *Ananke*, must be added to the immortal part are those which we have already come to know in the *Phaedrus* and the *Republic*, namely, the θυμός (*thumos*) or θυμοειδές (*thumo-eides*), and the ἐπιθυμητικόν (*epithumetikon*) or appetitive part. We have learned that the former of these is that part of the soul which is supposed to enable the immortal, rational part to control the *epithumētikon*. It corresponds to the second class of Plato's ideal state, the military guardians, which is subordinate to the class of philosopher kings and is characterized by the virtue of bravery (ἀνδρεία, the element of force in government).

In their formation of the human body, the celestial gods see to it that the mortal parts of the soul are given a place in the body where they will not be able to pollute the divine, immortal part, which resides in the head, any more than its confinement in the material body necessitates in accordance with *Ananke*.[1] To this end they made the neck as a partition and boundary between the head and the breast. The *thumos*, being the higher of the two mortal parts of the soul, was given its seat in the heart, between the neck and the midriff, and thus closer to the head than the appetitive part. As Timaeus explains in accordance with the rational form motive, the purpose of this is that the *thumos* "might be able to listen to the reasoning of the *nous* and, in concert with this, forcibly restrain the power of the desires, whenever these do not willingly obey the command from the cita-

---

τὸ μετὰ τοῦτο θνητὸν σῶμα αὐτῇ περιετόρνευσαν ὄχημά τε πᾶν τὸ σῶμα ἔδοσαν. ("They [i.e., the celestial gods], imitating him [the demiurge], after they had received from him the immortal principle of the soul, clothed it with a mortal body and gave it the whole body as a vehicle.")

1 *Ibid.*, 69 D-E: καὶ διὰ ταῦτα δὴ σεβόμενοι μιαίνειν τὸ θεῖον, ὅτι μὴ πᾶσα ἦν ἀνάγκη, χωρὶς ἐκείνου κατοικίζουσιν εἰς ἄλλην τοῦ σώματος οἴκησιν τὸ θνητόν ("And now, since they were no doubt afraid to pollute the divine part by these [mortal parts], insofar as this was not altogether necessary [in accordance with *Ananke*], they housed the mortal apart from this in another place in the body.")

del" (i.e., the head as the seat of the *anima rationalis*).[1] According to Plato, the rational part of the soul, as the headquarters of sense perception, is the first part to become aware of wrong behavior in a particular region of the body. It thereupon sends a message to the part of the soul residing in the heart. This sets the blood boiling and, flowing out through all the veins, it passes on to every sentient part of the body the message from reason that they must obey the latter.[2]

The appetitive part of the soul, which is set on food and drink and everything else that is necessary for life, is assigned its seat in the belly, where the stomach is set up as a sort of manager for the body's sustenance. Timaeus graphically describes how the appetitive part is here "tethered like a wild animal, which, since it is firmly joined to us, must still be provided for if a mortal race is to be able to exist. In order that, always feeding at the manger and dwelling as far as possible from the deliberative part of the soul, it might cause the least possible tumult and clamor and allow the higher part to deliberate in peace concerning what is beneficial for the welfare of the whole – for these reasons they [i.e., the celestial gods] stationed it there."[3]

---

1 *Ibid.*, 70 A: ἵνα τοῦ λόγου κατήκοον ὂν κοινῇ μετ᾽ ἐκείνου βίᾳ τὸ τῶν ἐπιθυμιῶν κατέχοι γένος, ὁπότ᾽ ἐκ τῆς ἀκροπόλεως τῷ τ᾽ ἐπιτάγματι καὶ λόγῳ μηδαμῇ πείθεσθαι ἑκὸν ἐθέλοι. (Translation in text.)

2 *Ibid.*, 70 A-B: τὴν δὲ δὴ καρδίαν ἅμμα τῶν φλεβῶν καὶ πηγὴν τοῦ περιφερομένου κατὰ πάντα τὰ μέλη σφοδρῶς αἵματος εἰς τὴν δορυφορικὴν οἴκησιν κατέστησαν, ἵνα ὅτε ζέσειε τὸ τοῦ θυμοῦ μένος τοῦ λόγου παραγγείλαντος, ὥς τις ἄδικος περὶ αὐτὰ γίγνεται πρᾶξις ἔξωθεν ἢ καί τις ἀπὸ τῶν ἔνδοθεν ἐπιθυμιῶν, ὀξέως διὰ πάντων τῶν στενωπῶν πᾶν ὅσον αἰσθητικὸν ἐν τῷ σώματι τῶν τε παρακελεύσεων καὶ ἀπειλῶν αἰσθανόμενον γίγνοιτο ἐπήκοον καὶ ἕποιτο πάντη καὶ τὸ βέλτιστον οὕτως ἐν αὐτοῖς πᾶσιν ἡγεμονεῖν ἐῷ ("The heart, then, the knot of the veins and the fountain of the blood, which courses impetuously through all the members, they established as a guardhouse, in order that, when the *thumos* should boil with anger at a message from reason that something wrong is happening in the members, whether this comes from without or from the desires within, then every sentient member in the body might, through all the narrow channels, swiftly perceive the commands and threats and hearken completely, and thus suffer the best part to be leader among them all.")

3 *Ibid.*, 70 D-71 A: τὸ δὲ δὴ σίτων τε καὶ ποτῶν ἐπιθυμητικὸν τῆς ψυχῆς καὶ ὅσων ἔνδειαν διὰ τὴν τοῦ σώματος ἴσχει φύσιν, τοῦτο εἰς τὸ μεταξὺ τῶν τε φρενῶν καὶ τοῦ πρὸς τὸν ὀμφαλὸν ὅρου κατῴκισαν, οἷον φάτνην ἐν ἅπαντι τούτῳ τῷ τόπῳ τῇ τοῦ σώματος τροφῇ τεκτηνάμενοι· καὶ κατέδησαν δὴ τὸ τοιοῦτον ἐνταῦθα ὡς θρέμμα ἄγριον, τρέφειν δὲ ξυνημμένον ἀναγκαῖον, εἴπερ τι μέλλοι ποτὲ θνητὸν ἔσεσθαι γένος. ἵν᾽ οὖν ἀεὶ νεμόμενον πρὸς φάτνῃ καὶ ὅτι πορρωτάτω τοῦ βουλευομένου κατοικοῦν, θόρυβον καὶ βοὴν ὡς ἐλαχίστην παρέχον, τὸ κράτιστον καθ᾽ ἡσυχίαν περὶ τοῦ πᾶσι κοινῇ ξυμφέροντος ἐῷ βουλεύεσθαι, διὰ ταῦτα ἐνταῦθ᾽ ἔδοσαν αὐτῷ τὴν ταξιν. (Translation in text.)

c. *The Liver as the Seat of* μαντεία *(Divination).* Theoria's
Depreciation of Prophecy

In this connection, a special function is assigned to the liver. The appetitive part of the soul is unable to understand the reasoning of the rational part. Even if it should somehow become aware of this, it would not be in its nature to take heed, whereas by day and night it constantly lets itself be guided by *eidōla* (sensible images) and phantasms. In view of this, the liver was formed as a seat for the art of divination.

The intention here was that the influence emanating from the reason would make impressions of its thoughts upon this organ, which would receive them like a mirror and reflect back visible images. This influence strikes fear into the appetitive part, "when, making use of the liver's inherent bitterness, with threatening severity it suffuses this throughout the whole liver, causing bilious colors to appear in it, and by contracting this organ produces pain and loathing. On the other hand, when an inspiration from the mind evokes contrary images of gentleness, then making use of the sweetness that is likewise inherent in the liver, it puts the part of the soul that resides in the region of the liver into a gentle and joyful mood and makes it by night to pass its time sleeping in the tranquil exercise of divination by dreams, since it has no part in intelligence and rational understanding."[1] Timaeus argues that "we have good reason to believe that the art of divination is actually a divine gift to human unwisdom, since no one in his normal, rational consciousness [ἔννους] partakes of divine and true divination, but only when his power of understanding is chained in sleep or he is made delirious by disease or divine possession [ἐνθουσιασμός]."[2]

The high regard in which Plato continued to hold the art of divination [μαντεία] in the *Phaedrus*,[3] where he placed it in the same class with poetry, *erōs*, and philosophy itself as a 'form of divine madness,' has therefore declined sharply, although he still grants it a certain useful function in reason's mastery of sensual desire. Now Platonic *theōria* can only view the prophetic gift as an expression of sensuous fantasy that is tied to the matter principle. As such it belongs to the lowest part of the soul, and its only use is to curb sensual desires, which are altogether impervious to understanding and rational discourse.

In surveying the theory of the soul developed in the *Timaeus*, one is im-

---

1 *Ibid.*, 71 A ff. As I see it, the phrase τὴν περὶ τὸ ἧπαρ ψυχῆς μοῖραν lends no support to Galen's often cited assertion that Plato regarded the liver as the seat of the appetitive part of the soul. See Galen's commentary on the *Timaeus*, published by Schröder.
2 *Ibid.*, 71 E: ἱκανὸν δὲ σημεῖον, ὡς μαντικὴν ἀφροσύνη θεὸς ἀνθρωπίνη δέδωκεν· οὐδεὶς γὰρ ἔννους ἐφάπτεται μαντικῆς ἐνθέου καὶ ἀληθοῦς, ἀλλ' ἢ καθ' ὕπνον τὴν τῆς φρονήσεως πεδηθεὶς δύναμιν ἢ διὰ νόσον, ἢ διά τινα ἐνθουσιασμὸν παραλλάξας. (Translation in text.)
3 *Phaedrus*, 244 B.

mediately struck by its dual relation to the *Republic's* conception. In its trichotomistic construction it ties in with the latter; but at the same time it departs from it in principle by conceiving the immortal part of the soul as a composite or mixed structure. In the manner that it conceives the relation between the immortal form-soul and the earthly, material body, the *Timaeus'* theory of the soul also forms a distinct continuation of the Orphic-Pythagorean line. We have been able to trace this conception ever since the *Phaedo*. The three parts of the soul are not conjoined into a unity by the bond of a divine *harmonia*, for in terms of its *ousia* (ontic form) only the immortal part of the soul is a mathematical harmony. Its mixture with the mortal parts of the soul is conceived as a result of *Anankē*, which is inimical to the pure form principle and causes the pollution and defilement of the *anima rationalis*. And it is the incarnation of the immortal soul in an earthly body subject to the matter principle that makes this mixture necessary.

d. The Timaeus' *Theory of the Soul Is More Fruitful for Empirical Science Than the Thomistic-Aristotelian Theory*

In spite of his still primitive knowledge of the physical-chemical, anatomical, physiological, and psychological aspects of temporal human existence, Plato, in his trichotomistic understanding of the soul's construction, is nevertheless on the track of an important truth regarding the complicated structure of the human being's temporal form of existence. Only his lack of insight into the fundamental religious unity – the immortal soul in its scriptural sense – prevents him from giving a correct scientific interpretation of this state of affairs.

Plato's theory of the soul stands in contrast to the Scholastic, Thomistic conception, which I shall later discuss at length. On the latter view, the human soul, in the sense of *anima rationalis*, is held to be an immortal simple substance that, as the sole form of the material body, must also perform all the sentient-psychical and vegetative functions. If one compares these two theories, one cannot but recognize that the Platonic conception, notwithstanding its lack of strict metaphysical rigor, is beyond question more penetrating and scientifically fruitful. That is to say, Plato can do far more justice to the diverse structures of temporal human existence than the monistic theory of the soul of Thomistic Scholasticism can. Any notion, however, that the Platonic theory in the *Timaeus* is capable of being accommodated to the Christian conception of the soul, as Augustinian Scholasticism attempted to do, betrays a lack of insight into the indissoluble connection between this theory and the religious ground-motive of Greek thought.

e. The Timaeus' *Theory of the Soul against the Background of the Homeric Conception*

We may recall how a distinction could be perceived as early as Homer (partly following Onians' interpretation) between the *psychē*, in the sense of the intangible, individual shadow form (*eidōlon*) of the human personality that continues to exist in Hades, the *thumos*, as the breath-soul endowed with intelligence and feeling that resides in the breast, and the blood-soul, which forms the principle of vitality. In view of this, Cornford is very likely correct in thinking that Plato's trichotomistic conception is rooted in this primeval religious picture and has merely transformed the latter in accordance with Platonic *theōria*. This entire conception bears the impress of the form-matter motive.

f. The Maladies of the Soul under the Influence of Ananke

In the final part of the dialogue, Plato's spokesman Timaeus sets forth how the human soul can be induced by *Ananke*, which has joined it to the material body, to fall into a condition in which the rational part is no longer capable of guiding human action. Conversely, a soul that is too strong for the particular body to which it is joined can make the latter ill through intense intellectual activity.[1]

In speaking of the inability of some men to restrain their profligate desire for sensual pleasure, Timaeus appeals to the Socratic adage that no one is voluntarily bad.[2] Sexual intemperance, for example, thus arises largely from the condition of one particular material (the marrow, the substance of sperm in Plato's primitive conception), which floods the body with moisture owing to the porosity of the bones. "And in nearly every case that is called incontinence in pleasure, the reproach that men act this way voluntarily is unjustified. No one is voluntarily bad, but man be-

---

1 *Ibid.*, 87 E-88 B: ὡς ὅταν τε ἐν αὐτῷ ψυχὴ κρείττων οὖσα σώματος περιθύμως ἴσχῃ, διασείουσα πᾶν αὐτὸ ἔνδοθεν νόσων ἐμπίπλησι, καὶ ὅταν εἴς τινας μαθήσεις καὶ ζητήσεις ξυντόνως ἴῃ, κατατήκει, διδαχάς τ' αὖ καὶ μάχας ἐν λόγοις ποιουμένη δημοσίᾳ καὶ ἰδίᾳ δι' ἐρίδων καὶ φιλονεικίας γιγνομένων διάπυρον αὐτὸ ποιοῦσα λύει, καὶ ῥεύματα ἐπάγουσα, τῶν λεγομένων ἰατρῶν ἀπατῶσα τοὺς πλείστους, τὰ ἀναίτια αἰτιᾶσθαι ποιεῖ· σῶμά τε ὅταν αὖ μέγα καὶ ὑπέρψυχον σμικρᾷ ξυμφυὲς ἀσθενεῖ τε διανοίᾳ γένηται, διττῶν ἐπιθυμιῶν οὐσῶν φύσει κατ' ἀνθρώπους, διὰ σῶμα μὲν τροφῆς, διὰ δὲ τὸ θειότατον τῶν ἐν ἡμῖν φρονήσεως, αἱ τοῦ κρείττονος κινήσεις κρατοῦσαι καὶ τὸ μὲν σφέτερον αὔξουσαι, τὸ δὲ τῆς ψυχῆς κωφὸν καὶ δυσμαθὲς ἀμνηνόν τε ποιοῦσαι τὴν μεγίστην νόσον ἀμαθίαν ἐναπεργάζονται. ("When the soul in it [i.e., the living being] is too strong for the body and of a fiery temperament, she convulses the whole body and fills it inwardly with ailments; she destroys it, when she throws herself intently into learning and research, just as, in teaching and disputation, whether public or private, she inflames and consumes it through the quarrels and rivalry that thereby arise, and by bringing on rheums deludes most so-called physicians, since they seek to blame the blameless part. On the other hand, when a large body, too strong for the soul, is joined to a small and feeble mind, then, since the desires natural to man are of two kinds – viz., desire of food for the body and desire of rational discernment for the divine part in us – the motions of the stronger part prevail and, by increasing their own power, while they make that of the soul dull, slow to learn, and forgetful, produce in the soul the worst of all maladies, namely, stupidity.")

2 *Ibid.*, 86 D.

comes bad because of a certain faulty condition of his body and a poor education, and such things come upon him against his will as hateful disorders."[1]

It is not Plato's intention here to argue for a moral fatalism, much less a modern, materialistic determinism. His whole argument can be understood solely in the light of the Greek form-matter motive. The rational part of the soul is by nature good, since it owes its origin entirely to the form-power of the divine *nous*. Nevertheless, its attachment to the material body, and the combination with the two mortal parts of the soul that this necessitates, subject it to influences from *Ananke* that can render it wicked and diseased beyond the will of either the human being or the demiurge. Plato is of the opinion that a proper bodily *paideia* can be beneficial in the cases in question. In this context, one is again struck by his surprisingly acute observation of the facts – at least in view of the state of biological and medical knowledge at that time – coupled with his complete lack of insight into the religious root of evil.

6. *Ananke* as the Errant Cause and the Persuasive Power of the Divine *Nous*. The Conception of the Good and the Evil World-Soul in the *Laws* and the *Epinomis*

a. Ananke *as Blind Causality and the Modern Concept of Mechanical Causation*

Once he has completed, in the second part of the dialogue, his detailed account of everything in the cosmos that can be attributed to the divine *nous* and the formative causality of its *idea tou agathou* (τὰ διὰ Νοῦ δεδημιουργημένα), Plato turns to the second great theme of his inquiry, namely, the matter principle, which in opposition to the form principle serves as the autonomous origin of the disorderly motions (the πλανωμένη αἰτία). *Ananke*, in its original religious sense of incalculable destiny, now makes its entry in his argument.

The cosmos is born of a mixture, a "systasis" [σύστασις] of *Ananke* and *nous*. "The divine *nous* rules over *Ananke* [only] by persuasion, whereby he induces it to lead the majority of things that come into being to the best possible state."[2]

As a demiurge, however, this *nous* is nothing more than a form-giver.

1 *Ibid.*, τὸ δὲ ἀληθές, ἡ περὶ τὰ ἀφροδίσια ἀκολασία κατὰ τὸ πολὺ μέρος διὰ τὴν ἑνὸς γένους ἕξιν ὑπὸ μανότητος ὀστῶν ἐν σώματι ῥυώδη καὶ ὑγραίνουσαν νόσος ψυχῆς γέγονε. καὶ σχεδὸν δὴ πάντα ὁπόσα ἡδονῶν ἀκράτεια καὶ ὄνειδος ὡς ἑκόντων λέγεται τῶν κακῶν, οὐκ ὀρθῶς ὀνειδίζεται. κακὸς μὲν γὰρ ἑκὼν οὐδείς· διὰ δὲ πονηρὰν ἕξιν τινὰ τοῦ σώματος καὶ ἀπαίδευτον τροφὴν ὁ κακὸς γίγνεται κακός, παντὶ δὲ ταῦτα ἐχθρὰ καὶ ἄκοντι προσγίγνεται. (Translation in text.)

2 *Timaeus*, 47 e-48 a: Τὰ μὲν οὖν παρεληλυθότα τῶν εἰρημένων πλὴν βραχέων ἐπιδέδεικται τὰ διὰ νοῦ δεδημιουργημένα· δεῖ δὲ καὶ τὰ δι᾿ ἀνάγκης γιγνόμενα τῷ λόγῳ παραθέσθαι. μεμιγμένη γὰρ οὖν ἡ τοῦδε τοῦ κόσμου γένεσις ἐξ ἀνάγκης τε καὶ νοῦ συστάσεως ἐγεννήθη· νοῦ δὲ ἀνάγκης ἄρχοντος τῷ πείθειν αὐτὴν τῶν

He is not the Creator, whose omnipotence is confronted by no autonomous opposing power. Being a divine "engineer," he is in need of a "material," and this has its own irrational, blind nature (*physis*) and sets limits to his power to actualize the good. In accordance with the nature (*physis*) of matter, the working of *Ananke* follows *tuche* (chance) and proceeds without law or order, plan or objective.[1]

The modern concept of a law of nature, which arose under the influence of the humanistic science ideal and has been abandoned again in the most recent development of natural science, implies that phenomena are completely determined. This conception is as intrinsically foreign to Plato's conceptual domain as it was to that of all his predecessors. For Plato, the concept of law and order (*nomos kai taxis*) is completely bound up with the form principle, which operates according to a rational, purposive plan.[2] The causality that stems from *Ananke* is characterized as a "cooperative cause" (ξυναιτία). Although the demiurge makes use of this in order to actualize the *idea* of the good as much as possible in the cosmos, it retains its own character and origin.[3]

γιγνομένων τὰ πεῖστα ἐπὶ τὸ βέλτιστον ἄγειν, ταύτῃ κατὰ ταὐτά τε δι᾿ ἀνάγκης ἡττωμένης ὑπὸ πειθοῦς ἔμφρονος οὕτω κατ᾿ ἀρχὰς ξυνίστατο τόδε τὸ πᾶν. εἴ τις οὖν ᾖ γέγονε, κατὰ ταῦτα ὄντως ἐρεῖ, μικτέον καὶ τὸ τῆς πλανωμένης εἶδος αἰτίας ᾗ φέρειν πέφυκεν. ("The foregoing presentation, except for a few trifles, has displayed what has come about due to the formative power of *nous*. But we must now set forth next to this the things brought forth by *Ananke*. For the generation of this cosmos was a mixed result of the combination of *Ananke* and *nous*. The divine *nous* ruled over *Ananke* by persuading it to lead the greatest part of the things that come into being to their best condition; in this manner and on this principle, consequently, this cosmos was fashioned in the beginning by the victory of rational persuasion over *Ananke*. If, then, someone really is to explain how the universe came into existence on this basis, he must work into his explanation also the nature of the chaotic [disorderly] cause – in what manner it is able by its nature to cause motion.")

1 *Ibid.*, 46 D-E: τὸν δὲ νοῦ καὶ ἐπιστήμης ἐραστὴν ἀνάγκη τὰς τῆς ἔμφρονος φύσεως αἰτίας πρώτας μεταδιώκειν, ὅσαι δὲ ὑπ᾿ ἄλλων κινουμένων, ἕτερα δὲ ἐξ ἀνάγκης κινούντων γίγνονται, δευτέρας. ποιητέον δὴ κατὰ ταῦτα καὶ ἡμῖν· λεκτέα μὲν ἀμφότερα τὰ τῶν αἰτιῶν γένη, χωρὶς δὲ ὅσαι μετὰ νοῦ καλῶν καὶ ἀγαθῶν δημιουργοὶ καὶ ὅσαι μονωθεῖσαι φρονήσεως τὸ τυχὸν ἄτακτον ἑκάστοτε ἐξεργάζονται. ("But a lover of *nous* [thought] and knowledge must necessarily first investigate the causes that belong to the rational nature, and only in the second place those belonging to things that are moved by others and in accordance with *Ananke* set others in motion. We too, then, should proceed accordingly; we must speak of both kinds of cause, but distinguish those causes that work by means of *nous* and, by lending form, produce what is good and beautiful, from those which, destitute of rational discernment, have their several effects according to *tuche* and without order.")
2 As Cornford rightly observes, *op.cit.*, p.167.
3 *Timaeus*, 46 C: ταῦτ᾿ οὖν πάντ᾿ ἔστι τῶν ξυναιτίων, οἷς θεὸς ὑπηρετοῦσι χρῆται τὴν τοῦ ἀρίστου κατὰ τὸ δυνατὸν ἰδέαν ἀποτελῶν. ("These all belong, then, to the cooperative causes, which God employs as means in order to actualize [in his work]

b. Reason Is Not the Unique Source of Motion. Cornford's Incorrect View

Plato is only concerned to combat his predecessors' view that this cooperative factor is the *sufficient* cause or origin of the entire cosmos.[1] The notion advanced by Cornford in his commentary, which otherwise evinces a fine study of detail, is therefore incorrect. There Cornford defends the view that Plato sought the unique cause of motion in the world-soul, as that which moves itself, a notion on which the Cambridge professor also bases his hypothesis of the purely mythological character of the demiurge.[2] In this view, Plato has the disorderly causes originating in the irrational workings of the world-soul. Rather than supporting all this, however, the text in fact contradicts it.[3] For Plato clearly states that the disorderly cause produces motion in accordance with its own nature, and this statement is worked out in detail in his further exposition. It would seem that Cornford approached the dualistic

the *idea* of the best as far as possible.")

1 *Ibid.*, 46 D: (directly continuing the previous quotation): δοξάζεται δὲ ὑπὸ τῶν πλείστων οὐ ξυναίτια ἀλλ᾽ αἴτια εἶναι τῶν πάντων, ψύχοντα καὶ θερμαίνοντα πηγνύντα τε καὶ διαχέοντα καὶ ὅσα τοιαῦτα ἀπεργαζόμενα. λόγον δὲ οὐδένα οὐδὲ νοῦν εἰς οὐδὲν δυνατὰ ἔχειν ἐστί. ("But most men think that that which has the power to cool and to heat, to compact and to make flow, and everything that has similar effects, is not a cooperative cause, but the [sole] cause of all things. This [opinion], however, is devoid of all sense and understanding.")

2 Cornford, *op.cit.*, p. 197.

3 In the same passage, Cornford maintains that it follows from *Timaeus* 46 D that the unique source of motion in the cosmos lies in the world-soul. This is not at all evident in the passage cited, however. The text reads as follows (directly continuing the previous quotation): τῶν γὰρ ὄντων ᾧ νοῦν μόνῳ κτᾶσθαι προσήκει, λεκτέον ψυχήν· τοῦτο δὲ ἀόρατον, πῦρ δὲ καὶ ὕδωρ καὶ ἀὴρ καὶ γῆ σώματα πάντα ὁρατὰ γέγονε. τὸν δὲ νοῦ καὶ ἐπιστήμης ἐραστὴν ἀνάγκη τὰς τῆς ἔμφρονος φύσεως αἰτίας πρώτας μεταδιώκειν, ὅσαι δὲ ὑπ᾽ ἄλλων κινουμένων, ἕτερα δὲ ἐξ ἀνάγκης κινούντων γίγνονται, δευτέρας. ("We must rather call that which alone can properly acquire knowledge of beings soul. But this is invisible, whereas fire, water, air, and earth are visible bodies. He who aspires to knowledge [*nous*] and science, however, must investigate the primary causes of the nature that works rationally, while that which imparts motion by means of other things in accordance with *Anankē* belongs among the secondary causes.") Plato thus makes an explicit contrast in this passage between the nature that works with understanding, the primary cause of whose motion can lie only in the soul, and the visible bodies – fire, water, air, and earth – which are set in motion by something else and themselves (in accordance with *Anankē*) set other things in motion. That which is moved by something else naturally cannot be a primary cause or source of motion. It is precisely in the continuation of Plato's account, however, that it is made clear that the source of the disorderly, chaotic motion is to be sought in a principle that is itself invisible, but still remains in complete antithesis to the *nous*. Plato expressly teaches that the visibility of bodies itself originates in the divine form-giving process. The fallacy of Cornford's interpretation is thus evident here.

theory of the *Timaeus* in terms of the conception put forth later in the *Laws* and the *Epinomis*; but the text resists this interpretation.

c. The Description of Chaos

Plato now moves on to the second principle of origin in his inquiry into the genesis of the world. He undertakes to describe the chaos, where fire, air, water, and earth were still found in an incorporeal and disorderly condition and presented a semblance of the cyclical flux of opposites as Heraclitus had conceived this.[1] The actual principle of life is absent here, however, since Plato explicitly ascribes the origin of this to the soul; and Heraclitus' doctrine of *logos* is likewise eliminated.

In this chaotic stage, according to Plato, we actually cannot yet speak of fire, air, water, and earth as bodies having definite form. All that is present is "something like this" (τὸ τοιοῦτον; cf. 49 B) that is subject to continual change. At this point there are as yet no things, but only powers (*dunameis*) without form (*eidos*) and number, which do indeed display a few characteristics traits (ἴχνη) of their own proper nature, "but are found altogether in a condition such as we may expect in the absence of form-giving divine *nous*."[2]

d. The Chōra as the Third Genus of That Which Comes into Being

One may ask whether in this chaos, with its constant fluid progression through contrary states, there is nothing that is abiding and permanent.

---

1 *Ibid.*, 49 B-C: πρῶτον μὲν ὃ δὴ νῦν ὕδωρ ὠνομάκαμεν, πηγνύμενον, ὡς δοκοῦμεν, λίθους καὶ γῆν γιγνόμενον ὁρῶμεν, τηκόμενον δὲ καὶ διακρινόμενον αὖ ταὐτὸν τοῦτο πνεῦμα καὶ ἀέρα, ξυγκαυθέντα δὲ ἀέρα πῦρ, ἀνάπαλιν δὲ πῦρ συγκριθὲν καὶ κατασβεσθὲν εἰς ἰδέαν ἀπιὸν αὖθις ἀέρος, καὶ πάλιν ἀέρα ξυνιόντα καὶ πυκνούμενον νέφος καὶ ὁμίχλην, ἐκ δὲ τούτων ἔτι μᾶλλον ξυμπιλουμένων ῥέον ὕδωρ, ἐξ ὕδατος δὲ γῆν καὶ λίθους αὖθις, κύκλον τε οὕτω διαδιδόντα εἰς ἄλληλα, ὡς φαίνεται, τὴν γένεσιν. ("First we see what we just now called water, when it is compacted, becoming (as we imagine) stone and earth, but this very same thing again, when it is rarefied and dissolved, becoming vapor and air; inflamed air becoming fire; fire, when condensed and extinguished, passing back again into the form of air, but air, by coming together and being compacted, into clouds and mist; from these, when they are compressed still more, flowing water, and from water once more earth and stones; and thus, as it appears, the passage of one into the other is effected by a circle.")

2 *Ibid.*, 53 A-B: καὶ τὸ μὲν δὴ πρὸ τούτου πάντα ταῦτ᾽ εἶχεν ἀλόγως καὶ ἀμέτρως· ὅτε δ᾽ ἐπεχειρεῖτο κοσμεῖσθαι τὸ πᾶν, πῦρ πρῶτον καὶ ὕδωρ καὶ γῆν καὶ ἀέρα ἴχνη μὲν ἔχοντα αὐτῶν αὐτά, παντάπασί γε μὴν διακείμενα ὥσπερ εἰκὸς ἔχειν ἅπαν ὅταν ἀπῇ τινος θεός, οὕτω δὴ τότε πεφυκότα ταῦτα πρῶτον διεσχηματίσατο εἴδεσί τε καὶ ἀριθμοῖς. ("And before that, all these [i.e., fire, air, water, and earth] were without proportion and measure. But when [the divine *nous*] undertook to put the universe in order, at first fire, water, air, and earth, which were already distinguished by certain character traits, were altogether in a condition as one can expect for anything when the deity is absent from it. Such being their nature at that time, it first molded them by means of shapes and numbers.")

Plato holds that there is, and he now introduces the well-known but highly mysterious χώρα (*chōra*) as a third genus (*genos*) in the process which brings the cosmos into being. The first genus is the eternally self-identical, intelligible form-world of the *eidē*, ungenerated and imperishable, which neither receives anything into itself from without nor itself enters into anything else, and is invisible – the *Gegenstand* (object) of theoretical thought alone.

The second genus is the world of the visible, generated forms of our cosmos, which bear the same names as their eidetic models and are copies of them. These are perpetually subject to motion and change, to coming into being in a certain place and passing away out of it, and they apprehend solely by *doxa* (opinion and belief), which involves sense perception. The third genus is the χώρα (chōra), which is everlasting and imperishable; it provides a seat for all that comes into being, but is itself invisible, accessible not to sense perception, but "only to a sort of bastard concept, and hardly an object of belief."[1]

Just before this Plato has called the *chōra* the "receptacle" and the "mother of all that comes into being," while the *eidos*, as the model for sensible forms, is compared with a "father," and that which comes into being with the "offspring" of these two.[2] The *chōra* remains always the same, and in this selfsame existence it therefore never takes on the features of things that come into being within it.[3] Of itself it has no visible qualities, but in this nonsensible mode of existence it "partakes in some puzzling way in the intelligible and is very difficult to grasp."[4] In other words, the *chōra* is not an object of sense perception, but of theoretical ab-

1　*Ibid.*, 51 E-52 B: τούτων δὲ οὕτως ἐχόντων ὁμολογητέον ἕν μὲν εἶναι τὸ κατὰ ταὐτὰ εἶδος ἔχον, ἀγέννητον καὶ ἀνώλεθρον, οὔτε εἰς ἑαυτὸ εἰσδεχόμενον ἄλλο ἄλλοθεν οὔτε αὐτὸ εἰς ἄλλο ποι ἰόν, ἀόρατον δὲ καὶ ἄλλως ἀναίσθητον, τοῦτο, ὃ δὴ νόησις εἴληχεν ἐπισκοπεῖν· τὸ δὲ ὁμώνυμον ὅμοιόν τε ἐκείνῳ δεύτερον, αἰσθητόν, γεννητόν, πεφορημένον ἀεί, γιγνόμενόν τε ἔν τινι τόπῳ καὶ πάλιν ἐκεῖθεν ἀπολλύμενον, δόξῃ μετ᾽ αἰσθήσεως περιληπτόν· τρίτον δὲ αὖ γένος ὃν τὸ τῆς χώρας ἀεί, φθορὰν οὐ προσδεχόμενον, ἕδραν δὲ παρέχον ὅσα ἔχει γένεσιν πᾶσιν, αὐτὸ δὲ μετ᾽ ἀναισθησίας ἁπτὸν λογισμῷ τινὶ νόθῳ, μόγις πιστόν. (Substance of passage translated in text.)

2　*Ibid.*, 50 D: καὶ δὴ καὶ προσεικάσαι πρέπει τὸ μὲν δεχόμενον μητρί, τὸ δ᾽ ὅθεν πατρί, τὴν δὲ μεταξὺ τούτων φύσιν ἐκγόνῳ ("and therefore it is fitting to compare the receptacle to a mother, the model to a father, and the nature that comes into being between these two to the offspring.")

3　*Ibid.*, 50 B: ταὐτὸν αὐτὴν ἀεὶ προσρητέον· ἐκ γὰρ τῆς ἑαυτῆς τὸ παράπαν οὐκ ἐξίσταται δυνάμεως. ("it [i.e., the receptacle] is to be characterized as always self-identical, for it never departs from its own nature.")

4　*Ibid.*, 51 A: ταὐτὸν οὖν καὶ τῷ τὰ τῶν πάντων ἀεί τε ὄντων κατὰ πᾶν ἑαυτοῦ πολλάκις ἀφομοιώματα καλῶς μέλλοντι δέχεσθαι πάντων ἐκτὸς αὐτῷ προσήκει πεφυκέναι τῶν εἰδῶν, διὸ δὴ τὴν τοῦ γεγονότος ὁρατοῦ καὶ πάντως αἰσθητοῦ μητέρα καὶ ὑποδοχὴν μήτε γῆν μήτε ἀέρα μήτε πῦρ μήτε ὕδωρ λέγωμεν, μήτε ὅσα ἐκ τούτων μήτε ἐξ ὧν ταῦτα γέγονεν· ἀλλ᾽ ἀνόρατον εἶδός τι καὶ ἄμορφον, πανδεχές, μεταλαμβάνον δὲ ἀπορώτατά πῃ τοῦ νοητοῦ καὶ δυσαλωτότατον αὐτὸ

straction, even though it cannot be grasped in a genuine concept.

e. The Chōra *Is Not Empty Space (Bäumker)*

What did Plato mean by this *chōra*? Bäumker thought that it can only be understood as empty space, and many have adopted this position.[1] Plato's description of the chaos, however, where "something like" fire, air, earth, and water are in constant, disorderly, and unbalanced motion, is of itself a sufficient refutation of this interpretation; for without question the *chōra* is completely filled with these powers, which in their chaotic state are yet indeterminable. Plato states the matter explicitly. As clearly distinct visible bodies, the four elements have their intelligible models in the eternal world of the *eidē*;[2] but in their unordered state they belong to the *chōra* and cannot be detached from it.[3]

In *Timaeus* 50 C, Plato expressly calls the *chōra* an ἐκμαγεῖον, that is, a neutral plastic "stuff" in which impressions are made. This "stuff" is set in motion and altered by the corporeal forms that enter it, and on account of these forms it appears at one time in one way and at another time in an-

---

λέγοντες οὐ ψευσόμεθα. ("In the same way, that which is destined to receive faithfully, through its whole being and many times over, the likenesses of all intelligible and eternal ontic forms, is properly in its own nature free of all these [visible forms]. For this reason, then, the mother and receptacle of all that has come into being visible and wholly perceptible to the senses must not be called earth or air or fire or water, nor given the name of anything that has arisen from these or from which these have arisen. But we shall not speak falsely if we maintain that it is an invisible and formless nature [*eidos*], all-receiving, which partakes in some puzzling way of the intelligible [the objects of thought] and is most difficult to grasp.")

1 Clemens Bäumker, *Das Problem der Materie in der griechischen Philosophie: Eine historisch-kritische Untersuchung* (Munich: Aschendorf, 1890), p.177.

2 *Timaeus* 51 B-E: Cf. *Sophist*, 266 B, where the following products of the form-power of the divine *nous* are listed: ourselves and all other living beings, and the elements of the latter – fire, water, and the like.

3 According to Cornford, *op.cit.*, p. 190, Plato regarded even the four yet unformed qualities as copies of the eidetic models of fire, water, earth, and air. For the elementary geometric form of the pyramid, which the demiurge gives to fire, is invisible, while Plato explicitly speaks of the fire in the *chōra* as a quality such as can be seen. This interpretation serves as its own refutation, however. Plato argues time and again that a sensible copy of an eidetic form is always the product of the form-giving activity of the divine *nous*. In the chaos, however, he already has "something like" fire, air, water, and earth appearing, which in this chaotic state are still without *eidos* and number. Although these do display a few characteristic traits of their own nature, they are all found together in such a condition as may be expected in the absence of the divine *nous*. The copies of "fire in itself" are always corporeal, and this corporeal nature indeed arises only through the imparting of geometric form. The elementary geometric corpuscles may be invisible, but in the macrodimension of corporeal fire, their combination results in a corporeal form that becomes perceptible to the senses.

other way to the senses. Plato also explicitly remarks in this connection that these things that pass into and out of the *chōra* are always copies (μιμήματα) of the ontic forms (*eidē*) having true being.[1] He then states in 51 A that the receptacle may be called neither earth, nor air, nor fire, nor water, nor anything that has arisen from these elements, but is rather an "invisible and unformed [amorphous] nature [*eidos*] that receives all things into itself and partakes in some puzzling way of the *noēton* [the intelligible]."[2]

Timaeus 52 E has this in addition to say about the *chōra*, that it is filled with *dunameis* (powers) that are unlike and out of balance with one another. Because of this, there was no equipoise in any of its parts, but it was shaken throughout and by its own motion in return set these *dunameis* in (disorderly) motion. Consequently, the latter were continually being separated and carried in different directions, "just as in a winnowing basket and other instruments for sifting grain, where the heavier ingredients fall in one place, while the lighter (the chaff) are thrown elsewhere."[3] In the same manner, fire, air, water, and earth in their still chaotic and unformed state were shaken by the *chōra*, which had the motion of a winnowing basket, sifting apart the most unlike *dunameis* and forcing together those which were most like one another.[4]

---

1 *Timaeus*, 50 C: δέχεταί τε γὰρ ἀεὶ τὰ πάντα καὶ μορφὴν οὐδεμίαν ποτὲ οὐδενὶ τῶν εἰσιόντων ὁμοίαν εἴληφεν οὐδαμῆ οὐδαμῶς· ἐκμαγεῖον γὰρ φύσει παντὶ κεῖται, κινούμενόν τε καὶ διασχηματιζόμενον ὑπὸ τῶν εἰσιόντων, φαίνεται δὲ δι᾽ ἐκεῖνα ἄλλοτε ἀλλοῖον· τὰ δὲ εἰσιόντα καὶ ἐξιόντα τῶν ὄντων ἀεὶ μιμήματα, τυπωθέντα ἀπ᾽ αὐτῶν τρόπον τινὰ δύσφραστον καὶ θαυμαστόν, ὃν εἰσαῦθις μέτιμεν. ("For it is always receiving all things, and it has never, in any way whatever, taken on any feature that is like any of the things that enter it. For by its nature it is the plastic stuff for everything, which is moved and transformed by the things that enter it, and on account of these it appears different at different times. But the things that pass in and out are always copies of the eternal ontic forms, modeled after them in a hard to express and wonderful manner; we shall pursue this later.")
2 *Ibid.*, 51 A-B.
3 *Ibid.*, 52 E-53 A.
4 *Ibid.*, 52 D-53 A: οὗτος μὲν οὖν δὴ παρὰ τῆς ἐμῆς ψήφου λογισθεὶς ἐν κεφαλαίῳ δεδόσθω λόγος, ὄν τε καὶ χώραν καὶ γένεσιν εἶναι, τρία τριχῆ, καὶ πρὶν οὐρανὸν γενέσθαι· τὴν δὲ γενέσεως τιθήνην ὑγραινομένην καὶ πυρουμένην καὶ τὰς γῆς τε καὶ ἀέρος μορφὰς δεχομένην καὶ ὅσα ἄλλα τούτοις πάθη ξυνέπεται πάσχουσαν παντοδαπὴν μὲν ἰδεῖν φαίνεσθαι, διὰ δὲ τὸ μήθ᾽ ὁμοίων δυνάμεων μήτε ἰσορρόπων ἐμπίπλασθαι κατ᾽ οὐδὲν αὐτῆς ἰσορροπεῖν, ἀλλ᾽ ἀνωμάλως πάντη ταλαντουμένην σείεσθαι μὲν ὑπ᾽ ἐκείνων αὐτήν, κινουμένην δ᾽ αὖ πάλιν ἐκεῖνα σείειν· τὰ δὲ κινούμενα ἄλλα ἄλλοσε ἀεὶ φέρεσθαι διακρινόμενα, ὥσπερ τὰ ὑπὸ τῶν πλοκάνων τε καὶ ὀργάνων τῶν περὶ τὴν τοῦ σίτου κάθαρσιν σειόμενα καὶ ἀνικμώμενα τὰ μὲν πυκνὰ καὶ βαρέα ἄλλη, τὰ δὲ μανὰ καὶ κοῦφα εἰς ἑτέραν ἵζει φερόμενα ἕδραν· ("This, then, in my judgment is the conclusion of my reasoning: there were being, the *chōra*, and becoming – three things differing in three ways – even before the heaven [the cosmos] came into being. Now the nurse of becoming, suffused with water and fire and receiving the qualities of earth and air, and being

f. The Chōra *as* Hulē

In my view, all of these mutually supplementary descriptions point to a single conclusion. As a matter of fact, Plato understands the *chōra* as a *hulē*. That is, he conceives it as an unformed matter in the typically Greek sense of the word, a matter that has an original, disorderly motion by virtue of the chaotic powers dwelling within it.

This interpretation is fully in keeping with Aristotle's report that the oral tradition regarded the receptacle of the *Timaeus* as nothing other than the great and the small.[1] The *chōra* then is simply a further elaboration of the *apeiron* in the *Philebus*. It displays a surprising likeness to Anaximander's conception of *physis* as *archē*, but with the fundamental difference that Plato de-deifies the *apeiron* and renders it soul-less in accordance with his dualistic conception of the religious ground-motive.

We should take special note of the fact that Plato's use of the term *chōra* here has a demonstrable connection with *chōrein* (χωρεῖν), a verb he continually uses to denote the Heraclitean conception of the matter principle, both in the *Cratylus* and the *Philebus*, and in the *Timaeus* itself.[2] In no case may the *chōra* be understood as geometric space, as even Cornford continues to do, even though for him it is "filled" space. This is clearly evident from the opening of Plato's account of the granting of corporeal form to fire, earth, water, and air by means of stereometric figures. For these figures have not only length and breadth, but also depth (βάθος), and since these three dimensions have a formal character within the cosmos that has come into being, they cannot as such belong to the *chōra*.[3]

One can say at most that the *chōra*, as the plastic material for the divine

---

subject to all the other conditions that accompany these, had every sort of diverse appearance to the sight; but because it was filled with powers that were neither alike nor in balance with one another, there was no equipoise in any part of it; it was rather itself everywhere shaken unevenly by these powers, and by its motion shook them in return. And these powers, thus set in motion, were constantly being separated from one another and carried in different directions, just like that which is shaken and sifted by means of winnowing baskets and other instruments for cleaning grain, where the firm and heavy particles fall in one place, while the loose and light ones are carried elsewhere.")

1 Aristotle, *Physics*, 209 b 13.
2 Cf Plato, *Cratylus*, 402 A: Λέγει που Ἡράκλειτος ὅτι πάντα χωρεῖ καὶ οὐδὲν μένει; cf. also Diels-Kranz, I; 22 [12]* Heraclitus, A.Fragm. 6, A. Fragm. 1, 8 and B.Fragm. 49 A and 91. Cf. *Philebus*, 24 D: προχωρεῖ γὰρ καὶ οὐ μένει (*Translator's note:* Here Dooyeweerd has used the second number, 12, instead of 22, when referring to Diels-Kranz. A.Fragm. 6 is a direct reference to Plato's *Cratylus* and concerns what Dooyeweerd quotes. B.Fragm. 49 a and 91 have to do with the latter part of the sentence from the *Cratylus*, about the inability to step in the same river twice.)
3 *Timaeus*, 53 C: Πρῶτον μὲν δὴ πῦρ καὶ γῆ καὶ ὕδωρ καὶ ἀὴρ ὅτι σώματά ἐστι, δῆλόν που καὶ παντί. τὸ δὲ τοῦ σώματος εἶδος πᾶν καὶ βάθος ἔχει. τὸ δὲ βάθος αὖ πᾶσα ἀνάγκη τὴν ἐπίπεδον περιειληφέναι φύσιν. ("In the first place, it is obvious

317

form-giving process, has to possess a certain (unformed) extended quality that is inherent in its nature. As we have also seen in the earlier cited quotations of Aristotle concering Plato's theory of the idea-numbers in his final period, one could speak of three as yet indeterminate demensions of this *hulē*: longer-shorter, broader-narrower, and higher-lower. All that Plato meant by this, however, is that the corporeal forms, as it were, leave their impressions at various places in the neutral plastic stuff, just as he compares the *chōra* to the gold in which diverse, changeable figures can be formed.

Plato's conception of the *chōra* is actually the direct precursor of the Aristotelian conception of so-called prime matter (πρώτη ὕλη), that is, matter that is still completely unformed. The difference between these two lies solely in the fact that Aristotle denies any real existence to prime matter, since in his line of thought matter, as pure potentiality (*dunamis*), can only come into actual existence through the ontic form. For Plato, by contrast, the fundamental separation (*chōrismos*) between the intelligible world of forms and the sensible world of changing figures forbids any substantive combination between the principles of form and matter in the cosmos that has come into being. Because of this, Plato found himself compelled to conceive *hulē* not just as a *dunamis* but also as a reality that exists in its own right. In this latter ever self-identical quality, it is the *chōra*, which remains always the same throughout all changing forms that it receives. Moreover, since the *Sophist* recognized identity as a fundamental form of *intelligible* being, Plato says that the *chōra* "partakes in some puzzling way in the intelligible," even though it is conversely the dialectical opposite of the form principle.

In his mature conception, Aristotle too speaks of a *hulē noētē*,[1] understanding this as *hulē* in the abstract category of quantitative extension. And just as Plato says that the nature of *hulē* can be grasped only in a "bastard concept," Aristotle expresses the same idea by making *hulē* in itself accessible only to an analogical concept. I shall return to this matter at length in my account of the Aristotelian-Thomistic ontology.

g. *The Inner Antinomies in the Conception of the* Chōra. *Plato and Anaxagoras*

That his conception of the *chōra* is obscure and intrinsically antinomic can be attributed to nothing else than the internal dialectic of the religious ground-motive of Greek thought. The principles of form and matter are the dialectical, religious (and therefore absolute) opposites of each other; but they nevertheless cannot be grasped in isolation from

---

to everyone that fire, earth, water, and air are bodies. But every form of body also has depth. Moreover, it is absolutely necessary that depth include in itself the nature of the plane.")

1 *Translator's note*: Intelligible matter.

each other. As soon as Plato attempts to describe matter in itself, that is, matter completely apart from the form principle, he falls into the same antinomies as Anaxagoras, whose notion of the original chaos underlies both the Platonic and the mature Aristotelian conceptions.

Plato himself clearly perceived these antinomies. He endeavors to escape them by withholding from the *dunameis* of the *chōra* – fire, air, water, and earth – the character of sharply defined, corporeal elements that Empedocles had given them. Instead, he merely calls them "something like this," just as Anaxagoras had qualified the *chrēmata* as only seeds (*spermata*) of corporeal objects with form. But in the chaotic movement of the *chōra*, members of these *dunameis* that are "alike" are nevertheless thrust together and those that are "unlike" are driven in a different direction. Because of this, fire, air, water, and earth, even though they may not properly be given these names in their unformed condition, must still already "display a few characteristic traits of their own nature." All distinctness and likeness, however, is due to ontic form alone. How then is it possible that the totally unordered and formless *dunameis* of the *chōra* already possess a few characteristic traits of the nature of the four elements?

h. The Chōra *and the Aristotelian Conception of Prime or Absolute Matter*

In order to evade this antinomy, Aristotle broke in his mature conception with the Platonic *chōrismos* between the intelligible world of forms and the sensible world of phenomena. Within the generated cosmos itself, he has form and matter enter into a substantive conjunction, which makes it impossible in this cosmos for matter ever to have real existence apart from a self-subsistent form (*forma substantialis*). I shall later demonstrate in detail, however, that the internal dialectic of the Greek ground-motive prevented Aristotle from removing the Platonic *chōrismos* entirely, and that he too was at a loss to find a veritable synthesis between form and matter as antagonistic principles of origin. This antinomy could not fail to emerge in his anthropological conception as well, and, in combination with Christian conceptual motives, it would later undergo a further dialectical course of development in the Scholastic theory concerning the relation between soul and body.

i. The Divine Reason's Persuasion of Anankē *in Aeschylus'* Oresteia *Tragedy*

All that remains for us here is to note that Plato's description of the relation between the form-giving divine *nous* and the *Anankē* of the matter principle displays a surprising, and almost verbatim, agreement with that presented by the Greek tragic poet Aeschylus in the third part of his renowned *Oresteia* trilogy. In the superb epilogue to his *Timaeus* commentary, a work to which I have referred often, Cornford has pointed this out in detail.

In the *Timaeus*, as we have seen, the generated cosmos is said to be a product of the cooperation between the form-giving divine *nous*, guided by the *idea* of the good and beautiful, and dark *Anankē*. The divine demiurge can rule *Anankē* only by persuasion, and even then the latter does not relinquish any of the original, blind causality that belongs to it.

The generated cosmos is the child of a father and a mother that correspond with heaven (*Ouranos*) and earth (*Gē* or *Gaia*), the first divine parental couple in the Greek theogony. The father, who comes "from above," is Olympian, while the mother, coming "from below," is the mother earth and has *Anankē* as one of her names. Already in Homer, both Zeus, as the supreme celestial god, and the other Olympian deities are confronted by a power that they are unable to subdue, namely, *Moira* or *Heimarmenē tuchē*. Like Plato's demiurge, the Homeric culture gods are not omnipotent, and it does not seem possible to infer from the statements of Homer and Hesiod any satisfactory conception of the relation between the will of these Olympians and the eternal opposition of blind destiny. Homer and Hesiod left behind here an unresolved problem that was taken up by both Aeschylus and Plato.

It is no accident that Aeschylus' greatest dramatic work culminates in the reconciliation of Zeus and *Anankē* and that this reconciliation is accomplished by the divine *nous* in the person of the Olympian goddess Athena. When Orestes is pursued by *Anankē*, Athena persuades the wild goddesses of vengeance, the daughters of *Anankē*, to cooperate in advancing her benevolent purpose of setting him free.

Submitting to the yoke of *Anankē*, Agamemnon has sacrificed his daughter, and in retaliation for this he is killed by his wife Clytemnestra. Their son Orestes retaliates in turn by slaying his mother, and he is aquitted of guilt by Apollo himself. But Orestes is then pursued by the wild Furies, the daughters of *Anankē*. In the final part of the trilogy, the *Eumenides*, the denouement of this dramatic conflict between *Anankē* and the Olympian deities comes when a tribunal meets on the Areopagus, or Hill of Ares. Apollo himself appears in order to plead the case of Orestes, and he releases an avlanche of curses and derision upon the Furies. Neither party is willing to make any concessions, however, and a tie vote prevents the human jurors from reaching a decision. Athena then casts her vote for acquittal. Apollo vanishes, having nothing more to say, and Orestes is released.

The wild goddesses of vengeance, daughters of Night or Mother Earth, are unappeased, however, and they remain on the stage opposite Athena, the "motherless child of the father (Zeus)." The divine Reason, personified in Athena, stands face to face with blind *Anankē*. In wild confusion, the Furies threaten to blight the soil of the city of Athens and to poison the springs of life. Athena then turns to them, and her first words are: "Let me persuade you." She offers the goddesses of vengeance an altar and cultic worship in a cave under the Hill of Ares, where they can be transformed into powers of fertility and blessing. But the Furies continue to cry out for *Dikē* and vengeance. Athena patiently repeats her offer. She reminds them that she alone knows the keys to the chamber where Zeus' thunderbolt is stored, but "there is no need for that." Violence cannot repair a situation that violence has created. The Furies then suddenly give in when Athena addresses their leader as follows:

> I will not weary in speaking good words. Never shall you say that you, the elder goddess, were driven dishonored from this land by me, the younger, and by my mortal citizens.
> No, but if you have any respect for unstained *Persuasion*, the appeasement and the soothing charm of my tongue – why then stay here.

The daugthers of *Anankē* at last succumb to this persuasion. The tragedy ends with a song in which they promise fertility to the soil and to the citizens of Athena's land, and with the triumphant cry:

> Thus Zeus and *Anankē* are reconciled.[1]

This once again confirms the theory that I have advanced, that the religious ground-motive not only controls the course of development of theoretical thought, but is also determinative of the entire spiritual structure of a cultural community.

j.   The Conception of the Good and Evil World-Souls in the
Laws *and the* Epinomis

It would appear, however, that ultimately Plato could not be satisfied with the *Timaeus'* dualistic conception of the principle of origin. In his old age, he wrote the much-disputed dialogues entitled *Laws* (*Nomoi*) and the *Epinomis*, which was a supplement to the *Laws*. In an intense struggle with the Greek ground-motive, the aged thinker returns here once more to the conception he had developed earlier in the *Phaedrus*, that the soul is the cause of *all* motion in the cosmos that has come into being. He thereby evidently discards *Anankē* as a second causative principle. Thus, he must seek a different solution to the question as to the origin of the disorderly and formless motions in the cosmos, a problem that the *Phaedrus* had left unresolved. He must now look for a solution that appears to be compatible with a causality that resides exclusively in the soul.

This attempt at solution brought Plato to a new impasse, however. In order to make it possible to attribute also the disorderly motion rooted in the matter principle to the soul conceived as the exclusive causative principle, he now introduces an irrational world-soul alongside the rational one.[2] The antagonism between the *chōra* and the divine *nous* is thereby trans-

---

1   See F. M. Cornford, *Plato's Cosmology*, London: 1937, p. 363.
2   *Laws*, 896 D-E: ΑΘ. Ἆρ᾽ οὖν τὸ μετὰ τοῦτο ὁμολογεῖν ἀναγκαῖον τῶν τε ἀγαθῶν

posed into a struggle between a good and an evil world-soul, which the *Epinomis*, 988 E, says must end with the triumph of the good.[1]

This, of course, offers no real solution; for the world-soul belongs among the first products of becoming, and these in turn require an ultimate cause. If this ultimate cause is the form-giving power of the *idea tou agathou* in the divine *nous*,[2] the evil world-soul cannot be a product of the form-giving principle of origin. The matter principle is then merely embodied in a second world-soul that conforms to all the features of the ground-motive of Greek nature religion. There remains one difference, however, in that the conception of this evil world-soul is gained in conscious opposition to the conception of the material body. Yet, it must be noted, the conception of the world-soul is supposed to precede the latter.

αἰτίαν εἶναι ψυχὴν καὶ τῶν κακῶν καὶ καλῶν καὶ αἰσχρῶν δικαίων τε καὶ ἀδίκων καὶ πάντων τῶν ἐναντίων, εἴπερ τῶν πάντων γε αὐτὴν θήσομεν αἰτίαν; Λ. Πῶς γὰρ οὔ; ΑΘ. υχη ᾽ν δὴ διοικοῦσαν καὶ ἐνοικοῦσαν ἐν ἅπασι τοῖς πάντῃ κινουμένοις μῶν οὐ καὶ τὸν οὐρανὸν ἀνάγκη διοικεῖν φάναι; Λ. Τί μήν; ΑΘ. ίαν , ἢ πλείους; πλείους, ἐγὼ ὑπὲρ σφῷν ἀποκρινοῦμαι. δυοῖν μήν γέ που ἔλαττον μηδὲν τιθῶμεν, τῆς τε εὐεργέτιδος καὶ τῆς τἀναντία δυναμένης ἐξεργάζεσθαι. ("*Athenian*: Must we not therefore of necessity admit the following, that the soul is the cause of good and evil, beautiful and ugly, just and unjust, and of all such contraries, if we want to assert it as the cause of everything? *Cleinias*: How could we not? *Athenian*: Must we not likewise say that the all-controlling soul inhabiting everything that moves in any direction also controls [the motion of] the heavens? *Cleinias*: Of course. *Athenian*: One or more? More than one, I will answer on your behalf. Fewer than two, at least, we may not assume – one beneficent, and one capable of the contrary effect.")

1   *Epinomis*, 988 D-E: διὸ καὶ νῦν ἡμῶν ἀξιούντων ψυχῆς οὔσης αἰτίας τοῦ ὅλου καὶ πάντων μὲν τῶν ἀγαθῶν ὄντων τοιούτων, τῶν δὲ αὖ φλαύρων τοιούτων ἄλλων, τῆς μὲν φορᾶς πάσης καὶ κινήσεως ψυχὴν αἰτίαν εἶναι θαῦμα οὐδέν, τὴν δ᾽ ἐπὶ τἀγαθὸν φορὰν καὶ κίνησιν τῆς ἀρίστης ψυχῆς εἶναι, τὴν δ᾽ ἐπὶ τοὐναντίον ἐναντίαν, νενικηκέναι δεῖ καὶ νικᾶν τὰ ἀγαθὰ τὰ μὴ τοιαῦτα. ("Therefore, since we now maintain that the soul is the cause of the whole cosmos and of all good of like nature, while evil has a nature different from this, it is no wonder that the soul is the cause of every revolution and every motion, that the revolution and motion directed to the good is proper to the best soul, but that directed to the opposite is proper to the contrary soul, and that the good has triumphed and must triumph over that which has a different nature.")

2   The fact that the *Laws* implicitly maintains this conception from the *Timaeus* is clearly evident in 904 A ff. Plato speaks there of "Him who takes care of everything," the "supreme Ruler," who, "since he saw that all our actions originate in the soul and have both much virtue and much vice in them, and that what has come into being composed of body and soul is imperishable, but not, by the laws ruling among the gods, eternal ... took thought ... to ensure the triumph of virtue over evil in the universe." This passage also makes a clear distinction between the divine demiurge and the numerous celestial gods who, according to 886 E, are themselves "of divine origin."

Thus Plato's attempted solution does not eliminate the basic religious dualism between the principles of form and matter. It still remains in force here; it has only found an alternate expression. Although one may call Plato's attempted solution "spiritualistic" it has by no means transcended this dualism.

Commentary on the Text[1]

1. Hesiod's Chaos

Page 9, text and note 1. In part, my conception of the meaning of the word *chaos* (χάος) in Hesiod, *Theog.* 116, follows Nilsson, *Geschichte der griechischen Religion* (Munich, 1941), I. 587. There he has the reading "formless and shapeless matter." Nevertheless, Nilsson undoubtedly goes beyond any defensible reading of the text when he has Hesiod say that from *chaos* arise "broad-breasted earth," dark Tartarus, and *Erōs*, the lord of gods and men.

The text itself reads: ἦ τοι μὲν πρώτιστα Χάος γένετ᾽, αὐτὰρ ἔπειτα Γαῖ᾽ εὐρύστερνος, etc., which expresses a merely chronological and not a genetic order. Yet, Hesiod explicitly states in *Theog.* 123 that *chaos* gave rise to darkness and night, and from this I concluded that *chaos* cannot mean "yawning *empty* space."

What I actually objected to in this now widely accepted position was not the interpretation of *chaos* as a "yawning abyss," an interpretation in which the word χάος is brought into connection with the verb χάσκω (to yawn). Rather, I quite specifically opposed the notion that this yawning is merely an *empty space* in the modern sense of the word empty. In any case, the *chaos* is a genetic potentiality, and in itself it can be understood quite well as a yawning in the sense of an as-yet-formless confusion.

The yawning must then be regarded as empty of *form*, not as an empty space in the modern sense of the word. In his *The Theology of the Early Greek Philosophers* (Oxford, 1947), p. 13, Werner Jaeger supports the latter conception by appealing to Aristotle, *Physics Δ* 1, 208 b 31, where Hesiod's *chaos* is spoken of as τόπος (place). In fact, however, this proves nothing; for Plato's *Timaeus* likewise understands the *chōra* as place, but precisely in the sense of a formless, plastic matter (ἐκμαγεῖον), not of empty space, as Aristotle himself observes in *Physics Δ* 1, 209 b. Damascius, the neo-Platonist, understood Hesiod's *chaos* as non-intelligible *physis* existing in complete unity (Diels-Kranz, I, 10; Orpheus, 1 [66], B 12). This indeed points strongly toward the original Greek conception of matter, and in any case it proves that my understanding of the word *chaos* cannot be un-Greek. Jaeger subsequently made the rash assertion

---

1 Although I completed this work for the most part during the Second World War, it was at press for more than two years after that. In consequence, I have written these comments not only to incorporate references to more recent literature but also to revise, wholly or in part, a number of views in the text concerning which doubts arose in my mind after I had submitted the manuscript. (*Editor's note*: In some instances the citations of the *Commentary* are not complete.)

that the "common idea of *chaos* as something in which all things are wildly confused is quite mistaken; and the antithesis between *chaos* and *cosmos*, which rests on this incorrect view, is purely a modern invention." This statement must be countered with the observation that Thomas Aquinas, who studied Aristotle's original writings, already accepted the view of *chaos* that Jaeger objects to here as the one current among the Greeks. See Thomas' *De principiis naturae*, opuscula XXXI: "dicitur materia prima, propter hoc quod ante ipsam non est materia alia; et haec etiam dicitur ὕλη, hoc est *chaos* vel *confusio graece*."

The view, therefore, that this interpretation is only a modern invention cannot be maintained. As I have shown in my sketch of the development of the form-matter motive, the contrast between a chaotic, formless initial state and a cosmos that has arisen from this solely due to divine influence is completely Greek. In Anaxagoras and in Plato's *Timaeus*, this contrast is worked out in detail. All we can grant to Jaeger is that neither thinker used the word *chaos* for the confused, initial state; but this word is indeed used by Nichomachus, the neo-Pythagorean.

In retrospect, however, I must admit that it cannot be proved that Hesiod's *chaos* is an expression of the Greek matter motive proper, a passing assumption of mine on page 66. This would indeed be the case if the text supported Nilsson's interpretation that the earth, underworld, and *Erōs, originated* from *chaos*. Since it does not, however, it is perhaps safer to regard Hesiod's *Erōs*, the principle of procreation, as the embodiment of the motive of the ever-flowing stream of life. In this connection, note the comparison made by Aristotle in *Metaphysics* A 4, 984 b 27 ff. between the roles that *Erōs* plays in Hesiod and Parmenides (in the second part of his didactic poem) as the principle of combination and movement.

2. The Lutheran Dialectic between Law and Gospel

Pages 36-37, text. I am well aware of the fact that, in the light of modern Luther research, it appears rash to speak without qualification of a dialectical opposition between "law" and "gospel" in Luther himself and generally to dissociate the German Reformer too much from Calvin. More recent critical investigation has shown that some of the fundamental differences that have long been assumed (particularly following Troeltsch) to exist between Luther and Calvin are either nonexistent or merely relative in character. In Calvinistic circles it is particularly my Viennese friend Josef Bohatec who has contributed greatly toward a better understanding of Luther and Calvin in their mutual interrelation.

All the same, my own earlier research in Luther's works has led me to hold fast to my view that his thinking indeed exhibits a dialectical tension between law, in the sense of the order for sinful nature, and gospel. This tension also comes to expression in the opposition between Christian faith and natural reason. It is rooted in a dualistic conception of the ground-motive of nature and grace.

Luther himself calls the law the "dialectic of the gospel" (*die Dialektik des Evangeliums*).[1] He no doubt taught the so-called *usus tertius legis*, that is, the didactic use of the decalogue, even though he did emphasize the so-called *usus politicus* in a very one-sided way, as can be seen, for instance, in his commentary on *Galatians*. Nevertheless, if what is in view is law in its comprehensive sense of the order for temporal life, it is placed in a veritable dialectical tension with the evangelical liberty of the Christian. He assigns law in this broad, inclusive sense to reason (*Vernunft*), which in matters of faith is "stone blind."[2] The great Reformer doubtless did not go so far as later Lutherans, however, who divorced the worldly ordinances entirely from the divine commandment[s].

The same dualism also comes to expression in Luther's standpoint on philosophy. Although he declared in 1518 that "Credo quod impossibile sit ecclesiam reformari, nisi funditus canones, decretales, scholastica theologia, philosophia, logica, ut nunc habentur, eradicentur et alia instituantur,"[3] he did not at all have in mind an inner reformation of philosophical thought. His only aim was to break the authority of Aristotle in philosophy, since this was a "weapon of the papists." In fact, he was so far removed from any notion of an inner connection between the Christian faith and philosophy, that he even inclined toward the Averroistic doctrine of a double truth. Thus he states that "the Sorbonne has advanced the highly objectionable teaching that whatever is established truth in philosophy must also count as truth in theology."

Since the law, in the sense of the order for created reality, is indissolubly bound up with the creation itself, the internal tension between law and gospel implies the presence of a dialectical tension between Luther's respective views of creation and redemption in Christ Jesus.

One may ask whether there is warrant for the view I expressed in the text that Luther's position has been influenced in some way by Marcion's contrast between the Old Testament God of creation and the New Testament God of redemption. I believe that there is, provided one does not accuse Luther of adopting this dualism consciously. Luther would naturally have kept a great distance between himself and Marcion's heresy; but a certain tension between creation and redemption is nonetheless undeniably present in his outlook. In his book *Het Christelijk Leven*,[4] G. Brillenburg-Wurth similarly establishes that there is a certain affinity be-

---

1 De Wette, *Luther*, IV, 46.

2 Cf. also Karl Holl, *Gesammelte Aufsätze zur Kirchengeschichte* (6th ed., revised; Tübingen: J.C.B. Mohr), I, Luther (1932), 473.

3 Luther, *Epist.* ed. De Wette, I, 64. "I believe that it is impossible for the church to be reformed unless the canons, decretals, scholastic theology, philosophy, and logic, as they now exist, are fundamentally uprooted, and others are established."

4 G. Brillenburg-Wurth, *Het Christelijk Leven* (Kampen: Kok, 1949), p. 87.

tween the conceptions of Marcion and Luther regarding the relation between Christ and Moses.

Emil Brunner's noted book *The Divine Imperative*, pp. 140 ff., in my view, contains undeniable evidence of this implicit tension between creation and redemption in Luther's view of law. He writes, "It is characteristic of our present existence (as an actuality created by God, and yet sinful) that it is embedded in a framework of orders of a most varied kind."[1] He writes further, "It is true that the *Lex* itself is not what God wills, but is absolutely controlled by the Divine Command. ... Thus the believer finds himself involved in a curious situation: from obedience to God he has to obey the *Lex*, in spite of the fact that the latter does not express what God himself wills."[2] In full accord with this, Brunner also teaches that natural life has its own autonomy (*Eigengesetzlichkeit*) and that the gospel's commandment of love intrinsically breaks through the law.

A further account of this appears in my essay in the quarterly journal *Antirevolutionaire Staatkunde* on Brunner's book.[3]

3. The Origin of the Word "Elements" (στοιχεῖα)

Page 44, text. In the first paragraph of this page, the words "since Empedocles" are dropped out after "which had been considered to be 'elements'." It is evident that one cannot yet properly speak of "elements" in the case of the early Milesian nature philosophers, since they assumed there was only a single constant *archē*. According to Simplicius (*Phys.*7, 13) the term element (στοιχεῖον) did not even originate until Plato.

4. The Meaning of Anaximander's Apeiron. Is This Apeiron Conceived as Ensouled?

Page 43-44, text. In *Physics*, *Γ* 4, 203 b 6, Aristotle remarks concerning Anaximander's *apeiron* that it encompasses and governs all things (καὶ περιέχειν ἄπαντα καὶ πάντα κυβερνᾶν) and that he calls it the "divine" because it is immortal (ἀθάνατον) and indestructible (ἀνώλεθρον). In another passage (*Phys.*, *Γ* 7, 207 b 35 – 208 a 4), Aristotle explicitly states that the *apeiron* of the early nature philosophers is the *hulē* (matter) of things. Consequently, he believes it is incorrect to say that it encompasses all things. Rather, we must say that the *apeiron* is encompassed by all things, or that all things contain it.

---

1 Emil Brunner,, *The Divine Imperative* (tr. Olive Wyon; Philadelphia: Westminister Press, 1947), p. 140. Original German: *Das Gebot und die Ordnungen: Entwurf einer protestantisch-theologischen Ethik* (Tübingen, J.C.B. Mohr, 1932).

2 *Ibid.*, p. 142.

3 Herman Dooyeweerd, "De Wetsbeschouwing in Brunner's boek *Das Gebot und die Ordnungen*," *Antirevolutionaire Staatkunde* (quarterly journal), vol. IX (1935), pp. 334-374.

Jaeger thinks (*op.cit.*, p. 30) that this critical remark is clear evidence that Aristotle misunderstood the ancient Milesian thinker. He thus writes that "Anaximander's *apeiron* is not to be understood in terms of the Aristotelian concept of mattter. He has not yet distinguished between Being as matter and Being as form, and his *apeiron* is not simply something which, as matter, is enveloped by form. It is rather the thing which encompasses all things and governs all things, something active, indeed the most active thing in the world."

What shall we say to this? Could Aristotle have failed to grasp that Anaximander conceived his *apeiron* not as mere "passive matter," but as an active (vital) power? This is hardly plausible. After his remark in the first passage mentioned above, that the *apeiron* is held to "encompass" and "govern" all things, Aristotle immediately adds: "as those assert who do not set alongside the *apeiron* other causes, such as *nous* [Anaxagoras] or *philia* [Empedocles]." Aristotle was therefore definitely aware that Anaximander regarded his *apeiron* as a moving and governing cause. Nevertheless, he criticizes him in terms of his own dualistic conception of the form-matter motive, where the form of things can no longer find its origin in matter. In his view, therefore, form can not be encompassed by matter. On the contrary, matter is necessarily encompassed by form, since it is only the latter that lends it actual existence.

It is equally implausible that Anaximander had not yet himself perceived the difference between matter and form. For him, however, the world of forms contains nothing but the objects of sense perception, and these are subject to the guilt of existing separately in individual, transitory shapes. Note in this connection Stenzel's observation that Ionian nature philosophy can be characterized as a process that strips the world of its form.[1] In Anaximander's thought the matter motive is present in its original sense. It is the invisible, ever-flowing divine fountain of life that cannot be limited by any individual form, and for this reason it is designated the *apeiron*. In Aristotle's thought this original sense of the matter motive has been adulterated, since for him the religious primacy belongs to the form motive of the culture religion. The *apeiron* is no mere *spatial* infinity, as Gigon has asserted in connection with his interpretation of Hesiod's *chaos*. Rather, the fragment that has been preserved from Anaximander's book shows that the *apeiron* is a stream which is both formless and material, and although everlasting, also temporal. And, further, it contains in itself a rigid law of justice (*dikē*), a motif that will later be taken up by Heraclitus.

One might ask whether Aristotle's undoubtedly reliable report that the *apeiron* "governs" all things does not force us to conclude that actually,

---

1 J. Stenzel, *Die Metaphysik des Altertums*, in *Handbuch der Philosophie* (1929), pp. 34, 36, 47.

for Anaximander, the divine *archē* is already a "thinking mind" as it will later be for Anaxagoras. This can in no way be the case. On the basis of his dualistic standpoint Anaxagoras could never have subscribed to Anaximander's statement that individual things return to the divine *apeiron* from which they originate, even though he does apply the latter's qualification of the divine as *apeiron* to his pure *nous* in a different sense. In addition, the matter motive no longer has its original meaning of "divine stream of life" in Anaxagoras' thought.

In the Anaximander fragment, as I see it, κατὰ τὸ χρεών must without question still be understood as the ineluctable stroke of death, the *Anankē* of the ancient nature religions. As I have observed in the text, however, the ground-motive of the culture religion has caused this *Anankē* to be partially rationalized into a law of *Dikē*, a law that maintains a proportionality or harmony among the contrary qualities that break loose from the formless *archē*, implacably avenging the unjust existence of individual forms that can arise only at the expense of others. The *apeiron* does indeed govern all things by means of this *Dikē*. Nevertheless, its control is not exercised according to a *free project*, and it thus cannot be equated with the sovereignty over the cosmos (at least in princple) that, under the influence of the form motive of the culture religion, Anaxagoras will grant to the divine *nous*.

In the ancient Ionian thinkers, *Dikē* still exhibits clear traces of the dreadful character of ancient *anankē*. Heraclitus, who adopted this motif from Anaximander, gives the Erinyes, the wild goddesses of vengeance of the ancient nature religion, to *Dikē* as its handmaidens. In Jaeger's remark (*op.cit.*, p. 36) that "to him [i.e., Anaximander] everything that happens in the natural world is rational through and through and subject to a rigid norm," the word "rational" therefore can only be used guardedly. It certainly may not be understood in the modern sense of natural scientific thought, and indeed, Jaeger himself emphatically warns against this.

Kurt Schilling's observation in his *Geschichte der Philosophie*[1] is very appropriate in this context:

> It is not enlightenment, and not the beginning of science in its modern sense, with its free disposal over nature, when men like these Ionian nature philosophers suddenly abandon the ancient, traditional myths and beliefs of their people and seek a full explanation of the world in terms of a fundamental principle ... Philosophy is here ... the passionate knowledge of the world. But, again, this is not in the modern sense. It is not knowledge for its own sake, or for the sake of controlling nature. Rather, its aim is to attain knowledge of the palpable, corporeal character and the exter-

---

1 Kurt Schilling, *Geschichte der Philosophie* (Munich, 1943), vol.1, p. 56.

nal aspect of this true god, to approach him directly in the investigation and contemplation of the world.

This indeed accords with Jeager's own view of ancient nature philosophy as in essence a natural theology, and even a *theodicy*. Both of these scholars thus contradict K. Reinhardt's claim (*Parmenides*, pp. 256-257) that fragment B 2 may not be understood religiously, but is merely intended as an "image."

5. Anaximenes and Anaximander. Anaximenes' Statement Concerning the Human Soul and the Divine Pneuma

According to Aetius, Anaximenes fully subscribed to Anaximander's notion that things return into the bosom of the divine Origin from which they rise. Cf. Diels-Kranz, Anaximenes B. Frag. 2: ἐκ γὰρ τούτου πάντα γίγνεσθαι καὶ εἰς αὐτὸν ἀναλύεσθαι. However, he conceives Anaximander's *apeiron* as *air*, which by condensation and rarefaction is changed into other substances. In this connection, Aetius has also preserved for us the following well-known utterance of Anaximenes: "Just as our *psychē*, which is air, rules us and holds us together, so do breath and air envelop the whole cosmos." Aetius also adds the comment that "air and breath [πνεῦμα] here are used synonymously" (οἷον ἡ ψυχή, φησίν, ἡ ἡμετέρα ἀὴρ οὖσα συγκρατεῖ ἡμᾶς, καὶ ὅλον τὸν κόσμον πνεῦμα καὶ ἀὴρ περιέχει · (λέγεται δὲ συνωνύμως ἀὴρ καὶ πνεῦμα)).

I share Jaeger's view (*op.cit.*, p. 207, note 62) that there is no convincing basis for the doubt expressed by Reinhardt, in his noted book *Parmenides* (Bonn, 1916, p. 175) concerning the authenticity of this fragment. According to him, the fragment "word for word and in its main idea" originated later. It is another question, however, whether we can grant to Jaeger that Anaximenes was the first to conceive the *apeiron* as "ensouled," and that he therein clearly felt that the divine nature of the *apeiron* should include the *power of thought*, indispensable for ruling the universe (p. 36). Regarding the first point, there can be no doubt that Anaximander conceived his *apeiron* not as a mere spatial infinity of lifeless matter, but as the boundless and ever-flowing source of life, and in this sense as "ensouled." If he had not, the motif of *Dikē* and time with its *taxis* (τάξις), which are explicitly accentuated in the preserved B fragment, would not make sense, and the notion that the deity governs the world would be even further out of the question. The modern, natural scientific concept of energy can in no way be ascribed to the ancient Milesians. For them, life and the principle of motion were still one and the same. As for Jaeger's second point, I believe that he approaches Anaximenes' "air god" too much in terms of the later conception of Diogenes of Apollonia. The latter interpreted Anaximines' concept of the deity on the basis of Anaxagoras' theory of *nous*.

One thing is certain. As long as the matter motive has the primacy in Greek thought, no trace can be found of a divine *demiurge* who *imparts form* to yet formless matter, following a *free project*, and arranges the cosmos in accordance with *rational ends*.

We should thus note that in B fragment 2, quoted above, Aetius does not have Anaximenes say that the divine *pneuma rules* the cosmos, as our soul rules us and holds us together, but only that it *encompasses* the cosmos. A comparison of this utterance with the above-cited testimony of Aristotle (*Physics, Γ* 4, 203 b 6) concerning Anaximander's *apeiron* makes it reasonable to assume that the περιέχειν spoken of here involves a κυβερνᾶν, a steering of the world, but not a typical κρατεῖν, a sovereignty in accordance with freely chosen ends, such as Anaxagoras will later in principle reserve for his pure *nous*.

If we only keep this in mind, the question whether Anaximenes also ascribed the power of thought to his divine *pneuma* actually becomes secondary. For the conflict between the earlier nature philosophy and the thinkers inspired by Anaxagoras and Socrates was concerned precisely with the question of whether or not the cosmos must be viewed as a universe that is ruled by a divine cultural power and is therefore organized in terms of a purposive, rational plan. As soon as the ground-motive of the culture religion receives consistent philosophical expression in this sense, it requires a divine power of thought that is unmingled with matter. Even Jaeger unreservedly admits that neither Anaximander nor Anaximenes had such an intelligence in mind. On the other hand, we can then acknowledge that in the Ionian thinkers the matter motive has been partially rationalized. In view of this, it is not a priori out of the question that they ascribed a certain power of thought to the divine *physis*. One could perhaps even say that this was a necessary condition for conceiving blind *Anankē* as *Dikē*, a cosmic law of retribution guided by the rational standard of proportionality. In the case of Heraclitus, the extant fragments remove all doubts on this score.

6. Textual Correction on Page 46. The Meaning of the Word νόμος in the Fragment Quoted in Note 1

On page 45-46 (text and note 1), I have used the words "rational world-law (*nomos*) and nature (*physis*)" to translate νόμος καὶ φύσις in the fragment from the pseudo-Hippocratic writing Περὶ διαίτης, appearing in note 1. My translation of the term νόμος was based on Diels-Kranz, I, 176: Heraclitus, B. Fragm. 114: ξὺν νόωι λέγοντας ἰσχυρίζεσθαι χρὴ τῶι ξυνῶι πάντων, ὅκωσπερ νόμωι πόλις, καὶ πολὺ ἰσχυροτέρως. τρέφονται γὰρ πάντες οἱ ἀνθρώπειοι νόμοι ὑπὸ ἑνὸς τοῦ θείου· κρατεῖ γὰρ τοσοῦτον ὁκόσον ἐθέλει καὶ ἐξαρκεῖ πᾶσι καὶ περιγίνεται.

> "Those who speak with rational insight must strengthen themselves with what is common to all, just as a city strenghtens itself by its law, and even much more strongly [than this]. For all hu-

man laws are nourished by the one divine law. For this holds sway as far as it will, and suffices for all, and prevails in all."

Jaeger comments here (*op.cit.*, p. 115) that "this is the first time that the idea of 'law' has appeared in philosophic thought; what is more, it is now regarded as the object of the highest and most universal knowledge; *the term is not used in the simple political sense but has been extended to cover the very nature of reality itself*" (my italics). This idea is developed more fully by Jaeger in his study *Praise of the Law.*[1]

Reinhardt likewise says that Heraclitus' θεῖος νόμος is the φύσις that "triumphs over all" and whose power "reaches into human statutes" (*Parmenides*, p. 215). In this connection, he discusses the statement from Περὶ διαίτης that I have quoted and cites the words that directly follow this, which I overlooked in my presentation: νόμον μὲν ἄνθρωποι ἔθεσαν αὐτοὶ ἑωυτοῖσιν, οὐ γιγνώσκοντες περὶ ὧν ἔθεσαν, φύσιν δὲ πάντων θεοὶ διεκόσμησαν· ("For men themselves established the *nomos* for themselves, not knowing over whom they established it; but gods put in order the *physis* of all things"). It is quite evident here that in this fragment νόμος cannot mean θεῖος νόμος (divine law), and I therefore have to correct my translation at this point.

Reinhardt himself gives the word νόμος an epistemological meaning in this context and applies it to the opinions of men who do not get beyond the external aspect of phenomena. Consequently, νόμος would contradict the true nature (φύσις) of things, inasmuch as human opinion finds a contradiction where in reality there is harmony and unity. This conception hardly seems convincing to me, however. In his book *Heracleitos von Ephesos*, p. 55, Diels translates νόμος in this passage as "lingual usage" (*Sprachgebrauch*).

It is most natural, it seems to me, to understand law here in its *political* sense. This interpretation also fits in very well with Diels-Kranz, Heraclitus, B. Fragm. 114, if θεῖος νόμος is there understood as *physis*. In this interpretation, what the passage means is that human laws are indeed tied to the divine world-order in nature, but human legislators have no knowledge of this *physis*. Neither Reinhardt's nor Diels's translation of νόμος does justice to the element of correspondence between νόμος and φύσις that is explicitly brought out in the fragment.

7. The Dialectical Combination of the Rational World-Order and the Incalculable (Irrational) in Heraclitus' Thought

It can be shown from Heraclitus, B. Fragm. 124 that the passage from Περὶ διαίτης discussed in point 6 lies completely in the line of Heraclitus; also in its dialectical identification of the *irrational* and the

---

1 W. Jaeger, "Praise of Law. The Origin of Legal Philosophy and the Greeks" in *Interpretations of Modern Legal Philosophies*: *Essays in Honor of Roscoe Pound* (New York: Oxford University Press, 1947), pp. 359 ff.

rational in nature. This fragment is taken from Theophrastus' quotation from the thinker of Ephesus in *Met.* 15 p.7 a 10: ὥσπερ σάρμα εἰκῆ κεχυμένων ὁ κάλλιστος κόσμος ("like a heap of things poured out at random, the fairest world-order.")

Diels-Kranz comments here as follows: "Probable meaning: thus it appears to the multitude, who do not comprehend the *logos.*" This interpretation, however, does not at all do justice to the typical Heraclitean dialectic, and the context of the quotation in Theophrastus makes it unmistakably clear that he himself understood the passage differently. For he ascribes to Heraclitus the irrational notion that, although the universe does exist in a rational order (ἐν τάξει καὶ λόγωι), none of this is present in the *archai*. In Heraclitus' divine *archē*, the irrational and the rational are indeed conceived dialectically as one and the same.

Heraclitus' dialectic has a deep, irrationalistic root in the matter motive. In his thought, the θεῖος νόμος, i.e., the supreme divine order, wisdom, and beauty, springs dialectically from the ever-flowing, incalculable divinity. The well-known utterance in Heraclitus, B. Fragm. 123, φύσις κρύπτεσθαι φιλεῖ ("*physis* loves to conceal itself") is also in keeping with this.

8. The More Recent Interpretation of Heraclitus. Is the Theory of Eternal Flux Attributable to Heraclitus?

The older interpretation of Heraclitus' thought, put forward in particular by Zeller and Burnet, was wholly in line with the view of Plato and Aristotle that was later propounded by the ancient doxographers from Themistius to Nemesius of Emesa. These writers placed Heraclitus completely within the line of Milesian nature philosophy.

Cornford already took exception to this view in the work discussed in the text, *From Religion to Philosophy* (1912). Nevertheless, he did not object to the notion deriving from Plato's *Cratylus* (402 A) that Heraclitus taught that all things are in eternal flux. On the contrary, he brought this doctrine into connection with the Dionysian motif of the ever-flowing stream of life, as I also have done, and interpreted Heraclitus' thought as a mystical philosophy of the oneness of all life.

Reinhardt, in the extremely interesting book that I have often mentioned, *Parmenides und die Geschichte der griechischen Philosophie* (Bonn, 1916), was the first to turn against Plato's interpretation of Heraclitus' philosophy as a "theory of flux." He calls it a fundamental misunderstanding to think that πάντα ῥεῖ (all is in flux), the statement that Plato ascribes to Heraclitus, lays hold of the latter's basic idea. According to Reinhardt (*op.cit.*, pp. 206-207), Heraclitus taught the exact opposite of this, namely, the constancy of *physis* throughout all change. And further, against the view deriving from Aristotle (*Met.*, A 3, 984 a 8) that Heraclitus identified fire as the *archē* instead of Thales' water and

Anaximenes' and Diogenes' air, Reinhardt observes that the Heraclitean counterpart to the *apeiron* of Anaximander and the ὄν of Parmenides is not fire, but the ἓν τὸ σοφόν (the one Wise). In this connection, he has in mind particularly Diels-Kranz I, Heraclitus B. Fragm. 108 and 32. The latter fragment will be discussed below, while the former reads: ὁκόσων λόγους ἤκουσα, οὐδεὶς ἀφικνεῖται ἐς τοῦτο, ὥστε γιγνώσκειν ὅτι σοφόν ἐστι πάντων κεχωρισμένον. ("Of all those whose doctrines I have heard, no one attains to the realization that the Wise is something separate from all things.")

Reinhardt claims that Heraclitus could only have developed this conception of a divine unity which maintains itself within the contrary elements of the *physis*-process against the background of Parmenides' rigid oneness of being and in opposition to it. According to him, the obscure thinker from Ephesus had here found the way to preserve the multiplicity present in the world of becoming in the face of Parmenides' argument by conceiving of the unity in a fundamentally different way. In this manner, Reinhardt reverses the traditionally accepted chronological order of Parmenides' and Heraclitus' philosophies; but both Jaeger (p. 123) and I find such an hypothesis unprovable.

As for Reinhardt's attitude toward the Platonic interpretation of Heraclitus' philosophy as a theory of flux, it appears to me that his opposition to this is just as one-sided as Plato's representation of Heraclitus' theory of eternal flux in his *Cratylus*. Indeed, it is true that the statement πάντα ῥεῖ does not occur in literal form in Diels-Kranz's Heraclitus B. fragments. Nevertheless, the teaching that all things are eternally in flux does come through clearly in B. Fragm. 12, 49 a, and 91. When he takes issue with this theory in the *Cratylus* and the *Theaetetus* (189 E), Plato for his part ignores Heraclitus' conception of the constancy of the divine unity within the process of eternal flux and also his idea of the θεῖος νόμος. In consequence, he is actually doing battle more with Protagoras' and Cratylus' skeptical version of Heraclitus' theory of eternal flux than with Heraclitus himself, and this probably was his intention. For that matter, I have shown in the text how Protagoras deliberately severed Heraclitus' matter principle from his theory of the divine *nomos* in order to undermine the whole philosophy of nature in an epistemological manner. Reinhardt's claim (*op.cit.*, p. 88) that Protagoras' theory of knowledge ties in, not with Heraclitus, but with Parmenides' epistemological relativism in respect of *doxa*, once again is hardly given a convincing basis.

All the same, the original nucleus of Heraclitus' theory cannot have been his conception of a constant divine unity that maintains itself amidst the oppositions present in the process in which visible phenomena are involved. This was no innovation with respect to the theories of Anaximander and Anaximenes, for these thinkers taught the same.

As I have argued in the text, the unique character of Heraclitus' philosophy rather lies in the fact that it deliberately gives expression to the religious dialectic of the form-matter motive by means of a theoretical dialectic. I can agree with Jaeger's interpretation to this extent, that we are here indeed confronted with a mystical philosophy of life, which takes up the new religious problems raised by the Milesian nature philosophers regarding the status of individual (formal) existence over against the divine primordial ground, and works these out dialectically into a rule of life in which conscious submission to the $\theta\epsilon\hat{\imath}o\varsigma$ $\nu\acuteo\mu o\varsigma$ becomes the highest practical wisdom. In contrast, I have already noted in the text that the actual cosmological questions of the Milesians remain in the background and are only dealt with in part by Heraclitus. It is then also my view that Heraclitus' fire can only be regarded as the visible, physical manifestation of the invisible divine unity.

But, then, how are we to understand this divine unity? This question can only be answered in terms of the dialectic of the Greek ground-motive itself, a dialectic to which Cornford, Reinhardt, Jaeger, and Gigon were all blind. Heraclitus' deity, like those of Anaximander and Anaximenes, is conceived primarily in terms of the Greek matter motive in its original sense. It is the ever-flowing stream of life that cannot be circumscribed by any form. For Heraclitus, therefore, the deity is identical with the process of *physis*, as is made unmistakably clear in B. Fragm. 67: "God is day night, winter summer, war peace, satiety hunger. But he changes just as fire, which, when it is mixed with incenses, is named after the aroma of each." B. Fragm. 108, which I have cited above, does not conflict with this. If we bear in mind that this deity cannot be limited by any form, it becomes evident that the Wise (the divine unity) is separate from all transitory things appearing in contrary visible forms. This however does not mean, as Jaeger supposes (p. 125), that it is not present in everything but rather transcends all things. Heraclitus' deity is not the one God of Xenophanes, who indeed transcends visible nature since he is essentially a form-god with a supersensible character.

In his important book *Untersuchungen zu Heraklit*,[1] Olof Gigon develops the idea that Heraclitus' theology is a foreign element in his philosophy. In his view, it stands in peculiar contrast to his cosmology and must have originated in Xenophanes' concept of the deity. This view is indefensible, however. In fact, Jaeger himself rejects it. The mere fact that Heraclitus passes an unfavorable judgment on Xenophanes in B. Fragm.40 makes Gigon's thesis extremely improbable. Jaeger fails to explain, however, how Heraclitus' deity can then be conceived as transcendent.

---

1   Olof Gigon, *Untersuchungen zu Heraklit*, (Leipzig, 1935), pp. 135 ff.

In my view, it is necessary to realize that the characterization of this deity as the ever-flowing stream of life, in which "the way up and down is one and the same" (B Fragm. 60), leaves something unsaid. In the dialectical theology of the obscure Ephesian, the matter motive once again calls forth the form motive of the culture religion, and it is fully in keeping with his dialectical mode of thought to look for the unity of the polar opposites in this theology as well. This offers a natural explanation of the meaning of B. Fragm. 32, 33, and 64:

B. Fragm. 32: ἓν τὸ σοφὸν μοῦνον λέγεσθαι οὐκ ἐθέλει καὶ ἐθέλει Ζηνὸς ὄνομα.
("The one, the only Wise, is unwilling and yet willing to be called by the name of Zeus.")
B. Fragm. 33: νόμος καὶ βουλῆι πείθεσθαι ἑνός.
("Law is also to obey the will of a One.")
B. Fragm. 64: τὰ δὲ πάντα οἰακίζει Κερουνός
("But the universe is steered by the thunderbolt.")

This last utterance must be understood as speaking of the thunderbolt of Zeus, who himself is symbolized in fire.

It is then also easy to understand that, in Heraclitus' conception of the deity, the matter motive has been strongly rationalized. This rationalization definitely proceeds further here than with the Milesians, although *physis* still retains here a deep, irrationalistic substratum. The wisdom of Zeus, the supreme god of the culture religion, is transferred to the divine stream of life and elaborated in the θεῖος νόμος. At the same time, the anthropomorphic limitation that this god had received in the Olympian religion is done away with. This wisdom, however, is not the wisdom of a demiurge.

9. The Interpretation of Parmenides, B. Fragm. 3

Reinhardt has emphatically established (*op.cit.*, p. 30) that in the didactic poem of Parmenides, *being* and *thought*, and also *appearance* and *doxa*, are conceived as one and the same. He observes in this regard:

Indeed, if one looks more closely, a separation between thought and being (or appearance and representation) simply cannot be carried through in the fragments. Parmenides begins the [path of] *doxa* (δόξα) by telling (Fragm. 8, 53) that men have agreed to give names to two different forms, but he does not set forth, as one should expect, how they produced their worldview from the two forms. Rather, the content of thought at once takes on a life of its own. Darkness and light join together and constitute the world; from the theory of knowledge there springs, to our surprise, a cosmogony; what was nothing but a name, a bare asser-

tion, an *onoma* (ὄνομα), enters into physical relationships and finally gives birth even to man himself along with his cognitive
acts.

In his *Der Ursprung der griechischen Philosophie, von Hesiod bis
Parmenides* (B. Schwabe & Co., 1945, p. 267), Gigon takes the same
view.

10. The Religious Interpretation of Parmenides' Ontology

Page 54, text. Various modern writers (particularly Burnet, Reinhardt,
and Gigon) have attached undue importance to the fact that the preserved fragments of Parmenides' didactic poem do not explicitly style
being as a deity or call it divine. Reinhardt, whose book on Parmenides
is especially important because of the new light it has shed on the extremely fragmentary remnants of the second part of the poem, thinks
(pp. 250 ff.) that Parmenides' ontology may be characterized as a "free"
logic – i.e., free in the sense of "lacking all admixture of theology" – a
logic in which a method of pure conceptual thought is supposedly developed. According to Reinhardt, Xenophanes was the first to give a
theological interpretation to Parmenides' concept of being. In the main,
Gigon has followed him in this view (see my critique of this bold hypothesis on page 62, note 2).

As far as Reinhardt is concerned, this view of Parmenides' ontology
does not stand alone. Within pre-Socratic philosophy, according to him,
Anaximander, Parmenides, Anaxagoras, Empedocles, and Democritus all
stand equally outside the sphere of religious thought. Only in the case of
Pythagoras and Heraclitus will he grant that the striving for pure scientific
knowledge is interlaced "in a strange manner" with a basic mystical-religious interpretation of the world.

Jaeger (*op.cit.*, chapter 6) arrives at a completely different view of
Parmenides' metaphysics, one that is much closer to my own. He stresses
the fact that in his solemn *prooemium* Parmenides, like Hesiod, appeals to
a special divine revelation that discloses to him the path of Truth. "His
mysterious vision in the realm of light is a genuine religious experience"
(p. 96), and Jaeger claims that the prototype for this religious experience
is to be sought in the mysteries and the initiation ceremonies. Nevertheless, since being is not explicitly named as a deity, Jaeger too does not
venture to give a theological interpretation to Parmenides' metaphysics.
He rather concludes that "the religious element lies more in the way the
man has been affected by his discovery, and in his firm and decided han-
dling of the alternatives of truth and appearance, than in any classification
of the object of his research as divine" (p. 107). It seems to me that this
statement once again attaches too much weight to the formal question of
names. To my mind, it is much more important to focus on *predicates* that
the Eleatic thinker attributes to being, for these acquire distinctively divine overtones in their polar antithesis to the predicates taken from the

matter motive which Milesian nature philosophy assigned to the divine *archē*.

As I have argued in the text, Parmenides, B. Fragm. 8 42-44 (see note 2, p. 56 text) in particular must be considered here in its full religious significance. Because of his lack of insight into the religious ground-motive of Greek thought, Jaeger was no more able to do justice to this fragment than were the other, later writers whom I consulted. He regards Parmenides' idea of being as a conception in which the endeavor of the Ionian nature philosophers to strip the world of its form is carried to its ultimate conclusion by depriving it even of its character as a world. "When Parmenides asserts that the Existent is equidistant on all sides like a sphere (an obviously Pythagoreanizing comparison), this is, so to speak, its one last vestige of world-form which he has not succeeded in removing; and even in this passage he makes it plain that he is dealing merely with a comparison" (pp. 106-107).

This statement is rife with misunderstanding! In point of fact, the entire fragment only receives its meaning from the religious *form motive*, and in the uranic, Pythagorean-Orphic conception that this motive has here, it stands diametrically opposed to the religious matter motive as this came to expression in the Milesians' idea of the deity.

The ascription of the spherical form to "true being" in this fragment cannot be based on a mere comparison. This is clearly evident from the fact that Parmenides directly attributes a *geometric* property to this being, namely, that it is "equally curved on every side outward from the center." The comparison applies solely to a sphere as a body perceptible to the senses (the *mass* of a globe). This latter fact is disregarded by Burnet, Ueberweg-Praechter, et al., who thought that Parmenides identified the form of being with a *material* globe. The latter writer thus comments: "According to his clear words, he rather really pictures being as a mass that fills space and is spatially bounded."[1] But what the fragment says points clearly in another direction, namely, that the spherical form of the true being is called only *comparable* to the ὄγκος, the mass, of a well-rounded globe.

It would appear that this ὄγκος refers back to the visible, fixed heavenly dome treated in Parmenides, B. Fragm.10, 5 (οὐρανὸν ἀμφὶς ἔχοντα). This is shaped like a globe, and it is constrained by *anankē* (which here again is akin to the cosmic *Dikē* of the *prooemium*) to keep the stars within the limits of their courses. In his *Der Ursprung der griechischen Philosophie*, 1945, p. 279, Gigon follows the current view in supposing that this heavenly dome must have consisted of pure fire, for Parmenides makes a corresponding claim that the earth is a mass composed of sheer

---

1 Ueberweg-Praechter: *Grundrisz der Geschichte der Philosophie des Altertums* (12th ed., 1926), p. 84.

night or darkness. "If the symmetry and equilibrium of the two forms that fill the cosmos [viz., fire and night] is to be preserved, it is obvious that the heavenly dome cannot also consist of night. For then there would be more night than light in the cosmos, and what is more, this would be contrary to all appearance."

Now, Cicero relates in his *De natura deorum*, I, 11, 28 (cf. Diels-Kranz, I, 224; Parmenides A Fragm. 37) that Parmenides claimed that the heavens are surrounded by a ring of light ("lucis orbem qui cingit caelum"), which he called God (quem appellat deum). He then adds "in quo neque figuram divinam neque sensum quisquam suspicari potest." It is evident from Aetius' account in the same A fragment that this ring of light – of which Cicero says further: "coronae simile efficit ($\sigma\tau\epsilon\phi\acute{\alpha}\nu\eta\nu$ appellat)" – is not identical to the fiery dome of the visible heavens themselves, but rather lies beyond this. It is only in this context that the connection with Parmenides, B. Fragm. 8, 42-44, becomes fully clear. Parmenides' sphere of being is indeed conceived in a religious sense as a sphere of light, and this is represented within the visible cosmos by the material fiery celestial dome with which the above B fragment says it is comparable.

In this connection Gigon makes the following comment (p. 280): "In terms of its form, the outermost layer of fire is the counterpart of the tenebrous earth. It is also the representative of being, whereas the earth is the representative of non-being. But this is not all. It is also the divine, which stands opposite the abode of men. It is the deity itself and the province of the deity, which therefore indeed is also called 'the outermost Olympus' in 28 B 11.[1] If anywhere, it is here that we find the influence of Xenophanes' theology, which was absent in Parmenides' ontology. In the outermost ring of fire encircling the cosmos and ... beyond the cosmos, which is called God, Xenophanes' spherical deity is taken into the cosmos of opinion ..."

This conception too, however, leaves no place for the supersensible sphere of being that B. Fragm. 8, 42-44 expressly sets forth. Gigon writes, "Being is beyond the possibility of perception and is therefore only comparable to the sphere. The cosmos of semblance, which still contains a part of being, is a sphere" (p. 275). He too ignores, therefore, the subtle distinction made in the above fragment. What is more, if the "divine sphere of light" spoken of by Cicero indeed must be accounted to the cosmos of semblance, it is altogether unclear how this actual God relates to the *daemōn* who, in B. Fragm. 12, is said to "steer all things" ($\mathring{\eta}\ \pi\acute{\alpha}\nu\tau\alpha\ \kappa\upsilon\beta\epsilon\rho\nu\mathring{\alpha}\iota$). Gigon concedes that this *daemōn* is a mixture of light and darkness and supposes that her abode lies in the lunar sphere. But what function would then remain within the visible cosmos for a pure, spherical god of light?

---

1 Diels-Kranz, I, 241: Parmenides, B. Fragm. 11.

*11. The Orphic Myth of Dionysus Zagreus. The Pantheistic
Tendency in the Ancient Orphic Cosmogomies*

Pages 59-61, text. The Orphic myth of Dionysus Zagreus exhibits a clear pantheistic trait that is typical of Orphic theology as a whole and is connected with the so-called "theocrastic" tendency, in which the divine forms are intermingled.

This pantheism comes out very clearly in the well-known verses from the pseudo-Aristotelian writing *De mundo*, c. 7. In his noted collection of Orphic fragments, Franz Kern has classed this under the "Fragmenta veteriora," and the second line has now been included by Diels-Kranz, I (Heraclitus, B. Fragm. 6, at the end), among the attested ancient witnesses. The verses read:[1]

> Zeus became the first and he is to the last the lord of the thunderbolt; Zeus is the head and the middle; everything has come into being through Zeus; Zeus is the foundation of earth and heaven, which is strewn with stars; Zeus took on human form; Zeus became an immortal nymph; Zeus is the breath of all; Zeus rules in the glow of the flickering fire; Zeus is in the depth of the sea, in the beams of the sun, and in the light of the moon; Zeus is the king and the lord of all, the lord of the thunderbolt; he hid everything in himself; then he brings it again to friendly light. Heavenwards, out of his holy breast, by means of famous deeds.

This pantheistic tendency also finds clear expression in various fragments from the Orphic cosmogonies. 7 B. Fragm. 3 (Diels-Kranz, I, 48) thus says of Pherecedes' cosmogony: "Pherecedes says that when Zeus purposed to form the world, he changed into *Erōs*, because he was combining the cosmos from the opposite [elements] into harmony and love and was sowing the same endeavor in all things, and unity that pervades all." It is known that Pherecedes of Syros (died ca. 540 B.C.), who already displays the clear influence of Milesian nature philosophy, proposed as the eternal *archai Zas* (Zeus, i.e., the aether or light), *Chthonie* (the earth), and *Chronos* (time). The Orphic dualism between the heavenly sphere of light and the earthly sphere of darkness is maintained here. Pherecedes, however, has *Zas* and *Chthonie* unite in marriage, just as the Orphic myth of Dionysus has the latter enter into the process of ever-flowing *physis*, where he is torn apart into a multiplicity before his return into the divine luminous unity. In another ancient Orphic cosmogony, *Chronos* brings forth the "world-egg," the top part of which became *Ouranos* and the bottom part *Gē* (the earth). Here again there follows a marriage between heaven and earth (see 1 A. Fragm. 13).

It seems to me that the undeniably pantheistic trait in Orphic theology is an important indicator of the relative character of the ancient Orphic belief

---

1   *De mundo*, tr. E.S. Forster. *The Works of Aristotle Translated into English*, ed. W.D. Ross, vol.III (Oxford: Clarendon Press, 1931).

in the immortality of the individual soul. In the text I have repeatedly called attention to this Orphic belief, as it occurs in the ancient Pythagoreans and in Empedocles.

12. The Third Path in the Second Part of Parmenides' Poem

On page 59 of the text I wrote that in the second part of Parmenides' didactic poem, the goddess *Dikē* undertakes to expound the *second* path of inquiry. In this I was following the words of Parmenides, B. Fragm. 2 and 6. Reinhardt (*op.cit.*, p. 36) has rightly pointed out, however, that the poem actually sets out three paths: (1) being *is*; (2) being *is not*; (3) being *is and is not*. He supports this by referring to Gorgias's treatise *On Non-Being.*[1]

The path that is expounded in the second part of the poem is then, as a matter of fact, not the second [one] but the third one. See also under 13.

13. The Interpretation of Parmenides, B. Fragm. 8, 50 ff.

In an important article on Parmenides' didactic poem, which appeared in the magazine *Gids* in 1948, Peter Brommer gave the words τῶν μίαν οὐ χρεών ἐστιν in Parmenides, B. Fragm. 8, 54 an interpretation that departs from the prevailing view.[2] According to him, they mean that a single form is not sufficient for explaining the visible phenomena of nature, but that two forms are necessary. Of course, such an interpretation alters the entire meaning of this fragment. It seems to me, however, that this view is difficult to maintain, even for linguistic reasons alone. To my knowledge, the words οὐ χρεών ἐστιν can never mean "is not sufficient." The word χρεών means either "what is necessary" or "what is proper."

Brommer's interpretation favors the attempts that have recently been made to grant a more positive meaning to the second part of the poem. Some have found it difficult to believe that the great Eleatic thinker could have denied the reality of the phenomena of nature, and that – as would necessarily follow from a purely logical interpretation of the first part of the poem – the summation of his entire wisdom could be found in the logical judgment of identity, "being is." For this reason, an attempt was made to give Parmenides' ontology a role in explaining the process of becoming similar to that played by the *archē* of Milesian nature philosophy (cf., e.g., Kurt Reizler, *Parmenides*, Frankfurt, 1934, pp. 50 ff.). Brommer felt, however, that this interpretation, which is also rejected by Jaeger (*op.cit.*, p. 105), results in a total distortion of Parmenides' ontology that is contradicted by the fragments themselves. He looks for a solution, therefore, in the view that the first part of the poem presents more of a directly felt *experience* of the absolute unity of being under the guidance of divine revelation, while the second part offers an explanation of the world that is ac-

---

1 Cf. Diels-Kranz, II, 279-280. Sext Emp. *adv. math*, VII, 65 ff.

2 Dooyeweerd did not give any further reference information to the work of Brommer.

commodated to human *mental representation* and *conceptual thought*, which is always compelled to divide the unity asunder into plurality.

From this latter point of view, light and darkness are two necessary, mutually supplementary aspects of being. "We men at any rate do not escape the irresistible necessity of 'conceiving' reality in a twofold series of concepts; that is the necessary 'form' in which we are condemned to understand being."

It is evident that Brommer's translation of the words οὐ χρεών ἐστιν already implies a complete theory concerning the relationship between the first and second parts of the poem. This theory was formulated, however, without taking into consideration the dialectical religious ground-motive of Greek thought; and it therefore could apply equally well to a modern philosophical system that contrasts the intuitive, ontological contemplation of the absolute with the discursive, conceptual thought in which what is only relative is grasped.

Even though Aristotle expressly affirms that light and darkness represent being and non-being, respectively, Brommer dismisses this with the remark, "Listen to Parmenides' sharp censure of the two-headed persons (fr. 6, 5, and 8) who caused Being and Non-Being to cooperate equally in the foundation of the universe, and then say whether it is likely that he here, and under the guidance of the goddess no less, could have taken recourse to the same weakness." But if one reads fragment 6 in its entirety, what becomes clear is that, in this "censure of the two-headed," the goddess is disclosing to Parmenides precisely the third path that is pursued in the second part of the poem only to keep the philosopher from being ignorant of the deceptive, illusory opinions of men (frag. 1, 31-32), and their *doxa* from outstripping his own (frag. 8, 61).

According to Brommer, however, the path followed in the second part of the poem holds that the one being is conceived in the two contrary forms of light and darkness. In support of this he appeals to the Pythagorean table of opposites, which in his view also is not concerned with the opposition between being and non-being. Rather, the distinction that it makes allegedly lies within the bosom of being, in this case within the bosom of number itself. "The Void, as Non-Being, indeed has a function in number for the Pythagoreans, but then in all numbers; it serves to make possible the distinction of points, which is what constitutes the essence of number; but it plays no role at all in valuing the opposites."

Thus, if I understand him rightly, Brommer perceives in the method followed in the second part of the poem a *fourth* path, which indeed would have to be distinguished from the path indicated in B. Fragm. 6, lines 8 and 9, namely, that "Being and Non-Being are to be considered the same and not the same," and that "all things follow the path of a circle" (παλίντροπος κέλευθος). But what would this distinction be? I am unable to see that there is one. Besides, if indeed the method followed in the second part of the poem differs fundamentally from the one condemned in B. Fragm. 6, lines 8 and 9, it would have to be regarded as a completely new approach that has not at all been critically prepared for in the first part. This view has little to commend it. The introduction to the second part of the poem (B. Fragm. 8, 55) does state that "they divided the form [of *physis*] into two opposed [forms]"; but those who do this must of necessity be reckoned among the mortals whom B. Fragm. 6 censures as "two-headed." For one cannot split being into opposites without saying that being and non-being are the same and not the same.

If one accepts Brommer's interpretation of τῶν μίαν οὐ χρεών ἐστιν – ἐν ὧι πεπλανημένοι εἰσίν, the words that directly precede the above quotation from B. Fragm. 8, he is then immediately faced with the question as to which predecessors of Parmenides taught that the visible cosmos can be explained in terms of a single principle, and without the appearance of pairs of opposites in the visible forms. For it cannot be that Parmenides' critique is here aimed at the unity of the divine principle of Origin, which the Milesians had postulated and which is also found in the Pythagorean *Monas*. This unity, considered by itself, apart from the eternal flux in the process of becoming, could be accepted by the Eleatic thinker without reservation. His critique was of necessity directed exclusively against the *combination* of form and matter, being and non-being (becoming), a combination which neither the Milesians nor Heraclitus nor the Pythagoreans could bring about without resorting to *opposition*.

And now, all the predecessors of Parmenides unanimously taught that the one Origin is manifested within the visible cosmos in pairs of opposites. The opposition between light and darkness, which receives Parmenides' particular mention here, is of Orphic-Pythagorean lineage. In view of this, the additional remark in B. Fragm. 8, 54, "at which point they have fallen into error," would be senseless if Brommer's translation of the words τῶν μίαν οὐ χρεών ἐστί were correct. In opposition to this, Gigon expresses the generally accepted interpretation, which was first articulated by Aristotle, in his comment:

> The remark that the one of the two forms ought not to have been given a name is decisive. The other therefore has its name rightly. The latter thus stands for being, the former for non-being. The error of men is that they give a name also to non-being. The pair is fire and night, thus, the same pair that in Anaximander proceeded from the unlimited and there constituted the starry heavens.[1]

---

1   Gigon, *op.cit.*, pp. 271-272 (English translation by translator).

14. Parmenides' Pythagorean-Orphic Conception of the Soul

Page 60, text and note 2. Parmenides' statement, reported by Simplicius, that souls are sent from the visible to the invisible, and then back again from the invisible into the visible, is interpreted by Gigon (*op.cit.*, p. 281) – in my view correctly – entirely in terms of B. Fragments 12 and 13. He then observes: "[This] is nothing other than the unending rhythm of Pythagorean immortality, the alternation of death and reincarnation. This teaching too surely falls into line with the principle of the two forms. The alternation takes place between light and night ... The inescapable question is then: what is light and what is night? Earthly being will not be 'light,' for the earth is indeed out of night. ...

"There is a passage that without question supplements this one. 28 A. 1 says that according to Parmenides 'man descended originally from the sun.' Hence, the luminous being of man, or the soul, in the pure, fiery region of the sun is an obvious transformation of the Pythagorean view already referred to which holds that the abode of the soul is in the stars. At the same time, we see once again how the equation 'night = non-being = world of opinion = world of morality' continues to operate even in the details of the cosmic structure.

"The earth not only consists of the form of night in physical terms. It is also the true region of the dead in which the souls are buried, and Empedocles later depicted it as such in his poem of *Purifications*."[1]

15. The Form Motive in Xenophanes' Idea of God

Pages 60, 61, and 66, text. In several of the Diels-Kranz, A fragments (cf. Xenophanes, A. Fragm. 28, 31, and 33) we are told that Xenophanes described the deity as σφαιροειδές (like a sphere). If these *testimonia* can be considered reliable on this point, we are thus confronted with the same problem in Xenophanes' idea of the divine form that we met with in Parmenides' divine form of being. It indeed seems highly improbable that Xenophanes would have identified the divine form with the *material* celestial dome, which according to the *testimonia* was first spoken of by Anaximander.

Gigon has correctly pointed out that the fragments of Xenophanes' poem on nature delineate a picture of the world that altogether excludes the possibility of a cosmos that is spherically bounded. He further notes that the comparison of the deity to a sphere can only be an indication of Pythagorean influence, which according to Gigon dates from a later stage in Xenophanes' development than the extremely primitive notions in his philosophy of nature. In my view, we here again have to regard this sphere as a supersensible, purely mathematical form; otherwise the word σφαιροειδές would have no meaning. In this case, however, we are left without any clear indication such as that provided by Parmenides, B.

---

1 *Ibid.*, p. 281 (English translation by translator).

Fragm. 8, 42-44, something that was also the cause of Aristotle's uncertainty in *Metaphysics* A 5, 986 b 21 (see page 57, text and note 2).

The fact that Xenophanes' conception of the deity has no connection at all with his philosophy of nature once again underscores the position taken in the text that no trace of a metaphysical theory concerning the relationship between principles of form and matter can be found in his thought.

B. Fragm. 23 and 25, quoted in note 2 on page 66, remain highly significant for Xenophanes' idea of God. The latter fragment says that the one God without toil shakes or stirs (κραδαίνει) all things by the thought power of his mind. Gigon here makes the comment: "Xenophanes calls the world rule κραδαίνειν, "shaking." We can gather from this not only that God stands opposite the cosmos and is completely distinct from it, but also that this rule is still described by means of mythological notions, which regarded the quaking of the earth as one of the foremost manifestations of divine presence."[1] In my opinion, the fragment indicates more than this. It shows that Xenophanes' religious form motive, like that of Parmenides, still cannot be the pure form motive of the culture religion. In the *testimonia* from the A fragments cited above, the κραδαίνειν spoken of by Xenophanes has already been replaced – perhaps partly due to the influence of Plato and Aristotle – by a κρατεῖν. For his part, Xenophanes instead thought of the divine world rule in terms of the notions of nature religion and merely rationalized and intellectualized these. As I have observed in the text on page 62, he can for this reason only be regarded as the forerunner of Anaxagoras' theory of *nous*.

The *nous* of Xenophanes' deity is neither a theoretical intelligence, as is the case in Parmenides, nor a practical power. It is rather an intelligence which in its governance of the visible events of nature is manifested only as *action*, without following any definite cultural plan in this.

16. Xenophanes' Theological Skepticism

Page 61, text. I can fully concur with Gigon in his observation that Xenophanes' theological skepticism can only be understood against the background of the deity's omniscience, in comparison with which all human knowledge is nothing more than *doxa*. I too am inclined to interpret B. Fragm. 34 in this sense. However, I would not go so far as to restrict Xenophanes' doubt to his cosmology, which he developed early on, and to grant his doctrine of God (which Gigon says arose later under Pythagorean influence) the status of true and certain knowledge. The fragment contains no evidence whatsoever for such a distinction.

---

1 *Ibid.*, p. 189 (English translation by translator).

17. The Original Pythagorean Theory of Numbers

Page 66-66, text. The Pythagoreans' original, *dynamic* conception of number is still preserved in the definition given by Nicomachus, the Neo-Pythagorean, which holds that number is "a flow of quantity made up of units" (ποσότητος χύμα ἐκ μονάδων συγκέιμενον; Nicomachus, *Introd. arith.* A 7. 1, quoted by Sir Thomas Heath, *A History of Greek Mathematics*, Vol. I, 1921, p. 70).

Aristotle (*Met.* M 7, 1080 b 18, 32) explicitly states that the Pythagoreans constructed the entire heavens out of numbers, but not out of monads, since they held that numbers have magnitude (extension). For them the *Monas* was not itself a number, but rather the *archē* or principle of all numbers. In *Metaphysics* N 5, 1092 b 10, Aristotle provides an illustration of how the Pythagoreans used sensible points in order to denote the units of a number having a particular form: "Eurytus determined which number belongs to which thing (e.g., this is the number of man, that of horse) and imitated the forms of living things with pebbles, like those who arrange numbers in the forms of a triangle or a square" (see further, Heath, *op.cit.*, pp. 76 ff.).

18. Alcmaeon's Conception of Logical Thought as the Core of the Human Soul. His Great Physiological Discovery

Page 75, note 1, cf. the discussion in the text. It appears from various *testimonia* (Alcmaeon, A. Fragm. 10 and 11) that Alcmaeon taught that the brain is the seat of logical thought, a view that Plato adopted in his *Timaeus*. This insight was closely related to his great physiological discovery.

According to Chalcidius (in his commentary on Plato's *Timaeus*, Alcmaeon, A. Fragm. 10), Alcmaeon was the first person to perform dissection, and he did this upon living animals (see Julius Hirschberg, *Archiv für Opthalmologie*, 105 [1921], pp. 129 ff., and *Vorlesungen über hippokratische Heilkunde* [Berlin, 1922], pp. 19 ff.). In doing this he observed that nerve pathways (as we call them) depart from our sense organs and lead into the brain at certain points. He thus discovered that the brain is the central organ of sense perception. What is more, he laid out for the first time a complete physiology of sensation, in which his explanation of the process of optic perception in particular has drawn special notice. He apparently conceived the glass-like body of the eye as a kind of mirror that reflects objects in the outside world, producing "images" that are conveyed to the brain through the "light-conducting paths" (i.e., the optic nerves).

Theophrastus says that Alcmaeon was one of those who denied that perception can be explained in terms of the action of like upon like. On this point, we therefore must regard him as a precursor of Anaxagoras.

19. The Meaning of the Psychē *in Homer and in the Branch of Greek Philosophy Influenced by Orphism*

Page 78, text. Rohde's conception of the Homeric *psychē*, which prevailed until the publication of W. Otto's book *Die Manen oder von den Urformen des Totenglaubens* (1923), is summarized in his statement: "In the Homeric conception a human being has a twofold presence: his perceptible manifestation, and his invisible likeness that is first set free at death. This and nothing else is his *psychē*."[1] Along the lines of Spencer's and Tylor's animistic theory, he explained this notion of a "second ego" or "double" (*psychē*), which lies dormant for the duration of human life and is only released at death, on the basis of our experience of a seemingly dual life in dreams, in ecstasy, and in unconsciousness.

Otto has once and for all refuted this "dream theory." Indeed, Rohde betrayed a lack of critical insight when he sought support for his interpretation of the Homeric conception of the *psychē* in the following poetic utterance of Pindar:

And all men's bodies follow the call
of over-mastering death;
And yet there will remain behind
A living *eidōlon* of the living,
For this alone comes from the gods.
It sleeps while the members are active,
But to those themselves asleep,
It reveals in myriad visions
The approach ordained by fate
Of doleful things or joyful.

What these verses give expression to is the influence of the Orphic dualism between the soul, which originates in the heavens, and the earthly material body; and of course there can be no thought of this in Homer. Nevertheless, we shall see presently that there is, in fact, a certain connection between the way the *eidōlon* is conceived in Homer and in Pindar; but this naturally does not mean that Homer's conception can be interpreted on the basis of Pindar's. On the contrary, the conception of Pindar must at a certain point rather have tied in with the Homeric view.

As I have observed in the text, Otto himself (*op.cit.*, pp. 18, 26, 32) identifies Homer's "life-soul" with the *thumos*. He emphatically denies that the *psychē* ever means life-soul in this poet. According to him, the *psychē* of the living person in Homer never stands for an independent entity like the *thumos*. Rather, it simply means "life." But Otto himself weakens the force of the basic contrast he has made here when shortly

---

1   Rohde, *Psyche*, I, 5.

thereafter he admits that *thumos* and *psychē* in Homer often equally denote life.

It seems to me that the question as to what ψυχή meant for Homer cannot be answered by considering how it should be translated into a modern language. A modern person has learned to distinguish the organic aspect, that of life, from the psychical aspect. But for the Greek, and a fortiori for a Greek from Homer's day, all life was pervaded by soul. In the text I have understood the *psychē* of the living person in Homer as a blood-soul or life-soul and this is wholly in keeping with the notion in the *Odyssey*, XI, that the shadows in the underworld can temporarily regain earthly consciousness and memory (both of which are tied to bodily life for Homer) only by drinking blood. This *psychē*, however, is not at all conceived as having an individual, personal form. Within the framework of the Greek form-matter motive, it is rather an impersonal matter-soul animating everything that has life.

Jaeger (*op.cit.*, p. 84), who on first consideration seems to agree with Otto's interpretation of Homer's "*psychē*" of the living," in fact understands this differently. Otto explicitly states (p. 26) that "in Homer this *soul of the living* is called the θυμός." He then further elucidates this life-soul as the invisible being that in the belief of many peoples is harbored within man "as the sustainer of his life and the bearer of his psychical and mental functions." In other words, Otto regards the *thumos* as both the life-soul and the seat of the psychical and mental functions. Jaeger, by contrast, makes a distinction between the *psychē*, the life-soul which deserts the body at death but has neither thought nor feeling, and the *thumos* or conscious soul. However, unlike Onians, the Cambridge professor to whom I have referred in the text, he connects the *psychē* etymologically with the breath and the *thumos* with the smoking blood that is poured out in offerings (θύω).

In the first of these derivations Jaeger follows Ernst Bickel, who in his treatise *Homerischer Seelenglaube* (1925) seeks a satisfying answer to the question of how Homer could have used the one word, ψυχή, for both life and the ghost of the dead (the shadow of the lifeless body), a problem that Otto had left unresolved. Just as I do, Bickel contests Otto's idea that the ψυχή is the abstract concept "life." He understands it rather as the "breath-soul," which according to him was the basic etymological meaning of the word (cf. Homer's use of the verb ἀποψύχω to mean "exhale"[1]). On this basis, Jaeger now comments (*op.cit.*, p. 81): "It was then fairly easy to think of the breathsoul that escaped at death as identical with what primitive belief held to be the one thing remaining from the dead person which could under certain circumstances become an object of human

---

1   Otto rejected this etymological approach to the problem, which in his view is irrelevant.

sense perception – namely, the ghost." In my view, this cannot offer a so-lution to the above problem if one continues to accept Otto's notion, which is based solely upon his own interpretation of ethnological material, that the *eidōlon*-soul in Homer is nothing more than the shadow of the dead body conceived in purely material terms.[1] Otto appeals to the fact that this belief in ghosts, along with the uncanny fear that accompanies it, is found in all ages and exists even today; but I have grave doubts that what is in-volved in this is merely an immaterial double of the material dead body. This certainly is not the case with Samuel's ghost, which rises up in the cave of Endor at Saul's request and foretells his coming defeat and death. As for Homer himself, one can point to the *Iliad*, XXIII, 65, where the ψυχή of Patroclos, the very likeness of the man himself in all respects, his stature, his lovely eyes, and his voice, appears to his friend Achilles and adjures him to attend to his cremation and burial without delay. This epi-sode does not at all fit Otto's picture of the *eidōlon*-soul. Patroclos' *psychē* evidently still has the ability to feel and think, although it will lose its earthly faculty of memory at its entrance into Hades because its bond with the earth will then have been severed. The ghost that appears to Achilles is therefore indeed the individual shadow-form of the *whole human being*, including his earthly *psychē* and *thumos*. Even the shades in Hades appar-ently still have a shadow-*soul*, for they forbid Patroclos' entrance to Hades before he has been cremated, and they move about.

To my mind, the scholarly debate that Otto's slender volume gave rise to has neglected this point all too much. Otto himself dealt with it (*op.cit.*, pp. 32 ff.), but only in order to make it fit into his theory. In his explana-tion of this episode of the appearance of Patroclos' ghost, the shadow sup-posedly still has a soul by virtue of its contact with the uncremated body. But is not this body bereft of the *psychē* and *thumos*? The shadow could thus hardly draw its consciousness from there. Besides this, cremation did not exist in pre-Homeric times, and Rohde has shown in detail that at that time the dead were buried with great care. Nevertheless, Otto maintains that the notion of the "ghost of the dead" has remained the same through-out all periods, from primitive peoples until today.

Otto has correctly demonstrated that Rohde's conception of the *psychē* in Homer is subject to the reproach of being under the spell of the aprioris-tic animistic constructions of Spencer and Tylor. But, in like manner, Otto's own theory of the ghost of the dead can justly be accused of being in

1   It is inconceivable to me how Otto, after he has first vigorously defended this notion, can write on page 66: "According to the ancient beliefs which the Homeric Greeks and other civilized races as well shared with primitive peoples, that which lives on after death as a shadow is the whole person, not a part of him, even though this be the most important part." And how then can he conclude directly after this: "It is a soulless body in a 'spiritualized' state"? Surely this latter is not the "whole person"? (English translation by translator.)

thrall to the no less aprioristic and speculative – notwithstanding the fact that it styles itself "positivistic"– theory of Lévy-Bruhl, the student of Durkheim, which conceives the "primitive mentality" as a "pre-logical mentality." According to Otto, "This scholar has shown precisely in the case of the belief in souls that a series of concepts, which we, following the example of primitive peoples themselves, designate by the name 'soul', is no more than an expression of a feeling of affinity, whether this be with animals, with places, or with objects; and it is not likely that our intellectual approach will ever be capable of explaining such connections on its own terms."[1] In his book *Het primitieve denken in de moderne wetenschap* (1933, p. 48), T.S.G. Moelia rightly notes that this theory of the prelogical mentality has been elevated almost to a dogma, and he subjects it to a thoroughgoing critique on the basis of the ethnological evidence itself.

In my view, it is perilous in the extreme to use such an ethnological dogma as the basis for one's interpretation of Homer's concept of the *eidolon-psychē*. The problems of life and death are inescapably religious in character. Even though one might accept Otto's thesis that the notion of the "ghost of the dead" is grounded in certain recurring experiences of ghostly apparitions, one must never forget that the assimilation and interpretation of these experiences is always religiously determined and may not be construed for all times and for all peoples in accordance with the scheme of Lévy-Bruhl's prelogic. For this reason, in my view, Homer's conception of the soul must be approached in terms of the *Greek* religious ground-motive. Of course, the few remarks that I was able to devote to this matter in the text can in no way be considered an adequate treatment of this difficult question. Before that could be done, one would have to undertake a detailed critical examination of all the passages in Homer where the term *psychē* occurs, and that would lie entirely beyond the scope of this book. My study of the argument of Bickel and Jaeger has led me to think that Homer does not make such a sharp contrast between the blood-soul and the breath-soul as Onians and Cornford supposed. The life-soul can be situated in the blood as well as in the breath.

I still believe, however, that my conception of the *eidolon*-soul as the individual, supersensible shadow-form of the whole person, including the living *psychē* and the *thumos*, is in full agreement with the passages that Otto himself has adduced. Over against this, Otto's explanation of the appearance of Patroclos' *psychē* proved to be incompatible with his own theory. This *eidolon* is then actually the polar counterpart-in-death of the divine *eidolon* of the Olympian culture gods, who enjoy immortal life in a supernatural, nonsensible individual form in which there is just as little evidence of any dualism between body and soul.

---

1 Otto, *op.cit.*, p. 79 (English translation by translator).

In Pindar's later use of the word *eidōlon* for the soul of the living person, which as the immortal form of a person originates in the heavens, the form motive of the culture religion has been divorced from corporeal existence due to the influence of the Orphic dualism. The Homeric *eidōlon-psychē* has thereby lost its original meaning. The *eidōlon*-soul now belongs to the celestial region of light, and no longer to the nocturnal sphere of Hades. In dualistic fashion, it is set over against the earthly, corporeal manifestation of man, although it still partakes equally of *physis*, the ever-flowing stream of earthly life. The Orphic dualism also underlies the fundamental change in the Homeric conception that is involved in Plato's identification of the *eidōlon-psychē* with the thinking soul in his *Phaedo*. It is this that I had in mind on page p. 78 of the text, where I remarked that in Plato's *Phaedo*, a dialogue betraying Orphic influence, the Homeric *eidōlon*-soul is identified with the thinking subject of cognition. Such an identification naturally only became possible when the Homeric conception had been transformed fundamentally. And to achieve this transformation it was not sufficient, as Jaeger supposed, that the Homeric conceptions of the *psychē* (as the life-soul) and the *thumos* merely coalesce into a unified conception of the human soul.

It seems to me that the crux of the matter lies in the conception of the *eidōlon* as the individual, supersensible shadow-form of a person, which the Orphics detached from the earthly body and transported from the dark realm of death to the celestial sphere of life. This transformed *eidōlon* could then become the seat of thought and, as the case may be, feeling and life, functions which Homer divided between the *thumos* and the *psychē*. The connection I have traced between the Homeric and the Orphic conceptions of the *eidōlon-psychē* can still be clearly observed in Plato's *Gorgias*, 523 A ff. (see note 1, page 141), a passage where he describes, completely in the vein of Pindar's second Olympian ode, the judgment of the souls after death. The judge here inspects the soul that appears before him and perceives in it such deformities as can also be observed *on the body*, both while it is alive and after death. An even stronger argument for the connection I have drawn here can be found in the completely new meaning that Plato gives to the Homeric Hades, the abode of the dead, in his *Phaedo*. Hades there becomes Ἀΐδης, a supersensible, invisible realm of light to which Socrates' immortal *psychē* is destined to ascend and there behold the radiant *eidē*. See also my comments on page 153 of the text.

An Orphic transformation of the Homeric Hades already comes out in the portrayal that Empedocles' poem *Purifications* (*Katharmoi*) gives of the sorrowful world in which the fallen souls are clothed in earthly bodies (Empedocles, B. Fragm. 118 ff., especially 120-123). The poet here takes as his example the Homeric *Nekyia*, the descent of Odysseus into Hades. Just as Odysseus beholds in the underworld the hosts of the shadows (*eidōla*) of those who have died, the fallen souls of Empedocles see in the dark, "vaulted cavern" of our own world the hosts of spirits that are at work there, and both here and in Homer's *Nekyia* these are systematically enumerated. In Empedocles' poem, the fallen soul in its earthly prison is the Orphic counterpart of the Homeric *eidōlon*-soul, and here again the connection is drawn consciously and deliberately.

The difference between this and the conception of the *eidōlon* in Pindar and Plato is presumably related to the fact that, in Empedocles' Orphic conception, the individual soul's immortality remains limited to its sorrowful Dionysian wanderings in the earthly sphere, where it must stay so long as it is chained to the wheel of birth and rebirth. At its return to the celestial sphere of light it is once again absorbed into the divine all-encompassing unity. On account of this, the connection with the Homeric *eidōlon-psychē* is even more direct here than in the case of Pindar and Plato. For Empedocles, Hades remains the realm of darkness and gloom. It is possible that his *Katharmoi* even provided the inspiration for Plato's celebrated myth of the cave in his *Republic*.

Our conclusion can only be that the connection made by Rohde between the *eidōlon-psychē* of Homer and that of Pindar's Olympian odes, in spite of the uncritical approach that he took, contained a kernel of truth that Otto utterly failed to appreciate.

20. The Relationship between Empedocles' Purifications and His Poem on Physis

Pages 84 ff., text. The view which long held sway that Empedocles' *Katharmoi* or *Purifications* and his poem on *physis* intrinsically contradict each other was strongly influenced by the interpretation of the latter as a "mechanistic physics." The starting point for this interpretation lay once again in the modern humanistic science ideal (see, e.g., Eduard Zeller-Nestle, *Philosophie der Griechen* [6th edition], I, p. 1001). The presumed conflict had to be imported into the *Purifications* itself, however, because it could not be denied that the role played by the four elements, along with love and hate, is just as essential there, just as in the poem on nature. Herman Diels (*Über die Gedichte des Empedokles*, Berlin Akademie, 1898, pp. 396 ff.) and Jean Bidez (*La biographie d'Empédocle*, Ghent, 1894) attempted to remove this difficulty by assigning the two poems to successive periods of Empedocles' life.

Jaeger (*op.cit.*, pp. 128-155) agrees with my own conception to the extent that he, following the important work *Empedocle* (Turin, 1916) by the Italian scholar Ettore Bignone, perceives basically the same spirit in both poems. This harmonizing viewpoint rests on his judgment that the poem on nature is no less mythological in character than the *Katharmoi*. For him it is actually nothing but a cosmological theology, which describes in the world of "nature" the operation of the same divine powers that the *Purifications* sees at work in the "soul." But when Jaeger proceeds to expand on this interpretation, which to me seems correct, he departs considerably from the analysis that I have given in the text, since here again he is blind to the dialectical character of the religious ground-motive of Greek philosophy. He thus maintains that the problem of God for Empedocles is nothing more than the problem of the divine *form*: "And this is the angle from which he approaches it as a student of nature. What he finds in nature is no single form but a manifold revelation of the Divine, such as the Greek mind has found there all along" (p. 153). Because of this, Jaeger was unable to detect any basic difference between the divine nature of the four elements and that of love and hate, and he regards the *Sphairos* as still another deity, the highest God, who is akin to Xenophanes' "one God."

For the first of these points he appeals to Empedocles, B. Fragm. 17, 27 ff.: "All these are equal in power and of the same age ..." (see note 1, p. 88 and the corresponding translation in the text). Whereas Diels and W. Capelle (*Die Vorsokratiker*, p. 196) hold, in my view correctly, that the word $\tau\alpha\hat{v}\tau\alpha$ (these) here refers only to the four elements, Jaeger follows Kranz in thinking that it includes *philia* and *neikos* as well. All these forms of the divine then would have an equal status, and Jaeger regards this as a cosmological reflection of the democratic ideal of government which Empedocles had championed in the political struggle of his native city Acragas. Thus Empedocles is allegedly taking a position here that is opposed in principle to the theogonic hierarchy of Hesiod.

If one reads the above B fragment in its context, however, this "democratic" interpretation proves to be untenable. For it is not possible that both the elements *and* the two motive forces of love and hate should in turn "gain the upper hand." Fire's coming into power is necessarily coupled with the supremacy of love, and the "upper hand" of the other elements is necessarily linked with the predominance of hate; for love and hate are in fact the *causes* of the elements' motion. In addition, it seems to me that the word $\tau\iota\mu\dot{\eta}$, which Diels-Kranz translates as "office," would better be rendered as "value" or "rank."

Neither in the poem on nature nor in the *Purifications* are love and hate represented as corporeal forms of being. The only passage in the first of these poems that has been taken to support this incorrect notion is Empedocles, B. Fragm. 17, 18-21, where *neikos* and *philotēs* are named in direct connection with the four elements, and a geometric, spatial property is seemingly attributed to love itself ($\check{\iota}\sigma\eta \mu\hat{\eta}\kappa\acute{o}\varsigma \tau\epsilon \pi\lambda\acute{\alpha}\tau o\varsigma \tau\epsilon$, i.e., "equal in length and breadth"). But the fact that these words are immediately preceded by $\acute{\epsilon}v \tau o\hat{\iota}\sigma\iota v$ ("in them," i.e., the elements) undermines this whole interpretation. Love, as a driving force, is manifested only *within* the elements, equally according to their length and their breadth, while *neikos* or hate is said to be separate from the elements and "everywhere equal in weight" ($\acute{\alpha}\tau\acute{\alpha}\lambda\alpha v\tau o v \acute{\alpha}\pi\acute{\alpha}v\tau\eta\iota$). In other words, *philia*, as a *daemon* or divine soul-force, completely interpenetrates the basic corporeal forms; but it can do this only because it is *not* a corporeal form itself. Empedocles, B. Fragm. 16 accordingly brings love and hate into connection with the infinite *time* of life's existence, which always will be filled with them. Thus they are clearly seen here to be a psychic counterpart to the corporeal elements, which similarly fill *space* without leaving any void.

In the text, I have demonstrated in detail that the divine *sphairos* is simply the corporeal form that is *produced* by the divine *philia* when its unification of the elements is no longer counteracted by *neikos*. Therefore, it cannot at all be the case that the *sphairos* is an independent manifestation of the divine that exists alongside, or perhaps above, the polytheistic series formed by the four elements and love and hate. Love is the highest deity conceived as an eternally flowing soul-force, and the *sphairos* is merely its appropriate corporeal form. In both of Empedocles' poems this love is identified with the goddess Cypris or Aphrodite. Speaking of the golden age, Empedocles, B. Fragm. 128 (from the *Purifications*) says that at that time neither Ares, nor Cydoimos, nor Zeus, nor Poseidon was God, but only Cypris the Queen. From this it is very clear that the Dionysian matter motive in its Orphic reinterpretation still retains the religious primacy in Empedocles' thought.

In speaking of a "broad oath" by which hegemony is alternately assigned to hate and love, Empedocles, B. Fragm. 30 brings to expression the same thought that is encountered in B. Fragm. 115 of the *Purifications*, where we read of the "decree of *Anankē*, an ancient and eternal edict of the gods, sealed with broad oaths." The divine *philia*, the highest god, whose appropriate corporeal form is the *sphairos*, is impotent in the face of *Anankē*, which has also appointed for discord and hate their fixed time in the cycle of the world process. Nowhere in the two poems, however, is it said that the good and evil driving forces are equal in value, just as B. Fragm. 17, 28 does not say this of the elements. The only thing that appears is that they are all equally ancient in origin and equal in power. The characteristically democratic principle of equivalency is therefore not to be found here. According to the clear words of B. Fragm. 27, *philia*, when it comes to its full manifestation in the *sphairos*, does away with the elements in their discrete formal limitation.

Another weighty argument against the thought that the elements must be put on a par with the driving forces of love and hate can be found in Empedocles' epistemological ideas. Whereas the poet teaches (Empedocles, B. Fragm. 4, 9 ff.) that one should rely on sense perception when it comes to corporeal things, he expressly states in B. Fragm. 17, 21 that love has to be contemplated with the *nous* (τὴν σὺ νόωι δέρκευ). Evidently, *philia* is not perceptible to the senses, since it is itself incorporeal in nature. Further, in response to Jaeger's remark on page 137 that "Empedocles' elemental principles are imbued with the very life-breath and essence of divine powers," it must be objected that there is no instance where this poet-thinker represents the elements *themselves* as imbued with the breath of life. The only things that "imbue" them are *philia* and *neikos*, which by their antagonistic activity first make possible the fluid process of life in the intermingling of the elements. The statement in Empedocles' B. Fragm. 102 that "everything has received breath and smell" clearly refers to the *cosmos*, not to the elements as such.

All these objections must also be brought to bear against Walter Kranz. In his recently published important work *Empedokles: Antike Gestalt and romantische Neuschöpfung,* he writes: "It has rightly been observed that the term 'psyche' does not occur in the preserved word of Empedocles. Moreover, according to his theory of nature it could not at all have designated a particular entity, since in his view there is nothing that is in itself psychical."[1] In the poem on nature, however, we found that only *philia* and *neikos* are characterized as *daimones*, and in the *Purifications* the word *daimōn* unquestionably denotes a *psychē* existing apart. Appealing to Aristotle, Kranz maintains nevertheless (p. 42) that each of Empedocles' elements is also a soul.

Finally, we can take note of the description of the Pythagorean Apollo given in B. Fragm. 134, "he is only a mind, holy and ineffable, which darts through the whole cosmos with swift thought." Here he is doubtless conceived as a divine mind that cannot be perceived by the senses. Is this Apollo identical to *philia*, which is given its appropriate, transitory corporeal form in the *sphairos*, but as an eternal psychical power still remains distinct from this corporeal nature? Because of the lack of relevant passages this cannot be determined, although in light of the Orphic "theocrastic" tendency (see above, point 11) it seems very likely.

21. Anaxagoras' Theory of the Nous and the Spermata

Pages 99 ff., text. Just as Parmenides, in the extant fragments of his didactic poem, does not expressly call his supersensible sphere of being God, the extant B fragments concerning Anaxagoras' theory of *physis* nowhere explicitly grant this appellation to the *nous*, which reigns sovereign over the whole physical process. The modern, materialistic interpretation that Burnet has given to Anaxagoras' theory of *nous*, which denies that it differs in any essential way from the Milesian nature philosophers' conception of the principle of origin, is based partly on this fact. For this reason, I find it all the more surprising that Jaeger, who regards the absence of the name God in Parmenides' ontology as crucial, does not have the same objection to a theological interpretation of Anaxogaras' *nous*. In the work that I have frequently cited, *The Theology of the Early Greek Philosophers* (1947), pp. 161 ff, he finds it absolutely certain that the thinker from Clazomenae regarded the *nous* as

---

1 Walter Kranz, *Empedokles: Antike Gestalt und romantische Neuschöpfung* (Zürich, 1949), p. 63. (English translation by translator.)

God. He bases this conclusion both on the hymnic style of Anaxagoras, B. Fragm. 12 and on the epithets that Anaxagoras explicitly confers on his world-ruling *nous*. Had Jaeger applied these same criteria to the first part of Parmenides' poem, he could not have avoided coming to the same conclusion there.

All the same, Jaeger's further analysis of Anaxagoras' theory of *nous* entirely confirms the view I advanced in the text, that the pure form motive of the culture religion comes to the fore here for the first time in the philosophy of nature. Jaeger himself, however, did not discern this religious ground-motive as such. With regard to the providential world-plan that Anaxagoras ascribes to the divine *Nous* (B. Fragm. 12), he observes: "The idea of this preconceived world-plan is quite worthy of the rational physics of the fifth century; it is peculiarly fitting in a period that ascribes decided significance to τέχνη in all realms of being and even finds it present in nature itself. ... The fact that he made the divine Mind guide the vortex in a specific direction gave his physics its new theological aspect" (*op.cit.*, p. 163). That τέχνη has typically cultural meaning is clear. As soon as *physis* is regarded under this aspect, a veritable revolution takes place in the Greek view of nature. The form motive of the culture religion now becomes ascendant, and it also makes its presence felt in theological terms. Between Xenophanes' and Empedocles' conception of the deity and that advanced by Anaxagoras there is a profound, unmistakable difference.

The interpretation of Anaxagoras' conception of the original *mixis* that I defended in the text accords fully with Aristotle's interpretation. In *Metaphysics Λ* 2, 1069 b, he makes the following observation concerning the initial state of *hulē* in this Ionian thinker: "And this potential [δυνάμει ὄν] is the 'one' of Anaxagoras – that is a better expression for 'all things together' – and the mixture of Empedocles and Anaximander, and is meant in the statement of Democritus: 'all things were together potentially, but not actually.' Hence they must have sought with these concepts to indicate or comprehend *hulē*." A few lines later he criticizes Anaxagoras' theory of the *spermata*: "One might ask, however, from what sort of non-being generation takes place; for non-being is threefold in character [viz., absolute non-being, *sterēsis* or privation of being, and *hulē* as potential being]. The answer is: from potential non-being, if such a thing exists; but still, a thing does not arise from an arbitrary potentiality, but different things come into being from different potentialities. To say 'all *chrēmata* were together' is therefore inadequate, for they differ as to their *hulē*. Why else should they be infinite in number and not one? For the *nous* is just one, so that, if *hulē* also were merely one, only that would have come to be in actuality for which hulē was in potentiality."

That Anaxagoras did in fact grant to the chaotic state of *hulē* a real existence before the form-giving work of the divine *Nous* took place is confirmed by the following information from Diogenes Laertius, 2, 6

(Anaxagoras, A. Fragm. 1, 6-7): "All things were together; then, *Nous* came and gave order to them." The same is indicated by Aristotle's testimony in *Physics*, VIII, 250 b 24: "When all *chrēmata* were together and at rest for a measureless length of time, [Anaxagoras says that] *Nous* introduced motion among them and separated them from each other."

It is clear from B. Fragm. 10 how Anaxagoras arrived at his theory of the *spermata*. There it appears that he pondered the question of how the most diverse parts of an organic body (i.e., hair, nails, veins, nerves, bones) could spring from the same seed, unless they were all contained within the *spermata* from the outset. Simplicius (*ad Arist. Phys. Γ* 4, 203 a 19 ff.) likewise corroborates the view that Anaxagoras' starting point was the problem of the nourishment and growth of organic bodies. Jaeger has correctly observed (pp. 157 ff.) that the theory of mixture, which we first encounter in the extant works of Alcmaeon, the physician from Croton, was medical in origin.

Anaxagoras' Anthropological Ideas

Aristotle testifies (*De partibus animalium*, *Δ* 10, 687 a 7 ff.) that the thought that the human hand is evidence of special rational ability is found already in Anaxagoras. He notes further (*De Anima*, A 2, 405 a 13 ff.) that although Anaxagoras seems to distinguish between *nous* and *psychē*, in other statements he treats them as one and the same. Nevertheless, it is beyond question that the fundamental distinction between *nous* and *psychē* is a necessary consequence of Anaxagoras' conception of the *nous* as an unmixed intelligence that has sovereignty over all other things. For this conception entails that *nous* cannot be affected by material things, i.e., that it is *ἀπαθής*, elevated above all emotional influence (as Aristotle himself observes, Anaxagoras, A. Fragm. 56), and is therefore also distinct from sensation. Moreover, only the *nous* can be called *autokratēs*, i.e., possessed of a power that is borrowed from nothing else (see the beginning of B. Fragm. 12).

22. The Relationship between the Divine and the Human Nous *in Anaxagoras*

On page 105 of the text I wrote, "Thus, the human mental faculty (*nous*) is evidently not regarded as an independent form, divorced from matter." Further reflection compels me to take this back, since toward the end of Anaxagoras, B. Fragm. 12 it is clearly stated, "and all *nous* is alike, both the greater and the smaller." B. Fragm. 11, to which I appealed on page 105, must be interpreted therefore in accordance with this statement. According to B. Fragm. 117, Anaxagoras thought that feeling, intelligence, and discernment belong also to plants. This would thus mean that *all* living beings on this earth (plants, animals, and human beings) partake to a greater or lesser degree of *nous*. Jaeger observes (p. 164) that Anaxagoras regarded the human *nous* as the divine in a person.

23. The Relationship between Diogenes of Apollonia and Anaxagoras

Page 105, note 3. The fundamental change that Diogenes of Apollonia brought about in Anaxagoras' theology by identifying the divine *nous* with Anaximenes' air-god is clearly illustrated in Diogenes, B. Fragm. 5 (from a treatise on *physis*), where he says of the divine *archē*: "And by this all men are also governed, and it rules them all. For it is precisely this, it seems to me, that is god, and is present to everything and arranges all things, and inheres in everything. And there is not one thing which does not partake of it."[1]

In this fragment, one is first of all struck by the use of the two verbs κυβερνᾶν and κρατεῖν. In addition to the κυβερνᾶν, the *governing* of the world that Anaximenes had ascribed to the deity, Diogenes finds it necessary to specify, as a separate epithet that is clearly distinct from the first, the κρατεῖν, or *rational sovereignty* over the world, that Anaxagoras had reserved for the divine *nous*. This confirms my observation under point 4.

In the second place, it is evident that Diogenes broke in principle with Anaxagoras' dualistic conception of the relation between the divine and *physis*. Diogenes' god is *in* everything (ἐν παντὶ ἐνεῖναι), and for him all that is one *partakes* of the deity (μετέχει τούτου). The latter part of B. Fragm. 5 says that in accordance with the diverse forms (τρόποι) of change (ἑτεροίωσις) present in the divine origin, by which diverse kinds of beings are generated, the latter all have varying grades of νόησις; but they nevertheless all live, see, and hear, and take all other forms of νόησις, from one and the same principle of origin (the air). Anaximenes regarded the change of air into water, fire, and earth as taking place through condensation and rarefaction. In Diogenes' conception, Parmenides' critique of the combination of the principles of form and matter within a single principle of origin is therefore disregarded. He says in B. Fragm. 7: "And this itself [i.e., the deity] is an eternal and immortal being; but the other things are such that some come into being, while others pass away."

Nevertheless, Diogenes was the first person to unfold Anaxagoras' idea of a purposive, divine world-plan by interpreting specific phenomena of nature from this point of view (see Diogenes, B. Fragm. 3). This is what Jaeger means by the spirit of enlightenment, which asserted itself in the fifth century B.C. view of nature and led in particular to the understanding of living organisms as mechanisms constructed according to a technical plan.

More recent research (W. Theiler, *Zur Geschichte der teleologischen Naturbetrachtung bis auf Aristoteles* [Zurich, 1925], and even before that the dissertation by S.O. Dickerman, *De argumentis quibusdam apud*

---

1 καὶ ὑπὸ τούτου πάντας καὶ κυβερνᾶσθαι καὶ πάντων κρατεῖν· αὐτὸ γάρ μοι τοῦτο θεὸς δοκεῖ εἶναι καὶ ἐπὶ πᾶν ἀφῖχθαι καὶ πάντα διατιθέναι καὶ ἐν παντὶ ἐνεῖναι. καὶ ἔστιν οὐδὲ ἓν ὅ τι μὴ μετέχει τούτου (English translation by AW).

Xenophontem, Platonem, Aristotelem obviis e structura hominis et animalium petitis [Halle, 1909]), has shown that it is very likely that Socrates' teleological view of nature, which has been passed down to us in Xenophon's *Memorabilia* and Plato's *Philebus*, was directly influenced by the development which Diogenes gave to Anaxagoras' theory of *nous*. Theophrastus relates (Diogenes, A. Fragm. 19) that Diogenes made a distinction between the internal air (*ὁ ἐντὸς ἀήρ*) within man and the air outside. The first of these, through which human sense perception takes place, he calls "a small portion of God" (*μικρὸν μόριον θεοῦ*), i.e., of the cosmic air. This "internal air" is obviously the human *psychē*. As Theiler (p. 21) has convincingly demonstrated, Socrates' physico-teleological proof for the deity, presented in Xenophon's *Memorabilia*, A, 4, 8, and Plato's *Philebus*, 29 a and 30 a, could indeed have its foundation here. The reader may compare pages 251 ff. in the text with this.

It must not be forgotten, however, that Socrates and Plato did not at all accept Diogenes' *pantheistic* conception of the divine *nous* as a demiurge, and especially not his identification of God with the air conceived as the *archē*. In *Philebus* 30 a, the only inference drawn from the human soul is that a world-soul exists; but this in turn finds its own origin in the divine *nous* as demiurge. In both Xenophon's *Memorabilia* and Plato's *Philebus*, Socrates' sole aim is to prove that the presence of a rational soul is not confined to human beings alone.

24. The Conception of the "Void" in Leucippus and Democritus

Pages 105 ff., text. I was pleased to discover that the view I have taken in the text regarding the *kenon* (void), as the founders of the atomist school conceived this, is found also in Wilhelm Capelle.[1] The writer gives no arguments for his position, however. The relevant passage from his introduction to the Leucippus fragments reads as follows: "For the second basic presupposition of the atomistic physics is precisely the hypothesis of empty space (this being understood as space filled only with air)." Capelle, however, draws no conclusions from this regarding the origin of the disorderly motion. According to him, the primordial motion of the atoms was nothing but a *metaphysical axiom* for Leucippus, which in his view needed no further justification. The founder of atomism allegedly considered this primordial motion to be an original property of matter itself, and, unlike Empedocles and Anaxagoras, did not find it necessary to specify an immaterial cause for this. Capelle thus remarks that "here he is evidently influenced by his recollection of the basic notion of his great Milesian intellectual forebears, who regarded matter as being self-moved. And thus, the problem seemed to be solved in an amazingly simple manner: the atoms, of their own accord, are in perpetual motion."[2]

---

1 Wilhelm Capelle, *Die Vorsokratiker: Die Fragmente und Quellenberichte übersetzt und eingeleitet* (Leipzig, 1935), p. 286.

2 *Ibid.*

Capelle forgets, however, that the atoms are something vastly different from the "divine primal matter" of the Milesians. He too approaches the Greek atomists in terms of the modern, natural scientific concept of matter and is altogether blind to the dialectical ground-motive of Greek thought, where the principles of form and matter stand in polar opposition. On account of this, he did not even perceive the problem that is contained in his (in my view correct) understanding of Leucippus' and Democritus' void, for the air as a *kenon* naturally cannot be identical with the air *atoms*.

In the A fragments, however, one can in fact find strong evidence for my view that the atoms take their original, disorderly motion from the *kenon* conceived as a fluid stream of air. Aristotle's words in *Physics Δ* 6, 213 a 27 ff. (Leucippus, A. Fragm. 19) thus have prime importance for Leucippus' and Democritus' conception of the *kenon* as formless air: "But people understand the void as a spatial interval [διάστημα] in which no body perceptible to the senses [σῶμα αἰσθητόν] is present. Believing, however, that all that *is* is body, they say that that in which there is nothing at all is the void. *Therefore what is full of air is held to be void*" (my italics).

The Evidence That the Motion of the Atoms Stems from the Surrounding Fluid Air-Matter

My view that, for Leucippus and Democritus, motion does not originate in the atoms themselves but rather is first imparted to them from without (from the "form-empty" air) is based above all on the following *testimonia*:

Simplicius, *ad Arist. Phys.* 42, 10 (Democritus, A. Fragm. 47): "Democritus says that the atoms by nature are unmoved and are [first] set in motion by an impact." And further, Aetius, in Democritus, A. Fragm. 47: "Democritus declared that there is one kind of motion, that due to striking [παλμός]."

Democritus, A. Fragm. 128 (Aetius, *Δ* 19, 3) is also very important: "Democritus says that by sound the air is broken up into atoms of like shape, and that it moves along (like a flowing undulation) together with the fragments split off by the sound." This fragment would make no sense at all if the air, as flowing matter, were not distinguished from the air-atoms that are separated out from it as forms of beings. For how else could it move along as a flowing stream *together with* its atoms, which are driven asunder by sound?

Alexander of Aphrodisias, *ad Arist. Met.*, 36, 21, (Leucippus, A. Fragm. 6): "Aristotle speaks of Leucippus and Democritus. For they assert that the atoms are set in motion when they strike each other or are struck against one another. But whence the *natural* motion takes its origin, this they do not say. For the motion resulting from their striking each other is a violent motion [βίαιός ἐστι κίνησις] and not natural [οὐ κατὰ φύσιν]; the violent [imparted from without] motion, however, is later than the natural [determined by the intrinsic nature]."

Simplicius, *ad Arist. De caelo Γ* 2, 300 b 8 (583, 20), (Leucippus, A. Fragm. 16): "They asserted that the primary particles which they speak of, i.e. the atoms, are in eternal motion within the unbounded void due to violence." Democritus, A. Fragm. 37: "He [Democritus] thinks that they [the atoms] are intertwined with one another and stay together until a *strong compulsion, which acts upon them from the surrounding air* [ἐκ τοῦ περιέχοντος], shakes them together and separates and disperses them" (my italics). In Leucippus and Democritus, the περιέχον always denotes the *apeiron* or *kenon*, and this has great significance in the present fragment, since the περιέχον here is distinguished from *all* atoms.

Other *testimonia* state that this περιέχον exerts pressure on the fire atoms of bodies that breathe and that it expels them. Compare Aristotle, *De anima* A 2, 404 a 1 ff. (Leucippus, A. Fragm. 28), and especially Aristotle, *De respiratione Δ* 4, 471 b 30 (Democritus, A. Fragm. 106): "But he [Democritus] asserts that the soul and the hot [i.e., fire] are the same, namely, the spherical primary particles. Hence when these are forced together by the surrounding [air], which would squeeze them out, inhalation intervenes to help them. *For in the air there are a large number of those atoms* which he calls *nous* and *psychē* [my italics]. Thus, when a person inhales and the air [thereby] enters in [into that person's body], these [fire-] atoms supposedly enter the body along with it and, by counteracting the expulsion [of the soul-atoms that are still within], prevent the soul that dwells in the living being from passing out of the body. For this reason, life and death supposedly depend on inhalation and exhalation. For when the surrounding air gains the upper hand in the compression [that it causes in the soul-atoms], and the atoms entering from without no longer are able to counteract it, since breathing has become impossible, then death supposedly comes to the living beings. For death is held to be the departure of such atoms from the body owing to the expulsive pressure of the surrounding air." The importance of this fragment lies in the fact that it shows clearly that Leucippus and Democritus considered the soul-atoms to be suspended in a formless and fluid air-matter. For, as is plainly evident in the penultimate sentence of the fragment, the air spoken of here is invariably the περιέχον, i.e., the *kenon*, not the air-atoms.

Do the Soul-Atoms Have a Natural, Inherent Self-Movement?

In spite of this, it cannot be denied that Aristotle repeatedly gives the impression that the fiery soul-atoms, unlike the other atoms, were granted a *natural*, eternal self-movement by Leucippus and Democritus. See, for example, *De anima* A 3, 406 b 15 ff. (Democritus, A. Fragm. 104): "Some even say that the soul moves the body in which it dwells in the same way that it moves itself. Thus, for example, Democritus ... For he asserts that the spherical atoms by their movement – since *it is their nature* never to come to rest – draw along and set in motion the whole body." In De *anima* A 2, 404 a 1 ff. (Leucippus, A. Fragm. 28) he also states: "Democritus declares that the soul is a sort of fire or heat. For among the countless forms or atoms, he calls the spherical ones fire and soul, just like the so-called motes that can be seen in the beams of light coming through windows...."

If this had indeed been Democritus' view, it would indicate that his conception of the fire-atoms was actually closely related to the Orphic-Pythagorean notions of the soul. For we may recall that in the old Pythagorean school the motes visible in sunbeams were regarded as souls in perpetual self-movement. In this case, the atoms of fire would be the only atoms that do not have their primary motion imparted to them externally by the fluid stream of air, and Democritus' atomic theory would then in fact betray a kind of Orphic dualism. But can we accept this on Aristotle's authority alone? In the discussion of Democritus' theory of atoms in his *Metaphysics*, he does not make the above distinction. At any rate, it is certain that Democritus absolutely rejected the Orphic belief in the immortality of the soul and a judgment after death. In Democritus, B. Fragm. 297 he thus says: "Some men, knowing nothing of the dissolution of mortal nature, vex their conscience [συνειδήσει] about the evil things they have done in life, living their entire lives in anxiety and disquiet, because they invent false tales about the time after death."

The Connection between the Atomists' *Kenon* and Empedocles' Theory of the Pores

I now come to the last important argument for my view that the *kenon* of Leucippus and Democritus does not denote space that is absolutely empty, but rather formless air-matter. Here we shall examine the connection between the atomists' conception of the void and Empedocles' theory of pores.

Outside of a brief exchange between Socrates and Meno in Plato's *Meno* 76 c our information on this subject comes from the extremely important account given by Aristotle in *De generatione et corruptione* A 8, 325 b 6 ff. (Leucippus, A. Fragm. 7): "Empedocles too has to take approximately the same position as Leucippus. For he must say that there exist certain solid [particles of elements] that are indivisible – unless on all sides there are continuous pores [πόροι]. But that is impossible; for then nothing solid would exist at all, but only pores, i.e., only a void. It is necessary, therefore, that the contiguous particles [of bodies] be indivisible, while the intervals, which Empedocles calls pores, must by contrast be void. And Leucippus speaks similarly concerning the action and passion [of substances]."

According to another passage from this same work of Aristotle (A 8, 324 b 26 ff.), Empedocles held that substances intermingle because as effluences from corporeal things, they penetrate into one another's pores.

Aristotle says that these pores are considered too small to be seen, but are closely packed and arranged in rows. Only those substances intermingle which have pores that are symmetrical in relation to one another. Philoponus makes the following observation in his commentary on this passage (Empedocles, A. Fragm. 87): "We know that those students of nature who suppose there are pores [in bodies] do not regard these as empty spaces, but as filled with a finer substance such as air." Shortly before this he says: "The pores differ from [absolutely] empty space, because those who introduced pores denied the existence of empty space."

From these *testimonia*, it is clear that Leucippus and Democritus developed their theory of the *kenon* and the atoms partly as a *logical inference* from Empedocles' theory of the pores. They therefore conceived the void itself in the sense of this pore theory, i.e., as filled with nonsolid, flowing air. The only inference they drew was that the acceptance of such a *kenon* necessarily implied that the existence of indivisible, infinitesimal atoms or forms of being also had to be assumed.

25. Protagoras' and Democritus' Philosophy of History

Pages 118 ff., text. Because Protagoras' evolutionistic philosophy of history shows such astonishing similarities with the fragmentary remnants that Diodorus, et.al., have preserved of Democritus' view of history, it is highly probable that Democritus was somewhat dependent here on the founder of Sophism. In an excellent study in *Hermes*: 47 (1912, pp. 509 ff.), Karl Reinhardt demonstrated the authenticity of these fragments, which Diels-Kranz has included under Democritus, B. Fragm. 5, numbers 1-3.

Protagoras' influence on Democritus can be established with great likelihood on the basis of other fragments as well. Democritus' statement on formative education (*paideia*), for example, is very telling in this regard. See Capelle, *Vorsokratiker*, p. 461: "Nature and education have a certain similarity. For education also transforms man, but by this transformation it creates a [second] nature" (248, Fragm. 33); See also p. 459: "Poverty in a democracy is as much better than so-called 'good fortune' under despots as freedom is better than the life of a slave" (239, Fragm. 251).

26. Self-Knowledge in Socrates and Heraclitus.

Pages 120 ff., text. When I made my claim in the text that critical self-reflection in Greek thought began with Socrates, I was not at all unaware that Heraclitus had already spoken of self-knowledge. Thus he says in Heraclitus, B. Fragm. 101, ἐδιζησάμην ἐμεωυτόν ("I searched myself out") and in B. Fragm. 116, ἀνθρώποισι πᾶσι μέτεστι γιγνώσκειν ἑωυτοὺς καὶ σωφρονεῖν ("It is the portion of all men to know themselves and to think rationally").

It is difficult, however, to regard this self-knowledge of Heraclitus as the true critical turning point in Greek philosophical thought. In the pantheistic dialectic of the great Ephesian thinker, man had not yet been dissociated from ever-flowing *physis*. He still seeks his identity here in the boundless depth of the divine stream of life, even though the latter has become dialectically united with the divine *logos*, the hidden unity of opposites that imposes a fixed measure and proportionality upon coming into being and passing away. Heraclitus' utterances on the soul must also be understood in this sense: "You could not in your going find the boundaries of the soul, even though you should search out every path: so deep is its *logos* " (B. Fragm. 45), and "The soul has its own *logos*, which increases itself" (B. Fragm. 115).

27. The Chronological Problem in the Phaedrus' Theory of the Soul

Pages 159 ff., text. In his introduction to the *Phaedrus* (*Platon, Oeuvres complètes*, vol.IV, part 3, 1947), Léon Robin has once again argued at length (pp. iv ff.) for the view that this dialogue had to be written *after* the *Republic*, and he applies this also to its conception of the soul. According to him, the *Phaedrus* must have been written at about the same time as the *Theaetetus*.

Thinking to perceive a measure of uncertainty in the *Republic's* treatment of the problem of immortality, Robin claims it would be very strange that this should be found *after* the proof given in the *Phaedrus*, since at the end of his life Plato still maintained this proof in the *Laws* (X, 894 E – 895 C, 896 A-B). In this view, the eschatology of the *Phaedrus* would remain a puzzle at certain points apart from the corresponding material in the tenth book of the *Republic*. And finally, he holds that the "supra-celestial sphere" (τόπος ὑπερουράνιος) in the *Phaedrus* is nothing but a "mythical counterpart of the intelligible realm of the Republic."

The strength of these arguments escapes me. I feel that Robin too has come too much under the influence of the pre-conceived view which regards the *Phaedrus* in its present form as "all of a piece," and then makes the dialectical part of this dialogue, which appears to have been written later, pivotal for proving the later date of its conception of the soul. The *Phaedrus'* theory of the soul differs profoundly from that presented in the later dialogues. Plato's continued adherence in the *Laws* to the *Phaedrus'* proof for immortality does not diminish this fact, since in the interim the conception of what in the soul is immortal had been fundamentally modified. I find it unthinkable that Plato, after having first developed the tripartite concept of the soul in a completely dialectical theory, should then present it in a purely mythological form, without theoretical foundation. It seems to me that the same consideration applies to the relationship between the purely mythological description of the *topos huperouranios* in the *Phaedrus* and the theoretical-dialectical account of this in the *Republic*.

28. Plato's Oration On the Good

Pages 270 ff., text. After I had completed this book an important study of Plato's oration *On the Good* was published by Paul Wilpert under the title "Platons Altersvorlesung über das Gute" (*Philosophisches Jahrbuch*, vol. 59 [1949], pp. 1-14, where a reference is made to an earlier essay in *Hermes* [1941, pp. 225-250]). The importance of this study, which in my view also contains a number of mistaken notions, lies in its disclosure of the inner connection between the final phase of Plato's theory of idea-numbers and his earlier views. Wilpert takes his cue here from an extensive account of the Pythagorean theory of numbers written by Sextus Empiricus.

29. Roman Catholic Objections to a Few Points in My Account of the Thomistic Doctrine of Creation

Pages 35 ff., text. After this book had gone through the press, there appeared in the journal *Studia Catholica* (vol. 23, no. 2 [1948] and vol. 24 [1949]), a pair of articles by professor Dr. H. Robbers, S.J., respectively entitled "The Nature-Grace Scheme as the Religious Ground-Motive of Scholastic Philosophy" ("Het natuur-genade-schema als religieus grondmotief der scholastieke wijsbegeerte") and "The Calvinistic Philosophy of the Cosmonomic Idea in Dialogue with Thomism" ("De Calvinistische Wijsbegeerte der Wetsidee in gesprek met het Thomisme"). In these articles Prof. Robbers objects to my account of Thomas' doctrine of creation in *Philosophia Reformata*, vols. VI (1941) and VIII (1943) at two different points, which are also treated summarily on page pp. 35 ff. of the present book. He takes exception to my following observations: (1) that the scriptural notion of God's *activity* has been lost in Thomas' idea of creation; (2) that in Thomas' thought the principles of form and matter are both withdrawn from God's sovereignty as Creator.

I have already promised Prof. Robbers that I shall give serious consideration to these objections and shall return to them at a later point. This will take place as a matter of course in the second volume of this work, where Scholastic philosophy will be subjected to a transcendental critique. For the present, I can only convey my initial impression that Prof. Robbers apparently has misunderstood the purport of my remarks and that I myself am likely to blame for this because I did not state them with enough precision. There is no doubt in my mind that Thomas sincerely *intended* to make Aristotle's metaphysics square with the church's doctrine of creation. The only question is whether this was possible within the framework of an accommodated Aristotelian philosophy. Accordingly I hope to return to this point in detail later on.

Index of Subjects

Index of Persons

Printed in the USA
CPSIA information can be obtained
at www.ICGtesting.com
LVHW090835180824
788594LV00029B/637